DATE DUE			

THE RUMP PARLIAMENT
1648-1653

THE RUMP
PARLIAMENT
1648-1653

BLAIR WORDEN
Fellow and College Lecturer in History
Selwyn College, Cambridge

CAMBRIDGE UNIVERSITY PRESS

Published by the Syndics of the Cambridge University Press
Bentley House, 200 Euston Road, London NW1 2DB
American Branch: 32 East 57th Street, New York, N.Y.10022

© Cambridge University Press 1974

Library of Congress Catalogue Card Number: 73–77264

ISBN: 0 521 20205 1

First published 1974

Printed in Great Britain by
Alden & Mowbray Ltd
at the Alden Press, Oxford

CONTENTS

Contents

For Hamish

ACKNOWLEDGEMENTS

This book grew out of a doctoral thesis submitted at the University of Oxford in 1971. For the first two years of my research I was assisted by a grant from the Department of Education and Science. The research was completed, and both the thesis and the book were written, during my tenure of a Research Fellowship awarded me by the Fellows of Pembroke College, Cambridge. I shall always remember my time there with gratitude and affection. In rewriting my thesis for publication I have benefited much from the perceptive suggestions of my editor, Mrs Christine Linehan, and of Professor Geoffrey Elton. I am also indebted to the Duke of Northumberland, to the Marquess of Bath and to Major Ralph B. Verney for their kindness in allowing me to read and to cite manuscripts in their ownership. A section of this book is a revised version of an article published in the *English Historical Review* in 1971; I am grateful for permission to reproduce it here.

Readers of Professor David Underdown's *Pride's Purge* will recognise my debt to that excellent book. What they will not be aware of is the thoughtfulness with which, from the early stages of my research, Professor Underdown has kept me supplied with sound advice, precious information and welcome encouragement. His help has made a considerable difference. No two historians studying related subjects will reach identical conclusions, but the minor differences which will emerge in these pages are, I think, peripheral to the broad area of agreement between us. Many other seventeenth-century scholars, too, have unselfishly given to me of their time, knowledge and historical understanding. I am especially grateful for the trouble taken on my behalf by Dr Valerie Pearl, whose own work has done so much to illuminate the politics of the 1640s, and by Professors Gerald Aylmer and Austin Woolrych, who are engaged on studies likely similarly to illuminate those of the 1650s. For their valuable assistance on general or specific points I wish also to thank Dr Toby Barnard, Mr John Cooper,

Mrs Mary Cotterell, Dr John Morrill, Mr Malcolm Oxley, Mr Conrad Russell, Dr Barbara Taft, Professor Mick Williams and Mr George Yule. I alone, however, am responsible for the arguments and the errors of the book.

I leave my greatest debts until last. For to Dr Anne Whiteman, who supervised my thesis with unfailing vigilance and kindness, and to Professor Hugh Trevor-Roper, whose interest in my research has always been so generous and so stimulating, I owe–as their other pupils will understand–far more than I could say.

Cambridge, 1972   A.B.W.

AUTHOR'S NOTE

In writing this book I have tried to picture a reader who has an outline knowledge of seventeenth-century English history, and who wishes to learn more about a particular part of it. But I have also had a more specialised audience in mind, and most of the book is based on specialised research. There are therefore many footnote references; and because of the nature of the available evidence, the footnotes are often bulky. I have tried to keep them to manageable length by making use of abbreviations and (after the first reference to the work concerned) of shortened titles. The former are listed on p. xii: the extended versions of the latter, with a list of manuscript locations and classmarks, may be found in the bibliographical guide at the end of the book. When citing pamphlets and newspapers whose pagination is erroneous, I have usually supplied corrected pagination in parentheses. I have given the place of publication only in the case of works not published in London.

In quoting from seventeenth-century sources I have modernised spelling, punctuation and the use of capital letters, except where to do so would be to impair the sense, or to destroy the flavour, of the original. Dates are given in Old Style, but with the year regarded as beginning on 1 January.

The collection of essays edited by G. E. Aylmer, *The Interregnum: The Quest for Settlement 1646–1660* (1972) appeared after work on this book was completed. A number of the essays, especially that by J. P. Cooper on 'Social and Economic Policies under the Commonwealth', bear directly on my subject. So does Dr Christopher Hill's book *The World Turned Upside Down* (1972), which likewise appeared too late for me to take adequate account of its findings.

LIST OF ABBREVIATIONS

Add.	Additional (MS)
B.M.	British Museum
C.C.A.M.	*Calendar of the Committee for Advance of Money*
C.C.C.	*Calendar of the Committee for Compounding*
C.J.	*Journal of the House of Commons* (printed version)
C.J. (MS)	Journal of the House of Commons (manuscript fair copy, House of Lords Record Office)
C.S.P.D.	*Calendar of State Papers Domestic*
E.H.R.	*English Historical Review*
H.M.C.R.	*Historical Manuscript Commission Report*
N.L.W.	National Library of Wales
SP	Public Record Office classmark

INTRODUCTION

On the evening of 19 April 1653, Oliver Cromwell convened a meeting between representatives of the House of Commons and leading army officers at his lodgings in Whitehall. The subject discussed was a bill concerning parliamentary elections, a measure which the House intended to pass the following morning in the face of strong opposition from the army. There was little chance of agreement at the meeting, where tempers soon deteriorated; but Cromwell, using his position as both member of parliament and Lord General, pressed hard for a compromise. When the gathering dispersed, he believed that he had secured an undertaking from the most influential M.P.s to postpone completion of the bill until further talks with the officers had been held. He was therefore surprised to learn, next morning, that parliament was proceeding with the measure 'with all the eagerness [it] could'. Once the news was confirmed he left for Westminster, where he stationed a troop of musketeers at the door of the Commons before entering and taking his seat. For a while he listened quietly to the debate. Then, as the House prepared to put the motion, he rose to intervene. Pacing the floor, he delivered one of the most extraordinary speeches of his career. Bulstrode Whitelocke, who was among the members present, recorded the scene in an unusually vivid passage of his journal. Cromwell, wrote Whitelocke, 'told the House, that they had sat long enough . . . that some of them were whore-masters . . . that others of them were drunkards, and some corrupt and unjust men and scandalous to the profession of the gospel, and that it was not fit they should sit as a parliament any longer'. The angry protest drawn by this unparliamentary language was silenced by the appearance of Cromwell's musketeers, who met little resistance in clearing the chamber. The Long Parliament, which had met in November 1640 and which had sat for twelve and a half years, was no more. 'Thus', reflected Whitelocke, 'was this great parliament, which had done so great things . . . this assembly, famous through the world for its undertakings, actions, and successes, wholly at this time routed.'[1]

The enthusiasm professed by Whitelocke and other M.P.s for the achievements of the Long Parliament was coloured by retrospect and by indignation at the manner of the House's dissolution. Of the magnitude of those achievements, however, there could be no doubt. The years 1640 to 1653 were a period of profound transformation in English politics. Before 1640, parliaments had met only for short periods and at long intervals; and since 1629 they had not met at all. Like other representative institutions in Europe they had felt themselves to be fighting for survival against the growth of absolutist monarchy. They had exerted little direct influence on the policies, and held no direct share in the executive powers, of governments which could dismiss them at will. The divine authority of kingship was unchallenged before 1640, the inauguration of a republic unthinkable. Yet a republic was precisely what the Long Parliament achieved. Charles I lost to the House of Commons his prerogatives in 1641, the civil war by 1646, and his head in January 1649. Four weeks before his execution the Commons declared 'that the people are, under God, the original of all just power', and 'that the Commons of England, in parliament assembled . . . have the supreme power in this nation'. These startling claims rendered redundant not only Charles I but the House of Lords as well, and in March 1649 the upper house, like the institution of monarchy, was formally abolished, the Commons thereafter assuming the title of 'the parliament' and a monopoly of both legislative and executive power. In May the Commons resolved that 'the people of England . . . shall from henceforth be governed as a Commonwealth and free state by the supreme authority of this nation, the representatives of the people in parliament'.[2] For the next four years England experienced a period, unique in its history, of supreme parliamentary government.

The political achievements of the Long Parliament brought with them equally remarkable developments in. religious, military and diplomatic history. Before 1640 English puritans, like the parliaments they had so effectively colonised, had been on the defensive, struggling to contain the repressive policies of Laudian Anglicanism, a movement whose affinities with the Counter-Reformation in Europe they were

[1] W. C. Abbott, *Writings and Speeches of Oliver Cromwell* (4 vols., Cambridge, Mass., 1937–47), ii. 637–42, iii. 59–60; Bulstrode Whitelocke, *Memorials of the English Affairs* (4 vols., 1853), iv. 6.

[2] *C.J.* 4 Jan. 1649; S. R. Gardiner, *Constitutional Documents of the Puritan Revolution* (1958 edn.), pp. 384–8.

quick to notice. The 1640s, in religion as in politics, reversed the tendencies of the previous decades. Laud was executed by the Long Parliament, bishops were abolished, and a Calvinist form of church government was introduced, with new forms of worship to replace the Book of Common Prayer. Puritans had regarded the foreign policies of the early Stuarts, who had failed to defend the cause of European Protestantism in the Thirty Years War, as a catalogue of military, naval and diplomatic humiliation. The Long Parliament, in striking contrast, created an army and a navy that were justly the envy of Europe, obliged the mighty Catholic powers of France and Spain to compete for England's favour, successfully challenged the commercial and maritime supremacy of the Protestant Dutch, and reduced Scotland and Ireland to military conquest and political union. Behind these revolutionary events lay a marked change in the function of members of parliament. Before 1640, parliaments had provided their members with only brief respites from the provincial landscape: in the Long Parliament, a number of M.P.s became full-time politicians at a national level, spending most of the year in London, tirelessly attending debates in parliament or sitting on the overworked parliamentary committees appointed to finance and organise the war effort. In the process they acquired political skills, administrative experience, a taste for power and a sense of their own importance which made a lasting impression on English politics. Puritanism might be defeated by the restoration of Charles II in 1660, but parliaments would never be the same again.

It is worth reviewing the achievements of the Long Parliament as a whole in order to understand the attitudes of the men who were turned out of power in April 1653. A majority of the M.P.s who had assembled at Westminster in November 1640, however, were turned out much earlier. Fewer than a fifth of the members sitting at the beginning of the parliament were still sitting at its end. In 1640 M.P.s had been almost united in their condemnation of government policies, but they would have been appalled by the prospect of taking up arms against their king, let alone of executing him. When war did break out in 1642, over two hundred members of the Commons, out of a total of just over five hundred, committed themselves to the king's side and were consequently expelled from parliament. Most of them were eventually replaced through 'recruiter' elections held in their constituencies between 1645 and 1648; but although several of the recruited M.P.s were more amenable to revolutionary persuasion than were the

3

members they joined in the House, only a small minority in parliament was ever prepared to countenance the king's execution.[1] Before Charles could be brought to trial another bout of exclusions was necessary, and this, in the operation known as Pride's Purge, was forcibly accomplished by the Cromwellian army in December 1648, less than two months before the king's death. The remnant of the Commons which was allowed to sit after Pride's Purge, and which remained in power until April 1653, has always suffered an unsavoury reputation. Described in 1649 by the purged M.P. Clement Walker as 'this fag end, this veritable Rump of a parliament with corrupt maggots in it',[2] it became popularly known as the Rump when, for a few chaotic months, it was restored to power in 1659–60. It is with the politics of the Rump from December 1648 to April 1653 that this book is concerned.

Historians used to describe the divisions which beset the Long Parliament during the civil war in terms of a fairly straightforward split between two opposing parties. One, the peace party, was conservative, regretting the outbreak of the war, prosecuting it with minimal vigour, and hoping for a settlement which would restore the king, if not to his former power, then at least to honour and authority. The other, the war party, was radical, wishing to fight the war to a finish, to bring the king to his knees, and to impose on him a settlement of its own making. When, after Charles's defeat in 1646, parliament had to decide what to do with him, the peace and war parties were succeeded, according to this view, by the presbyterian party and the independent party respectively. The presbyterians aimed at the king's honourable restoration and were expelled from parliament at Pride's Purge: the independents connived at Charles's execution and sat in the Rump. With these political attitudes, it was assumed, went corresponding religious ones. The presbyterians, as conservative in religion as in politics, wanted to replace the Anglican hierarchy with a form of church government equally centralised and equally intolerant of dissent: the independents, as radical in religion as in politics, advocated a decentralised church and religious toleration.

The researches of Professor Hexter, and more recently of Dr Pearl

---

[1] E. L. Klotz, 'List of members expelled from the Long Parliament', *Huntington Library Quarterly*, ii (1938–9); D. E. Underdown, 'Party management in the recruiter elections', *E.H.R.*, lxxxiii (1968).
[2] Clement Walker, *Complete History of Independency* (4 vols., 1661), ii. 32. Cf. *ibid.* ii. 115.

and Professor Underdown, have undermined this interpretation of the
parliamentary politics of the 1640s.[1] The 'two-party' view, although
not always as simple as a brief summary necessarily suggests, set up an
essentially static model which left little room for the fluidity of politics
or for the vagaries of politicians confronted with constantly changing
issues. It was inevitable that subsequent historians, undertaking more
microscopic research on the Long Parliament, should find such an
interpretation too superficial. Yet the rejection of the two-party view
involved more than the mere process of refinement always applied by
historians to the work of their most respected forerunners. Professor
Hexter, although confirming the existence in the earlier 1640s of the
war and peace parties, uncovered a third party, the 'middle group',
opposed to the more extreme policies of the other two and propound-
ing a distinctive programme of its own. Equally important was
Hexter's repudiation of his predecessors' use of the term 'party'. The
rigid distinction between war and peace parties, and the implication
that every M.P. belonged to one of them, reflected a view of seventeenth-century parliaments derived from the experience of those of the
later nineteenth and earlier twentieth centuries. The development
during the last hundred years of modern party machinery, with whips
and constituency organisations, has made it difficult for a candidate to
secure election to parliament unless he belongs to one of the main
political parties. This notion of party is very different from that
prevalent in the seventeenth century, when such party organisation as
existed was makeshift and informal. The pattern of electoral patronage
was then set by social rather than by political affiliation, and M.P.s were
elected more often because of who they were than because of what they
thought. Allegiance within parliament, formed by the common response of a group of individuals to a particular issue, was usually
flexible and transient. Instead of two large parties there were several
smaller ones, frequently overlapping and re-forming as different issues
arose. Hexter showed that those who during the civil war belonged to
any of the three parties which he examined formed only a small
minority of the House's total membership. Debates in the House of

[1] J. H. Hexter, *The Reign of King Pym* (Cambridge, Mass., 1941), and 'The problem of the
Presbyterian Independents', published in the *American Historical Review* (1938) and in
Hexter's *Reappraisals in History* (New York, 1963 edn.); V. Pearl, 'Oliver St. John and
the "Middle Group" in the Long Parliament', *E.H.R.*, lxxxi (1966), and 'The "Royal
Independents" in the English Civil War', *Transactions of the Royal Historical Society*,
5th series, xviii (1968); D. E. Underdown, *Pride's Purge. Politics in the Puritan Revolution*
(Oxford, 1971).

Commons were a struggle for the votes of the majority, the back-benchers who owed allegiance to no party. When the House divided on a motion relating to the prosecution of the war, each member had to commit himself to one or other of two opposing sides; but men who voted on opposing sides on a particular motion did not thereby become members of opposing parties.

Yet if we can no longer think of the war and peace parties as parties in the modern sense, it is still possible to see them as polarities, against which the opinions of individual M.P.s can be measured. The king's defeat in 1646, by removing the external threat which had imposed some coherence on parliamentary politics, produced a much more complex situation; and the use of the terms 'presbyterian' and 'independent' has provoked a vigorous debate, conducted in the pages of learned journals, whose convolutions and technicalities must recently have bewildered or wearied the non-specialist reader still more than the argument about who, at the end of the seventeenth century, were respectively the whigs and the tories. Yet no one writing about Rump politics could, or should, avoid reference to the issue, and it is necessary to create some kind of order from the apparent chaos surrounding it.[1]

When the terms presbyterian and independent were first widely used in the 1640s, they had religious connotations. Contemporaries used them to describe opposing views about the church settlement which was to be substituted for the Anglican hierarchy abolished by the Long Parliament. The central issue was state control. Presbyterianism, in its classical or 'high' sense, implied the replacement of the Anglican state church by a puritan one: instead of bishops there would be a rigid Genevan hierarchy, with local churches responsible to and supervised by regional ones, and with regional organisations responsible to and supervised by a national one. Independency, by contrast, properly meant the voluntary association of autonomous local congregations, without necessary reference either to a national church or to each other. If these were the strictly correct meanings of the terms, however, contemporaries frequently used them much more loosely. Sometimes they used them to describe views on church government only approximately similar to the pure presbyterian and independent positions. Sometimes they adapted them to describe views on religious issues which ran parallel to that of church government and which

[1] The bibliography of the controversy was surveyed by S. Foster, 'The Presbyterian Independents exorcised', *Past and Present*, 44 (1969). Foster's own arguments were challenged in the 'Debate' section of the same journal, no. 47 (1970).

usually, but by no means always, divided men along similar lines. Forms of worship were one such issue: another, far more inflammatory, was religious toleration. Those who wanted a strong state church tended also, not surprisingly, to be opposed to toleration, while those who favoured a decentralised church tended to advocate it; and the terms presbyterian and independent were often employed to describe the opponents and the advocates of freedom of worship respectively.

Why were contemporaries so unhelpfully indiscriminate in their use of these labels? We might equally ask why, today, we so indiscriminately label those with whom we disagree as either 'right' or 'left' wing. We often adopt these terms to describe political temperament rather than political belief, or as blanket phrases covering a multitude of persuasions. As such, they often have a general usefulness. So, for a study of the 1640s, do the words presbyterian and independent; but they, too, became terms of abuse, and in consequence were frequently abused. The debate over church government and over the problems relating to it, although often conducted at the level of intricate theological detail, was not a merely academic one. The issue of religious toleration, in particular, raised fundamental religious questions, turning as it did on the rival claims of will and obedience, of conscience and authority, of subjective and objective faith. It brought to the surface men's most deeply held beliefs about the nature of religion. Equally, in a society in which politics and religion were intimately related and in which the church was the prime instrument of social cohesion, it brought to the surface their deepest social and political convictions. Passions are rarely conducive to terminological rigour.

Few of the M.P.s described by contemporaries as presbyterians wanted either presbyterian church government in its strictest form or uncompromising religious intolerance. Still fewer of the M.P.s described by contemporaries as independents wanted a complete end to state supervision of religion or unlimited toleration. The extreme positions were held, on the whole, by groups outside parliament; most M.P.s looked for something between the two. There was a variety of positions which they could adopt, and many people in parliament changed their minds more than once. The two-party model again obscures the gradations of individual opinion. Where, then, did the dividing line between presbyterian and independent M.P.s rest? Different people, naturally enough, had different answers. An M.P. who sought a compromise between the two extreme forms of church government, or who argued for a limited toleration, might be regarded

7

by a devotee of classical presbyterianism as an independent; to an advocate of wholly autonomous congregations he might appear to be a presbyterian. When, today, we are told that a particular politician is either 'reactionary' or 'radical', we obviously need to consider the views not only of the politician concerned but of the person who has applied the label. Similar caution is needed in the face of contemporary usage of the terms presbyterian and independent. They, like the terms war and peace party, are valuable if we regard them as polarities against which the opinions of individual M.P.s can be measured. They are useless, and indeed quite misleading, if we infer from them that the Long Parliament was split down the middle between advocates of two opposed and clearly defined positions.

The heart of the problem of presbyterianism and independency, however, is that it provides us not with one set of polarities but with two. So far we have considered presbyterianism and independency as religious positions. Contemporaries, unhappily for the cause of historical understanding, did not only give the terms religious connotations. They gave them, at least as frequently, political connotations as well. Politicians were often described as presbyterians not because of their religious views but because they wanted to offer generous terms to the king. Others were called independents because they wanted to take a strong line against him. It is not hard to understand the development of such usage. M.P.s who favoured strong state control in religion were often among those most anxious for peace with Charles. M.P.s who wanted less state control were, still more often, among those prepared to impose harsh terms upon him. Often: but not necessarily, and not always; and if we presuppose an automatic correlation between political and religious affiliations we quickly land ourselves in confusion. If we can satisfy ourselves with a particular definition of political independency, for example, we find that a number of those whom we are thus obliged to describe as political independents were much more sympathetic to classical religious presbyterianism than to any of the different forms of religious independency.

Even if we use the terms presbyterian and independent in an exclusively political sense, we find again that the two-party model crumbles on inspection, and that the views of most M.P.s, if they remained constant long enough for us to identify them, lay at various and numerous points between two extremes. This does not mean that parliamentary politics in the later 1640s were so fragmented as to defy

Introduction

understanding, or that no two politicians can helpfully be placed together in a single category. Indeed, as the Long Parliament grew older, many of the groupings within it were fortified by the growing enmity of other groups, so that hostilities between some factions out-lived the issues which had given rise to them. A number of antipathetic factions, however, are not the same thing as two major political parties. Just as, during the civil war, M.P.s had often been obliged to support or to oppose motions calling for a thorough prosecution of military campaigns, so in the later 1640s they had frequently to vote for or against proposals to restore the king to power; but, again as in the war years, both sides in such divisions were *ad hoc* coalitions, strengthened by the support of backbenchers who, if circumstances changed, might vote the other way next time round. There were, of course, many M.P.s who did vote consistently for a single policy, but the cooperation of such men was dependent on the prevalence of particular political circumstances. Once those circumstances ceased to prevail, alliances which had been created by them could quickly collapse. Pride's Purge made this clear. Some of the M.P.s who before the purge had been commonly known as presbyterians went over to the royalist side after December 1648; others withdrew into a sulky retirement from politics; others still sat in the Rump. The independents found themselves equally divided. Dr Pearl and Professor Underdown have shown that what has traditionally been described as the 'independent party' existed in any sense only between 1646 and 1648, and that even then it was the most fragile of coalitions, held together by hatred of the Scots and by a fear that others in parliament, in negotiating with the king, would betray the cause for which the Roundheads had fought.[1] Some members of the alliance, heirs to the 'middle group' of the civil war period, were moderate constitutionalists, 'royal independents' who wanted to restore the king and who opposed Pride's Purge. Others, who had more in common with the war party of earlier years, were prepared, if necessary, to do without Charles altogether.

Nothing, indeed, has so impeded understanding of Rump politics as the assumption that Pride's Purge divided the Long Parliament between presbyterians, who then ceased to sit, and independents, who continued to do so. To equate membership of the Rump with either religious or political independency (let alone with both) is to put blinkers over our eyes. If all members of the Rump had been religious independents,

[1] Pearl, 'The "Royal Independents"'; D. E. Underdown, 'The Independents again', *Journal of British Studies*, viii (1968), 86–8, and *Pride's Purge*, pp. 76–105.

9

the religious policies which the Rump pursued would be distinctly puzzling. They appear less puzzling when we examine the views of the M.P.s who sat after Pride's Purge, views rarely close to the pure independent position and often much closer to the pure presbyterian one. Equally, the politics of the Rump period are incomprehensible if we imagine that all those who sat after Pride's Purge held common political attitudes, whether we call those attitudes 'independent' or not. The split within the Long Parliament brought about by the purge was an artificial, not a natural one; and there is no more striking feature of the Rump Parliament than the variety of opinions held by those who sat in it.

It is always easy for historians, in undertaking the detailed research made possible by the pioneering labours of their predecessors, to show that things were less simple than those predecessors imagined; and there is always the corresponding danger that in showing how complicated things were we may blur clear narrative outlines or belittle both the importance and the drama of political confrontations between men of directly opposing views. The terms presbyterian and independent are frequently necessary and, if discriminately used, often helpful. If adopted by historians, however, they are bound to mean, as they meant to contemporaries, different things at different times. When discussing religion in this book I have explicitly used both terms in their religious senses. In discussing politics, however, I have normally avoided the term independent, which in a study of the Rump would obscure far more than it would illuminate. (The exception to this rule is the use of the term 'royal independent' to describe the heirs to the 'middle group'. The royal independents earn their title as a specific and identifiable group of individuals rather than merely as representatives of a general attitude of mind.) The term presbyterian, in its political sense, appears more frequently, although in general sparingly. It is used to denote that section of opinion which had supported the parliamentary cause in the civil war but which was alienated by, and which steered clear of politics after, Pride's Purge and the execution of the king. This usage is justified by contemporary parlance. The Rump, when formulating its policies, was always profoundly conscious of a body of opinion which had formerly supported the Roundhead cause but which strongly opposed the events which brought the Commonwealth into being; and 'presbyterian' is the best description of that opinion. If, however, this book had been about the people who are described in it as presbyterians, the use of the term presbyterian would have been as inappropriate as would the use of the term independency to describe, in a book about the Rump, the political attitudes of its members; for the term presbyterian can be justified only as a form of shorthand, describing men whom contemporaries, between 1648 and 1653, were able to fit into a single category, and who together presented the Rump with a common problem, but who were no more united in their attitudes than were those who sat in the Rump. The application to politics of the term presbyterian in this book is consistent, but two points relating to it should be borne in mind. First, although political and religious presbyterianism were not necessarily interrelated, there was frequently a very strong connection between the two; and the intimate interdependence of politics and religion often makes it difficult to distinguish between political and religious opposition to the regime. The term presbyterianism is thus often bound to refer to both at once. Secondly, many of those who sat in the Rump, and who are therefore not described in this book as presbyterians, shared a number of attitudes with those who did not sit after December 1648 and who thus are so described. As the Rump period progressed, indeed, the artificiality of the breach within the parliamentary party caused by the purge became increasingly apparent. In religion, too, the events of the Rump period led to an increasing awareness of the areas of agreement, rather than of disagreement, between many men generally known as religious presbyterians and many usually regarded as religious independents.

The Rump began and ended with armed force, and lived constantly under its shadow. The emergence of the parliamentary army in the later 1640s as a radical and almost autonomous political force added a new dimension to the revolution. The army had its own proposals for ending the conflict with Charles, and had no intention of disbanding until its wishes were implemented. Its political pretensions were useful to many M.P.s seeking a counterweight to the parliamentary strength of rivals in the House, for in the turmoil of the later 1640s politicians sought their allies where they could; but those pretensions ran directly counter to the tradition on which the parliamentary case against the king rested. Ingrained in the minds of most members were the principles of constitutional propriety, parliamentary privilege, and the rule of law. If, in the 1640s, M.P.s were willing to sacrifice means to ends and so to bend those principles themselves, they were not prepared to allow others to break them. If anything alarmed most members more than the prospect of a restored absolutist monarchy, it was the threat of arbitrary military rule. M.P.s were representatives of the nation; the army, in their view, was the servant of parliament, employed to win battles, not to propound its own notions of political reform. Pride's Purge, although removing from the Commons the army's most vigorous opponents, served nevertheless to increase ill-feeling between parliament and its forces. The brazen use of force to truncate the Commons shocked even M.P.s who were allowed to remain in the House and who viewed the execution of the king with relative equanimity. The central conflict of the 1640s was between crown and parliament: the central conflict of the 1650s was between parliament and army; and the outrage provoked by the Rump's dissolution in April 1653 overshadowed the remaining course of Interregnum politics.

The enmity between parliament and army reflected a profound difference of political perspective between them. To parliament, the revolution was about political and religious issues: to the army, it was also about social ones. The civil war had been a split within the governing classes represented in parliament. Both sides had been obliged to employ men from outside the governing classes to fight their battles for them, but neither had questioned the divine right of those classes to govern or had imagined that the war had anything to do with the remedy of social inequalities. The demand for social reform advanced by the parliamentary army, and especially by Cromwell's increasingly prominent New Model forces, transformed the nature of the revolution. The troops, grievously underpaid, exhorted by their officers and their chaplains to regard themselves as God's chosen instruments of victory, provided fertile ground for the dissemination of social radicalism. The pace-setters of the reform movement were the Levellers, who in 1647 infiltrated the army rank-and-file just as earlier they had infiltrated the Baptist congregations of London. Despite the panic-stricken assertions of their enemies, John Lilburne and his fellow Leveller leaders (unlike some of their supporters) advocated neither anarchy nor an assault on the established social hierarchy. They simply opposed what they regarded as the man-made, artificial inequalities – political, legal and economic – which separated the rich from the poor. Yet the vocabulary and the political theory with which they so forcefully supported their demands, and their ability to articulate and to channel the grievances of men hitherto accustomed to speak to their superiors only when spoken to, produced mounting alarm in parliament. The civil war had seemed to most M.P.s an appalling, in-comprehensible breach with the natural order of things, perhaps a prelude to social dissolution. They had seen order collapse, an experi-ence not easily understood by those who have not lived through similar circumstances. The growth of Leveller organisation and doctrine seemed to confirm parliament's fears. Debates in the Commons about peace terms with the king took on social implications. John Maynard, one of the M.P.s most anxious to restore Charles, spoke for most of his colleagues when he attacked republican notions in January 1648: 'if the argument (some have gone upon) hold, that there was another government before that of kings, etc., so husbandmen was before gentlemen, and they before lords, etc., and so we must come to the Levellers' doctrine'.[1]

Lilburne and his friends chose their issues well. The demands which they most frequently advanced were for a reform of the legal system, to make its workings less inequitable and less baffling to poorer clients; for a widening of the social base of the electorate and for stronger ties between parliaments and their electors; for an end to the monopolies held by wealthy trading companies; for the redress of various agrarian grievances; for extensive religious toleration; and for the abolition of tithes, the financial pillar of the established church ministry. Of all the Leveller demands, none seemed more alarming than those for religious change. In the 1640s, in religion as in politics, the abandonment by the ruling classes of traditional forms of government appeared to have opened the way to anarchy. 'No bishop, no king', James I had said, with European example to support him. In the 1640s, when James was proved right, it seemed that no bishop might also mean no gentry. The Long Parliament's attack on the Anglican hierarchy was followed by the emergence of numerous religious sects, each of them professing notions more extreme than the last, and many of them committed to social and political as well as to religious radicalism. The call for the abolition of tithes was interpreted as a threat to property, order and godliness. The fears aroused by the demand for religious toleration were well exploited, but not much exaggerated, by the clergyman Thomas Edwards in 1646: 'Oh! let the ministers . . . oppose toleration . . . possess the magistrates of the evil of it, yea and the people too, showing them how if a toleration were granted, they should never have peace in their families more, or ever after have command of

---

[1] D. E. Underdown (ed.), 'The Parliamentary Diary of John Boys', *Bulletin of the Institute of Historical Research*, xxxix (1966), 156.

wives, children, servants!'[1] In the later 1640s and in the earlier 1650s, social revolution frequently seemed imminent. The threat may have been largely illusory, but it was not for that reason any the less alarming.

The army's enemies sometimes claimed that the radicals who spoke in its name were unrepresentative of rank-and-file opinion.[2] Certainly Cromwell was able to suppress with singular ease, as well as with characteristic ruthlessness, Leveller attempts to subvert army discipline. As the events of December 1648 and January 1649 were to show, there were limits to the hold exerted on the troops by Leveller doctrine. The army officers were nevertheless occasionally obliged, for the sake of army unity, to give at least tacit support to the Leveller programme. Besides, they often sympathised with it. Cromwell and his son-in-law Henry Ireton, the two most influential army politicians, although keenly sensitive to any threat to the social hierarchy and much more cautious than the Levellers in advancing reform proposals, shared their concern to remedy social abuses. There were times, indeed, when the two men seemed more interested in social amelioration than in political settlement. In 1647 they even offered the king, in return for guarantees of social reform, terms more generous than those proposed by parliament.[3] The reform movement was not monopolised by extremists. Radical arguments frequently filter through the innate conservatism of more moderate politicians. When they have done so, however, continued radical agitation tends to reduce rather than enhance the reformers' prospects of success. In the Rump period the clamour of sects and soldiers outside the House weakened the position, and diminished the enthusiasm, of those who wished to achieve moderate reform within it. Only after the fall of Barebone's Parliament in December 1653 did a programme of piecemeal change, effected from within, have much hope of success.

The threat of social revolution was but one of the developments which made the 1640s so wretched a decade for the overwhelming majority of Englishmen of all classes. The war set neighbour against neighbour, brother against brother, father against son. Trade was dislocated; judicial proceedings were interrupted; social upstarts seized power on

---

[1] In Edwards's *Gangraena* (1646): quoted by H. N. Brailsford, *The Levellers and the English Revolution* (ed. C. Hill, 1961), p. 42.

[2] See e.g. *The Substance of a Speech made by Wil. Prynne* (1649), p. 58; M. Sylvester (ed.), *Reliquiae Baxterianae: or, Mr. Richard Baxter's Narrative of . . . his Life and Times* (1696,) pp. 50–1, 53, 56.

[3] Gardiner, *Constitutional Documents*, pp. 316–26 ('Heads of the Proposals').

the hated county committees appointed by parliament to control the localities; and free quarter and high taxation were among the manifold inconveniences of military occupation.[1] Parliament, rebelling against arbitrary government, had assumed powers far more arbitrary and far more extensive than those of Charles I. By 1648, most Englishmen seem to have longed for peace and stability at almost any price. The first civil war had been a revolt of the provinces against the Stuart court: the second civil war, in the summer of 1648, was a revolt of the peace-seeking provinces against the parliament.[2]

The events of 1648 hardened the divisions on the parliamentary side, until there seemed no middle course between restoring the king with honour and bringing him to judicial account. M.P.s who had advocated moderation now found themselves obliged to choose between the hawks and the doves. A majority chose the doves; and in the autumn of 1648, despite the army's efficient suppression of the rebellion, parliament reopened negotiations with the king at Newport in the Isle of Wight. In the army, by contrast, the feeling in favour of bringing the king and his leading adherents to justice, of cleansing the land of the blood which had been shed in it, was intensified by the second civil war. When, at the beginning of December, the parliamentary commissioners returned from Newport to inform the Commons of the outcome of the negotiations, the army marched on London and occupied Whitehall. On the morning of 5 December the House, defying military threats, voted by 129 votes to 83 in favour of further negotiations with the king. Next morning, members coming to the House found their way blocked by a troop of soldiers under the command of Colonel Pride. About forty of them were arrested. The remainder were allowed to enter; but in the days which followed about sixty or seventy more M.P.s were forcibly prevented from doing so, most of them being turned away on the 7th, a few as late as the 14th. The Rump of the Commons which survived the purge offered little resistance to the army's determination to try the king. On 4 January the House passed an ordinance setting up the High Court of Justice, which began its sessions four days later. On 27 January Charles, charged with 'a wicked design to erect and uphold in himself an unlimited and tyrannical power to rule according to his will, and to overthrow the

---

[1] On those inconveniences see J. S. Morrill, 'Mutiny and discontent in English provincial armies 1645–1647', *Past and Present*, 56 (1972).

[2] This point is well brought out in A. M. Everitt, *The Community of Kent and the Great Rebellion 1640–60* (Leicester, 1966).

rights and liberties of the people', was found guilty of high treason. Three days later he went to the scaffold.[1]

The narrative outline of British history from 1648 to 1653 was established eighty years ago in S. R. Gardiner's *History of the Commonwealth and Protectorate*. Anyone who studies the period quickly learns to appreciate the magnificent depth and breadth of Gardiner's scholarship, and there are times when it is possible to do no more than modify or elaborate upon his account. He paid relatively slight attention, however, to the parliamentary politics of the Rump, which provide the more limited theme of this book; and subsequent historians, although devoting thorough and fruitful research to the earlier years of the Long Parliament, have also shied away from the subject. We know much more than Gardiner did about the backgrounds and beliefs of the M.P.s who came to sit in the Rump,[2] but little more about what they did when they got there. If there has been no substantial study of Rump politics, however, there have been two brief accounts to whet the appetite. Professor Trevor-Roper, in an essay concerned mainly with later Interregnum parliaments, has illuminated the Rump period in passing, and there is an astute chapter on the Rump in Professor Underdown's recent book, *Pride's Purge*.[3]

The relative neglect of Rump politics has as its main cause the shortcomings of the available evidence. There are apparently no extant parliamentary diaries for the Rump period, and the information supplied by letters and memoirs, although not negligible, is nevertheless scanty. In consequence there are severe limits to what can be learnt about the Rump; but even if we cannot learn as much as we would like, it is still worth trying to learn as much as we can. Careful study of the institutional evidence, and especially of the *Journal of the House of Commons*, suggests techniques of investigation which often prove surprisingly revealing. Equally rewarding is a study of the pamphlets, and particularly of the weekly newspapers, of the period. The reader who

[1] *C.J.* 5 Dec. 1648, 4 Jan. 1649; Gardiner, *Constitutional Documents*, p. 372. The events leading up to the execution are best described in Underdown, *Pride's Purge*, pp. 143–200, and in C. V. Wedgwood, *The Trial of Charles I* (1964). There is little to add to Professor Underdown's lucid narrative of parliamentary developments during these weeks.

[2] D. Brunton and D. H. Pennington, *Members of the Long Parliament* (1968 edn.), pp. 38–52; M. F. Keeler, *The Long Parliament 1640–1641* (Philadelphia, 1954); G. Yule, *The Independents in the English Civil War* (Cambridge, 1958); Underdown, *Pride's Purge*, esp. pp. 208–56, 361–98.

[3] H. R. Trevor-Roper, *Religion, The Reformation and Social Change* (1967), pp. 357–61; Underdown, *Pride's Purge*, pp. 258–96.

comes to this book for specialist purposes, who proposes to delve among the footnotes, or who is merely interested in or sceptical of the ways in which historians deduce information from the material available to them, may wish to consult the 'note on sources' at the end of the book.

If the sources relating to the Rump period are restricted in kind, they are certainly not wanting in volume. Much more could be learnt about the Rump than I have been able to discover in a study of this scope or to convey in a book of this size. It is primarily a book about politics rather than about government. I have selected for detailed study those of the Rump's policies, in the fields of social and religious reform, which seem to me best to illustrate its politics; but such selection inevitably leaves large gaps. Historians of politics are nowadays often told that their preoccupations are outdated, isolated from broader and (although it is not clear to what) more 'relevant' historical concerns. Yet the study of politics, which are both a reflection and a determinant of men's thoughts, beliefs, economic activities and social attitudes, can tell us as much about a past age as can research into its other aspects. Historians who study politics and historians who study other things are engaged in a common enterprise. The problem of the political historian is not that he is working in a vacuum, but, on the contrary, that in seeking to understand political events he is seeking to understand the society which gave rise to them: he needs to know not about too little but about too much. What I have tried to do in this book is to clear a path through a forest hitherto largely unexplored; but I am very conscious that there are subjects which I have had to ignore and others in which, to use a different metaphor, I have kept to safe but shallow waters rather than plunge out of my depth. I have also omitted from discussion the period of the Rump's brief restoration to power in 1659–60. The years between the dissolution of the Long Parliament in 1653 and Cromwell's death in 1658 profoundly altered the political perspectives of many members of the Rump, and the politics of the period between Cromwell's death and the return of Charles II were extraordinarily complicated. To include an account of the restored Rump as an *addendum*, as the mere rump, of a study of the earlier Rump period, would be unsatisfactory and misleading.

In another way, too, this is perhaps an old-fashioned book. Much of it is cast in narrative form. It is impossible to know why things happened until we know how they happened, and without a narrative backbone no sensible study of Rump politics can be undertaken. Narrative may also forestall the strongest temptation created by the limitations of the evidence. The course of Rump politics, as of all politics, was shaped largely by the daily, complex interaction of personalities. The available sources only rarely allow more than a glimpse of such interaction, and it is usually possible to relate political developments only in terms of weeks and months rather than of days. This would be no excuse for writing as if the interaction of personalities did not occur, or for imposing on the period simplified patterns which ignore development through time. Analysis without narrative would be as distorting as narrative without analysis would be uninteresting.

The narrative of the Rump period divides naturally in two. First, there is the period beginning with Pride's Purge and Charles I's execution and ending with the battle of Worcester in September 1651. During this time the Commonwealth was severely threatened by the survival of royalist ambitions, expressed partly in attempted conspiracy in England but more alarmingly in plans for an invasion, led by Charles II, from Ireland or Scotland. The Rump consequently found itself engaged in prolonged military campaigns in both countries. The struggle for survival, involving the financing and organising of a huge army and navy, reduced all other issues to secondary importance. Although there were sometimes bitter conflicts, this was a period of relative homogeneity within the government, to be explained partly by external pressures towards unity, partly by the preoccupation of army officers with military campaigns, and partly by the cooperation of a small but powerful group of 'grandees' in the Rump. These men, whose success owed much to the acquiescence of radicals both inside and outside the Commons, sought to play down the Rump's revolutionary origins, to repudiate the policies of its most radical supporters, and to emphasise the moderation and respectability of the new regime. Calling for an extended period of domestic tranquillity, they aimed to woo, or at least to appease, that 'presbyterian' opinion which had been alienated by the purge and the king's execution, and thus to dissuade presbyterians from going over to the royalists. This programme, improvised rather than preconceived, served adequately until the final defeat of Charles II's forces in September 1651. The second part of the Rump's history, from Worcester to the dissolution, presents a quite different story. With the return to active politics of the leading army officers, differences of temperament and disagreement about the nature of the correct political settlement exposed the Commonwealth as an uncomfortable alliance of diverse interests. Conflict between parliament and army came to overshadow all political developments. Failing to act with sufficient speed either to abdicate or to inaugurate a righteous reformation, and devoting much of its time and energy to the costly naval war against the Dutch, the Rump became the target of increasingly aggressive radical criticism until its forcible expulsion in April 1653.

The architect of the Rump regime was Oliver Cromwell. His complex political temperament, and in particular the paradox of his desire for both constitutional propriety and godly reformation, had a decisive influence on Rump politics. Even when, at a late stage, he agreed to the trial and execution of the king, he ensured that the settlement which followed would be as respectable as possible, and that power would remain in the hands of unrevolutionary men. Enthusiasm for godly reformation was not the criterion he adopted when he sought to determine the character and composition of the Rump government. When he later demanded such reformation of the Rump, it not surprisingly declined to grant it.

PART ONE

THE RUMP AND THE RUMPERS

I

MEMBERSHIP, ATTENDANCE AND ALLEGIANCE

Pride's Purge deprived the House of Commons of well over half its membership. Although only about 110 M.P.s seem to have been forcibly prevented by the army from entering the House, these were a minority of the members whose active participation in the Long Parliament came to an end in December 1648. Many withdrew at the purge of their own initiative, either out of distaste for the army's proceedings or because they suspected that attempted entry would be fruitless or dangerous. Others, whether because of disillusionment or old age, had long since ceased to take their seats with any regularity, and were merely confirmed in their abstinence by the purge. Of the 470 or so M.P.s qualified to sit at the beginning of December 1648, the purge permanently removed about 270. Temporarily it removed nearly 100 more, who stayed away from parliament in the weeks between the purge and the king's execution and who returned to join the Rump only in or after February 1649. It is impossible to determine exactly how many members sat in parliament during the Rump period, but the number is unlikely to have been significantly smaller or larger than 211. Of these members, nine – unlike their colleagues – were elected to parliament only after the purge, as a result of by-elections held on the deaths of certain of the excluded members. The nineteen members of the Rump who died between December 1648 and April 1653 were not similarly replaced.[1]

On 5 December 1648, the day on which the Commons voted in favour of further negotiations with the king, three M.P.s and three army officers met to draw up a list of the members who were to be excluded from the House. Edmund Ludlow, one of the three M.P.s, recalled later that those present at the meeting 'went over the names of the members one by one, giving the truest character we could of their inclinations, wherein I presume we were not mistaken in many'.

---

[1] For this paragraph, see Appendix A. On the membership of the Long Parliament before December 1648 see Underdown, *Pride's Purge*, pp. 361–98.

Clearly, however, they were mistaken in some: as a supporter of the purge admitted, the army 'kept out some good and kept in some bad members'.[1] At least four of the M.P.s forcibly 'secluded' (John Ashe, John Barker, Samuel Gardiner and Sir John Hippisley) were subsequently admitted to the Rump, while some of those who by contrast escaped Pride's clutches were at least as hostile to the army's cause as were the bulk of those refused admission. William Pierrepoint, one of the most influential politicians of the Long Parliament and a firm opponent of the purge, survived the coup but voluntarily led his followers away from the House almost immediately after it. Thereafter he vigorously denounced the members who retained their seats, but he was unable to dissuade William Ashhurst, another of the army's more outspoken opponents who had survived the purge, from entering the Commons on 19 December.[2]

On 20 December, however, the House at last took steps to define and to restrict its membership. From that date all M.P.s who wished to retain their seats were expected to declare that they had dissented, or that had they been present they would have dissented, from the vote passed on 5 December in favour of further negotiations with Charles. This was not, in itself, a particularly stiff test. To register dissent was not necessarily to imply support for the subsequent moves to bring the king to justice, or even, it could be argued, for the purge itself; and in any case a number of members contrived to remain in the House without dissenting at least for some weeks.[3] Everyone, nevertheless, knew who the chief advocates of the motion of 5 December had been, and no one who had then voted for further negotiations could honourably have taken the test. The decision of 20 December removed from the House those of the army's most voluble opponents who, like Ashhurst, still retained their seats. The tactic of dignified voluntary withdrawal adopted by men like Pierrepoint and Ashhurst was, of course, not available to the M.P.s who had been forcibly secluded, some of whom loudly demanded readmission even after the imposition of the test. One of them contrived briefly to take his seat on the day before Charles's

---

[1] C. H. Firth (ed.), *Memoirs of Edmund Ludlow* (2 vols., 1894), i. 209–10; N.L.W., MS 11,434B, fo. 3.

[2] *Mercurius Elencticus* 5–12 Dec. 1648, p. 33; W. Prynne, *A Full Declaration of the true State of the Secluded Members Case* (1660), p. 18; W. Ashhurst, *Reasons against Agreement with . . . The Agreement of The People* (1648); Underdown, *Pride's Purge*, pp. 160, 175, 216n., 218.

[3] For the test of dissent, and for the dissenters, see Underdown, *Pride's Purge*, pp. 160, 165–6, 213–16.

execution, and a few more managed occasionally to take their places at some of the Rump's standing committees in the weeks thereafter.[1] These, however, were the last flickerings of a lost cause. Many M.P.s remaining in the Commons after 20 December were unsympathetic to the moves against the king, but none, at least at this stage, was prepared to oppose them openly. In this book I use the inelegant but inescapable term 'rumper' to describe anyone recorded as sitting in the House of Commons between 20 December 1648 and the parliament's dissolution on 20 April 1653.

The immediate success of the test of dissent was reflected in the army's decision early in January to leave future discussion of the House's membership to the House itself. A change in procedure on 1 February, two days after Charles's death, made it much easier for M.P.s to register dissent and tacitly allowed those who had voted in favour of the motion of 5 December to change their minds and to resume active membership. It seems to have been believed, probably with some justice,[2] that members who dissented after rather than before the king's execution would not, in the event of a royalist counter-revolution, be regarded as accomplices to the act of regicide; and the test's political significance was now seriously reduced by the willingness of so many members to subscribe to it. At least sixty-six M.P.s, and perhaps as many as seventy-five,[3] took the test in the first three weeks of February, including a number who had sat without dissenting between the purge and the execution. Thereafter the restrictions on the Rump's membership were again tightened. Only about fifty members were readmitted at any point after 22 February 1649, all but seven of them by early August of the same year.

Pride's Purge has always been rightly regarded as a decisive turning-point in the revolution. From this there is, however, no need to infer – as historians have frequently done – that those M.P.s who continued to sit after the purge were different kinds of people from those who did not. The Rump did not usually think of itself as a corporate political entity distinct in membership, aims and character from the Long Parliament of the 1640s. Indeed, it continued to describe men denied admission after the purge as 'members of parliament', a sophism

---

[1] *Ibid.* p. 158; below, pp. 61, 179.
[2] G. F. Warner (ed.), *The Nicholas Papers* (4 vols., 1886–1920), i. 139.
[3] There are problems of identification: see Underdown, *Pride's Purge*, p. 214n. In cases where there can be no certainty, I have usually (but not invariably) followed Underdown.

indicative of the hope entertained by many rumpers that their excluded colleagues would be readmitted. The purge destroyed many political alliances among M.P.s, but few private friendships. The distinction between rumpers and non-rumpers was the product of specific and complex historical circumstances, not of any natural cleavage among the members of the Long Parliament. There were a number of different reasons for wanting to sit in the Rump. Some M.P.s did so because they supported the events of December 1648 and January 1649, or even because they hoped that those events would prove merely the prelude to even more revolutionary changes. Others, however, had distinctly unrevolutionary reasons for sitting: principally a desire to moderate the course of events by influencing them from within, a wish to pre-serve power in civilian rather than military hands, a sense of obligation to constituents, a relish for political activity, or the hope of financial advantage. The Rump was an uneasy coalition of interests whose members shared little beyond a willingness to sit in it. Despite its assumption of executive powers, the parliament was not in practice the same thing as the government. The House soon divided between frontbenchers and backbenchers, between court and country, between professional politicians and M.P.s who paid only occasional visits to Westminster. The terms in which even members relatively active in the House sometimes resisted government actions conflicting with their own views or interests suggest that not everyone equated membership of the Rump with involvement in, or responsibility for, the functioning of the executive;[1] and the members who regarded activity at West-minster as their main concern were always in a minority.

The parliamentary energies of the rumpers, indeed, varied consider-ably. Attendance at the House, the Council of State or parliamentary committees was an almost full-time occupation for about thirty members, and the major occupation for thirty or forty more. These sixty or seventy men, forming about a third or the Rump's total membership, were at any one point more likely than not to be actively engaged in parliamentary politics. The remaining members of the Rump were essentially part-timers. Thirty or more of them did attend often enough to play a significant part in the House's deliberations, but the other hundred or so, comprising about half the Rump's member-ship, made only brief and sporadic appearances at Westminster, some attending for perhaps two or three brief spells every year, others

[1] See e.g. *C.C.A.M.*, pp. 257, 338, 530–1, 589, 621, 643; *C.C.C.*, p. 2084; Folger Library, Add. MS 494, p. 1656; R. N. Worth (ed.), *The Buller Papers* (Plymouth, 1895), p. 112.

making no more than one or two recorded appearances in the House throughout the Rump period. Among the less active members were some, it is true, who held weighty administrative responsibilities in the provinces, the most notable examples being Thomas Mackworth, governor of Shrewsbury, Sir William Constable, regicide governor of Gloucester, Thomas Birch, regicide governor of Liverpool, and John Pyne, whose self-appointed role as the Rump's *intendant* in Somerset brought him into prolonged and acrimonious conflict with the central government.[1] Many other rumpers who rarely appeared in parliament were also useful to the regime in their localities, if usually to a more modest extent. In the main, however, the M.P.s who made only rare appearances at Westminster during the Rump period seem otherwise to have lived quietly at home.

The Rump was beset from the start by division; and it would be convenient if we could discern among its members distinctive and tightly knit factions, warring in the House for supremacy. The truth is much more complex. Factions certainly existed in the Rump, as they exist in all political assemblies, but they were flexible, often ephemeral, and rarely mutually exclusive. Men who came together over particular issues found themselves divided over others, just as particular events could temporarily unite hardened enemies. On numerous occasions M.P.s who had acted as tellers on the same side in one debate found themselves tellers for opposing sides in another. There were nevertheless more enduring ties – based on kinship, friendship, patronage, regional association or common interest – whose importance should not be underestimated. Yet it is much easier to overestimate their significance. Many members of the Long Parliament had owed their election to the influence of patrons or relatives; but the parliamentary experience of the 1640s, providing M.P.s with ample opportunities to earn independent political prominence and to form new friendships and alliances, was bound to reduce the importance of electoral connections, just as the major crises of the parliament were certain on occasion to break them.

The massive electoral network controlled by Philip Herbert, fourth Earl of Pembroke, was a case in point. The earl himself, elected as a commoner in April 1649, sat in the Rump. So did his eldest son, his relation Henry Herbert, his secretary Michael Oldsworth, and another client William Stephens. Another of his sons, by contrast, had been

---

[1] Underdown, *Pride's Purge*, pp. 301–2, 313; *C.C.C.*, as indexed under Pyne.

27

expelled from parliament as a royalist, and two more ceased to sit at the purge. Sir Benjamin Rudyerd and Sir Robert Pye, both clients of the earl, were among the members imprisoned by Pride. By the time of the purge, Pembroke was among the least respected members of his political empire. The Rump was glad to secure his allegiance, but many of those who had owed their election to him had by that time gone their own way. Similarly Thomas Fairfax, Lord General of the army until 1650, opposed the king's execution and kept clear of the Rump. Seven of his relations had been elected to the Long Parliament through the influence of his father; all of them sat in the Rump, and three of them signed Charles's death warrant.[1] Brothers, too, were divided by the purge, like the Nelthorpes of Yorkshire and the Hays of Sussex. So many M.P.s were related to or electorally connected with so many others that political groupings inevitably cut across such loyalties. Ties formed outside parliament achieved political significance only when they brought and kept together men who influenced each other's judgements or who found that they shared certain convictions. When there was no such agreement extra-parliamentary allegiances counted for nothing. The most important of the groupings to emerge in Rump politics owed little to electoral or family relationships and much more to friendships formed either in the later 1640s or after the inauguration of the Commonwealth.

Allegiances originating outside parliament did, nevertheless, play a large part in the daily political round of many M.P.s, and could occasionally be galvanised for effective political action. As Clement Walker acidly observed, 'it were endless to name the father and the son, brother and brother that fills this house; they come in couples more than unclean beasts to the ark'.[2] Walker was writing before Pride's Purge, but the Rump had its share of close family relations often engaged in political cooperation, like the two Vanes,[3] the two Stricklands, the two Darleys and the three Ashes. Still more consistent, and more influential in Rump politics, was the support given to Sir Arthur Heselrige by his cousin George Fenwick,[4] to Thomas Chaloner by his brother

[1] Cf. Underdown, *Pride's Purge*, p. 48.
[2] Walker, *History of Independency*, i. 173.
[3] 'Vane', in this book, refers to Vane the younger.
[4] On the use of the available evidence to detect parliamentary allegiances, see below, pp. 400–01. For Heselrige and Fenwick see *C.J.* 15, 17 Feb., 12, 19 Mar., 6 Apr., 2, 22 Nov. 1649, 5 May 1650; SP: 23/5, fos. 71, 75, 83, 86; 23/6, p. 3; 23/7, pp. 11, 28; 23/9, fos. 6, 8, 11ᵛ, 13, 14ᵛ, 24ᵛ, 25&ᵛ; 28/77, fo. 870; *C.C.C.*, pp. 170, 329, 1180, 2253; *Several Proceedings in Parliament* 18–25 Sep. 1651, p. 387; *Mercurius Politicus* 19–26 Aug. 1652, p.

James,[1] and to Cornelius Holland by his son-in-law Henry Smyth.[2] Members from a particular county frequently joined forces in the Rump over national as well as over purely local issues. John Nutt, for example, slavishly followed the lead of his Kentish colleague Augustine Garland,[3] just as Sir Thomas Mauleverer was firmly in the tow of another Yorkshire M.P., Sir William Allanson;[4] and both Kent and Yorkshire were represented in the Rump by men who had often worked together in the House. The same was true of Buckinghamshire, Westmorland, Somerset, Dorset and Sussex.[5] Among the Dorset rumpers there were, in particular, two old and firm allies, John Bingham and William Sydenham, and two cousins long accustomed to joint political action, John Trenchard, father-in-law to both Bingham and Sydenham, and John Browne.[6] Yet allegiances between members from particular counties rested on little more than habit and loyalty. They sometimes fostered agreement on political issues, but they did not always do so. Although they could often be mobilised in debate, they rarely constituted pressure groups taking the initiative in the House. There was, however, one important exception to this rule. Herbert Morley, M.P. for Lewes and one of the ablest parliamentary managers of the Rump period, controlled a network of members from Sussex and the Cinque Ports. His brother-in-law John Fagge, like William Hay, was simply his creature in parliament, while John Baker, Roger Gratwick, Sir Henry Heyman and Anthony Stapley could usually be expected to rally to his support.[7]

1293; *Complete Writings of Roger Williams* (7 vols., New York, 1964), vi (ed. J. R. Bartlett), 255; Roger Howell jr., *Newcastle-upon-Tyne and the Puritan Revolution* (Oxford, 1967), p. 188 and n.; Underdown, *Pride's Purge*, p. 49.

[1] *C.J.* 2, 6 Jan., 6, 20 Apr., 25 May, 6 June, 13 July, 15, 16, 22 Aug. 1649, 22 July, 26 Dec. 1651, 11 June 1652; B.M., Add. MS 36,792, fo. 13; *Mercurius Pragmaticus* 12–19 Dec. 1648, p. 8.

[2] *C.J.* 15 Dec. 1648, 3 Jan., 7 Sep., 22 Nov. 1649, 7, 11 Feb. 1651; SP 23/6, p. 181; Underdown, *Pride's Purge*, pp. 52, 130.

[3] *C.J.* 24 May 1650, 14, 24 Jan. 1651, 13 Aug. 1652. (Nutt made only four other recorded appearances in the Rump.)

[4] *Ibid.* 25 Nov. 1648, 5 Feb., 28 Nov. 1649, 27 Dec. 1650, 31 Dec. 1651, 21 Jan. 1652. (These were Mauleverer's only recorded appearances in the Rump.)

[5] Cf. Underdown, *Pride's Purge*, pp. 32–4, 93, 308.

[6] C. H. Mayo (ed.), *Minute Book of the Dorset Standing Committee* (Exeter, 1902), pp. 488, 493, 570; W. D. Christie, *A Life of Anthony Ashley Cooper, First Earl of Shaftesbury* (2 vols., 1871), vol. i, Appendix i, at pp. ii, li; *C.C.C.*, pp. 144, 1135, 1166, 1168, 2304; Underdown, *Pride's Purge*, pp. 33, 313; Brunton and Pennington, *Members of the Long Parliament*, pp. 160–1.

[7] *C.J.* (MS) xxxiii, pp. 645, 648; *C.J.* 1 Mar. 1648, 3, 6 Jan., 12 Apr., 8 May, 14, 20, 21 July, 7, 9 Nov. 1649, 9, 18 Feb., 14 Mar., 8, 28, 31 May, 20 Dec. 1650, 10 Jan., 13 Feb., 10

The limitation of Morley's organisation was that, in common with the other allegiances which have been mentioned, it could only serve to link relatively inactive members of the Rump with more active ones. It was the least energetic rumpers who, when they appeared at Westminster, tended to turn most readily to the guidance of more prominent members. The more frequently an M.P. attended parliament, the less likely was he to be inhibited by extra-parliamentary loyalties or to content himself with the role of parliamentary satellite. In this respect local and family allegiances differed from two impressive groupings in the Rump, both based on common interest and both including a number of M.P.s in regular attendance at Westminster. The first consisted of the House's professional lawyers, who acted in a close cooperation strengthened by their common opposition to proposals for reform of the legal system and by the extensive responsibility given them by parliament for drafting legislation and supervising committees. Bulstrode Whitelocke and Sir Thomas Widdrington were the best known pair of lawyer allies, but Nicholas Lechmere of Worcestershire and Lislibone Long of Somerset must have formed, in the ears of advocates of law reform, an equally sinister alliterative duo. Long was also remarkably close to two other west-country lawyer members, Roger Hill and the Commonwealth's attorney-general Edmund Prideaux. Augustine Garland, William Say, John Corbet and the Commonwealth's solicitor-general Robert Reynolds were other energetic rumpers who can often be seen working with their fellow lawyers in the House.[1]

The second organised interest group consisted of M.P.s with special interests in commercial matters or in the politics of the city of London. Three pairs of allies were especially impressive in their cooperation: John Venn, who had organised radical puritan agitation in London in

Apr., 3 Dec. 1651, 13 May, 15 July, 27 Aug., 15 Sep. 1652, 14 Apr. 1653; SP: 18/5, 18/12, 18/17, 18/30, *passim*; 24/8, fo. 10; 24/10, fo. 9; 28/61, fo. 861; 28/76, p. 461; 28/81, fos. 447, 866ff.; 28/91, fo. 231; 22/F2, *passim*; Clarendon MS 34, fo. 94; Bodleian MS 328, pp. 13, 14, 136, 377, 417, 426, and MS 329, pp. 447, 547; J. T. Rutt (ed.), *Diary of Thomas Burton* (4 vols., 1828), ii. 202–3; C. Thomas-Stanford, *Sussex in the Great Civil War and the Interregnum* (1910), pp. 219, 288; Underdown, 'Party management in the recruiter elections', p. 240, and *Pride's Purge*, pp. 34–5, 49.

[1] For the lawyers' cohesion, see *C.J.* 1649: 3, 6, 10, 30, 31 Jan., 1, 2, 7, 8, 9, 16, 22 Feb., 9 Mar., 3, 6, 12, 13, 14, 20 Apr., 9, 18, 25, 28, 29 May, 19, 22 June, 5, 6, July, 2, 7, 8 Nov., 11, 21 Dec.; 1650: 4, 17, 29 Jan., 2, 8 Feb., 15 Apr., 14, 23, 28, 31 May, 7, 18, 21, 22, 27 June, 30 July, 9, 24, 25 Oct., 15 Nov., 20, 26, 27 Dec.; 1651: 10, 28 Jan., 8, 18, 25 Apr., 13 June, 1 July, 5, 7 Aug., 9, 25 Sep., 19 Nov., 3, 9, 23, 26 Dec.; 1652: 1, 21, 22 Jan., 3 Feb., 20 May, 3, 11 June, 15 July, 6, 12 Oct., 29, 31 Dec.; 1653: 6, 8 Jan., 2 Feb., 1 Mar. See also Whitelocke, *Memorials*, i. 283, 288, iii. 31.

the 1640s, and his fellow regicide Miles Corbet;[1] Isaac Pennington, M.P. for London and one of the most influential politicians in the city, and Thomas Atkins, a Norfolk cloth merchant who had been a London alderman since 1638;[2] and, most strikingly of all, Francis Allen and Richard Salwey, who combined political and commercial interests in the city with considerable financial expertise, and whose alliance was as intimate and consistent as that of any two rumpers.[3] In each of these three cases there is a remarkable similarity between the two men concerned of political energy, interest and attitude. All six M.P.s frequently cooperated with each other and also with members of similar experience and interests like Rowland Wilson, George Snelling, George Thomson, William Leman, John Dove, Edmund Harvey (who was especially close to Venn)[4] and John Ashe. Also notable for their cooperation, if slightly less active in the Rump, were three west-country merchants with London connections, Thomas Boone, Gregory Clement and Nicholas Gould, all of whom worked also with the Cornish member John Moyle.[5] Boone was, too, a loyal ally of Thomas Chaloner,[6] an M.P. keenly interested in trade who was largely responsible for coordinating members with mercantile concerns. John Ashe

[1] *C.J.* 15, 29 Dec. 1648; 2, 6 Jan., 4 Oct., 22 Nov. 1649, 14 Mar. 1650 (Venn died in late June or early July 1650); SP 18/5, fos. 36, 48, 60, 62, 76; Rawlinson MS A224, fo. 92; and see *Persecutio Undecima* (1648), pp. 33–5.

[2] *C.J.* 23, 28 Dec. 1648, 10 Feb., 9 Apr., 28 May, 28 June, 18 July 1649, 28 Jan., 29 Mar., 26 Dec. 1650, 2 May, 4 Sep. 1651, 18 Mar. 1653; C.J. (MS) xxxiii, p. 490; *C.C.A.M.*, p. 1151; *Perfect Occurrences of Every Day's Journal in Parliament* 1–8 June 1649, p. 1094; Clarendon MS 34, fo. 94; C. H. Firth and R. S. Rait (ed.), *Acts and Ordinances of the Interregnum* (3 vols., 1911), ii. 38, 153.

[3] *C.J.* 6 Apr., 8, 9, 27 June, 17 July, 5 Sep. 1649, 17 Jan., 23 Feb., 9 Mar., 6, 25 Apr., 28 May, 22 June, 23 July, 28 Aug. 1650, 14 Jan., 23 Apr., 15, 27 July 1652; *C.S.P.D.* 1651, pp. 50, 56; C. H. Firth (ed.), *The Clarke Papers* (4 vols., 1891–1901), iii. 2; Journal of the London Common Council xli, fo. 13ᵛ; SP: 18/17, fo. 292; 23/9, fo. 8; 28/91, fos. 530, 558, 560; 28/92, fo. 292. Much valuable biographical information about M.P.s with city connections can be found in V. Pearl, *London and the Outbreak of the Puritan Revolution* (Oxford, 1961).

[4] *Mercurius Pragmaticus* 3–17 October, 1648; B.M., Add. MS 22,546, fos. 28, 30, 35; C.J. 13, 29 Dec. 1648, 9 May, 30 June 1649, 18 Feb. 1650.

[5] *C.J.* 1, 6, 12, 15 Jan., 10 Feb., 9 Mar., 11 June, 6 July, 3 Aug., 23 Nov. 1649, 9 Feb., 9 Mar., 13, 25 Apr., 19, 27 June, 6, 25 July, 5, 12 Sep., 24 Oct. 1650, 24 Jan., 4 Feb., 10 Apr., 20, 29 May, 17 June, 9 Sep. 1651, 1 Jan., 19 Mar., 27 Apr. 1652; SP: 18/5, fos. 90, 96; 18/7, fos. 161, 165, 167, 169, 172, 206; 18/12, fos. 235, 282; 23/7, p. 87; 23/9, fos. 33ᵛ, 34; 24/10, fos. 69ᵛ, 70ᵛ, 74ᵛ, 80&ᵛ, 90, 122, 147ᵛ, 150ᵛ, 167, 193ᵛ; Whitelocke Letters (Longleat) xi, fo. 83; Brunton and Pennington, *Members of the Long Parliament*, p. 59; Rawlinson MS A224, esp. fos. 3ᵛ, 4ᵛ, 10ᵛ, 13&ᵛ, 14, 18.

[6] *C.J.* 4 Mar. 1648, 17 Jan., 25 July 1649, 17 Jan., 9, 16 Mar., 20 June, 25 July, 22 Aug., 20 Dec. 1650, 13 Feb., 9 Sep. (James Chaloner) 1651, 11 Mar., 13 Apr., 26 Nov., 1652; C.J. (MS) xxxiii, p. 625.

and the merchant M.P. for King's Lynn, Thomas Toll, were likewise particularly close to Chaloner, and Toll was also a frequent ally of Boone.[1] Among both the lawyer and the merchant groups were men of diverse political views and private interests; and there was nothing new in the Rump's practice of referring to lawyers and merchants matters which they were specially qualified to discuss.[2] Nevertheless, the experience derived from such discussion often led members of both groups to ally on matters of more general importance. Both lawyers and merchants were heavily outnumbered in the House by rural land-lords, but because of their parliamentary energy and their capacity for cohesion the two groups were able to exert an influence on Rump politics disproportionate to their numerical strength.

[1] Ashe: *C.J.* 4 Dec. 1648, 12 Mar., 25 July, 18 Aug. 1649, 16 Mar., 20 June 1650; Toll: *ibid.* 4 Mar. 1648, 13 Apr., 7, 17, 25 July, 4, 5 Sep. 1649, 4 Feb. 1650 (Toll made only four other recorded appearances in the Rump); B.M., Add. MS 22,546, fos. 17, 19; Rawlinson MS A224, *passim*; SP 18/5, fos. 34, 40, 46, 52, 78, 86, 107, 109.
[2] Brunton and Pennington, *Members of the Long Parliament*, p. 53.

2

THE LIMITS OF REVOLUTION

The Rump's enemies, mocking its occasional difficulty in its early stages in raising a quorum (a problem to which the Long Parliament was in fact well accustomed), have bequeathed the impression that only a hard core of extreme radicals sat in the House between the purge and the execution of the king.[1] Yet well over a hundred rumpers seem to have taken their seats at some point during these weeks,[2] and not all of them can in any sense be described as radical. Nearly forty of them, indeed, failed at this time either to register dissent from the vote of 5 December or to commit themselves in any way to the moves against Charles. Some, whose behaviour in the wake of the purge resembled that of Pierrepoint and Ashhurst, made only one or two recorded appearances before withdrawing from parliament. Unlike Pierrepoint and Ashhurst they later returned to join the Rump, but not for several weeks and in some cases not for several months. Richard Aldworth of Bristol, who returned in April 1649, and Edmund Harby of Northamptonshire, who returned in July, were two examples. Another was Lislibone Long, who made clear his opposition to the purge on 7 December, withdrew on the 25th, and did not resume active membership until February. Sir Richard Lucy, M.P. for Old Sarum, made his sole recorded appearance between the purge and the execution on 20 December, when the test of dissent was introduced and when he demonstrated his hostility to the army's actions.[3] He did not reappear until July. Other rumpers who failed to dissent between the purge and the execution sat more frequently in these weeks but were equally unhappy about the events which occurred during them, like the Speaker, William Lenthall, who kept to his post,[4] or the inseparable trimming

[1] Walker, *History of Independency*, ii. 34; *Mercurius Elencticus* 12–19 Dec. 1648, p. (539); W. H. Coates (ed.), *The Journal of Sir Simonds D'Ewes from the First Recess of the Long Parliament to the Withdrawal of King Charles from London* (New Haven, 1942), pp. 11, 49.
[2] *C.J.* 6 Dec. 1648–30 Jan. 1649, *passim*. On attendances in the Rump period see Appendix A, below.
[3] *C.J.* 7, 20, 25 Dec. 1648.   [4] Whitelocke, *Memorials*, ii. 495.

lawyers Bulstrode Whitelocke and Sir Thomas Widdrington, who oscillated with comic indecisiveness between taking their seats and keeping well away from the House. Whitelocke opposed the purge, the execution and the abolition of the House of Lords. So did Widdrington, who like Whitelocke continued to work within the regime but who retained strong reservations about the actions which had brought it to power.[1]

The refusal of M.P.s like Whitelocke and Widdrington to register dissent before the execution was consistent with their previous political attitudes. More surprising was the failure to take the test at this time of M.P.s who had hitherto possessed revolutionary credentials but who now, although continuing to sit in the House, proved lacking in revolutionary fibre. Fewer members dissented before the execution than had voted against the motion of 5 December, and the weeks following the purge exposed the limits of either the radicalism or the courage of a sizeable number of M.P.s. Sir Peter Wentworth, for example, had advocated severe methods against royalists throughout 1648. Early in January 1649 he was named by the well-informed newspaper *Mercurius Pragmaticus* as one of the revolutionary leaders. Before the execution, however, he withdrew to the country, complaining of the 'want of air and exercise' in London. He stayed in retreat until April, stranded no doubt by the 'sprains and bruises' which 'disabled me from pulling on a boot'.[2] John Gurdon of Suffolk, described by Clement Walker as 'a man hot enough for his zeal to set a kingdom on fire', instigated the move to compel M.P.s to dissent from the vote of 5 December. Yet he probably failed to register his own dissent during these weeks. On 20 December, the day of the test's introduction, he acted as teller in favour of a motion critical of the purge.[3] He made no recorded appearance in the House between late December and early February. John Weaver of Lincolnshire, who had a still more radical record, was another rumper to be afflicted at this time by either scruples or cold feet.[4] So was Richard Salwey, who although in the thick of the

[1] *Ibid.* ii. 471, 478, 484–5, 487, 491, 493, 521; B.M., Add. MS 37,344, fos. 232, 236, 239, 240ᵛ–242ᵛ, 250–252ᵛ, 265 (and cf. *ibid.* fo. 198ᵛ); C. H. Firth, *The House of Lords during the English Civil War* (1910), pp. 210, 211; Clarendon MS 34, fos. 12ᵛ, 73: newsletters, 21 Dec. 1648, 12 Jan. 1649.
[2] 'Parliamentary Diary of John Boys', p. 158; *Mercurius Pragmaticus* 26 Sep.–3 Oct. 1648, p. (4), 26 Dec. 1648–9 Jan. 1649, p. (7); Tanner. MS 57/2, fo. 539: Wentworth to Speaker Lenthall, 24 Feb. 1649.
[3] Walker, *History of Independency*, i. 96, 98, ii. 38; *C.J.* 20 Dec. 1648; *Mercurius Pragmaticus* 10–17 Oct. 1648, p. (4), 12–19 Dec. 1648, p. (5); Underdown, *Pride's Purge*, p. 214n.
[4] *Mercurius Pragmaticus* 26 July–1 Aug. 1648, pp. (6), (7), 10–17 Oct. 1648, p. (4); Underdown, *Pride's Purge*, pp. 103n., 109.

revolutionary movement until early January 1649 did not dissent until May.[1] Edmund Prideaux's failure to register dissent in these weeks, when he was in regular attendance in the House, is also surprising. He seems to have been in touch at this time with Denis Bond, another Dorset rumper with an equally radical past and an equally influential future. It is possible, but unlikely, that Bond registered dissent in December.[2] He made no recorded appearance in parliament between the purge and the execution, but with Prideaux continued to attend one of its standing committees.[3] He was back in the House early in February, when he was appointed to the Rump's first Council of State; but he soon withdrew again, reappearing only in June and failing to take his seat on the council until November.[4]

Between the purge and the execution there were, then, many members who sat in the Rump without in any way committing themselves to supporting it. More than sixty rumpers, nevertheless, did take the test of dissent before the king's death, including all but seven of the forty-three who took the much bolder step of signing his death warrant; and it was from among the regicides and early dissenters that the M.P.s most prominent during these weeks came. Who were they? The chief ringleader, it is clear, was the regicide Thomas Scot, a Buckinghamshire attorney who had risen to prominence, and won election to parliament as a recruited member, through his administrative work on the county committee. He was in close touch with the army at the time of the purge, took over from John Gurdon the measure requiring M.P.s to register dissent, and became the 'belweather of the king-killing committee'. After Charles's death he was appointed to the small Rump committee which nominated members to the first Council of State.[5] Quickly emerging as one of the Rump's most able and industrious administrators, he was (with Cromwell, Sir Arthur Heselrige and

[1] 'Parliamentary Diary of John Boys', p. 156; Underdown, *Pride's Purge*, p. 220; *C.J.* Dec. 1648 and Jan. 1649, esp. 4 Jan.

[2] Underdown (*Pride's Purge*, p. 214n., where the evidence is discussed) inclines to the view that Bond probably did dissent before the king's execution: I suspect that he did not.

[3] *Mercurius Pragmaticus* 5–12 Dec. 1648, p. (4), 12–19 Dec. 1648, p. (4); SP 28/58, fo. 80. Prideaux and Bond can often be seen cooperating during the Rump period.

[4] *C.J.* 13 June 1649; *C.S.P.D.* 1649–50, council attendance tables.

[5] A. M. Johnson, 'Buckinghamshire 1640–1660' (Swansea M.A. thesis, 1963), p. 106; J. Lilburne, *The Legal, Fundamental Liberties of the People of England* (1649), p. 33; *Journal of the House of Lords*, 12 Dec. 1648; T. Scot, *A Pair of Crystal Spectacles* (1648); *C.J.* 7 Feb., 3 Mar. 1649; D. M. Wolfe (ed.), *Leveller Manifestoes of the Puritan Revolution* (1967 edn.), p. 81. For all the regicides and early dissenters mentioned in this and the following three paragraphs, see also their numerous appearances in *C.J.* for Dec. 1648 and Jan. 1649.

Sir Henry Vane) one of the four members who had most influence in the formulation of its policies. Two other regicides, Henry Marten and Thomas Chaloner, were almost equally prominent in the weeks following the purge. They provided the republican formula adopted by the Rump in January 1649, and their close friendship was to reap many political rewards during the Commonwealth.[1] Marten had rashly suggested as early as 1643 that kingship was unnecessary, and had in consequence been expelled for a time from the House.[2] In January 1648 he declared 'that he would not have us stick to any government because it's that we found, unless it be good, and for the safety of the people'. Later in the same year he scandalised parliament by raising a Leveller regiment in his native Berkshire, formed to fight 'not for kings, or parliament, but for the people'. Ignoring the House's summons to explain his behaviour, he returned to London only at the beginning of December.[3] On the 7th, the second day of the purge, he made his first recorded appearance in the House since May, calling flamboyantly for a vote of thanks to Oliver Cromwell, who was also appearing in the House after a long absence. It was a rare moment of harmony between the two men.[4] Marten subsequently inspired the motto on the Commonwealth's Great Seal, drawn up 'in the first year of freedom, by God's blessing restored'.[5] In the Rump period he had only limited time for the administrative chores essential to the government's survival, and he made more enemies than friends. Yet in debate he was magnificent, time and again winning support for the most outspoken of motions. John Aubrey described him as

of an incomparable wit for repartees; not at all covetous; humble, not at all arrogant, as most of them were; a great cultor of justice, who did always in the House take the part of the oppressed. His speeches in the House were not long, but wondrous poignant and witty. He was exceedingly happy in apt instances. He alone has sometimes turned the whole House.

Chaloner, thought Aubrey, was 'a well bred gentleman, and of very

[1] Lilburne, *Legal, Fundamental Liberties*, pp. 28, 33; *Mercurius Pragmaticus* 26 Dec. 1648–9 Jan. 1649, p. (4); *C.J.* 4 Dec. 1648, 4 Jan. 1649 (and cf. *ibid.* 1 May 1649); C. M. Williams, 'The Political career of Henry Marten' (Oxford D. Phil. thesis, 1954), pp. 255–6.

[2] Hexter, *Reign of King Pym*, p. 148.

[3] 'Parliamentary Diary of John Boys', pp. 149, 158; B.M., Verney MS (microfilm) 636, 9: Burgoyne to Verney, 17 Aug. 1648; *Perfect Weekly Account* 29 Nov.–6 Dec. 1648, p. 300; Williams, 'Political career of Henry Marten', pp. 369–72.

[4] Underdown, *Pride's Purge*, pp. 150–1; Verney MS 636,9: Burgoyne to Verney, 7 Dec. 1648.

[5] *C.J.* 6, 8 Jan. 1649; Underdown, *Pride's Purge*, p. 204.

good parts, and of an agreeable humour . . . neither proud nor covetous, nor a hypocrite: not apt to do injustice, but apt to revenge'.[1] A Yorkshireman who had suffered financially from the northern policies of Thomas Wentworth (later Earl of Strafford), Chaloner was noted in the 1640s for his hawkish views. Like his friend Henry Neville, who was to be admitted to the Rump in October 1649 and who was likewise a close ally of Marten, Chaloner had travelled on the continent and had become interested in the differing forms of government to be found there.[2] He had evidently been feeling his way towards a republican position as early as 1646, when he argued that parliament should 'first settle the honour, safety and freedom of the Common-wealth, and then . . . of the king, so far as the latter may stand with the former, and not otherwise'. In 1647 he was accused of 'homespun slovenly malice' towards Charles, of recommending the king's deposition by parliament, and of claiming that 'the Houses are accountable to none but God Almighty'.[3] This estimate of his radicalism was probably accurate, although it was generally agreed that God Almighty occupied as small a place in Chaloner's thoughts as He did in Marten's or Neville's.

Scot, Marten and Chaloner stand out as the major parliamentary figures between the purge and the execution, but other regicides were also well to the fore in these weeks. The most prominent were John Blakiston of Newcastle, probably a close follower of Scot, as also of Sir Henry Vane the younger;[4] Thomas Harrison's sectarian ally John Carew;[5] the M.P. for Malmesbury Sir John Danvers; the Nottinghamshire member Gilbert Millington; those inseparable allies Humphrey Edwards of Shropshire and Sir Gregory Norton of Hampshire;[6] John Venn and Miles Corbet, whose alliance was noted earlier; the

[1] O. Lawson Dick (ed.), *Aubrey's Brief Lives* (1949): Marten and Chaloner.
[2] Cf. W. Cobbett (ed.), *The Parliamentary History of England* (36 vols., 1806–20), iii. 994.
[3] T. Chaloner, *An Answer to the Scotch Papers* (1646), pp. 4, 7–8, 14–15; *Lex Talionis* (1647), pp. 6–7; *Mercurius Pragmaticus* 3–10 Oct. 1648, p. (8).
[4] Lilburne, *Legal, Fundamental Liberties*, p. 15; *Mercurius Pragmaticus* 25 July–1 Aug. 1648, p. (6), 10–17 Oct. 1648, p. (11), 24–31 Oct. 1648, p. (9); Walker, *History of Independency*, ii. 48–9; Underdown, *Pride's Purge*, pp. 103n., 109, 161; Roger Howell jr., 'Newcastle's Regicide: The Parliamentary Career of John Blakiston', *Archaeologia Aeliana*, 4th series, xliii (1964).
[5] *The Traitor's Perspective Glass* (1662), pp. 23–4; B. S. Capp, *The Fifth Monarchy Men. A Study in Seventeenth-Century English Millenarianism* (1972), as indexed under Carew.
[6] For their cooperation see: *C.J.* 29 Jan., 19 Apr., 21 (x 3), 23 Dec. 1648, 1, 2, 6 (x 4) Jan., 8 Feb., 14 Apr., 29 May, 2, 14 July 1649; SP: 19/6, 19/7, 19/8, *passim*; 28/59, fo. 319; 28/60, fos. 70, 78; 28/269, fos. 268ᵛ, 269, 307, 312; *C.C.C.*, p. 1797; Clarendon MS 34, fo. 18ᵛ: newsletter, 29 Dec. 1648.

elderly William Purefoy, who had played a major part in organising the war effort in Warwickshire and who became a formidable politician in the Rump; Augustine Garland, elected in 1648, who had probably never sat in the Long Parliament before the purge but who after it seems to have attended more debates than any other member except the Speaker, becoming the Rump's most assiduous committeeman and toiling incessantly over the drafting of legislation; Lord Grey of Groby, a Leicestershire magnate still in his twenties during the Rump period, who acted as Pride's right-hand man at the purge; and of course Oliver Cromwell, to whose behaviour at this time, as to that of his fellow rumpers, regicides and army officers Henry Ireton and Thomas Harrison, we shall return. The Wiltshire regicide Edmund Ludlow, that dour opponent of arbitrary government, made less direct impact in parliament during these weeks, but there is no doubt of his deep involvement in the purge and in the events which followed it.[1]

The regicides supplied a majority of the parliamentary leaders between the purge and the execution, but not all of them. A number of men who were among the early dissenters but who did not sign the death warrant were also well to the fore. Among the most important were two former courtiers to Charles I who had undergone much-derided political conversions and who frequently made common cause during the Rump period, Sir Henry Mildmay of Essex and Cornelius Holland, M.P. for Windsor.[2] Mildmay, tireless on committees, pressed eagerly during the Commonwealth for harsh measures against royalists, and did much to help the intelligence system run by Thomas Scot.[3] Holland earned a reputation in late December 1648 as 'link-boy' between parliament and army.[4] Other early dissenters prominent in these weeks were Sir James Harrington of Rutland, singled out by *Mercurius Pragmaticus* as one of the revolutionary leaders,[5] and another pair of allies, John Lisle and Nicholas Love, both lawyers, both M.P.s

---

[1] Clarendon MS 34, fo. 86; *C.J.* 4 Dec. 1648.

[2] *C.J.* 23 Dec. 1648, 14 June 1649, 14 May 1651; *C.S.P.D.* 1649–50: committees appointed 5 June, 14 Aug., 31 Oct., 21 Nov., 4 Dec.; 1650–1: 23 Feb., 10 Apr., 11 June, 24 Sep., 1 Jan.; SP 28/269, fos. 268ᵛ, 320, 325, 331, 332, 354; Stowe MS 184, fo. 239; Clarendon MS 34, fo. 18ᵛ; Robert Bacon, *A Taste of the Spirit of God* (1652), pp. 22–3. See also G. E. Aylmer, *The King's Servants* (1961), pp. 382, 384–5.

[3] Walker, *History of Independency*, ii. 257, iii. 23; *Mercurius Pragmaticus* 5–12 Dec. 1648, p. (5), 12–19 Dec. 1648, p. (4); *Mercurius Elencticus* 10–17 Sep. 1649, p. (5); Enoch Grey, *Vox Coeli, containing Maxims of pious Policy* (1649), p. 35.

[4] Lilburne, *Legal, Fundamental Liberties*, pp. 28, 33; W. Haller and G. Davies (ed.), *The Leveller Tracts, 1647–1653* (Gloucester, Mass., 1964 edn.), p. 206; *Mercurius Pragmaticus* 14–21 Nov. 1648, p. (3), 12–19 Dec. 1648, p. (7).

[5] *Mercurius Pragmaticus* 26 Dec. 1648–9 Jan. 1649, p. (7).

for Winchester, and both entrusted with the formulation of many of the Rump's early republican measures.[1] Three other early dissenters who, for varying reasons, sat only rarely between the purge and the execution were nevertheless renowned for their radical sentiments, Sir Thomas Wroth of Somerset, Luke Robinson of Yorkshire, and Alexander Rigby of Lancashire. In January 1648 Wroth – or 'Wrath', as his enemies appropriately spelt him – had demanded 'any government rather than that of kings . . . from devils and kings good Lord deliver me'. He was thought to be Edmund Prideaux's 'fool'.[2] Robinson, whose views seem to have been similar to Wroth's, took the boldly radical step in 1651 of agitating publicly on behalf of freemen opposing the monopoly of an overseas trading company, an action which testified to his growing proximity to Henry Marten and which probably cost him his seat on the Council of State. In 1652, while acting as a J.P. in Yorkshire, he succumbed to the influence of the Quaker leader George Fox, although four years later, when he had recovered from the experience, he was anxious to protect his fellow justices from similar temptation.[3] Rigby, like Marten, Chaloner and Holland, was one of the tiny handful of M.P.s with Leveller connections. He had been among the king's most vigorous critics in the Long Parliament's early stages, displaying at the same time a zeal for law reform, and a concern to protect the poor against the rich, remarkable among M.P.s before the later 1640s.[4]

Although Pride's Purge drove large numbers of M.P.s away from Westminster, it also brought others back to it. Men who in 1648 had ceased to hope for any good from parliament, or who had preferred to assist the cause in the provinces rather than in London, returned to the House in large numbers either shortly before or shortly after the purge. Six of the regicides and early dissenters had, before December, made no recorded appearances in parliament throughout 1648, and twenty-

[1] *C.J.* 4, 21 Dec. 1648, 6, 9, 10, 23, 30, 31 Jan., 5 Feb. 1649; SP: 28/269, fos. 330, 342, 346; 23/113, p. 623; Clarendon MS 34, fo. 90; Walker, *History of Independency*, ii. 48–9.

[2] 'Parliamentary Diary of John Boys', pp. 145, 155; *Mercurius Pragmaticus* 17–24 Oct. 1648, p. (3), 5–12 Dec. 1648, p. (4), 12–19 Dec. 1648, p. (8); Walker, *History of Independency*, i. 71; *Arbitrary Government Displayed* (1682), p. 3; and see *C.J.* 14 Apr., 8 Oct. 1649, 21 May 1651.

[3] B.M., 669 f. 15, fo. 71 (petition of Greenland traders), with which cf. below, p. 249, and M. James, *Social Problems and Policy in the Puritan Revolution* (1930), p. 171; J. C. Nickalls (ed.), *Journal of George Fox* (Cambridge, 1952), pp. 86, 118, 507; *Diary of Thomas Burton*, i. 172.

[4] Haller and Davies, *The Leveller Tracts*, pp. 204, 211; *Master Rigby's Speech in answer to the Lord Finch* (1641); and see *C.C.A.M.*, p. 47.

five more had made very few.[1] Some of them withdrew again into relative obscurity after the king's execution, but most remained among the more energetic rumpers.

Pride's Purge, the execution of the king and the abolition of the House of Lords excited widespread optimism among radicals outside parliament. A regime capable of such actions, it was believed, would be anxious to instigate changes still more revolutionary. The act of regicide was celebrated as a symbol of liberation, as the triumph of a newly won freedom over immemorial slavery. The cleansing of political institutions, it was held, would be followed by the cleansing of society at large. The Levellers, who opposed both the purge and the execution, were admittedly more sceptical, but they found themselves increasingly isolated among the agitators for reform. Religious sects were particularly forthcoming with expressions of support for, and goodwill towards, the new regime, but they were not alone in their enthusiasm. As late as January 1650 Gerrard Winstanley, leader of the communist 'Digger' group which in the previous year had attempted to excavate St George's Hill, was convinced of the Rump's willingness to initiate radical changes.[2]

Such hopes were to be sadly disappointed. The inauguration of the Commonwealth proved to be the end, not the beginning, of the Long Parliament's revolutionary measures, and the regime left in its wake a trail of disillusionment and resentment among the advocates of social and religious reform. Parliament did, it is true, make occasional gestures to the radicals, but only in the autumn of 1650, with the conversion of legal proceedings into the English tongue, and with the act, passed with little enthusiasm and less grace, for the repeal of statutes enjoining church attendance on Sundays, did its concessions begin to appease the radical clamour. There were other minor adjustments to the legal system, but neither these nor the remainder of the Rump's religious legislation afforded much consolation to reformers outside the House. Monopolies were in general protected rather than

---

[1] The six: Alured, J. Chaloner, Clement, Constable, Fry, Garland. The twenty-five: Anlaby, Apsley, Blagrave, Bourchier, Carew, Cawley, Cromwell, Dixwell, Dove, Downes, H. Edwards, G. Fleetwood, Harrison, Heveningham, Holland, Hutchinson, Ireton, J. Jones, Ludlow, Millington, G. Norton, Oldsworth, Pickering, Robinson, H. Smyth. A few of these men had, of course, been absent on military duty or other government business, or (like Blagrave and Garland) had only secured election to parliament in 1648.

[2] G. E. Aylmer (ed.), 'England's spirit unfolded' (by Winstanley), *Past and Present*, 40 (1968), 5, 6, 9–11.

undermined; agrarian grievances received no redress; and the problems of poverty were met, but never solved, by piecemeal and usually traditional relief measures.[1] The Rump did agree to various proposals for electoral reform, but here again its resolutions took the sting out of radical demands.

Why were the expectations of reformers so grievously disappointed? Professor Underdown, whose book *Pride's Purge* has done so much to illuminate the attitudes and behaviour of members of the Long Parliament, draws from his research an impressive explanation of the radicals' failure. The revolution was defeated after January 1649, he believes, because the rumpers 'who were committed supporters of the revolution' were outnumbered by 'those who merely climbed on the band-wagon after the event'. The 'committed supporters of the revolution' he defines as the seventy or so M.P.s who signed Charles's death warrant or registered dissent before his execution. These men Underdown describes as 'revolutionaries'. Those who, by contrast, failed thus to commit themselves to the new regime until February 1649 or later, the men who 'climbed on the band-wagon', he describes as, at best, 'conformists'. The failure of the reform movement after January 1649, he argues, was the victory of the 'conformists' over the 'revolutionaries'.[2]

There is, it should be said at once, much to be said for this view; and frequent use of the terms 'revolutionary' and 'conformist' will be made in this book. With very few exceptions, the rumpers who were likely to favour reform measures were regicides or early dissenters, and the return of the 'conformists' to parliament after Charles's execution certainly reduced the prospects of social and religious change. It is also true that on many of the issues which divided the Rump a 'revolutionary' or radical attitude conflicted with a 'conformist' or moderate one. Indeed, the readmission of the 'conformists' after January 1649 provoked among many 'revolutionaries' a jealousy which pervaded much of the earlier Rump period and which caused repeated conflicts between the two groups. Underdown's description of the 'conformists' as men generally uninterested in or even opposed to revolutionary change is beyond dispute, and to it we owe a major insight into the politics of the Long Parliament. Where reservations are perhaps needed is in relation to his discussion of the 'revolutionaries', not all of whom were as revolutionary as his thesis suggests. Sometimes indeed he says as

[1] Cf. Underdown, *Pride's Purge*, pp. 281–3.
[2] *Ibid.* pp. 4–5; and cf. *ibid.* pp. 262, 265, 276.

much,[1] but he evidently regards the limits to the reforming ambitions of the 'revolutionaries' as only a secondary explanation of their failure. It will be argued here that the return to parliament of so many 'conformists' did not so much defeat a revolutionary programme as expose, as indeed it was made possible by, the absence among the 'revolutionaries' of any common or continuing revolutionary purpose.[2]

Had there been such a purpose, there ought to have been ample opportunity to implement it. It is true that the 'revolutionaries' were outnumbered among the Rump's total membership by a majority of about two to one, but in terms of parliamentary activity they more than held their own. Of the sixty or seventy members in regular attendance at Westminster during the Rump period, the 'revolutionaries' supplied at least half. By contrast, fewer than a quarter of the hundred or so members who only rarely attended the Rump were 'revolutionaries'. Tellers appointed during the Rump period were nominated noticeably more often from among the 'revolutionaries' than from among other members, although it is also true that 'revolutionaries', when they acted as tellers, were marginally more likely to be on the losing than on the winning side.[3] Parliamentary committees set up during the Rump period tended to include slightly more 'revolutionaries' than other members. 'Revolutionaries' also secured considerably more than their fair share of appointments to the Rump's annually elected Councils of State, and when thus appointed attended council meetings more frequently than their colleagues.[4] Admittedly their impact both in the House and on the council, if measured in such terms, lessened slightly as the Rump period progressed, but this decline was indicative less of diminishing opportunity than of their failure to act as a concerted

[1] Underdown, *Pride's Purge*, pp. 5, 173–4, 206, 296.
[2] Lest the purpose of what follows be misunderstood, it should be made clear that Underdown, in distinguishing between 'revolutionaries' and 'conformists', is concerned only partly with the course taken by Rump politics. He makes use of his categories for interesting and valuable statistical investigations: at no point does he imply that categories drawn up for statistical purposes correspond to rigid party groupings in the Rump. I refer so frequently to his argument about the failure of the reform movement in the Rump not out of any wish to quibble but because a discussion of his thesis has seemed the best peg on which to hang my own. There are many reasons for this, the chief one being not that Underdown seems to me wrong but that he seems to me so nearly right.
[3] There were four tellers at each division. At divisions held during the Rump period, the 'revolutionaries' averaged 2.28 tellers, other members 1.72. 'Revolutionaries' were on the losing side on 52% of the occasions on which they acted as tellers.
[4] 'Revolutionaries' supplied rather more than 50% of the members on the first two councils, rather fewer than 50% on the other three, and almost exactly 50% on the average council. On average, 'revolutionaries' on the council attended thirteen council meetings a month, other councillors eleven.

political party. For if the feelings engendered by the conflict of December 1648 and January 1649 survived into the Interregnum, the conflict itself did not. During the first two years of the Rump period the 'revolutionaries' were given an intermittent sense of common identity by the memory of the past, but not by any agreed policy for the present. The conflict between 'revolutionaries' and 'conformists' dominated debates only when the Rump discussed the problem of its own membership, and particularly the readmission of members who were neither regicides nor early dissenters. Although the membership issue persisted well into the Rump period, the key decisions relating to it had been taken by July 1649. Thereafter it must often have been hard for rumpers to remember whether their colleagues had been among the early dissenters or not. The regicides' claim to notoriety was unlikely to be so easily forgotten, but even for them the distinction between 'revolutionaries' and 'conformists' became submerged beneath new issues and new divisions.

What distinguished both the regicides and the early dissenters was their willingness to sign a particular piece of paper at a particular point in time. Their signatures tell us about their actions, but not, in themselves, about their intentions. In one sense, of course, the intentions do not matter: however various men's motives in killing the king, the king was killed nonetheless. Once he was dead, however, the variety of motives which had led men to commit themselves to the Rump in its early stages became increasingly apparent; and the politics of the Rump period remain inexplicable unless we look beyond the common actions of Underdown's 'revolutionaries' to their varying intentions. As anyone knows who has ever given his name to a document signed also by many other people, pieces of paper can temporarily and artificially unite men of very different views.

In considering intentions we are often, of course, dealing with intangibles. It is tempting, in the face of severely limited evidence, to belittle the complexity and the individuality of politicians by attributing their behaviour to simple and clear-cut motives. The temptation needs to be resisted. In general we know little about the fluctuations of opinion evidently experienced by many rumpers between the purge and the execution, about the ways in which M.P.s influenced each other at this time, or about the extent to which political convictions were fortified by courage or weakened by cowardice. At least three members, Thomas Waite, Simon Mayne and John Downes, probably signed the death warrant only after they had been bullied into doing so,[1] and Waite and Mayne withdrew from parliament soon after the execution to remain among the least active rumpers. Others with radical records would doubtless have signed had they had the courage to do so. Others still, like Wentworth, Gurdon, Weaver, Salway and Prideaux, surprisingly failed even to register dissent before the execution of the king. We do not really know why, and we know still less of the personalities of many other members who had to decide whether to commit themselves to the Rump in its early stages. What we can show, however, is that there was a variety of purely political reasons for joining the regicides and early dissenters. The intellectual equipment of most M.P.s would no doubt be flattered by the assumption that they chose particular courses of action in accordance with precise and clearly defined principles. More probably, they tended to cling to the principles which accorded best with their political instincts. Nevertheless those principles, as professed by members who sat between the purge and the execution, provide a useful guide to their thoughts.

Recent research has demonstrated the importance during the English revolution of 'loyalism', the sentiment, doubtless strengthened by the vagaries of the revolution's course, which encouraged men to accept, and if necessary to pledge support for, regimes of which they disapproved.[2] In the Rump period loyalism was elevated to the status of a political theory by propagandists concerned to justify government by conquest; but it also reflected the widespread feeling among less articulate men that bad government was better than no government, and that it was wiser to square one's conscience with allegiance to an unwelcome regime than to leave the management of affairs solely in the hands of one's enemies. Loyalist theories, which seem to have influenced the political outlooks of many rumpers,[3] and which anticipated the cult of 'trimming' widespread later in the century, played a major part in the controversy which followed the Rump's attempt in 1649–50 to impose an engagement of loyalty on the nation. They may also have led some men to take the test of dissent before the king's

[1] Wedgwood, *Trial of Charles I*, p. 101.
[2] Q. Skinner, 'History and ideology in the English revolution', *Historical Journal*, viii (1968); J. M. Wallace, 'The engagement controversy 1649–1652', *Bulletin of the New York Public Library*, 68 (1964), and *Destiny His Choice. The Loyalism of Andrew Marvell* (1968), esp. chapter 1.
[3] See e.g. Whitelocke, *Memorials*, ii. 495, 526, and *Journal of the Swedish Embassy* (2 vols. 1855), i. 323; Williams, 'Political career of Henry Marten', p. 539; H. Vane, 'A Healing Question Propounded', in John Lord Somers, *A Collection of scarce and valuable Tracts* (13 vols., 1809–15: ed. W. Scott), vi. 305; *Diary of Thomas Burton*, iii. 99.

execution, just as they influenced many who dissented only after it. Certainly a number of 'revolutionaries' seem to have committed themselves to the Rump in its early stages for reasons quite as unrevolutionary as those which subsequently impelled the 'conformists' to join them; and a glance at the behaviour of individual rumpers reminds us how much the two categories had in common.

The Suffolk rumper William Heveningham frequently took his seat in the weeks following the purge. He did not register dissent at this time, and so is classified by Underdown as a 'conformist'. Yet he had been a teller in July 1648 in favour of a hard line against the king, and on 7 December, the second day of the purge, in favour of proceeding with the army's programme. He was much more sympathetic than most M.P.s to army demands for pay. In February 1649, alone among the 'conformists' who were appointed to the Rump's first Council of State, he swore approval of Charles's trial and execution. As late as October of the same year Lilburne, spurned by 'revolutionary' rumpers, was writing respectfully but optimistically to him for support. As Heveningham's papers make clear, however, his interest in the army, and his willingness to condone its policies, stemmed from a desire to keep power in parliamentary and out of military hands, and so out of reach of 'the lower kind of people'. This resolve kept him active in the House until March 1649. By then, however, the civilian character of the new regime had been established, and thereafter his parliamentary energies declined rapidly. In January 1650 he had even to be persuaded, by 'loyalist' arguments, of the virtues of the Rump's engagement of loyalty. By 1651 and 1652 he was being appointed to only three parliamentary committees a year.[1] Bulstrode Whitelocke, another rumper who sat between the purge and the execution, wrote of those who at that time feared – as he did – that too small an attendance in the House would provoke a forced dissolution, 'and thereby the whole power ... given up into the hands of the army'. They therefore 'consulted about settling the kingdom by the parliament, and not to leave all to the sword'.[2]

[1] *C.J.* 25 July, 7 Dec. 1648; *The Trial of Lieut. Colonel John Lilburne* (1649), pp. 155–8; Holkham MS 684 (Bodleian Library microfilm): unfoliated papers beginning 'Sir, who can doubt' and 'If he that rules yield anything', and (in the same MS) letter of John Goodwin to Heveningham, 2 Jan. 1650; *C.S.P.D.* 1649–50, pp. xlviii, 9; and see *An Exact and most Impartial Account of the ... Trial ... of Twenty-Nine Regicides* (1660), p. 270.
[2] Whitelocke, *Memorials*, ii. 475, 481. Cf. *ibid.* iii. 102, and B.M., Add. MS 37,344, fos. 189, 325ᵛ–6.

Whitelocke, like Heveningham, did not register dissent until February 1649, but the attitudes expressed by these men were not confined to 'conformists'. Some of the 'revolutionaries' seem to have been equally determined to ensure that government remained under civilian control. The regicide Colonel Hutchinson, according to his widow Lucy, 'infinitely disliked' the army's 'arrogant usurpations' at the purge 'upon that authority which it was their duty rather to have obeyed than interrupted'. He and his friends, she believed, stayed in the House because they 'thought it better to sit still and go on in their duty than give up all, in so distempered a time, into the hands of the soldiery'.[1] Mrs Hutchinson was writing from jaundiced hindsight, but she did not shrink from recording her husband's radicalism on other matters (not least the execution of the king), and her account of his indignation at the purge has a ring of truth. Although Ludlow attempted to gloss over the point,[2] feeling against the army ran high in parliament after the purge and even after the withdrawal of men like Pierrepoint in the days which followed it. On 14 December the Commons voted by a majority of almost two to one to demand the readmission of all members 'against whom [the army] have no charge', and sent a committee to inquire of Fairfax 'upon what grounds the members of the House are restrained from coming to the House by the officers and soldiers of the army'. Fairfax failed to reply, but on the 20th, the day on which the Rump introduced the test of dissent and so took the issue of parliamentary membership out of the army's hands and into its own, a motion to renew the message to the Lord General was carried by an almost equally impressive majority – and this in a thin House numerically dominated by 'revolutionaries'. Among the tellers in favour of the motions of 14 and 20 December were two regicides, John Carew and William Purefoy, and one of the first members to register dissent, Purefoy's Warwickshire colleague and ally Godfrey Bosvile.[3] The House spent most of Christmas Day debating a proposal to readmit the purged members.[4] Early in January the officers at last responded to the Rump's demand for a formal explanation of the purge, but although their answer, emphasising the dangers of readmitting untrustworthy members but yielding the issue

1 C. H. Firth (ed.), *Memoirs of Colonel Hutchinson Governor of Nottingham by his Widow Lucy* (1906), p. 269.
2 *Memoirs of Edmund Ludlow*, i. 211.
3 *C.J.* 14, 20 Dec. 1648; Whitelocke, *Memorials*, ii. 475. Purefoy and Bosvile can often be seen cooperating during the Rump period, especially on standing committees.
4 *The Moderate* 19–26 Dec. 1648, p. 224; Whitelocke, *Memorials*, ii. 481.

of parliamentary membership to the House itself, was courteous enough, the House approved only the 'substance' of it.[1] The Rump's discussions, probably encouraged by Cromwell, of proposals to readmit the purged members may have been prompted as much by embarrassment at the low attendances in the House as by resentment against the army's actions.[2] Even so, the willingness of so many 'revolutionaries' to protest against the purge is a further pointer to the limits of their radicalism.

The desire to preserve power in parliamentary hands was often associated with another unrevolutionary attitude which encouraged some members, whether 'revolutionaries' or 'conformists', to take their seats between the purge and the execution. Even the M.P.s who spent most of their time at Westminster remembered their duty to the constituents who had elected them and whose interests required continuing representation in the House. The behaviour of the corporation of Hull, which in the 1640s and 1650s sought the patronage of a number of M.P.s in order to guarantee a hearing for its interests, reminds us of the importance placed by electors on the presence in parliament of men aware of their needs.[3] The 'conformist' Whitelocke, who after the purge was urged to remain in the House by so moderate a figure as the judge John Rolle, explained his continued membership by the 'trust' reposed in members by their constituents; so did the regicide Colonel Hutchinson.[4] The correspondence of the early dissenter Thomas Atkins, revealing his constant concern for his constituents' interests and his mounting anger at the failure of his fellow M.P. for Norwich to assist him by regular attendance, suggests one reason why he, at least, wished to retain his seat. Despite his early dissent, Atkins displayed no recorded enthusiasm for the purge and was dismayed by the breach within the parliamentary party which it caused.[5]

[1] *The Humble Answer of the General Council ... to the Honourable the Commons of England* (1649); Prynne, *A Full Declaration*, p. 22.
[2] Underdown, *Pride's Purge*, pp. 160, 165–6; B.M., Add. MS 37,344, fo. 239.
[3] T. Wildridge (ed.), *The Hull Letters* (undated: 1887?), pp. 48, 69, 85; F. W. Brooks (ed.), 'The first order book of the Hull Trinity House', *Yorkshire Archaeological Society Records* (1942), pp. 92, 93, 95, 115; Hull Corporation MSS, L: 491–8, 505–22, 558. Cf. e.g. F. R. Raines and W. C. Sutton (eds.), *Life of Humphrey Chetham* (Chetham Soc., 1903), pp. 168, 169, 175–6, 177, 179; M. Stocks (ed.), *Records of the Borough of Leicester* (Cambridge, 1923), pp. 386–7, 396.
[4] Whitelocke, *Memorials*, ii. 472, 475, 494; *Memoirs of Colonel Hutchinson*, pp. 268–9. For Whitelocke see also B.M., Stowe MS 333, fos. 55&ᵛ, 80&ᵛ, 115ᵛ.
[5] B.M., Add. MS 15,903, fos. 61, 67, 71, and Add. MS 22,620, fos. 45, 50, 54, 56, 60, 66, 69, 94, 111, 115, 119, 121, 135, 137, 139, 140, 146, 150, 156, 162, 182 (all letters of Atkins to Mayor of Norwich).

Eventually he stayed away from the House for the whole of January 1649. Although appointed one of Charles's judges, he never attended the trial. One purged M.P., George Booth of Cheshire, felt it necessary to explain to his constituents that force alone prevented him from continuing to serve their interests in parliament.[1] Such arguments could no doubt be adopted for public consumption or self-justification, but they provide further warning of the dangers of automatically associating early commitment to the Rump with enthusiasm for the army's policies.

Instinct and principle played their parts in persuading men unsympathetic to the purge to take their seats, and if necessary to register dissent, before the execution of the king. So, apparently, did force of habit. Remarkably often, the extent of a member's parliamentary activity was simply unaffected by the purge. The overwhelming majority of rumpers were about as energetic or unenergetic in parliament during the Rump period as they had been in the year preceding it.[2] Many of them doubtless continued to sit because they enjoyed or were accustomed to doing so. Some M.P.s seem to have regarded dissent as a price worth paying to remain at the centre of events; others contrived to sit between the purge and the execution without at that time dissenting; others still, who stayed away from the House between the purge and the execution, thereafter merely resumed the former rhythm of their parliamentary attendances.

As Underdown emphasises, not all those who registered dissent before the end of January 1649 supported the execution of the king.[3] One of the earliest dissenters, Edmund Harvey, stormed away from the regicide court in protest against its refusal to allow Charles to defend himself. Another, Sir James Harrington, helped to create a political crisis in February 1649 by declining to approve the court's work when he was elected to the Council of State.[4] All that dissent expressed on paper was a belief that it would have been mistaken to negotiate further with the defeated king. Before December 1648 this view would have implied no more than that parliament should impose its own terms on Charles. By the time of the purge, admittedly, the alternatives to further negotiations had become more revolutionary. Yet, as we have seen, it

---

[1] *Clarke Papers*, ii. 136–8.
[2] The main exceptions were those listed above, p. 40, n. 1. The only others of note were John Feilder, who was more active in the Rump period than in 1648, and Oliver St John, who was less so.
[3] Underdown, *Pride's Purge*, p. 186.
[4] Whitelocke, *Memorials*, ii. 559; below, p. 180.

is often difficult to detect much difference of attitude between those who dissented and those who did not dissent before the execution. But what of the forty-three regicide M.P.s, the men who risked their lives by condemning the divinely appointed king? They, surely, were 'revolutionaries' if anyone was. Yet there were limits even to their revolutionary appetites. We naturally think of the execution of the king as the perilous achievement of an extremist minority: we tend to forget that many people saw it as the only means of restoring peace. The regicide Thomas Scot recalled in 1659, with pardonable exaggeration, that 'it was impossible to keep [the king] alive ... So long as he was above ground, in view, there were daily revoltings among the army, and risings in all places.'[1] But for such considerations Cromwell, who would have liked to keep Charles alive and who agreed to his trial only after lengthy hesitation, would probably not have agreed to the execution. This does not mean that either Cromwell, who seems never to have regretted signing the death warrant, or Scot, who was evidently proud of having done so,[2] acted from expediency rather than from conviction. Far from it: the desire for peace, often expressed in a belief that a purgative act of justice was necessary to cleanse the land of the blood which had been shed during the 1640s, was deeply held, and the experience of the second civil war in the summer of 1648 had convinced many that civil strife would never end so long as Charles remained alive.

Regicides who had opposed Pride's Purge, like Purefoy and Hutchinson, were not the kind of men to take easily to revolutionary courses. Purefoy, one of Thomas Scot's most influential allies,[3] cooperated with him in January 1649 to try to preserve the House of Lords, and in February to place 'conformists' in positions of power.[4] Throughout the Rump period Purefoy took a consistently hard line against royalists, of whose misdemeanours he seems, like most regicides, to have been unable to think dispassionately; nevertheless, like Hutchinson and others, he evidently regarded the act of regicide, the culmination of the conflict between crown and parliament, as less revolutionary than the

[1] *Diary of Thomas Burton*, iii. 110.
[2] *Dictionary of National Biography*: Thomas Scott (*sic*); *Diary of Thomas Burton*, iii. 109–11, 275–6.
[3] *C.J.* 27 May 1648, 6, 9 Jan., 2 Feb., 19 Apr., 19 June 1649, 19, 20 Feb., 19 Mar., 11 June, 9 Dec. 1652; B.M., Egerton MS 2618, fo. 40; SP: 28/61, fos. 97, 102, 306; 28/62, p. 713; 28/63, p. 285; 28/81, pp. 488, 507, 904ff.; 28/86, fo. 515; 28/88, fo. 400; 28/89, fo. 162; 28/90, fo. 162; *C.S.P.D.* 1649–50: pp. 154, 224, 392, 469, 490, 491, 508, 511; 1650–1: pp. 10, 17, 173; 1651: pp. 32, 53, 85, 458; 1651–2: pp. 4, 34, 192, 290; 1652–3: pp. 7, 22, 48.   [4] *C.J.* 9, 18 Jan., 19 Feb. 1649.

army's invasion at the purge of the sacred representative. To oppose the purge and yet to sign the death warrant may appear inconsistent, for an unpurged parliament would never have set up the High Court of Justice; but Hutchinson, for one, seems to have given serious thought to the issue of regicide only when the army made it an imminent possibility. Then, after much heartsearching, he agreed to it. In his view the king was guilty, as the court decided he was, of the treasons of which he was accused and of the 'murders, rapines, burnings, spoils, desolations, damages, and mischiefs to this nation' committed during the civil wars; and he must die for his crimes. Yet it is hard to believe that Hutchinson would have signed the warrant had not the court received parliamentary as well as military sanction, and had not a majority of his fellow regicides been M.P.s.[1]

Others who signed the death warrant had contemplated the king's death for much longer. A few, like Marten, Chaloner and Ludlow, had for some time been moving towards republican theory.[2] It is not clear how far they had got, but what is evident is that in their republicanism they were in a small minority among the regicides, let alone among the rumpers as a whole.[3] Most of those who signed the death warrant, if they were aware of the distinction, opposed not the office of kingship but the person of the king.[4] Once the decision to proceed against Charles had been taken, the House was obliged to search for political theories to justify its actions. Marten and Chaloner were glad to supply those theories, but their views received little convinced support at this stage. The famous resolution by the Commons on 4 January 1649, declaring that power lay originally with the people, was adopted only because the pitifully small remnant of the House of Lords refused to agree to the moves against the king; and even then, as Underdown observes, the resolution's republican bite was removed by the Rump's parallel announcement that popular sovereignty was subsumed under the sovereignty of the Commons.[5] It was not until

[1] *Memoirs of Colonel Hutchinson*, pp. 268–72; Gardiner, *Constitutional Documents*, pp. 373–4. Cf. *The Speeches and Prayers of the late King's Judges* (1662), p. 7.
[2] We might be better equipped to understand the parliamentary radicalism of the later 1640s if we knew what Ludlow meant by his various references in his *Memoirs* to the 'Commonwealthsmen'. It seems possible that his use of the term was anachronistic; and in any case he may at times have been referring to men who were not M.P.s.
[3] Cf. below, pp. 172–7.
[4] Marten was clearly an exception to this rule: see Williams, 'Political career of Henry Marten', pp. 408–9.
[5] Underdown, *Pride's Purge*, pp. 201, 263; and see *Perfect Occurrences* 29 Dec. 1648–5 Jan. 1649, p. 782; *C.J.* 3 Jan. 1649.

well after the execution of the king, when it became clear that the body politic could survive the loss of its head, that more than a small minority of rumpers decided that the republic was an admirable form of government.

The events of December 1648 and January 1649 revealed the intellectual limitations as much as the spiritual dedication of many regicides. More M.P.s wanted to be rid of the king, or even of kingship altogether, than knew what they wanted instead. The political attitudes of most regicides had been both formed and limited by the struggles between crown and parliament. Once the king was dead, what were the M.P.s who had sanctioned his execution to do with themselves? The radicalism of a regicide like Ludlow, fortified by a vivid historical memory and by a belief that a majority of those who had opposed the king had subsequently betrayed the cause,[1] looked to the past rather than to the future. The sense of mission displayed by regicides made possible what seems to us the most revolutionary event in English history, but it was inadequate to promote, let alone to sustain, a coherent radical programme once the emotions roused by the execution had subsided. Mrs Hutchinson wrote of the days following the king's death that 'every man almost was fancying a form of government, and angry that his invention took not place': Whitelocke that 'everyone almost ... endeavoured or expected to have his private fancy put in motion'; 'there were everywhere too many talkers, and few with much judgement'.[2] The rumpers most heavily committed to the moves against the king, as the jibes chosen by their enemies to describe them suggest, were often distinguished by their temperaments rather than their opinions: 'hot spirits' rather than cool-headed reformers. Ludlow's persistent but myopic resentment against the 'corrupt interest' of 'the lawyers and clergy'[3] was no substitute for practicable reform proposals. Nor was his naive republicanism, which never seems to have come down to earth. Seventeenth-century English society stood even less chance of reformation at the hands of the M.P. for Queenborough, the 'quarrelsome and maladjusted' regicide Sir Michael Livesy.[4] Opposed in 1648 to concessions to the king, Livesy vaunted throughout the Rump period his hostility to royalists, papists and titular honours, to the undue preeminence of a 'single person' as

---

[1] See e. g. *Memoirs of Edmund Ludlow*, i. 9, 38, 96.
[2] *Memoirs of Colonel Hutchinson*, p. 272; Whitelocke, *Memorials*, ii. 486, iii. 79.
[3] *Memoirs of Edmund Ludlow*, i. 246, 333–4, 365, 366, 368, 388, ii. 75, 133, 156, 161, 204.
[4] The phrase is Underdown's: *Pride's Purge*, p. 31.

president of the Council of State, and to those who failed quickly to subscribe the Rump's engagement of loyalty. The only feature of pre-revolutionary society he seems actively to have supported was the rotten boroughs – specifically his own.[1] When it came to formulating reform proposals he, like Ludlow, seems to have had nothing to offer. It would be a mistake to regard all or even a majority of the regicides as hot-headed zealots scornful of political realities. Nevertheless, Professor Trevor-Roper's suggestion that the salient characteristic of the radical M.P.s was that 'they knew what they hated, what they wanted to destroy' is borne out all too often by the events of the Rump period.[2] Cromwell, in a reference to the failure of Barebone's Parliament, was to lament that 'our passions were more than our judgements'.[3] He might have extended the same criticism to his fellow regicides during the Rump period. The most radical among them, mistaking in December 1648 and January 1649 the sensation of revolution for the substance, found after Charles's death that they had been outwitted by men of more moderate persuasion, who were able to show how little had in fact been changed by the execution.

This is not to suggest that the 'conformists' were as a whole politically more sophisticated than the 'revolutionaries'. Among them, however, was a small but extremely influential group of M.P.s who provided the House with its most skilful and experienced leadership, and whose presence, far more than that of the diehard radicals, set the tone of Rump politics. What the failure of the radicals in the Rump demonstrated, above all else, was the absence among those whom the revolution brought to power of a positive and clearly defined ideology. The 'grand rebellion' is often seen as the first of the great national revolutions of the western world; but in terms of ideological precision it fell far short of its successors.

The failure of the 'revolutionaries' in the Rump was, then, largely of their own making. Yet if they had merely been in want of an ideology they might still have been expected to achieve something, if only by

[1] *C.J.* 15, 19 Feb., 25, 28 Apr. 1649, 23 Feb., 23 Aug., 19 Nov. 1650, 30 June 1652, 16 Mar. 1653; 'Sir Roger Twysden's Journal', *Archaeologia Cantiana* iv (1861), 189–90; Everitt, *Community of Kent and the Great Rebellion*, pp. 276–7.
[2] H. R. Trevor-Roper, 'The Gentry 1540–1640', *Economic History Review*, Supplement 1 (1953), p. 42. Marten, on whom Professor Williams's dissertation throws much light, and whose republicanism was always a positive force, is again an obvious exception to this rule.
[3] Abbott, *Writings and Speeches*, iii. 435.

way of destruction. So perhaps they would have done, had they all wanted to destroy the same things; but with the execution of the king, or at least with the abolition of the House of Lords, many of them evidently felt that they had destroyed quite enough already. The 'revolutionaries', in fact, proved as divided over the central issues facing the new regime as in their motives for committing themselves to it in the first place. The main political conflict of the Rump period was quite different from that of the 1640s. The 'revolutionaries' were distinguished by their willingness to take a hard line against the king and thus to countenance a radical alteration in the balance of power among those traditionally accustomed to political activity at a national level. After the execution of the king, however, the prime issue was not political reform but the demand, made still less palatable to most M.P.s by its espousal by the army, for social reform; and radicalism against the king did not necessarily betoken radicalism on social issues. There may at first sight seem to be socially revolutionary implications in the conviction held by regicides that God had given 'his saints honour to bind kings in chains, and nobles in fetters of iron',[1] but cruelty towards kings and nobles, at least as practised by the Rump in the early months of 1649, involved only a redistribution of power within the governing classes. Oblivious as many radicals outside parliament seem to have been to the fact, this was a very different matter from questioning the social privileges of those classes as a whole.

Historians have argued for decades about the social origins of members of the Long Parliament and about the relationship between their social status and their political behaviour. Some of the propositions advanced during the controversy have been exhaustively tested by Professor Underdown, who shows that his 'revolutionaries' were, as a group, men of 'lower rank, lower income and more unstable fortune' than the M.P.s, taken as a whole, who were qualified to sit in the Commons at the beginning of December 1648.[2] He demonstrates, for example, that only about half the 'revolutionaries' whose incomes can be identified were worth over £500 a year before the civil war, compared with almost two-thirds of the Roundhead M.P.s still alive on the eve of the purge. Similarly, only about a quarter of the 'revolutionaries' whose incomes can be identified, compared with nearly half

[1] See e.g. Joseph Mayer, 'Inedited letters of Cromwell, Colonel Jones, Bradshaw and other regicides', *Transactions of the Historical Society of Lancashire and Cheshire*, new series, i (1860–2), p. 184.
[2] Underdown, *Pride's Purge*, p. 245.

of all members sitting before the purge, were worth more than £1,000 a year; and the relative poverty of the 'revolutionaries' was aggravated by their readiness, much greater than that of other Roundhead M.P.s, to advance money to the parliamentary cause during the civil war. The proportion of 'revolutionaries' known to have been heavily in debt even before the war (about seventeen per cent) was almost twice as high as that of all M.P.s able to sit in 1648.[1] There is plenty of ammunition here for those who like to see political radicalism as a reflection of economic insecurity; and if political radicalism had been the same thing as social radicalism, or economic insecurity the same thing as exclusion from the governing classes, the optimism of reformers who expected major changes from the Rump might have been justified. They were not, however, by any means the same things. Indeed, as Underdown points out, over half the 'revolutionaries' (about fifty-three per cent, as opposed to about fifty-eight per cent of all members able to sit in 1648) were drawn from 'the traditional governors of the kingdom', either from what he calls the 'greater gentry', who exercised extensive influence in the counties in which their estates lay, or from the 'county gentry', who stood only a little lower in the social hierarchy.[2] Revolutions are not made by differences between fifty-three and fifty-eight per cent. It is true that nearly a third of the 'greater' or 'county' gentry families which supplied 'revolutionary' M.P.s, compared with fewer than a quarter of all those which supplied M.P.s able to sit before the purge, had either risen to social eminence relatively recently or were of declining economic fortunes.[3] As the Rump period was to demonstrate, however, men in the upper reaches of an ancient social hierarchy are unlikely to attack that hierarchy simply becaues their position within it is novel or fragile. They are at least as likely, indeed, to do the opposite. 'Revolutionaries' who did not come from the more prominent landed families – whether 'lesser gentlemen' like Cromwell or merchants like John Venn – shared the social convictions of those who did, and never imagined that there was any alternative, other than a hideous anarchy, to the hierarchy to which they were accustomed. There was every difference in outlook between even the socially least distinguished rumpers and the urban craftsmen and artisans who, outside parliament, provided the social base of the radical reform movement. Whatever happened in parliament in December 1648 and January 1649, it was not a class struggle.

[1] These figures are taken or deduced from Underdown, *Pride's Purge*, pp. 405–7.
[2] *Ibid.* pp. 239–40, 405.   [3] *Ibid.* pp. 238–9, 405.

Underdown's decision to combine regicides and early dissenters in the single category of 'revolutionaries', which we have seen to be a sometimes unsatisfactory guide to political developments, is also a slightly misleading yardstick for analysing the relationship between social status and political behaviour. For if we look instead only at the regicides, whom we might expect to have been socially even less eminent than the 'revolutionaries' as a whole, we find that on the contrary they were rather more so. Of the fifteen 'revolutionaries' from greater gentry families, fourteen were regicides; and it was to the socially more exalted 'revolutionaries' that other radical M.P.s tended to turn for leadership in the weeks between the purge and the execution. Fifteen of the forty-three M.P.s who signed the death warrant were identified earlier in this chapter as the regicides most prominent in parliament in December 1648 and January 1649. Not only were these fifteen socially much more impressive than the 'revolutionaries' as a whole; they also included a higher proportion than had the entire membership of the Commons before the purge of men who meet Underdown's various criteria of high social status. Six of them (Hutchinson, Carew, Norton, Lord Grey of Groby and the republicans Marten and Chaloner) were 'greater gentry'; another four (Ludlow, Purefoy, Edwards and Corbet) were 'county gentry'; and four (Hutchinson, Marten, Ludlow and Edwards) were among the M.P.s who sat for the coveted English county seats, which carried so much more social prestige than did the boroughs.[1] Fifteen is, of course, much too small a total to justify ambitious sociological speculation, but it is large enough to suggest what a study of the Rump period as a whole confirms, that the socially more exalted rumpers stood a better chance than their colleagues of winning political prominence. It is also notable that Sir James Harrington, the only 'greater gentleman' among the M.P.s who dissented before the execution without signing the death warrant, was to become the most influential of such members in the Rump.

The 'revolutionaries' had undergone widely differing social and political experiences, and they often held widely differing views. Some of them were men of the world, established merchants or lawyers whose interests centred on London. The majority, however, spent most of their lives in the countryside, displaying when they came to Westminster the dogged, humourless provincialism that was for centuries so marked a feature of English parliaments. Unable to forget

---

[1] Cf. *ibid.* pp. 366–90.

the political enormities and humiliations of the 1620s and 1630s, let alone to bury the passions of the 1640s, they had, many of them, become by the Rump period angry old men, their attitudes hardening with their arteries. They tended to dislike lawyers, who in that extraordinarily litigious age took so much from their pockets and seemed to accomplish so little in return, and clergymen, who presumed to tell them how to worship and what to think; but their hostility to both professions stopped well short of criticism of the social order of which law and church were integral parts. What chance was there of radical reform, indeed, when among the very few M.P.s ever sympathetic to the Levellers were Edmund Ludlow, who, like another regicide William Purefoy, was reluctant during the civil war to lead an armed force raised in his own county to the defence of another, 'foreign' shire; Alexander Rigby, who in the summer of 1648, as the revolution moved towards its crisis, was arranging dancing classes for his *débutante* niece; and Oliver Cromwell, who as Lord Protector was to be appalled by the notion that property was not one of the 'badges of the kingdom of Christ'?[1] The 'revolutionaries' were not the stuff of which social radicalism is made.

Of all the Rump's supposed failings, none has seemed more reprehensible to present-day historians than its failure to implement a programme of social reform. This dismay reflects the priorities of modern scholars, but not those of the Rump. Seventeenth-century parliaments were never the most eager of reforming institutions. The great reformers of the earlier seventeenth century, Cranfield, Bacon and Strafford, were all broken by parliaments. Cromwell, as Lord Protector, came – like Strafford before him – to rely on administrative rather than on legislative reform, and achieved it only when parliament was in abeyance.[2] The reforms demanded by the parliamentary army, very different from those for which Bacon, Cranfield and Strafford had called, were of a kind even less likely to win support in the Rump.

It would be fashionable to view the resistance of gentry M.P.s to demands for social reform simply as an expression of class interest. Such, at root, it may have been; but to assume that that is all it was would be as naive as the contrary (and now unfashionable) fallacy

[1] Underdown, *Pride's Purge*, p. 26; C. A. Holmes, 'The Eastern Association' (Cambridge Ph.D. thesis, 1969), p. 3; *H.M.C.R. Kenyon*, p. 64; Abbott, *Writings and Speeches*, iii. 438.
[2] Cf. C. R. Niehaus, 'The issue of law reform in the Puritan revolution' (Harvard Ph.D. thesis, 1957), chapter 5.

which invests the past with visions of unbroken feudal harmony. To attack the social hierarchy was to threaten the gentry's economic interests and their social status; it was also, in their eyes (and not in the gentry's eyes alone), to jeopardise the survival of a whole way of life and a whole form of civilisation, to call in question the bonds of order, stability and decency and the landmarks which enabled men to distinguish between good and evil. Values frequently transcend, and even come to exist independently of, the social circumstances which give rise to them. And yet, it might be asked, were the implications of the reform movement really so cataclysmic? Would all the reforms demanded by the Levellers in fact have undermined the social fabric? Perhaps not; but whether or not the fabric was seriously threatened, what mattered was that in the Rump period, still more than in the 1640s, M.P.s believed that it was. If it had been possible, in a political vacuum, to invite the views of individual rumpers on specific reform proposals, it may be that many would have expressed a measure of support for them. There were certainly a number of M.P.s who, at least intermittently, favoured a rationalisation of the legal system or of the distribution of parliamentary constituencies, or who were sometimes prepared to advocate a modest degree of religious toleration and a more satisfactory solution to the problem of financing ministers than the tithe system. But politicians do not operate in a vacuum. They are continually subject to pressures and emotions which deflect them from policies or which distort particular issues. Such pressures and emotions worked against the advocates of reform almost throughout the Rump period. Between Pride's Purge and the execution of the king the imminence of anarchy was widely proclaimed, and the army's enthusiasm for social reform at this time may have increased the willingness of M.P.s to try to stem the radical tide by taking their seats in parliament. The traumatic popular reception accorded the king's execution likewise encouraged caution rather than experiment. Thereafter the need to appease the presbyterians, and to prevent them from going over to the royalists, impressed on even the most 'revolutionary' M.P.s, as it impressed on the leading army officers, the importance of emphasising the respectability of the new government's intentions. Once the royalists had been defeated, as they were by September 1651, social radicalism outside parliament became ever more extreme and ever more vociferous. Outlandish schemes, increasingly favoured by the more radical members of the army, were advanced for a wholesale assault on what M.P.s saw as the pillars of society: law, church and ministry. When rumpers, appalled by the army's political ambitions, not surprisingly joined hands in defence of the social order, the cause of moderate reform was lost. Army pressure for reform was not entirely fruitless. Indeed, as we shall see, the Rump gave serious consideration to reform proposals only when the strength of army demands obliged it to do so. Yet demonstrations of army feeling tended to weaken rather than strengthen the reformers' prospects of success – especially after Worcester, when moderate reform proposals were sacrificed to political enmities. Even in the earlier Rump period only four M.P.s, Rigby, Ludlow, Holland and Marten, were willing to work hard and consistently for social reform. By the later Rump period Rigby was dead, Ludlow in Ireland, Holland a spent force, and Marten often preoccupied with other matters. Rumpers with politically radical records were prepared to unite with their more moderate colleagues against the threat of social disruption. Regicides like Cromwell, Scot, Purefoy, Hutchinson, Ireton, Blagrave and Danvers, as well as other 'revolutionaries' like Mildmay, Wroth and Pyne, turned on the Levellers during the Rump period with energy and with an uninhibited sense of conviction.[1] Danvers and Purefoy, the latter a persistent opponent of Marten, were two of the Rump's boldest opponents of reform proposals.[2]

The growth of extreme radicalism outside parliament was not the only reason for the failure of reform proposals within it. Seventeenth-century politicians, unlike their twentieth-century counterparts, did not normally look to state legislation as the obvious instrument of social amelioration. The manner in which M.P.s administered poor relief in their localities, for instance, may indicate a less callous attitude to the needy than is suggested by the Rump's discussions of the poverty problem in the spring of 1649.[3] More important, the Rump was beset from the start by massive fiscal and economic problems and by the need to overhaul naval administration in order to keep its enemies at bay. Barely had it outlived these difficulties when it found itself responsible for lengthy and costly military campaigns, first in Ireland

[1] *C.J.* 12 May, 25 Oct. 1649, 6 Feb. 1652; *The Humble Petition and Advice of John Feilder* (1651), pp. 19, 30; Wolfe, *Leveller Manifestoes*, p. 67; *Perfect Occurrences* 1–8 June 1649, p. 1082; Whitelocke, *Memorials*, iii. 43; *Memoirs of Colonel Hutchinson*, p. 272; *Clarke Papers*, ii. 212–13.

[2] For Danvers: *C.J.* 14, 19, 27 July, 25 Oct. 1649. For Purefoy: *ibid.* 9, 18 Jan., 6, 19 Feb., 18 May, 14 July, 4 Sep. 1649, 9 Aug., 21 Nov. 1650, 31 Jan., 14 Mar., 12, 15 Aug. 1651, 6, 27 Jan., 13 Feb., 8, 24 June, 8, 22 July 1652; Williams, 'Political career of Henry Marten', p. 432n.

[3] Cf. A. L. Beier, 'Poor relief in Warwickshire, 1630–1660', *Past and Present*, 35 (1966).

and then in Scotland. Administrative and financial pressures, and the government's despairing attempts to keep pace with them, relegated reform to the secondary issue which most rumpers in any case considered it to be. When, after the defeat of the royalists, the Rump adopted a policy of naval conflict with the Dutch, its administrative burdens were admittedly the product of choice rather than necessity, but by that time the army's behaviour had made continued warfare, for parliament, a welcome alternative to discussion of reform.

Administration was, after all, the activity in which most of the more energetic M.P.s had distinguished themselves in the 1640s. Where bureaucrats are wanted bureaucrats will always come forward, and the Rump period was no exception. A number of the regicides, absorbing themselves in administrative responsibilities rather than facing up to the practical problems raised by demands for reform, achieved far more as organisers than in the cut and thrust of political debate. Augustine Garland, for example, the most industrious M.P. in the Rump, never acted as a teller in debates or secured appointment to the Council of State. The same was true of another very active committee-man, Daniel Blagrave of Reading. Miles Corbet, an extremely energetic rumper, played a central role in the Rump's early naval reorganisation; yet he acted as teller on only two occasions.[1] Like his friend John Venn, Corbet played a more important part in implementing than in formulating policies. Venn, when he died in the summer of 1650, was succeeded as chairman of the hard-pressed Committee for the Army by another ceaselessly industrious regicide, John Downes, who – apart from being hostile to religious toleration[2] – seems to have taken no interest in reform issues. Not all the 'revolutionaries', of course, were faceless bureaucrats, and not all the Rump's bureaucrats were 'revolutionaries'; but few of the regicides and early dissenters matched the most influential 'conformists' in political acumen. It is indicative of the limits to both the cohesion and the commitment to reform of the 'revolutionaries' that the three main exceptions to this rule, the regicides Scot and Purefoy and the early dissenter Sir James Harrington, all emerged in the Rump period as instruments of moderation. The preoccupations of the 'revolutionaries' as a whole are illustrated by a study of the active membership of the Rump's standing committees, whose main tasks required sustained administrative diligence but little

---

[1] *C.J.* 15, 19, 29 Dec. 1648, 5, 11, 13, 17, 19 Jan., 14 Feb. 1649, 9 July 1650; *Mercurius Pragmaticus* 12–19 Dec. 1648, p. (7); SP 18/5, fos. 24ff.
[2] Whitelocke, *Memorials*, iii. 291; John Fry, *The Accuser Shamed* (1649), pp. 14–17.

in the way of imagination. With one exception, these bodies were dominated by 'revolutionaries' and especially by regicides: this was especially true of the committees whose tasks were related to the exaction of fines and compositions from royalists. The exception, the Committee for Plundered Ministers, was the only one responsible for the formulation of social policy as well as for purely administrative decisions.

To describe as 'revolutionaries' all those who signed Charles's death warrant or who dissented before his execution is, then, both to exaggerate the political radicalism of many M.P.s and to blur the distinction between political radicalism and social radicalism. The Rump's failure to reform is to be explained as much by the behaviour and attitudes of the 'revolutionaries' as by the obstruction provided by the 'conformists'.

MODERATION AND CONFORMITY

On 29 January 1649, when 'one of the late secluded members' managed to take his seat, the Rump resumed discussion of the question of readmitting M.P.s. It decided to adhere to the principle previously adopted of excluding those who had voted the wrong way on 5 December: they 'should not be readmitted, but disabled to sit any longer members for the future'.[1] On 1 February, however, two days after Charles's execution, the House again 'spent much time about reception of members, that so they might go on without interruption, in the intended settlement. Divers members having, since the death of the king, intimated a desire to come in, and some before', the Rump 'at last' resolved on a change of policy. Those who had voted for further negotiations on 5 December were to be allowed to acknowledge the error of their ways and, after registering dissent, to resume active membership. On the same day thirty or more M.P.s dissented accordingly, and a large committee was set up to receive further assurances of dissent from members who would then be allowed to take their seats without official approval from the House itself. Those who failed to dissent by the end of February were, admittedly, to be subjected to much closer scrutiny, but it is likely that at least another forty members had dissented by the 22nd, making a total of about seventy since the king's death.[2] In the three weeks after the execution, the Rump's active membership grew almost daily.[3]

It would be innocent to attribute the sudden 'desire' of so many members to resume their seats to any spontaneous or unsolicited enthusiasm for the new government. Robert Reynolds, who returned to parliament in mid-February, and Henry Oxinden, who after anguished consultation with his friends decided about the same time

[1] *A Perfect Diurnal of some Passages in Parliament* 29 Jan.–5 Feb. 1649, p. 2313.
[2] *The Moderate Intelligencer* 1–8 Feb. 1649, p. (1876); C.J. (MS) xxxiii, pp. 624–7, 631–734; and see Underdown, *Pride's Purge*, p. 218n.
[3] Cf. *Perfect Occurrences* 2–9 Feb. 1649, p. 826, 16–23 Feb. 1649, pp. 860, 864; T. Carte (ed.), *A Collection of Original Letters and Papers . . . 1641 to 1650* (2 vols., 1739), i. 228.

61

to keep away from it, both recorded attempts to persuade them to resume their seats,[1] and they cannot have been the sole recipients of such attentions. The dissent of over thirty members on the very day of the House's change of policy suggests extensive backstage organisation. So, still more, does the return to the House in February of so many members who had played little part in parliament at least since 1647 and who nevertheless now came to Westminster, if rarely for very long, to take their seats. Three of them, indeed, had made no recorded appearances in parliament for at least thirteen months: Robert Brewster of Suffolk and Roger Gratwick of Sussex, both of whom dissented on 1 February, and John Dormer, M.P. for Buckingham, who dissented on the 22nd. Other returning members who had played minimal roles in the House during the previous year included Benjamin Weston (son of the Earl of Portland) and William Armyne (son of the more prominent rumper Sir William), both of whom dissented on 2 February; William Masham, another son of a more important rumper; Robert Blake, later famous as the Commonwealth's General-at-Sea; John Lowry, Cromwell's fellow member for Cambridge and apparently an absentee from parliament since January 1648; and John Feilder, M.P. for St Ives in Cornwall, who had made no recorded appearance since April 1648 but who, alone among these hitherto truant M.P.s, was to follow his reappearance with sustained attendance in the House. He was to prove one of the most conservative influences in the Rump. The return of such absentees testifies to the widespread feeling in February 1649 that the country could be saved from disaster only if men of moderation were prepared to help govern it.[2]

Also among the February dissenters were most of the M.P.s who had continued to sit – at least intermittently – between the purge and the execution but who had managed to avoid taking the test during that time. Thomas Boone, William Lord Monson, Edmund Prideaux, John Trenchard, Rowland Wilson, Bulstrode Whitelocke and Sir Thomas Widdrington, all of whom had sat frequently in December and January, dissented on 1 February. So did five members who had also taken their seats at various points between the purge and the execution, but who had done so less frequently: Sir Edmund Baynton of Wiltshire, who had expressed opposition to the purge on 7 Decem-

---

[1] B.M., Add. MS 28,002, fo. 117; *Diary of Thomas Burton*, iii. 207–9; D. E. Underdown, 'The Independents reconsidered', *Journal of British Studies* iii (1964), 71, and *Pride's Purge*, p. 197.

[2] For the parliamentary activity of these members before the purge see *C.J.* Jan.–Nov. 1648, *passim*.

ber; Francis Lascelles of Yorkshire; Lawrence Whitaker of Devon; John Weaver of Lincolnshire; and, much the most important, Sir Henry Vane the younger.[1] Other members who had likewise attended only rarely between the purge and the execution registered dissent later in February. They included Herbert Morley of Sussex, who in January had defended the House of Lords against the arguments of the abolitionists;[2] Alexander Popham of Somerset, one of the most conservative rumpers,[3] who dissented with his brother Edward; Sir Gilbert Pickering, that intimate and unshakeably loyal ally of Cromwell;[4] the Southwark merchant George Thomson; and the sons of the Earl of Leicester, Algernon Sidney and Philip Lord Lisle, both of whom had withdrawn from parliament in protest against the king's impending execution.[5]

The qualifications which have been applied to Professor Underdown's identification of the 'revolutionaries' in no way detract from, and if anything underline, the fundamental and incontrovertible point to emerge from his work on the Rump's membership: that to sit in the Rump was not in itself an indication of enthusiasm for the events which had brought it to power or of anything that can usefully be described as political radicalism. Underdown's portrait of his 'conformists', of whom he is evidently not fond, as men 'who merely climbed on the band-wagon' after the king's execution is perhaps unnecessarily pejorative. Some of them had more positive motives than a desire to climb on a band-wagon, and as band-wagons go the new government was not a particularly comfortable one to join. Trimming is rarely an attractive activity, but it is not always a disreputable one. If the aims of the 'conformists' were often more positive than Underdown allows, however, they were certainly not more radical. Some of the 'revolutionaries', I have argued, were impelled by such unrevolutionary aims as a desire to restrain radical tendencies by influencing the course of events from within, to preserve power in civilian hands, to serve the interests of constituents, or merely to remain active in politics. Such considerations were still more apparent among

[1] Cf. Underdown, *Pride's Purge*, pp. 196–7; *Diary of Thomas Burton*, iii. 174, 176; *C.J.* 19 Dec. 1648, 6, 20, 29 Jan. 1649.

[2] *C.J.* 18 Jan. 1649.

[3] See e.g. *ibid.* 1 Mar. 1650, 14 Mar. 1651.

[4] For their cooperation see e.g. B.M., Add. MS 31,984, fos. 161&^{v}, 204^v, 221; Whitelocke, *Journal of the Swedish Embassy*, i. 7–20; SP: 25/40, pp. 8, 27; 25/66, pp. 265, 595.

[5] *H.M.C.R. De Lisle and Dudley*, vi. 580, 584; R. W. Blencowe (ed.), *The Sydney Papers* (1825), p. 237; Underdown, *Pride's Purge*, pp. 187–8. The precise date of Sidney's dissent is unclear: Underdown, *Pride's Purge*, p. 218n.

the 'conformists', many of whom had, as Hyde observed, been generally regarded before the purge as political presbyterians.[1] There were, it is true, a small number of 'conformists', like Wentworth, Gurdon and Weaver, who in 1648 had tried as hard as anyone to steer parliament in a revolutionary direction and whose failure to dissent before the execution is therefore surprising; and there were rather more among them who had been prepared in 1648 to impose harsh terms on the king but who had drawn back in the face of the execution. In the main, however, the 'conformists' had long shown, and in the Rump period continued to show, a pronounced lack of revolutionary zeal. The M.P.s who failed to commit themselves to the new government before the act of regicide, between them comprising about two-thirds of the Rump's membership, were in general men among whom the purge and the execution had aroused no support and, in many cases, considerable unease.

The civil war was a conflict about how the country should be governed. It was not a conflict about why the country should be governed. Most M.P.s, whether Cavaliers or Roundheads, were apolitical in outlook, regarding political differences as of secondary importance to the preservation of the ordered world they knew, and sharing conventional and non-partisan assumptions about the ends of government. The 'conformist' Whitelocke took it for granted that 'government is a well ordering, managing and guidance of persons and affairs, that men may live well and happily. It is called the art of reason, to keep men in such order that they may live peaceably and plentifully.'[2] Bewildered and dismayed by the events of the 1640s, Whitelocke viewed the revolution as an affront to nature. Had it not occurred he, like other rumpers, would never have troubled his head about the issues it raised, or have found himself keeping radical company.[3] As it was, he joined the Rump. If order, peace and plenty were the ultimate concerns of politics, it made sense to trim with events, to influence them from within, and so help ensure the survival of traditional forms of social and political organisation. The conformists who returned to the Commons in February 1649 were in no sense taking sides against the M.P.s who continued to boycott it. They were not consciously committing themselves to 'the Rump'; they were merely resuming their places in a parliament in which they had long been accustomed to

[1] *Nicholas Papers*, i. 141.
[2] B.M., Stowe MS 333, fo. 73.
[3] Cf. Whitelocke, *Memorials*, iii. 80.

sit. They were making decisions about their immediate responsibilities, not about future and unforeseeable party loyalties: only later did it become evident that the events of late 1648 and early 1649 had created a distinction between rumpers and non-rumpers, between the Rump and the Long Parliament before it. The distinction did not correspond to any natural division of opinion among M.P.s.

The members who sat frequently between the purge and the execution, but who dissented only in February, contributed much to the character of Rump politics. In general, however, the most important February dissenters were those who had played a consistently active role in parliament before the purge but who had kept completely clear of the House in the weeks which followed it. Returning in February, they exercised a decisive and moderating influence on government policies. Sir William Armyne of Lincolnshire, one of the most respected if not always one of the most industrious rumpers, was one example: others were the elder Thomas Pury of Gloucestershire, an energetic administrator in the Rump's early stages; Sir William Masham of Essex, member of a distinguished East Anglian connection which in the 1640s had consistently advocated moderating policies;[1] Sir William Brereton, the Long Parliament's supremo in Cheshire; and Robert Reynolds, the Rump's solicitor-general, who 'had no hand in, nor heart for, trying the king', and who later recalled how in February 1649 'I came to town, and was importuned to come into the House. I thought I might do some good. To take off free quarter, and excise of ale and beer was no ill deed; and, seeing I must sit here, I would keep up as much of the people's rights as I could.'[2] Such dampening sentiments were characteristic of the Rump's conservative lawyers, all of whom shared Reynolds's tendency to swim with events of which they disapproved. Most of them likewise dissented in February: Whitelocke, Widdrington, Hill, Long, Erasmus Earle, and finally Nicholas Lechmere, whose political testament reveals his dislike of all forms of radicalism, and especially of military radicalism. His two main political concerns seem to have been to protect his own profession from the demands of reformers, and to restrict the punitive treatment of royalists.[3] There was nothing radical, either, about two ageing but influential February dissenters, Sir Henry Vane the elder and Francis Rous.

[1] Hexter, *Reign of King Pym*, pp. 87, 89n.; Abbott, *Writings and Speeches*, i. 54, 119.
[2] *Diary of Thomas Burton*, ii. 207–9; Underdown, 'The Independents reconsidered', p. 71.
[3] E. P. Shirley, *Hanley and the House of Lechmere* (1883), pp. 28, 31; *H.M.C.R. Lord Hatherton*, p. 298; *C.C.C.*, pp. 2229, 2867, 2870, 3056.

Rous went into print in the earlier Rump period, using openly 'loyalist' arguments to urge other members to return to parliament and so to influence from within a government of which they, like he, could not approve. The only alternative, Rous believed, was an anarchy which would 'level the rich with the poor'.[1]

Easily the most influential member returning in February, however, was Sir Arthur Heselrige. Of a prominent Leicestershire family, he had been one of the 'five members' before the civil war, a leader of the war party during it, and the organiser of the 'flight to the army' in 1647, creating for himself in the meantime an impressive political empire in the northern counties. A man of quick temper and wearisome obstinacy, he was nevertheless one of the most skilful (if hardly one of the most constructive) politicians of the English revolution. Despite being nominated as one of Charles's judges, he remained during the weeks following Pride's Purge at his post as governor of Newcastle.[2] Within a few days of the execution he left for London, ostensibly 'upon some extraordinary occasion in relation to the [Newcastle] garrison',[3] but in reality upon a much more important mission. He made a well-advertised return to the Commons in mid-February, to be quickly joined by his cousin and ally George Fenwick, who had likewise kept out of the way in December and January.[4] Regarded by the Rump's conservative enemies as a bulwark against radical tendencies in the new government,[5] Heselrige sought immediately after his return to London to broaden the base of its support. He subsequently confirmed his opposition to Pride's Purge, with which, as he said, he had had 'nought to do'.[6] Oliver St John described Heselrige and Vane the younger as the 'well-head' of the new government.[7] He was right. Although Heselrige spent much of the Rump period helping to keep the peace in the northern counties,

[1] Underdown, *Pride's Purge*, pp. 263–4; Wallace, 'The engagement controversy', pp. 384–5, and *Destiny His Choice*, pp. 45–6.

[2] Underdown (*Pride's Purge*, p. 188n.) notes that Heselrige's signature appears on an Army Committee warrant dated 2 January 1649, but concludes that 'either the warrant must be misdated' or Heselrige 'signed it retrospectively'. A study of Army Committee warrants as a whole, and especially of those for January 1649, shows that the latter explanation is the correct one. Heselrige was certainly in Newcastle on 27 January: SP 28/58, fo. 142^v.

[3] *Perfect Diurnal . . . Parliament* 5–12 Feb. 1649, p. 2325.

[4] *C.J.* 12, 15, 17 Feb. 1649; *Perfect Occurrences* 9–16 Feb. 1649, p. 848.

[5] *A Brief Narration of the Mysteries of State carried on by the Spanish Faction in England* (The Hague, 1651), pp. 109–10; and see *Complete Writings of Roger Williams*, vi. 255.

[6] *Diary of Thomas Burton*, iii. 96, iv. 78.

[7] J. Nickolls (ed.), *Original Letters and Papers of State addressed to Oliver Cromwell* (1743), p. 48.

his political influence during his extended stays in London, and even during his spells away from it, can scarcely be exaggerated. Nor, at least until 1651, can the influence of Vane, the doyen of financial, naval and diplomatic affairs during the Commonwealth. Like Heselrige he had been one of the most important politicians of the 1640s; like Heselrige he had established a strong political base in the north; like Heselrige he was a renowned enemy of the Levellers; and like Heselrige he sought in February 1649 to place moderates in positions of power. In the 1640s, while Charles was still alive, both Heselrige and Vane had been regarded as uncompromising radicals: in the earlier 1650s, when the army's political pretensions and its demands for social reform had so altered the nature of the revolution, they seemed nothing of the kind.

Who organised the return to parliament of so many of its members during the first three weeks of February? The large number of M.P.s who reported the individual dissents of other members to the House suggests that many rumpers, perhaps often on their own initiative, were involved in the process of persuasion. There can be little doubt, however, which of them took the lead. In the autumn of 1648 Oliver Cromwell had remained on military duty in the north, 'waiting on God', undergoing one of those periods of prolonged introspection which usually preceded his more decisive political interventions. Long resisting suggestions that he should return to Westminster, he contrived to reach London only on the evening of 6 December, the day on which the purge had begun.[1] Among the soldiers at Whitehall he 'was most joyfully received . . . with many pious compliments', and when told of the purge replied disingenuously 'that he had not been acquainted with this design; yet since it was done he was glad of it, and would endeavour to maintain it'.[2] In the following month he did quite the reverse. Blunting the radical edge of army policies, he discreetly sought to postpone the trial of the king and to preserve the House of Lords, and wooed the members who had voluntarily withdrawn from the House. He also spread the word in the city of London that he had been opposed to the purge, and sent his trusted ally Robert Tichborne to try to secure the cooperation of the city divines who were protesting so vigorously against the army's actions. Between 18 and 25 December he was at the centre of moves to undo the purge and spare the king, inviting Whitelocke 'to frame somewhat in order to the restitution of

[1] Underdown, *Pride's Purge*, pp. 119, 148–50.
[2] *Mercurius Elencticus* 5–12 Dec. 1648, p. 528; *Memoirs of Edmund Ludlow*, i. 211–12.

the secluded members'.[1] The failure of Whitelocke's subsequent initiative drove the trimming lawyer to his country seat at Henley-on-Thames, but John Owen, later chaplain to Cromwell and probably already under his wing, went after him to persuade him to return to Westminster.[2] When, early in January 1649, it became clear that army feeling in favour of executing Charles was too strong to resist, Cromwell temporarily abandoned the policy of conciliation and devoted both his political and his spiritual energies to bringing the king to justice;[3] yet it was Cromwell, more than anyone else, who amidst the rubble of monarchical government was to shape the essentially unrevolutionary character of the Rump regime.

Owen, in his pursuit of Whitelocke, preached before him 'two excellent sermons. And upon discourse concerning the present affairs of the army he seemed much to favour them, and spoke in dislike of those members who voluntarily absented themselves from the House, having no particular force upon their persons.' This was on 31 December.[4] On 31 January, the day after Charles's execution, Owen delivered to the Commons a fast sermon of similarly unrevolutionary import. Passing quickly over the events of the previous day, he, like his fellow preacher John Cardell, urged parliament to woo 'fainters in difficult seasons', in other words those who after the purge had voluntarily withdrawn from political activity. The new government should 'be not too hasty in laying further burdens' upon 'such, as for want of light, want of faith, sit down and sigh in darkness . . . Labour to recover others, even all that were ever distinguished and called by the name of the Lord, from their late fearful returning to sinful compliance with the enemies of God and the nation.'[5] Whether or not Owen was acting as

---

1 Underdown, *Pride's Purge*, pp. 158, 166–70; Clarendon MS 34, fo. 73ᵛ; *Mercurius Pragmaticus* 26 Dec. 1648–9 Jan. 1649, pp. (5), (8); *A Modest and Clear Vindication of the Serious Representation* (1649), p. 9; *Brief Narration of the Mysteries of State*, p. 65.

2 B.M., Add. MS 37,344, fo. 240&ᵛ. Cf. *ibid.* fo. 189&ᵛ. The usual view that Cromwell and Owen did not even know each other until April 1649 or even early 1650 rests on the most slender of evidence, and is intrinsically improbable. Owen was already a prominent figure by December 1648 and was in close touch with a number of M.P.s. See e.g. J. Asty (ed.), *A Complete Collection of the Sermons of the Reverend and Learned John Owen, D.D.*, p. 270; E. Hockliffe (ed.), *The Diary of the Rev. R. Josselin* (Camden Soc., 1908), pp. 43, 48, 84–5. See also Asty, *op. cit.* p. 234.

3 Underdown, *Pride's Purge*, pp. 184–5.

4 B.M., Add. MS 37,344, fo. 240&ᵛ.

5 Asty, *Sermons of John Owen*, esp. pp. 270, 278, 280, 281, 309; J. Cardell, *God's Wisdom Justified and Man's Folly Condemned* (1649), esp. pp. 13–14, 30. Cf. J. Milton, *The Tenure of Kings and Magistrates* (ed. W. T. Allison, New York, 1911), pp. 4–5. My view of the political purpose of these sermons differs from those advanced by Professor Trevor-Roper (*Religion, The Reformation and Social Change*, p. 337) and by other historians.

Cromwell's mouthpiece (and it is hard to believe that he was not), Cromwell certainly pursued the policies which Owen advocated. He was said to have persuaded Vane the younger to return to the House in February,[1] when he also did all he could to ensure that 'conformists' held influential positions in the government. In April 1649, as in the previous December, he sought to secure the readmission to parliament of all the purged members. The failure of this move did not weaken his resolve to heal the breach within the parliamentary cause which the events of December 1648 and January 1649 had brought about, and for the rest of the Rump period he tried to persuade members who had withdrawn at the purge to return to the House.

The more we learn about individual rumpers, the harder it is to draw a convincing distinction between 'revolutionaries' and 'conformists'. The task becomes impossible when we consider Cromwell, the rumper about whom we know most. It would indeed be hard to exaggerate the influence of the ambiguities of Cromwell's political temperament on Rump politics. A conservative by social instinct and early political training, he was inspired to spiritual radicalism by his role as God's instrument of victory in the civil war, by his intimacy with his troops, and by his informal but weighty responsibilities as patron of the religious sects.[2] What resulted was (to simplify) a kind of ideological schizophrenia, setting him on an almost predictable course of political self-destruction. Whenever the social order seemed in peril, whenever the spectre of anarchy was raised, he would expound the virtues of harmony and property and set about repairing the damage; but when he had done so, and when inevitably the cause then strayed once more from the paths of righteousness and reform, he would inveigh against the soullessness of his more temperate colleagues, and destroy the good-will he had so scrupulously fostered. Endlessly patient in building political unity, Cromwell was sudden and terrible in its destruction. So it was with the Rump government, which he took such pains to create and which he was so dramatically to shatter.

That so many 'conformists' were allowed to return to parliament in the weeks after the king's death is a striking testament to the lack of cohesion displayed by the 'revolutionaries' and to the limits of their revolu-

---

[1] *A Vindication of that prudent and honourable Knight Sir Henry Vane* (1659), p. 7. Cf. Lilburne, *Legal, Fundamental Liberties*, p. 16.
[2] See e.g. Abbott, *Writings and Speeches*, i. 80, 136, 258, 344, 360, 377, 408, 428, 432, 434, 452, 619, 638, 646, 697–8; *Reliquiae Baxterianae*, pp. 50–3, 56–7.

tionary aims. By 22 February, however, those who between the purge
and the execution had 'run the utmost hazard' were becoming resentful
of the 'many members' who 'had been absent for many months in the
country, and had not appeared in the late transactions of parliament,
for abolishing the House of Lords, or for trial of the late king; and did
now endeavour to come to the House, after the storm is over, to
receive the honour and benefit of those great undertakings.'[1] On 23
February it was accordingly resolved that members who had not sat
since the end of the previous month, 'except such as have been upon
martial employments, etc.', should be denied entry until further notice.[2]
Two more members were readmitted on 28 February; six, who were
still in the provinces, were excused for their failure to meet the deadline
for dissent set for the same day; and one, William Carent, was allowed
back on 5 March. Carent's admission, however, was the last for more
than a month. Also on the 5th, the large committee previously appointed to receive dissents was replaced by a five-man 'Committee for
Absent Members', with power to interrogate candidates for admission.[3] The committee members, as William Prynne observed, were
'some of the most eminent dissenters . . . and so not very inclinable to
receive satisfaction, from other M.P.s.[4] Ludlow, who was on the committee, recalled that members who came before it were asked not
merely, as the members hitherto readmitted had been, to disavow the
vote of 5 December, but to declare that 'they approved of the proceedings against the king . . . and . . . would engage to be true to a Commonwealth government'. For

> we apprehending such extraordinary expulsions as had lately been used, to be
> extremely hazardous to the public safety, made it our endeavour to keep those
> from a readmission, who might necessitate another occasion of using the like
> remedy. And therefore, though all possible satisfactions were given in words, we
> did, by weighing the former deportment of every particular member who
> presented himself, desire to be in some measure assured, that they would be
> true to what they promised, in case the Commonwealth interest should come
> to be disputed, before we would report their condition to the House.

One M.P., refused membership of the Rump after such examination,
later referred to his interrogators as the 'committee of inquisition'.[5]

[1] *Memoirs of Colonel Hutchinson*, p. 271; *Perfect Diurnal . . . Parliament* 19–26 Feb. 1649,
p. (2344).
[2] C.J. (MS) xxxiii, p. 736.
[3] *C.J.* 28 Feb., 5 Mar. 1649; Underdown, *Pride's Purge*, p. 217.
[4] Prynne, *A Full Declaration*, p. 26.
[5] *Memoirs of Edmund Ludlow*, i. 226; *Diary of Thomas Burton*, iii. 214.

Yet the inquisitors did not have it all their own way. Prynne believed that the House, in setting up the Committee for Absent Members, had intended to facilitate the readmission of more M.P.s than the committee was prepared to allow, and conflict soon developed between those rumpers who wished to expand and those who wished to restrict the House's membership. The committee was instructed by the House to meet regularly, and thirty-six more M.P.s were able to resume their seats between early April and early August.[1] A few of these, like Richard Salwey (who had helped draft the republican resolution of 4 January) and William Sydenham (who early in February had acted as teller in favour of a motion to save the House of Lords) had previously appeared in the Rump.[2] They had evidently failed to dissent by the end of February, however, and so had been obliged to apply to the Committee for Absent Members before securing readmission. The others had not sat since the purge, and most of them, for all the difference they made to Rump politics, might just as well have stayed permanently away. Of all the members readmitted between April and August, Salwey alone was one of the sixty or seventy rumpers who during the Rump period regarded parliamentary activity as their main occupation. Of the others, Sir John Trevor (once a close friend of John Hampden and in the Rump period one of Herbert Morley's most distinguished allies), Sydenham, Charles Fleetwood, Henry Darley (an important 'middle group' politician in the 1640s), John Moyle and Sir William Strickland all at various points made an impact on political developments. The rest, however, were among the hundred or so rumpers who attended parliament only rarely. As a group, the men who returned between April and August were of higher social rank and greater wealth than their colleagues.[3] Many of them were prosperous country gentlemen putting in occasional appearances at Westminster, just as their ancestors had put in occasional appearances at Westminster for generations. Among the rumpers returning between April and August, but thereafter playing a minimal role in the House, was the Cheshire judge Thomas Fell, who had protected his royalist father from sequestration. According to a report sent to a regicide M.P. in February 1649, Fell 'hath deserted the parliament, and was none of those that were secluded, but ran into the country because he would not join with you

[1] *C. J.* 23 Mar., 6, 18, 27 Apr., 7, 14, 22 May, 2, 4, 6, 19, 21, 29 June, 6, 23 July, 5 Aug. 1649.
[2] *C. J.* 4 Jan., 6 Feb. 1649.
[3] Cf. Underdown, *Pride's Purge*, p. 405.

that took this great work upon you; [and] lurks in the country to see
the event of things, that so he may come in smoothly when the coast
is clear'.[1] Others were the lawyer William Ellis, who after Pride's
Purge had sued for a writ of habeas corpus on behalf of the army's
prisoner William Prynne;[2] Francis Pierrepoint, William's much less
influential brother, later said by Mrs Hutchinson to have been involved
in a 'presbyterian' plot against the Rump;[3] and Sir Peter Temple,
accused in the House early in 1652 of conspiring with royalists: the
charge did not stick, but it is interesting that it was taken seriously.[4]
Some of the M.P.s given permission to return in the summer of 1649 –
like Francis Bacon, who seems to have been no friend to the Rump[5] –
may in fact never have resumed their seats.[6]

Only seven members were readmitted to the House after August
1649. Two of them were allowed back in November 1650, one, Hugh
Rogers, making no recorded appearance thereafter, the other, Richard
Edwards, making only one recorded appearance thereafter, and that
when he was specially summoned to attend.[7] Another four members
were permitted to return, probably through Cromwell's influence, in
the autumn of 1651, Thomas Westrow, Richard Norton, Sir Thomas
Wodehouse and John Stephens.[8] All of them had opposed the purge
and the execution. The seventh was the Northamptonshire magnate
Sir John Dryden, admitted in April 1652. He made no recorded
appearance thereafter, although he did occasionally attend meetings of
the Committee for Plundered Ministers.[9] The Rump's membership
was completed by the election of nine members returned in by-elections held to replace some, but not all, of the excluded members who
died between 1648 and 1653. One of the nine, Henry Neville, was
returned for Abingdon, formerly the seat of his close friend Henry
Marten, who came to Neville's defence when the latter's election was
disputed in the House. So did Algernon Sidney, who like Marten and
Neville was to become one of the most famous republicans produced

[1] SP 19/118, no. 53.
[2] Underdown, *Pride's Purge*, p. 194.
[3] *Memoirs of Colonel Hutchinson*, p. 284; cf. A. C. Wood, *Nottinghamshire in the Civil War* (1937), p. 161.
[4] *C.J.* 21 Jan., 3 Feb. 1652.
[5] Holmes, 'The Eastern Association', p. 274.
[6] Cf. *C.J.* 6 June 1649 with *Perfect Occurrences* 25 May–1 June 1649, p. 1092; and see William Salt Library (Stafford), Salt MS 454 (Swynfen), no. 6: John Trevor to John Swynfen, 9 Jan. 1651.
[7] *C.J.* 20, 26 Nov. 1650, 24 Jan. 1651.
[8] *C.J.* 17 Oct., 26, 27 Nov. 1651.
[9] SP 22/F2, fos. 405, 408ᵛ, 412, 432.

by the revolution.[1] Also returned in by-elections, after the Rump's decision to permit the election of peers as commoners, were Lord Howard of Escrick and the Earls of Pembroke and Salisbury. The admission of 'this unsavoury trio', as Brunton and Pennington have called them, increased the considerable contempt in which they were already held by their fellow peers.[2] Their behaviour in the Rump deservedly lowered their reputations still further. The admission of peers to the lower house no doubt afforded Marten and his republican friends a pleasurable sense of condescension, but it did nothing to increase the radical vote.

The fact that so few active or influential members were allowed to return after February 1649 may look at first like a victory for the diehard 'revolutionaries'. The damage to the revolutionary cause, however, had already been done by the end of February. For it is probable that the overwhelming majority of those who actively sought readmission after the king's execution were granted it. About twenty-five M.P.s who appeared before the Committee for Absent Members between March and July 1649 were almost certainly refused admission, but it is unlikely that many other non-rumpers applied.[3] Four members, Sir John Barrington, Sir Thomas and Sir Nathaniel Barnardiston and Thomas Cholmeley, were given every opportunity to resume their seats and yet declined to do so.[4] The pressure put on them, and on other members reluctant to join the Rump like the Bacon brothers, suggests that as many rumpers were keen to persuade unrevolutionary members to sit as were anxious to keep them out. The conflict between the Rump and its Committee for Absent Members was, however, of secondary importance in determining the character of the regime. It was the February readmissions, enabling so many influential and energetic members to return, which mattered. The battle between 'revolutionaries' and 'conformists' was won and lost in the three weeks or so following the execution of the king. If the 'conformists' emerged as clear winners, then many 'revolutionaries' were evidently glad to be on the losing side.

[1] *C.J.* 11 Oct. 1649.
[2] Brunton and Pennington, *Members of the Long Parliament*, p. 105. Cf. Underdown, *Pride's Purge*, p. 168, and *H.M.C.R. Southampton and King's Lynn*, p. 182.
[3] Verney MS 636,10: newsletter 3 May 1649; Walker, *History of Independency*, ii. 210; and cf. *C.J.* 23 July 1649 with *A Perfect Summary of an Exact Diary of some Passages in Parliament 9–16 July 1649*, p. (105), with *A Perfect Diurnal of some Passages and Proceedings of, and in relation to, the Armies 9–16 July 1649*, p. (8), and with *A Tuesday's Journal of Perfect Passages in Parliament 17–24 July 1649*, pp. 7–8.
[4] Underdown, *Pride's Purge*, p. 218n.; *C.J.* 23 July 1649.

SOLDIERS AND CLERGYMEN

Cromwell, although preeminent among the army leaders when he chose to be, did not become Lord General until June 1650, when Fairfax resigned his command rather than lead an army into Scotland. Fairfax, admitted to the Rump with his fellow army officer Nathaniel Rich after a disputed election, seems never to have taken his seat. Opposed to the purge and the execution, he, like so many others, remained at his post as long as he felt able to moderate the revolution's course.[1] Other army officers who took their seats in the Rump included Richard Ingoldsby, a regicide who rarely attended the House, Philip Skippon, who played a central role in Pride's Purge but who was nevertheless always one of the more moderate army leaders, and Charles Fleetwood, a 'conformist' who enjoyed Cromwell's confidence. More important were two other army M.P.s, Henry Ireton and Thomas Harrison, who had provided the radical initiative in the Council of Officers in the autumn of 1648. In December and January both men underwent changes of mind, with profound consequences for the character of the Commonwealth regime.

Harrison, later to emerge as the leader of the Fifth Monarchists and as the focus of the army's most radical aspirations, had in November 1648 been as anxious as anyone to dissolve the Long Parliament, if necessary by force. Yet, at the height of the crisis between the purge and the execution, he acknowledged that the day of the saints had not yet dawned, and conceded that power must remain in the hands of the existing parliament.[2] Ireton's submission to the Rump's survival represented an equally marked and even more consequential change of policy. In the autumn of 1648 he had struggled hard, and eventually successfully, to persuade his fellow officers to acknowledge the need for the Long Parliament's speedy dissolution. In the event, bowing to the arguments of M.P.s like Ludlow, he contented himself with a purge,

[1] Underdown, *Pride's Purge*, pp. 189–93.
[2] A. S. P. Woodhouse (ed.), *Puritanism and Liberty* (1938), pp. 176–8.

'thereby preserving the name and place of the parliament'.[1] It was probably the most critical decision of his career. His revolutionary zeal steadily declined thereafter, until by the spring of 1649 he was evidently reconciled to the entrenchment of the Rump's authority. In the summer he left for Ireland, where he stayed until his death in December 1651. His departure deprived the army leadership of its most talented and clear-headed radical thinker, but his day as revolutionary leader had already passed with his acceptance of the Rump's survival.

The behaviour of Harrison and Ireton after Pride's Purge indicated the pressures on the radical leadership both inside and outside parliament towards moderation. It also exposed contradictions in radical views. Ireton wanted political revolution and social reform; he was also an astute politician who saw that revolution, to succeed, must appear as respectable as possible, and that the Levellers, with many of whose sentiments he sympathised, constituted a major embarrassment to his programme. In the autumn of 1648 a tactical contest had developed between Ireton, who as Lilburne complained was at that time the army's 'alpha and omega',[2] and the Leveller leadership. The march on London at the beginning of December, central to Ireton's plans, was opposed by Lilburne and his friends, who feared that the officers might exercise a power as arbitrary as that of Charles I. Less interested in political revolution than in social reform, they were anxious to secure formal commitment from the officers to the *Agreement of the People*, the manifesto defining their programme, before consenting to an armed assault on the political establishment. Ireton, knowing that king and parliament bent on a treaty would not wait for the army to resolve its differences, wanted to march on London first and to worry about the *Agreement* afterwards. Believing that such divisive issues as the religious toleration demanded by the Levellers must not be allowed to deflect the army from its immediate purpose of trying the king, he continually emphasised his colleagues' respect, which he fully shared, for the social order and the rights of property.[3] The moves against king and parliament, he emphasised, would involve only a temporary suspension of 'magistracy'. Prynne, the most eloquent of the army's opponents in parliament before the purge, exalted 'the beauty of order and golden reins of discipline': the army, under Ireton's guidance,

---

[1] Underdown, *Pride's Purge*, pp. 132–3; *Memoirs of Edmund Ludlow*, i. 206.

[2] Lilburne, *Legal, Fundamental Liberties*, p. 31.

[3] *Ibid.* pp. 31, 34–5; Woodhouse, *Puritanism and Liberty*, pp. 129–33, 148–50, 152, 154–6, 161–3, 166–74.

protested 'the real love they bear to the silver cords of amity and concord'.[1] The outcome of Ireton's conflict with the Levellers was a triumph for his political skill. As Lilburne put it, Ireton and the officers 'undertook merely to quiet and please us (like children with rattles) till they had done their main work; viz. either in annihilating or purging the House to make it fit for their purpose, and in destroying the king'.[2] In the decisive period from late-November to mid-January, Leveller energies were absorbed in the framing of an *Agreement of the People* which barely influenced the ensuing settlement. The officers, having diluted the *Agreement*, finally presented it to the Rump on 20 January, with a tepid preamble making clear that they did not expect the House to implement it. The House listened only to the preamble and laid the *Agreement* itself aside, 'it being long'.[3]

The defeat of the Levellers enabled Fairfax to lead a united army on London. It also showed the limits of the influence exerted by Leveller doctrine on soldiers more readily attracted by the prospects of pay, justice and revenge. These enticements were skilfully dangled by the army leaders before troops who might be expected to share Lilburne's scruples at the march on the capital. The form taken by the purge can be at least partly explained by the officers' willingness, in their desire to preserve army unity, to give satisfying vent to the resentments of the soldiery. So, too, can the contradictions and confusions of an aggressive document handed in to the Commons by the army on 6 December.[4] The troops were evidently given to believe that a march on London would provide access to large sums of money stored in the city treasuries, and that the M.P.s who were to be imprisoned had been largely responsible for withholding their pay.[5] The prisoners were subjected to scandalous indignities at the soldiers' hands immediately after the purge, when the story was circulated that they were to be

---

[1] *A Remonstrance of . . . Fairfax . . . and . . . the General Council* (Nov. 1648), pp. 3, 5–6; *His Majesty's Declaration and Remonstrance* (1648), p. 3; W. Prynne, *A Vindication of the Imprisoned and Secluded Members* (1649), p. 18.

[2] Lilburne, *Legal, Fundamental Liberties*, p. 37. Cf. his *The Second Part of England's New Chains Discovered* (1649), p. 13; Clarendon MS 34, fos. 12, 72&ᵛ; *A Perfect Diurnal . . . Parliament* 8–15 Jan. 1649, p. 2272.

[3] *A Petition from . . . Fairfax and the General Council . . . concerning the Draft of an Agreement of the People* (1649), esp. pp. 5–6; Whitelocke, *Memorials*, ii. 499.

[4] J. Rushworth (ed.), *Historical Collections* (8 vols., 1659–1701), viii. 1354–5. One of the document's inconsistencies is noted in S. R. Gardiner, *The History of the Great Civil Wars* (4 vols., 1893–4), iv. 271 and n. There are many others.

[5] *Kingdom's Weekly Intelligencer* 28 Nov.–5 Dec. 1648, p. 1175; Walker, *History of Independency*, ii. 31.

tried by court-martial.[1] Thereafter the officers, as perceptive critics understood,[2] were able to contain the demand for pay by emphasising the alternative attraction of reprisals against the army's enemies. The purge, the troops were given to understand, had been merely the opening stage in a process of 'executing of impartial justice upon king, lords, and commons, and all others (even from the highest to the lowest)'.[3]

Too little is known of the varieties of opinion within the Council of Officers to explain satisfactorily the vacillations of army policy in December 1648. Yet, if compared with the army's rhetoric, the purge itself was an almost tame affair. It was certainly much tamer than the forcible dissolution which had previously been planned would have been. Only after the refusal of the M.P.s admitted to the House on 6 December to yield to army pressure did the officers resort to the exclusion of more than forty-one M.P.s, and even then it seems to have been widely believed that the purge was intended as a temporary measure, designed to bar hostile members from the House only until Charles had been executed.[4] Despite the ill treatment at first meted out to the imprisoned M.P.s, the officers soon became embarrassed by the arrests they had sanctioned. Some of the prisoners were quickly released, while others, aware of the political capital to be made by remaining in a captivity which in any case became increasingly less uncomfortable, were urged almost apologetically to go home. Sixteen of them were even given the army's blessing to resume their seats in parliament.[5] This move, which doubtless enjoyed Cromwell's approval but which probably did not have the support of the Council of Officers as a whole, was quickly defeated by the imposition of the test of dissent, but not before the limits of the army leaders' commitment to revolution had been exposed. Some officers may even have believed – and hoped – that the prisoners, now released, would readily take the test. The army's willingness, both before and after the purge, to put out feelers to such eminently unrevolutionary figures as Whitelocke, Lord Lisle and the Earls of Pembroke and Warwick provides an instructive

---

[1] *The Staff set at the Parliament's own Door* (1648), p. 8.
[2] B.M., Thomason MS E537(8), fo. 1&ᵛ; *The Faithful Soldier* (1649), p. 4.
[3] *His Majesty's Declaration and Remonstrance*, pp. 3-4.
[4] *Kingdom's Weekly Intelligencer* 19–26 Dec. 1648, p. 1195; *Buller Papers*, p. 110; Raines and Sutton, *Life of Humphrey Chetham*, p. 163; N.L.W., MS 11,434B, fo. 2.
[5] Walker, *History of Independency*, ii. 31, 49; Whitelocke, *Memorials*, ii. 478; Clarendon MS 34, fo. 19&ᵛ; *Mercurius Elencticus* 12–19 Dec. 1648, p. 539; Underdown, *Pride's Purge*, pp. 153–4.

contrast to the radicalism of its public utterances.[1] The purge, satisfying the soldiery's crudest political instincts, also set up a smokescreen behind which more moderate purposes were at work. Once the smoke had cleared, it became evident that the revolutionary enthusiasm of the senior officers was confined within the same limits as those which inhibited the zeal of the 'revolutionaries' in parliament. At first sight the purge looks like a decisive break with the constitutionalist programme pursued by parliament in the 1640s. In fact, it served to preserve that tradition. No more conservative solution to the conflict between parliament and army in the later 1640s can be readily imagined than the Rump.

The members who survived the purge were frequently described by their enemies as 'Pride's juncto', as mere schoolboys obedient to every whim of their masters in the army.[2] Certainly the army exerted much more influence, and commanded much more attention, in parliament after the purge than before it. Once the officers had agreed on the need for the Rump's survival, however, the army became as dependent on parliament as was parliament, at war with the royalists in Ireland and Scotland, on the army. For what alternative to the Rump was there? After the purge the officers had at first demanded that parliament dissolve itself by the end of April 1649.[3] Fresh elections, however, were likely simply to restore to power those against whom the army had rebelled in the later 1640s. Military rule, in any case so unpalatable to Cromwell and indeed, at this stage, to most of the officers, would alienate still further those who had already been appalled by the purge and the execution and perhaps drive them into the hands of the royalists. What the officers needed was time, time to live down the trauma of the execution, time to set the regime's finances and its navy in order. Increasingly they found themselves emphasising the moderation of the new government and, in consequence, entrusting as much power as they dared to civilian hands. The Rump's survival, and the return of the 'conformist' members to the House, were the best advertisements for the respectability of the army's intentions. One day, perhaps, the new regime might win its place in the affections of moderates. If so, fresh elections might then bring to power men who

---

[1] B.M., Add. MS 37,344, fos. 231, 233ᵛ; Clarendon MS 34, fos. 12ᵛ, 19; *Kingdom's Weekly Intelligencer* 19–26 Dec. 1648, p. 1196; *Perfect Occurrences* 19–26 Dec. 1648, p. 787.

[2] See e.g. Lilburne, *Legal, Fundamental Liberties*, preface and p. 37, and *Second Part of England's New Chains Discovered*, p. 12; Walker, *History of Independency*, ii. 30–3, 38, 104; Clarendon MS 34, fo. 73ᵛ.

[3] Gardiner, *Constitutional Documents*, p. 359.

had thus become sympathetic to proposals for social and religious reform. In the meantime, to insist on fresh elections would be disastrous; and when, in the spring of 1649, the Levellers mutinied against the Rump and demanded its dissolution, Ireton was quick to commit himself to their suppression.

To consider parliament and army as separate bodies is in a sense misleading, since their personnel overlapped. Apart from the regular officers who were also M.P.s, there were many rumpers who had been colonels of regiments during the civil war, who had then learnt something of military problems, and who retained their military titles. Some even retained their regiments, leaving parliament to take charge of them at times of military crisis. There were broad areas of cooperation between army and parliament, and particularly between the Council of Officers and the Rump's Committee for the Army, which worked together on a number of financial and administrative matters. Yet, even though the army officers in the House rarely acted as a concerted pressure group after the manner of the lawyer and merchant M.P.s, parliament and army still seemed to themselves and each other to be distinct and often opposing institutions. Between the purge and the execution, when only a few M.P.s provided even muted opposition to the moves against Charles, parliament followed rather than led the army, although even at this stage the House's expressions of resentment against the purge dispel the notion of its fawning servility. Parliament's reply on 20 January to the *Agreement of the People*, thanking the officers for 'your faithful and great service to the kingdom, in standing in the gap, for their preservation',[1] made clear that the House intended the period of military supremacy to be a short one; and after Charles's death the Rump began to assume the initiative. The pointed omission from the Commonwealth's first Council of State of Ireton and Harrison, the chief villains of the purge, gave a strong indication of the House's feelings: the fact that it got away with it was evidence of its growing strength. The incident was not the only sign of tension between parliament and army in the Commonwealth's early stages, and little love was lost between the two. Yet most of the time both sides remembered, in the service of their common interests, to hide their differences from public view and to project an image of harmony. The officers' revolutionary bravado at the time of the purge gave way to discreet and private persuasion. Only after the defeat of the royalists in September 1651, which destroyed the base of the alliance between

[1] *C.J.* 20 Jan. 1649.

parliament and army, did the conflict between them emerge into the open.

The army's self-imposed political restraint during the earlier Rump period did not diminish its desire for reform. The need to assuage the reform movement was, indeed, always one of parliament's most serious problems. Unhappily, it conflicted with the House's equally pressing need, to conciliate that 'presbyterian' opinion, shared by many rumpers, which had been so profoundly alienated by the purge and the execution. Attempting to balance the two requirements, the government was eventually left stranded between them.

Because of the variety of political perspectives among its members, the House was perhaps even more vulnerable than most governments to outside pressures. Among both its radical and its conservative critics there were, admittedly, many who were prepared to hold their peace, at least for a time. Others, however, were immediately vociferous in their opposition. The Levellers, so embarrassing to the Rump in 1649, acted as the repository of the radical conscience, but the forthright hostility supplied by presbyterians was more enduring. Clement Walker, one of the M.P.s briefly imprisoned at the purge, was perhaps the most troublesome example. Before the purge he had styled himself the champion of the 'middle and disengaged men' in the Commons, casting a plague on presbyterians and independents alike;[1] after it he addressed his hostility exclusively to the latter. The Rump's problem was to prevent men like Walker, in their disgust at the purge and execution, from lending support to the royalists. Perhaps the danger was not as great as it seemed. As Hyde quickly saw,[2] the gap between the presbyterians, who had fought against Charles in the civil war, and the royalist party of the 1640s was still a wide one. The bitter memories of warfare ensured that it remained so. Yet all the M.P.s who favoured negotiations with the king in December 1648, and whose participation in the Long Parliament ended with the purge, became thereafter in some sense royalists. As one of the Rump's enemies noted in February 1649, 'presbytery' was 'kingified now'.[3] Frustration and opposition can create curious alliances; and many of the Rump's policies were determined by its anxiety to isolate royalists from presbyterians. Although the government earned little love from presbyterians, it did succeed in procuring passive sufferance from most of them. It did so by pursuing the moderating policies to which many rumpers were in any case inclined, and by eschewing anything which might be interpreted

[1] C. Walker, *The Mystery of Two Juntoes* (1647), p. 17.
[2] *Nicholas Papers*, i, 143.   [3] *A Thunder Clap to Sion College* (1649), p. 6.

as an attack on property or the social order. The strength of presbyterian feeling outside the House thus diminished still further the prospects of those who advocated measures of social reform.

If the Rump succeeded in appeasing many presbyterian laymen, however, it had less success with presbyterian clergymen. It was in the pulpit, which played a continuously irritant role in Rump politics, that political and religious presbyterianism were most effectively combined. Ministers in London, declining Cromwell's offer of negotiation, conducted a vigorous and well-organised campaign, which they extended to the provinces and which had the support of purged M.P.s,[1] against the moves to bring Charles to justice.[2] The king's death by no means ended the protests.[3] The presbyterian clergy proved resourceful in their techniques of opposition. Fast days enjoined by the Rump were ignored[4] or, worse, were used for counter-fasts, at which ministers prayed for the success of Charles II or of the forces fighting in Scotland for his restoration.[5] Clerical opposition proved especially troublesome to the government in two areas, first in Lancashire and Cheshire, where ministers sustained a chorus of opposition to the Commonwealth and were suspected of corresponding with its enemies in Scotland,[6] and secondly in London, where a well-known group of divines, notably Christopher Love, Thomas Watson, Thomas Cawton and Thomas

---

[1] *Diary of the Rev. R. Josselin*, p. 63; *Kingdom's Faithful Scout* 26 Jan.–2 Feb. 1649, p. 1; *The Moderate* 9–16 Jan. 1649, p. (259), 26 Jan.–2 Feb. 1649, p. 307; B.M., Loan MS 29/176 (Harley Papers), fo. 63: Annesley and others to Cranford, 16 Jan. 1649.

[2] Underdown, *Pride's Purge*, pp. 176–7; *Mercurius Melancholicus* 1–8 Jan. 1649, p. 16; *Mercurius Pragmaticus* 26 Dec. 1648–9 Jan. 1649, pp. (5), (8); *The Army's Modest Intelligencer* 9–16 Jan. 1649, p. 3; John Price, *Clerico-Classicum* (1649), pp. 4, 6, 7, 11–12, 15, 30–1; *Brief Narration of the Mysteries of State*, pp. 65–7, 82, 86, 90; Walker, *History of Independency*, ii. 67; *A Modest and Clear Vindication, passim*; Clarendon MS 34, fos. 12ᵛ, 73ᵛ, 86ᵛ.

[3] For a useful but brief survey of the presbyterian clerical opposition to the Rump see L. H. Carlson, 'A history of the Presbyterian party from Pride's Purge to the dissolution of the Long Parliament', *Church History*, xii (1942). See also G. Abernathy, 'The English Presbyterians and the Stuart Restoration, 1648–1663', *Transactions of the American Philosophical Society*, new series, 55 part 2 (1965).

[4] See e.g. *Brief Narration of the Mysteries of State*, p. 97; Whitelocke, *Memorials*, iii. 159, 250, 281; *The Moderate* 17–24 Apr. 1649, p. (436), 21–28 Aug. 1649, pp. 677–8; *Kingdom's Faithful Scout* 6–13 July 1649, p. 191; *Great Britain's Painful Messenger* 23–30 Aug. 1649, p. 21; *Mercurius Politicus* 1–8 Aug. 1650, p. (132).

[5] See e.g. *Perfect Weekly Account* 25 July–1 Aug. 1649, p. 559; *Mercurius Aulicus* 28 Aug.–3 Sep. 1649, p. 21; *Mercurius Pragmaticus* 1–8 Jan. 1650, p. 313; *Mercurius Politicus* 12–19 June 1651, p. 865; Whitelocke, *Memorials*, iii. 157; *C.S.P.D. 1651*, p. 279.

[6] See e.g. *C.S.P.D. 1649–50*, p. 62; 1650–1: pp. 20–1, 49–50, 78; *Mercurius Politicus* 6–13 June 1650, p. 4, 2–9 Oct. 1651, pp. 1121–2; *Moderate Intelligencer* 1–8 Feb. 1649, p. (1181); *Mercurius Pragmaticus* 13–20 March 1649, p. (8); *The Moderate* 20–27 Mar. 1649, pp. (374), (375); *H.M.C.R. Leybourne-Popham*, p. 59.

Juggard, was continually in trouble with the regime.[1] The west country, especially Exeter and Taunton, was also a serious problem.[2] But from everywhere came reports of sermons, prayers, or exhortations to magistrates all directed in opposition to the Rump.[3] This was especially frustrating to those of the Commonwealth's supporters who regarded the clergy's hostility as the sole obstacle to the acceptance of the new regime by moderate opinion. From all sides it was reported that the conciliatory tendencies of laymen, and in particular their willingness to take the Rump's engagement of loyalty, were countered by ill-feeling stirred from the pulpit.[4]

Religion presented itself to the Rump primarily as a political problem, and it was as a political problem that the Rump, characteristically, dealt with it, by attempting to draw a distinction between private scruples about the regime, which it would tolerate and which indeed many of its members shared, and public opposition, which it could not allow. Two measures were passed in 1649 with the purpose of reducing the political power of the presbyterian clergy. First, an ordinance modelled on a recent edict in the United Provinces provided for the punishment of clergymen who interfered in politics. Secondly, the act for the monthly fast-day, passed early in 1642, was repealed, on the grounds that the fasts had been 'for divers years past, in most places of this Commonwealth, wholly neglected', and that, where they were still held, they had 'declined by degrees from that solemnity wherewith the same was at the first institution thereof entertained'.[5] Such criticisms were widespread. Some rumpers, Whitelocke probably among them, 'held

[1] See e.g. *C.S.P.D.* 1649–50: pp. 19, 24–7, 526; 1650–1: p. 254; *Perfect Occurrences* 13–20 Apr. 1649, p. 944, 25 May–1 June 1649, p. 1054; *Perfect Summary* 9–16 Apr. 1649, p. 119; *The Moderate* 6–20 Mar. 1649, pp. (357), (369); *Mercurius Politicus* 25 July–8 Aug. 1650, pp. 126–7, 159; *H.M.C.R. Leybourne-Popham*, p. 15; *A Book without a Title* (1649), pp. 7, 17, 25.
[2] See e.g. *Mercurius Politicus* 20–27 June 1650, pp. 38–9, 1–8 Aug. 1650, p. 132, 12–19 Sept. 1650, p. 232; *C.S.P.D.* 1650–1, p. 78; Whitelocke, *Memorials*, iii. 158–9, 229, 241, 276, 362; *Perfect Diurnal . . . Armies* 18–25 Nov. 1650, p. 642, 24 Feb.–3 Mar. 1651, p. 861, 9–16 Feb. 1652, pp. 1669–70.
[3] See e.g. John Goodwin, *The Obstructors of Justice* (1649), pp. 1–2; John Price, *The Cloudy Clergy* (1650), pp. 4ff.; Clarendon MS 39, fo. 80; *The Impartial Scout* 12–19 July 1650, p. 243; *H.M.C.R. Leybourne-Popham*, p. 51; *C.S.P.D.* 1649–50: p. 549; 1650–1: pp. 250, 254, 415, 426, 428, 432; 1651: pp. 27, 42, 49, 51, 52, 55, 65, 93, 149, 180, 201, 210, 224, 225, 277, 281, 282, 304, 384, 440, 503; 1651–2: pp. 20, 21, 73–4.
[4] See e.g. *The Moderate* 20–27 Mar. 1649, p. (375); *Perfect Diurnal . . . Armies* 25 Feb.–4 Mar. 1650, p. 102, 20–27 Jan. 1651, p. (781), 24 Feb.–3 Mar. 1651, p. 861. Cf. *ibid.* 24–31 Dec. 1649, pp. 22, 23; *Original Letters . . . addressed to Oliver Cromwell*, p. 83; J. Latimer (ed.), *Annals of Bristol* (Bristol, 1900), p. 229.
[5] Trevor-Roper, *Religion, The Reformation and Social Change*, pp. 339–40.

the course of keeping a monthly fast to be not so proper, but savouring of too much formality, and that it was fitter to appoint days of public humiliation upon special occasions'.[1] There were, however, less exalted and more pressing reasons for the act's abolition, which enabled the government thereafter to time public celebration and lamentation to suit its political convenience. A regime with so narrow a base of support, anxious to create a sense of stability and tranquillity, was in general less inclined than the Long Parliament before it to exhort its countrymen to organised spiritual fervour. The Rump's policies to-wards recalcitrant clergymen, too, were indicative more of political embarrassment than of moral indignation. Instead of treating presby-terians – as its most radical supporters would have liked to see them treated – as agents of Antichrist, the Rump dealt with the issue of clerical disaffection as primarily one of security: most cases were referred to the Council of State, which in turn entrusted them to its security committee. Action was occasionally taken, depriving a minister of his living or leading to his temporary imprisonment, but the Rump seems to have been principally concerned to create as little unrest as possible.[2] Normally, indeed, it appears to have taken action against ministers only in those areas, like the south-west, where the radical press had regular correspondents and where the misconduct of clergymen was thus brought to public attention. Another trouble-spot was Hull, where two clergymen refused, as did so many ministers throughout the country, either to take the Rump's engagement of loyalty or to cele-brate Cromwell's victory over the Scottish presbyterians at Dunbar. Their recalcitrance earned them the hostility of the Hull garrison and of the radical preacher John Canne. The Council of State's initial response to this dangerous affair was one of righteous anger; later, when the dispute became laboriously protracted, it came to admit almost bluntly that its prime concern was the political loyalty and stability of a port of such strategic importance.[3] Sedition from the pulpit was bound to

---

[1] Whitelocke, *Memorials*, ii. 517. Cf. William Gouge, *The Right Way* (1648), pp. 29–30, 32; *Diary of the Rev. R. Josselin*, p. 19; John Bond, *Eschol* (1648), p. 17; John Cardell, *Morbus Epidemicus* (1650), pp. 28–9; Mayer, 'Inedited letters', p. 238; Asty, *Sermons of John Owen*, pp. 281, 438, 527.

[2] See e.g. *C.S.P.D.* 1650–1, pp. 17, 73, 92, 188, 475; *Brief Narration of the Mysteries of State*, pp. 99–100; Price, *The Cloudy Clergy*, pp. 5, 14; *Mercurius Politicus* 6–13 June 1651, p. 863; *Kingdom's Faithful Scout*, 13–20 April 1649, p. 89; *The Moderate* 6 Mar.–10 Apr. 1649, pp. (35), 325, 399; *Great Britain's Painful Messenger* 23–30 Aug. 1649, p. 21; *One Blow More at Babylon* (1651), ep. ded. p. (3); Gardiner, *History of the Commonwealth and Protectorate*, ii. 7–8.

[3] *C.S.P.D.* 1649–50: p. 312; 1650–1: pp. 213, 385, 399, 452; 1651: pp. 22, 243; 1651–2:

create unrest among both supporters and opponents of the Rump, which therefore tried to remove troublesome ministers from towns and especially from areas near garrisons, where they were likely to provoke the soldiery to counter-measures. Occasionally, panic at reviving royalist hopes led the Rump to condemn dissent from the pulpit in trenchant terms. Yet, to the dismay of radicals who called for harsh punitive steps, the government's strenuous assertions of repressive intent were rarely followed by decisive action.[1] As Thomas Scot made clear in September 1649, the Rump would have been prepared to leave the misguided souls of presbyterians in peace if the ministers

had only remained passive, and been contented to have let others carry on the work of religion in its purity, though they themselves held back; but this would not serve their turn, unless they flew in the face of the visible authority in this nation, and took upon them to be judges, whether we were a lawful magistracy or not; as if that were within their line, and committed to them to determine.[2]

Troublesome as clerical opposition to the Rump was, however, not all presbyterian ministers were politically disaffected. Some cooperated with their independent brethren on a number of occasions in attempts to build bridges between parliament and those who in December 1648 had ceased to sit in it. Both clergymen and politicians who declined to commit themselves to the Rump nevertheless often recognised that its members were, in the main, as unrevolutionary as they. Yet the new government remained tainted throughout its history by its revolutionary origins. Pride's Purge and regicide were rarely forgiven and never forgotten. To political presbyterians, the rule of the Rump was the victory of force over legality. The fact that the Long Parliament surprisingly survived for so long after the spring of 1649, and that so much power consequently remained in civilian rather than in military hands, made little difference. The events of December 1648 and January 1649 directly contradicted every principle for which presbyterian M.P.s had gone to war; and the frequent and forceful presbyterian criticisms directed against the Rump returned again and again to the

pp. 9, 31, 99, 100, 123, 141, 172, 187, 211; *Mercurius Politicus* 17–24 Oct. 1650, pp. 327–8, 333–5. There are numerous letters relating to the incident in the Hull Corporation MSS.
[1] See e.g. *Reliquiae Baxterianae*, p. 66; *The Weekly Intelligencer of the Commonwealth* 22–29 Oct. 1650, p. 39; *Original Letters . . . addressed to Oliver Cromwell*, p. 23; *H.M.C.R. Leybourne-Popham*, p. 78.
[2] Cobbett, *Parliamentary History of England*, iii. 1323. Cf. Milton, *Tenure of Kings and Magistrates*, pp. 40–1; Marchamont Nedham, *The Case of the Commonwealth of England Stated* (1650), p. 75.

theme of illegality. Presbyterians also believed that the Rump, whatever the limits to its radicalism, would never break free of its dependence on the army or be in a position to renounce the army's aims. It is
thus understandable that many of the M.P.s whose participation in the
Long Parliament ended at the purge seem thereafter to have isolated
themselves from politics and to have regarded the rule of the Rump with
gloomy resignation. Some, like Samuel Gott, decided that 'happiness'
was to be found in withdrawal from the public stage into rural medita-
tion – although Gott's 'happiness' seems to have been a somewhat
sombre affair.[1] There were, of course, presbyterians who recognised, as
did the Suffolk J.P. Thomas Edgar in the spring of 1649, that 'those in
public employment to a Commonwealth must not desert government
because the way or form doth not like them. Though one kind of government be better than another, yet take that is next rather than none.'
Edgar's argument was similar to that expounded about the same time
by rumpers like Rous and Francis Thorpe:[2] the Rump, whatever its failings, could always be seen as an alternative to anarchy, and as time went
by the House's hostility to social radicalism became increasingly apparent.
But if fear of anarchy could encourage among presbyterians a spirit of
passive sufferance, their quietude represented no mass conversion
among them to loyalist principles. The initiatives undertaken during the
Rump period towards reconciliation between presbyterians and independents, in both politics and religion, clearly had influential support
on both sides; yet they rarely seem to have got off the ground. Only in
the last year of the Rump period, when hostility between parliament and
army became increasingly overt and when the Rump could thus be
seen as a positive alternative to military rule, did it seem likely that the
breach within the parliamentary party might be healed.

[1] S. Gott, *An Essay of the True Happiness of Man* (1650).
[2] Underdown, *Pride's Purge*, pp. 263, 299.

5

COMMITMENT AND CORRUPTION

The nature of the surviving evidence, which tells us much more about the views of individual rumpers after the Rump's dissolution than before it, tempts us to misunderstand the attitude of its members towards the parliament at the time of its sitting. The dissolution, driving large numbers of M.P.s from power for six years, profoundly changed the political attitudes of many of them. Around Cromwell's usurpation of power a mythology developed, leading to retrospective glorification of the Rump's achievements which disguised the limits of its members' earlier enthusiasm for their government. Such glorification repays close inspection. It came sometimes from men like Edmund Ludlow, who had in fact turned a blind eye to the dissolution of the Rump until Cromwell's assumption of the title of Protector in December 1653.[1] In the later 1650s rumpers became especially proud of the military, naval and diplomatic accomplishments of their rule, but often their protestations of enthusiasm for the Rump either referred to the Long Parliament as a whole rather than merely to its tail, or were closely associated with resentment at Cromwell's usurpation of power and at military intervention at the time of the dissolution.[2] When less concerned to vent their bitterness at the events of April 1653, rumpers could be more modest about their glorious past. Heselrige at one such moment made clear the improvised, defensive nature of the republican settlement which had followed Charles's death. With the execution of the king and with the abolition of the House of Lords, he recalled, two of the three estates had been destroyed: 'then, for the third, that (God knows!) had been much shattered and broken. Force was much upon us. What should we do? We turned ourselves into the Commonwealth.' The Long Parliament had been 'a glorious parliament for pulling down', but no more. Vane apparently agreed. The

---

[1] *Memoirs of Edmund Ludlow*, i. 356–7, 373–8.
[2] See e.g. Whitelocke, *Memorials*, iii. 475–7, iv. 6; *Diary of Thomas Burton*, ii. 376, iii. 111–12; *Memoirs of Colonel Hutchinson*, p. 292.

Rump, he thought, had had its virtues in its early stages, when there had seemed no alternative other than anarchy, but thereafter its usefulness had ended; 'the parliament showed that . . . shackles were broken. It did not oblige further. That it was famous and had power: that was the Israelites' argument for worshipping the sun and moon.'[1] Henry Marten and Henry Neville, who had been among the few convinced republicans in the Rump, seem to have been acutely conscious of its failings.[2] Most of those who agreed to sit in the Rump recognised that, at least for the time being, the new government was the only possible solution which would not leave the army in full control. Few of them, however, displayed any enthusiasm for the expedient which they found themselves adopting; and when, in 1649–50, the Rump campaigned for the support of alienated moderates, it gladly encouraged the use of 'loyalist' arguments which conceded the government's illegitimate origins.

Failing to usher in the godly reformation, and yet tainted from the start by military intervention and regicide, the Rump could never hope for popularity. During its brief restoration to power in 1659–60 it became little more than a laughing-stock, the butt of hatred and contempt. When it finally fell from power in February 1660, rumps were roasted by the dozen in the streets of London, while catchpenny poets entertained the city populace with cumbrous anal witticisms. The Rump has suffered severely for the prurience of its patronymic, which has encouraged historians to accept without close examination the charges levelled at it by contemporaries. This is not surprising, for the Commonwealth government, so detested at the time, has little obvious attraction for scholars of any particular political persuasion. Historians often assume, but rarely attempt to demonstrate, that the Rump was oligarchical, dilatory and corrupt.[3] Many contemporaries thought the same, but they, too, rarely specified or substantiated their claims, which tell us more about the political perspectives of those who made them than about the Rump itself. The trouble with the term oligarchy is that it can be, and has been, used in two different ways, one precise and objective, the other vague and subjective. The first usage belongs to the vocabulary of political theory, the second to the

---

[1] *Diary of Thomas Burton*, iii. 27, 97, 178.

[2] Williams, 'Political career of Henry Marten', iii. 545; *Diary of Thomas Burton*, iii. 134. There is an instructive contrast, too, between Milton's condemnation of the Rump in 1654 and his praise of it in 1659; see F. A. Patterson (ed.), *The Works of John Milton* (18 vols., New York, 1931–8), vi. 102, viii. 221.

[3] For a modern view see Yule, *The Independents in the English Civil War*, p. 74.

vocabulary of political abuse. Among contemporaries using the term in the former sense were Henry Neville, who like many others claimed that the Rump government was a commonwealth in name only, and Thomas Hobbes, who thought that the Rump became an oligarchy when it expelled the members purged by Colonel Pride.[1] Neville and Hobbes evidently understood by an oligarchy a kingless government presided over by a few and lacking a broad base of support. Although both men disapproved of the Rump's oligarchical tendencies, their consternation did not deflect them from terminological precision, and the usage they adopted was fully warranted. Some historians have been equally scrupulous; but the term has also been used, in a looser and more purely pejorative sense, to convey the impression that the Rump was a small, wealthy clique governing solely in its own interests and for the purpose of its own perpetuation. This book will show the inaccuracy of the charge. To call the Rump an oligarchy does not help us to understand, and may encourage us to misunderstand, the character of the Commonwealth government.

The claim that the Rump was dilatory is equally hard to test. It could certainly be dilatory when it wanted to be, skilfully spinning out debates on bills which it had considered in the first place only in response to pressure from the army. Committees discussing controversial business contrived to postpone meetings for months on end, and, when they did meet, to put off further discussion for equally long periods.[2] The overriding impression of Rump politics, however, is one not of sloth but of bustle. Time and again parliament, weighed down by its administrative responsibilities, failed to keep pace with the demanding timetable it was obliged to set itself. In this there was, however, nothing new, as a glance at the records of other seventeenth-century parliaments will show; and the diary of Sir Symonds D'Ewes suggests that the frustrations facing those who wished to steer measures through the Commons quickly had been as acute in the early stages of the Long Parliament as they were after 1648.[3] The sheer quantity of

---

[1] Cf. e.g. *Original Letters . . . addressed to Oliver Cromwell*, p. 31; *A Letter written to a Gentleman in the Country* (1653), p. 5; T. Hobbes, 'Behemoth', in F. Maseres (ed.), *Select Tracts relating to the Civil Wars in England* (2 vols., 1815), i. 605–6; *Diary of Thomas Burton*, iii. 134. Cf. e.g. Clarendon MS 34, fos. 17, 72ᵛ; Patterson, *Works of John Milton*, viii. 221.

[2] Samuel Chidley, *A Remonstrance to the valiant and well-deserving Soldier* (1653), pp. 12–14; *Letter written to a Gentleman in the Country* (1653), pp. 4–6.

[3] W. Notestein (ed.), *The Journal of Sir Simonds D'Ewes from the Beginning of the Long Parliament to the Opening of the Trial of the Earl of Strafford* (New Haven, 1923), pp. 96, 109, 111, 121, 517–18; Coates, *Journal of Sir Simonds D'Ewes*, p. 518. Cf. *Hull Letters*, pp. 48, 114.

business undertaken by the Rump, the Council of State and the innumerable parliamentary committees is astonishing, a tribute to the formidable industry of the leading rumpers. Parliamentary government was clearly not an ideal form of decision-making, but this was no more true of the 1650s than of the 1640s. The real problem was that M.P.s could not be in more than one place at once. In its early stages the Rump, anxious to sit six days a week, found it hard to find time for council and parliamentary committee meetings.[1] Eventually it yielded to common sense, sitting, except at certain times of crisis, only three or four days a week, and then sometimes for only two or three hours a day. Early in 1650, too, the House began a slow and uncompleted process of handing over the duties of some of its more hard-pressed standing committees to commissioners who were not M.P.s. Yet, jealous of its executive authority, it still supervised more administrative work than it could reasonably be expected to handle. Occasionally the Rump, which seems to have spent less time than most seventeenth-century parliaments debating private bills, banned all discussion of private business for a specified period. Such measures were unlikely to satisfy those radicals who declared that the Lord's work could not wait upon the need of mortals for occasional relaxation, and who demanded that parliament sit all day every day;[2] but politicians who give much of their time to mundane administrative tasks cannot be expected to sustain an unrelieved sense of apocalyptic urgency for more than four years. Judged by human standards, or at least by the standards of other seventeenth-century governments, the Rump was certainly not idle. It was dilatory only when it chose to be, which was when radicals outside the House forced it to debate issues it did not wish to debate.

The press of business could, nevertheless, create appalling backlogs. This was especially unfortunate in the case of petitions to parliament, which often went unheard for months or even years. In this respect, as in many others, parliament's burdens had been increased by the abolition of Star Chamber and of the Privy Council. The Fifth Monarchist preacher Vavasour Powell, writing in 1652, colourfully claimed that

---

[1] See e.g. *C.J.* 23 Feb., 8 Mar., 2 Apr. 1649; *C.S.P.D.* 1649–50, p. 158; *Perfect Weekly Account* 7–14 Mar. 1649, p. 418.

[2] Chidley, *Remonstrance to the valiant and well-deserving Soldier*, p. 14; *Letter written to a Gentleman in the Country*, p. 5; *The Flying Eagle* 4–11 Dec. 1652, p. 13. For more measured complaints of dilatoriness see e.g. Patterson, *Works of John Milton*, viii. 221; *H.M.C.R. Leybourne-Popham*, p. 56; *Mercurius Politicus* 6–13 Nov. 1651, p. 1190, 9–16 June 1653, p. 2505. Cf. *Memoirs of Colonel Hutchinson*, p. 292.

'the petitions of poor sufferers are used only to light tobacco', and there were many other, more plausible complaints about the Rump's failure to give adequate attention to the claims of petitioners. One of the House's better informed critics even claimed that it ignored ten thousand petitions brought before it. No seventeenth-century parliament could have dealt with ten thousand petitions, and there are signs that by the later Rump period the whole problem had got out of control. Members entering the House or committee rooms were daily approached by petitioners, many of whom, representing either soldiers or civilian radicals, had reduced the techniques of supplication to a fine and relentless art.[1] Not surprisingly, the Rump's intolerance of petitioners hardened with time; and when petitions did come before parliament, the House occasionally displayed irritation at the distraction from public affairs which they caused. Yet the neglect of genuine grievances was probably brought about as much by the press of business as by indifference. When Cromwell, who regularly championed the causes of individual petitioners and who was not used to having his wishes crossed in such matters, complained during the hectic summer of 1650 that Edmund Prideaux had failed to bring a private motion before the House, Prideaux replied indignantly that want of opportunity, and not want of endeavour, had prevented him from doing so; and in November 1652 Cromwell himself admitted in a similar case that 'the important affairs of the Commonwealth are so numerous that we cannot find opportunity to move parliament in it'.[2]

The accusation of dilatoriness was frequently accompanied by charges of factiousness, divisiveness and absenteeism. All these claims were of course accurate if measured against the standards of an ideal political assembly, but less impressive if set against those of other seventeenth-century governments. It may be true, for instance, that 'oppositions and conjunctions' of debates were sometimes rigged in the Speaker's chamber beforehand.[3] Men who had sat in previous parliaments would perhaps have been surprised had they not been. The Rump was certainly divided; yet, to use the only available yardstick, it

[1] C.C.C., pp. 543, 567; *Letter written to a Gentleman in the Country*, pp. 4–6; Chidley, *Remonstrance to the valiant and well-deserving Soldier*, pp. 12–13, 16; *A Perfect Account of the daily Intelligence from the Armies* 21–28 Jan. 1652, p. 447; B.M., Add. MS 22,620, fos. 131, 171, and Add. MS 35,863, p. 2; T. Richards, *A History of the Puritan Movement in Wales* (1920), p. 271.

[2] SP 23/101, fo. 1037; Abbott, *Writings and Speeches*, ii. 593.

[3] *Letter written to a Gentleman in the Country*, pp. 4, 6; cf. Raines and Sutton, *Life of Humphrey Chetham*, p. 184.

was only in 1652 that anything like as many motions were put to the vote as during any of the three years before Pride's Purge.[1] Absenteeism, in an age when most M.P.s were part-timers, was a persistently troublesome and often a deeply embarrassing problem during the Rump period. Yet it was unrealistic to expect members to attend more often than they did. In any case, although only about fifty-five rumpers were present at the average division of the House, attendances over particular periods were in general considerably higher than the numbers present at divisions suggest. The lists of members appointed to parliamentary committees provide a better guide, but even they, especially in the later Rump period, probably tend at times to give too gloomy a picture of parliamentary attendances. Further, there were several M.P.s who, although rarely present in the house, were much more active on parliamentary committees.[2] The purge did deplete the effective strength of many of the Long Parliament's standing committees, which often found difficulty in the weeks thereafter in raising quorums.[3] Low attendances at parliamentary committees, however, were not new. In the 1640s standing committees had similarly been carried on by small numbers,[4] and they may have functioned the better for it. Again, although the number of members who attended particular meetings of standing committees was usually small, the rumpers showed a remarkable ability to share among themselves the administrative tasks for which such committees were responsible and to involve even members who rarely attended parliament in the processes of government. Nearly three-quarters of the rumpers can be seen to have attended one or more standing committees at some time during the Rump period, and the proportion may have been even higher.[5]

In one sense, however, those who accused the Rump of dilatoriness were correct. In its early stages the regime displayed remarkable energy and industry, and it continued to do so in all times of emergency.

---

[1] Divisions:

1646: 106	1650: 56
1647: 130	1651: 73
1648: 110	1652: 122
1649: 52	1653: 22 (Jan.–Apr.)

(Figures for 1646–8 from V. F. Snow, 'Attendance trends and absenteeism in the Long Parliament', *Huntington Library Quarterly*, 18 (1954–5), 302; others from *C.J.*)

[2] Cf. below pp. 393–4; Snow, 'Attendance trends and absenteeism', p. 303.

[3] See e.g. SP: 19/6, fos. 133, 135; 23/5, fos. 35ᵛ, 36ᵛ, 46; 28/57, fos. 290–369; Underdown, *Pride's Purge*, p. 158.

[4] This is clear from their order and minute books. And see Henry Scobell, *Memorials of the Method and Manner of Proceedings in Parliament in Passing Bills* (1689), p. 47.

[5] 149 rumpers can be identified as so attending; and not all committee records survive.

Whitelocke, who drove himself hard in politics, has left an awed and stirring tribute to the zeal and efficiency of the Council of State during the Scottish invasion in the summer of 1651.[1] In calmer times, however, M.P.s refused to be hurried by army pressure or to exhaust themselves merely to accommodate the wishes of the army. If no crisis demanded immediate attention, rumpers resolved to proceed at their own pace; and the more aggressively the army demanded reforming legislation, the slower that pace became. After the summer of 1649 there is a steady decline in the amount of legislation passed,[2] in the number of committees appointed[3] and, to a lesser extent, in the frequency with which the House sat. Attendances at the Council of State also tended to fall slightly as the Rump period wore on, and it is possible that parliamentary attendances, especially after the first half of 1649, did the same.[4] Once the royalist threat had faded, the bond which had held the regime together simply snapped. As army pressure for reform increased, business and legislation became ever more bogged down in parliamentary dissension, until long delays became the norm rather than the exception. Division and delay promoted each other, and the decline in the number of committees appointed was closely paralleled by an increase in the number of occasions on which motions were put to the vote. Even Whitelocke admitted that, in its last months, the Rump became 'slow' in enacting legislation.[5] The government had run out of steam. Yet the inertia which afflicted the Rump in its later stages is to be explained more by the conflict between parliament and army than by any endemic resistance to hard work on the part of the rumpers.

[1] Whitelocke, *Memorials*, iii. 332–3.
[2] Bills passed (excluding private bills):

    1649: 124   1652: 44
    1650: 78   1653: 10 (Jan.–Apr.)
    1651: 54

Annual average 1640–8: 119
Annual average 1646–8: 97

Many of the bills passed in the 1640s were administrative measures answering needs no longer present in the Rump period. (Calculations based on the table of bills in Firth and Rait, *Acts and Ordinances*, vol. iii.)

[3] Committees appointed:

    1649: 152 (of which 110 appointed between Feb. and July)
    1650: 98
    1651: 61
    1652: 51
    1653: 12 (Jan.–Apr.)

[4] Cf. below, pp. 393–4.
[5] Whitelocke, *Memorials*, iii. 475.

The failure of contemporaries to specify or substantiate the charge of corruption is revealing to the historian, but also frequently exasperating. There is no topic about which it is easier to jump to conclusions or harder to ascertain the truth. Seventeenth-century history is littered with charges and counter-charges of corruption, most of them impossible either to confirm or to refute. Politicians writing memoirs or apologias almost invariably assured their readers that they, unlike so many of their colleagues, had never yielded to corrupt practices, a precaution which would hardly have been necessary had such practices not been familiar. Sometimes, one feels, politicians protested too much. Yet the charge of corruption is extraordinarily difficult to pin down, partly because the term was often used so nebulously and so indiscriminately. Fifth Monarchists and army radicals, who in 1653 laid the most bitter charges of corruption against the Rump, seem at times to have meant no more than that its members were worldly (or unrevolutionary) rather than saintly (or revolutionary). If we are to understand the Rump's behaviour, it once more seems wiser to compare its habits with those of other seventeenth-century governments than with the apolitical and sectarian standards of the saints. Yet what criteria of public morality do we apply to a society in which patronage and perquisites served the functions nowadays fulfilled by competitive appointment and regular salaries? The seventeenth century had its own unspoken rules on the subject, but they were not constant and they are often hard to identify – especially in the Rump, which, replacing the Stuart court, had to improvise its own public morality. Any seventeenth-century government was bound to centre on a court, to favour those who belonged to it and to deny rewards to those who opposed it. It would be naive to take offence because a parliament which controlled the executive adopted practices which had been habitual under the early Stuarts. In terms of sinecures and extravagance the Rump was much less 'corrupt' than, say, the government of James I. Yet, although it toyed with proposals to replace fees by regular salaries, it never challenged the notion that those who worked hardest on the government's behalf were entitled to the pickings of place, patronage and financial opportunity. It would have seemed entirely proper to the Rump, for example, that Heselrige and Vane were considerably richer men at the end of the revolution than at the beginning.[1] It also seemed

[1] Howell, *Newcastle-upon-Tyne and the Puritan Revolution*, p. 346; V. A. Rowe, *Sir Henry Vane the Younger* (1970), p. 270.

natural to M.P.s to use their 'interest and favour in the House' to secure appointments for their relatives and clients.[1] At what point in such cases did private interests endanger the public good? Some of the Rump's opponents drew up lists to show how its members had helped themselves to profitable employments, although most of the M.P.s concerned had secured their posts well before the Rump came to power. A few rumpers, like Prideaux as postmaster-general, certainly seem to have gained large sums for little work.[2] What was an appropriate ceiling for such gains? The decision of some (although probably not many) members to sit in the Rump, or even to join the 'revolutionaries', may well have been influenced by their desire to retain offices.[3] Were such members, for that reason, corrupt? Most men are susceptible in some way to political passions or to arguments based on political principles. They are also subject to worries about their jobs and their finances. The relationship between such concerns is rarely clear-cut or stable, and it would be unwise to assume that more than a small number of rumpers stayed in politics after the purge either with complete disregard for their own interests or in shameless pursuit of them. Such regicides as John Downes and Daniel Blagrave certainly gained lucrative employment by committing themselves to the Rump,[4] and White-locke, congratulating himself on the high principles which had prompted him to steer clear of the High Court of Justice, suggested that regicide had been a road to favour.[5] Yet to sign the death warrant was also, more obviously, to invite reprisals in the event of a counter-revolution. Rumpers like Sir Henry Mildmay, Cornelius Holland, John Dove, Sir Peter Wentworth and Edmund Harvey attracted reputations as sharks,[6] yet they devoted the overwhelming preponderance of their political activity to matters which could in no way advance their material interests.

To discuss the charge of corruption in terms of motive may ulti-mately be fruitless. Corruption could, however, carry the more specific and more sinister charge of embezzlement or bribery. It seems likely (although the evidence is not conclusive) that John Dove, John Wylde, Sir William Constable, Lord Grey of Groby and Thomas Birch, as well as some government officials, trafficked during the Common-

---

[1] B.M., Add. MS 37,345, fo. 5ᵛ. Cf. *ibid.* fos. 14&ᵛ, 101ᵛ, 209, and B.M., Add. MS 37,344, fos. 314ᵛ, 316&ᵛ.

[2] *Arbitrary Government Displayed*, p. 94; Walker, *History of Independency*, ii. 167.

[3] See Underdown, *Pride's Purge*, pp. 49–53, 250–3.

[4] *Ibid.* pp. 50–1, 53.   [5] Whitelocke, *Memorials*, ii. 487.

[6] Underdown, *Pride's Purge*, pp. 52–3, 58, 138, 241.

wealth in the thriving trade of forged debentures for fee-farm rents.[1] Other rumpers, for all we know, may have indulged in similar practices. Speaker Lenthall and his rumper son were believed to take bribes, but no proof was supplied. Immediately after the dissolution of the Rump the army threatened reprisals against those of the Commonwealth's treasurers who insisted on remaining at their posts. They would, it was said, be 'squeezed' of their ill-gotten gains. Yet no one (except for one writer who, apparently on the strength of mere gossip, aimed the ridiculous figure of £70,000 in the direction of Francis Allen) said what the gains were, and no one explained how they had been gotten. One rumper, probably Henry Marten, vigorously denied the charges of corruption levelled at the Rump by the army after the dissolution, and urged Cromwell to particularise them.[2] The political uses of baseless slander were considerable in such circumstances. Other accusations, on the other hand, were clearly well founded. The only M.P. against whom a charge of corruption was successfully brought before the Rump was Lord Howard of Escrick, the former chairman of the Committee for Advance of Money, who in the summer of 1651 was convicted by the House of taking bribes. He was fined £10,000 and sent to the Tower. There were purely political reasons for so stiff a sentence, which nevertheless testified to the Rump's sensitivity on the subject of corruption.[3] The committee which Howard had chaired, reforming its procedures in February 1650, had hinted that the practice of allowing M.P.s who were not members of the committee to consult its records had afforded opportunities for peculation.[4] There are other occasional hints of malpractice. Philip Jones, who attracted charges of corruption throughout the Interregnum, was plausibly accused during the Rump period of embezzling funds from sequestered Welsh estates. Similar charges were levelled at Jones's fellow Commissioners for the Propagation of the Gospel in Wales.[5] Harrison, the commissioners' leader, was also to be the hero of the Fifth Monarchists; if it would be hard to show that the Rump was more corrupt than other seventeenth-century governments, it would be still harder to show that its members were more corrupt than the men who at the time accused it of corruption. Army leaders grew quite as rich from the revolution as did

---

[1] I. J. Gentles, 'The debentures and the military purchases of crown land' (London Ph.D. thesis, 1969), pp. 98–9, and the sources there cited.
[2] Williams, 'Political career of Henry Marten', p. 544.
[3] Below, p. 243.
[4] *C.C.A.M.*, p. 81.
[5] *C.C.C.*, pp. 1770, 2177, 2178.

most M.P.s, and two of the Rump's most severe critics, the radical and sectarian allies Colonel Pride and Samuel Chidley, advanced from penury to landed wealth with a rapidity which must have been the envy of many rumpers.[1]

It was, admittedly, not only radicals who brought charges of corruption against M.P.s during the Rump period. Even so, at a time when arrangements for the distribution of public funds were often chaotic, the offences of which rumpers were accused were mainly venial. Thomas Atkins, for example, held on to £27 and to some silver spoons to which he may not have been entitled, and Augustine Garland may have retained for an unwarrantably long time books belonging to the deanery of Winchester. William Say, as attorney to the Marshal's Court at Southwark, drew a small annual salary which, it was claimed, should properly have gone to the state. John Browne and John Trenchard may have sequestered an estate under false pretences and held on to the proceeds, while Sir Henry Mildmay was accused of wrongly taking for himself the profits of a confiscated estate in Shropshire. A few other rumpers were accused of similar offences, but although the evidence seems impressive in a handful of cases it looks much less convincing in others.[2] Too rarely do we get a glimpse of the other side of the story; when we do, evidence which has seemed impressive suddenly looks worthless. A savage feud between John Pyne and others of the Rump's supporters in Somerset, for example, in which accusations of embezzlement were monotonously advanced and denied by both sides, is almost impossible to disentangle.[3]

Some rumpers, like Isaac Pennington and Sir John Hippisley, seem to have adopted the technique of seeking protection from the House when fair claims were made against them. The Rump absolved Pennington from certain debts, while Hippisley, who improperly retained a sum of £58 during the Rump period, was forced to surrender it after the dissolution.[4] It was only after the Rump's expulsion, too, that a threat by the Commissioners for Compounding to levy the estate of Sir John Danvers, who had failed to pay debts owed to the government,

[1] Gentles, 'Debentures and military purchases', pp. 125, 265, 324.
[2] C.C.C., pp. 400, 408, 416–17, 465–9, 523, 531, 532, 542, 956–8, 1257, 1586, 1781, 1796, 2463, 2482; C.C.A.M., pp. 1290–1.
[3] C.C.C., and C.C.A.M., as indexed under Pyne. On this and similar matters the documents in the Public Record Office are often more revealing than the Calendars in which they are summarised. The evidence against Pyne becomes weaker when it is realised that, in one instance, the word 'money' in the Calendar is an inaccurate transcription of 'mercy' (C.C.C., p. 221; SP 23/118, p. 892).
[4] C.J. 21 Dec. 1648; C.C.A.M., pp. 572–3; C.C.C., pp. 523, 1716.

was implemented, and a similar threat against Lord Howard of Escrick
was enforced only when he was expelled from parliament.[1] The Earls
of Pembroke and Salisbury likewise escaped payment of debts to the
state while they remained M.P.s.[2] In general, however, the commissioners who in 1650 assumed responsibility for all matters relating to
debts owed to the government kept a sharp eye open for such abuses.
It should also be noted that many of the M.P.s who held on to money
or land which should have gone to the state were owed sums by the
government which they found difficulty in procuring. Some rumpers
may even have declined to accept payment of debts owed them by the
state rather than deplete the government's already strained finances.[3]
Bulstrode Whitelocke, whose political loyalties Professor Underdown
believes to have been influenced by a desire to retain the post of Commissioner of the Great Seal, calculated privately that his tenure of the
office during the Rump period cost him, through the loss of his legal
practice, more than it gained him.[4]

The financial interests of at least half the rumpers were considered
at some stage by the Rump or by its committees. The cases which arose
often emerged in the routine course of business rather than as a result
of initiatives by the members concerned, and the private concerns of
M.P.s took up no higher a proportion of parliament's time during the
Rump period than in the 1640s. Yet it is certainly true that members
who did not sit after the purge stood much less chance than those who
did of a hearing for their interests in the Rump. Between April and
October 1649 the House, by dispensing largesse to M.P.s who had
already taken their seats, issued a hint to members who might thus be
persuaded to join the Rump.[5] The grants of land or money which the
House awarded were not, however, indiscriminate. They were occasionally made as rewards for services, like the gifts made to the Speaker,
to the president of the Council of State, to Cromwell and to other
army officers; but in most instances they were merely orders for the
repayment of long-standing and properly audited loans contributed to
the parliamentary cause during the civil war. Many of the rumpers,
and especially of the 'revolutionaries', were among the M.P.s who had

[1] C.C.C., pp. 657, 687, 725; C.C.A.M., pp. 109, 459ff., 749, 832–3, 942. See also Underdown, *Pride's Purge*, p. 246n.
[2] C.C.A.M., pp. 954–5; C.C.C., pp. 1930, 1931, 2036.
[3] See e.g. C.C.C., pp. 288, 290, 1835, 2262.
[4] Underdown, *Pride's Purge*, pp. 52–3; B.M., Add. MS 37,344, fo. 278&ᵛ.
[5] C.J. e.g. 24, 25, 26 Apr., 16 May, 6, 19, 23, 25, 30 June, 17, 19, 20, 21, 24, 25 July, 1, 14,
16, 24 Aug., 5, 6, 13, 14, 21, 28 Sep., 17 Oct. 1649.

contributed most generously to the war effort and who had been financially most embarrassed in consequence.[1] What is surprising is less the Rump's recognition of such claims than the difficulties facing most of the members who sought repayment. The usual course was to 'discover' concealments or undervaluations of royalist estates subject to composition or confiscation by the state. Many rumpers had to make such discoveries before they could hope for even partial repayment of the debts owed to them, and the discoveries which they presented were not always ratified. The search for discoveries cannot have increased the sum of human happiness, or at least of royalists' happiness. It is hard to avoid dismay at the rapidity with which some rumpers settled into the London mansions of royalist magnates, or bought, sometimes below the market price and sometimes after jumping the queue of purchasers, royalist estates confiscated by parliament.[2] Lord Craven, whose lands were seized on the basis of decidedly unconvincing evidence, and who had obviously checked his information, claimed that the rumpers who bought his estates were those who had pressed hardest in the House for their confiscation.[3] Heselrige, who had extensive powers relating to compositions both in the north and at Westminster, and whose cousin and ally Edmund Winslow became one of the Rump's seven Commissioners for Compounding, evidently amassed considerable quantities of land for himself.[4] The scale of his purchases was, however, much larger than that of most rumpers. It can certainly be shown that some rumpers secured repayment of their debts through discoveries, and that in this respect they were more fortunate than men to whom the state was equally indebted; but this is a very different matter from suggesting that the Rump simply handed out vast and unearned fortunes to its members. Apart from anything else, its precarious finances made such wanton generosity unthinkable.

The most common (if also the most harmless) manifestation of M.P.s' regard for their own interests seems largely to have escaped contemporary observation. The recorded appearances in parliament of some of the less active rumpers coincided strikingly with the House's consideration of their debts or private concerns. A few examples will illustrate the point. John Dormer was uncharacteristically busy in parliament in late

[1] Underdown, *Pride's Purge*, pp. 245–8, 407.
[2] *Ibid.* p. 249; *C.C.A.M.*, p. 530; *C.C.C.*, pp. 184–5, 465, 496, 657, 1116, 1247, 1257, 1429, 1580, 1624, 1625, 1714, 1785, 2183, 2304, 2424, 2426, 2463, 2533–4, 2766.
[3] *C.C.C.*, p. 1618; *C.J.* 3 Aug. 1652.
[4] Numerous references in *C.C.C.* and *C.C.A.M.*, as indexed. For Heselrige and Winslow see also *Complete Writings of Roger Williams*, vi. 255.

December 1651 and in January 1652, but his brief burst of activity ended abruptly on 21 January, the day after he had succeeded in presenting a request for an annuity to the Commissioners for Compounding.[1] Thomas Hussey, after a long absence from parliament, reappeared on 15 September 1652 and presented a financial request on the same day. The case dragged on until the Rump's dissolution, during which time Hussey was much more active in parliament than in any other period since Pride's Purge.[2] Colonel Hutchinson's appearances in the House frequently kept time with his private interests until May 1651, when one of his requests for land was granted. Thereafter he withdrew from Rump politics to his native Nottinghamshire, there to suppress alehouses and to contemplate the portraits he had salvaged from Charles I's collection.[3] John Lenthall, rarely seen in parliament, became temporarily more active in August 1650, when he petitioned parliament for land.[4] The elder Thomas Pury, so industrious a politician in the Rump's earlier stages, made his sole recorded appearance between February 1652 and January 1653 on 27 July, the day on which he was awarded money for a discovery.[5] George Searle put in a brief and extremely rare appearance in September 1649, when the House made him mayor of Taunton and when the Committee for Advance of Money granted him an admittedly small contribution towards a sum owed him by the state since 1646.[6] George Snelling's participation in Rump politics came to a sudden and permanent halt on 20 September 1650, the day on which the House acceded to his request for payment of a debt.[7] Thomas Waite made three of his rare recorded appearances in the Rump in November and December 1649, but withdrew again as soon as he had been granted certain rents for which he had petitioned. His short spell of parliamentary energy in July 1650 was doubtless related to his presentation of a petition for land in the same month.[8] The parliamentary appearances of at least twelve other relatively inactive rumpers seem also to have coincided remarkably with discussion of their interests by the government.[9] It is not always possible to tell,

---

[1] *C.C.C.*, p. 2939. For Dormer and all the other rumpers mentioned in this paragraph, see also *C.J.* for the appropriate dates and periods.
[2] *C.C.C.*, p. 3017.
[3] *C.C.A.M.*, pp. 215, 882, 942; *C.C.C.*, pp. 1708, 1709, 2108, 2339; *Memoirs of Colonel Hutchinson*, pp. 288, 293, 295–6.
[4] *C.C.C.*, p. 962.
[5] *C.J.* 27 July 1652; *C.C.A.M.*, pp. 1335, 1336.
[6] *C.C.A.M.*, p. 1504.　　　　　[7] *Ibid.* p. 1403.　　　　　[8] *C.C.C.*, p. 2303.
[9] Andrews, Jervoise, Moore, Moyle, G. Norton, Pierrepoint, A. Popham, Philip Lord Herbert (fifth Earl of Pembroke), H. Salwey, Sydenham, Sir P. Temple, Wallop.

however, whether such members came to London simply to secure a hearing for their private affairs, or whether, deciding in any case to make one of their rare visits to Westminster, they merely sought repayment of money owed them while they were about it.

There are four rumpers, nevertheless, whose behaviour does leave a decidedly unpleasant taste in the mouth. The most prominent politician among them was Sir John Danvers. According to Aubrey, Danvers was

a great friend to the king's party and a patron to distressed and cashiered Cavaliers. But to revenge himself of his sister, the Lady Gargrave, and to ingratiate himself with [Cromwell] to null his brother, Earl of Danby's, will, he, contrary to his own natural inclination, did sit in the High Court of Justice at the king's trial.[1]

Danvers certainly made a determined effort during the Rump period to procure his sister's estate, forcing lengthy debates in parliament on the subject; and Aubrey's claim that Danvers, who signed Charles's death warrant, sat in the High Court of Justice to please Cromwell was probably accurate.[2] Danvers was a strange political animal. In May 1648, when a number of M.P.s had been added to the Long Parliament's Derby House Committee, he had been the only nominee whose candidacy was formally challenged in the House: in February 1650 he was the only active member of the Rump's first Council of State who failed to secure election to its second.[3] His unpopularity was probably connected with his ruthless pursuit of his private interests in the House, a trait which might have been less unattractive had he not also failed to repay the large sums he owed to the state.[4] Equally pressing for consideration of their claims, and equally unforthcoming with their own debts to the government, were Lord Howard of Escrick and two M.P.s from Hampshire, Sir Thomas Jervoise and Robert Wallop. Jervoise and Wallop, who worked in unison, and whose financial interests were tied up with those of Danvers, rarely honoured the House with their presence except when their insatiable requests were under discussion.[5] These four rumpers, like many others whose interests were considered by the House, were, it is true, deeply in debt on all sides; but Henry Marten, another heavily indebted member, was not prevented by his

[1] *Aubrey's Brief Lives:* Danvers.
[2] *C.S.P.D.* 1649–50, p. 63; *C.J.* 17 May 1649.
[3] *C.J.* 30 May 1648; below, p. 221.
[4] *C.C.C.*, e.g. pp. 1563, 1638, 1974, 1975.
[5] *Ibid.* pp. 271, 348; *C.C.A.M.*, pp. 202–5, 461–3.

difficulties from consistently opposing the award of large sums of money to individual M.P.s – although even he, at a time when the Rump was anxious to isolate him from the Levellers, could not resist a long over-due repayment which eased his financial position.[1]

By the late 1640s it was felt, by people of widely differing views, that the Long Parliament had already sat much too long for its own good. Its members knew each other too well to retain illusions about their colleagues, and the sense of purpose and idealism prevalent in the early 1640s, the respect for parliament as the embodiment of the public conscience, had often turned sour. In debates, the less exalted sides of human nature came increasingly to the surface. The loyalist sentiment which emerged in the Rump period was born of a disillusionment at times almost amounting to cynicism. Yet the sense of political *malaise* often evident in the later 1640s and early 1650s sets traps which the historian needs to avoid. Puritans were often a disconcerting mixture of intense idealism and intense materialism. Many of them spent more time contemplating the salvation of their souls and trying to keep economic-ally afloat than present-day politicians could afford to spend on either. To castigate puritans, whether or not they were rumpers, because they were obsessed by both God and money would be inappropriately to export the attitudes of the twentieth century to the seventeenth. It is easy, but also pointless, to describe as 'corrupt' politicians who did not behave as frugally or selflessly as one would like them to have behaved. Politicians rarely do. The Rump's seedy reputation derives primarily from its failure to do what radicals, who are mainly responsible for the legend of corruption, wanted it to do. The rumpers, radicals believed, had betrayed the revolution, dashing the hopes raised by the purge and the execution. Yet the Rump itself had done little to raise those hopes, and no one who knew its members well, or who understood why they had gone to war with Charles I, could have believed that it would inaugurate the kind of reformation for which radicals were impatient. The Rump was vilified not because it betrayed obligations but because it failed to live up to the groundless expectations radicals held of it. The parliament left behind by Pride's Purge contained a fair proportion of sharks and even, probably, a small handful of crooks; but to suppose that in this respect it differed from other seventeenth-century govern-ments, or to suggest that its members were a bunch of unprincipled self-seekers, would be to misjudge the whole tenor of Rump politics. The Rump spent most of its time governing the country and arguing

[1] Below, p. 198.

about how best to govern it. The private interests of its members took up a very small proportion of the parliamentary timetable. However unscrupulously or unattractively individual politicians behaved, it is hard to think of a major policy decision in which the Rump's concept of the public interest was sacrificed to private ends. It does not help, in studying the Rump, to presuppose that its members were an unusually nefarious body of politicians.

PART TWO

THE RUMP AND REFORM

6

LAW REFORM

The Rump's discussions of the army's reform programme were strongly influenced by the particular circumstances which gave rise to them, and which will be considered in the narrative section of this book. Before we turn to narrative, however, it will be well to consider some of the issues involved in the three main subjects on which the reform movement touched: the law, religion, and the relationship between parliament and electorate.

Few features of English society were subjected to such sustained and voluble criticism during the revolution as the legal system. The common law was predominantly the product of the medieval world, its character determined by the needs of a relatively static society. The increased social mobility of the sixteenth and seventeenth centuries, and the consequent growth in the tendency to litigation, placed novel strains on the common law. These it could meet only by sporadic, haphazard patterns of accretion which left its workings more unwieldy than ever. In many cases the old local courts had yielded jurisdiction to the central courts at Westminster, which had in turn to be supplemented by the expanding equity and prerogative courts; but all these courts developed their own abuses which many found intolerable. The abolition of the prerogative courts by the Long Parliament, although removing political grievances, increased the burdens which the common law already had to bear and to which the chaos of civil war could only add still further.[1]

Criticism of the legal system was not new. Most of the reform demands voiced during the revolution had also been heard before 1640.

[1] There are informative studies, based mainly on pamphlet material, of the law reform movement by C. R. Niehaus, 'The issue of law reform', and by Donald Veall, *The Popular Movement for Law Reform 1640–1660* (Oxford, 1970). The only detailed study of the political application of the reform proposals contained in the pamphlets is by Mary Cotterell, 'Interregnum law reform: the Hale Commission of 1652', *E.H.R.*, lxxxiii (1968).

Both literary and popular complaints against laws and lawyers were, indeed, almost as old as literary and popular anticlericalism. In the early seventeenth century king and parliament, encouraged by Bacon and Coke, showed a passing interest in the remedy of legal abuses. Yet little was done, and by 1640 the movement for law reform had vanished from political view. Since the parliamentary case in the civil war rested largely on a claim to defend the common law, M.P.s were unlikely to display enthusiasm for aggressive criticism of that law. It was left to the Levellers and their radical allies to revive, and to give coherence and urgency to, the movement for law reform. They found plenty of scope for criticism. The immoderate length of time it took to get a case first heard and then settled, and the exorbitant fees which had some-times to be paid in the process, were targets for particularly heavy attack. The blame for them was laid principally at the door of the lawyers, those 'verminous caterpillars' who, it was held, cared more for their own pockets than for the interests of their clients, more for legal technicalities than for the execution of justice. Others who were supposed to benefit from the abuses of the legal system were the swarms of court officials encountered by any plaintiff trying to secure a hearing, and the gaolers under whose supervision impoverished men languished in appalling conditions. If the workings of the law were cumbersome and corrupt, the law itself needed reform. Punishment, all too often, bore little relation to the deserts of the crime. There was growing hostility, too, to the land law, whose uncertainties could embitter the relationship between landlord and tenant. Arrangements surrounding the buying and selling of land afforded further opportunity for fraud.

Yet interest in law reform went beyond criticism of the law and its workings. It extended to the social evils which the failings of the legal system were held to reflect. The social implications of the radical reform movement can be seen in a number of the demands put forward: in the call, deriving from an anti-professionalism aimed not only at lawyers but at clergymen and sometimes even at physicians, for the abolition of the legal profession, or at least for an abrogation of its privileges; in the insistence that laws should be codified or abbreviated, so that everyone could understand them; or in the demand that all men, peers and commoners alike, should be equal before the law. Also suggestive of the reformers' social aims was the clamour for the reduction of the courts at Westminster and their replacement by county or even hundred courts. This proposal sounded reasonable enough when it came from men who lived far from London, but many of those who advocated it gave little thought to the practical difficulties, and the harm to the true interests of justice, to which their schemes might lead. Such demands at times reflected informed concern to remedy legal abuses, but in general they owed more to comprehensive dissatisfaction with social ones.[1]

The Rump devoted much time to discussion of law reform, and indeed on occasion committed itself to general criticism of legal abuses. Sweeping changes in the law were contemplated by the House in June and August 1649, and specific proposals received extensive discussion in parliament between November 1649 and March 1650. The House raised the expectations of reformers still further in the months after the battle of Dunbar in September 1650, and even more in the months following the battle of Worcester in September 1651. In the first half of 1652 a commission on law reform, set up by the Rump and chaired by the distinguished lawyer Matthew Hale, produced a formidable corpus of proposals for the removal of abuses and for a partial reconstruction of the court system. Yet, compared with the energy expended on the various schemes for reform laid before the House, the Rump's achievements were minimal. A few proposals did, it is true, reach the statute book. A series of piecemeal measures afforded some relief to impoverished debtors, while a bill to abolish writs of error secured, under Heselrige's guidance, a relatively easy passage in the winter of 1649–50.[2] The House's burst of activity on law reform after Dunbar led to the celebrated act for converting legal proceedings into the English tongue and for substituting ordinary handwriting for court hand. At about the same time the fee known as *damna clericorum*, or 'damage clear', widely condemned even by lawyers as 'a great and unreasonable burden to the client', was swept away.[3] Peers and M.P.s were stripped of their special privileges before the law.[4] Finally, twelve days before the dissolution, the Rump passed an act for probate of wills.[5] Yet these measures were small reward for the industry of reformers. Various proposals debated by the Rump, like the moves to reform the jury system, the bill to rationalise the proceedings of the Court of

---

[1] Veall, *Popular Movement for Law Reform*, chapter 3; Niehaus, 'The issue of law reform', chapters 1 and 2.

[2] *C.J.* 13, 23 Nov., 4, 11 Dec. 1649, 18 Jan., 1 Feb., 4, 11 Mar. 1650; Firth and Rait, *Acts and Ordinances*, ii. 357–8.

[3] *Certain Proposals of Divers Attorneys of the Court of Common Pleas* (1651), p. 6; *C.J.* 13 Dec. 1650, 17 Jan. 1651.

[4] Gardiner, *Constitutional Documents*, p. 388; *C.J.* 14, 16 Apr. 1649. Cf. *C.J.* 2 Aug. 1650; *The Moderate* 6–13 Mar. 1649, p. 349; *Perfect Weekly Account* 7–14 Mar. 1649, p. 413.

[5] Below, pp. 318–20.

Exchequer, and the list of suggestions submitted to the House by Henry Marten in December 1650, were quietly pushed aside. Some of Marten's proposals, admittedly, were subsumed under the recommendations of the Hale commission, but not one of the commission's proposals was implemented by the Rump.[1] Even the measures which did pass the House must in some instances have disappointed reformers by their caution. The act for probate of wills and, still more, the acts for reform of the debt law represented particularly serious dilutions of the radical proposals which the House had at first contemplated.

Why did law reform make so little headway in parliament? Frustrated contemporaries had a ready explanation. The failure of the reform movement, they argued, could be attributed to the influence of lawyer M.P.s. Forbid practising lawyers to sit in parliament or on its committees, they hinted, and reform measures would easily pass the House.[2] Lawyers attended parliamentary committees on law reform, it was claimed in 1651, 'for no other end . . . but either to obstruct, weather, or pervert the work'. Indeed, 'divers well meaning clerks have already been threatened and otherwise discouraged [from] giving their informations and propositions, and from attending' the Rump's committee on law reform 'by some lawyers now members of parliament'.[3] When the same committee was revived in November 1651, an army writer claimed that its report of the previous December was 'endeavoured to be laid aside by the lawyers'.[4] Such allegations, which have found frequent favour with historians, were widespread.[5] What truth was there in them? Dr Niehaus has argued that the charge that lawyers obstructed reform proposals 'should be consigned to the limbo of convenient but false explanations'.[6] So charitable a view rests upon the misconception that the mid seventeenth-century legal profession can be regarded as united in its reactions to reform proposals. It is true that a number of lawyers urged the need for at least moderate reform, and that the influence of such men, both generally in clearing the way for limited reform measures and particularly in their contribu-

[1] *C.J.* 21 May, 7 Nov. 1649, 13 Dec. 1650.
[2] Veall, *Popular Movement for Law Reform*, pp. 203–6; B.M., Add. MS 37,345, fos. 21ᵛ, 27ᵛ–8; *Some Advertisements for the new Election of Burgesses* (1645), p. 34.
[3] *To the Supreme Authority, the Parliament* (1651: B.M., 669 f. 15, fo. 78).
[4] Clarke MS. xx, fo. 10.
[5] See e.g. A. Warren, *Eight Reasons Categorical* (1653), p. 6; *Memoirs of Edmund Ludlow*, i. 333–4, ii. 161.
[6] Niehaus, 'The issue of law reform', p. 225.

tion to the work of the Hale commission, was considerable. In the main, however, the legal profession was as resistant in the seventeenth century as it always has been to reforms proposed by laymen. Reforming lawyers had to look over their shoulders at other members of the profession who, they thought, would regard their efforts with odium.[1] As Mr Veall has observed, few of the reformers came from the established and wealthy legal 'dynasty', from the men who rose, often as their fathers had done, to the top jobs in the legal profession.[2]

Such men were well represented in the Rump. Among them were two of the Commissioners of the Great Seal (Whitelocke and Lisle), a Chief Baron of the Exchequer (John Wylde), a Chief Justice of the Court of Common Pleas (Oliver St John), the Rump's attorney-general and its solicitor-general (Edmund Prideaux and Robert Reynolds), three other Commonwealth judges (Robert Nicholas, Alexander Rigby and Francis Thorpe), and Sir Thomas Widdrington. Of these, only two were 'revolutionaries': Lisle, whom Whitelocke dismissed contemptuously as being 'for all assays' and who was cold-shouldered by the legal establishment,[3] and Rigby, who played no part in the Rump after his promotion to the post of Baron of the Exchequer in June 1649. There were also in the Rump a number of prominent barristers, serjeants-at-law or future judges who displayed no symptoms of political radicalism, men like Nicholas Lechmere, Lislibone Long (significantly praised by Whitelocke as 'a very sober discreet gentleman, and a good lawyer'),[4] William Stephens, Nathaniel Bacon, Erasmus Earle and William Ellis. Eight other rumpers, Humphrey Salwey, Thomas Pury, Thomas Hussey, Robert Goodwin, Miles Corbet, Daniel Blagrave, Richard Edwards and Nicholas Love, held paid offices in the Courts of Chancery or Exchequer, Love enjoying a notorious sinecure as one of the Six Clerks in Chancery.[5] The two courts proved resourcefully resistant to change. Corbet and Blagrave were regicides, as were two other lawyers active in the Rump, Augustine Garland and William Say. In general, however, the weight of legal

[1] See e.g. J. March, *Amicus Republicae* (1651), ep. ded.
[2] Veall, *Popular Movement for Law Reform*, pp. 229, 233. Men who, by contrast, had failed as lawyers were often to be found among the advocates of law reform: see e.g. *The Anti-Levellers Antidote* (1652), pp. 1–2; *The Law's Discovery* (1653), p. 31.
[3] Whitelocke, *Memorials*, iv. 6. Cf. B.M., Add. MS 37,345, fos. 41ᵛ–2, 71ᵛ, 117ᵛ, 200ᵛ, 204, 267ᵛ, and Whitelocke Letters (Longleat) x, fo. 129.
[4] Whitelocke, *Memorials*, iv. 341.
[5] *Ibid.* ii. 279, 470; *C.S.P.D.* 1651–2, pp. 160, 162; *Proposals concerning the Chancery* (1650), pp. 9–13; *The Anti-Levellers Antidote*, p. 7; *C.C.A.M.*, pp. 386, 849; Veall, *Popular Movement for Law Reform*, p. 40.

expertise in the Rump lay with the forces of both political and social conservatism. In its legal patronage the Rump displayed the tastes which were also, as we shall see, evident in its ecclesiastical patronage: it promoted safe, conservative figures and left reformers aside.[1]

Those who demanded the exclusion of lawyers from the House usually overlooked the Long Parliament's dependence on its legal element for the drafting of legislation and the organisation of parliamentary business. On a wide variety of issues, 'all the lawyers in the House' were sometimes added as a group to committees or summoned to attend debates.[2] Some lawyers were of course more active as M.P.s than others, but those who did attend the House assiduously also took a keen interest, naturally enough, in debates on law reform. Of the nineteen M.P.s most frequently appointed to Rump committees on law reform, nine were or had been prominent lawyers;[3] and time and again it was the lawyers who secured control of such committees.[4] The cohesion of the lawyer M.P.s in the House has already been emphasised.[5] It could be used to devastating effect, as reformers found to their cost on three crucial occasions: in the summer of 1649, when the lawyers organised skilful opposition to the bill for relieving poor prisoners for debt; in the autumn of 1650, when Henry Marten planned major legal reforms; and in February 1653, when, after efficient cooperation by the lawyers, the Rump rejected the entire report of the Hale commission.[6]

Indeed, it is arguable not only that lawyers provided the main opposition to law reform, but that such reform as was achieved came only when fear, or an instinct for self-preservation, drove them to make concessions to reforming sentiment. Henry Robinson, a keen advocate of law reform who held office under the Rump, claimed after the dissolution that the lawyer M.P.s,

when they perceived and saw that they had outgone their own politics . . . began to acknowledge their own irregularities and exorbitances, even not to be longer endured, and promised reformation . . . and at last suffered [the Hale] commissioners to be chosen to consider of the regulation of the laws, and courts of

---

[1] Veall, *Popular Movement for Law Reform*, pp. 233–4.
[2] *C.J.* 6 July, 11 Dec. 1649, 15 Apr., 21, 22 June, 25 Oct. 1650, 28 Aug. 1651, 26 Jan. 1653. This tendency was not new.
[3] Lawyers: Garland, Hill, Lechmere, Lisle, Long, Prideaux, Reynolds, Say, Whitelocke. Others: Allen, Bond, T. Chaloner, Dove, J. Gurdon, Harrison, Holland, Marten, Mildmay, Vane jr.
[4] *C.J.* 20 Apr., 18, 23, 26 May, 23 June, 3, 7 Aug., 11 Dec. 1649, 18, 25 Jan., 11 Mar., 14, 23 May, 11 June, 25 Oct. 1650, 10 Jan., 14 May 1651, 2 Feb. 1653.
[5] Above, p. 30.   [6] Below, pp. 203–4, 238, 320.

justice, who that they might not be over charged with so great a task, they gave them half a dozen gentlemen of the same tribe, to save them that labour (I wish it proved so); and what fruit is produced is best known to themselves; but it seems the late parliament could not digest, but still grew worse until its dissolution.[1]

The lawyer Albertus Warren called in November 1649 for legal proceedings to be held in English, as 'the way to put [the law] into a capacity of winning her causeless enemies unto the obedience of her just sanctions'.[2] So long as there was a chance of moderate reform, achieved from within, Warren advocated change; but as the reform movement became more vitriolic, so he retreated into conservatism.[3] In December 1649 one lawyer sent a list of reform proposals to Whitelocke, designed to achieve 'the preservation of the law, from future ignorance, calumny, and ruin, which now much menace it, by making it cognoscible and practicable'.[4] There is other evidence, too, of lawyers attempting during the Rump period to anticipate radical demands by remedying glaring abuses. During 1649 the attorney-general, the Commissioners of the Great Seal, the Master of the Rolls and others held meetings to draw up proposals 'for reformation of proceedings in chancery'. The result was a manual on the court's procedure. Certain abuses were criticised, but these were implicitly blamed on the court's officials, who were instructed to mend their ways accordingly. There was no criticism in the document of the general principles on which the court was run or of the structure of office-holding dependent upon it. Two of the Commissioners of the Great Seal put their names to it, but the third, John Lisle, the only committed reformer among them, did not.[5] Meanwhile a series of meetings was held by 'divers attorneys of the Court of Common Pleas', who in May 1650 came forward with a comprehensive series of proposals, to which Whitelocke evidently attached importance, for the remedy of existing abuses in the workings of the legal system. Their recommendations were presented to the Rump's committee on law reform in December of the same year. The attorneys conceded that 'not the least of their ambitions' was to 'take away those aspersions that

[1] H. Robinson, *Certain Proposals in order to a new Modelling of the Laws* (1653), p. 3; Firth and Rait, *Acts and Ordinances*, ii. 180, 277, 362.
[2] A. Warren, *The Royalist Reformed* (1649), p. 39.
[3] Warren, *Eight Reasons Categorical*, and *A New Plea for the Old Law* (1653).
[4] Whitelocke Letters (Longleat) x, fo. 80: Peter Ball to Whitelocke, 22 Dec. 1649.
[5] B.M., Add. MS 37,344, fo. 281, and Add. MS 37,345, fos. 5ᵛ, 6ᵛ; *A Collection of . . . the Orders heretofore used in Chancery* (1649), esp. pp. 5–6, 28, 30–1, 48–9, 53–4, 78–9, 81–3, 91–2.

seem to blemish that law, the law of England, which they humbly conceive to be the most perfect law of any humane law in the world'.[1]

Yet if Dr Niehaus was mistaken in regarding the attitudes of lawyers as a false explanation of the failure of the movement for law reform, he was right to insist that it is an all too convenient one. Vested interests are always an easy target. We are fortunate in having, in Whitelocke's Annals, a record of the response of an established, prosperous lawyer to the growth of the reform movement. In the sixteenth and earlier seventeenth centuries lawyers became increasingly numerous, increasingly wealthy, and increasingly conscious of the distinctiveness of their profession;[2] and there are times, certainly, when Whitelocke's views are hard to stomach. Time and again he lectured the Rump on the unparalleled virtues of the English legal system. His scorn for proposals that lawyers should be excluded from the House, or that legal proceedings should be in English, and his attempts to daub the advocates of law reform with the smear of levelling, reflect at times no more than mere professional snobbery. But there also emerge more attractive traits, notably a vigilant concern for the maintenance of professional standards and for incorruptibility in the administration of the law without fear or favour. Even here Whitelocke's self-importance could get the better of him; but it was not mere pomposity which led him to view with dismay the inexperience of his fellow Commissioners of the Great Seal and the failings of other lawyers, or which provoked his outburst against his fellow rumpers when in February 1650 they sent three men to the pillory:

Thus they took upon them and exercised all manner of jurisdiction, and sentenced persons *secundum arbitrarium*. Which was disliked by many lawyers of the House (whereof I was one), and we showed them the illegality and breach of liberty in those arbitrary proceedings; and advised them to refer such matters to the legal proceedings in ordinary courts of justice; but the dominion and power was sweet to some of them, and they were very unwilling to part with it.[3]

---

[1] *Certain Proposals of Divers Attorneys*, esp. ep. ded. and p. 1; Whitelocke, *Memorials*, iii 194; *Perfect Diurnal . . . Armies* 20–27 May 1650, pp. 276–8.

[2] K. Charlton, 'The professions in sixteenth century England', *University of Birmingham Historical Journal*, xii (1966), 24. See also E. W. Ives, 'Social Change and the Law', in a collection of essays edited by the same author, *The English Revolution 1640–1660* (1968); *Some Advertisements for the new Election of Burgesses*, pp. 1–2.

[3] B.M., Add. MS 37,345, fos. 21ᵛ–25ᵛ, 27ᵛ–31ᵛ, 189ᵛ, 200ᵛ, 204, 239ᵛ–40, 267ᵛ; Whitelocke, *Memorials*, i. 269, ii. 440–7, 449–56, iii. 88, 146, 260–73, iv. 188, 191–207. In the (1853) printed *Memorials* some curious editorial liberties were taken with Whitelocke's account of his speeches on law reform in the autumn of 1649.

Whitelocke's contempt for proposals which smacked more of fashionable rhetoric than of concern for the true interests of justice was not entirely groundless. It is too easy to mock him for the unkind innuendo which he aimed at such advocates of law reform as Henry Ireton, John Lambert and Hugh Peter,[1] men with a smattering of legal knowledge in an age when, as has recently been suggested, a little knowledge of the law could be a dangerous thing in the hands of those who administered or sought to reform it.[2] Many reform proposals were ludicrously impracticable, yet they must have appealed readily to men whose lives were dogged by suspicion of lawyers and clergymen. Cromwell made a virtue of his amateur ignorance of the law. As he informed parliament in 1657, during one of his own pleas for law reform,

I confess, if any man would ask me, 'Why, how would you have it done?', I confess I do not know how. But I think verily at the least, the delays in suits and excessiveness of fees, and those various things that I do not know what names they bear, – I heard talk of 'demurrers' and such like things as I scarce know . . .

'I have as little skill in arithmetic', he boasted, 'as I have in the law!'[3] Whitelocke may have been mistaken in believing that Cromwell's policy of law reform during the Protectorate was designed simply to curry popularity, but his suspicions are understandable.[4] Whitelocke was not opposed to all reform proposals. He thought there was a case for itinerant courts which would spare people long treks to Westminster. He was sometimes prepared to back down to reformers, as over the bill in the autumn of 1650 to convert legal proceedings into English. In general, however, Whitelocke like many others believed English law and lawyers to be justly the envy of the world. The 'multiplicity of suits', he thought, was inevitable in a society economically more sophisticated than its neighbours, in which trade flourished and men were free. There were fewer law suits in such economically retarded and relatively enslaved societies as France and Sweden.[5] In this view there was at least an element of truth. However plentiful or shocking the vices of the legal system, it was unrealistic to suppose that the celebrated freedoms of Englishmen would be preserved by making the law less rather than more complex. The decentralisation of the law,

[1] Whitelocke, *Memorials*, ii. 162–3, iii. 388. But cf. *ibid.* iii. 371.
[2] W. Prest, 'The legal education of the gentry at the Inns of Court, 1540–1640', *Past and Present*, 38 (1967), 20–9, 35, 36.
[3] Abbott, *Writings and Speeches*, iv. 493, 496.
[4] Whitelocke, *Memorials*, iv. 182, 188.
[5] *Ibid.* iv. 139; B.M., Add. MS 37,345, fos. 24–5, 116ᵛ, and Add. MS 31,984, fo. 175.

favoured by reformers, would have led to a multiplicity of competing jurisdictions. These in turn would have made it much harder for many men to secure legal redress or payment of debts. They would also, in the view of Whitelocke and others, have damaged both national cohesion and national trade.[1] Ludlow's famous complaint, echoed by Cromwell, that during the Rump period the 'word "incumbrance" was so managed by the lawyers, that it took three months' time'[2] was probably accurate: the meaning of the term was a contentious issue in the drafting of the controversial bill for county registers which was introduced into the House three months before the dissolution and in which no progress was made. But was this mere recalcitrance on the lawyers' part? Matthew Hale, so sympathetic to reasonable reform proposals, had strong doubts about the desirability both of the compulsory county registers and of the county courts for which the proposals brought before the Rump in its last months provided.[3] Reasoned and detailed objections were put forward to the commission's proposals on the same subject,[4] and the demands of reformers who wanted county registers were in any case frequently confused.[5]

Vigorous hostility to lawyers, which became especially marked at those times when the Rump was under greatest pressure to reform, cannot have improved the lawyers' tempers, especially since such enmity had increasingly little to do with the practical reform issues which both parliament and the Hale commissioners had to face. To the radical saints who attacked the Rump in its later stages, the law was a symbol of social slavery. But who would take over from the sons of Zeruiah? Perhaps, when the Mosaic law were introduced, or when – as the saints frequently predicted – justice flowed as free and fast as a clear stream down a mountainside, human intermediaries would become superfluous. Not all the elect, however, seem to have thought so. When the Rump debated the question of county registers, the radical Welsh preacher Walter Cradock wrote to Cromwell that

that renowned ancient saint Mr. Rice Williams of Newport, being one who

[1] Cf. *Reasons against the Bill entitled an Act for County Registers* (1653), p. 32; William Leach, *Bills Proposed for Acts* (1651), p. 5; Warren, *Eight Reasons Categorical*, pp. 7–8; *Several Proposals for the General Good of the Commonwealth* (1651), pp. 1–2.
[2] *Memoirs of Edmund Ludlow*, i. 334; Abbott, *Writings and Speeches*, iv. 493.
[3] B.M., Add. MS 35,863, pp. 93–4, 134; Veall, *Popular Movement for Law Reform*, pp. 187, 223–4; Cotterell, 'Interregnum law reform', p. 698.
[4] *Reasons against the Bill entitled an Act for County Registers*, pp. 5–9; *A Supply to a Draft of an Act or System Proposed* (1653), pp. 11–12.
[5] Veall, *Popular Movement for Law Reform*, pp. 219–20.

hath served the state in many places, but not gained a penny therefrom, is pitched upon by the saints here a year ago for that place of registering deeds in this county . . . your favourable assistance is much desired therein by the godly of this county . . .

In a postscript Cradock added that one Richard Creed, 'late servant to Major General Harrison', was 'also commended unto you by the godly for registering of wills, the rather because his sufficiency in clerkship might make up what is wanting (as to that) in Mr. Rice Williams'.[1] Unfortunately for Williams the county registers were never introduced, although Harrison did secure a post for Creed as Clerk to the Rump's Admiralty Committee.[2] If there were those with a vested interest in preserving the legal system, then there were also those who stood to gain from changing it. Is it any wonder if Whitelocke believed himself to be a more reliable guardian of justice than Rice Williams, with his 'want of clerkship', or Richard Creed?

If the lawyers' position is defensible, however, it is surprising to find it so stoutly defended in the Rump. Particularly remarkable is the House's willingness to entrust so much power to its conservative lawyers during its debates on law reform early in 1653. The earlier attitudes of rumpers had been less flattering to the legal profession. Whitelocke recorded that in a debate on legal abuses in October 1649, an M.P.

did very bitterly reflect upon the profession of lawyers as the chief cause of these mischiefs, and the excessiveness of their fees, and that it was not fit that any lawyer that was a member of the House should plead any cause whilst he was a member, and that it was fit to have the law in our native tongue, that all might understand it, with much to the like purpose. I being in the House perceived many to smile at this invective, and to seem well pleased at it.

There was in the Rump, Whitelocke thought, a 'great pique against the lawyers'.[3] It must have been easy to stir anti-lawyer feeling among M.P.s like Ludlow, with their vigilant hostility to the 'corrupt interest' of 'the lawyers and clergy'. A number of M.P.s who seem to have favoured at least moderate law reform, including not only parliamentary radicals like Marten, Thomas Chaloner, Rigby and Harrison but also more moderate figures like Vane and Heselrige, frequently sat

[1] *Original Letters . . . addressed to Oliver Cromwell*, pp. 85–6; cf. *C.C.C.*, p. 246.
[2] SP 46/114, fo. 89. Cf. Richards, *History of the Puritan Movement in Wales*, p. 248, and Mayer, 'Inedited letters', p. 215.
[3] B.M., Add. MS 37,345, fos. 21^v, 27^v.

on committees on the subject.[1] The concern of Cromwell and Ireton for law reform is also well known.[2] What needs explaining, then, is the House's resistance to reform proposals, a resistance which cannot be explained solely by the number and cohesion of the lawyer M.P.s. Why did the lawyers, especially towards the end of the Rump period, win so much support in the Rump? Denis Bond and Francis Allen, who sat on numerous law reform committees, turned their faces against reform proposals at critical moments, as did two other influential rumpers, Sir John Danvers and Cromwell's friend Sir William Armyne. That staunch conservative John Feilder sat regularly on the Rump's later committees on law reform and helped to defeat their proposals.[3]

The Rump's conservatism on law reform, like its conservatism on other issues, is to be explained largely by its desire before the battle of Worcester to appease moderates and presbyterians, and largely by its hostility, after the defeat of the royalists, to the army. These are matters to which we shall return later in the book, when we shall see how such considerations influenced the House's debates on individual reform proposals. There were, however, two special factors which strengthened the House's resistance to the remedy of legal abuses, and which may be mentioned here. First, there was the Rump's embarrassment at its constitutional illegitimacy. Its determination to live down its origins made it particularly tender of lawyers' feelings, especially since the government found it so difficult to persuade judges to accept commissions after Charles's execution,[4] and since there were so many lawyers among the 'middle group' and 'royal independent' M.P.s whom many rumpers were anxious to reconcile to the new regime.

---

[1] Marten: *C.J.* 18, 21 May, 4 Aug. 1649, 4 Feb., 25 Oct., 13 Dec. 1650, 17 Jan. 1651, 12 Nov. 1652, 17, 31 Mar. 1653; Rigby: *ibid.* 20 Apr., 18, 25, 26 May, 5 June 1649; Harrison: *ibid.* 18, 25 July, 28 Nov. 1649, 25 Oct. 1650, 26 Dec. 1651, 19 Mar., 12 Nov. 1652, 2 Feb. 1653; Chaloner: *ibid.* 20 Apr., 18, 21 May, 17, 18, 25 July, 7 Nov. 1649, 25 Oct. 1650, 26 Dec. 1651; Vane: *ibid.* 17, 18 July, 7 Nov. 1649, 25 Oct. 1650, 19 Mar., 12 Nov. 1652, 2 Mar. 1653; Heselrige: *ibid.* 4, 11, 21 Dec. 1649, 18 Jan., 4 Feb. 1650, 2 Feb. 1653.

[2] Abbott, *Writings and Speeches*, iii. 439, iv. 493; Whitelocke, *Memorials*, ii. 162–3, iii. 371; J. Cooke, *Monarchy no Creature of God's Making* (1652), ep. ded. at p. (35). And see *Several Proceedings of State Affairs*, 6 July 1654.

[3] For Bond see *C.J.* 18, 25 July, 4 Aug., 28 Nov. 1649, 4 Feb. 1650, 26 Dec. 1651, 12 Nov. 1652, 17 Mar. 1653; Allen: *ibid.* 24 Apr., 21 May, 4 Aug., 11 Dec. 1649, 25 Oct. 1650, 26 Dec. 1651, 19 Mar., 12 Nov. 1652, 17 Mar. 1653; Danvers: *ibid.* 27 July, 28 Nov. 1649, 4 Feb. 1650, 12 Nov. 1652, 17 Mar. 1653; Feilder: *ibid.* 26 Dec. 1651, 19 Mar. 1652, 2 Feb., 31 Mar. 1653.

[4] Gardiner, *History of the Commonwealth and Protectorate*, i. 9; Underdown, *Pride's Purge*, p. 203.

The lawyers' notoriously 'strong fancy of a single necessary governor'[1] must have encouraged both political and social conservatism in the Rump.

Secondly, hostility between parliament and army became even more marked on the subject of law reform than on other reform issues. The civil war had produced a widely recognised conflict between soldiers and the lawyer 'gown men', not least because of the lawyers' resistance to all forms of innovation and their readiness to condemn the rule of the sword.[2] The issue of law reform became a focus of the quarrel between civilian and military. Colonel Pride, one of the army's most active proponents of law reform, declared in Westminster Hall 'that it would never be well in England until . . . mercenary lawyers' gowns were hung up by the Scotch trophies'.[3] Army pressure, although sometimes driving the Rump to take action on law reform, was more likely to provoke the House to obdurate resistance. This was especially true early in 1653, when parliament was called upon to debate measures, recommended by the Hale commission, for county land registers and for the probate of wills. These proposals were partly designed to prevent landlords from taking advantage of the obscurity of existing records to cheat their tenants; but such reforms would hardly have jeopardised the survival either of the landed classes or of the legal profession. Nor would any of the commission's other proposals.[4] Yet the political tension of the Rump's final months, when soldiers and saints lashed out at lawyers and clergymen, gave a disturbing social dimension to debates on reform. Henry Parker, discussing in November 1650 the probate bill at that time before the Rump, advanced an explanation of the House's opposition to the measure which might be applied to the whole movement for law reform:

The reason why the reforming of these things (though the state itself, and thousands of particular men, remain sufferers in the meantime) proves so dilatory, and difficult, is supposed to be: because most men are possessed with two contrary extreme opinions; and few there are that pitch upon the middle and more moderate way.[5]

The 'middle and more moderate way' stood a chance in the Rump

[1] Warren, *The Royalist Reformed*, p. 41.
[2] B.M., Add. MS 37,345, fos. 22&ᵛ, 116ᵛ; Whitelocke, *Memorials*, iii. 273, 379–80; Warren, *The Royalist Reformed*, p. 41; *H.M.C.R Leybourne-Popham*, pp. 77–8.
[3] *A New Year's Gift for England* (1653), p. 15.
[4] Cf. Veall, *Popular Movement for Law Reform*, pp. 237–8.
[5] H. Parker, *Reformation in Courts, and Cases Testamentary* (1650), p. 3.

only in rare intervals of political harmony. It stood no chance at all by the spring of 1653. Rumpers might have no great love for their lawyer colleagues, but the point came at which criticisms of the legal system appeared also to be attacks on the social system and on the commitment of most M.P.s to civilian rule. In such circumstances, reasoned discussion of specific proposals was as unlikely as moderation. In its discussions on law reform the Rump was eventually obliged to choose between the lawyers on the one hand and army and sectarian radicals on the other. It is not surprising that it chose the lawyers.

7

PURITANS AND POLITICIANS

The Rump, when it came to power, was widely expected to introduce immediate and radical religious change. Men had long feared that 'fierce and ignorant separatists', being 'set up and maintained as rulers both in church and state', would 'authorise ignorance' and destroy the fabric of church, state and society.[1] In the weeks between Pride's Purge and the execution of the king, heresy and schism seemed finally to have triumphed. So, at least, might anyone have believed who listened to the propaganda aimed at the new regime. The army, 'in all men's opinions being rather set for the dissolving, than the settling of religion', would, it was claimed, 'cut the reins of church government . . . We shall have as many religions, as there be men of different judgements. So farewell Protestant religion.'[2] Pamphleteers, depicting the purged parliament as the mere tool of the army, tarred soldier and M.P. alike with the brush of heresy: 'They turn the church topsy-turvy by an universal toleration of atheism, heresy and impiety, abolish tithes, the maintenance of the ministry, and level the estates of nobility and gentry.'[3] As John Owen told the House of Commons soon after the king's execution, 'it is the toleration of all religions, or invented ways of worship, wherein your constitutions are confidently antedated in many places of the nation', which 'almost everywhere is spoken against'; 'the thing itself withal being held out as the most enormous apprehension, and desperate endeavour for the destruction of truth and godliness'.[4]

If the Rump's enemies were eager to cast the parliament as the champion of heresy and the dreaded toleration, its more radical supporters were equally determined that the new government should live up to the same sectarian role. A revolution in 'civils', it was believed, would lead to a revolution in 'spirituals'. The accession of

[1] Walker, *History of Independency*, i. 162.
[2] *Memorandums of the Conferences held between the Brethren scrupled at the Engagement, and others who were satisfied with it* (1650), p. 3; *Mercurius Elencticus* 12–19 Dec. 1648, p. (6).
[3] *Mercurius Pragmaticus* 12–19 Dec. 1648, p. (6).
[4] Asty, *Sermons of John Owen*, pp. 271, 317.

the new government inspired among religious radicals widespread goodwill and high expectations. Equally important, it elicited from them a novel readiness to discretion. The radical minister Thomas Brooks, addressing the Rump shortly after Pride's Purge, and exulting in the course which the revolution had taken, issued a strong hint to both M.P.s and sects. As he told the house, 'you have many precious saints to take care of, use them kindly . . . I hope there be a generation that will not abuse that liberty, that shall be granted them according to the Word, but will in the midst of all their liberties, be faithful servants to peace and concord'.[1] A similarly tactful suggestion came in a tract of March 1649, which informed its readers that 'it hath pleased the Lord now at last to infuse . . . tenderness into the breasts of many conscientious, and well-affected people . . . who see . . . the deformity of the passionate proceeding of those who would ruin all men that agree not with them in belief'. In the previous month William Dell, soon to be regarded as an enemy of all order and learning, had expressed gratitude to the rumpers, who 'after a manifold apostacy and defection of your members, seem yet to remain as pillars in the house of God';[2] and in April William Sheppard, praising the Rump for its resistance to religious presbyterianism, reminded the House of 'the many thousands that love and honour you'.[3]

Compared with the Rump's actual performance on religious matters, the expectations both of its opponents and of its radical supporters seem curiously exaggerated. The House spent much of its time, and in particular many of its Fridays, discussing proposals for religious reform, but its achievements were as minimal as were its concessions to the movement for law reform. Acts were passed for the propagation of the gospel, the advancement of learning, or the maintenance of godly ministers in Wales, Ireland, New England, and a number of English towns and counties. In most cases, however, these were merely stop-gap measures, evidently inspired by M.P.s from the areas concerned. Their usual purpose was either to augment the stipends of local ministers or to solve some other local problem such as the unification or division of parishes.[4] The much-vaunted bill for the propagation of

[1] T. Brooks, *God's Delight in the Progress of the Upright* (1649), ep. ded.
[2] *Liberty of Conscience Asserted* (1649), p. 1; *Several Sermons and Discourses of William Dell* (1652), p. 139.
[3] W. Sheppard, *Of the Four Great, Last Things* (1649), ep. ded.
[4] Firth and Rait, *Acts and Ordinances*, ii. 197–200, 342–8, 355–7, 393–6; *C.J.* 20 Apr., 13 June, 17, 18, 19 July 1649, 1 Feb., 1, 8, 15, 29 Mar., 1, 19 Apr., 14, 17, 24 May, 7 June, 19 July 1650, 12, 21 Mar., 15 Aug. 1651; *Perfect Passages of Every Day's Intelligence*

the gospel at national level never passed the House. Only one of the Rump's measures for propagation seems to have provoked opposition among religious presbyterians, and this, the act for the propagation of the gospel in Wales, was revoked when its initial term expired. Sums of money were earmarked to increase the income of certain needy ministers, but tithes, far from being abolished, were ratified by the House in April 1652; and the acts for the augmentation of ministers' salaries were designed to reinforce rather than undermine the tithe system.[1] Many ministers were evidently grateful for the money they received,[2] but it is doubtful whether the augmentations were effective on a large scale.[3] In few areas was there a thorough purge of scandalous clergy. Such appointments as the Rump made to livings seem in the main to have pleased moderates or religious presbyterians and to have disconcerted radicals.[4] The toleration act of September 1650 did, it is true, pass the House during the period of radical celebration after the battle of Dunbar, but the measure aroused little enthusiasm in parliament. By contrast, severe legislation was enacted against various forms of moral licence and against the abuse of the sabbath. The presbyterian system of church government which had been set up in 1648, but which in most areas had made little headway, was never abolished by the Rump and came within one vote of receiving its official blessing.

The moderation of the Rump's religious attitudes is evident also in its clerical patronage. To which ministers did the House accord its especial favour? Not to Thomas Brooks, who so unhesitatingly championed Pride's Purge and the subsequent moves against Charles I. Brooks preached once more before the Rump, but by late 1652 he was in trouble with the Committee for Plundered Ministers for his radical views.[5] Not to John Goodwin, either. In the earlier Rump period

---

30 Aug.–6 Sep. 1650, pp. 67–8; Latimer, *Annals of Bristol*, pp. 227–8. And see Stocks, *Records of the Borough of Leicester*, pp. 399, 402, 404.

[1] Cf. Underdown, *Pride's Purge*, pp. 330–1.

[2] See e.g. *Diary of the Rev. R. Josselin*, p. 81; *The Cries of England to the Parliament* (1653), p. 6.

[3] See e.g. *Diary of Thomas Burton*, ii. 332 (speech of Sir John Thoroughgood, one of the Rump's most active trustees for the maintenance of ministers: Firth and Rait, *Acts and Ordinances*, ii. 143; Lambeth Palace, MS (e.g.) 1019, fos. 1–65). And see B.M., Add. MS 22,620, fos. 117–18. But this subject deserves much fuller investigation.

[4] See e.g. Abraham Browne, *The Clergy in their Colours* (1651), pp. 42–3; *Perfect Diurnal . . . Armies* 9–16 Feb. 1652, p. 1669; R. Parkinson (ed.), *Life of Adam Martindale* (Chetham Soc., 1845), pp. 80–1.

[5] Trevor-Roper, *Religion, The Reformation and Social Change*, pp. 333–4; Brooks, *The Hypocrite Detected, Anatomised, Impeached* (1650); Mayer, 'Inedited letters', p. 217.

Goodwin was indefatigable in his defence of the purge and the execution. In November 1649, after the incumbent of St Stephen's, Coleman
Street, had been ejected for preaching against the government, Goodwin returned to the congregation from which he had been dismissed
in 1645 for his separatist views on church government. There is no
indication, however, that the Rump showed favour to Goodwin on
any other occasion, and by May 1652 he had become discredited in
the government's eyes.[1] The Rump gave equally little support to
George Cockayne, who like Goodwin had gone into print to defend
the revolutionary achievements of December 1648 and January 1649.[2]
Hugh Peter, who had been at the centre of those events, was eventually
made an official preacher before the Council of State, but both parliament and the council gave prior attention to men who had failed to
commit themselves to the purge or the execution.[3] The first preacher
appointed by the council was Peter Sterry, who seems to have made
no recorded mention of Charles's execution and who was amicably
disposed to the more moderate religious presbyterians.[4] The council's
subsequent nominees were Thomas Goodwin, Joseph Caryl and John
Owen. Goodwin's dismay at the purge and the execution were widely
known. Like Caryl, who was on close terms with presbyterian divines
in May 1649 and who remained an active member of the presbyterian
Westminster Assembly, he wanted reconciliation between presbyterians and independents.[5] Owen and Goodwin preached consecutively
to the House in June 1649, gloating over the defeat of the Levellers,
and were handsomely rewarded for their pains by the Rump.[6] In the
previous month parliament had extended favour to two divines still
less enthusiastic about the events of December 1648 and January 1649,

[1] P. Zagorin, *A History of Political Thought in the English Revolution* (1954), pp. 81–6;
Holkham MS 684: letter of Goodwin to Heveningham, 2 Jan. 1650; E. Freshfield,
Some Remarks upon . . . the Records of St. Stephen's Coleman Street, in London (1887), pp.
8, 10–11; *Mercurius Aulicus* 28 Aug.–4 Sep. 1649, p. 20; *Several Proceedings* 13–27 May
1652, pp. 2166, 2182.
[2] Trevor-Roper, *Religion, The Reformation and Social Change*, pp. 330–1; G. Cockayne,
Flesh Expiring and the Spirit Inspiring (1648).
[3] For the council's appointments see *C.S.P.D.* 1649–50: pp. 239, 373, 374, 515; 1650–1:
pp. 53, 72, 241, 263; 1651–2: pp. 9, 56; 1652–3: pp. 7–8.
[4] V. de Sola Pinto, *Peter Sterry, Platonist and Puritan* (Cambridge, 1934), p. 19; Sterry,
England's Deliverance from the Northern Presbytery (1652), ep. ded.
[5] *Life of Adam Martindale*, pp. 85–6; T. Goodwin, *Christ the Universal Peace-Maker* (1651);
Dr Williams's Library, Minutes of the Westminster Assembly (transcript), pp. 364b,
366, 368b, 370, 370b. During the Rump period Caryl gave his *imprimatur* to a number of
pamphlets urging moderation in religious matters.
[6] *C.J.* 7, 8 June 1649; T. Russell, *The Works of John Owen* (21 vols., 1826), xvi. 281–305.

Philip Nye and Stephen Marshall.[1] Only seven ministers were invited on more than three occasions to preach before the Rump. They were Thomas Goodwin, Caryl, Owen, Nye, Marshall and two other equally safe divines, John Bond (like Caryl and Nye still a participant member of the Westminster Assembly), and William Strong.

The Rump's failure to measure up to the expectations of either its opponents or its radical supporters must be perplexing to those who still equate membership of the Rump with religious independency. The equation does not survive a study of the beliefs of individual M.P.s. There were at least as many rumpers whom we can confidently describe as religious presbyterians as there were rumpers who were clearly religious independents or sectaries.[2] Professor Underdown, admittedly, shows that there was a much higher proportion of independents and sectaries among his 'revolutionaries' than among the rumpers as a whole, a point which lends initial credence to his claim that the failure of the reform movement in the Rump represented the defeat of the 'revolutionaries' by the 'conformists'.[3] Yet the 'revolutionaries' whom he labels 'sectaries and independents' were (as he points out) men of diverse views. Among them there were, certainly, radical sectaries like Thomas Harrison and John Carew, but there were also religious independents whose beliefs were much closer to those of presbyterians than to those of the sects. There was Miles Corbet, for example, who vacillated between the presbyterian and independent positions;[4] or there was Thomas Atkins, who frequently lamented the 'sad divisions' between the Rump and its 'brethren', the Scottish presbyterians.[5] In the mid 1640s, perhaps, the gap between independents like Corbet and Atkins on the one hand, and sectaries like Harrison and Carew on the other, had not seemed so wide. Then, both groups had defied the more generally accepted views of the presbyterians and had argued for seemingly radical solutions to the problem of church government. Yet if the events of the mid 1640s had created a barrier between presbyterians and independents, the events of the

[1] *Perfect Occurrences* 27 Apr.–4 May 1649, p. 1007.
[2] See Underdown, *Pride's Purge*, pp. 233–6, 361–90, 404.
[3] *Ibid.* pp. 235–6, 404.
[4] See e.g. *The Traitor's Perspective Glass*, pp. 3–4.
[5] B.M., Add. MS 22,620, fos. 154, 170ᵛ, 176ᵛ, 178: letters of Atkins to the mayor of Norwich. Many of Atkins's letters are equally illustrative of the character both of his puritanism and of parliamentary puritanism in general: see esp. *ibid.* fos. 45, 48, 64, 94, 113, 160, 164, 172, and B.M., Add. MS 15,903, fos. 61, 67, 71.

Rump period served to bring them closer together. After 1649 the growing manifestations of extreme religious radicalism, although occasionally welcomed by the vocal but small minority of sectaries in parliament, alarmed and appalled most M.P.s, whether they were presbyterians or independents.

Attempts to classify M.P.s as either religious presbyterians or religious independents are fraught with inescapable difficulties. There is the danger that we may mistake a chance indication of a member's preference at a particular point in time for a lasting and exclusive commitment to either form. Often such classification can be safely made (although almost equally often it cannot),[1] but it is a mistake to regard presbyterianism and independency, in the forms in which most M.P.s subscribed to them, as opposing sides to one of which every M.P. necessarily belonged. The two shared more ground than might be supposed, and to many people the quarrel between them had long seemed trivial. In the Long Parliament, both before and after Pride's Purge, there were extreme or 'high' presbyterians, just as there were committed tolerationists, radical independents and sectaries; but those who held uncompromising views of either variety were always in a minority. What most M.P.s asked of a church settlement was a compromise between episcopacy on the one hand and separatism on the other. The majority found one in a makeshift, erastian presbyterianism, denuded of 'Scottified' clerical pretensions but preserving a cohesive, disciplined ecclesiastical structure and subjecting the clergy to lay rather than episcopal control. Others turned to a state-supervised independency which adhered to the principle of voluntary association but which firmly rejected separatism and the divorce of church from state. The two solutions had more in common with each other than either had with 'high' presbyterianism or with radical separatism. Indeed, as was increasingly realised during the Rump period, presbyterianism and independency might even be compatible if independent congregations could be tolerated within a national presbyterian system.

Church government, and the closely related issue of toleration, were matters of serious concern to all M.P.s and of obsessive interest to some; but they were matters which parliamentary puritanism came to face only late in life. They were critical issues about which individual M.P.s had to make individual choices and about which they sometimes quarrelled bitterly; but they were not what their puritanism was

[1] Underdown, *Pride's Purge*, p. 404.

essentially about. At times of political crisis, disputes about church government tended to recede into the background. As Sir Harbottle Grimston wrote to Sir Robert Harley during the debate on church government in the autumn of 1648, 'there is not a man amongst us that thinks it worth endangering the kingdom for'.[1] At root, parliamentary puritanism was non-denominational, sometimes bitterly dividing M.P.s but more often, and more profoundly, uniting them in awareness of a common purpose.[2] The rumper Sir James Harrington had in 1645 made a plea for 'agreement and union' between presbyterians and independents, who were 'two children contending in the womb of the same mother . . . both Jacobs, both the Israel of God'.[3] As Cromwell, scorning the claims to exclusiveness of the Scottish presbyterian kirk, asked in 1650: 'Is all religion wrapped up in that or any form? Doth that name, or thing, give the difference between those that are the members of Christ and those that are not? We think not so. We say, faith working by love is the true character of a Christian.'[4]

The developments of the Rump period inspired an increasingly impressive movement towards reconciliation between presbyterians and independents. The quarrel between them in the 1640s, often concerned with technicalities or confined within a small area of debate, had engendered a heat disproportionate to the issues involved. Only among extreme presbyterians and extreme radicals, both of whom were mainly to be found outside parliament, did the argument about church government reflect incompatible religious outlooks. In the Rump period, however, it was not the issue of church government which aroused the strongest feelings among presbyterian and independent M.P.s, but rather the emergence of new forms of religious radicalism unpalatable to both of them. However vigorously they had disagreed, presbyterians and independents in parliament had shared a respect for the orthodox puritan ministry and a commitment to the forms of worship laid down in the Puritan Directory by the Westminster Assembly and sanctioned by the Long Parliament. In one sense, clearly, the issue of religious reform differs from the other reform proposals brought before the Rump. Demands for law reform and for electoral reform raised questions wholly separate from those over which

[1] *H.M.C.R. Portland*, iii. 165.
[2] Cf. B. Worden, 'The Independents. A reprisal in history', *Past and Present*, 47 (1970), 121–2.
[3] Harrington, *Noah's Dove* (1645), p. 1.
[4] Abbott, *Writings and Speeches*, ii. 285. Cf. *ibid*. i. 677, and C. Hill, *God's Englishman. Oliver Cromwell and the English Revolution* (1970), p. 77.

parliament had gone to war with Charles I. Most M.P.s, on the other hand, were puritans who believed, often intensely, in the need for religious reform; and to that extent, at least, they were at one with radical reformers. Yet in the early 1650s puritan M.P.s, who in the previous decade had fought for religious changes which had then seemed far-reaching, found themselves uniting in defence of what had become an entrenched orthodoxy.[1]

Religious radicals were not without their successes in the Rump, where their proposals sometimes won considerable, if rarely decisive, support. Yet only limited attention should be paid to voting figures. In an assembly as lacking in political or ideological cohesion as the Rump, the most surprising moves may attract sizeable support. There were always those in the House who, in the heat of debate, could be relied upon to vent hostility to tithes, papists or presbyterians, or simply to oppose whatever view seemed to be prevailing. Few motions put to the vote during the Rump period were won or lost by an overwhelming majority. In the formulation of policy, however, the men who matter are those who, hemmed in by and facing up to political realities, will sit on endless committees and spend innumerable hours drafting legislation and steering it through the House. Who, then, were the Rump's 'experts' on religion? Five men stood out; and they operated with remarkable cohesion. There was, first, Sir James Harrington, a man with a keen interest in theological subtleties, whose concern to reconcile presbyterians and independents has already been noted and who was dismayed by the extravagant notions of the sects.[2] In the Rump he consistently opposed the aims of religious radicals. Secondly there was William Purefoy, a regicide whose hostility to social radicalism was noted earlier. He held conservative views on tithes, favoured a motion to condemn as scandalous a tract of the Socinian rumper John Fry, opposed the decision to remove a presbyterian divine from the post of Dean of Christ Church, Oxford, and resisted any wavering of repressive purpose in the drafting of the Rump's legislation against blasphemy. It is safe to describe as religious presbyterians both Purefoy and the third member of the group, John Gurdon. The two men acted together in August 1649 as tellers in favour of retaining the presbyterian church system. Like Harrington, they argued for leniency towards

---

[1] Cf. below, pp. 196, 233, 241, 296, 322–5.
[2] See, as well as his *Noah's Dove*, his *Certain Queries Proposed by the King . . . with an Answer Thereunto* (1647).

Christopher Love when that presbyterian divine was found guilty of treason in the summer of 1651. Nathaniel Fiennes described Gurdon as 'an honest religious gentleman, but a presbyterian throughout, though not of this man's fiery zeal, that cannot endure godly men if they differ in judgement from him'.[1] The other two members of the group were Nathaniel Bacon, a Suffolk lawyer whose father had studied under Beza at Geneva,[2] and Francis Rous. Both were religious presbyterians, although neither was at Westminster often enough to influence events as strongly as did the other three.[3] Despite his presbyterianism Rous, like Harrington and Gurdon, was of a tolerant disposition: 'let true Christians seriously consider', he exhorted in 1648, 'that union in Christ their head is a stronger root of love and unity than lesser differences can be of division'.[4] There were other assiduous members of the Rump's committees on religion who also seem to have favoured a presbyterian church settlement, like John Venn, Michael Oldsworth, Godfrey Bosvile, Philip Skippon and Gilbert Millington, the chairman of the Committee for Plundered Ministers.[5] John Weaver, who played a central role in the formulation of the Rump's legislation of 1650 against moral and religious licence, and who consistently advocated measures for the propagation of the

---

[1] *Vindiciae Veritatis* (1654), p. 131. On Fiennes's authorship of this pamphlet see Pearl, 'The "Royal Independents"', p. 93n.

[2] Holmes, 'The Eastern Association', p. 26.

[3] For the cooperation of these five men, see *C.J.* 3, 12, 26 Apr., 16, 21 May, 5, 7, 13 June, 26 July, 7, 16 Aug., 2 Nov., 20 Dec. 1649, 29 Jan., 12 Apr., 14 June, 23 Aug. 1650, 10 Feb., 10 Aug. 1652; and cf. *ibid.* 20 Dec. 1648. For Harrington, see also *ibid.* 9, 23, 26 Feb. 1648, 6 Jan., 28 Feb., 14 Apr., 30 Nov. 1649, 29 Mar., 26 Apr., 4 July, 9 Oct. 1650, 27 Feb., 30 May, 9, 15 July, 16 Aug., 5, 9 Sep. 1651, 28 Jan. 1653. For Purefoy, see also *ibid.* 18 May, 14, 29 June, 18 July, 30 Nov. 1649, 8, 15 Feb., 7 June, 9 Aug. 1650, 31 Jan., 14 Mar., 5 Sep. 1651, 30 June 1652, 6 Mar. 1653. For Gurdon, see also *ibid.* 23 Feb. 1648, 10, 28 Mar., 29 June, 18 July, 30 Nov., 4 Dec. 1649, 15, 29 Mar., 7 June, 31 Dec. 1650, 4 Mar., 11 July 1651, 6 Jan. 1653. For Rous, see also *ibid.* 17 Mar. 1648, 8 Feb., 15 Mar., 31 May, 27 Sep. 1650, 1 June 1652. For Bacon, see also *ibid.* 23 Feb., 29 May, 21 June 1648. See also Underdown, 'The Independents again', pp. 89–90.

[4] F. Rous, *The Balm of Love* (1648), p. 10. G. Yule ('Presbyterians and Independents: some comments', *Past and Present*, 47 (1970), 131) seems to me to mistake, in both Rous and Gurdon, a tolerant disposition for a commitment to the principle of religious toleration: Rous does not, in *The Balm of Love*, 'advocate toleration'.

[5] Underdown, *Pride's Purge*, pp. 361–90, and 'The Independents again', p. 90. For Venn see *C.J.* 31 Mar. 1648, 26 Apr., 13 June, 7 Aug., 30 Nov., 26 Dec. 1649, 29 Jan., 15 Feb., 15 Mar., 7, 14 June 1650. For Oldsworth see *ibid.* 14 Apr., 18 July, 30 Nov., 21 Dec. 1649, 23 Aug. 1650, 30 June 1652, 6 Jan. 1653. For Bosvile see *ibid.* 24 May 1648, 6 Jan., 26 Apr., 24 May, 13 June, 18, 26 July, 30 Nov., 21 Dec. 1649, 23 Aug. 1650. For Skippon see *ibid.* 21 May, 21 Dec. 1649, 29 Jan., 26 Apr., 24 May 1650, 11 July 1651, 21 Apr. 1652, 6 Jan. 1653. For Millington see *ibid.* 8 Feb., 8, 15, 22, 29 Mar., 12 Apr., 31 May, 4 July, 31 Dec. 1650, 23 May 1651, 10 Feb., 26 Mar., 2 Apr. 1652, 6, 7 Jan., 3 Feb. 1653.

gospel, especially in Ireland, was probably at least as close to a presbyterian position as to an independent one.[1]

There were, of course, other M.P.s who took a keen interest in the Rump's discussions of religious matters and who might properly be described as uncompromising religious independents or as sectaries. There was Cornelius Holland, for example, an unstinting advocate of religious toleration and a loyal defender of religious radicals when they were threatened with prosecution.[2] There was Richard Salwey, who like Cromwell seems often to have been torn between an instinctive tendency towards political moderation and a susceptibility to the persuasions of radical millenarians.[3] There was Henry Marten, to whom theology was 'a matter for a university, perhaps, not for a kingdom',[4] and who in the Rump period consistently defended the principle of religious liberty and opposed parliament's harshness towards moral licence, of which he was believed to be a frequent practitioner.[5] In a puritan assembly, however, the allegiance of this worldly playboy may not have been an unmixed blessing to the tolerationists. Similarly Thomas Harrison, who organised a small but prominent group of religious radicals in the Rump but who was sadly wanting in the arts of political strategy, usually managed to alienate his parliamentary audience.[6] Sir Henry Vane was firmly committed to the principle of religious toleration and uncompromisingly opposed to any intervention by the magistrate in matters spiritual. According to his laudatory but well-informed contemporary biographer, he detested all 'popish and superstitious forms in religion', and did what he could 'for the reconciling all sorts of conscientious men (whatever variety of persuasion he found them in)'.[7] Yet his rigid divorce of church from state, coupled with an opacity of belief which brought him friendship with mystical divines but which puzzled lesser mortals, limited his contribution to religious reform. Although Vane could always be relied upon

[1] *C.J.* 26 Jan., 31 Mar., 27 Oct. 1648, 3 Apr., 29 June, 16 Aug., 30 Nov., 3 Dec. 1649, 15, 29 Mar., 14, 21 June, 5, 19 July, 13, 27 Sep. 1650, 5 Jan. 1653.
[2] *Ibid.* 26 Apr., 21 May, 13, 29 June, 7, 18 July, 16 Aug., 30 Nov. 1649, 29 Jan., 24 May 1650, 10 Feb., 21 Apr., 9 July 1652, 6 Jan. 1653; Fry, *The Accuser Shamed*, pp. 13–14; 'Parliamentary Diary of John Boys', p. 150; H. J. McLachlan, *Socinianism in Seventeenth-Century England* (Oxford, 1951), pp. 240–1.
[3] Mayer, 'Inedited letters', pp. 187, 196; below, pp. 184, 270, 339.
[4] H. Marten, *The Independency of England Endeavoured to be Maintained* (1648), p. 12.
[5] *C.J.* 26 Apr. 1650, 1, 30 June 1652; Whitelocke, *Memorials*, iii. 190; Anthony à Wood, *Athenae Oxoniensis* (3 vols., 1692), ii. 294.
[6] Cf. Capp, *Fifth Monarchy Men*, p. 99.
[7] *Life and Death of . . . Sir Henry Vane Knight*, p. 9; Rowe, *Sir Henry Vane the Younger*, pp. 195, 197–201.

during the Rump period to defend religious liberty when conflict arose on the subject,[1] there is no sign that he ever took the initiative in the House for any measure of toleration. It would be hard to imagine three men more different than Marten, Harrison and Vane, who if they were agreed about the need for religious toleration were agreed about little else. The Rump's religious radicals, all of them outside the mainstream of parliamentary puritanism, never pursued a common programme in the House. Almost invariably the initiative for measures of religious toleration came not from within parliament but from outside it: from the Cromwellian army and, in particular, from Cromwell himself.

Cromwell's role as patron of the sects, and his timeless statements in favour of liberty of conscience, are well known. What has attracted less attention is the support his views on toleration enjoyed among civilian M.P.s, some of them of most unrevolutionary political persuasion. This support derived from sentiments which were closer to the heart of parliamentary puritanism than were the aspirations of religious radicals, and which afforded the tolerationists a greater prospect of success. To understand these sentiments, we need for a moment to look forward from the politics of the Rump period to those of the second protectorate parliament of 1656–7. It was then that the Bristol Quaker James Nayler, a sorry lunatic accused of imitating Christ, was brought before the Commons on a charge of blasphemy.[2] The full and vivid surviving account of the debate which followed,[3] contrasting so markedly with the dearth of similar evidence for the Rump period, tempts one to regard the Nayler case as a set-piece on the issue of toleration. It would be dangerous to do so, for Nayler's 'offence', committed at a time when the numbers of Quakers seemed to be growing with alarming speed,[4] was an extreme one which shocked even M.P.s anxious to save him from severe punishment. Further, the incident raised legal and constitutional problems which complicated politicians' responses to Nayler's crime. The debate nevertheless exposed attitudes which seem in many cases to have derived from deep-seated views on toleration; and much can be learnt

---

[1] *C.J.* 9 Aug. 1650, 31 Jan. 1651, 1 June 1652.
[2] For a brief discussion of the Nayler affair see T. A. Wilson and F. J. Marli, 'Nayl[e]r's case and the dilemma of the Protectorate', *University of Birmingham Historical Journal*, x (1965–6).
[3] In *Diary of Thomas Burton*, esp. i. 10–264.
[4] *Ibid.* i. 25, 96, 128, 169, 171, 173.

about the religious attitudes prevalent in the Rump from some of the statements made during the Nayler debate by its former members.

Some rumpers were among the most outraged of Nayler's critics. There was Sir William Strickland, who had been a noted opponent of the tolerationists in the 1640s, who during the Rump period had stoutly defended the compulsory payment of tithes, and who at about the time of the Nayler debate was promoting a stiff bill for their enforcement.[1] As he said of the Nayler case, 'I would not have our zeal in this business . . . to meet with the least damp or coldness . . . It is sunshine makes these horrid things grow. I wish they were not tolerated.'[2] Philip Skippon agreed: 'It has always been my opinion, that the growth of these things is more dangerous than the most intestine or foreign enemies. I have often been troubled in my thoughts to think of this toleration . . . I was always of opinion in the Long Parliament, the more liberty the greater mischief.'[3] Another of Nayler's fiercest critics was Sir Thomas Wroth. During the Nayler dispute he tried one morning to take the House by storm, opening the day's debate with the words: 'Seeing Nayler must die, I desire to know what manner of death it must be.' When this ploy failed, he adopted a different tactic. 'Slit his tongue, or bore it', he cried, 'and brand him with the letter B.'[4] Strickland had been on the conservative wing of Rump politics, Wroth on the radical wing. The issue of toleration cut across political allegiances. Other ex-rumpers who wanted Nayler to be severely punished were three religious presbyterians whose strong influence in the formulation of the Rump's religious policies was discussed earlier (Rous, Bacon and Purefoy), two other religious presbyterians (Edmund Prideaux and Peter Brooke), and Denis Bond, who had figured prominently on Rump committees on religion.[5]

If, among the ex-rumpers, these were Nayler's leading opponents, then who were his defenders? They were, principally, the court party, the Cromwellians, united on the issue of toleration by personal conviction as well as by the court's need for political cohesion. Above all there was Cromwell's old and faithful friend Sir Gilbert Pickering. 'I

[1] *Diary of Thomas Burton*, ii. 165–6; *Hinc Illae Lachrymae* (1649), p. 10; *C.J.* 6 Aug. 1649.
[2] *Diary of Thomas Burton*, i. 33, 220. Cf. *ibid.* i. 28, 35, 45–6, 247–8.
[3] *Ibid.* i. 24–5, 218. Cf. *ibid.* i. 35, 48–50, 101, 153.
[4] *Ibid.* i. 53, 153. Cf. *ibid.* i. 66, 91, 168, 169.
[5] For Rous see *ibid.* i. 27, 37, 66, 156. For Bacon see *ibid.* i. 34–5, 66, 126, 131–3, 164, 246. For Purefoy see *ibid.* i. 262. For Prideaux see *ibid.* i. 29, and Underdown, 'The Independents again', p. 89. For Brooke see *Diary of Thomas Burton*, i. 171. For Bond see *ibid.* i. 28, 35, 118, 173, and *C.J.* 13, 29 June, 18 July, 2, 30 Nov. 1649, 29 Jan., 8 Feb., 15 Mar., 24 May, 7, 14 June 1650, 22 Aug. 1651, 30 June 1652.

hope', Pickering said, 'there is none here but desires [Nayler's] repent-
ance rather than his ruin. I speak my heart in this thing, though none
second me.'[1] Other courtiers who came to Nayler's defence were
Bulstrode Whitelocke[2] and Walter Strickland, They, like Pickering,
had been among the latecomers to the Rump. Strickland, cousin to
Sir William, was a shrewd and experienced diplomat, politically pliant,
a man of the world, and far removed in both belief and temperament
from the Rump's religious radicals. Yet he took a thoughtful interest
in religious reform, and in the Nayler debate he argued:

Where most power of the gospel, most prodigies of heresies and opinions;
which will happen always, unless you restrain the reading of the scriptures ...
Heresies are like leaden pipes underground. They run on still, though we do not
see them, in a Commonwealth where they are restrained. Where liberty is,
they will discover themselves, and are come to punishment.[3]

The sentiment is reminiscent more of the eighteenth-century enlighten-
ment than of seventeenth-century puritanism.

Whitelocke, like Strickland, was a trimmer in politics. Yet he
defended the principle of religious toleration with singular consistency,
in the Long Parliament before Pride's Purge, in the Rump (where
among other things he came to the defence of John Fry and – with
Cromwell, Pickering and Walter Strickland – seems to have advocated
the readmission of the Jews to England), and in the Protectorate.[4]
After the Restoration he drew up a compendious 'History of Persecu-
tion', to which elevated theme he brought his relentless brand of
turgidity.[5] What was it that led this pompous, *arriviste* lawyer to view
with such distaste intolerance towards the opinions of others? It was
certainly not any form of radicalism, to which he was consistently
immune. Nowadays it is rightly considered improper to talk of a
'middle class' in the English revolution, but if anyone in mid seventeenth-century England was middle-class it was Bulstrode Whitelocke.
Appalled by 'the vanity and uncertainty of ... earthly palaces and

[1] *Diary of Thomas Burton*, i. 36. Cf. *ibid.* i. 24, 27, 35, 43, 48, 53, 64–5, 66, 150, 153, ii. 131–2.
[2] *Ibid.* i. 32, 58, 125, 128–31, 150, 164, 216, 219; Whitelocke, *Memorials*, iv. 282.
[3] *Diary of Thomas Burton*, i. 88. Cf. *ibid.* i. 28, 56, 87–8, 164, 173, 219. Walter Strickland's temperament is well illustrated by his letters in T. Birch (ed.), *A Collection of the State Papers of John Thurloe* (7 vols., 1742), i. 113ff.
[4] Whitelocke, *Memorials*, ii. 80, 88, 559, iv. 201, 212–13, 312, 313, 315; B.M., Add. MS 37,345, fo. 194&ᵛ; *C.S.P.D.* 1651: p. 472; 1652–3: p. 138; *C.J.* 31 Jan. 1651. And see Bacon, *A Taste of the Spirit of God*, p. 23.
[5] Whitelocke Letters (Longleat), xxvii, *passim*.

mansions', he reflected that 'all the cities and palaces of this world are without foundations; they are built of earthly materials, and by mortal hands; they must decay and come to rubbish'. This perception did not prevent him from tirelessly ingratiating himself with members of the peerage, from buying his way to landed respectability, or from eventually purchasing a house which, to the amusement of Dorothy Osborne, was 'such a one as will not become any thing less than a lord'.[1] In general, however, Whitelocke liked his architecture 'handsome, without curiosity' and 'homely without loathsomeness', a taste which reflected his respect for the 'golden mean', the 'middle kind of life' between riches and poverty, display and self-negation. He admired the members of George Cockayne's congregation, who lived 'not riotously, yet plentifully'. Hunting and drinking were excellent in moderation, disgraceful in excess. It was agreeable to celebrate Christmas with one's family (even though many radicals both inside and outside parliament regarded the feast as popish), but improper to celebrate one's birthday.[2] Whitelocke's puritanism resembled that of another rumper with a fondness for the middle way, William Heveningham, who also shared Whitelocke's ability to combine a distaste for 'the golden and glittering bugles of honour and preferment' with a shrewd application of the techniques of self-advancement.[3]

Whitelocke's belief in moderation is one of the three keys to his commitment to the principle of religious toleration. The second is his growing ability to divorce religion from politics. In the Rump period, when theology became for him a hobby of increasing fascination,[4] he like other M.P.s began to prefer private to public worship, attending services at a wide variety of churches but spending more and more of his Sundays at home in devotions with his family.[5] The bitter religious controversies of the 1640s often encouraged, by way of reaction, a distinction between the private and the public man, and a preference

[1] B.M., Add. MS 31,984, fo. 102ᵛ; K. Hart (ed.), *The Letters of Dorothy Osborne to Sir William Temple* (1968), p. 87. Cf. Whitelocke Letters (Longleat) x, fo. 35; xi, fos. 32, 66, 72, 76, 87ff.; xii, fos. 59, 61, 142, 152; B.M., Add. MS 37,344, fos. 256, 263, 264, 266, 267&ᵛ, 274, 284ᵛ, 291ᵛ, 308ᵛ, 320, and Add. MS 37,345, fos. 2, 4, 5, 14, 17, 20ᵛ, 35ᵛ, 36ᵛ–37, 37ᵛ, 74ᵛ.
[2] B.M., Add. MS 31,984, fos. 48–54, 102–3ᵛ, 138ᵛ–144, 176–182, and Add. MS 37,345, fos. 140, 173ᵛ, 224–235ᵛ, 244–53, 254ᵛ–67.
[3] Holkham MS 684: 'Precepts of Wm. Heveningham to his Son'. See also, in the same MS, 'Observations upon the Scriptures' and 'Reasons why any man cannot swear not to alter the Government in the Church by Bishops'.
[4] B.M., Add. MS 37,345, fos. 150ᵛ–155, 190–198ᵛ, 209–213, 220–222, 300&ᵛ.
[5] *Ibid.* fos. 196ᵛ–7, and the entries for each Sunday in the same volume. Cf. *Diary of Thomas Burton*, i. 267–8.

for a personal, contemplative, uncombative religion. Whitelocke's interest in two developments during the Rump period is especially revealing. First, he was the patron of the astrologer William Lilly,[1] whose moonspun predictions earned a large following under the Commonwealth. Lilly made himself unpopular, however, with the clergy, and in 1651 he was hauled before the Committee for Plundered Ministers for his *Annus Tenebrosus*, a tract containing politically infelicitous prophecies. Lilly knew who his enemies were. He was detested both by the 'churlish presbyterians' and by regicides like John Bradshaw, William Cawley, Miles Corbet, Gilbert Millington and Thomas Scot. His defenders were men with more moderate political reputations, like James Ashe, Sir Arthur Heselrige, Robert Reynolds, Richard Salwey, Speaker Lenthall, and Whitelocke himself. Lilly was also assisted by Cromwell and by that other tolerant ex-rumper of the protectorate court, Walter Strickland.[2] A pamphlet published in Lilly's defence in 1652 appealed for support to 'you that are rational and moderate'.[3] Secondly, Whitelocke developed during the Rump period a favourable interest in lay-preaching – provided, of course, it was practised in moderation.[4] After the Restoration he inflicted a series of his own sermons on his family, delivered in his inimitable and interminable vein.[5] He, like other rumpers, had harsh words for the 'dumb preachers' among the clergy. 'A child of eight years old', he believed, could manage what usually passed for preaching, viz.

the writing of a sermon in a pocket book, then conning it by heart, and re-peating it to the congregation, as a schoolboy repeats his part to the school-master ... It is the powerful expressions of the preacher, with lively and apt words, suited to the present occasion, and the pressing upon the consciences of men ... which will make the Word to be the more imprinted in the hearts of the hearers, and work upon their spirits and memories: whereas a dead dream-ing repetition, or reading, passeth away with the sound of it, and is like the seed sown by the wayside.[6]

---

1 C. H. Josten (ed.), *Elias Ashmole 1617–1692* (5 vols., Oxford, 1966), ii. 497, 522; Ashmole MS 421, fos. 198ᵛ, 199, 205, 207ᵛ, and MS 423, fo. 168&ᵛ: Society of Astrologers to Whitelocke.
2 Ashmole MS 421, fos. 200–1, 203ᵛ, 205, 207ᵛ, 209–10. Cf. Keith Thomas, *Religion and the Decline of Magic* (1971), pp. 371–2.
3 *Philastrogus Knavery Epitomised* (1652), p. 12.
4 B.M., Add. MS 37,345, fos. 156ᵛ–161ᵛ.
5 B.M., Add. MS 53,728, *passim*.
6 B.M., Add. MS 31,984, fos. 54&ᵛ, 56ᵛ–57ᵛ.

The rumper Luke Robinson agreed: 'Ministers tell us our faults. It is fit we should tell them theirs. Their reading of sermons makes their voice lower. I doubt we are going to the episcopal way of reading prayers, too.'[1] The authentic voice of parliamentary puritanism is nowhere heard more clearly than in the detestation of 'formality' in religion and of the clergy's addiction to it.

Laicism, indeed, provides the third key to Whitelocke's tolerance. The sixteenth century had seen not only the fracture of the medieval religious orthodoxy but the effective challenge by laymen to the intellectual monopoly of the clergy. In the earlier seventeenth century the clergy fought back, seeking a return to both intellectual orthodoxy and clerical control. Hence, largely, the puritan hatred of 'Arminianism' and of Laud, and hence the venom of the *Root and Branch Petition* against 'the encouragement of ministers to despise the temporal magistracy, the nobles and gentry of the land'. The first specific demand of the *Grand Remonstrance* was for a reduction of the bishops' 'immoderate power usurped over the clergy', and soon afterwards the House passed a clerical disabilities act, intended to prevent bishops and clergy from 'intermeddling with secular jurisdictions'.[2] The puritan hatred of Laudian clerics was of course largely political in inspiration, and puritan laymen were happy to ally with puritan clergymen to defeat the Anglican establishment. Throughout the revolution most politicians recognised the interdependence of magistracy and ministry, and those who were anxious to preserve the former also saw the virtue of protecting the latter. Yet the relationship between M.P.s and the clergymen who supported them was often a tense one. Lay opinion, self-confident and diverse, became increasingly resentful of clerical interference. Cromwell's scorn during the Rump period for the ministers of Ireland and Scotland displays all the assured superiority of the lay Englishman. Ireland was ruled, he thought, by 'a company of silly ignorant priests' with their 'senseless orders and traditions'. He attacked the Catholic clergy in Ireland for drawing a distinction between themselves and their flocks:

I wonder not at differences in opinion, at discontents and divisions, where so Antichristian and dividing a term as clergy and laity is given and received; a term unknown to any save the Antichristian church ... It was your pride that begat that expression, and it is for filthy lucre's sake that you keep it up, that by making the people believe that they are not so holy as yourselves, they might

[1] *Diary of Thomas Burton*, i. 359.
[2] Gardiner, *Constitutional Documents*, pp. 138, 204, 242.

for their penny purchase some sanctity from you; and that you might bridle, saddle and ride them at your pleasure.[1]

Whitelocke, whose suspicions of the clergy were reinforced by the habitual anticlericalism of the legal profession, for his part recalled with horror the days when, under Laud, 'the spiritual men began ... to swell higher than ordinary, and to take it as an injury to the church that any thing savouring of the spirituality should be within the cognizance of ignorant laymen'.[2] Whitelocke played an important part in the successful moves to deny the presbyterian church government established by the Long Parliament the *iure divino* authority which the clergy had hoped for it. He consistently opposed attempts to give what he called 'an arbitrary power to the presbytery'. He was particularly resistant to any proposal which might permit clergymen to threaten the property rights of laymen.[3]

Such concerns as anticlericalism, belief in lay preaching or interest in astrology were also prevalent among men of more radical religious views than the courtiers of the protectorate, and there was much common ground between moderates and radicals. M.P.s of such diverse beliefs and temperaments as St John, Cromwell, Ireton, Harrison, Scot, John Jones and Richard Salwey often spoke the same saintly language and could be united in a sense of common spiritual purpose.[4] Yet, although the strands of moderation and radicalism could intertwine, they were – or became – separate strands nonetheless. Men like Whitelocke and Walter Strickland differed from many radicals by not only preaching toleration but, when they found themselves in power, practising tolerance. By doing so, they cut themselves off from the proselytising element in the puritan tradition. The form taken by their tolerance, indeed, was largely a reaction against the conflicts to which, in the 1640s, crusading puritanism had given rise. Cromwell, although still vulnerable to radical persuasion, disowned those who demanded toleration for everyone but who proved to want it only for themselves.[5] His famous statement of 1652 that 'he had rather that Muhammetanism were permitted amongst us, than that one of God's children

[1] Abbott, *Writings and Speeches*, ii. 197, 201.
[2] Whitelocke, *Memorials*, i. 67. Cf. *ibid.* i. 292. The similarities between Cromwell's and Whitelocke's statements on religious matters are frequent and remarkable.
[3] *Ibid.* i. 208–9, 291–4, 327, 504–8, 559; B.M., Add. MS 31,984 fo. 108ᵛ, and Add. MS 37, 345, fo. 194&ᵛ; *Diary of Thomas Burton*, i. 7, ii. 166, 263.
[4] This is well illustrated in a number of the documents printed in Mayer, 'Inedited letters' and in *Original Letters . . . addressed to Oliver Cromwell*.
[5] See e.g. Abbott, *Writings and Speeches*, ii. 459.

should be persecuted' was made as an indignant rebuke to an M.P. who chose 'zealously to argue against a Laodicean, and lukewarm indifferency in religion'.[1] Cromwell's commitment to toleration was a function not only of his tolerance but of what might almost be called his liberalism. In the 1650s tolerance and radicalism increasingly went separate ways, until, for the proponents of the former, being sincere became almost as important as being right. The 'triumph of reason' and the emergence of religious *laissez-faire* in the seventeenth century were intimately connected, and in their combined development Cromwell and the protectorate courtiers played a full if often unwitting and often unwilling part. The spirit of Cromwell's tolerance can be discerned in the pronouncements of his friends: in Ireton's warning during the Whitehall debates on toleration, for instance, that 'from the convincing of one another with light and reason we are fallen to an eager catching of that which is our own opinion';[2] or in Stephen Marshall's argument, in a sermon delivered in 1652, that 'men who hold dissenting opinions in ... lesser points' should be 'content to ... have their faith, in these, to themselves, before God ... and so be quiet. I can be no advocate for such people, if they judge the spreading of their opinions to be a duty.'[3] Cromwellians, insisting on moderation and the golden mean, were eventually obliged to draw up boundaries to their tolerance. Sir William Armyne, for example, trying to steer a path between repression and anarchy, opposed 'a jostling spirit of domination', was 'very indulgent to a real tender conscience', and advanced godly ministers to livings; but he 'well knew the bounders and mere-stones betwixt rule and liberty', and was 'as great an enemy as any of those wild exorbitances rife' in the early 1650s.[4] St John, another of Cromwell's most valued friends, extolled after Dunbar the virtues of 'God's peculiar, excluded on the one hand from papists and atheists, and from sectaries on the other'.[5] Thomas Westrow, another rumper on terms of spiritual intimacy with Cromwell, earned on his death a panegyric from his friend the poet George Wither for 'The Christian liberty he did profess / Without allowing of licentiousness.'[6]

[1] *The Fourth Paper, presented by Major Butler* (1652), preface.
[2] Woodhouse, *Puritanism and Liberty*, p. 142. Cf. Abbott, *Writings and Speeches*, i. 482.
[3] S. Marshall, *A Sermon preached to the ... Lord Mayor ... tending to heal our Rents and Divisions* (1653), p. 31.
[4] Seth Wood, *The Saints Entrance into Peace and Rest by Death* (1651), pp. 19–21. Cf. C.J. 31 Jan. 1651.   [5] *Original Letters ... addressed to Oliver Cromwell*, pp. 25, 48.
[6] G. Wither, *Westrow Revived* (1654), pp. 8–9.

Licentiousness, however, was the problem with which parliament had increasingly to deal. Before the battle of Worcester, the danger of a royalist–presbyterian alliance inhibited rumpers of moderate disposition from advocating a course of extensive religious reform; after it, the rising tide of religious radicalism had the same effect. The predicament confronting Cromwellian advocates of religious toleration during the Rump period is well illustrated by the sermons of Cromwell's chaplain, John Owen, who was driven increasingly to emphasise the necessary limits of tolerance. The language of Owen's sermons to the Rump is always dramatic, the imagery always intense. The millenarian setting, the prospect of the 'tremendous, total destruction of Babylon', is faithfully stressed. There are countless reminders of the perils of 'backsliding', and equally frequent assurances that unrelenting faith, untarnished by private interest, will provide a shelter against the fiercest political storms. Yet as early as February 1649 Owen was pleading for reconciliation between presbyterians and independents, whose areas of agreement were 'broad' and whose differences were 'minute', and castigating men 'to whom forbearance is indulged in by-paths of their own' and who 'make it their way to cast dirt on the better ways of truth'. In April of the same year he urged the Rump to exercise patience in its enthusiasm for the godly reformation: 'though a tower may be pulled down faster than it was set up, yet that which hath been building a thousand years is not like to go down in a thousand days'; and

As for such, who from hence do, or for sinister ends pretend to fancy to themselves a terrene kingly state unto each private particular saint, so making it a bottom ... for everyone to do that which is good in his own eyes, to the disturbance of all order, civil and spiritual; as they expressly clash against innumerable promises, so they discreetly introduce such confusion and disorder, as the soul of the Lord doth exceedingly abhor.

As the Rump period advanced, Owen became ever more alarmed by 'a perverse spirit' of 'giddiness' in 'the broaching of many opinions'. At the beginning of the Rump period he scorned as unnecessarily repressive the notion that the state should impose 'fundamentals' in religion: by 1652 he was seeking to impose them himself. In October 1652, distressed by the shrill cries of soldiers and sects, who were 'almost taking upon' themselves 'to prescribe to the Almighty', Owen could only present the Rump with evidence of his own confusion. By this time he almost seemed to sympathise with the House's inaction on reform issues. For Owen, as for so many others, the religious radicalism of the early 1650s seemed directly to contradict the premises on which the puritan revolution had been conducted. All he could urge in such circumstances was restraint and patience. Few rumpers, he warned, would live to see the Lord's reforming purposes fulfilled: 'God will proceed [at] his own pace.'[1] Thus far had Owen been obliged to retreat from the radical millenarianism of early 1649.

[1] Asty, *Sermons of John Owen*, pp. 312, 326, 336, 436–7; Russell, *Works of John Owen*, xvi. 300; J. Owen, *Of The Death of Christ* (1650), ep. ded. Cf. W. M. Lamont, *Godly Rule* (1969), pp. 139–40.

8

ELECTORAL REFORM[1]

Nothing better illustrates the limits of seventeenth-century English radicalism than the faith displayed by reformers of almost every variety in the institution of parliament. The army reform programmes of the later 1640s are an ample testimony to that faith. It was the reverence of the army leaders for parliament, too, which late in 1648 persuaded Ireton to abandon his plan for a forcible dissolution and to settle instead for a mere purge, a decision which ensured the prolongation rather than the destruction of the Long Parliament and consequently the defeat of the army's reforming ambitions. Men who were willing to undertake so revolutionary a step as the execution of the king were nevertheless prepared to leave the Rump in power. By 1653, when the Rump had become wholly discredited in radical eyes, the Fifth Monarchists were prepared to do away with parliamentary institutions; yet even Barebone's assembly which succeeded the Rump was modelled, as far as was compatible with the saintly programme, on previous parliaments. When it met it immediately gave itself the title of parliament and scrupulously observed traditional parliamentary procedures.[2] In the later 1640s and early 1650s it should have been obvious that the Long Parliament would never fulfil the army's reforming hopes, yet time and again radicals met the problem not by challenging the institution of parliament but by demanding changes in the manner in which parliaments were elected. They called persistently for frequent parliamentary elections as the cure to all evils, but rarely seem to have asked themselves what kind of men parliamentary elections would return. It was not only frequent elections, however, that reformers demanded. Elections themselves, they argued, must be reorganised on the basis of a new franchise and a new distribution of seats. The Rump, which achieved so little in the spheres of legal and religious change, proved much more receptive to some of the army's proposals for electoral reform. In accordance with the wishes of the

[1] See also Appendix B.   [2] *C.J.* 4–6 July 1653.

army officers the House made provision for biennial elections, for a wholesale redistribution of seats, and for a revision of the franchise. Although the Rump was dissolved before its plans could be implemented, enough evidence has survived to give a clear indication of its intentions. The decision to hold biennial elections will be discussed later in the book. Here I shall consider the Rump's plans for the reform of electoral procedure, and in particular for the redistribution of parliamentary constituencies.

In the sixteenth and earlier seventeenth centuries the size and nature of the membership of the House of Commons changed markedly. In 1500 there were two hundred and ninety-six members. By 1600 there were four hundred and sixty-two, and the creation of forty-five more seats under the early Stuarts brought the total to five hundred and seven by 1640. Throughout this period the English county constituencies continued to return only two members each. Except for the enfranchisement of the Welsh counties and of the two universities the new seats went entirely to the boroughs, which by 1640 provided over eighty-two per cent of the members of the House. The new boroughs, whose creation fostered a belief that the Commons' membership was too large, sprang up in a haphazard fashion which bore little relation to the size, population or taxable capacity of the areas concerned. By 1640, as Ludlow complained in words very similar to those used by Lilburne and other reformers,

some boroughs that had scarce a house upon them chose two members to be representatives in parliament (just as many of the great cities in England, London only excepted), and the single county of Cornwall elected forty-four, when Essex and other counties bearing as great a share in the payment of taxes, sent no more than six or eight[1] . . .

In the later sixteenth and earlier seventeenth centuries, the crown began to view the new creations with unease. Elizabeth I created seats more sparingly than had her Tudor predecessors and, parsimonious here as elsewhere in her old age, created none after 1586. James I had similar scruples. Swept along by the tide, he did agree to several new creations, 'because it seemed reasonable'; but he drew the line at what was perhaps the most reasonable request of all, that for the enfranchisement of Durham, 'because, he sayeth, our number in the lower house is already too great . . . some decayed towns, as Old Sarum, must first be

---

[1] *Memoirs of Edmund Ludlow*, i. 334; J. Lilburne, *London's Liberty in Chains Discovered* (1646), p. 53, and *Rash Oaths Unwarrantable* (1647), p. 49; Cockayne, *Foundations of Freedom Vindicated*, p. 3.

deprived of their numbers before this can be passed'. The number of
seats went on growing, however, to the pleasure of the parliamentary
opposition of the 1620s, which was so much more adept than the
crown at influencing the opinions of backbenchers and hence also of
their constituents. Yet although Pym, Eliot, Hampden and Hakewil
were glad to take advantage of the pressures for new seats, they did not
create those pressures, which derived rather from local ambitions and
rivalries. Membership of parliament was becoming an increasingly
important source of social prestige. The borough seats may have been
less glamorous than the county ones, but there were many who eagerly
coveted them. Burgesses were supposed by statute to be residents of
their constituencies, but this stipulation was blatantly ignored. The
main social feature of the new creations was the invasion of the borough
seats by the gentry and the establishment of large networks of electoral
patronage in the hands of the great landowners.[1]

In the 1640s a strong movement emerged in favour of reforming
the electoral system. The decayed boroughs, it was argued, should be
swept away; parliamentary representation should be more equitably
apportioned; and the membership of the House of Commons should
be reduced. The demand for the redistribution of seats was, admittedly,
peripheral to the main political conflicts of the 1640s. Civil war
politicians argued more about the power and frequency of parliaments
than about the manner of their election. Although opposition to the
continued enfranchisement of rotten boroughs was sometimes expressed, the Long Parliament made only sporadic assaults before 1649
on an electoral system which it used to such effect in the recruiter
elections.[2] Besides, general electoral reform foreboded general elections. Since those who called most loudly for the reapportionment of
constituencies coupled their demands with pleas for the speedy dissolution of the existing parliament and for the holding of annual or
biennial parliaments thereafter, they could expect little enthusiasm
from an assembly reluctant to terminate its own authority. The impulse
for change came from the Cromwellian army. It won nevertheless a
sympathetic hearing in the Rump, and the composition of the protectorate parliaments was determined by electoral arrangements which
put into reverse, however briefly, the broad electoral tendencies of the

[1] J. E. Neale, *The Elizabethan House of Commons* (1963 edn.), chapter 1 and pp. 133–4, 139–40, 147, 151, 156; E. de Villiers, 'Parliamentary boroughs restored by the English House of Commons, 1621–41', *E.H.R.*, lxvii (1952).
[2] Underdown, 'Party management in the recruiter elections', *passim*.

previous century and a half. In this change the Rump played a critical role.

To understand the Rump's contribution it is necessary to set the proposals which it countenanced in the context of the movement for electoral reform as a whole. The army's call for the redistribution of seats had first become audible in 1647. Ireton was probably a moving spirit behind it, and his ideas quickly won influential support.[1] Cromwell accepted them, agreeing 'that the elections, or forms of choosing the parliament are very unequal'.[2] Hugh Peter, in the social programme which he advanced in 1647, asked that 'burgesses of parliament may be better proportioned, six, four or two for shires, and some for great cities'.[3] The army's *Heads of the Proposals*, also of 1647, demanded the abolition of decayed boroughs and the redistribution of seats 'according to some rule of equality or proportion', while in the same year the Levellers' *Agreement of the People* asked for parliamentary seats 'to be more indifferently proportioned'.[4]

Between Pride's Purge in December 1648 and the inauguration of the protectorate in December 1653, four concrete plans were advanced for the redistribution of seats. The first two appeared between the purge and the king's execution. In December 1648 the Levellers, under Lilburne's leadership, drew up a scheme which is to be found in their version of the second *Agreement of the People*.[5] It will be referred to here as the Leveller plan. The army officers, in framing their own version of the same *Agreement* for submission to the Rump in January 1649, modified the Leveller proposals.[6] Their version will be described as the officers' plan. The third scheme was formulated by a Rump committee and laid before parliament in January 1650.[7] This will be called the 1650 plan. Fourthly, the parliaments of 1654 and 1656 were elected according to a redistribution of seats laid down by the *Instrument of Government*.[8] This will be referred to as the 1653 plan. These four schemes were by no means identical in their provisions, or even in the premises on which they rested. Some of the illuminating differences between them will be

---

[1] Woodhouse, *Puritanism and Liberty*, p. 85.
[2] *Ibid.* p. 98.
[3] H. Peter, *A Word for the Army* (1647), p. 12.
[4] Gardiner, *Constitutional Documents*, pp. 317, 333.
[5] Wolfe, *Leveller Manifestoes*, pp. 295–7.
[6] Gardiner, *Constitutional Documents*, pp. 359–63.
[7] *C.J.* 9 Jan. 1650. Cf. Gardiner, *History of the Commonwealth and Protectorate*, i. 242–3.
[8] Gardiner, *Constitutional Documents*, pp. 407–9.

examined here. It is nevertheless important to stress at the outset the community and continuity of ideas which informed all of them. Without exception they looked forward to a radical geographical redistribution of parliamentary representation, to the abolition of at least a substantial majority of the rotten boroughs, and to a massive increase in the number of county seats.

The Leveller plan of December 1648 was strikingly comprehensive. It provided for a reduction in the total number of seats from over five hundred to three hundred, of which only forty-one (under fourteen per cent, as opposed to over eighty-two per cent in 1640) were to go to boroughs. These borough seats were to be distributed among the main centres of population. All the decayed boroughs were to vanish. The remaining seats for which the Leveller scheme provided were to be shared among the counties, in proportion to their respective populations. The result of the scheme would have been to curtail drastically the representation of the traditionally over-represented areas, the south-east and the south-west, and to increase considerably the representation of the midlands, the home counties and East Anglia.

The officers' plan of January 1649 proposed a number of changes to the Leveller scheme. These alterations must now be examined if the proposals countenanced by the Rump are to be properly understood. The most obvious change, the increase in the total number of seats from three hundred to four hundred, was probably the least important. The officers' divergence from the Leveller position was in this instance pragmatic rather than ideological. A total of four hundred still represented a sizeable inroad into the House's existing membership. The difference was that the officers wanted a gradual rather than a root-and-branch reduction in the number of seats. Their *Heads of the Proposals* had asked for 'an equal representative' only 'as near as may be'; again, reapportionment of seats was to be equitable '(at present), as near as may be'.[1] Similarly, the officers had stipulated in November 1648 that in succeeding parliaments there should be 'as near as may be, an equal representative'.[2] Leveller demands were hedged by no such qualifications. The figure of three hundred was not, however, sacred to the Leveller leaders. As late as October 1646 Lilburne had been content with the prospect of a membership of five or six hundred,[3] and in May

[1] *Ibid.* p. 317.
[2] *Remonstrance of . . . the General Council of Officers*, p. 66. Cf. Abbott, *Writings and Speeches*, i. 559.
[3] Lilburne, *London's Liberty in Chains Discovered*, p. 54; C.B. Macpherson, *The Political Theory of Possessive Individualism* (Oxford, 1964 edn.), p. 133.

1649 he and his imprisoned colleagues settled for the officers' figure of four hundred.[1] In any case, although the officers' plan envisaged a total of four hundred members, it made specific provision for only three hundred and fifty-one. The others were to be assigned by future parliaments, 'if they see cause', to 'such counties as shall appear in the present distribution to have less than their due proportion'. The 'present distribution' was only a slightly modified version of the Leveller scheme. The boroughs were now to have twenty rather than fourteen per cent of the seats, but again it was the principal towns which would be rewarded. In the counties, too, the officers made some concessions to the *status quo*, showing themselves marginally more generous than the Levellers to areas traditionally over-represented. They also gave a curiously large number of seats to Wales, possibly because they hoped to take electoral advantage of the political machinery established there by radical preachers.[2] The overall similarity between the Leveller and officer schemes is nevertheless remarkable. The significance of the alterations to the Leveller plan effected by the officers lay less in the respective provisions of the two schemes than in the differing premises on which the two sides seem to have proceeded.

In neither scheme was the criterion of redistribution stated. In 1647, however, the Levellers and the officers had drawn up their respective positions on the issue: the Levellers (although they had initially considered alternative proposals[3]) decided to use population as the basis of reapportionment, whereas the officers consistently argued that the index of redistribution should be the burden of taxation borne by the various counties.[4] This is one of the points on which the 1647 Leveller *Agreement of the People* differed from the officers' *Heads of the Proposals*,

---

1 Vernon F. Snow, 'Parliamentary reapportionment proposals in the Puritan revolution', *E.H.R.*, lxxiv (1959), 400.

2 Snow (*op. cit.*, pp. 414–15) suggests that the officers may have been influenced by the electoral influence in Wales of the Herbert family and by 'the prosperity of the Welsh counties due to both the New World trade and the colonisation of Ireland'. But the officers were hard on Wiltshire, the Herberts' main electoral stronghold, while Snow's latter premise is left unsupported. On the Herberts see V. A. Rowe, 'The influence of the Earls of Pembroke on English parliamentary elections', *E.H.R.*, l (1935).

3 See e.g. Lilburne, *London's Liberty in Chains Discovered*, p. 54, and *Rash Oaths Unwarrantable*, p. 49.

4 Dr Cannon assumes – if I understand him correctly – that the Leveller scheme of December 1648 was designed in accordance with the principle of apportionment by tax burden rather than by population, but I cannot discern his grounds for doing so. (John Cannon, *Parliamentary Reform 1640–1832* (Cambridge, 1973), p. 10. This book, whose opening chapter is devoted to the movement for electoral reform during the English revolution, was published after my own book was completed.)

and the conflict came to the surface in the 1647 army debates. We do not know how the Levellers intended to assess the distribution of population, and it may be that when they formulated the December 1648 scheme they in fact paid at least as much attention to taxation as to population: certainly the disagreement between Levellers and officers seems to have made little practical difference when the two sides framed their respective schemes. Yet neither side ever publicly abandoned the position it had adopted in 1647, and the assertions of differing principles are revealing. During the 1647 army debates Ireton implied disingenuously that population was too fluctuating to provide a reliable guide,[1] but there were deeper reasons for favouring a fiscal index. Taxation was a matter to be arranged between the government and the landed interest, affectionately described by Ireton as the 'interest . . . that is permanent and fixed'.[2] To take account of the claims of population rather than of property would be to imply the existence of popular rights in elections, and would thus involve a concession of principle to the Levellers on the inflammatory issue of the franchise. In fact, as Ireton made clear, the officers favoured taxation as a convenient rather than as an ideal guide to reapportionment.[3] When it came to framing specific proposals, they paid as much attention to geographical size as to taxable capacity, giving far more seats both to the north and to Wales than the burden of taxation borne by either area could justify. The officers nevertheless continued to profess commitment to the principle of apportionment by taxation, which provided them with a defensible alternative to the radically suggestive proposals of the Levellers.

Beneath the surface similarity of the two schemes lay another subtle but important conflict of premise. Both Levellers and officers took it for granted that the unit of redistribution should be the county, the provincial focus of the social and political ambitions of the governing classes. The Levellers, however, treated the county unit with none of the awe accorded it by the officers. Unlike the army leaders they were prepared to divide the county into smaller electoral districts, stipulating that any county awarded more than three seats should be divided into smaller units, none of which was to return more than three members. An elaborate scheme was drawn up providing for meetings to be held in each county between locally elected commissioners, who were to

[1] Woodhouse, *Puritanism and Liberty*, p. 85. See also Gardiner, *Constitutional Documents*, pp. 317, 333.
[2] Woodhouse, *Puritanism and Liberty*, p. 82.　　　　　　　　　[3] *Ibid.* p. 85.

decide how the shire was thus to be divided. This proposal may have
been partly intended, as Mr Snow suggests,[1] to exclude outside
interests from elections. It also, however, emphasised the responsibility
of each member to his constituents. In 1647, in much the same way, the
Leveller leader Richard Overton had devised a scheme whereby
locally elected commissioners would keep a strict watch on the parliamentary activities of their representatives and call them to account for
misdemeanours.[2] The officers' plan, on the other hand, would merely
have made more equitable the demonstrations of local standing and
privilege which county elections customarily comprised. The elections
envisaged by the Levellers, with the extended franchise for which they
also called, would have been very different affairs. The community
revered by Lilburne and his colleagues was not the county but the
'hundred, lath, or wapentake' into which, by their scheme, each of the
more generously represented counties was to be divided for electoral
purposes. Again, county sub-divisions would have made it easier for
those whom the Levellers hoped newly to enfranchise to record their
votes.[3]

The officers' response to the Leveller plan for the sub-division of
counties was evidently at best lukewarm. Although they did not jettison the proposal that counties should be divided, they remodelled it in
a fashion which was unlikely to encourage its implementation and
which divested it of its more overt social implications. Instead of
locally elected commissioners the officers nominated for the task a
group of their friends, notably among the independent congregations
of London.[4] Although the officers might have been happy to allow
these men to subdivide the city, it seems unlikely that they would
have wanted them to carry out their brief for the counties. The
elaborate scheme for partitioning advanced by the officers bears the
contrived and implausible appearance of a political dummy.

In March 1649 the Rump 'spent some time to consider of elections of
members, to be equally laid over the nation, and not to be engrossed
in a few corporations unequally'.[5] In May a parliamentary committee

[1] Snow, 'Parliamentary reapportionment proposals', p. 410.
[2] Wolfe, *Leveller Manifestoes*, pp. 189–90.
[3] This seems to me the point of the passages from Lilburne's pamphlets in which Macpherson (*Political Theory of Possessive Individualism*, pp. 133, 135) discerns a different significance.
[4] Gardiner, *Constitutional Documents*, pp. 365–7. Cf. Whitelocke, *Memorials*, ii. 495.
[5] *Kingdom's Weekly Intelligencer* 13–20 Mar. 1649, p. 1296.

was set up to consider the whole question of electoral reform and future parliaments,[1] and by November the outlines of a reapportionment scheme had been decided upon.[2] Vane the younger laid the committee's report before the House in January 1650.[3]

The 1650 scheme accepted the premises which had been adopted by the officers in revising the Leveller plan. In some instances, indeed, it took them further; as *Mercurius Politicus* observed of the 1650 plan, ' 'Tis not the wild levelling representative.'[4] As in the officers' scheme, there were to be four hundred rather than three hundred seats;[5] representation was to be based on tax contribution rather than on population; and the county unit was to be preserved intact. The 1650 plan also made explicit what had been implicit in both the earlier schemes, that borough seats were to be regarded as contributing to the total representation of the counties in which they lay: except in the case of London, whose representation was to be reduced slightly from its pre-war level, the committee's report left it to the House to decide whether, and how far, seats allotted to individual counties should be awarded to boroughs within those counties. The compromises which the officers, in revising the Leveller plan, had made with electoral tradition became still more marked in the 1650 scheme, which was more generous to the south-west, the south-east and the north, and less generous to the midlands, East Anglia and the home counties, than had been the officers' plan. A direct comparison of the 1650 scheme with that of the officers is, however, a little misleading, for in 1649 the Rump had redistributed the burden of the assessment tax in a more equitable fashion.[6] To gauge the fairness of the 1650 scheme we need, therefore, to compare its provisions not with those of the officers' plan but with the new distribution of taxation. In other words, we have to set side by side the number of seats awarded to each county by the 1650 scheme and the number of seats to which that county, on the basis of its new share of national taxation, was entitled. The correlation is in the main impressive. One particularly marked change corrected a glaring anomaly in the officers' plan: the Rump increased the tax contribution of Wales and awarded it fewer seats than had the officers. In the 1650 scheme Wales received precisely the number of seats to which its contribution to national taxation now entitled it.[7]

[1] Cf. below, p. 194.   [2] *H.M.C.R. Hodgkin*, p. 47.   [3] *C.J.* 9 Jan. 1649.
[4] *Mercurius Politicus* 6–13 June 1650, p. 16.   [5] *H.M.C.R. Hodgkin*, p. 47.
[6] Firth and Rait, *Acts and Ordinances*, ii. 24–57, 285–515.
[7] Cf. *Perfect Diurnal . . . Parliament* 26 Mar.–2 Apr. 1649, pp. 2399–2400. For mathematical illustration of my arguments about the Rump's redistribution schemes, see Appendix B.

There were, however, exceptions to the overall fidelity of the 1650 plan to the principle of apportionment by taxation. In most cases they were trifling, but they are still revealing. The scheme was even more un-warrantably generous than that of the officers to the northern counties. Perhaps this can be partly explained by the influence in the Rump of Vane and Heselrige, both stout defenders of the interests of the northern counties, or by the presence of Ireton and Richard Salwey, M.P.s for Appleby in Westmorland, on the committee from which Vane reported.[1] There were other anomalies, too. The committee's report, addressing itself to the demand for the Rump's dissolution, recommend-ed that the M.P.s who had already joined the Rump should retain their seats, and that recruiter elections should be held in constituencies un-represented since the purge. It was thus incumbent on the committee, in planning a redistribution of seats, to protect the electoral bases of the Rump's existing membership. To only two counties, Dorset and Wilt-shire, did the committee fail to award as many seats as there were rum-pers representing constituencies within those counties; elsewhere the committee tended to look favourably on counties strongly represented in the Rump. Although some counties weakly represented after the purge, like Devon and Lancashire, were kindly treated by the plan, generosity was more usually accorded to counties like Yorkshire, Cumberland, Westmorland, Buckinghamshire and Hampshire, which supplied relatively large numbers of rumpers. Other counties relatively under-represented in the Rump, like Surrey, lost out slightly in conse-quence. These, however, were only minor aberrations in a scheme which, like its predecessors, would have revolutionised the electoral system.

Mr Snow, author of the only substantial account of the various schemes for redistribution, writes that 'the subsequent history of this proposal ... was one of failure ... [Despite] the time and energy devoted to the measure ... the Rump reached no definite conclusions. The proposal appears to have died a slow, natural death in the decaying Rump Parliament.'[2] On the contrary, it was still showing vigorous and unmistakable signs of life in March 1653, when the House debated the bill, whose projected passage brought about the parliament's dissolution a month later, for a new representative. The *Journal of the House of Commons*, which becomes increasingly scanty towards the end of the Rump period, gives details only of those clauses in the bill

[1] Cf. Underdown, 'Party management in the recruiter elections', p. 242.
[2] Snow, 'Parliamentary reapportionment proposals', p. 417.

which occasioned dispute in parliament, but there are enough of these
to make clear the exact nature of the bill's provisions for redistribution.
As Ludlow twice claimed,[1] the scheme for reapportionment incorporated in the *Instrument of Government* in December 1653, and implemented
in the elections to the two protectorate parliaments, was taken in its
entirety from that very bill for a new representative whose other provisions so angered Cromwell.[2]

The 1653 plan, that contained both in the bill for a new representative
and in the *Instrument of Government*, was evidently modelled on that of
1650, whose premises it retained. Again, taxation was to be the
criterion of distribution; again, there were to be four hundred seats for
England and Wales;[3] again, the county unit (except in the instance of

---

[1] *Memoirs of Edmund Ludlow*, i. 386, ii. 48.

[2] The disputed amendments are in *C.J.* 2, 9, 16, 23 and 30 Mar. 1653. On 2 March the
Rump rejected a proposal to give thirty-three seats to Ireland and thirty-seven to
Scotland, and decided instead to give them both thirty seats – the number they received
in the *Instrument of Government*. On 9, 16 and 23 March the House debated the distribution of English seats, and its many resolutions on this point may likewise be compared
with the identical provisions of the *Instrument*. (In two cases, the similarity of the two
schemes may not be immediately apparent. First, the Rump decided at one point to give
two seats to Southampton and none to Andover. In the following week, however, it
resolved to give them both one seat, as was to be the case in the *Instrument*. Secondly,
there is the instance of Surrey. In the *Instrument* the county received ten seats, of which
six went to the shire and four to boroughs within it. In March 1653 the House had
resolved to give Surrey only five county seats. But this apparent discrepancy can, be
easily explained. In reaching its previous decisions the House had determined which
boroughs were to be represented in a particular county before deciding the number of
seats which were to go to the shire. In the case of Surrey, however, an objection was
raised after the House had resolved to give Surrey only five seats, and it was successfully
moved that Kingston-on-Thames, which had been given a seat in the original scheme,
should be denied it. On the principle accepted by the Rump that the grant of a borough
seat reduced by one the number of county seats to be awarded to the shire in which the
borough lay, the logical course was to give Kingston's seat to the county, which would
thus have had six seats (as in the *Instrument*). This move should have been a mere formality, and we need not be disconcerted by the failure of the *Journal of the House of Commons*,
which was becoming increasingly thin by this stage, to record it. Even if the rumpers
omitted to take the action to which their own logic pointed, then the officers, in giving
Surrey six seats, were merely taking it for them.) If the *Instrument* and the Rump were
agreed over the numerous disputed amendments (which involved all the most novel
and distinctive features of the 1653 plan) it seems legitimate to assume that they were
also agreed about constituencies over which there was no recorded disagreement in the
Rump in March 1653.

[3] *Memoirs of Edmund Ludlow*, i. 354; Abbott, *Writings and Speeches*, iv. 487. Dr Cannon
(*Parliamentary Reform 1640–1832*, chapter 1 and appendices 1 and 2: cf. above, p. 144
n. 4) notes the interesting correlations between the various redistribution schemes of
1648–53 and the distribution of the ship money assessments of 1636; and he provides
(p. 268) a table comparing the *Instrument's* reapportionment provisions with the ship
money distribution. It is in fact clear that the 1653 scheme was based rather on the
Rump's assessment taxes, a point which becomes evident when it is realised that the

Yorkshire, which was to be subdivided into its separate Ridings) was to be preserved; again, borough seats were to count towards their counties' total representation. In contrast to the 1650 plan, however, the 1653 scheme listed the boroughs which were to be represented. Here the new plan was more conservative than those of the Levellers and the officers; it reprieved fifty-nine borough seats which had been condemned by both army schemes.[1] The 1653 plan also reduced the representation which the officers had proposed to award to major seaports, giving seats instead to lesser coastal towns. The ratio of county to borough seats in the 1653 plan was, as near as mathematically possible, two to one. As this was also the ratio adopted both in the Rump's proposals for the enfranchisement of Scotland and in the subsequent Cromwellian ordinance for Scottish elections,[2] it seems likely that such a formula had won general acceptance. The resolution to give thirty seats to both Scotland and Ireland, in addition to the four hundred seats claimed by England and Wales, was a novel feature of the 1653 plan.

The scheme made slightly more concessions to electoral tradition in the south-east and south-west than had either the officers' or the 1650 plan, but reduced the unwarrantably high representation given by both of them to the northern counties. In the case of two counties, Hampshire and Wiltshire, the 1653 scheme took further than that of 1650 the tendency to award an undeservedly high number of seats to counties strongly represented in the Rump, but in most other such counties the bill for a new representative accorded a more equitable distribution than had the previous scheme. It is in the distribution of borough seats that the rumpers' concern to feather their electoral nests, or to protect the interests of their constituents, is more noticeable. The partisan element in the scheme can be discerned in the names of the tellers appointed during the debates on the redistribution proposals. Thus the tellers in favour of reprieving Queenborough, which was to be abolished as a decayed borough after 1654, were Sir Michael Livesy,

scheme was framed by the Rump, not by the army officers. Even so, Dr Cannon's suggestion provides interesting food for thought about the relationship between the ship money distribution and the distribution of the Rump's assessment taxes: cf. Abbott, *Writings and Speeches*, iii. 384–5. The proportion of the Rump's assessments required of each county remained exactly consistent from the assessment reform of 1649 to the end of the Rump period, although there are hints that the reform may not have been fully implemented: see e.g. *Perfect Diurnal . . . Armies* 16–23 Feb. 1652, pp. 1684–5.

[1] These preserved boroughs are listed by Snow, 'Parliamentary reapportionment proposals', p. 422 and n.

[2] *C.J.* 25 Mar. 1652; Gardiner, *Constitutional Documents*, pp. 422–3.

who sat for it, and the Earl of Salisbury, an electoral magnate who had good reason to support the preservation of decayed boroughs. Speaker Lenthall, whose own decayed borough was due to come up for consideration immediately afterwards, gave his casting vote in Queenborough's favour. Lord Monson, a powerful Surrey magnate, acted as teller for the reprieve of Kingston-on-Thames, just after the reprieve of his own nearby seat at Reigate.[1] Suspicion must also centre on the award of seats to three small coastal towns as well as Queenborough (Dunwich, Rye, and the newly combined constituency East and West Looe), and to three small inland towns as well as Reigate (Arundel, East Grinstead and Woodstock). These eight boroughs supplied eleven rumpers among them. Woodstock, Speaker Lenthall's seat, was another of the decayed boroughs to be abolished after 1654.[2] Leicester, to which the officers had proposed to give only one seat, was given two in 1653, one of which was won in the following year by Sir Arthur Heselrige. Other rumpers whose seats were condemned by both army schemes but reprieved by the 1653 plan included Sir Henry Mildmay, Henry Neville, Oliver St John and Thomas Scot.[3]

Of course, the concern of such men to protect their own or their constituents' interests cannot be held responsible for the formulation of the 1653 scheme or for the Rump's decision to implement it: rumpers who sought to preserve their own boroughs were aiming not to strengthen their electoral bases but rather to shelter them from a scheme which threatened all vested electoral interests, including those of rumpers. In any case the play of local or self-interest in determining the provisions of the 1653 scheme had only a marginal effect on the scheme as a whole, and those who framed the *Instrument of Government* evidently did not think it worth the trouble to reallot the seats which rumpers had successfully protected. Indeed, one of the most remarkable

[1] *C.J.* 16, 23 Mar. 1653; L. Stone, 'The electoral influence of the second Earl of Salisbury', *E.H.R.*, lxxi (1966).
[2] *Diary of Thomas Burton*, i. cxi. Of course, the Rump did also reprieve boroughs represented by non-rumpers. The problem is to find a criterion for a borough's rottenness. Snow ('Parliamentary reapportionment proposals', pp. 436–42) singles out, as rotten, boroughs which were to be abolished in 1832, a superficially bizarre but on closer inspection (and with obvious exceptions) a not unreasonable guide. Apart from the eight boroughs mentioned above, only three seats which were to be abolished in 1832 had been condemned by both army plans but reprieved by the 1653 scheme; and these three boroughs supplied three rumpers between them. (On the decayed state of seventeenth-century Dunwich, see *Salus Populi, desperately ill of a Languishing Consumption* (1648), p. 5.)
[3] For the members of the 1654 parliament, see Cobbett, *Parliamentary History of England*, iii. 1428–33.

features of the whole movement for parliamentary reapportionment is
the willingness of all the reformers, whether in the army or in parliament, to favour schemes which in personal or party terms offered
them few if any advantages and many disadvantages. The appropriation of the Rump's 1653 scheme by the planners of the protectorate
bears striking witness to the continuity of ideas which underlay the
politics of the 1650s, and which become apparent when we study the
policies of the decade rather than the ambitions and tempers of those
who wielded them.

Why was the Rump, which was so unreceptive to demands for legal
and religious reform, at the same time willing to accept wholesale
redistribution of constituencies? There is no subject in which the
deficiencies of the evidence available for a study of Rump politics are
more frustrating. From the action which the Rump took we can see
that its members, like the army reformers, took the redistribution
issue seriously; but its reasons for taking it seriously are largely hidden
from us. The dearth of evidence on this point does not, however, discourage Mr Snow, who provides an ambitious explanation of the
various reform schemes. In his view,

> the political and economic centre of Puritanism – the East – assumed the rôle
> in the Puritan-planned House of Commons which had previously been played
> by the southwest ... The Puritans ... reshaped the power structure to fit
> social and economic realities. Since the older agrarian economy with its static
> status hierarchy was giving way to a commercial economy with a sliding social
> scale, the constitution and parliamentary institutions should likewise be re
> formed by those elected by God to usher in the new order.[1]

I have found no evidence to suggest that this was what the reformers
had in mind. The notion, indeed, that a stubborn provincial landowner like Edmund Ludlow, who helped to draft the 1650 scheme and
who later wrote enthusiastically of the Rump's redistribution proposals,
was the champion of a new social order and a 'sliding social scale' is
likely to constitute an insuperable imaginative hurdle to anyone who
has read Ludlow's *Memoirs* or studied the outlooks of members of the
Long Parliament. In any case, Snow's reasoning rests on a misleading
premise. Attempting to explain the intentions behind the various
schemes, he places prime emphasis on the contrast between the
number of seats enjoyed by a particular county or region in 1640 and

[1] Snow, 'Parliamentary reapportionment proposals', pp. 430, 431; and see *ibid.* pp. 413–14, 424–6.

the number awarded it by the various schemes of 1648–1653. Such a comparison, although interesting and helpful, is no basis for proclaiming the triumph of novel social attitudes. The social and economic reorientation of the electoral system may have been merely a consequence, rather than the purpose, of the changes which the reformers proposed. Those who formulated the schemes for reapportionment planned to redistribute seats on the basis of specific criteria of population or taxation. Prosperous regions, usually more populous and more heavily taxed than poorer ones, benefited accordingly from the reform proposals; but such gains may have been purely incidental to the reformers' intentions. If we wish to use the reapportionment schemes as guides to the social or economic preferences of those who framed them, it may be more profitable to examine the points at which, in drawing up their proposals, the reformers either bent or failed to live up to the criteria of redistribution to which they had committed themselves. None of the three schemes based on tax distribution (the officers' plan and those of 1650 and 1653) gave to either London or East Anglia – 'the political and economic centre of Puritanism' – anything like as many seats as their contributions to national taxation warranted. By the same criterion the three schemes were excessively generous to the 'backward parts', the north (especially in 1650) and (in 1649 and 1653) Wales.

Geographical redistribution was, however, only one half of the reformers' achievement. The other was the huge reduction in the number of borough seats and the corresponding increase in the number of county seats. Professor Trevor-Roper has discussed the significance of the *Instrument of Government*'s provisions for electoral redistribution – provisions which, as we have seen, were taken from the Rump's bill for a new representative. To him, the replacement of borough by county seats was the successful outcome of a revolt by the 'country gentry' against the 'borough gentry'. The 'country gentry', as represented in parliament, were backbenchers whose attitudes anticipated those of the 'independent country gentlemen' of the eighteenth century: the 'borough gentry', a more cosmopolitan breed, were those through whom courtiers and magnates had customarily established networks of electoral clientage.[1] This is the most plausible explanation of the reformers' intentions which has been advanced, and such evidence as we have of the attitudes of rumpers towards the unreformed electoral system suggests that it is an accurate one. At least some of the

[1] Trevor-Roper, *Religion, The Reformation and Social Change*, pp. 371–4.

M.P.s most prominent in the Rump wished to reform electoral arrangements because those arrangements compromised the independence of judgement of the men elected. Henry Neville complained during a Commons debate of 1659, in one of his imaginative forays into the past, 'Heretofore the Lords' House paid this. There were so many blue coats in our fathers' remembrance, that sat in this House, as we could see no other colours there. Near twenty parliament men would wait upon one lord, to know how they [should] demean themselves in the House of Commons.'[1] Vane, Cromwell and Marten seem likewise to have resented the abuses to which aristocratic electoral patronage could lead.[2] Marten, like Neville, would always have been ready to decry the political privileges of the peerage; and to read Cromwell's speeches to the first protectorate parliament, to watch his attempts to play on and to identify himself with backwoods attitudes, is to be reminded of the extent to which the 1653 scheme worked to the advantage of independent country gentlemen and to the disadvantage of electoral patrons and clients.

Convincing as Professor Trevor-Roper's explanation is, however, it is not a comprehensive one. It does not touch on the similarities between the 1653 scheme and the Leveller proposals; and even the most moderate of the Leveller leaders can hardly be regarded as conscious representatives of the country gentry interest. Professor Trevor-Roper's argument also highlights a problem which it does not solve, namely the willingness of the numerous electoral patrons and clients who sat in the Rump to agree to the 1650 and 1653 schemes. We are also left with the question why the Rump concerned itself not merely with the proportion of county to borough seats but also with the geographical distribution of constituencies. None of these problems admits of easy solution, and it is here possible only to suggest some of the considerations which may have helped to shape the Rump's attitudes.

Among these considerations were some, no doubt, of mundane political calculation. In particular, discussion of the reapportionment schemes made it possible for the House to avoid debating other, more contentious, issues. Under pressure from radicals to dissolve, the House quickly saw that it could stall on the timing of the dissolution by insisting that prior attention be given to the accompanying demand for a

[1] *Diary of Thomas Burton*, iv. 26

[2] *Life and Death of Sir Henry Vane Knight*, p. 99; *Diary of Thomas Burton*, iv. 24–5; Williams, 'Political career of Henry Marten', pp. 522–3; Trevor-Roper, *Religion, The Reformation and Social Change*, p. 239.

redistribution of seats. Only when reapportionment had been achieved, after all, would it be possible to hold elections of the kind which radicals demanded. In March 1649, when 'it was much pressed to set a time for dissolving this parliament', the House responded by debating 'the matter touching the equal distribution of the next representatives'.[1] Having discovered the advantages of this delaying tactic, the Rump frequently repeated it. There were, as we shall see, reasons of sound political sense, rather than of mere selfishness, for postponing the Rump's dissolution; and the frequent postponements should not be taken for evidence that the Rump lacked concern for the electoral injustices which its reapportionment schemes were designed to correct. Debates on redistribution, nevertheless, played a useful part in prolonging the Rump's tenure of power. The House's willingness to discuss redistribution was probably also connected with its disinclination to debate the other, more controversial, aspect of the movement for electoral reform, the demand for an extension of the franchise. During the 1647 army debates Ireton had been able to divide the Levellers by sidetracking them from the redistribution issue on to that of the franchise:[2] the Rump steered discussion away from the Leveller demand for an enlargement of the franchise by debating proposals for redistribution.

It is also possible that the decision to draw up the 1650 and the 1653 schemes was connected with the 1649 reform of the distribution of the assessment. That reform, like the redistribution schemes, was no doubt partly brought about by the feeling that it was inherently desirable: again as with the redistribution schemes, more pragmatic considerations may have been involved. Previously, the government claimed in 1649, there had been 'much inequality' in the distribution of the tax, leading 'to the obstructing and retarding the getting in thereof'.[3] The relationship between assessment burden and parliamentary representation was a sensitive issue in the provinces, especially during the Rump period when so few counties were still strongly represented in the House, and the Rump's schemes for the redistribution of seats may have been partly intended to reconcile particular areas to the increased share of national taxation which they now had to bear.

Influential as these considerations of political strategy may have been, however, they are not in themselves adequate to explain the

[1] Cf. below, pp. 188–9.
[2] Woodhouse, *Puritanism and Liberty*, pp. 52, 443–4.
[3] Firth and Rait, *Acts and Ordinances*, ii. 24–7. Cf. *H.M.C.R. Hodgkin*, p. 47.

impulse behind the Rump's redistribution proposals. It is, indeed, impossible to explain the movement for reapportionment solely in terms of the political calculations or the social and economic interests of the reformers. No one would suggest that the Rump's decision to proceed with redistribution was born solely of a respect for the principle of equity, but it is equally hard to see how the decision could have been taken had the principle not been widely accepted. The fact that reformers felt so little need to indicate the reasoning behind their schemes, that they took it for granted that the abuses of existing electoral arrangements were plain for all to see, is instructive. All that reformers said was that the geographical imbalances of the pre-war electoral system, and the surfeit of decayed boroughs, made the system less representative than it ought to have been. We may take this criticism at its face value. It seems to have won general acceptance in the 1640s, when ideas about representation were freely circulated, when many of the client M.P.s in the Long Parliament became increasingly independent of the patrons who had secured their election, and when the prestige of the House of Lords sank low. William Prynne and others did continue to oppose the movement for reapportionment, largely on the ground that it constituted a threat to the ancient rights and charters of boroughs, but in general reformers do not seem to have been confronted with the theoretical vindications of the traditional system which faced their nineteenth-century counterparts. Clarendon thought that the 1653 scheme was popular, and even devoted one of his rare and grudging expressions of admiration for Cromwell on the subject of the *Instrument of Government*'s provisions for reapportionment.[1] There is no sign that anyone in the Rump resisted the principle of reapportionment.[2] Unfortunately, broad agreement in the House was always an impediment to the survival of useful historical evidence. The *Journal of the House of Commons* is much more forthcoming about issues which provoked conflict than about those which did not. For this reason the inspiration behind the 1650 and the 1653 schemes is hard to identify. Ireton and Ludlow, both warm advocates of redistribution, were on the small committee which drew up the 1650 plan,

---

[1] W. Prynne, *Brevia Parliamentaria Rediviva* (1662) ep. ded.; Ashhurst, *Reasons against Agreement*, pp. 1–2; W. D. Macray (ed.), *Clarendon's History of the Rebellion* (6 vols., Oxford, 1958 edn.), xiv, section 43: cited by Snow, 'Parliamentary reapportionment proposals', pp. 435–6.

[2] There was, however, some resistance – ineffective but interesting – to the substitution in the schemes of the term 'representative' for 'parliament': Abbott, *Writings and Speeches*, iv. 467, with which cf. *Mercurius Pragmaticus* 12–19 Dec. 1648, p. (6).

although Ireton's departure for Ireland must have prevented him from playing any direct part in the committee's deliberations after July 1649, while Ludlow was added to the committee only late in its life.[1] Vane, the chairman of the committee, was probably a warm advocate of the plan, and Scot, too, seems to have favoured the Rump's redistribution proposals.[2] Yet those proposals, which occasioned much less dispute outside parliament than did the Rump's debates on other reform issues, probably neither received nor needed any large show of enthusiasm in the House. Any movement for social reform is likely to produce individual proposals which will earn the quiet approval of men dismayed by the movement as a whole, and the schemes for reapportionment seem to have received such approval. We have seen how, on other reform issues, the Rump tended to react against proposals which could be interpreted as attacks on the social order or which became involved in the conflict between parliament and army. Neither fate overtook the 1650 or the 1653 reapportionment scheme, partly because the officers had already taken the social sting out of the Leveller proposal (with the result that the Rump was asked to consider only a redistribution of political power within the governing classes rather than an extension of that power to other social groups) and partly because the Rump committed itself to the principle of reapportionment as early as 1650. On other reform issues, most of the Rump's critical decisions were taken only in 1652 or 1653, when the hostility between parliament and army, and the growth of extreme radicalism in the army and among the religious sects, gave to all discussions of reform a dimension of political and social conflict. The reapportionment schemes were relatively successful in the Rump because, although radicals favoured redistribution, it was the issue about which they created least unrest: on other reform issues, radical passion was the greatest obstacle to radical achievement. The fact that the Rump was prepared to revise the distribution of constituencies reminds us that its members had no innate hostility to reasoned and moderate reform proposals, and that many rumpers were willing, when the political temperature was low, to support them. The fact, too, that the Rump was prepared to take the demand for electoral reform so seriously is worth remembering when we consider, later in the book, the bill for a new representative in which the 1653 scheme was contained. The provisions of the bill for a new representative, it will be argued, show the rumpers to have been

[1] *C.J.* 15 May, 11 Oct. 1649; *Memoirs of Edmund Ludlow*, i. 334, 386, ii. 48.
[2] *Diary of Thomas Burton*, iii. 73, iv. 93–4.

concerned much more with the rights and interests of the electorate, and much less with their own political advantage, than historians have tended to suppose.[1]

The Rump managed to evade the issue of the franchise until the last weeks of its existence. Here again, however, the provisions of the *Instrument of Government* were identical with those of the bill for a new representative.

The county franchise, established in the reign of Henry VI, gave the vote to the forty-shilling freeholder.[2] By the seventeenth century, in Professor Plumb's words, 'Inflation ... had reduced, almost to triviality, the property qualification ... of -voters in the county electorates [and had] brought the Parliamentary franchise not to hundreds but to thousands of small farmers, shopkeepers, craftsmen, and owners of modest freeholdings.'[3] At the same time, as an army officer complained in 1647, 'there are men of substance in the country with no voice in elections'.[4] It was argued, especially in the later 1640s and especially by the Levellers, that the outdated standard of the forty-shilling freehold should make way for a more equitable qualification which would give the vote to 'men of substance', including prosperous copyholders.[5]

The Rump does not seem to have discussed the franchise until March 1653. In the first version of the bill for a new representative it was proposed that the forty-shilling freehold be retained as the prime electoral qualification, but that the vote be extended to certain categories of tenants, provided they were clearly residents of the constituencies in which they were to exercise their votes. On 30 March 1653 this

[1] The customary claim that the bill provided for the 'recruitment' of new members to join the rumpers in the House, rather than for wholly fresh elections, is challenged in Part Five, below. The 1653 redistribution scheme would, in any case, have made recruitment a very complex operation; and it is worth noting that neither Wiltshire nor Buckinghamshire was given as many seats in 1653 as there were rumpers holding seats in those counties. Similar difficulties would have attended any attempt to co-ordinate recruitment with the 1650 redistribution scheme: one wonders whether the rumpers ever envisaged such coordination as a concrete or imminent possibility.

[2] Cf. Goronwy Edwards, 'The emergence of majority rule in English parliamentary elections', *Transactions of the Royal Historical Society*, 5th series, xiv (1964), 176.

[3] J. H. Plumb, *The Growth of Political Stability in England, 1675–1725* (1967), p. 27. On the franchise see also Plumb, 'The growth of the electorate in England from 1600 to 1715', *Past and Present*, 45 (1969), and R. L. Bushman, 'English franchise reform in the seventeenth century', *Journal of British Studies*, iii (1963).

[4] Woodhouse, *Puritanism and Liberty*, p. 64.

[5] See e.g. *ibid.* p. 73; Wolfe, *Leveller Manifestoes*, p. 317.

cautious proposal, favoured by Vane, was dropped in favour of one supported by Heselrige and Morley, and it was resolved 'that all persons seized or possessed, to his own use, of any estate, real or personal, to the value of two hundred pounds, shall be capable to elect members to serve in parliament for counties'.[1] A newswriter suggested two days later that the change was made 'to please the army',[2] and the army's *Instrument of Government* made the same franchise provisions.

The Rump ignored the more sensitive issue of the borough franchise, but the county franchise assumed a new importance with the massive increase in 1653 in the number of county seats. The provisions of the bill for a new representative and of the *Instrument of Government* must have been hard to enforce, and the rumper Lislibone Long, referring in 1657 to the £200 qualification, observed that 'there is no way to try that, and many strange elections have happened upon it'.[3] What was the purpose of the change? An official apologia for the *Instrument of Government* claimed that, as a result of the franchise provisions of the 1653 plan,

the liberty of that kind is drawn forth to a greater latitude than in the days of kings, when this privilege was exceedingly curtailed, and communicated to those alone who were to be called freeholders, as if they alone had been the men that ought to be free; but now we conceive it is circumscribed with such prudence and caution, that it sits neither too straight nor too loose, to the body of the nation.[4]

Would the abolition of the forty-shilling freehold and the substitution of a £200 property qualification in fact have increased the electorate? Or (as would seem much more likely) did those who framed the 1653 plan want, like Milton, to keep the 'rude multitude' out of politics and so to confine the vote to those of 'a better breeding',[5] men of sufficient property to enable them to form their political judgements independently? Was the abolition of the forty-shilling freehold in fact observed? These are questions which could only be answered, if at all, by research at a local level.[6] What is clear is that the franchise

[1] *C.J.* 30 Mar. 1653. Cf. Gardiner, *Constitutional Documents*, p. 411.
[2] Clarendon MS 45, fo. 222ᵛ: newsletter, 1 Apr. 1653. The newswriter inaccurately gave the figure as £100.
[3] *Diary of Thomas Burton*, ii. 138–9.
[4] *A True State of the Case of the Commonwealth* (1654), p. 31. Cf. Patterson, *Works of John Milton*, viii. 221.
[5] Z. S. Fink, *The Classical Republicans* (Evanston, 1945), p. 114.
[6] Cf. Hill, *God's Englishman*, pp. 209, 291. Mr Derek Hirst, of Trinity Hall, Cambridge, is studying the workings of the franchise during the earlier seventeenth century.

provisions of the 1653 scheme were quite as effective as were both the officers' and the Rump's schemes for the redistribution of seats in sidestepping the social implications of the reforms which the Levellers had propounded. It is certainly feasible that the House, which was under considerable political pressure from the officers at the time, changed the franchise 'to please the army', but if so it was only because the change for which the officers called, and which was to be incorporated into the *Instrument of Government*, was of relatively small consequence.

The overall failure of the movement for social and religious reform can only be fully understood in the light of the circumstances in which reform proposals were debated in parliament; and it is now time to turn to the political narrative of the Rump period. Reform provided the major issue of conflict in the Rump, but it was the wishes of the army, not those of parliament, which made it so. Sympathetic as many rumpers were to individual reform proposals, reform remained incidental to their prime political concerns. As Peter Sterry, preaching before the Rump after the victory at Dunbar, lamented: 'Alas! I fear that, whatever there is of true reformation, and powerful sanctification among us, lies in a narrow compass, in some little corner of a very few hearts.'[1]

[1] P. Sterry, *The Comings Forth of Christ* (1650), p. 32.

PART THREE

THE STRUGGLE FOR SURVIVAL, FEBRUARY 1649–SEPTEMBER 1651

9

PROBLEMS AND POLICIES,
FEBRUARY 1649

The Rump, surrounded by enemies both at home and abroad, was faced from the start by problems of daunting magnitude. When governments have survived crises, it is sometimes difficult to realise how grave the crises were. The Commonwealth's survival between 1649 and 1651 was a remarkable, and to contemporaries often a surprising, achievement.

The thrill of horror which ran through England at the execution of Charles I spread quickly to the continent, where the previous decade had likewise been one of acute political instability, and where rulers were understandably alarmed by the murder of one of God's anointed kings. Unhappily for Charles II's exiled court, resolved to regain the throne and anxious for continental support for an invasion, the expressions of grief and condolence proffered by European governments were not matched by supplies of arms, money or men, let alone by open declarations of hostility to the new republic.[1] Such parsimony, although politically and financially unavoidable, could hardly be predicted, and could certainly not be taken for granted, by the infant Commonwealth. Indeed, although France and Spain remained at war, and consequently were unable to contemplate open aggression towards England, the conclusion of the Thirty Years War in 1648 left the new government diplomatically isolated, perilously exposed, and struggling for formal recognition by European powers. If the conduct of continental governments towards the Rump was a matter for worried speculation, the behaviour of its enemies in Ireland and Scotland presented a more immediate threat. In Ireland, the news of the moves against Charles I made possible, in January 1649, an ominous alliance between the king's Lord Lieutenant, the Earl of Ormonde, and the Confederate Catholics of Ulster, who were regarded by Englishmen as responsible for the

[1] C. V. Wedgwood, 'European reaction to the death of Charles I', in C. H. Carter (ed.), *From the Renaissance to the Counter-Reformation. Essays in Honour of Garrett Mattingly* (1966).

notorious Irish massacre of 1641. In Scotland, Charles II's succession was proclaimed as soon as accounts of his father's death reached the north. The Scottish envoys in London, who had promoted what resistance they could to the king's trial, and had thereafter issued a bold condemnation of the new regime, were deported by the Rump late in February.[1]

Charles II learnt of the execution at the court of his father's ally, William of Orange. Although there were those who advised him to wait quietly for better days, he soon decided to bid for restoration to the Stuart throne. Once the notion of a European crusade, fought by fellow monarchs on behalf of the Stuart dynasty, had been exposed as illusory, two alternative strategies were open to him. The first, which may be called the 'presbyterian' policy, was to seek the alliance of all those in England or Scotland who might in certain circumstances be tempted to prefer a Stuart restoration to the continued rule of the Rump. In England this policy would mean conspiring with the presbyterian organisation in the city of London, major political and religious concessions to presbyterian sentiment, an appeal to those on the parliamentary side who in the autumn of 1648 had wanted a treaty with the royalists on the lines proposed at Newport, and an implicit acknowledgement that Charles I had been wrong to decline the Newport terms. Still greater concessions would be necessary in Scotland, where feelings between royalists and presbyterians ran even higher than in England, and where the presbyterian kirk, in full cry early in 1649, was prepared to countenance Charles II's accession only in return for rigid religious guarantees. Much depended on the renowned political dexterity of the Marquess of Argyle, whose commanding position rested on presbyterian support. He had been willing, in the autumn of 1648, to negotiate with the heretical rebels south of the border. He showed himself equally prepared, early in 1649, to reach an understanding with the Scottish royalists. The question was whether, in pursuit of either policy, he could carry his clerical storm-troopers with him.

The presbyterian policy was firmly, and for a long time successfully, resisted by Hyde, one of Charles II's most influential courtiers. Only in the short term, Hyde believed, could anything be gained by compromising with presbyterians, whom he held to be fundamentally as opposed

---

[1] Remarks about royalist activity and policy between 1649 and 1651, and about the situations in Ireland and Scotland, are based on the excellent accounts in Gardiner, *History of the Commonwealth and Protectorate*, and in D. E. Underdown, *Royalist Conspiracy in England* (Yale, 1960).

to the true interests of monarchy as were the rebels left in power in England. Hyde's own policy, which seemed to his friends more far-sighted and to his enemies unrealistic, and which may be called the 'Cavalier' policy, was to invite the support only of men who in the 1640s had been unswervingly loyal to the royalist cause. In Scotland the obvious recipient of royalist trust was the Earl of Montrose, but he, for all his courageous dedication to the Stuart house, stood little chance against the combined strength of Argyle and the presbyterians. If the Cavalier policy were to be preferred to the presbyterian one, it made sense to use Ireland, rather than Scotland, as the base of a projected invasion of England. In Ireland, royalist hopes could be entrusted to Ormonde and to his alliance, so disagreeable to presbyterians every-where, with the Ulster Catholics. Meanwhile negotiations with the Catholic powers of Europe, and even with the Papacy, could be set in motion. At the exiled court, support for Hyde's views was increased by the tough bargaining of the Scottish presbyterians, whose unwilling-ness to put forward terms acceptable to Charles had become clear by March 1649. The Cavalier, Irish-based policy received Charles's blessing from March until autumn of the same year, when its failure became manifest. Also in March the Rump, quick to detect the drift of royalist policy, resolved to send an army to Ireland. The expedition was long delayed, but not because anyone in parliament underestimated the threat which Ormonde presented. By May, when he was making major military advances, the Commonwealth's survival seemed to depend on its ability to withstand his progress.

The main obstacle facing the royalists was the parliamentary army; but the same army was also the Rump's greatest political liability, necessitating huge taxation, free quarter, and intense unpopularity. The narrower the base of the government's support, the greater the forces needed to defend it; and the greater the forces, the narrower the base of support was likely to be. The army had grown considerably in response to the needs of the second civil war, but it was still not large enough to meet the combined needs of the Commonwealth's internal security and the dispatch of a major expedition to Ireland. The number of soldiers under parliament's command seems to have risen from about forty-seven thousand in March 1649 to about seventy thousand in 1652.[1] So sizeable a force presented massive financial problems. Since 1646 parliament, reluctant to impose still higher taxation, had treated the issue of army pay with a negligence interpreted by the troops as

[1] C. H. Firth, *Cromwell's Army* (1962 edn.), pp. 34–5.

contemptuous indifference.[1] Vast arrears had mounted up; present wages went unpaid; and free quarter, the inevitable substitute for pay, was as bitterly resented by the troops as by those on whom they were quartered. Financial grievances were at the heart of military unrest in the later 1640s, and in the spring of 1649 the army's discontent grew to unprecedented proportions. Payment of the troops, a problem which the army officers were no longer prepared to see shelved, was an urgent political necessity.

Equally urgent was the need to reorganise the navy. Prince Rupert exploited one of the most effective instruments of opposition available to the royalists by directing a piracy campaign based on Ireland. England was already engaged in a nascent, unofficial piracy war with France, and soon the Portuguese government was to lend support to Rupert's campaign. English trade, both foreign and domestic, depended heavily on coastal shipping, and in the grim economic circumstances of the spring and summer of 1649 the protection of merchant ships from the depredations of pirates was one of the government's most immediate priorities. The civil wars, and a succession of bad harvests, had created the most serious poverty problem for many years. Acute dearth – perhaps even starvation – was widespread, especially in the long-suffering northern counties.[2] All seventeenth-century governments acknowledged a duty to alleviate poverty, and none of them, certainly not one as precariously situated as the Rump, could afford to ignore the possibilities of social and political unrest which poverty created. The Rump brought little that was new to poor relief, relying in the main on the methods adopted since Elizabeth's reign, but in the spring of 1649 the government became especially solicitous of the needs of the poor at those moments when the Levellers seemed most likely to incite rebellion. It was not only the poor, however, who stood to suffer from interruptions to maritime trade. A revival of commerce was an essential precondition of the Rump's acceptance by the nation in general, and by the merchant community in particular.

From December 1648 to April 1649 the Rump was busily engaged in organising a strong fleet, 'for guard of the narrow seas, protection and preservation of trade, reducing of the revolted ships, and for the necessary defence of England and Ireland'.[3] The eventual dispatch of

[1] Cf. Gentles, 'Debentures and military purchases', chapter 1.
[2] Underdown, *Pride's Purge*, p. 281. There are numerous references to the widespread poverty in the newspapers.
[3] Firth and Rait, *Acts and Ordinances*, ii. 9–14, 18.

the fleet, although regarded by many as sadly belated,[1] was a considerable administrative achievement, for hitherto the navy had been
heavily beset by disorganisation, disrepair and divided political loyalties. The Earl of Warwick, brother of a royalist peer executed in
March 1649, had remained in charge of the Admiralty, and had continued to attend Navy Committee meetings, until the middle of the
previous month.[2] After angling for his support for a time, the government decided instead to dismiss him and to bring the direction of the
Admiralty under the Council of State. Three Generals-at-Sea, Robert
Blake, Edward Popham (both rumpers), and Richard Deane, were
appointed in Warwick's place. Legislation was passed to quash disaffection in the fleet and to encourage naval recruitment; army
officers and a committee of city merchants were closely consulted
about the reorganisation of the fleet; and measures were taken to reform the administration of the customs, always an important source of
naval finance. It would have taken more than the customs, however, to
solve the most alarming problem raised by the Rump's naval programme: a navy budget for the coming year of £300,000.[3]

Finance, indeed, was at the heart of the new government's difficulties.
Inheriting a vast deficit, and finding 'the receipts of public monies . . .
through the former improvident and evil managing of the public
treasury . . . clogged with vast anticipations charged upon them',[4] the
Rump was soon committed to even higher expenditure than the Long
Parliament had been before Pride's Purge. How was the money to be
raised? Three main methods were available to the government; it took
advantage, and suffered the disadvantages, of all of them. The first was
through taxation, and especially through the principal financial expedients produced by the civil war, the assessment on property and the
excise. The assessment, profoundly unpopular and likely to become
more so, was notoriously difficult to collect. The government tried to
render it more palatable by claiming that it was a substitute for free
quarter, and by asserting that free quarter had ended in those areas
where the assessment was fully paid.[5] Such arguments were unlikely to

[1] *Kingdom's Faithful Scout* 16–23 Feb. 1649, p. 378; *Moderate Intelligencer* 15–22 Mar. 1649,
p. 1945; *Perfect Weekly Account* 21–28 Mar. 1649, p. 432.
[2] Rawlinson MS A224, fos. 1–18.
[3] *C.J.* 14, 15 Dec. 1648; *Perfect Occurrences* 5–12 Jan. 1649, p. 790, 16–23 Feb. 1649, p. 849;
Perfect Weekly Account 31 Jan.–7 Feb. 1649, p. 378, 21–28 Mar. 1649, pp. 431–2; *Perfect
Diurnal . . . Parliament* 19–26 Feb. 1649, p. 2399; Whitelocke, *Memorials*, ii. 519.
[4] Firth and Rait, *Acts and Ordinances*, ii. 25.
[5] See e.g. *ibid.* ii. 24–7; *Perfect Diurnal . . . Parliament* 1–8 Jan. 1649, p. 2256.

prompt spontaneous payment of the huge sums which the Rump was obliged to demand. In March 1649, when the previous assessment act expired, parliament imposed a new levy of £90,000 a month. High as the figure was, the Rump admitted that it would have had to be at least a third as high again to have met the military needs which it was designed to answer; already the government was compromising between financial and political necessities.[1] The excise was if anything more hated than the assessment, especially during an economic depression, but it had obvious attractions for a government desperate for the support of the landed classes and consequently willing to broaden the social distribution of taxation. The Rump favoured the excise as 'the most equal and indifferent way that can be laid upon the people', and in June 1649 demanded 'the people's due conformity to the payment of the excise, as the only way ... to take away assessments and other taxes, and to ease the great burden of free quarter'.[2] Excessive reliance on the excise, however, was likely to provoke social unrest, and in the summer of 1649 the Rump professed itself resolved to reform the tax so as to ease the burden on the poor.[3] Its resolution proved short-lived.

If the Rump could not survive without money, it could only hope to exploit the second obvious channel of finance, a loan from the city of London, when it had displayed its ability to survive. The city also demanded financial security, and it was to this end that the Rump turned to the third method of raising money, the sale of confiscated estates. The problem, as the government found, was to persuade people to purchase them.[4] Even if they were bought their sale could only be a short-term expedient, and the potential yield would soon be exhausted. Besides, land sales could be politically unpopular, even if paraded, as the Rump paraded them, as alternatives to higher taxation. Perhaps this was why the government was so slow to undertake confiscations of royalist estates, which could be financially profitable only if undertaken on a huge scale. Royalists who failed to compound for their estates were treated, until 1651, with surprising leniency.[5] Instead, the government turned to the dean and chapter lands, which it opened to sale at the end of April 1649, and to the crown lands,

---

[1] Firth and Rait, *Acts and Ordinances*, ii. 26.
[2] *Ibid.* ii. 213–35; *Perfect Diurnal ... Parliament* 11–18 June 1649, p. 2587.
[3] See e.g. *England's Moderate Messenger* 18–25 June 1649, pp. 68–9. The newspapers contain much information about the Rump's early financial policies and difficulties.
[4] See e.g. *C.C.C.*, pp. 198–9, 408.
[5] See e.g. *C.J.* 14, 17 Mar., 19, 23, 26, 27 May 1649.

which it saw as the answer to the problem of soldiers' arrears. The aim was to free to the state's use vast sums hitherto charged as debts on the excise.[1]

Financial difficulties ate heavily into the parliamentary timetable throughout the Rump period, but never more so than in the months after Charles's execution. Only when the difficulties had been resolved could the army leave for Ireland, and in July 1649, on the eve of the army's departure, the government's fiscal energies reached their peak. The promise of a loan was at last secured from the city, and the act for the sale of crown lands was pushed through after urgent parliamentary sessions of unusual length.[2] Once the army had left, the Commonwealth could afford to take its second wind. The respite was a short one, and the problems of supplying and paying both army and navy, combined with the continuing incidence of free quarter, haunted the Rump throughout its history. Yet, compared with the expressions of army feeling before 1649, complaints that soldiers went unpaid were thereafter generally isolated and restrained. If the Rump never solved the financial problems which it inherited, it nevertheless made notable inroads upon them. The level of army pay was raised in 1649; and thereafter the administration and hence the yield of the assessment were strikingly improved, until in some areas the tax was fully paid.[3] The army was grateful for the act for the sale of crown lands and cooperated fully in its implementation.[4] It says something for the government that the question of army pay, although still a sore point, seems to have played a relatively small part in the enmity between parliament and army which so dominated the politics of the later Rump period.

Such, briefly, were the pressures, diplomatic, military, naval, economic and financial, which faced the Government after its assumption of power and which consumed so much of its time. Without exception, they were pressures towards moderation. There was little opportunity for detailed discussion of social reform, and little inclination, even among parliamentary radicals or army officers, to offend moderate opinion by discussing it. Radical sentiment in parliament, however, was not suppressed, although it was deflected towards secondary

---

[1] Firth and Rait, *Acts and Ordinances*, ii. 168–91.
[2] Whitelocke, *Memorials*, iii. 66, 67; *Perfect Diurnal . . . Parliament* 9–16 July 1649, p. 2654.
[3] See Johnson, 'Buckinghamshire 1640–1660', pp. 134, 391; M. Ashley, *Financial and Commercial Policy under the Cromwellian Protectorate* (1962 edn.), p. 79.
[4] See e.g. *Perfect Weekly Account* 3–10 Oct. 1649, p. 629; Whitelocke, *Memorials*, iii. 118, 125, 127, 129.

targets. Sudden gusts of radical feeling, prompted by speeches critical of tithes, clergymen, lawyers, papists or royalists, could sweep unexpectedly through the chamber, obstructing or reversing carefully formulated and previously agreed policies. The Rump, which few individuals or parties were ever able to dominate for long, was the least predictable of assemblies, given to intemperate and often irrational moods of optimism or pessimism, aggressiveness or defensiveness, radicalism or reaction. If we look at the day-to-day activity of the House, we often seem to be watching a closely fought battle between radicals and moderates, even if radicalism and moderation meant different things at different times to different people. Only when we look at the broader pattern do we see how one-sided the conflict was.

Although the radicals were not without their successes in the Rump, their achievements were primarily negative, victories of containment rather than of initiative. After the abolition of kingship and the House of Lords, there were four periods when they went on to the attack. The first was in the summer of 1649, when Marten drew up a list of reform proposals to which the Council of State apparently agreed but which the House successfully evaded. The second was in late 1649 and early 1650, in the wake of Cromwell's victories at Drogheda and Wexford. Again it was Marten who took the radical lead; again he was defeated. He was more successful in the third period of radical initiative, which followed the defeat of the Scottish presbyterians at Dunbar in September 1650, but even here the reformers' success was short-lived, giving way to a spell of unyielding reaction. The fourth period followed the battle of Worcester in September 1651, when the army's hopes of reform were severely disappointed. In each of the four instances radical exertion in parliament was supported, and probably prompted, by the army. Radicals never achieved anything in the Rump without the army's assistance. Yet, equally, army pressure – at which the House was quick to take offence – was often counter-productive.

The radicals' victories of containment were more impressive. 1649 saw the defeat of a number of conservative proposals designed to restore the unity of the parliamentary party. Debates took place on schemes for the preservation of kingship and the House of Lords, for the readmission of all the members secluded at the purge, for official confirmation of the presbyterian church settlement, and for an act of oblivion for the Rump's enemies. All these moves failed; and their failure owed much to radical vigilance in the House. Yet, once again, it owed still more to army feeling. Republicanism, religious independency, and a determination to uphold the effects of the purge were all strong in the army, but they commanded only small numerical support in the House. The victories of containment were possible because, although the Rump was usually unwilling to agree to army demands for reform, it was much more wary of affronting the army by challenging the *status quo*. In consequence, most of the Rump period was characterised by political stalemate, in which both those who wished to undo the revolution of December 1648 and January 1649, and those who wished to take it further, suffered endless frustrations. It is against this background that the gradual deterioration of relations between parliament and army must be seen.

The continuing influence of the army gives a misleading impression of the balance of power within the House. The Rump was a much more conservative body than its concessions to army feeling might suggest, and it was only rarely that radicals held the initiative. When they did, the limitations of both their numbers and their outlooks were exposed. In the early spring of 1649, for example, when the central issue was the struggle for control of the new government, they were sidetracked on to the more emotive but in political terms much less significant issue of the number of Charles I's leading adherents to be executed. Three prominent royalists died in March, and a fourth followed in April; but their executions, however satisfying to radicals, scarcely affected more fundamental issues like the readmission of 'conformist' M.P.s to the House or the composition of the first Council of State. After the royalist executions, radicals turned their attention to the equally emotive and equally secondary problem of the five M.P.s, imprisoned at the purge, who had not thereafter been released. The prisoners remained in gaol, but hopes that they would be tried for treason were not fulfilled. The radicals, concentrating on symbolic acts of destruction, fighting the battles of yesterday, were trounced in the struggle for control of the Rump.

Their defeat was not immediately apparent. In the days after Charles's execution, indeed, revolutionary ardour seemed to carry all before it. On 31 January, the day after the execution, Henry Marten secured the appointment of a parliamentary committee to investigate one of the most sensitive subjects raised by the movement for law reform, the plight of poor prisoners gaoled for debts they were unable to pay. On 2 February Marten's freelance regiment, whose behaviour had so scandalised parliament in the previous year, was accorded official status within the army, and the order for the trial of five royalist peers was given. On the 5th the Commons debated the future of the House of Lords.[1] Cromwell and Whitelocke, both of whom had stoutly defended the upper house during a debate in January, now repeated their arguments, hoping to preserve for the peers either a judicial or a consultative role. When the 'long and smart' debate was resumed on the 6th, however, Marten persuaded the Commons to defeat (by forty-four votes to twenty-nine) a motion that it should 'take advice of the House of Lords, in the exercise of the legislative power'. It was resolved that 'the House of Peers in parliament is useless and dangerous, and ought to be abolished'. A committee was set up to draft an abolition bill, Whitelocke, to his chagrin, being put in charge of the drafting. This question settled, the Commons quickly moved on to a still more fundamental issue, debating 'what government' should be 'set up', and 'whether kingship should be abolished or not'. Next day, the 7th, monarchy was voted down. The act for its abolition was eventually passed on 17 March, two days before that for the abolition of the House of Lords.[2]

The resolutions of 6 and 7 February testify to the revolutionary daring of some rumpers, but much more to the absence of a plausible alternative policy. There was little to be said for propping up a House of Lords deserted by the overwhelming majority of its members. The retention of monarchy was no more practicable. Its abolition did not betoken the sudden conversion of large numbers of rumpers to republican principles, any more than had the execution of Charles I. Indeed, the fact that after Charles's death it took the Commons a week even to ask itself whether or not kingship should be abolished indicates the limits to republican feeling at this time.[3] Both the resolution and the act abolishing kingship proclaimed, with an ambiguity so blatant that it must have been contrived, the proven dangers of 'the office of a king in this nation, and to have the power thereof in any single person', a form of wording which left the door open for the mixed monarchical solution long desired by many M.P.s. Not until May 1649, at a time of acute discontent in the army, did the government decide that England 'shall from henceforth be governed as a Commonwealth and free state

[1] See *C.J.* for dates mentioned.
[2] Firth, *The House of Lords during the English Civil War*, pp. 205–14; Gardiner, *History of the Commonwealth and Protectorate*, i. 3; Whitelocke, *Memorials*, iii. 519, 521; Clarendon MS 34, fo. 73ᵛ; B.M., Add. MS 37,344, fo. 256; *Perfect Weekly Account* 31 Jan.–7 Feb. 1649, p. 378; *C.J.* 6, 7 Feb. 1649; Gardiner, *Constitutional Documents*, pp. 384–8.
[3] Cf. *Perfect Occurrences* 2–9 Feb. 1649, p. 830. And see the shrewd and sensible observations by P. Zagorin, *A History of Political Thought in the English Revolution* (1954), p. 148.

by the supreme authority of this nation, the representatives of the people in parliament . . . and that without any king or House of Lords'. In any case, as was often pointed out, England had long been described as a Commonwealth. The term, although popular with republicans, was in itself compatible with monarchy. 'Free state' had a valuable emotional content, but not a theoretical one; no doubt it was useful as a substitute for the more revolutionary term 'republic', which in the earlier Rump period the government usually, although not always, contrived to avoid. The republicanism of the Rump in 1649 was, in fact, a mere improvisation, triumphant by default, unconvinced and largely unprofessed. Until May the country did not even have a 'form of government' at all, ruled as it was by an *ad hoc* coalition brought about by arbitrary historical circumstances. Yet however strong the resistance to a complete repudiation of monarchy, there was little chance at this stage of restoring it. The divisions created by the purge and the execution ran too deep. Even if the army could have been persuaded to accept a proposal for restored kingship, which is most unlikely, any such move would have reopened all the questions which the army's actions of December and January had been designed to close, and which would now have been still harder to answer. Such stability as Cromwell achieved in February 1649, based as it was on so frail a coalition of interests, was bought at the expense of monarchy. Any attempt to reinstate the crown, whatever the proposed constitutional formula, would very probably have renewed the warfare of 1648. Only when the royalist threat had been eliminated did it again become practicable to advance proposals for some form of monarchical settlement. Cromwell was then among the first to air them.

The decisive debates on kingship and the House of Lords were held first in early February 1649, when many 'conformists' had still to return to the House, and then in the middle of March, when most of them, dismayed by the new government's difficulties, had temporarily withdrawn once more. It is interesting to speculate what might have happened had the debates taken place in the interim. Yet when, after Worcester, Cromwell and the lawyers argued for mixed monarchy, their proposals seem to have won little support in parliament. There is, indeed, no evidence to suggest that the subject of kingship, which might be expected to have provided one of the principal issues dividing parliament and army between Worcester and the Rump's dissolution, was ever discussed in the House during that time. No doubt this was largely because any challenge to the *status quo* during the Rump period was likely to raise more problems than it solved; as Cromwell admitted, the restoration of kingship would have been 'a business of more than ordinary difficulty'.[1] Willing as the Rump often was to resist the army, it was usually reluctant to provoke it, and the army would certainly have regarded a proposal to restore monarchy as provocative. Despite the House's silence on the kingship issue after Worcester, there is no reason to think that republican doctrine ever made much headway in the Rump. Such progress as it did make is probably to be largely explained by the government's exploits in the sphere of foreign policy. When the Commonwealth achieved in Europe what generations of monarchy had failed to achieve, and when England began to challenge effectively the commercial supremacy of the envied Dutch republic, it was natural for the architects of the Rump's diplomacy – men like Heselrige, Scot, Morley, Marten, Neville, Chaloner and John Bradshaw – to postulate a connection between republicanism and national prestige. Certainly one can detect a growth of republican feeling outside parliament after the defeat of the Scots at Dunbar in September 1650 and with the Commonwealth's subsequent discovery of its new-found diplomatic strength. The movement became even stronger after Worcester. Yet what flourished inside parliament was less republicanism than a belief – inconceivable in 1640 – in the right of the House of Commons to political supremacy. The two things, although often connected, were not necessarily the same.

The experience of the Long Parliament served at every turn to nourish respect for the House of Commons and assertion of its political rights. The fickleness of Charles I strengthened the hand of those who argued that the Commons had the right to dictate its own peace terms. The frequent conflicts between Lords and Commons during the 1640s encouraged opposition to the upper house, and the purging and subsequent absenteeism of its membership led often to contempt for it. The Commons' resolution of 4 January 1649, declaring that power lay originally with the people as represented in the lower House, may have been adopted for reasons of pragmatism, but men who adopt theories as justifications for their actions often, with the passage of time, become convinced by them. After the abolition of kingship and the House of Lords the need of rumpers to believe in their right to political supremacy became even greater. Yet if the theories adopted by the Rump were defensive, the emotional commitment which lay behind

[1] Cf. below, p. 276.

them was more positive. The 1640s had shown that parliament, hitherto an outlet for provincial grievances, could govern. Indeed, it was clearly capable of governing more efficiently than the Stuart monarchy. Whether it could govern for long, and without the support of a standing army, was one of the central issues of the Rump period. In our preoccupation with such matters as the social backgrounds and outlooks of M.P.s, we tend too often to forget that the course of politics is largely determined by such matters as morale, vanity, self-doubt and self-confidence. These matters were all affected by the Long Parliament's experience of governing. The achievements of its rule, and the sentiments to which those achievements gave rise among the M.P.s responsible for them, were at least as important in shaping the notion of the Commons' right to supremacy as was the theoretical apparatus with which parliament justified its actions against crown and Lords. It tells us much about the outlooks of M.P.s that many of them – presbyterians and rumpers alike – were more deeply angered by Pride's Purge than by the execution of the king. It is not clear when the idea of Commons' supremacy first won the support of more than a small minority of M.P.s, but it is notable that Whitelocke, recording that twenty-two members of the Rump's first Council of State refused to approve the act of regicide, observed that all but one of them nevertheless 'confessed ... the Commons to be the supreme power of the nation, and that they would live and die with them in what they should do for the future'. (The single exception was a peer.)[1] Whitelocke, himself one of the councillors who acknowledged the Commons' supremacy in February 1649, believed in the 1650s that monarchy should be restored only on parliament's terms and only at parliament's bidding. To observe Whitelocke's conversion to the principle of Commons' supremacy is not to challenge Carlyle's assertion that he remained 'a secret-royalist in the worst of times'.[2] He, and other rumpers, plainly regarded parliamentary supremacy and kingship as compatible. Few M.P.s were persuaded by the events of the Rump period that monarchy was undesirable. What many of them do seem to have come to believe, especially after 1650, was that monarchy was unnecessary. Political theorists had long argued that without kingship there could only be anarchy. In the Rump period, and especially after the defeat of the Scots, it became clear that the state could after all exist without a

---

[1] Whitelocke, *Memorials*, ii. 536.
[2] Whitelocke, *Journal of the Swedish Embassy*, i. 309–11; Thomas Carlyle, *Cromwell's Letters and Speeches* (3 vols., 1846 edn.), iii. 374; and see Abbott, *Writings and Speeches*, ii. 591–2.

king; and political theorists, impressed by the Commonwealth's survival and by its military, naval and diplomatic accomplishments, revised their ideas accordingly.

The Rump's belief in parliament's right to govern was strengthened further, and perhaps above all, by the conflict between parliament and army. Military claims to political influence could only increase the House's readiness to describe itself as the representative body of the nation, its resolve to defend parliamentary privileges, and its pride in the customary procedures of debate. Yet there was a paradox here, for parliament's emphasis on the sanctity of what went on within its walls could diminish its responsiveness to opinion outside them. The Rump, indeed, claimed to represent a nation which neither was nor wished to be represented by it. Bedfordshire was not represented by a single rumper, and many counties were represented by only one. Oxfordshire, Devon, Cheshire and Lancashire, all centres of opposition to the Commonwealth, were among the counties seriously under-represented after the purge. As time went by the Rump was increasingly urged by constituencies to remedy their 'great and pressing want of burgesses'.[1] The House made numerous attempts to expand its membership, and made provision, as we have seen, for a more equitable distribution of constituencies. Rumpers knew very well that parliaments derived their authority solely from the trust reposed in them by the electorate. Embarrassed by the rows of empty seats, the Rump consistently regarded parliamentary elections as the ultimate solution to its difficulties.[2] Yet such elections, at least before Worcester, were likely to prove politically disastrous. Any radical change in the House's membership would have upset the delicate equilibrium created early in 1649 between parliament and army, between 'revolutionaries' and 'conformists'. To justify its tenure of power the Rump was obliged to argue, especially in its earlier stages, that the M.P.s who had ceased to sit at the purge had betrayed their trust. Later, at least some members may have come to believe that they governed by right of conquest. But if rumpers convinced themselves that their rule was justifiable, they never seem to have believed that it represented an intrinsically desirable form of government. The royalist threat before Worcester, and the political exertions of the army after it, impressed on parliament the need to

[1] Journal of the London Common Council lxi, fo. 53ᵛ. Cf. *ibid.* fos. 53, 65, 66ᵛ, 67; *Mercurius Politicus* 15–22 May 1651, p. 803; Isaac Pennington jr., *The Fundamental Right, Safety and Liberty of the People* (1651), pp. 26–7. For the geographical distribution of rumpers, see Appendix B, Table 1.
[2] Cf. below, Part Five.

postpone elections until domestic stability had been achieved. In consequence, the Rump remained in power for much longer than any of its
enemies wished; but we should not infer from this that it ever saw
itself as anything other than an interim solution. A belief in the
supremacy of parliaments was not the same thing as admiration for the
bastardised parliament left behind by Pride's Purge.

This is to look ahead; we must return now to the struggle for control
of the new government in February 1649. What happened to kingship
in that month was less important than what happened to parliament,
whose benches, with the return of so many 'conformist' M.P.s, were
filling rapidly. The army officers, alarmed by continuing Leveller
unrest, could not afford to retract publicly their demand that the
Rump dissolve itself by the end of April 1649. Yet still less, as parliament well knew, could they afford to press for speedy elections, which
in the present climate of opinion would be suicidal. The Rump was
thus able to anticipate a longer tenure of power than had seemed possible in December, and on 7 February, the day of the resolution against
kingship, it felt strong enough to assert both its staying power and its
control of the executive. A small committee, consisting of Thomas
Scot, Edmund Ludlow, Luke Robinson, John Lisle and Cornelius
Holland (the men who were later to comprise the Committee for
Absent Members) was set up to draft instructions to, and to nominate
members of, a Council of State. On the 13th Scot reported the instructions, which met with the House's approval; and on the 16th he
reported the names.[1] The ensuing struggle over the council's composition proved decisive in the formation of the regime's character. The
course and outcome of the conflict showed how far, within three weeks
or so of Charles's execution, revolutionary purposes had already been
weakened. Both supporters and opponents of the Rump agreed that
'divers gentlemen of the best quality' were appointed to the council,
'but not to the content of all that pretended merit in destroying the
former government'.[2] The achievement, and evidently the aim, of
Scot's committee was to nominate the most broadly based and the least
radical body that could be persuaded to serve, and that the 'revolutionaries' could be prevailed upon to accept.

[1] See *C.J.* for dates mentioned.
[2] T. Carte (ed.), *A Collection of Original Letters . . . 1641 to 1650* (2 vols., 1739), i. 224;
The Moderate 20–27 Feb. 1649, p. 330; Walker, *History of Independency*, ii. 129; *Memoirs
of Colonel Hutchinson*, p. 272.

Forty-one candidates were nominated, thirty-four of them M.P.s. The inclusion of the seven men who were not M.P.s provides the clue to the committee's intentions. One, John Bradshaw, who had presided over the trial of Charles I, was a regicide, but the views of the other six were decidedly unrevolutionary. Five were peers: Lord Grey of Wark, who alone of the committee's nominees refused to serve; the Earl of Mulgrave, who by attending a parliamentary committee late in January 1649[1] had raised hopes that he would support the Rump, but who never in fact appeared at a council meeting; and the trimming Earls of Denbigh, Pembroke and Salisbury, all of whom attended Rump committees after the abolition of the House of Lords and played their parts on the council.[2] The appointment of five peers to the council, scarcely a week after the abolition of the House of Lords, is a further reminder of the boundaries of the Rump's revolutionary zeal. The seventh nominated councillor who was not an M.P. was the 'loyalist' judge John Rolle.[3] His appointment was recommended with that of two other judges, Oliver St John and John Wylde. Both were M.P.s, but until June 1651 they took voluntary advantage of a Commons resolution of October 1648 disqualifying judges from attending parliament. The refusal of six of the twelve high court judges to serve after Charles's execution was a grave blow to the government, which hastened to protest its concern for the 'fundamental laws' and to ensure the uninterrupted continuation of judicial proceedings.[4] The appointment of eminent lawyers to the Council of State was another illustration of the Rump's determination to secure respectability in the eyes of the legal profession. St John's inclusion on the council was especially significant, even though he rarely attended it. His opposition to the purge and the execution, and his dislike of military intervention in politics, were widely known,[5] and his scruples, combined with recurrent ill-health,[6] restricted his role in the Rump. Behind the scenes, however, he was a prominent member of the 'royal independent' group which had broken with the parliamentary radicals in 1648 and which Cromwell was anxious to reconcile to the Commonwealth. St John was the only member of the group to sit in the Rump, but the

[1] SP 23/5, fo. 49.   [2] SP (e.g.) 23/5, fos. 51, 56, 62^v.   [3] Cf. above, p. 47.
[4] Gardiner, *History of the Commonwealth and Protectorate*, i. 9.
[5] *The Case of Oliver St. John* (1660), esp. pp. 3–5, 10, 12. The political philosophy of St John and his allies is admirably described in Pearl, 'Oliver St. John and the "Middle Group" ', and 'The "Royal Independents" ', *passim*.
[6] B.M., Add. MS 10,114, fo. 32; *Mercurius Politicus* 3–10 Apr. 1651, p. 713, 10–17 Apr. 1651, p. 725; *Several Proceedings* 22–29 Apr. 1652, p. 2094.

others, the most prominent of whom were Nathaniel Fiennes, John Crewe (like Fiennes briefly imprisoned at the purge), Sir John Evelyn, William Pierrepoint and St John's cousin Samuel Browne, remained close to him and to each other. Fiennes, Crewe and Pierrepoint signed warrants of the Army Committee in March 1649, a month after the Commons had ordered the exclusion of non-rumpers from its committees.[1] If ever Cromwell were to undo the events of December 1648–January 1649, it was the 'royal independents' whom he would have to approach, and it was through St John that he would have to approach them. But for the loss of two pages from the diary of John Harington, a friend of St John's who did not sit in the Rump, we should probably be able to learn much more than we can of the activities of the 'royal independents' in the earlier Rump period; but the pages which do survive provide telling evidence of their importance later on.[2]

St John was not alone among Cromwell's intimate friends in both opposing the developments of December 1648 and January 1649 and securing appointment to the council. Sir William Armyne, Sir William Masham and Sir Gilbert Pickering, 'conformist' M.P.s who enjoyed Cromwell's trust, were almost equally significant appointments. Other 'conformists' chosen included Alexander Popham, Robert Wallop and Philip Lord Lisle, men of pronounced conservative views, extensive landed wealth, and limited political stature. By contrast, industrious and prominent regicides like John Blakiston, John Carew and Thomas Chaloner were not appointed. It is thus easy to understand the dissatisfaction with the council's composition felt by 'those that pretended merit in destroying the former government'. Twenty 'revolutionaries', fourteen of them regicides, did admittedly secure nomination, including Cromwell, Scot, Ludlow, Marten, Grey of Groby, Mildmay, Lisle, Harrington, Ireton and Harrison. Yet these men could hardly have been omitted from the list of nominees. In the middle of February 1649, when so many 'conformists' had either yet to return to the Rump or yet to exert their full influence within it, the 'revolutionaries' enjoyed a clear majority of the most active and energetic rumpers. The representation accorded them on the council, although flattering enough if compared with their percentage of the Rump's total membership, was in fact a serious setback. Their frustration, however, was self-inflicted. Scot's nominating committee was almost as 'revolutionary' a body as could have been appointed. No doubt it was sub-

---

[1] SP 28/66, fos. 461, 465 (Army Committee warrants bound in 1650 collection).
[2] Cf. below, pp. 277–8.

jected to pressures from other members, not least from Cromwell, but its list of candidates, like the readmission to the House of the 'conformists', is clear evidence of the readiness of the 'revolutionaries' to welcome back their more lukewarm colleagues to positions of influence. Rather than remain an isolated and embarrassingly small minority, they committed the singularly human error of looking for friends. Only when the vital decisions had been taken did they wake up to, and vent ineffectual discontent at, their tactical defeat.

When the committee's nominations were brought before the House, Marten unavailingly opposed the choice of Pembroke and Salisbury. The only other formal challenge to the list of nominees was more successful, indicating the Rump's lingering resentment against Pride's Purge and its determination to confine power to civilian hands. What seems to have been an attempt to exclude all army officers from the council failed, and Fairfax, Skippon, Cromwell and Sir William Constable, all army leaders who were also M.P.s, were duly elected; but the House overruled the committee's nomination of Ireton and Harrison, the officers most responsible for the purge. The only two members of the nominating committee not included on its list of proposed councillors, Holland and Robinson, were appointed in their stead. Ireton's omission rebounded on the army's opponents. He responded to the slight by demanding that elected councillors be required to swear full approval of the judicial proceedings against Charles I and of the abolition of the House of Lords. At first the Rump agreed to his proposal, which seemed fatally to have damaged Cromwell's policy of conciliation. Only nineteen of the forty-one elected councillors were prepared to take Ireton's oath. Fortunately for Cromwell, however, the refusal of the other twenty-two, who included the peers, the judges, and all but one of the 'conformist' M.P.s appointed, was couched in terms so obsequious and so flattering to the government as to make clear their willingness to bargain for a milder oath. They drew the line only at retrospective vindication of events from which they had deliberately kept clear: the peers declined to sanction the abolition of the House of Lords, while Whitelocke, playing safe as ever, ingeniously discovered that he could hardly 'fully approve' the proceedings against the king since, not having attended the High Court of Justice, he did not know what those proceedings had been.

The split among the councillors over Ireton's oath led Cromwell to instigate delicate negotiations between the subscribing and the non-subscribing members which worked to the latter's advantage. On 22 February he proposed to parliament an alternative oath, which would require councillors to declare only their willingness to 'adhere to this present parliament in the maintenance and defence of the public liberty and freedom of this nation as it is now declared by this parliament'. The proposal, coming at the very time when the most committed 'revolutionaries' were rebelling against the return to parliament of so many 'conformists', provoked one of the most bitter debates of the Rump period. Heselrige and Vane, both of whom had declined Ireton's oath, came to Cromwell's support. So did Algernon Sidney, who argued that Ireton's test 'would prove a snare to many an honest man, but every knave would slip through it'. Lord Grey of Groby 'took great exceptions to this', claiming that Sidney 'had called all those knaves' who had taken Ireton's oath; 'upon which', Sidney subsequently recalled, 'there was a hot debate, some defending, others blaming what I had said'. Marten was able to restore the peace, but not before Sidney had earned from the radicals a personal animosity for which he was to suffer two years later. Vane, too, achieved lasting unpopularity among some rumpers by his support of Cromwell's strategy. Eventually Ireton and Marten demanded the restoration of a retrospective clause, but their motion was defeated by thirty-six votes to nineteen, Heselrige and Sir William Masham leading the opposition. As a concession to republican sentiment a substitute clause was inserted, requiring councillors to agree to 'the settling of the government of this nation for future in the way of a republic without king or House of Peers'. This, however, proved only a minor setback which the hitherto non-subscribing councillors did not scruple to overcome. Through Cromwell's initiative a council was thus formed over half of whose members had declined to endorse the events which had brought the Rump to power.[1]

The creation of the council, which was modelled on the Committee of Safety and the Derby House Committee of the 1640s, and which had much in common with the Privy Council of the early Stuarts, was not an especially innovative step.[2] Until May 1649, when its sessions

[1] C.J. (MS) xxxiii, pp. 732–4; C.J. 16 Feb. 1649; Whitelocke, *Memorials*, ii. 536; SP 25/62, pp. 2–4; B.M., Add. MS 37,344, fo. 264; Blencowe, *Sydney Papers*, pp. 238–9. (Gardiner's account (*History of the Commonwealth and Protectorate*, i. 6–7) is a little misleading.) The MS Journal contains much information not in the printed version about the struggle over the council's composition.

[2] The army's printed reform programmes of 1647 and 1648 had envisaged the creation of councils of state: Gardiner, *Constitutional Documents*, pp. 320, 368.

were transferred to Whitehall, the council continued to meet at Derby House. It quickly settled to a routine, meeting in the afternoon of each week-day and occasionally, in times of urgency, holding additional sessions in the early morning before parliament assembled. Instructions by the House to the council, and reports by the council to the House, were major and frequent features of day-to-day politics. The council established in February 1649 was authorised to hold office for a year, 'unless it were otherwise ordered by parliament': the Rump, evidently, had already decided to sit well beyond the deadline of April 1649 set by the army. There were annual council elections throughout the Rump period, a procedure which enhanced the House's control over the executive. The Rump, so sensitive in its early stages on the subject of 'single persons', at first instructed the council to operate without a president. Common sense soon prevailed, Bradshaw, who enjoyed considerable influence in the weeks after the king's execution, filling the presidential office. Throughout the Rump period he attended council meetings with astonishing and unrivalled diligence. Whitelocke, always critical of the failings of less eminent lawyers, complained that Bradshaw, whose job as chairman was 'only to gather the sense of the council, and to state the question', 'seemed not much versed in such businesses', and 'spent much of their time in urging his own long arguments'.[1] Certainly Bradshaw had his enemies, and he eventually lost his job as president when a monthly rota system, sharing the office among a number of councillors, was introduced.

The council was given responsibility by the Rump for the execution of all business relating to defence, the army, the encouragement of trade, and foreign policy; and a blanket clause permitted it to 'advise and consult of any thing concerning the good of this Commonwealth'. The subordination of executive to legislature was nevertheless heavily stressed, more so, perhaps, than the press of business made advisable. Certainly the council, which like parliament was overworked and which came to rely increasingly on the work of its sub-committees, frequently displayed impatience at the slow pace at which the Commons proceeded. In the main, however, the boundaries of the two bodies' spheres of influence were understood and respected on both sides. Conflicts between parliament and council were rare, if only because the council displayed no more unanimity than did parliament. Politicians defeated at council meetings were able to challenge the council's

[1] Whitelocke, *Memorials*, ii. 552, 558.

decisions when they were brought before the House.[1] It is possible that the council, during its first meetings, saw a role for itself as the government's policy-making body,[2] but if so its illusions were soon dispelled. There were only two important occasions thereafter when the council was permitted to exceed the bounds of its office, the first in May 1649, when the Leveller mutiny made haste imperative and when the council called on the House to reach a decision on fresh elections, the second in a period of intense parliamentary in-fighting in the following month, when the radicals sought to take advantage of their relative numerical strength on the council to press the House into pursuing policies of social reform. The council's responsibility for foreign policy gave it much room for manoeuvre, but here again it was quickly established that all major decisions must have the House's approval. Only in the summer of 1652, when parliament and council quarrelled over negotiations with the Dutch ambassadors, did the two institutions clash head on.

If the House exercised a jealous control of its executive arm, it was nevertheless the council which provided much of the day-to-day initiative of government. Its resolutions could be opposed in parliament, but they were rarely superseded by alternative policies. The composition of the council was thus of considerable importance, and it was the council, as much as the House, which provided the political base of what Whitelocke called the 'juncto' which shaped government policy.[3] The term 'juncto' may be a little misleading, implying perhaps both a cohesion and an exclusiveness never achieved by the leading members of the government, who frequently opposed each other in parliament. There can be no doubt, however, who those leaders were, or about their broad agreement, created as much by daily habits of communication as by initially shared assumptions, on a general political strategy. At the hub, of course, was Cromwell, who despite his long absences in Ireland and Scotland continued to communicate with and to influence the other leaders. The position of Vane and Heselrige at the 'well-head' of the government has already been stressed.[4] Scot's importance would be equally hard to overestimate. Heselrige and Scot, indeed, have been portrayed as the joint rulers of the Rump, at least from 1651. To describe them so is slightly to exaggerate both their

[1] Cf. Gardiner, *History of the Commonwealth and Protectorate*, i. 8–9.
[2] Thus see below, p. 186.
[3] B.M., Add. MS 37, 345, fo. 80ᵛ.
[4] Above, pp. 66–7.

importance and their cooperation: they seem to have become an 'inseparable combine' only after the parliament's dissolution. When they did join forces in the Rump, however, they were a formidable pair.[1] Barely less important was Richard Salwey, whose political outlook was so similar to Cromwell's, and who had the confidence of Scot, Heselrige and Vane.[2] The juncto was completed by men whose cooperation with Cromwell, like that of Vane and Scot, was enhanced by personal and often by family friendship: St John, Sir William Armyne, Sir Gilbert Pickering, Sir William Masham, Whitelocke, and even Ireton, whose acceptance of the moderating policies pursued by the new government is one of the most obscure but also one of the most important political developments of 1649.[3] It is difficult to say exactly what any of these men wanted, and it is doubtful whether they themselves knew. Heselrige's political principles, beyond a zealous concern to protect parliamentary privilege, are virtually unfathomable. What all members of the juncto shared, however, was a determination to keep the Rump in being, to restore a sense of political stability, to emphasise the moderation and respectability of the new regime, and to play down its revolutionary origins. The desire to broaden the base of the government's support, and to dissuade presbyterians from joining hands with royalists, informed all their major decisions. Levellers, parliamentary radicals, royalists and politically recalcitrant clergymen were the chief obstacles to the implementation of the juncto's policies, and the juncto, if it was united by little else, was united in its resolution to overcome those obstacles. In the earlier Rump period, differences of opinion among the leading rumpers were for the most part submerged beneath the weight of business and the daily problems of survival. When the royalist threat eased, differing viewpoints came once more to the surface, and the juncto began to break up; until then, however, it was the juncto which shaped the broad policies, and set the tone, of the Rump government.

It was as well that the new regime had such capable men at the helm.

[1] Trevor-Roper, *Religion, The Reformation and Social Change*, pp. 358–60; Gardiner, *History of the Commonwealth and Protectorate*, ii. 10; *C.J.* e.g. 2 May, 11 Dec. 1649, 4 Jan. 1650, 1 Apr. 1651, 8 July 1652; below, p. 256. But cf. *C.J.* 10 June 2, Oct. 1651.
[2] See e.g. *C.J.* 14 May 1649, 23 Feb. 1650; SP: 23/7, pp. 11, 14, 90; 23/9, fos. 11ᵛ, 19, 32ᵛ, 35, 43ᵛ; Clarke MS xx, fo. (14); Mayer, 'Inedited letters', pp. 187, 192.
[3] The influence and cooperation of these men pervade the evidence for the Rump period as a whole; but some impression of the ties between them can be gained from *Original Letters . . . addressed to Oliver Cromwell*, pp. 8, 11, 16, 17, 19, 21, 24–6, 40, 41, 43, 48, 76, 84, 85; Abbott, *Writings and Speeches*, i. 707, ii. 315, 329, 397. On Vane's importance see also Rowe, *Sir Henry Vane the Younger*, pp. 139–90.

The inauguration of republican government took the rumpers into uncharted political territory, where policies had rapidly to be improvised, adjusted and revised. It may even be misleading to suggest that the government, at least before Dunbar, had any long-term policies at all. Tossed and buffeted by crisis after crisis, it instinctively turned to the ways of moderation and conciliation, making use of whatever instruments came to hand. Short-term programmes were designed to meet short-term needs, but in general the leading rumpers, in the earlier stages of their rule, did not so much formulate policies as clutch at straws. Out of the fluid situation of early 1649 there emerged a political institution which, in retrospect, we can isolate from the Long Parliament before it and call the Rump. In retrospect we can see, too, that the government's behaviour followed consistent patterns; yet these rarely amounted to preconceived or clearly defined programmes. As Professor Roots has written, the Rump was 'a government regarded from the start as a stop-gap, a mere expedient, never an experiment'.[1] It was also a government which, much of the time, did not know whether it was coming or going.

[1] Ivan Roots, *The Great Rebellion 1642–1660* (1966), p. 138.

10

THE PURSUIT OF RESPECTABILITY,
FEBRUARY–AUGUST 1649

Cromwell and Ireton were described by Whitelocke as 'very cheerful, and . . . extremely well pleased' on the Saturday evening of 24 February.[1] Their shared contentment at this stage is an interesting pointer to Ireton's change of mood, for Cromwell, as an advocate of moderation, had every cause for satisfaction. The benches of the Commons had filled remarkably in the course of the previous week, and the obstacles to the creation of a broadly based Council of State had been overcome. On the 24th, at one of its first full meetings, the council repaid Cromwell's efforts by giving notice of its moderating intentions, deciding that the government's first concerns should be a reduction of taxation and a general amnesty. These subjects were discussed in the Commons on the same day, when there were even 'some motions made' for the Earl of Warwick to be added to the council.[2]

Yet Cromwell's pleasure in his achievement was short-lived. On the 23rd the House had called a halt to the readmission of M.P.s; and in late February and early March the new ship of state found itself in troubled waters. The main problem was the revival of political unrest in the army, prompted by 'a dangerous petition set on foot in London, carried on by some discontented persons, some of whom are in the army'. On 26 February Lilburne presented a sharp petition to the House, attacking both the Council of Officers and the Council of State. On 1 March a further petition, drawn up by eight troopers, and equally critical of what Lilburne called 'new chains discovered', was brought before the officers. The army leaders acted swiftly, urging the House to end free quarter and to proceed with the sale of dean and chapter lands in order that arrears might be paid.[3] On 2 March the

---

[1] Whitelocke, *Memorials*, ii. 540; Gardiner, *History of the Commonwealth and Protectorate*, i. 7.
[2] *C.J.* 24 Feb. 1649; *C.S.P.D.* 1649–50, p. 18; *Perfect Occurrences* 23 Feb.–2 Mar. 1649, p. 860. Cf. *Perfect Summary* 5–12 Feb. 1649, p. 35.
[3] Gardiner, *History of the Commonwealth and Protectorate*, i. 29–36; *Kingdom's Weekly Intelligencer* 20–27 Feb. 1649, p. 1271; *Clarke Papers*, ii. 190–2; *Perfect Occurrences* 16–23 Feb. 1649, p. 864.

Council of Officers warned the Rump that although 'we have hitherto been very tender in reminding you of any further particulars in order to the peace and settlement of the Commonwealth, or army, lest by that means we should either hinder or distract your proceedings', their patience was not inexhaustible. Their petition, confining itself to military rather than political matters, was elsewhere respectful enough. It probably represented an attempt by the officers, who increasingly found themselves driven by Leveller disaffection into tacit submission to parliament, to isolate the Levellers by appeasing the rest of the troops. Certainly parliament chose to interpret the petition as a gesture of goodwill.[1] Yet the Rump could not afford to ignore the army's political concerns indefinitely. As the parliamentary newspaper *The Moderate Intelligencer* warned, 'if the workmen differ, the building is not like to go on so fast, nor to be made so strong, as otherwise it might'.[2] The admonition went unheeded by the Levellers, and the cashiering of five of the eight recalcitrant troopers, found guilty of attempted mutiny, provoked further demonstrations of disaffection in the army.[3] Matters were made worse by the behaviour of Henry Marten and Lord Grey of Groby, who between them had organised the resistance in parliament to Cromwell's bridge-building after the king's execution. Both men were achieving popularity among the lower-ranking officers, some of whom were said to want Grey as Lord General, and Marten as Lieutenant General, of the army. Marten and his regiment seem to have been instrumental in the spring of 1649 in provoking popular disturbances in Hampshire and perhaps elsewhere.[4]

After the imposition of restrictions on the Rump's membership on 23 February, parliamentary attendances began to fall sharply. Only thirty-two members voted in a division on 5 March. There was a thin House again on the 9th, and on the 10th the Commons failed to secure a quorum. On the 17th rumpers were ordered to attend daily, but to little effect.[5] Many members who had reappeared in February had now withdrawn once more; some of them soon returned, but others stayed

---

[1] *The Petition of the General Council . . . for the taking away of Free Quarter* (1649), esp. pp. 4–5, 14–15; Whitelocke, *Memorials*, iii. 544, 545.

[2] *Moderate Intelligencer* 22 Feb.–1 Mar. 1649, p. 1920.

[3] The Leveller unrest in the spring and early summer of 1649 is described by Gardiner in his *History of the Commonwealth and Protectorate*.

[4] Carte, *Original Letters*, i. 225, 229; *Mercurius Pragmaticus* 27 Feb.–5 Mar. 1649, p. 8, 13–20 Mar. 1649, p. 4; *Clarke Papers*, ii. 212–13. Cf. *Perfect Occurrences* 13–20 July 1649, p. 1184; *Perfect Diurnal . . . , Armies* 16–23 July 1649, p. 9; *Kingdom's Faithful Scout* 20–27 July 1649, p. 216; *The Moderate* 13–20 Mar. 1649, p. 372.

[5] *C.J.* 5, 17 Mar. 1649; Whitelocke, *Memorials*, ii. 548, 552.

away for a matter of months or even longer. A smallpox scare in London early in March cannot have helped,[1] but there were other reasons for the desertions, principally the Leveller troubles and the acrimonious debates on the fate of five royalists condemned to death by the High Court of Justice. To the dismay of many rumpers, the sentences on three of the five were confirmed by the House on 8 March.[2] Bitterness was increased by the final debates on the bills for the abolition of kingship and of the House of Lords. The government, Whitelocke noted at this time, was rent by 'most threatening divisions' and 'animosities'. By 12 March, the Leveller threat was reducing the government to a state of panic.[3]

The shaken parliamentary leadership responded to the growing sense of crisis by emphasising before the world the respectability of its intentions. On 1 March Whitelocke had begun work on a declaration in defence of the execution of the king and the inauguration of the new government. It eventually passed the House on the 17th, the same day as the act abolishing kingship. Even though certain rumpers, probably Marten and Chaloner, made the declaration 'much sharper', it remained a notably defensive document, recounting in familiar terms the tyrannous traits of Charles I, appealing to the sentiments which had formerly united the Long Parliament in opposition to him, and coming close to apologising for the fact that parliament had been 'necessitated' to undertake 'the late alterations in the government'. The Rump's respect for law, its reluctance to offend foreign states, and its determination to end free quarter were emphasised, and the declaration ended with a remarkably gentle request for the acceptance of the new regime.[4] The Rump also discussed at this time the issue, restored to the limelight by Leveller unrest, of its own tenure of power. 'It was much pressed to set a time for dissolving', perhaps within twelve months, perhaps by the end of April 1650; 'but most of the House disliked to set a time, as dangerous'. The Rump did, however, promise to terminate its rule 'so soon as may possibly stand with the safety of the people', and it was resolved that 'after this House hath settled the business touching the navy, monies, and free quarter, this House will take into

---

[1] B.M., Add. MS 37,344, fo. 269ᵛ.

[2] Whitelocke, *Memorials*, ii. 547; *Memoirs of Colonel Hutchinson*, pp. 273–5.

[3] Whitelocke, *Memorials*, ii. 553–4, 555, 557.

[4] *Ibid.* ii. 554, 555; B.M., Add. MS 37,345, fo. 267&ᵛ; *C.J.* 14, 16, 17 Mar. 1649; *The First Part of the Last Will . . . of . . . Pembroke* (1649); James Harrington, *The Censure of the Rota upon Mr Milton's Book* (1660), p. 5. The declaration, which was also published in foreign languages, is in Cobbett, *Parliamentary History of England*, iii. 1292–1304.

consideration the matter touching the equal distribution of the next representatives'.[1] This announcement, allowing ample scope for delay, also introduced the tactic, which the Rump was to find so useful, of insisting that the issue of fresh elections could only be discussed once the Leveller demand for the redistribution of seats had been met.

Leveller disaffection, which not only endangered army unity but delayed plans for the expedition to Ireland, became increasingly serious in the spring and early summer. The activities of Winstanley's Diggers on St George's Hill, and appalling reports of starvation in the north, strengthened fears of popular insurrection. On 28 March Lilburne and his fellow Leveller leaders were brought before the Council of State, which committed them to the Tower. On 17 April, when the choice of the regiments to serve in Ireland was announced, it became clear that many of the troops were determined not to cross the Irish Channel until their grievances had been met. On 18 April a petition on behalf of the imprisoned Leveller leaders, attracting a huge number of signatures, impressed the Rump sufficiently to elicit a relatively mild response: 'the parliament will yet exercise patience towards you, conceiving that divers well meaning men may [have been] deluded into your miscarriages'. 'By this forbearance', it was hoped, 'such may come to see their own error.' On 19 April, however, John Warren, preaching before the Rump, warned that 'that which men call liberty is often our bondage'; and other Leveller representations to parliament received short shrift. When a Leveller petition was presented by some women on the 24th, the House 'desired them to go home, and look after their own business, and meddle with their housewifery'.[2] If Leveller wives could be safely ignored, however, Leveller husbands could not. On 27 April the trooper Richard Lockyer was shot for attempted mutiny, but once again harsh measures succeeded only in provoking wider unrest. On 1 May there appeared a revised version of Lilburne's *Agreement of the People*, evidently designed, like other of Lilburne's ventures of 1649, to appeal to his former friends in the Rump against the officers' treatment of the army dissidents. In the following fortnight disaffection turned to outright mutiny, crushed by Fairfax and Cromwell only after a brief but dramatic military campaign in the Cotswolds. Thereafter the Levellers were a broken force, but the threat

---

[1] Whitelocke, *Memorials*, ii. 555; *Impartial Intelligencer* 14–21 Mar. 1649, p. 21; *Kingdom's Weekly Intelligencer* 13–20 Mar. 1649, p. 1295; *C.J.* 16 Mar. 1649; Gardiner, *Constitutional Documents*, pp. 386–7.

[2] *Perfect Occurrences* 13–20 Apr. 1649, p. 952; J. Warren, *The Potent Potter* (1649), p. 20; Whitelocke, *Memorials*, iii. 20, 21, 22.

which they had presented in May 1649 should not be obscured by their relative impotence thereafter.

The Leveller disturbances strengthened the Rump's inclination towards moderation. They had a similar effect, if such were needed, on Cromwell, who towards the end of March found himself under pressure from his fellow officers to take command of the Irish expedition. He was reluctant to do so, fearing lest his absence might imperil his political achievements of the previous two months: 'I think there is more cause of danger from disunion amongst ourselves than by any thing from our enemies.'[1] On 28 March, when the Leveller leaders were brought before the Council of State, he was fiercely critical of Lilburne and his colleagues. According to Lilburne, Cromwell told the council that

you have no other way to deal with these men but to break them . . . [or] they will break you; yea, and bring all the guilt of the blood and treasure shed and spent in this kingdom upon your heads and shoulders; and frustrate and make void all that work that, with so many years' industry, toil and pains you have done, and so render you to all rational men in the world as the most contemptiblest generation of silly, low-spirited men in the earth to be broken and routed by such a despicable, contemptible generation of men as they are; and therefore . . . I tell you again, you are necessitated to break them.

Although some of these phrases sound authentically Cromwellian, others seem suspiciously Lilburnian. When Lilburne's statements can be checked against other evidence they usually appear to be reliable, but it is curious that Ludlow, who according to Lilburne came to his defence at the council, is not listed in the council's order-book among the councillors present at the meeting. Lilburne's statement that a proposal to grant the Leveller leaders bail was defeated by only one vote is therefore likewise suspect.[2] What is beyond doubt is Cromwell's determination to crush the Levellers, a task to which he devoted much of his energy in the weeks which followed.

The Leveller problem was magnified by the threat from Ireland. On 30 March Cromwell, submitting to the arguments of his fellow officers, agreed to take command of the Irish expedition, although some members of the Rump, which had come to depend on his guidance, may have doubted the wisdom of the appointment. Cromwell's eventual enthusiasm for the expedition was, as he admitted, not unmixed with 'carnal' – and, indeed, singularly astute – calculation. If there

[1] Abbott, *Writings and Speeches*, ii. 36–9.
[2] Haller and Davies, *The Leveller Tracts*, p. 204; SP 25/62, pp. 125–7.

was one thing which could be relied upon to unite the majority of Englishmen, it was hatred of the Irish and the Scots. These barbarous races were the enemies of the nation rather than merely of the Rump, and campaigns against them offered the government its best hope of securing the tolerance, if not the support, of presbyterian opinion in England. In Cromwell's words,

I had rather be overrun with a Cavalierish interest than of a Scotch interest; I had rather be overrun with a Scotch interest than an Irish interest . . . the quarrel is brought to this state, that we can hardly return unto that tyranny that formerly we were under the yoke of . . . but we must at the same time be subject to the kingdom of Scotland, or the kingdom of Ireland, for the bringing in of the king. Now that should awaken all Englishmen, who perhaps are willing enough he should have come in upon an accommodation, but not [that] he must come from Ireland or Scotland.[1]

Cromwell's determination to appease English presbyterians was soon to become still more evident. In April he launched a major political initiative which, although unsuccessful in the short term, had a lasting effect on Rump politics. He urged in parliament that 'the presbyterian [church] government might be settled, promising his endeavours thereto . . . he likewise moved that the secured and secluded members might again be invited into the House'. A group of clergymen, led by Stephen Marshall, Philip Nye and Joseph Caryl, all of whom had taken exception to the purge and the execution, was dispatched into the city of London to negotiate with both political and religious presbyterians. One of the tactics they adopted was to remind purged M.P.s that presbyterians, as much as rumpers, could expect to pay the price for past misdeeds if Charles II were restored. Clement Walker objected that Cromwell's promise of a presbyterian church counted for little when presbyterianism meant such different things to different people, and Cromwell would never have accepted a presbyterian settlement without at least a measure of toleration for the sects. Nevertheless, his gesture was a remarkable one.[2] It was no doubt connected with attempts made at the same time to secure a loan to the government from the city, the House assuring its potential creditors that

---

[1] Abbott, *Writings and Speeches*, ii. 38–9.

[2] Walker, *History of Independency*, ii. 57; Wood, *Athenae Oxoniensis*, ii. 236; *Brief Narration of the Mysteries of State*, p. 100. Gardiner (*History of the Commonwealth and Protectorate*, i. 64) and, still more, Abbott (*Writings and Speeches*, ii. 52–3) make curiously little of this episode. Walker, the chief source, was closely involved in the city presbyterian network, and he is unlikely to have invented a story implying that the tyrant regicide Cromwell was sympathetic to presbyterians. The story ties up with other evidence: see below, pp. 196–7.

the Irish enterprise would be conducted on behalf not merely of the Rump's interest but of the united Protestant interest, in which presbyterians of all kinds were involved.[1]

Cromwell's strategy made considerable headway in parliament. A declaration was drafted 'to settle religion according to presbytery, and a full maintenance to the ministers'. According to an army newspaper, 'the presbyterian government is to be wound up into one bottom, only an admission to be given to such other churches which profess the advancement of the gospel of Jesus Christ, that they may be free from disturbance'. Other accounts made less of the Rump's willingness to give protection to dissenters, and it is not clear precisely what the House intended. What is evident is that the declaration, had it been passed, would have firmly identified the Rump with the cause of moderation and respectability in religion. It was with the same end in view that the Rump earmarked sums of money for needy orthodox clergymen, and drew up a plan to give formal sanction to tithes until a more satisfactory solution to the problem of financing ministers were found.[2] *Perfect Occurrences*, the government's official mouthpiece, discreetly advertised the continuing good work of the presbyterian Assembly of Divines. It also published a letter, sent by a presbyterian minister in Yorkshire to two of the county's rumper M.P.s, which noted with pleasure that 'the parliament answers oft times with silence to such demands as would shake the foundations of church and state'. In consequence, 'the veil which did a little interpose to obscure our beholding of you is removed'.[3] Other developments in April also testified to the Rump's growing moderation. The House gave a further reminder of its opposition to military intervention at Pride's Purge by making an exaggerated fuss of a petition from Oxfordshire, which described the Rump as 'that remnant that God hath pleased to preserve to this day; and we may say, had there not been a remnant, we had been as Sodom and we had been as Gomorrah'.[4] On the 16th the Earl of Pembroke, whose candidacy had been 'cried up' almost immediately after the abolition of the House of Lords, made a triumphal entry into

---

[1] Gardiner, *History of the Commonwealth and Protectorate*, i. 40.

[2] *C. J.* 4, 17, 18, 20, 23, 25, 26, 29 Apr., 2, 18, 29 May, 6, 16, 22, 24, 25 June, 2, 6, 7 July 1649; Whitelocke, *Memorials*, iii. 8, 12, 26; *Kingdom's Faithful Scout* 6–13 Apr. 1649, p. 82; *Perfect Occurrences* 30 Mar.–13 Apr. 1649, pp. 934, 963; *Impartial Intelligencer* 11–18 Apr. 1649, p. 56; *Kingdom's Weekly Intelligencer* 3–10 Apr. 1649, p. 1313; *Perfect Weekly Account* 4–11 Apr. 1649, p. 440; *Perfect Diurnal . . . Parliament* 2–16 Apr. 1649, pp. 2410, 2423; *The Moderate* 3–10 Apr. 1649, p. 398.

[3] *Perfect Occurrences* 30 Mar.–25 Apr. 1649, pp. 925, 986, 990, 1051.

[4] *C. J.* 6 Apr. 1649.

the House after his return in a by-election as a commoner.[1] Meanwhile the House's active membership was growing once more, as members who had withstood the scrutiny of the Committee for Absent Members began to resume their seats. On the 28th, 'for the better settling of peace in the nation, and giving satisfaction to the late king's party', Whitelocke followed the wish of both parliament and Council of State by drafting a bill of pardon, 'to put into oblivion all rancour, and evil will, occasioned by the late troubles'.[2]

The Leveller mutiny dictated the course of Rump politics in the latter part of April and in the first half of May. Heselrige, whose influence within the government was already firmly established, now took impressive command. He found timely support for his policies from his old friend Edmund Prideaux, the Rump's attorney-general, and from Ireton. There were reports that Ireton was upset by, and that he quarrelled with Cromwell over, the suppression of the Levellers,[3] but he was closely involved in the moves taken by both parliament and army to crush them. Heselrige's strategy, with which Ireton seems fully to have concurred, was two-edged. First, by persuading the House to pass a severe treason act, he provided the government with a stick with which to beat the Levellers. Secondly, he sought to isolate them from the army rank-and-file by promoting measures suggestive of parliament's responsiveness to peaceable reforming idealism. An act was passed to take off free quarter; attention was given to the woes of the poor, of prisoners for debt and of soldiers' widows; the mooted act of pardon was held out to Levellers as well as royalists; and government supporters, emphasising the differences between the parliament preceding Pride's Purge and the parliament left behind by it, urged the soldiers to count their blessings.[4] Two issues which were long to embitter relations between army and parliament were also discussed by the House with a view to placating the troops: the claims of soldiers on

---

[1] *Perfect Occurrences* 16–23 Feb. 1649, p. 861; *H.M.C.R. De Lisle and Dudley*, vi. 586; *The Moderate* 10–17 Apr. 1649, p. 424.

[2] Whitelocke Letters (Longleat) x, fo. 5&ᵛ; B.M., Add. MS 37,344, fos. 285ᵛ, 286; *A Modest Narrative of Intelligence* 21–28 Apr. 1649, p. 32; *Moderate Intelligencer* 26 Apr.–2 May 1649, pp. 2013–14; *Perfect Occurrences* 6–13 Apr. 1649, p. 959; *Perfect Diurnal . . . Parliament* 23–30 Apr. 1649, pp. 2246–7.

[3] See e.g. Walker, *History of Independency*, ii. 180.

[4] Firth and Rait, *Acts and Ordinances*, ii. 110–18; *England's Moderate Messenger* 7–14 May 1649, p. 21; *Perfect Summary* 14–21 May 1649, p. 147; *Overton's Defiance of the Act of Pardon* (1649), p. 7; W. Bray, *Innocency and the Blood of the Slain Soldiers and People* (1649), pp. 9–10; *C.J.* 4, 9, 14, 15 May 1649; *Perfect Occurrences* 11–18 May 1649, pp. (1039)–1042; *Kingdom's Faithful Scout* 18–25 May 1649, pp. 134–5.

the public faith, and the fate of royalists to whom the army, but not parliament, had granted amnesty under articles of war. On 9 May Heselrige brought from the Council of State a list of proposals requiring the House's immediate attention. Among them were measures for the payment of soldiers' arrears, the treason act, and 'a declaration for putting a period to this parliament'.[1] Next day a group of six prominent lawyers, consisting of two Chief Justices, two Commissioners of the Great Seal, Attorney-General Prideaux and Serjeant Thorpe, met at Whitelocke's chamber and 'perused two bills, one concerning the settlement, and the other to declare what shall be treason'. The bill 'concerning the settlement' was that declaring England to be a Commonwealth and free state.[2] The question of the Rump's dissolution, a subject on which Leveller feelings ran especially high, was debated for four hours on the 11th and for 'many hours' on the 15th, when a committee was set up under Vane's guidance to discuss the matter further.[3]

Also on the 15th, however, came news of the decisive defeat of the Levellers at Burford. Discussion of the dissolution issue was immediately dropped, and most of the other proposals designed to placate the army were likewise soon forgotten. So complete was the change of mood that on the 17th, two days after the news of the Leveller defeat, the House felt able to devote most of its attention to a property dispute involving one of its members, Sir John Danvers.[4] Vane's committee on elections did not report until January 1650, and in the meantime the pro-government newspaper *A Modest Narrative* instructed its readers in the dangers of holding elections before the Commonwealth had achieved widespread popularity.[5] After the defeat of the Levellers the government felt free, for the first time since its inception, of a sense of imminent crisis. For the next three weeks or so, cheered further by

[1] For the cooperation and prominence of Heselrige, Prideaux and Ireton at this time, and for the measures debated and the policies pursued, see Walker, *History of Independency*, ii. 197–8; *C.J.* 6, 10, 11, 12, 13, 18, 20, 23, 25, 27, 30 Apr., 1, 4, 5, 8, 9, 12, 14, 15, 16, 17, 19, 22, 23, 28 May 1649; Firth and Rait, *Acts and Ordinances*, ii. 110–18, 120–1; *Mercurius Militaris* no. 3 (1649), pp. 26, 30–1; J. Nayler, *The Foxes Craft Discovered* (1649), p. 4; T[homas] M[ay], *An Anatomy of Lieut. Col. John Lilburne's Spirit and Pamphlets* (1649), p. 11; Haller and Davies, *The Leveller Tracts*, p. 205; Whitelocke, *Memorials*, iii. 31; *The Moderate* 1–8 May 1649, pp. 9–10; *Perfect Diurnal . . . Parliament* 30 Apr.–7 May 1649, pp. 2481–2; *England's Moderate Messenger* 7–14 May 1649, p. 21; *Perfect Summary* 14–21 May 1649, p. 147.   [2] Whitelocke, *Memorials*, iii. 31.
[3] *C.J.* 1, 4, 5, 11, 15 May 1649; Whitelocke, *Memorials*, iii. 33; *Overton's Defiance of the Act of Pardon*, p. 7; *Modest Narrative* 5–12 May 1649, p. 48; *Moderate Intelligencer* 10–17 May 1649, p. 2046; *Mercurius Pragmaticus* 1–8 May 1649, p. 4.
[4] *C.J.* 17 May 1649.
[5] *Modest Narrative* 5 May–2 June 1649, pp. 41, 49, 65–6; Gardiner, *History of the Commonwealth and Protectorate*, i. 59.

what was probably the first spell of hot weather for two years,[1] it displayed a buoyant optimism and self-confidence.

Its morale was heightened further by a happily timed series of political successes. A purge of the Rump's enemies in the government of the city of London, initiated in the previous December, was now completed by the dismissal of the mayor, Abraham Reynardson. Supported by the city's presbyterian network, he had embarrassed parliament by refusing to proclaim the abolition of monarchy. The new city leaders welcomed prominent rumpers and army officers to a lavish banquet held to celebrate the Levellers' defeat. John Owen and Thomas Goodwin, invited to preach before the Rump, were asked to thank the Lord 'for reducing the Levellers', a request with which they readily concurred.[2] On 22 May Blake achieved the Commonwealth's first notable naval success, winning a skirmish with part of Rupert's pirate fleet. M.P.s who had either boycotted parliament since the purge, deserted it in February or March, or met initial resistance at the Committee for Absent Members, continued to return to the House. The Council of State, now able to anticipate with confidence a full term of office, moved from its improvised headquarters at Derby House to more imposing surroundings at Whitehall. Finally, parliament was at last able to complete its judicial bench by satisfactorily replacing the six high court judges who had resigned after the execution of the king.[3]

The Rump's treatment of the Levellers was watched carefully by presbyterians of all kinds as a pointer to the respectability or otherwise of its intentions. The firm suppression of the uprising thus considerably enhanced the government's standing. The Leveller defeat also left the Rump more prepared than ever to advance moderating and conciliatory policies. As the army newspaper *The Kingdom's Faithful Scout* observed, '*Roundhead* and *Cavalier* are almost forgotten, by reason of the new invented terms of *Independent* and *Leveller*.'[4] Certainly the independent congregations of the city of London, whose political fortunes were intimately connected with those of the Rump,[5] displayed brazen delight at the Levellers' humiliation. The opportunity

[1] Harleian MS 454, fo. 95ᵛ. The summer of 1648 had been one of the worst of the century: see Underdown, *Pride's Purge*, p. 106.
[2] *Perfect Summary* 28 May–4 June 1649, p. 200.
[3] Gardiner, *History of the Commonwealth and Protectorate*, i. 38–9, 57–8, 87.
[4] *Kingdom's Faithful Scout* 25 May–1 June 1649, p. 121. Cf. *Perfect Diurnal ... Parliament* 21–28 May 1649, p. 2530.
[5] J. E. Farnell, 'The usurpation of honest London householders: Barebone's Parliament', *E.H.R.*, lxxxii (1967).

for reconciliation between presbyterians and independents was widely appreciated. In June, for example, the Rump newspaper *A Modest Narrative* reported that 'the presbyterian party' of Gloucester

have lately had a disputation touching the present government of the discipline of the church of England; at which conference they declared great affection to the covenant, obedience to the parliament, but utterly detested against heresy, and the proceedings of Lieut. Col. John Lilburne and his party.

There were similar reports from elsewhere, and proposals for estab-lishing common ground between presbyterian and independent divines.[1]

The new political mood was energetically fostered by the govern-ment. A week after the Leveller defeat Heselrige departed for New-castle, there to mourn the death of a son;[2] but he left only after parliament had passed a letter, brought into the house by Vane, 'tending to a composure of things' with Scotland, and particularly with the less rigid of the Scottish presbyterians. *Perfect Occurrences* reported on the Rump's behalf that there was also a 'very great probability of a com-posure of things in England among those that fear God. And several things are in agitation thereunto' – including a proposal to release Thomas Cawton, a London presbyterian minister under arrest since February for preaching before the mayor a sermon in favour of Charles II, and the award of 'more liberty than they had' to the five secluded M.P.s who remained in prison. Further, 'the regiments of the army are purging from Levellers, Cavaliers etc. Now there is good hope of peace, if malice and madness prevent not that good which is now hoped for. And the members of parliament come in daily, so that the House is much increased, and are very unanimous.' Early in June, according to the same newspaper, 'a motion was made in the House concerning what some ministers had said [against the government] in their pulpits, and some named, and the place, etc. But the House being at this time upon a way of composing, and not aggravating, that debate was presently laid aside.'[3] The royalist *Mercurius Pragmaticus*, identifying the disaffected ministers as Love, Jenkins and Juggard, reported that

[1] *Modest Narrative* 9–16 June 1649, p. 87; *Kingdom's Faithful Scout* 25 May–1 June 1649, p. 141; *Impartial Intelligencer* 30 Aug.–6 Sep. 1649, p. 211; Grey, *Vox Coeli*, p. 9; Ellis Bradshaw, *An Husbandman's Harrow* (1649); *Mysterium Religionis Recognitum* (1649), esp. pp. 13–14; *Perfect Occurrences* 22–29 June 1649, p. 1093.
[2] *Impartial Intelligencer* 6–13 June 1649, p. 119.
[3] *C.J.* 22 May 1649; *A Declaration of the Parliament concerning . . . Scotland* (1649), pp. 25–6; *Perfect Occurrences* 18–25 May 1649, p. 1059, 1–8 June 1649, p. 1088.

when punitive action was suggested the rumpers John Gurdon, Miles Corbet, Thomas Atkins and Isaac Pennington

were all pleased to oppose this motion, because they have long been employed in the city among the presbyters, to accomplish the good work of a brotherly union; and said it would be too severe a proceeding to call the brethren in question, since that the chief of them having swallowed the great bait of tithes, it would be an easy matter to catch them, and the rest of the gudgeons.[1]

The names of the M.P.s singled out by *Mercurius Pragmaticus* give his story an authentic ring. Corbet, Atkins and Pennington were deeply involved in city politics, and Gurdon was one of the Rump's foremost advocates of religious presbyterianism. Atkins and Pennington were close political allies, while Corbet and Gurdon, who were cousins, likewise often acted in unison.[2]

In another way, too, the conflict with the Levellers strengthened the movement towards conservatism. It was becoming clear that the Levellers no longer commanded much support among other radicals. In April Hugh Courtenay, overcoming doubts about the Rump, agreed with his fellow radical millenarian Morgan Lloyd that Lilburne's tactics were 'exploded by all upright men', a view evidently shared by the leaders of the Anabaptists.[3] Still more important, the Leveller uprising elicited from regiment after regiment declarations of unanimous support for the Rump's continued existence and authority.[4] The army newspaper *The Kingdom's Faithful Scout*, hitherto occasionally critical of the Rump, now found itself supporting parliament's attempts to reconcile presbyterians and independents.[5] Clement Walker, usually reliable on such matters, recorded that the Leveller uprising had prompted a scheme to raise seven new regiments, 'which they call presbyterian regiments, and shall be raised by presbyterian com-

---

[1] *Mercurius Pragmaticus* 5–12 June 1649, p. 68. The 'great bait' was the House's proposal to give official confirmation to tithes, a plan widely interpreted as a design to secure the loyalty of presbyterian ministers: see e.g. *Mercurius Pragmaticus* 31 July–7 Aug. 1649, p. 8; *Perfect Weekly Account* 1–8 Aug. 1649, pp. 563–4; *Mercurius Politicus* 1–8 Aug. 1650, p. 132; Whitelocke, *Memorials*, iii. 159; *Brief Narration of the Mysteries of State*, p. 92; *A Gag to Love's Advocate* (1651), p. 19.
[2] *C.J.* 14 Apr. 1649; SP 19/8, p. 64; *C.C.A.M.*, pp. 155, 821; Holmes, 'The Eastern Association', pp. 3, 73–4; above, p. 31.
[3] N.L.W., MS 11,439D, fo. 17; *The Humble Petition of . . . Anabaptists* (1649), pp. 4–5.
[4] *The Declaration . . . of . . . Whalley and . . . his Regiment* (1649); *The . . . Remonstrance of . . . Overton's Regiment* (1649); *The Humble Representations . . . of . . . Cromwell's Regiment* (1649); *Perfect Diurnal . . . Parliament* 4–11 June 1649, pp. 2560–1, 2569–70; Whitelocke, *Memorials*, iii. 42.
[5] *Kingdom's Faithful Scout* 25 May–1 June 1649, p. 141.

manders.'¹ Although the officers retained their reforming ambitions after the suppression of the mutiny, they were always careful henceforth to convey them to the House with respect and caution. Whatever reservations the army leaders may have had about the quality of the Rump's membership, they kept them, until the battle of Worcester in September 1651, mainly to themselves.

The taming of radicals outside the House was paralleled within it. When Lilburne, who had retreated to the north after his tactical defeat in December 1648, returned to Westminster after the execution of the king,

> that which perplexed me most was that I found promotion and promised hopes of gain had very much changed the principles, and cooled the zeal of three or four of my familiar acquaintance and friends, that not long before had been the valiantest, stoutest, ablest champions for England's liberties and freedoms that I know in the nation.²

Lilburne's nose for betrayal was always excessively strong, and it is arguable that some of his friends, rather than double-crossing him, had merely dissociated themselves from his contempt for political realities. It is nevertheless clear that the experience of power had dulled the reforming enthusiasm of some of the parliamentary radicals. Among the rumpers with former Leveller connections, Cornelius Holland, now Cromwell's 'present darling', was the most blatant, if also the least surprising, defector.³ More significant was the behaviour of Marten and Grey of Groby. Although they retained their interest in reform, they were now evidently prepared to abandon their more outrageous tactics. The House gave generous consideration to the financial embarrassment of both Marten and Grey of Groby at a critical moment during the Leveller unrest of April 1649, and the Leveller leaders believed that the two men had been bought off. Marten's reputation for integrity in such matters makes this unlikely, but the Rump's generosity doubtless encouraged his growing inclination to work for reform from within.⁴ Alexander Rigby, another of the Levellers' former allies, energetically promoted reform measures in the Rump until June, but his parliamentary activities then ceased abruptly with his

---

¹ Walker, *History of Independency*, ii. 197–8.
² Lilburne, *Legal, Fundamental Liberties*, p. 65.
³ Lilburne, *An Impeachment of High Treason* (1649), pp. 7, 9; Haller and Davies, *The Leveller Tracts*, pp. 210, 414.
⁴ Carte, *Original Letters*, ii. 273; *Overton's Defiance of the Act of Pardon*, pp. 6–7; *Perfect Diurnal . . . Parliament* 18–25 June 1649, p. 2604. See also *C.C.C.*, pp. 1505, 1506, 1830.

rapid promotion first to the post of serjeant-at-law and then to that of Baron of the Exchequer. He retained Lilburne's affection thereafter, but by August the Leveller leader thought that he and Rigby were 'now positively engaged in two contrary interests'.[1] Also in August, at a time when army proposals for reform were being presented to the House, Edmund Ludlow was to be found on a hunting expedition on Bulstrode Whitelocke's estate, eager for the chase and informing his companions that 'his gelding on which he rode was as good as any in England'.[2] Ludlow, with Marten, consistently endeavoured to protect the Levellers from those rumpers who were mercilessly keen to crush them,[3] but the months after Charles's execution exposed the disparity between his aims and those of Lilburne. The death of John Blakiston in May deprived the Levellers of another possible source of parliamentary support. So long as the royalist threat remained, it was sound policy for even the most radical rumpers to eschew the divisive luxury of Leveller affiliation. By the time the royalists were defeated, such parliamentary enthusiasm as there had ever been for Leveller doctrine had become permanently dimmed. Radicals with Leveller connections were not the only 'revolutionary' M.P.s to temper their zeal in and after the summer of 1649. Sir Gregory Norton, for example, who had been one of the most committed 'revolutionaries' of December and January, and who had consistently attended the House in the months thereafter, lost interest in politics after the Leveller defeat, making only occasional appearances in parliament during the remainder of the Rump period. Perhaps he realised that there were no policies left for him to pursue. The regicide John Jones recognised, as did his friend and fellow radical millenarian Thomas Harrison,[4] that the implementation of the saintly programme must await the defeat of the royalists. In Jones's view, the earlier Rump period was to be seen as 'a time of ignorance whereat God winked'.[5]

Yet if radical enthusiasm was depleted by the Leveller humiliation, it was by no means extinguished; and the festive mood of Rump politics after the suppression of the mutiny soon passed. Despite the optimism

[1] *The Moderate* 3–10 Apr. 1649, pp. 398–9; *Perfect Weekly Account* 30 May–6 June 1649, p. 507; *C.J.* 5, 20, 23 Apr., 1, 5, 18, 21, 24, 25 May 1649; J. Lilburne, *Strength out of Weakness* (1649), pp. 22–3; *A Letter of . . . Lilburne to Mr. John Price* (1651), p. 3.
[2] B.M., Add. MS 37,345, fo. 7ᵛ. Cf. Whitelocke Letters (Longleat) x, fo. 28: Ludlow to Whitelocke, 11 Sep. 1649.
[3] See e.g. *C.J.* 25 Oct. 1649.
[4] Above, p. 74.
[5] N.L.W., MS 11,440D, p. 122: Jones to Lowry Gwyn, 25 May 1653.

of the Rump's newspapers, and despite its 'out-cry for a fresh supply of members',[1] attendances in the House failed to attain consistent respectability. Although some fifty M.P.s either reappeared in or were first admitted to the Rump in May, June or July, fewer than ten of them remained in London for long or played any regular part in Rump politics. It was the 'revolutionaries' who continued to provide the active core of the Rump's membership, and on 9 June two regicides, Harrison and Hutchinson, acted as tellers for a motion to refuse re-admission to all those 'who shall not first acknowledge and assert the just authority of this House, in making the act for erecting a High Court of Justice for trying and judging the late king'. Francis Allen and Richard Salwey were the tellers against. The battle between 'revolutionaries' and 'conformists', which had been so heated in February, was being fought again. Radical motions always fared best when attendances were thin, and there was a small house on the 9th. Although the motion was defeated, only five votes separated the two sides. The Rump agreed to an alternative scheme providing for the formal expulsion from parliament of all M.P.s who failed to satisfy the Committee for Absent Members by the end of June. Recruiter elections were to be held in the constituencies thus made vacant. Yet this plan, too, was never implemented. Cromwell, possibly sensing a threat to the coalition he had created, persuaded the House to abandon the scheme and to countenance instead a third proposal. The Rump was to push through pressing business and then to hold an adjournment, perhaps for six or seven weeks, perhaps for as long as three months.[2]

The reasoning behind the adjournment scheme is unclear. Low parliamentary attendances evidently provided the main motive, and it seems to have been believed, somewhat optimistically, that they would improve once members with duties on judicial circuit were free to resume their seats.[3] The adjournment proposal had first been mooted at the height of the Leveller crisis in May, and it may have been thought advisable to suspend the Rump's sittings until the army for Ireland had been safely shipped off.[4] Perhaps M.P.s, unused to acting as full-time statesmen, simply wanted a holiday in which to resume contacts, and

---

[1] *Mercurius Pragmaticus* 12–19 June 1649, p. 4.

[2] *C.J.* 9 June 1649; Gardiner, *History of the Commonwealth and Protectorate*, i. 86; Abbott, *Writings and Speeches*, ii. 79–80; Underdown, *Pride's Purge*, pp. 272, 295; *England's Moderate Messenger* no. 3 (1649), p. 22; and see *Modest Narrative* 9–16 June 1649, p. 88, and *Moderate Intelligencer* 5–12 July 1651, p. 2151.

[3] *Perfect Summary* 9–16 July 1649, p. 105.

[4] *England's Moderate Messenger* no. 3, p. 24.

explain government policies, in their constituencies.[1] There was a more partisan reason, however, for favouring an adjournment, which would have given the reforming radicals time and opportunity to draft detailed social legislation. Cromwell, for all his moderating intentions, had never lost sight of the need for godly reformation, and he may have felt at this time that the movement towards conservatism was going too far. Nothing more consistently destroyed the various initiatives undertaken by Cromwell during the Interregnum towards moderating the revolution's course than his own realisation that they might succeed. It was certainly the most enthusiastic of the reforming rumpers, Henry Marten, who was first to take advantage of the adjournment proposal, by drawing up a list of measures to be completed before the adjournment and of others to be prepared during it. The former included the act of pardon, specific proposals for law reform, and the repeal of statutes against 'pretended sectaries': the latter consisted of proposals to evaluate tithes throughout the country (so that they could be abolished and replaced by some alternative method of financing ministers), to advance a general programme of law reform, and to reach a decision on the dissolution of the Rump and the election of a new parliament.[2]

Of the measures for immediate consideration, only the bill for religious toleration, which had timely support from a petition by the Council of Officers, received serious attention in the Rump.[3] The others were comfortably evaded. By 12 July it was reported that 'the House being full enough to sit, it is probable they will not adjourn so soon as was expected they must'. Towards the end of July the benches of the Commons began, albeit temporarily, to fill once more. Eleven members were readmitted on the 23rd, and it was expected that others would soon be given permission to resume their seats. Their return, it was believed, would 'much more fill the House'. On 25 July it was accordingly announced that the proposed adjournment 'requires no great expedition'. It never took place.[4]

The ease with which Marten's reform plans were by-passed in the summer of 1649 is instructive. His defeat can be seen most clearly in the

[1] Cf. *Mercurius Pragmaticus* 25 Sep.–1 Oct. 1649, p. 5.
[2] *C.J.* 22 June 1649.
[3] *Perfect Diurnal . . . Armies* 9–16 July 1649, pp. 1–2; *Perfect Occurrences* 6–13 July 1649, p. 1101; *Moderate Intelligencer* 28 June–5 July 1649, p. 2128; Whitelocke, *Memorials*, iii. 65.
[4] *Perfect Summary* 9–16 July 1649, p. 105; *Perfect Diurnal . . . Parliament* 16–23 July 1649, pp. 2668–9; *C.J.* 23 July 1649; *Kingdom's Faithful Scout* 20–27 July 1649, p. 215.

outcome of the Rump's debates at this time on legal and religious reform.

In response to Marten's adjournment scheme, the House agreed that during the recess a committee should draw up measures for 'the regulating of the proceedings in law, and courts of justice and equity, for preventing the tediousness of suits, and abuses burdensome to the people'.[1] These were grand words, but they produced little action. Only one measure of law reform was passed in the summer of 1649, and this, an act for reform of the debt law, fell far short of the hopes of those who had pressed for it.

The debt law had long aroused strong passions, but never more so than in 1649.[2] Creditors were legally entitled to procure the indefinite imprisonment of debtors unable to meet their obligations. Consequently the prisons were crowded with men who had no hope of release, and whose squalid and impoverished condition, aggravated by the cruel treatment accorded them by extortionate gaolers, provoked strong resentment. The Rump was always aware of the social implications of proposals for reform of the debt law. It combined its discussions of the subject with debates on other problems of poverty, and in the spring of 1649 held out the prospect of reform to those who, it was feared, might be susceptible to the appeal of the Levellers.[3] A committee to investigate the debt law had been set up on the day after Charles's death. Dominated by radicals, it was headed by Cornelius Holland, Henry Marten, Grey of Groby, Holland's son-in-law and fellow Leveller associate Henry Smyth, the reforming lawyer John Lisle, and Cromwell, who after Dunbar was to urge the Rump to 'hear the groans of poor prisoners'. Also on the committee was John Anlaby, who sat on few other Rump committees but who was to demonstrate in Barebone's Parliament his concern to secure reform of the debt law. Alexander Rigby, although not on this committee, later supported the proposed reforms.[4]

Pressure for a bill to relieve poor prisoners for debt was sustained throughout endless discussions, both in the House and at committees, in the spring and summer of 1649.[5] The preachers of the fast sermons

[1] *C.J.* 22 June 1649.

[2] See e.g. *Perfect Diurnal . . . Armies* 30 July–6 Aug. 1649, p. 2686.

[3] *C.J.* 18 Apr., 26 May, 22, 28, 31 Aug. 1649, 27 Apr. 1652; *Kingdom's Weekly Intelligencer* 5–12 June 1649, pp. 1386–7; *Weekly Intelligencer* 27 Apr.–4 May 1652, pp. 1–2.

[4] *C.J.* 31 Jan., 20 Apr., 26 May, 5 June 1649, 20 July, 17 Aug. 1653; Haller and Davies, *The Leveller Tracts*, p. 420; Abbott, *Writings and Speeches*, ii. 325.

[5] *C.J.* 10 Mar., 18, 20 Apr., 23, 26 May, 4, 5, 22, 23 June, 7, 13, 16, 17, 23, 27 July, 8, 21,

delivered in the House on 29 August had 'the cries of poor prisoners . . . commended to us in papers, to be recommended to your grave considerations'. Yet the bill which passed parliament six days later showed how much sting the House had removed from the bill. As the Leveller newspaper *The Moderate* complained, 'it differs much from that which was first presented, having received many alterations in the most effectual parts thereof'.[1] The original version, although severe towards those who might try to defraud their creditors, had abandoned the whole principle of imprisonment for debt: the act of September 1649 preserved it. Two relatively minor amendments passed by the House showed where its sympathies lay. The measure was at one point to have provided for the release of all poor prisoners who could prove that the value of their goods did not amount to more than £10. In debate, the Rump reduced the sum to £5. Secondly, the provisions of the bill were denied to former royalists. As so often in the Rump, the question of the treatment of Cavaliers split the radical vote. Much more important, however, was the House's decision – which removed much of the measure's point – to tack on to the bill a proviso confining the privileges conferred by the act to those who were already in prison. The act made possible the release of a number of prisoners; it made no provision for those imprisoned in the future.[2]

There is clear evidence that the House's established lawyers provided the core of the opposition to the passage of a more comprehensive measure. A pamphleteer of August 1649 described the manoeuvres surrounding the bill, and the accuracy of his account is borne out by the *Journal of the House of Commons*. Whenever Marten, Rigby, or their reforming allies got hold of the bill, the pamphleteer recorded, speedy progress was made. Repeatedly, however, they were confronted by the Rump's conservative lawyers: by Nicholas Lechmere, in whose hands the measure 'was like to have been buried in everlasting silence'; by Robert Reynolds, who by 'unnecessary delays spun out the length and time of the last term in promises and repromises, protractions and rejoinders'; and by Bulstrode Whitelocke, who intervened decisively

22, 28, 30, 31 Aug., 4 Sep. 1649; *Perfect Diurnal . . . Parliament* 16–23 Apr. 1649, p. 2448; *Impartial Intelligencer* 20–27 June 1649, p. 134; *Kingdom's Weekly Intelligencer* 27 Feb.–6 Mar. 1649, pp. 1273–4, 22–29 May 1649, p. 1375, 5–12 June 1649, pp. 1386–7; *Perfect Weekly Account* 21–28 Mar. 1649, pp. 426–7; *Kingdom's Faithful Scout* 23 Feb.–2 Mar. 1649, p. 37, 22–29 Aug. 1649, p. 207; *Perfect Occurrences* 3–10 Aug. 1649, p. 1215. The newspapers are unusually informative on this subject.
[1] William Cooper, *Jerusalem Fatal to her Assailants* (1649), p. (34); *The Moderate* 28 Aug.–4 Sep. 1649, p. 691.
[2] *C.J.* 30 Aug., 4 Sep. 1649; Firth and Rait, *Acts and Ordinances*, ii. 240–1.

in a debate of 17 July. Finally, the bill's progress was impeded, 'as Mr. Lechmere affirmed', by the Speaker, who came to the defence of his elder brother John Lenthall, Marshal of the King's Bench. Impressive charges of corruption in the administration of the prisons under his command were later to be brought against John Lenthall.[1] The House, responding to army pressure in January 1653, ordered his interrogation on the same count.[2]

Nevertheless, the agitation for relief of poor debtors did achieve its temporary successes. The act of September 1649 was followed by similar measures in December 1649, April 1650 and April 1652, each designed to extend the duration, or to improve the equity, of the previous act.[3] All four acts were passed without preambles, a tactic which the Rump, to the annoyance of radicals outside the House,[4] frequently adopted when passing legislation for which it had little enthusiasm; but at least the acts were passed, in however tepid a form. By contrast, another proposal for reform of the debt law was wholly unsuccessful. Although the condition of impoverished prisoners had long aroused protest, there was a second target of radical criticism which, noted in the *Heads of the Proposals* in 1647,[5] had thereafter attracted growing attention, until by the Rump period it was seen as an almost equally grave issue. While poor men could not pay their debts, there were also wealthy debtors who would rather remain in gaol than pay up, and who, by suitably generous treatment of their gaolers, secured a comfortable existence for themselves while thwarting their creditors.[6] Criticism of this abuse may have had more profound social implications than the proposal to relieve poor prisoners, especially now that peers and M.P.s were liable to arrest. Marten must have enjoyed the letters which, as chairman of the committee investigating the debt question, he received on behalf of Lady Arundel, Lord Lovelace, the Earl of Portland and others, begging him to 'be as careful for debtors as for creditors'.[7] They need not have worried, for Marten, himself heav-

[1] *The Prisoners Remonstrance* (1649), esp. p. 4. See also *H.M.C.R. Loder-Symonds*, p. 396; *Tuesday's Journal* 31 July–7 Aug. 1649, p. 19; *Moderate Intelligencer* 26 July–2 Aug. 1649, p. 2181; *Perfect Weekly Account* 30 May–6 June 1649, p. 507.
[2] Veall, *Popular Movement for Law Reform*, pp. 16, 144; Clarke MS xxiv, fo. 107. Cf. *C.J.* 17 Aug. 1653.
[3] Firth and Rait, *Acts and Ordinances*, ii. 321–4, 582.
[4] Chidley, *Remonstrance to the valiant and well-deserving Soldier*, p. 13.
[5] Gardiner, *Constitutional Documents*, p. 325.
[6] Niehaus, 'The issue of law reform', p. 82; Veall, *Popular Movement for Law Reform*, p. 17.
[7] *H.M.C.R. Loder-Symonds*, p. 388.

ily indebted,[1] apparently showed no interest in the bill 'for relief of creditors' discussed by the Rump in the summer of 1649. A number of extremely wealthy men, some of them knights, were on the lists of indebted prisoners during the Rump period,[2] and there was clearly strong opposition in the House to the proposal to make liable to confiscation the estates of debtors who refused to meet their obligations. The pro-government newspaper *The Moderate Intelligencer* suggested that the creditors' bill required 'much more consideration' than the debtors' bill, 'as the making men poor is more than the relieving those not able to pay'.[3] Dropped in June 1650, it was revived but once more abandoned in July 1651. In April 1652 it appeared in a new form, when the Hale commissioners proposed that only those owing debts under the value of £4 should be covered by the act. Even this tame proposal was dropped at about the time the fourth bill for relief of debtors sailed easily through the House.[4]

Two other bills for law reform introduced in 1649 were accorded at best desultory treatment before the battle of Worcester. The first was for the registration of land transactions, the bill 'touching recording conveyances'. The main advocate of the measure was Daniel Blagrave, who seems to have looked to it for an office for himself. It took him five months to get it brought into the House, and even then he needed the cooperation of the conservative lawyer Roger Hill. The proposal was discussed at some length in January and February 1650, but thereafter interest declined, despite a reference to the issue in the House's resolutions on law reform in October 1650 and an attempt to revive discussion in the summer of 1651.[5] The other measure, for the probate of wills, had a similarly lukewarm reception in the House. The first (somewhat tame) version of the bill, supported by Roger Hill and opposed by the radicals Rigby and Holland, was rejected on 18 May 1649. It had provided for '24 courts to be in England, in nature with the old, commonly called spiritual, in every which court, a doctor of the civil law was to sit, who was to have his register etc.; this were to have before them the probate of wills'. Soon afterwards a measure less

[1] Williams, 'Political career of Henry Marten', pp. 435–7.
[2] Veall, *Popular Movement for Law Reform*, p. 17.
[3] *Moderate Intelligencer* 26 July–2 Aug. 1649, p. 218.
[4] *C.J.* 18 Oct., 28 Nov., 21 Dec. 1649, 11 Mar., 6 Apr., 14, 23 May, 6, 18 July 1650, 3 July 1651, 22, 27 Apr. 1652; John Lord Somers, *A Collection of scarce and valuable Tracts*, vi. 184.
[5] *C.J.* 7 Aug. 1649, 25 Jan., 1, 5 Feb., 25 Oct., 1 Nov. 1650, 20 May, 8 Aug. 1651; Josten, *Elias Ashmole*, ii. 556.

reminiscent of the days of popery and the civil law was introduced, by which England and Wales were now to be divided into twenty-two regions. Marten opposed discussion of the bill even in this form, possibly because it was still insufficiently radical or because he regarded the bill for poor prisoners, with which the bill for probate of wills was competing for attention, as more urgent. Although the adjournment scheme of June 1649 included a proposal for a probate act, the measure was subjected to endless delays and postponements.[1]

If advocates of law reform could take little comfort from parliamentary developments in the summer of 1649, religious radicals had equal cause for disenchantment. Marten's toleration bill was soon forgotten, as was his plea for the abolition of tithes. Instead, the Rump concentrated on legislation designed to enhance its standing with the orthodox ministry and to dissociate the government from radical demands. An act of June 1649, reserving £20,000 from the sale of dean and chapter lands to augment the incomes of needy clergymen, was clearly intended to strengthen rather than to challenge the tithe system.[2] By August, indeed, the Rump seemed more likely than ever to give its blessing to the presbyterian settlement of 1648. As the royalist newspaper *Mercurius Aulicus* noted ,'the juncto's votes run all for presbytery, so that some think the independent juncto will be turned again into a presbyterian parliament'. The same newspaper predicted that the five M.P.s imprisoned since the purge would be freed within a fortnight, and that if the Rump found 'their heat for monarchy abated' they would eventually be readmitted to the House.[3]

The release at this time of Thomas Cawton, the presbyterian minister under arrest since February for preaching on Charles II's behalf, gave colour to *Mercurius Aulicus*'s assertions. So, still more, did the reappearance in the House early in August of the declaration which had been drafted in April, and which had been frequently discussed thereafter, 'to settle religion according to presbytery, and a full maintenance to the ministry'. Seen by *Mercurius Pragmaticus* as an attempt to blunt the edge of presbyterian opposition to the government, the declaration sought to clear the regime of the 'unjust reproaches' which 'have been cast upon the parliament and particularly in reference to matters of

---

[1] *Moderate Intelligencer* 17–24 May 1649, p. 2055; House of Lords Record Office, Main Paper Series: 1649–50, fos. 81–91; Whitelocke, *Memorials*, iii. 36; *C.J.* 18 May, 22 June, 18, 23, 25, 27 July, 3, 4, Aug., 19 Dec. 1649, 18 Jan., 18, 23 Feb., 5, 11 June 1650, 10, 14 Jan., 14 May 1651.
[2] Firth and Rait, *Acts and Ordinances*, ii. 142–8.
[3] *Mercurius Aulicus* 14–21 Aug. 1649, pp. 3–4.

religion by such, who insinuate to the people that all thought is laid aside by the parliament by reason whereof popery is likely to take a deeper root than ever, and a door is opened to atheism, prophaneness, error and contempt of all piety and godliness'. On the contrary, it was the Rump's

> real intentions and . . . shall be their constant endeavour to advance religion in its purity, and to promote the sincere preaching and spreading of the gospel . . . And they will give all due encouragement and protection to all persons both who shall conscientiously serve and worship God in the purity of his ordinances and shall live peaceably and submissively under the present government.

Laws were promised for 'the suppressing of popery, superstition, idolatry, prelacy, atheism, and all manner of prophaneness', and there was to be a full maintenance for ministers from the sale of church and crown lands. Tithes were to be paid until a suitable substitute were found; and

> the public form of worship appointed by the directory and church government by presbyteries, and settled in several ordinances of parliament, are to be observed and put in practice throughout this Commonwealth of England and Ireland . . . which public form of worship and church government the parliament is resolved to give encouragement unto and to all the godly, religious and peaceable professors thereof.

At first the Rump seemed favourably disposed towards the declaration, which was brought into the Commons as a 'declarative ordinance', and which was described by a pro-government newspaper as an 'act' for 'payment of tithes'. The House passed 'the preamble declaring their resolutions for the propagation of the gospel, and establishing the presbyterian government, and the ministers to have sufficient maintenance'. But on the second day's debate, in a surprisingly thin House, parliament decided to leave aside the clause emphasising its determination to preserve tithes. By only the Speaker's casting vote, the passage committing the Rump to the presbyterian settlement was also rejected, despite a plea for its retention by two of the Rump's specialists in ecclesiastical legislation, Purefoy and Gurdon. The ordinance was eventually recommitted on the ground that it showed insufficient 'respect to tender consciences'.[1] No more was heard of it.

---

[1] Bodleian Library, Portland MS Dep. c. 175 (Nalson xxii), no. 58; *C.J.* 6, 7 Aug. 1649; *Mercurius Pragmaticus* 7–14 Aug. 1649, pp. 3–4; *Perfect Diurnal . . . Parliament* 30 July–6 Aug. 1649, p. 2685; *Perfect Occurrences* 3–10 Aug. 1649, p. 1213. The Portland MS, a draft of the declaration, contains a number of revealing deletions whose significance is open to various interpretations.

The parliamentary radicals, aided once more by low attendances, had once more held their ground; but their success inside the House was made possible by pressure from outside it. The army, at this time preparing to leave for Ireland, firmly reminded the Rump of its continuing hostility to religious presbyterianism. On 16 August the Council of Officers presented to the House, through the agency of Colonel Pride, a petition calling for the repeal of all statutes and ordinances 'whereby many conscientious people are molested, and the propagation of the gospel much hindered'.[1] Cromwell, again evidently anxious to restrict the swing towards presbyterianism, supported his officers with a farewell letter to the House, calling for an end to 'penal statutes that enforce the conscience[s] of honest conscientious men'.[2] Relations between the Rump and the leading officers had recently been strained, for early in August the House had tactlessly rebuked Colonel George Monck, later to become a prominent figure in Interregnum politics, for treating with the Confederate Catholics of Ulster. Monck's aim had been to break the dangerous alliance between the Catholics and Ormonde. In this he had evidently been supported by Cromwell, who was equally willing to court the Rump's less dangerous enemies in order to overcome the Irish threat, and who for that reason had recently made approaches to the former royalist Lord Broghil.[3] The army's resentment over the Rump's treatment of Monck seems to have been quelled, however, by the House's response to Cromwell's written request for an end to penal statutes. Discussion of the bill for religious toleration was revived on the day the letter was read. At the same time the House, to the dismay of presbyterian clergymen,[4] debated a proposal (never in fact implemented) to provide facilities in each county for the ordination of godly men unwilling to submit to the presbyterian service.[5] It was also in response to the army's valedictory proposals that the Rump instructed a committee on law reform to meet daily and to report with all speed. Now that the leading army officers were in Ireland, however, such gestures meant little. The reform proposals which had been debated as a concession to army pressure were soon allowed to languish.

---

1 *Kingdom's Faithful Scout* 10–17 Aug. 1649, p. 224.
2 Abbott, *Writings and Speeches*, ii. 104.
3 Gardiner, *History of the Commonwealth and Protectorate*, i. 95, 103–4.
4 See e.g. R. Bell (ed.), *Memorials of the Civil War: comprising the Correspondence of the Fairfax Family* (2 vols., 1849), ii. 99.
5 *C.J.* 21 Aug. 1649; Whitelocke, *Memorials*, iii. 91; cf. *Perfect Weekly Account* 15–22 Aug. 1649, pp. 571–2.

Cromwell sailed for Ireland on 13 August. He took care before leaving to raise the hopes of religious radicals, whom he encouraged not only by his letter to parliament but by private audiences. Yet the arguments advanced by the saints in these conversations had 'little success'.[1] Cromwell's departure marked the beginning of a period of prolonged political abstinence on his part which amounted to tacit approval of the moderating policies of the Rump's 'juncto', with which he remained in close touch. Firmly committed to the parliament's survival, he ignored complaints about its membership. 'I have heard computations made', he wrote to Lord Wharton at the beginning of 1650, 'of the members in parliament: good kept out, most bad remaining; it hath been so these nine years, yet what God has wrought. The greatest works last; and still is at work. Therefore take heed of this scandal.'[2] Between his departure for Ireland and the battle of Worcester, Cromwell showed himself in the main unwilling to interfere in the processes of parliamentary decision-making. Indeed, his failure to make 'more frequent addresses to the parliament' caused some offence.[3] He was evidently following his usual practice, in evidence again in 1653 and 1654, of patiently constructing a political assembly to his own specifications and then standing back in the hope that it would do his work without encouragement or interference.[4] Yet there was more to his strategy than this. When Cromwell delayed answering the Rump's 'invitation' early in 1650 to return from Ireland, the rumper Lord Lisle observed that 'there is some doubt of his coming, his interest, I believe, being in many respects to stay there'.[5] It is not clear what Lisle meant, but one inevitable consequence of Cromwell's absence was that his own political reputation became increasingly independent of the Rump's, a development which worked to his advantage in his relations with all parties. To presbyterians, he could appear as the man who had courageously advocated presbyterianism in April 1649 and who was now fighting on behalf of the united Protestant interest in Ireland. Among rumpers, his absence produced a tendency, increasingly marked as the government's fortunes slumped early in 1650, to regard him as a potential saviour.[6] His reputation was equally enhanced among radicals, both in the army, where he had returned to a full-time role as military

[1] *Original Letters . . . addressed to Oliver Cromwell*, pp. 58, 59.
[2] Abbott, *Writings and Speeches*, ii. 189.
[3] *Ibid.* ii. 321; *Original Letters . . . addressed to Oliver Cromwell*, pp. 40, 50–1.
[4] Trevor-Roper, *Religion, The Reformation and Social Change*, pp. 362–78.
[5] *H.M.C.R. De Lisle and Dudley*, vi. 472.
[6] Below, p. 226; Whitelocke, *Memorials*, iii. 183.

commander, and in the congregations. By sanctioning the Rump's survival, and by encouraging 'conformists' to return to it, he had placed himself in a potentially embarrassing position with those of his radical supporters who had regarded the execution of the king as merely the starting-point of godly reformation. Now, staying away from Westminster and smiting the heathen in both Ireland and Scotland, he could shine as divine instrument while doing no more to hasten the apocalypse than exhorting the Rump, in general terms, to take note of God's mercies. This policy earned him deserved mistrust, especially when he was suspected of reverting to his bad old ways of wooing the Scottish presbyterians, but in the main his martial exploits preserved him as the expected agent of sectarian and radical ambitions.[1] The willingness of reformers to be impressed by Cromwell's political postures, without looking too closely at his actions, is a remarkable tribute to his standing among them. Even a parliamentary radical like Ludlow gave an effusive welcome to Cromwell's vaguely worded assertion of reforming intent after the battle of Dunbar in September 1650.[2] The absence of the army officers in Ireland and Scotland, leaving the Rump free to develop its unrevolutionary tastes, was a major impediment to the hopes of reformers outside parliament. Cromwell's ability to retain their support, even when doing so little to advance their programme, played an important part in the containment of extra-parliamentary radicalism before the battle of Worcester.

1 *Original Letters . . . addressed to Oliver Cromwell*, pp. 18, 21, 29, 58, 82, 84; *H.M.C.R. De Lisle and Dudley*, vi. 485.
2 *Memoirs of Edmund Ludlow*, i. 254. Cf. Hill, *God's Englishman*, p. 125.

11

THE NADIR,
SEPTEMBER 1649–SEPTEMBER 1650

The departure of the Irish expedition freed parliament for a time from pressure to reform, although not from continuing reminders of the army's reforming concerns. It also deprived the government of Cromwell's guiding hand, which was to be sorely missed in the coming months. With Heselrige away in the north, the parliamentary leadership passed to Vane and Scot. Able as both men were, they missed Heselrige's powers of political manipulation and persuasion. They were left in command at a difficult time, for a series of reverses in September badly bruised the government's morale.

It was usual for parliamentary attendances to decline in the late summer and early autumn.[1] 1649 was no exception. Only fifty-six members can be shown to have taken their seats at any point during September, and only thirty-five and thirty-nine M.P.s respectively voted on the two occasions during the month on which the House divided.[2] John Moyle, five of whose seven Cornish colleagues had recently withdrawn from parliament to their native county, wrote from London urging them to return. He also expressed a hope that the House, in its present plight, might be persuaded to readmit members who had not sat since the purge: 'I verily believe that the parliament would most willingly receive into the House all such as could cordially own the parliament in that way which it now engageth of a free state.'[3] Such appeals had been tried before, however. The Rump had now to face the fact that its attempts during the summer of 1649 to increase its active membership had failed, partly because of radical opposition within the House, partly because so few of the latecomers to the Rump attended with any regularity, and partly because so few of the M.P.s absent since the purge showed any inclination to return. Renewed proposals for an adjournment, presumably until a time of the year

---

[1] Snow, 'Attendance trends and absenteeism', p. 304.   [2] C.J. 4, 12 Sep. 1649.
[3] Buller Papers, pp. 109–10; Folger Library, Add. MS 494, p. 165: Moyle to Bennett, 1 Sep. 1649.

when attendances were normally higher, were as usual resisted by a House anxious to retain control of the executive.[1] Adjournment, in any case, could only shelve the problem. With so few members present, there was little impetus for the formulation of detailed and urgently needed policies. Low attendances, so damaging to the government's self-esteem, undermined its claim to act as the representative body of the nation, and weakened both its hold on and its responsiveness to opinion outside parliament.

The obvious solution, which had been mooted in June and which attracted mounting support in September and the months which followed, was formally to expel all members who had not taken their seats since the purge and to hold recruiter elections to fill the seats thus left vacant. Yet the scheme had its drawbacks. Men who, like Cromwell, wished to rebuild the parliamentary party broken by the purge would lose the sole means available to them of rebuilding it: the only thing which the parliamentary party had in common, and which distinguished it from other people, was its membership of parliament. The more committed 'revolutionaries', who had fought so hard to limit the Rump's membership, were unlikely to agree to its expansion unless electoral qualifications were drawn up to ensure that only men with similarly radical views could be elected. 'Conformists', on the other hand, were unlikely to agree to such restrictions. Even if they did, the restrictions could only be enforced by military supervision, a prospect unwelcome to a parliament concerned to end military intervention in politics. Faced with this dilemma, the House characteristically discussed proposals for recruitment at considerable length and then did nothing about them. At various points during its tenure of power the Rump contemplated recruitment as a long-term possibility: rarely, if ever, did it consider it as an immediate one.

Low attendances were not the only problem to beset the Rump in September. 'We are hotly alarmed with the prince's landing at Jersey', wrote Vane on the 13th, referring to Charles II's preparations for participation in the Irish campaign.[2] There was growing evidence of royalist conspiracy in England. Three rumpers were among the members of the Hampshire county committee who believed that only their own vigilance prevented a major uprising in September, 'there appearing unto us such imminent dangers by the malignant parties

[1] *H.M.C.R. De Lisle and Dudley*, vi. 454; *Mercurius Aulicus* 21–28 Aug. 1649, pp. 12–13; *Moderate Intelligencer* 20–27 Sep. 1649, p. (2285).
[2] *H.M.C.R. Leybourne-Popham*, p. 30.

gathering together'.[1] There was more trouble from the presbyterian ministers in London, and early in the month the city divine Christopher Love was brought before a parliamentary committee. The interrogation was a fiasco: a 'rude company, in a tumultuous multitude' gathered at the door in Love's support, and the charge against him could not be proved.[2] There were new problems of foreign policy, too. Feelings in the unofficial piracy war with France had become so heated that late in August the French government had been driven to prohibit imports from England. Parliament responded in September by forbidding the admission to England of French wines and French woollen goods, and soon afterwards by sanctioning the issue of letters of marque to English ships wishing to challenge French pirates. Although neither government wished for open war, there were fears that it might prove unavoidable, a prospect which revived the ancient spectre of an alliance between France and England's enemies in Scotland. On the 19th came news of the expulsion of English merchants from Russia as a protest against the execution of Charles I; in consequence, it was reported, 'the merchant is grown malcontent' against the Rump.[3]

Most serious of all was the revival of unrest in the army. The Levellers, active once more, were helped by the absence of Cromwell and Ireton in Ireland. On 8 September there was a mutiny at Oxford. It was virtually the Levellers' last fling, but it seriously alarmed the Rump, as did rumours of an impending alliance between Levellers and royalists. The House repeated the tactics it had adopted in May, of trying to isolate the Levellers from the army rank-and-file by professing concern for the problems of poverty and for such matters as the needs of soldiers' widows. It also tried conciliatory tactics with Lilburne, arranging a series of meetings between M.P.s, army officers and Levellers 'for procuring a right understanding and making up all differences', and granting the Leveller leaders the liberty of the Tower. Lilburne's cultivated provocation, however, resulted in firmer measures, including the passage of the censorship act of 20 September.[4]

The army leaders remaining in England were likewise slow to crack

---

[1] SP 23/248, no. 69.
[2] *Mercurius Aulicus* 28 Aug.–4 Sep. 1649, p. 22; *Modest Narrative* 1–8 Sep. 1649, p. 184; *Moderate Messenger* 3–10 Sep 1649., p. 141; Whitelocke, *Memorials*, iii. 100.
[3] Whitelocke, *Memorials*, iii. 92, 107; Bell, *Memorials of the Civil War*, ii. 99.
[4] Whitelocke, *Memorials*, iii. 100, 101, 107; Bell, *Memorials of the Civil War*, ii. 102; *Perfect Occurrences* 7–28 Sep. 1649, pp. 1284, 1318; *Modest Narrative* 1–8 Sep. 1649, pp. 178, 182; *Kingdom's Faithful Scout* 14–28 Sep. 1649, pp. 246, 249; *Moderate Intelligencer* 6–13 Sep 1649, p. 2262; *Mercurius Pragmaticus* 11–18 Sep. 1649, p. (3); Gardiner, *History of the Commonwealth and Protectorate*, i. 164.

down on the Levellers, who were once more attracting support among the lower-ranking officers. The infection did not spread to the more senior officers, whose dismay at the prospect of social upheaval was becoming increasingly evident: the army newspaper *The Kingdom's Faithful Scout* observed at this time that 'The multitude are naturally desirous of novelty, and apt for every change, hoping for more than they should and enduring less than they ought . . . They consider not, that though they change their lord, their tenure is continued; and though they quit their old master, they are still in service.'[1] On 27 September the army kept a day of humiliation to lament the 'degrees of too much liberty' which had 'insensibly possessed some part of the army and many officers thereof'. 'It were well', a parliamentary newspaper tartly observed, 'if this had been done sooner.'[2] The Rump, for its part, spent most of the 27th debating its own rebuke to the disaffected, which took the form of a declaration almost certainly drawn up by Thomas Scot.[3] It was published on the 28th. Like the government manifesto of the previous March, which it much resembled, it was a singularly defensive document, emphasising the common ground which had united the parliamentary party in the 1640s and which, the declaration asserted, could now unite it once more. The 'sobriety and temperance' of the Rump's policies, and particularly of its religious policies, was emphasised. The government had 'continued those laws and ordinances that were already in force, for the good and furtherance of the work of reformation, in doctrine, worship, and discipline; and are still most willing to uphold the same, in order to suppress popery, superstition, blasphemy, and any manner of wickedness or prophaneness.' The declaration admitted that the rumpers 'do conceive themselves obliged' to 'remove and take away all obstructions and hindrances to the growth of religion, and power of holiness in the midst of us', and that they accordingly intended to repeal all such laws 'as they find penal and coercive in matters of conscience'; but the notion that the Rump was 'setting up and countenancing an universal toleration' was without foundation. Indeed, abuse of the liberty offered by the Rump would be vigorously punished. In wooing the Rump's passive enemies, or at least in urging them to remain passive, the document was strong in its criticism of the regime's active opponents; it attacked both Cavaliers and

[1] *Kingdom's Faithful Scout* 7–14 Sep. 1649, p. (249). Cf. *ibid.* 14–21 Sep. 1649, p. (241), and 21–28 Sep. 1649, p. 249; *Moderate Intelligencer* 6–13 Sep. 1649, p. 225.
[2] *Kingdom's Weekly Intelligencer* 25 Sep.–1 Oct. 1649, p. 1517.
[3] *C.J.* 26, 27 Sep. 1649; *C.S.P.D.* 1649–50, p. 319.

Levellers, attempted to prove collusion between them, and denounced the disaffected and still troublesome presbyterian clergy.[1]

Although the September mutiny had been crushed easily enough, the efforts of both army officers and M.P.s to stamp out Leveller agitation were unsuccessful. Feeling among the more junior officers also needed watching. On 11 October the Council of Officers, responding to demands from garrisons throughout England, decided to meet once a week to work out plans for law reform and for the abolition of tithes. Colonel Pride was, as usual, involved in the radical agitation.[2] On 25 October the government lost face when it failed to secure Lilburne's conviction for treason.[3] He was released early in November, but mutterings of Leveller discontent continued into December and January.[4] The rumper John Pyne, distressed by Lilburne's acquittal, wrote from Somerset on 17 November that 'I find his party to increase as well as insult and cry victory ... Now the soldier begins to grow discontented, being apt to turn Leveller, and the old deceitful interest of the presbyterian party begins to rejoice and practise their old designs.'[5] 'The times were licentious', observed Whitelocke of November 1649, 'and men took strange liberty to calumniate all in authority, and to clamour if they had not what themselves thought fit'.[6] In December, radical organisation in London secured the choice as common councillors of Colonel Pride and even of Lilburne, although the latter's victory was quashed by the Rump after a full day's debate.[7] Popular discontent against engrossers and excise-men reached alarming proportions, while early in 1650 the army newspaper *A Perfect Diurnal* provided a vehicle for radicals dissatisfied by the Rump's failure to act with due severity against its royalist opponents.[8] In these troubled times the government had one source

[1] Cobbett, *Parliamentary History of England*, iii. 1319–24; Gardiner, *History of the Commonwealth and Protectorate*, i. 173.
[2] *Perfect Occurrences* 5–12 Oct. 1649, p. 1348; *The Man in the Moon* 10–17 Oct. 1649, p. 210.
[3] Gardiner, *History of the Commonwealth and Protectorate*, i. 164–5.
[4] H.M.C.R. *De Lisle and Dudley*, vi. 466; Bell, *Memorials of the Civil War*, ii. 119.
[5] H.M.C.R. *Leybourne-Popham*, p. 51.
[6] Whitelocke, *Memorials*, iii. 100.
[7] Gardiner, *History of the Commonwealth and Protectorate*, i. 177–8; *Perfect Diurnal ... Armies* 17–24 Dec. 1649, p. 20; C.J. 26 Dec. 1649; Whitelocke, *Memorials*, iii. 133. Cf. *Several Proceedings* 2 Nov.–7 Dec. 1649, pp. 49–50, 66–7, 115–20; Journal of the London Common Council xli, fos. 18ᵛ–19.
[8] Whitelocke, *Memorials*, iii. 56; *Several Proceedings* 31 Jan.–7 Feb. 1649, pp. 257–8; *Man in the Moon* 6–13 Mar. 1649, pp. 367–8; *The Royal Diurnal* 11–19 Mar. 1649, p. 5; *Perfect Diurnal ... Armies* 28 Jan.–18 Mar. 1649, pp. 68, 74, 77, 109, 111, 127.

of comfort. Cromwell's task in Ireland had been lightened by an unexpected victory at Dublin before his arrival, a success which he compounded with his cruel but crucial victories at the strategic towns of Drogheda and Wexford. All historians mourn these dreadful massacres; all equally agree that Cromwell's attitude towards the Irishmen he slaughtered was no different from that of most of his countrymen. The Rump, certainly, showed no disposition to regret the price in life and suffering paid for victories which rescued it from a seemingly desperate situation. The temporary subsidence of the royalist threat, however, had the usual disadvantage to the Rump of encouraging radicals at home to express themselves more volubly.

Meanwhile the government remained plagued by problems of finance. The assessment act of March 1649 was due to expire in December, and parliament, still determined to broaden the base of its support, was anxious to reduce the monthly levy from £90,000 to £60,000 for the next six months. On 5 November, however, the Rump received from its Committee for Compounding a dispiriting estimate of the probable consequences of such action. Even if, as the committee suggested and as the House eventually resolved, the figure were reduced to £60,000 for only the second half of the six month period, parliament would still need to find more than £250,000 from other sources in order to procure 'the certain pay of the army'. The government was owed a larger sum than this from fines and compositions charged on royalist estates, but there was little hope of collecting more than a small proportion of it in the foreseeable future.[1] Turning to other possible sources of income, the Rump devoted much time in November to proposals for reforming the excise, but it was unable to overcome 'so much reluctance and averseness . . . in most of the nation to the paying of that tax'. The excise remained 'very far charged beforehand with very great sums of money'. Only in September 1650, after which the yield (as well as the unpopularity) of the excise seems to have increased considerably, did the Rump complete its plans for reform of the tax.[2] Meanwhile various attempts were made to improve the administration of other sources of government income, and in April 1650 the fee-farm rents were opened to sale. They proved to be popular purchases. Yet such measures merely tinkered

[1] SP 23/9, fo. 58&ᵛ; Firth and Rait, *Acts and Ordinances*, ii. 285–319.
[2] *H.M.C.R. Sutherland*, p. 180; *H.M.C.R. De Lisle and Dudley*, vi. 463; Firth and Rait, *Acts and Ordinances*, ii. 422–3.

with the problem. After the battle of Dunbar in September 1650 the government was still 'urgent for money', and in the autumn of 1650 it was obliged to increase the monthly assessment to the enormous sum of £120,000.[1] Finance was the unsolved problem which overshadowed Rump politics from beginning to end.

Although the government's attempts in November 1649 to reform its finances and to reduce taxation were unavailing, they testified to a renewed sense of vigour and purpose in parliament. The low attendances of the previous months had prompted a 'call' of the House to summon truant rumpers. The call had to be postponed because of the embarrassing failure of many sheriffs to issue the appropriate instructions to members in the localities, but attendances nevertheless rose appreciably in November.[2] They remained, by the standards of the Rump period as a whole, unusually high until February 1650. Most encouraging of all was the return of Heselrige, who had earlier been detained by his responsibilities in the north. Back at Westminster by 24 October, he played a decisive role in the House until leaving once more for Newcastle in April 1650. His influence in the House, if anything even stronger than in the previous April and May, was especially impressive between November and January. It was much needed, for the House's renewed energy, and the greater sense of security accorded the government by Cromwell's victories in Ireland, opened the way for further conflict in parliament.

Two opposing tendencies revealed themselves. On the one hand, the willingness of so many 'conformist' M.P.s to resume active membership at this time reflected a growing feeling that the policy of conciliation might now succeed. During the crisis of September John Moyle, writing to one of the Cornish M.P.s who had declined to sit since the purge, and urging him to return to Westminster, had warned that 'there is nothing that doth more embolden the malignant . . . than this, that we which professed ourselves for the parliament are divided, and . . . rent into divers pieces'. If the parliament

by your and others' desertion of it be ruined, we shall not perish alone, but let the most neutral in this kingdom understand that if the adverse party prevails you and us will surely sink into one common ruin . . . Since therefore we are all embarked in one common bottom, let us all join hands and hearts together

---

[1] *C.C.C.*, pp. 313, 430; *Original Letters . . . addressed to Oliver Cromwell*, p. 28; Firth and Rait, *Acts and Ordinances*, ii. 456–90; *Letters from Roundhead Officers . . . to Captain A. Baynes, July 1650–June 1660* (Edinburgh, 1856), p. 7.
[2] *H.M.C.R. Hodgkin*, p. 47; *H.M.C.R. De Lisle and Dudley*, vi. 462.

to preserve ourselves and the Commonwealth of which we are all members, and in whose good or ill ours is wrapped up.[1]

Other rumpers seem to have made similar appeals, for towards the end of October a government supporter, calling for 'an act of oblivion to end all former miscarriages', urged all men 'unanimously to close in with the present overtures, and promote, by all means and faithfulness, the government set up by the parliament'. They should lay aside 'all particular animosities, and . . . less differences'.[2] Among those who evidently responded to the 'present overtures' were Sir Thomas Widdrington, who now declared himself reconciled to the Commonwealth regime, and the Earl of Warwick, who on 1 November attended a thanksgiving sermon delivered to the House by his client Stephen Marshall in celebration of the recent successes in Ireland. The Earl, it was said, was 'making his approaches' to the government.[3] A royalist, writing on 9 November of the divisions on the parliamentary side, noted that 'two parties endeavour a conciliation'.[4]

The other, opposing tendency at this time was for the growing radical agitation outside parliament to spill over into the House. There were 'many debates about reformation of things, according to the late petitions';[5] and the autumn of 1649 saw the emergence for the first time in the Rump of an effectively coordinated radical party. The common feature of the group was its republicanism, a characteristic which set it apart from most M.P.s and which gave it its cohesion and identity. The basis of its organisation – friendships between Henry Marten, Edmund Ludlow, Cornelius Holland, Henry Smyth, Lord Grey of Groby and the Chaloner brothers – had existed at least since the beginning of the Rump period, but it was only now that separate pairs of allies began to join forces for regular parliamentary cooperation. On 11 October Marten's republican friend Henry Neville, returned in a by-election for Marten's former seat at Abingdon, was admitted to the House. Marten, Neville and Thomas Chaloner soon formed the centre of the most closely knit political grouping in the Rump. Ludlow, Grey and James Chaloner shared their republican sympathies and, like Holland and Smyth, were ready supporters of Marten. So were two other republicans, Augustine Garland and Luke

1 *Buller Papers*, pp. 109–10.
2 *A Short Discourse between Monarchical and Aristocratical Government* (1649), p. 8.
3 *H.M.C.R. De Lisle and Dudley*, vi. 461, 462; *C.J.* 2 Nov. 1649.
4 B.M., Loan MS 331, fo. 2.
5 Whitelocke, *Memorials*, iii. 118.

Robinson ('a most fierce man against the king'); their cooperation with him was especially remarkable from 3 August 1649, when the three men inspired a measure to remove the royal arms from public places. Algernon Sidney, closely involved in Neville's introduction to Rump politics, was on the fringe of the group, as for a time was John Jones.[1] Yet in late 1649 and early 1650 Marten, despite his following, saw his reforming ambitions thwarted once more. Far-reaching proposals for legal, religious and electoral reform, although extensively debated, were eventually set aside. Marten's defeat was Heselrige's victory. Quickly involving himself in debates on reform,[2] Heselrige steered discussion away from the more controversial issues. Only measures which would earn the approval of moderates, and which he was therefore prepared to promote, were given much encouragement. Demands for the decentralisation of the legal system, for example, were deflected, and law reformers had to content themselves with further piecemeal legislation to help poor prisoners for debt and with the uncontroversial bill (which Heselrige sponsored) abolishing writs of error.

There was, however, one major proposal advocated by Marten and his friends which evidently had Heselrige's approval – even though, to the government's surprise, its implementation rebounded on the policy of conciliation. On 11 October, the day of Neville's admission to the Rump, Vane's committee for elections was revived; Ludlow and Robinson, two of Marten's closest allies, were added to it and, with Vane, given special responsibility for supervising its meetings; and it was resolved that all rumpers should take a 'test' or 'engagement' in the words: 'I do declare and promise, that I will be true and faithful to the Commonwealth of England, as the same is now established, without a king or House of Lords.' The engagement closely resembled the oath taken in the previous February by the 'conformist' members of the Council of State. On the 12th a committee, on which the Marten–

---

[1] *C.J.* 14, 15 Dec. 1648, 1, 3, 4, 6, 9, 12, 18, 31 Jan., 2, 3, 8, 10 Feb., 7, 16, 19, 27 Mar., 6, 14, 28 Apr., 8, 12, 18, 21, 28 May, 6, 20, 22, 29 June, 25, 27 July, 3, 7, 16, 22, 30 Aug., 4, 7, 12, 18, 19, 20, 25, 28 Sep., 4, 11, 12, 25 Oct., 2, 7, 9, 21, 22, 23, 27, 28 Nov. 1649, 4, 12, 20 Feb., 15, 18, 26 Apr., 14 June, 23 July, 30 Aug. 1650; SP: 25/62, pp. 42, 48, 52, 254, 339; 25/64, pp. 25, 191, 277, 385, 503; B.M., Add. MS 35, 332, fos. 169ᵛ–180ᵛ; *Memoirs of Edmund Ludlow*, i. 183, 200n.; Whitelocke, *Memorials*, iv. 410. *C.S.P.D.*: 1649–50, committees appointed 5 Feb., 21, 26, 27, 28, 29 Mar., 3, 7 Apr., 5, 7, 9, 12, 23, 28, 31 May, 5, 9, 20, 21 June, 1, 13, 14, 16 Aug., 3, 15, 19 Sep., 2, 6, 17, 31 Oct., 21 Nov., 4 Dec. 1649; 1650–1, committees appointed 15, 30 Apr.,15, 20 May, 8, 29 June, 16, 22 Aug., 19, 24 Sep., 17 Oct., 18 Nov., 26 Dec. 1650.
[2] *C.J.* 2 Nov., 11, 20 Dec. 1649, 18 Jan., 4 Feb., 1 Mar. 1650.

Neville–Chaloner group was strongly represented, was set up to ensure that all rumpers subscribed the test, which was also to be taken by any M.P.s admitted to the Rump in the future. Marten seems to have been pursuing a double aim. First, he wanted recruiter elections as a means of increasing the House's membership. Secondly, he sought to ensure, through the imposition of the engagement, that those returned by recruiter elections would share, or at least abstain from opposing, his republicanism. In the event, the engagement fulfilled a rather different function. Perhaps because of the ease with which rumpers were persuaded to take it, its application was soon extended to all public officials and members of the professional classes, and to clergymen in future applying for benefices. From here it was a short step to the decision to impose the engagement on the whole nation. Initially designed as a qualification on the Rump's membership, the test was thus adopted as a means of rooting out opposition to the government in the country at large. On 24 October a committee, headed by Thomas Chaloner, was set up to find ways of 'undeceiving' those who regarded the engagement as incompatible with previous political oaths, whether that of allegiance to Charles I or the Solemn League and Covenant of 1643.[1]

Although attendances in the Rump never attained consistent respectability, it was to be another three years before they again slumped as badly as in the late summer and early autumn of 1649. The filling of the benches in November ended all thought, for the immediate future, of appeals to M.P.s who had ceased to sit at the purge to resume their seats. The engagement, in any case, was likely to dispel any remaining enthusiasm such members might have had for returning. On 4 December the Rump resolved to exclude from parliament, during its tenure of power, all members who had not sat since the purge. It stopped short of formally expelling them, a penalty inflicted only on Richard Browne, who was supposed to have conspired with the Scots during the second civil war and who was one of the five M.P.s still in prison.[2] Even so, the decision of 4 December reflected a growing (if short-lived) self-confidence within the government. In September John Moyle had begged those of his Cornish colleagues who had not sat since the purge to apply for permission to resume membership: in December he wrote condescendingly that, even if they wished to return, it was now too late for them to do so.[3] The way was thus open for the proposed

[1] *C.J.* 11, 12, 24 Oct. 1649.   [2] *C.J.* (MS) xxiv, p. 531.
[3] Above, p. 211; *Buller Papers*, p. 111.

recruiter elections, and on 9 January 1650 Vane, perhaps stirred into action by the re-emergence of Leveller unrest, brought into the House the report ordered in the previous May. Recruiter elections, however, would have been a very different matter from the new representative demanded by the Levellers. They would have fortified, not terminated, the Long Parliament. The recruitment scheme, in any case, was effectively shelved by the House's decision, a repetition of its tactic of the previous March, to give prior attention to another Leveller demand, that for the redistribution of seats. Vane's report was frequently and lengthily debated in the months which followed, but to no effect;[1] for by February 1650, when the government was plunged once more in a sense of crisis, discussion of elections had become academic. Even Marten had evidently had second thoughts about the desirability of recruitment. According to a royalist report, he told the House

that he thought they might find the best advice from the scripture what they were to do in this particular: that when Moses was found upon the river, and brought to Pharaoh's daughter, she took great care that the mother might be found out, to whose care he might be committed to be nursed; which succeeded very happily. He said, their Commonwealth was yet an infant, of a weak growth and a very tender constitution; and therefore his opinion was, that nobody would be so fit to nurse it as the mother who brought it forth, and

that they should not think of putting it under any other hands until it had obtained more years and vigour.[2]

Caution was also apparent when the Council of State's term of office expired in February. Only three members of the first council were omitted from the second, which was likewise appointed for one year: the Earl of Mulgrave, who had never attended, the fourth Earl of Pembroke, who had recently died and who was replaced by his rumper son and heir, and Sir John Danvers, whose unpopularity had apparently been strengthened by his recent assertion, bitterly opposed by Marten, that the council needed greater independence of the House if it were to function effectively.[3] Lord Howard of Escrick replaced the Earl of Mulgrave, but Marten, long an enemy of Vane, combined with Lud-

[1] *C.J.* 9, 16, 23, 29, 31 Jan., 6, 10, 20, 27 Feb., 6, 13, 20, 27 Mar., 3, 10, 17, 24 Apr., 1, 8, 15, 22, 29 May, 5, 12, 19, 25 June, 3, 10, 16, 24, 31 July, 7, 14 Aug. 1650; Whitelocke, *Memorials*, iii. 141, 143, 155; *Several Proceedings* 18–25 Jan. 1650, p. 229; Bell, *Memorials of the Civil War*, ii. 118.

[2] Gardiner, *History of the Commonwealth and Protectorate*, i. 243–4. (Clarendon, in his *History*, wrote that Marten delivered this speech shortly before the dissolution of the Rump; but the newsletter on which Clarendon's information was based was written in February 1650.)

[3] Gardiner, *History of the Commonwealth and Protectorate*, i. 244–5; *C.J.* 15 Feb. 1649.

low to defeat a proposal to appoint Vane's father.[1] Instead, Thomas Chaloner became one of the four commoners newly appointed, the other three being John Gurdon,[2] with whom Chaloner seems to have struck up an understanding, Sir Peter Wentworth and Herbert Morley. Morley, who had first made his presence in the House fully felt in July 1649, was a major political figure thereafter. His growing friendship with Chaloner and with the Marten group generally was to have a decisive influence on the subsequent course of Rump politics. Like Chaloner's cooperation with Gurdon, it had already been partly responsible for the Rump's decision to adopt the engagement policy.[3]

The sense of crisis afflicting the government in the opening months of 1650 was largely caused by the emergence of royalist organisation in England, a development connected with Charles II's willingness to come to terms with the Scottish presbyterians. Drogheda and Wexford had destroyed the Irish-based, 'Cavalier' policy, and Charles, like Argyle, saw that the future must lie with the 'presbyterian' policy in Scotland. But the royalist–presbyterian alliance was achieved only after prolonged and underhand bargaining. It took a minor civil war in Scotland, culminating in the execution of Montrose at presbyterian hands, to persuade Charles to capitulate to the kirk's humiliating demands. He sailed for Scotland on 2 June 1650, and signed the Treaty of Heligoland with the Scottish presbyterians nine days later.

By February 1650, fears of a royalist coup in England were widespread. Papists and delinquents were ordered to leave London, and in March a new High Court of Justice was erected with the purpose of preventing 'a new and bloody war'.[4] The royalist–presbyterian alliance in Scotland increased the threat posed by the English presbyterian clergy, many of whom were now even more disposed than before to preach and pray for Charles's military success. In April 1650, as in April 1649, the Rump sought to quell clerical disaffection by means of both the carrot and the stick. On the one hand, it increased subsidies to

---

[1] *C. J.* 20 Feb. 1649.

[2] E.g. *ibid.* 14, 23 Dec. 1648, 16 Mar., 4 May, 24 Oct., 22 Nov. 1649, 25 Apr. 1650.

[3] E.g. *ibid.* 12 Apr., 18, 20, 21 July, 7, 9 Nov. 1649; SP: 28/70, fos. 405, 407, 425, 465; 28/76, fo. 461.

[4] Gardiner, *History of the Commonwealth and Protectorate,* i. 203, 236, 250; Underdown, *Royalist Conspiracy in England,* pp. 30–1, 40; M. Coate, *Cornwall in the Great Civil War* (1939), pp. 253ff.; *Perfect Diurnal . . . Armies* 28 Jan.–13 May 1650, esp. pp. 68–9, 76–7, 253–4; *Several Proceedings* 31 Jan.–4 Apr. 1650, esp. pp. 258–9, 386; *The Scots Remonstrance and Declaration* (1650), pp. 5–6; B.M., 669 f. 15, fo. 30 (act for a public humiliation on 13 June 1650); Firth and Rait, *Acts and Ordinances,* ii. 349–54.

orthodox, needy, and politically loyal ministers;[1] on the other, it launched a trenchant attack on ministers who remained politically troublesome. The latter, the Council of State announced,

> have been long forborne, hoping they might have come to themselves, seen their error, and desisted from those courses dangerous to themselves and the Commonwealth. But this forbearance hath added to their boldness, and they have gone on to such a degree as 'tis evident the Commonwealth cannot be safe if they be suffered, under the veil and disguise of their learning and knowledge and their pretended calling, to abuse and mislead the people.[2]

In May the city presbyterian minister Thomas Juggard was arrested. It was expected that he would be tried with Clement Walker, who had been seized during the previous autumn, 'because they will mix the blood of presbyter and royalist'. Early in July two other London clergymen were brought before the Rump's Committee for Plundered Ministers and strictly interrogated. Prynne, too, was arrested about the same time, and a close watch was kept on other M.P.s who had not sat since the purge.[3]

Faced with an apparently grave threat to its survival, the Rump at last took in hand the problem of local government.[4] The county committees, many of them either of doubtful loyalty or, if loyal, then ineffective, were reduced to impotence, and county administration was brought under more direct government control. The procedures of sequestration were also centralised, and the amalgamation in April 1650 of the Committee for Compounding and the Committee for Advance of Money, both now placed in the hands of industrious commissioners who were not M.P.s, was another part of a general tightening-up process.[5] In the summer there was a purge of J.P.s in many counties, while a number of M.P.s whose participation in the Long Parliament had ceased at the purge, but who in 1649 had continued to be named as assessment commissioners, were now dropped from the commission lists.[6] The regime's determination to bring the localities

1 Firth and Rait, *Acts and Ordinances*, ii. 369–78.
2 SP 25/95, p. 71. Cf. *C.S.P.D.* 1650–1, pp. 49, 73, 78, 150.
3 *Mercurius Pragmaticus* 21–28 May 1650, p. 8; Clarke MS xvi, fo. 123; *Man in the Moon* 13–20 Mar. 1650, pp. 369–70; *C.J.* 4 July 1650; *Mercurius Politicus* 27 June–11 July 1650, pp. 50–3, 66–7, 79; B.M., Loan MS 29/123, Misc. g: Mackworth to Harley, May 1650; and Loan MS 29/176, fos. 177ff.
4 For this paragraph see esp. Underdown, *Pride's Purge*, pp. 297–8, 299–302, 311.
5 *C.C.C.*, pp. xiii–xiv.
6 The assessment commissioners are listed in the assessment acts printed in Firth and Rait, *Acts and Ordinances*, vol. ii. A number of M.P.s who ceased to sit at Pride's Purge and who were removed from the commission lists in 1650 were restored to them in 1652.

under control was also reflected in the zealous creation of county militias, a development probably inspired, at a parliamentary level, by Herbert Morley.[1] These measures combined to produce a greater measure of domestic security and a higher yield from taxation.[2] But they did nothing to solve the problem which had made them necessary, the absence in the provinces of any broad base of government support. The changes in local government were not intended to enhance the prominence of radicals, but this was often their effect, since in many areas radicals were the only men prepared to work hard on the government's behalf. The Rump, indeed, was frequently embarrassed by the radicalism of those who wielded power on its behalf.

The first eight months of 1650 represented the nadir of the regime's fortunes, and the spirits of its members sank low. In December 1649 and January 1650 Whitelocke, whose wife had recently died, found himself 'full of melancholy and apprehensions of death'.[3] His mood was infectious. The rumper Thomas Hoyle, after an unsuccessful attempt a few months earlier, committed suicide on the first anniversary of Charles I's execution.[4] The death of Whitelocke's friend Rowland Wilson in February 1650 likewise followed a bout of depression concerning the events which had brought the Rump to power – although he, like Hoyle, had been implicated in neither the purge nor the execution.[5] A popular demonstration at Wilson's state funeral gave the government a taste of its unpopularity in London.[6] Also in February Fairfax, unable to square his conscience with the engagement, was said to be 'melancholy mad',[7] while the Council of Officers, dismayed by a series of deaths among their colleagues and by 'the present condition of this nation in general', wondered whether the hand of God might not be against them. Hugh Peter had similar apprehensions. The gloom was increased by doubts whether the Commonwealth would be able to supply an adequate fleet for the coming months.[8] 'We are now entangled in misery', wrote the son of the rumper Isaac Pennington at this time; 'after all our running from it, we are become involved in it.'[9]

[1] E.g. *C.J.* 28 May 1650 (with which cf. above, p. 29).
[2] Johnson, 'Buckinghamshire 1640–1660', pp. 282ff.; Ashley, *Commercial and Financial Policy*, chapter viii.   [3] B.M., Add. MS 37,345, fos. 38–40.
[4] *Mercurius Pragmaticus* 7–14 Aug. 1649, penultimate page (unpaginated); Keeler, *The Long Parliament*, p. 224.
[5] *Mercurius Pragmaticus* 5–12 Feb. 1650, p. 4; *Man in the Moon* 6–14 Feb. 1650, pp. 335–6.
[6] B.M., Add. MS 37,345, fo. 54.
[7] Staffordshire Record Office, D868/5, fo. 32: Langley to Leveson, 16 Feb. 1650.
[8] Whitelocke, *Memorials*, iii. 131; Clarendon MS 39, fos. 80ᵛ, 81.
[9] I. Pennington jr., *A Word for the Common Weal* (1650), p. 4. Cf. *ibid.* p. 14.

The black mood prevalent in February rarely lifted in the months
thereafter. Frequent reports testified to the government's 'languishing
condition' in the provinces, and especially in counties renowned, like
Devon and Lancashire, for their hostility to the Rump.[1] Particularly
disheartening was the realisation that the 'present overtures' of the
previous autumn had failed dismally, and that the engagement, the
source of huge public controversy, had been a major reason for their
failure. In March Whitelocke bemoaned the divisions which continued
to beset the nation, and early in April the city government lamented to
the Rump that the 'discontents, prejudices, scandals, and backslidings
of some (which once engaged with us) have, of late, so much appeared
to the hazard of our sad reducement into slavery, and superstition'.[2]
At the end of the same month Bradshaw was said to have complained
that 'all the fair or foul means we can use, yet not any one Cavalier is
heartily converted to us', while Vane was reported to have admitted
that the rumpers

were now in a far worse estate than ever yet they had been; that all the world
was and would be their enemies; that their own army and general [Fairfax]
were not to be trusted; that the whole kingdom would rise and cut their
throats upon the first good occasion; and that they knew not any place to go
unto to be safe.[3]

It is unlikely that the royalist correspondent who reported Bradshaw's
and Vane's remarks exaggerated much. In May the rumper Thomas
Mackworth, governor of Shrewsbury, had 'sorrowful thoughts in
regard of the division that was between honest men and those that had
heretofore from the beginning cordially joined against the common
enemy'. Mackworth described as 'very much to be lamented ... that
great disunion that is now amongst brethren in this Commonwealth. I
mean those that have heretofore, and yet I hope will, endeavour the
advancement of the parliament's interest in carrying on the public
cause.'[4] In the same month the Rump appointed a fast day 'in these our
sad times of distractions and troubles'.[5] In August came a tract from
John Dury, who mused wistfully on what might be achieved 'if the

[1] *Perfect Diurnal ... Armies* 4–11 Mar. 1650, p. 109; SP 23/249, no. 3. Cf. *Strange News from the North* (1650), p. 3.
[2] Whitelocke, *Memorials*, iii. 165; *Several Proceedings* 28 Mar.–4 Apr. 1650, pp. 383–4.
[3] Gardiner, *History of the Commonwealth and Protectorate*, i. 248, 249.
[4] B.M., Loan MS 29/123, misc. 39g: Mackworth to Sir Robert Harley, 8 May 1650.
[5] B.M., Add. MS 22,620, fo. 160: Atkins to the mayor of Norwich, 16 May 1650.

godly party would not divide, and strengthen the hands of enemies . . .
by their disaffectedness and jealousies'.[1]

Cromwell's return from Ireland, requested as early as January, became a matter of urgency in the following months.[2] There were
pressures within the army for a quick expedition to Scotland, so that
the enemy might be defeated before the summer was out. The stumbling block was Fairfax. 'Being hourly persuaded by the presbyterian
ministers and his own lady, who was a great patroness to them', he
eventually declined to take the engagement. Although he did what he
could to mitigate the consequences of his decision for the government,
his refusal was a serious setback. Yet it hardly came as a surprise, for his
distaste for the Commonwealth had always been thinly concealed.
Soon it became clear that he would refuse to lead an expedition into
Scotland against fellow presbyterians. Cromwell, at last returning to
London in June, visited Fairfax with Lambert, Harrison, St John and
Whitelocke. The delegation was agreed in its support for the proposed
invasion, but Fairfax could not be brought round. He resigned his
command and went into dignified retirement in Yorkshire. Cromwell,
the obvious choice, succeeded him as Lord General, and in July led the
expedition into Scotland.[3] The campaign, expected to be 'the work of
many years',[4] began inauspiciously. The days of the Commonwealth
seemed numbered, and it was with a sense of desperation that Cromwell's forces, both their supplies and their morale seriously depleted,
moved to Dunbar at the beginning of September to try to force the
Scots to a fight. The victory which followed, achieved against all the
odds, was as unexpected as it was spectacular.

The threat from Scotland, and the danger of an alliance between
Scottish and English presbyterianism, overshadowed all parliamentary
proceedings from January to September 1650. The defensive posture
into which the government was driven is well shown by its treatment
of the two main issues confronting it during this period: the engagement, and religious reform.

The proposal to enforce an engagement of loyalty to the Rump,

[1] J. Dury, *Objections against taking the Engagement answered* (1650), pp. 18–19.
[2] Cf. Bell, *Memorials of the Civil War*, ii. 118; *Original Letters . . . addressed to Oliver Cromwell*, p. 7.
[3] Gardiner, *History of the Commonwealth and Protectorate*, i. 256–64; Abbott, *Writings and Speeches*, ii. 267–72; Whitelocke, *Memorials*, iii. 206–11; H.M.C.R. *De Lisle and Dudley*, vi. 479.
[4] *The Perfect Politician* (1660), p. 210.

rumoured as early as March 1649, had been mooted again in August of the same year, when it seems to have been aimed principally at the Levellers.[1] When the act for the national subscription of the engagement was passed on 2 January 1650, it was probably the Levellers who entertained 'jealousies of the parliament's intent, by putting forth the engagement, to perpetuate themselves, and to bind up the hands of future representatives';[2] and the Leveller disturbances between September 1649 and January 1650 may have hardened parliament's determination to impose the engagement. Yet Lilburne took the test (for his own reasons), as did the Digger leader Gerrard Winstanley, who thought it 'well liked' by 'the generality of people'.[3] Radicals were only a secondary target. As finally passed, the act was aimed primarily at royalist and presbyterian opposition to the regime.

The preamble to the engagement act began:

Whereas divers disaffected persons do by sundry ways and means oppose and endeavour to undermine . . . this present government, so that unless special care be taken a new war is likely to break forth; for the preventing whereof, and also for the better uniting of this nation, as well against all invasions from abroad, as the common enemy at home; and to the end that those which receive benefit and protection from this present government may give assurance of their living quietly and peaceably under the same, and that they will neither directly nor indirectly contrive or practise any thing to the disturbance thereof . . .[4]

Rarely was the Rump so forthcoming about its motives. The engagement was imposed on the nation chiefly out of panic. The Council of State regarded the test as an indispensable security measure and consistently favoured it as a means of controlling opposition to the regime.[5] As John Moyle observed, the test was introduced 'to the intent we may know our friends and our foes, and of what power the malignant party is throughout the whole Commonwealth'.[6] Although the engagement was divisive in its consequences, it was far from divisive in its intentions: rather, as the preamble stated, it was designed 'for the better uniting of this nation'. The aim was to isolate the most committed

[1] Carte, *Original Letters*, i. 253; *The Moderate Messenger*, 27 Aug.–3 Sep. 1649, p. 132. And see *Mercurius Pragmaticus* 31 July–7 Aug. 1650, p. 5, and Wallace, 'The engagement controversy', p. 386.
[2] Whitelocke, *Memorials*, iii. 135. Cf. Bell, *Memorials of the Civil War*, ii. 119.
[3] *Perfect Diurnal . . . Armies* 24–31 Dec. 1649, p. 28; *The Engagement Vindicated* (1650); Winstanley, *England's spirit unfolded* (ed. Aylmer), esp. pp. 5, 6, 9–11.
[4] Firth and Rait, *Acts and Ordinances*, ii. 325–9.
[5] *C.S.P.D.* 1649–50, pp. 370, 387, 431, 436, 448, 451, 465; 1650–1, pp. 74, 147.
[6] *H.M.C.R. Hodgkin*, p. 47.

royalists from the Rump's other critics, and to create a bond between the government and the presbyterians. Admittedly there were rumpers who, like John Pyne, anticipated with relish the imposition of the engagement, 'which I think will make a notable discovery and indeed rout amongst all professions and callings whatsoever'.[1] Pyne himself zealously enforced the engagement in Somerset, and doubtless there were other areas where local officials were delighted to have a new stick with which to beat their presbyterian opponents. The test was probably also welcomed by some 'revolutionary' M.P.s who suspected their colleagues of being 'apostates' to the cause.[2] There were always those prepared to argue, in defence of the engagement, that there could be no middle course between active support for the regime and active opposition to it.[3] Most apologists for the test, however, were much less aggressive. The engagement was designed to broaden rather than to narrow the base of the government's support; and its wording required from subscribers what the Rump must have felt to be the minimum commitment for which it could afford to ask. Those who took the oath were not even obliged to 'swear' loyalty to the Rump: they were required only to 'declare and promise' it. Yet, well before the passage of the act, the Rump found itself at the centre of a furious controversy, in which the test was vigorously condemned as tyrannical and divisive.

The arguments advanced during the pamphlet war over the engagement by the Rump's apologists, and especially by Marchamont Nedham and John Dury, reflect the Rump's continuing embarrassment at its constitutional illegitimacy and its lack of commitment to the form of government which had emerged after the execution of Charles I. Nedham, a trimming journalist previously employed by royalists, had been arrested by the government for his misdemeanours. Through Bradshaw's influence, however, he had been spared from punishment in return for wielding his pen on the Commonwealth's behalf.[4] Neither he nor Dury attempted to demonstrate the Rump's moral fitness to govern; they dismissed the question as irrelevant. Nedham even abandoned the argument, on which the Rump's claim to sovereignty had rested since 4 January 1649, that the Commonwealth regime was representative of the people.[5] Dury, for his part, asserted

---

[1] *H.M.C.R. Leybourne-Popham*, p. 51.

[2] *Mercurius Pragmaticus* 16–23 Oct. 1649, p. 2.

[3] *Memorandums of the Conferences*, p 80; *Short Discourse between Monarchical and Aristocratical Government*, pp. 19–20.

[4] B.M., Add. MS 28,002, fo. 172: Nedham to Henry Oxinden, 19 Nov. 1649.

[5] Nedham, *The Case of the Commonwealth of England, Stated*, p. 22.

that the Rump should be obeyed even if its members had taken up power 'for some sinister ends'.[1] In the suggestion that it did not matter whether the Rump was good or bad lay an implicit acknowledgement that in some ways, at least, it was bad. The apologists for the engagement developed an amoral, secular, Hobbesian philosophy of subordination to a *de facto* government, urging those sceptical of the regime to keep out of politics.[2] They should, wrote Dury, 'quiet your mind according to your place, concerning the right which the present powers have to rule. Do not take upon you to define matters whereof you are no competent judge; you are made a competent judge only of your own actions which belong to you as a subject.' 'This or that outward form of government', he stressed, 'is wholly accidental . . . and . . . alterable, in respect of forms, as is most expedient.'[3] The virtues of expediency were frequently emphasised by the apologists. So were the rights which, they argued, accrued to the Rump by right of conquest. Parliament was evidently well pleased by the work of the authors who defended the test. The Council of State commissioned Dury to draw up an official apologia for the engagement; and although the House was understandably unwilling to give formal blessing to a document whose arguments were so little to its credit, it rewarded him handsomely for his pains, as later it rewarded Nedham.[4] On 26 October Francis Rous, whose own writings had anticipated the frank admission by the engagement theorists of the Rump's weaknesses, and Miles Corbet, one of the M.P.s who had been sent in the spring of 1649 to woo the city presbyterians, were added to the committee set up two days earlier to 'undeceive' the test's opponents, and there need be little doubt that a large number of rumpers favoured the tactics of Dury, Nedham and their colleagues.[5]

The apologists were not concerned solely to prove the Rump's right to govern. They also assisted the government in its continuing moves to conciliate both political and religious presbyterians. One government supporter, adopting the tone and the arguments of the *de facto* theorists, and conceding that 'of late . . . our affairs in this nation, for

[1] J. Dury, *Considerations touching the present Engagement* (1649), pp. 18–19.
[2] For illuminating comments on the engagement controversy, see the works by Q. Skinner and J. M. Wallace cited above, p. 44 n. 2. Dr Hill (*God's Englishman*, p. 291) suggests that these authors have treated the engagement theorists 'a little portentously'. This is, I think, unfair, but Dr Hill is certainly right to emphasise the 'very pragmatic' nature of the theorists' arguments.
[3] Dury, *Considerations touching the present Engagement*, pp. 5, 16.
[4] *C.J.* 25 Dec. 1649; Gardiner, *History of the Commonwealth and Protectorate*, i. 252–5.
[5] *C.J.* 24, 26 Oct. 1649.

the external, and circumstantial part of them, have not gone on . . . smoothly, or takingly unto every spirit', advertised the Rump's policy as a middle course between the designs of royalists and Levellers.[1] Another, arguing that the Rump could not be expected to achieve settlement so long as the country was torn by faction and division, sought to win over 'the party in the kingdom, that would moderate, but not destroy monarchy'.[2] There were many similar appeals to 'the spirits of all that were moderate'.[3] Another attempt was made to heal the breach within the parliamentary party through approaches to presbyterian divines, Dury offering the London Provincial Assembly a paper 'in order to an accommodation'.[4] On 15 and 22 February and 1 March 1650, a series of conferences was held in London 'between the brethren scrupled at the engagement' and 'others who were satisfied with it'. The stated premise of the meeting was that 'there are godly well-meaning men, who have walked together affectionately heretofore towards one and the same end, to advance a gospel reformation in religion, and to maintain the grounds of a just liberty in the nation', but who 'of late . . . are unhappily parted, and fallen at a distance'. It was proposed that, to mend the quarrel, a joint manifesto be drawn up by the two sides, condemning the purge and the execution as the work of 'a minor party', accusing the army of destructive aims, but by implication absolving the Rump from the misdeeds of those who had brought it to power. For the rumpers, being

betrusted with a right to see the government settled, were bound to take it up, and have a care for the management thereof towards the public good, which they have endeavoured faithfully to do by laying the foundations of religion and justice, and giving protection to those that be true and faithful to the common interest of necessary liberty; and although this had been done by them for no other design but common preservation, and that they had taken in the midst of great opposition their lives to settle peace and lasting quietness in the nation, they had cause to grieve that their upright meanings and faithful undertakings were otherwise interpreted and constructed by such who should have joined with them to carry on the work.

It was true that the presbyterian reformation had yet to be achieved, but the Rump had made an admirable start. Its *Declarations* were proof of the respectability of its intentions; and 'no man could rationally expect

[1] *Short Discourse between Monarchical and Aristocratical Government*, pp. 4, 20.
[2] *The Engagement Vindicated*, pp. 10, 11.
[3] Wallace, 'The engagement controversy', p. 387.
[4] Minutes of the London Provincial Assembly (typed transcript, Dr Williams's Library), pp. 70, 71.

The nadir

a full accomplishment of all such hopes in an instant', or indeed so long as the non-engagers held out. There is nothing to identify the political inspiration behind the conferences, but the attendant publicity suggests that the proposals advanced during them, giving so accurate a picture of the motives of 'conformists' in joining the Rump, must have had at least the approval of leading rumpers.[1]

Yet the conferences, like Dury's offer to the London Provincial Assembly, failed; and the engagement soon proved to have been a strategic error of the first magnitude. The clauses prohibiting non-subscribers from holding office or taking legal proceedings, and barring non-engaging clergymen from receiving tithes, no doubt persuaded many to sign.[2] The rumpers seem to have taken the test readily enough. So did army officers and soldiers, the garrisons of Heselrige and Fenwick taking the lead.[3] There were reports of almost universal subscription in many parts of the country. These, however, were primarily areas where active supporters of the Rump controlled the machinery of local government or where militia commissioners or soldiers could bully people into engaging. Elsewhere, if the engagement was even pressed, it does not seem to have made much headway, and it soon became evident that the test had failed in precisely those respects in which its advocates had most hoped for success. The Cavaliers, the principle target of the engagement, were widely reported to have taken it without heed or scruple, a circumstance which offered no guarantee of their future loyalty. 'Such oaths as are over-hastily swallowed', a newswriter commented, 'are the most easily vomited up again.'[4] On the other hand the presbyterians, and particularly the presbyterian clergy, provided the principal opposition to subscription.[5] Egged on

1 *Memorandums of the Conferences*, esp. pp. 1–3.
2 E.g. H.M.C.R. *De Lisle and Dudley*, vi. 464, 466, 598–9; Gardiner (*History of the Commonwealth and Protectorate*, i. 193) wrongly implies that the clause relating to legal proceedings appeared only in the draft of the act and not in the act itself.
3 B.M., Add. MS 22,620, fo. 139: Atkins to the mayor of Norwich, 29 Nov. 1649; H.M.C.R. *Hodgkin*, p. 47; Whitelocke, *Memorials*, iii. 125, 128, 134, 140, 142, 147, 163; *Perfect Diurnal . . . Armies* 17 Dec. 1649–25 Feb. 1650, pp. 1–2, 12, 59, 61, 75–6, 93. For Heselrige's support for the engagement see also *C.J.* 27 Nov. 1649.
4 Underdown, *Pride's Purge*, p. 310. Cf. H.M.C.R. *Sutherland*, p. 180; R. Parkinson (ed.), *Autobiography of Henry Newcombe* (Chetham Soc., 1852), pp. 24–5.
5 H.M.C.R. *De Lisle and Dudley*, vi. 472; Whitelocke, *Memorials*, iii. 141; H. Cary (ed.), *Memorials of the Great Civil War in England* (2 vols., 1842), ii. 239–49; *Some Considerations in relation to . . . the Engagement* (1650), p. 3; *Mercurius Pragmaticus* 19–26 Feb. 1650, p. 4; *Reliquiae Baxterianae*, p. 66; *Perfect Diurnal . . . Armies* 21–28 Jan. 1650, p. 59 (the same newspaper contains much information about the response to the engagement in the provinces in the first half of 1650, although its accounts are strongly prejudiced).

once more by purged M.P.s, ministers found in their former subscription to the Solemn League and Covenant an insuperable objection
to taking the engagement. Numerous clergymen who, had the engagement not been imposed, might have been expected to hold their peace
now organised meetings to debate its legality, denounced the government from the pulpit, and attempted to persuade soldiers of the
impropriety of the measure.[1] By May of 1650 the test was being
allowed to lapse in many areas; 'the great work ... is not so eagerly
pursued now', *Mercurius Pragmaticus* noted.[2] It was enthusiastically
revived in the period of optimism following Dunbar, but not for long.[3]

The other main political problem facing the Rump in the year
before Dunbar, overlapping the engagement question, was religious
reform. As the government supporter Thomas May warned in October
1649, much of the Rump's unpopularity stemmed from 'that unlimited
toleration of religion which is yet granted in this nation'; 'religion is a
sacred bond and tie upon men's spirits ... It is the fear of this unlimited
toleration makes many honest presbyterians stand at such a distance.'[4]
The House allowed the proposal it had discussed in August 1649 for
repealing the statutes against sectaries to lapse until after Dunbar.
Discussion centred instead on measures for the suppression of moral
licence and for the propagation of the gospel. Here the Rump's
principal concern was to dissociate itself from growing and alarming
manifestations of religious extremism. In December 1649 the government newspaper *A Brief Relation* felt it necessary to interrupt its
laconic chronicle of events overseas with a favourable reference to a
sermon preached by Peter Sterry before the House of Commons.
Sterry had asked 'whether a Christian in the days of his flesh may be
set free from the moral law; the mistake wherein, by many unstable
souls ... hath caused them to fall from their former profession of
religion and holiness and, without blushing, to maintain and practise
all licentiousness.'[5] The sect known as the Ranters, claiming that
'swearing, drunkenness, adultery, and theft were not sinful unless the

---

[1] Whitelocke, *Memorials*, iii. 131, 144, 147, 157, 158–9; *Life of Adam Martindale*, pp.
89–100; *Mercurius Politicus* 6–13. June 1650, p. 4; *Perfect Diurnal ... Armies* 24–31 Dec.
1649, pp. 22, 23, 4–18 Feb. 1650, pp. 77, 85, 4–11 Mar. 1650, p. 108.

[2] *Mercurius Pragmaticus* 30 Apr.–7 May 1650, p. 7.

[3] *Several Proceedings* 17–24 Oct. 1650, pp. 835–6; *Weekly Intelligencer* 22–29 Oct. 1650,
p. 40; *Perfect Diurnal ... Armies* 20–27 Jan. 1651, p. 781.

[4] May, *Anatomy of ... Lilburne's Spirit and Pamphlets*, ep. ded. Cf. *The Trial of Lieut.
Colonel John Lilburne*, p. 158.

[5] *A Brief Relation of some Affairs and Transactions, Civil and Military, both Foreign and
Domestic* 18–25 Dec. 1650, pp. 187–8.

person guilty of them apprehended them to be so', was beginning to
cause serious concern. It was believed that they 'maintain community
of women'.[1] At the beginning of February 1650 the Rump, after
ordering the suppression of a Ranter tract, decided to hold a fast day
for the contemplation of 'such crying sins, hideous blasphemies, and
unheard of abominations (and that by some under pretence of liberty,
and greater measure of light) as after all our wondrous deliverances do
manifest themselves to the exceeding dishonour of God, and reproach
of our Christian profession'. Parliament urged the need for 'duty and
obedience' in matters of religion, and expressed the hope that 'all
differences among brethren might be reconciled'.[2] The same spirit was
cultivated in the spring of 1650 by a series of pamphlets either urging
reconciliation between presbyterians and independents, denouncing
radical sects, or emphasising the need for a respected and orthodox
ministry.[3] In April the Rump passed its act against non-observance of
the sabbath. In May came the act, carrying the death penalty for the
first offence, against incest, adultery and fornication, 'wherewith this
land is much defiled'. In June an act was passed 'for the better preventing and suppressing of the detestable sins of prophane swearing
and cursing'. These were harsh measures, although they had been even
harsher before the House had amended them. The act against swearing
and cursing was aimed directly at the Ranters. So was the blasphemy
act of August, which attacked 'divers men and women ... most
monstrous in their opinions, and loose in all wicked and abominable
practices ... not only to the notorious corrupting and disordering, but
even to the dissolution of all humane society; who rejecting the use of
any gospel ordinances, do deny the necessity of civil and moral righteousness among men'.[4] S.R. Gardiner described the religious legislation passed by the Rump in the months before Dunbar as 'almost
presbyterian', designed to appeal to the 'common puritanism' of the

[1] Gardiner, *History of the Commonwealth and Protectorate*, ii. 2; Josten, *Elias Ashmole*, ii. 529.
For recent studies of the Ranters, see J. F. McGregor, 'The Ranters: a study of the free
spirit in English sectarian religion, 1648–1660' (Oxford B. Litt. thesis, 1968); A. L.
Morton, *The World of the Ranters* (1970); C. Hill, *The World Turned Upside Down* (1972),
esp. pp. 163ff.
[2] B.M., 669 f. 15, fo. 11 (act for fast day); *C.J.* 4 Feb. 1650.
[3] E.g. Lazarus Seaman, *A Gloss for the Times* (1650); I. Pennington jr., *A Voice out of the
thick Darkness* (1650); *The Muzzled Ox* (1650), esp. pp. 6–8; J. Blackleach, *Endeavours
aiming at the Glory of God* (1650), pp. 63–4.
[4] Firth and Rait, *Acts and Ordinances*, ii. 383–9, 393–6; Gardiner, *History of the Commonwealth and Protectorate*, i. 255–6; Whitelocke, *Memorials*, iii. 206; *C.J.* 1, 15, 22, 29 Mar..
12, 19, 26 Apr., 3, 10, 31 May, 7, 14, 21, 28 June, 5, 12, 19 July, 9 Aug., 6 Sep. 1650.

parliamentary party of the 1640s and so to woo presbyterians who might otherwise be tempted to support the royalist cause.[1] This was slightly to oversimplify, for there must have been much sectarian support for the new laws. The initial parliamentary pressure for measures for the propagation of the gospel came from Harrison, who by January 1650 was organising his cohorts in the House, the chief of whom at this stage were Nathaniel Rich, Charles Fleetwood and John Jones.[2] The bills against moral licence, too, began as concessions to radicals in the city. In essence, however, Gardiner was right.[3] By early February it was becoming clear that the House as a whole favoured measures of propagation less from a desire to spread the Word than from a determination to emphasise once more the government's respect for the established ministry. The Rump debated a series of proposals designed to solve problems either of church finance or of parochial organisation in areas represented by rumpers prepared to advance their claims. Like the act of April 1650 for improving the maintenance of ministers, the measures which ensued must have been attractive to orthodox puritans. Even the presbyterian hostility to the act of March 1650 for the propagation of the gospel in Wales was directed not at the act itself but at the use to which the active radical minority on the commission succeeded in putting it. No more penetrating criticism was made of the measure when it came up for renewal than that, by its own terms of reference, it had failed: too many Welsh flocks remained without shepherds.[4]

The call for the propagation of the gospel had long been central to the puritan movement. By 1650, however, aspiring propagators were running out of both energy and ideas. It was easy to clamour for the spreading of the Word, but harder to persuade ministers holding fat livings to betake themselves to the heathen wilds in order to spread it.[5] The movement for propagation had become caught up in political and social divisions. To orthodox puritans, propagation now principally meant the fortification of the established ministry against the attacks of

---

[1] Gardiner, *History of the Commonwealth and Protectorate*, i. 173, 246, 255, ii. 2, 3, 83–4.

[2] For the emergence of this group see e.g. *C.J.* 13 July, 23, 28 Nov. 1649, 17, 29 Jan., 5, 7, 15, 20 Feb., 1, 16, 29 Mar., 7, 22, 24 June, 3, 5 July 1650; B.M., Egerton MS 1048, fo. 107.

[3] *C.J.* 2 Nov., 4 Dec. 1649; Journal of the London Common Council xli, fos. 18ᵛ–19; and cf. D[aniel] T[aylor], *Certain Queries or Considerations, presented to the view of all that desire Reformation of Grievances* (1651), pp. 9–10; Samuel Duncon, *Several Propositions of Public Concernment presented to . . . Cromwell* (1652), p. 3.

[4] E.g. *Weekly Intelligencer* 6–13 Jan. 1652, p. 317; *Reliquiae Baxterianae*, p. 70; *Strena Vavasoriensis* (1654), p. 3; *C.C.C.*, pp. 495, 517.

[5] See e.g. Asty, *Sermons of John Owen*, pp. 352ff.; N.L.W., MS 11,440D, p. 75; Mayer, 'Inedited letters', pp. 188, 213, 241; Hugh Peter, *A Word for the Army* (1647), p. 12.

sectaries; to the sects, it now meant little more than the abolition of the tithe system, that insuperable obstacle to the advancement of truth, and the uprooting of ministers to whose views radicals objected. As the 1650s went by it was increasingly left to men with ecumenical aims, who sought to stand above party strife, to propose means of propagating the gospel in the sense in which the term had previously been understood. In parliament, concern for the promotion of the Word was a less effective stimulant to the interest of M.P.s in religious matters than was righteous indignation. The Rump's Committee for Plundered Ministers, which had a wide variety of duties, was attended by thirty-six M.P.s when the astrologer William Lilly was brought before it; at other times it found difficulty in raising a quorum of five.[1] In the second protectorate parliament, in much the same way, debates centering on the crimes of James Nayler tended to draw members to the House as quickly as detailed discussion of proposals for religious reform drove them away.[2]

Such enthusiasm as the Rump did display for the spreading of the Word was almost invariably linked with political considerations. Those who made representations to the House for the advancement of the gospel were careful to remind parliament of the equation between ungodliness and political disloyalty. The 'nineteen thousand at the least' petitioners who in 1650 called on the Rump to promote the gospel in South Wales pointed out that 'the preaching of the gospel is not the least and most inconsiderable means to secure and establish your government'.[3] Others, too, emphasised the need to send godly ministers to the backward parts, either 'to sweeten your new government to the people, and to allay the bitterness of the late years', or as 'a way of countermining the adverse party' which attacked the Rump from the pulpit.[4] In February 1650, at the time when its interest in the propagation of the gospel was at its height, the Rump prayed 'for the advancement of the kingdom of Christ, and propagation of His gospel throughout the same, and all the dominions thereof . . . that all designs, combinations and conspiracies of all wicked men (whether within or without us) to imbroil this nation in a new war, may be discovered

---

[1] Ashmole MS 421, fo. 209; *Life of Adam Martindale*, p. 87.
[2] *Diary of Thomas Burton*, i. 43, 297, 351.
[3] *The Humble Acknowledgement of the Inhabitants of South Wales* (1650), p. 4.
[4] *C.S.P.D.* 1650–1, pp. 21, 180. Cf. *Original Letters . . . addressed to Oliver Cromwell*, p. 48; *Mercurius Politicus* 6–13 June 1650, p. 5, 18–25 July 1650, pp. 107–8; *Perfect Diurnal . . . Armies* 22–29 Dec. 1651, pp. 1563–4; *Weekly Intelligencer* 23–30 Mar. 1652, p. 400; *C.C.C.*, p. 162.

and prevented.'[1] Hence, no doubt, the House's special concern for the spiritual welfare of Wales and the north of England, the strongholds of surviving royalism. The Rump's political and religious concerns were always intimately related. In the year before Dunbar they could hardly have been otherwise.

[1] B.M., 669 f. 15, fo. 11.

12

DUNBAR TO WORCESTER:
THE COALITION UNDER STRAIN,
SEPTEMBER 1650–SEPTEMBER 1651

Dunbar was celebrated by the Rump as a miraculous deliverance. Unhappily it did nothing to lighten the burden of taxation, which like the government's indebtedness continued to soar;[1] but the threat from Scotland, although by no means extinguished, was now at least in temporary abeyance. As Cromwell wrote to Heselrige the day after the battle, 'it's probable the kirk has done their do'.[2] The consequent euphoria among English radicals aroused once more the reforming ambitions which had lain dormant in the previous months. Cromwell himself gave the lead. George Fox claimed later that 'O.C. at Dunbar fight had promised to the Lord that if he gave him the victory over his enemies, he would take away tithes, etc.'; and on the day after the battle, in a letter to Speaker Lenthall, Cromwell exhorted parliament to 'relieve the oppressed' and to 'hear the groans of poor prisoners in England; be pleased to reform the abuses of all professions; and if there be any one that makes many poor to make a few rich, that suits not a Commonwealth'. The House was again instructed to 'relieve the oppressed' in a thanksgiving sermon delivered by Thomas Brooks on 8 October. It was in the autumn of 1650 that the Rump made its most important concessions to reforming sentiment.[3] Yet radical success was short-lived, and reform quickly provoked reaction. The overall effect of the year between Dunbar and Worcester, indeed, was to strengthen still further the Rump's inclination to woo both political and religious presbyterians.

Characteristically, parliamentary radicals devoted much of their energy after Dunbar to parliamentary in-fighting. The battle between 'revolutionaries' and 'conformists' was fought once more. In November

---

[1] E.g. Firth and Rait, *Acts and Ordinances*, ii. 456–90; *Original Letters . . . addressed to Oliver Cromwell*, p. 28; Journal of the London Common Council xli, fo. 37; *H.M.C.R. De Lisle and Dudley*, vi. 484, 485.
[2] Abbott, *Writings and Speeches*, ii. 327.
[3] Hill, *God's Englishman*, pp. 125–6, 133; Abbott, *Writings and Speeches*, ii. 325; Brooks, *The Hypocrite Detected*, ep. ded. and p. 23.

1650 the House debated a proposal that all rumpers be required to swear retrospective approval of the proceedings of the High Court of Justice which had condemned Charles I. An army writer thought the scheme 'like to make a great rout amongst those that were not at the trial', but not surprisingly it was rejected, the House contenting itself with formally congratulating the regicides. In January 1651 the Rump was persuaded to order a day of thanksgiving on the second anniversary of the king's death, a decision provocatively offensive to presbyterian opinion.[1]

Reform, however, also had its place in the radical programme after Dunbar. Strong pressure for reforming legislation was exerted from outside the House, particularly by the army. Plans for law reform, soon taken up in the House by Henry Marten, were abundant. On 22 October the House agreed to 'take into consideration the regulation of the proceedings of the laws, and of all delays and charges in courts of justice; as also of all exorbitant fees, and other grievances, for the better ease and benefit of the people'. On the 25th it was resolved that all legal proceedings should be conducted in English and in ordinary hand, and a committee, chaired by Marten, was appointed to consider 'the delays and unnecessary charges, in proceedings in the law; and to present one or more bills to the House, for redress thereof'. The committee was also 'to consider of the salaries and the fees of judges and officers; and what officers or fees are fit to be retrenched'. Soon the Rump was busy with a host of proposals for law reform. Marten's committee, however, was packed with conservative lawyers. With 'the rest of the members of the long robe', they were 'enjoined to give their constant attendance on this committee'. Ordered to report to the House every Friday, the committee did so only for the first two weeks of its existence. Not until mid-December did Marten make his report. The act for holding legal proceedings in English soon passed the House, but thereafter the movement for law reform again receded into the background.[2]

Radical success in the sphere of religious reform was equally dramatic but equally short-lived. On 27 September 1650 parliament passed its celebrated toleration act. The measure repealed Elizabethan statutes enjoining church attendances on Sundays, on the stated ground that 'by the said acts divers religious and peaceable people, well-affected to the prosperity of the Commonwealth, have ... been molested and im-

[1] *H.M.C.R. Leybourne-Popham*, p. 78; Underdown, *Pride's Purge*, p. 289; *C.J.* 12 Dec. 1650, 3 Jan. 1651.
[2] *C.J.* 22, 25 Oct., 1, 8 Nov., 13 Dec. 1650; above, pp. 107–8. Cf. *H.M.C.R. Leybourne-Popham*, pp. 77–8.

prisoned'. Here, it might be thought, was a shining testament to the true 'independency' of the Commonwealth regime. With the defeat of the Scottish presbyterians, it might be supposed, the Rump at last felt able to indulge a taste for radical religious reform, and to make a triumphant gesture towards the principle of liberty of conscience. Yet the welcome given to the toleration act by parliament's publicity machine was anything but triumphant. The act was the Rump's sole legislative concession to religious radicalism, and the House tried almost furtively to play down its importance. It was usual for the government press to give details of the Rump's more important legislation, and to support it by prompt and favourable comment. The treatment of the toleration act by certain parliamentary newspapers was a significant exception. On the day the act was passed, the Rump, making clear the limits to its enthusiasm for toleration, took further action to quell the activities of the Ranters. Neither *Mercurius Politicus* nor *A Perfect Diurnal* recorded the toleration act among the events of 27 September. Instead, they concentrated on the Rump's moves against the Ranters, 'the severity of which votes', *Mercurius Politicus* observed, 'may serve to stop the slanderous mouths of those that publish abroad such vile reports of this Commonwealth, as if [the Rump] intended to countenance impious and licentious practices, under pretence of religion and liberty'. *Mercurius Politicus* did not mention the act until 30 September. Nor did *The Weekly Intelligencer*, which even then took pains to stress that, in the act, 'it is provided that liberty be not abused'. This was a reference to the clause in the act which obliged everyone to attend some form of service on Sundays, 'to the end that no profane or licentious persons may take occasion by the repealing of the said laws (intended only for relief of pious and peaceably minded people from the rigour of them) to neglect the performance of religious duties'. *A Perfect Diurnal* failed to refer to the act until its next weekly edition, when it provided a terse summary emphasising the limits of the measure.[1] The Rump, far from rejoicing in the toleration act, seems to have been positively embarrassed by it. Perhaps radicals took the point, for there is little sign that they attached much importance to the measure.

The frosty reception accorded the toleration act by the government press was no isolated act of conservative defiance. Rather, it was a

---

[1] *C.J.* 27 Sep. 1650; Firth and Rait, *Acts and Ordinances*, ii. 423–5; Gardiner, *History of the Commonwealth and Protectorate*, ii. 3; *Mercurius Politicus* 26 Sep.–3 Oct. 1650, pp. 286–7 (with which cf. e.g. *ibid.* 9–16 Oct. 1651, pp. 1128–9); *Perfect Diurnal . . . Armies* 23–30 Sep. 1650, pp. 487–8, 30 Sep.–7 Oct. 1650, p. 543; *Weekly Intelligencer* 24 Sep.–1 Oct. 1650, p. 16.

symptom of a growing parliamentary hostility to the sects which played a central part in Rump politics between Dunbar and Worcester. The conflict with the Scots had now altered in character. The humiliation of the kirk at Dunbar strengthened the bargaining position of Charles II and the royalists in Scotland, and it was they, rather than the presbyterian clergy, who were now in control. Accordingly the Rump was now able to portray the war as a national rather than as a religious one, as a struggle against royalism rather than against presbyterianism. It was thus natural for the English government to increase its efforts to reunite the parliamentary party of the 1640s against the common royalist threat. Indicative of the changing mood were the tactics of *Mercurius Politicus*. Before Dunbar the newspaper had conducted a vicious, indiscriminate campaign against presbyterians of all kinds (whether English or Scottish), against the political pretensions of clergymen, and against 'the secluded members', while at the same time urging Cavaliers to submit passively to the republic. After Dunbar *Mercurius Politicus*, suddenly converted to the principles of religious respectability, announced a truce with the presbyterian clergy: 'now that they are down, they shall have our pity'. Although the newspaper still could not resist occasional anti-clerical jibes, its author now showed himself much more concerned to distinguish between English and Scottish presbyterians, appealing to the former for support while castigating Scotsmen of all kinds. Soon after Dunbar the newspaper announced that the Rump, in its determination to reunite the English nation, was planning an act of general pardon; and in April 1651 it argued that 'those gentlemen of the presbyterian opinion ought now, if not for love, yet in consideration of their own safety, to return and cast themselves in the arms of their old friends, rather than expose themselves to the malice of their old enemies'. In May 1651 *Mercurius Politicus* published in full a distinctly unrevolutionary petition from Cheshire, which lauded the Rump's 'presbyterian' legislation against moral and religious licence while making no mention of the toleration act. The petitioners received the thanks of the House; 'and well they deserved it', *Mercurius Politicus* noted, 'having given a noble pattern of resolution to the other counties, to detest the malignant interest'.[1] How much success this and other propaganda enjoyed in the country at large

---

[1] *Mercurius Politicus* 5–12 Sep. 1650, p. 210, 19–26 Sep. 1650, pp. 261–3, 15–22 May 1651, pp. 802–4. Cf. *ibid.* June 1650–Aug. 1651, pp. 2, 4, 5, 13, 17–18, 20, 26, 33–4, 38–9, 50–3, 56, 58–60, 65–6, 67–9, 70, 97–9, 116–17, 129–31, 144, 145–6, 148, 159, 174, 177, 178, 193–4, 199, 225–6, 232, 306–7, 381–2, 528, 655, 671–3, 703–4, 735–6, 783–4, 1012.

is unclear, but it is notable that both Fairfax and the purged M.P. Sir Richard Onslow, men much influenced by presbyterian divines, seem actively to have supported the Rump's military action against the invading Scots in the late summer of 1651. The lawyer Francis Thorpe, who may well have withdrawn his support for the Rump in the months before Dunbar, 'exchanged a gown for a sword' during the invasion. Lord Wharton, who had broken with Cromwell at the time of the purge and who opposed the Rump's decision to invade Scotland, found himself 'now satisfied because it is the old quarrel'. The Earl of Leicester, equally unenthusiastic about the Rump, wrote of the Scots at this time as 'the enemy'.[1] Cromwell's decision in August 1651 to allow the Scots to invade England, and there to meet the full blast of English hatred, was a shrewd one.

The political mood prevalent during the first half of 1651 provided the Rump with a timely opportunity to demonstrate once more its affection for the established puritan worship and ministry, and its dislike of those who sought to undermine them. It needed little encouragement. In February 1651 it expelled one of its members, John Fry, 'chiefly, as was conceived, upon a presbyterian interest'. Fry, author of cheerfully anti-clerical and anti-Trinitarian pamphlets, had been suspended on 26 January 1649 from the House of Commons and from the high court trying Charles I. Despite a firm hint by John Owen that he should remain excluded, however, he had been readmitted to parliament early in February 1649 as a concession to Leveller pressure for religious toleration. In March 1651 a tract appeared, under the auspices of one of the Rump's semi-official printers, attacking Fry and praising the work of the ministers who continued to sit in the Assembly of Divines.[2] It was but one of a host of pamphlets published between January and August 1651 with the aim either of boosting support for religious presbyterianism, of emphasising the amount of common ground between religious presbyterianism and religious independency, or of discrediting the sects.[3]

[1] *Perfect Diurnal . . . Armies* 1–8 Sep. 1651, p. 1268; *Mercurius Politicus* 14–21 Aug. 1651, p. 1000; *H.M.C.R. De Lisle and Dudley*, vi. 602–6; Underdown, *Royalist Conspiracy in England*, p. 38; G. F. T. Jones, *Saw-pit Wharton* (Sydney, 1967), p. 134.

[2] *C.J.* 26, 30 Jan., 3 Feb. 1649, 31 Jan., 20, 22 Feb. 1651; Whitelocke, *Memorials*, iii. 291; Asty, *Sermons of John Owen*, p. 311; *The Moderate* 30 Jan.–6 Feb. 1649, p. 293; Fry, *The Accuser Shamed*, and *The Clergy in their Colours* (1650); *Original Letters . . . addressed to Oliver Cromwell*, p. 81; *Divine Beams of Glorious Light* (1651), esp. p. 3.

[3] E.g. *Digitus Testium*; T. Hall, *The Pulpit Guarded*; T. Goodwin, *Christ the Universal Peace-Maker*; R. Culmer, *The Ministers Hue and Cry*; W. Prynne, *Independency Examined* (all published 1651).

A correspondent of Cromwell, dismayed by the 'prosecution' of Fry, found cause for still more aggrieved complaint. On 13 March three preachers delivered fast sermons to the Rump. One was Owen, who according to a government newspaper preached 'very excellently . . . in vindication of the present government', and who was promptly rewarded with the deanery of Christ Church, Oxford. The second preacher, Leigh, 'was very full and learned', and also earned the House's approval. The third preacher, however, was 'exceeding home in his application'.[1] This was Thomas Harrison's nominee John Simpson, 'commonly called the antinomian'. In his sermon, according to Cromwell's correspondent, Simpson

set up the spirit of God against humane learning, against that order of men who challenge to themselves the prerogative of dispensing it; he said the word Chemarim, used in Zephany, did properly signify black coats [i.e. clergymen] . . . He further said, he believed the Lord had more eminently blessed the preaching of the gospel by the soldiers of the army, than he had done the endeavours of the ministers, in many years together.

The result was a stormy debate, lasting over two hours and culminating in an implied rebuke to Simpson. Harrison was 'exceedingly reflected upon' for nominating Simpson to preach. Cromwell's correspondent noted 'the observations that are made of every little thing that is done here, as if done in favour to a presbyterian interest; and surely that interest is judged to be very thriving here'.[2] After the Simpson incident the formal expression of thanks to clergymen preaching before the House, and invitations to print them, became infrequent, a sign of the growing contentiousness of Rump politics.[3] On 21 March the Rump revived discussion of its bill for the propagation of the gospel at national level. By May it had become clear that the main concern of those who now promoted the measure was to secure the 'due payment' of tithes. It was probably also about May that a Rump committee took action against a group of religious radicals for 'pretended conventicling'. By June the House, its hostility to the sects now overt, was debating a bill 'touching the conformity in religion'.[4]

The Rump's mounting opposition to religious radicalism produced its own reaction, not least in the House itself. Political tension was

[1] *Perfect Account* 12–19 Mar. 1651, p. 77.
[2] *Original Letters . . . addressed to Oliver Cromwell*, pp. 82–3.
[3] Trevor-Roper, *Religion, The Reformation and Social Change*, p. 342 and n.
[4] *C.J.* 27 Feb., 21 Mar., 18, 25, 30 Apr., 1, 9, 20, 23 May, 26 June 1651; *Perfect Account* 30 Apr.–7 May 1651, p. 131; *The Humble Petition and Appeal of John Fielder*, p. 2.

increased by the now widespread evidence of royalist organisation in England, much of it uncovered during an attempted insurrection in Norfolk in December 1650. On 4 March 1651 the royalist Sir Henry Hyde was executed, as was Browne Bushell at the end of the same month. Thereafter the war in Scotland, now moving towards its second climax, cast its shadow once more over parliamentary politics, fortifying the convictions of those who opposed the movement for conciliation. Soon the government found itself split more profoundly than at any previous time. The first sign of serious trouble came late in May 1651, when the most radical of the government newspapers began to stir up social resentment against peers.[1] In June, at the instigation of Harrison, the House expelled Lord Howard of Escrick for succumbing to bribery, fined him £10,000 and imprisoned him in the Tower. The case had been brought to light at least as early as the previous July, but the Rump had evidently been reluctant to take action. One of Howard's sons, when he received news of his father's punishment, promptly went over to the royalists in the north. 'The riddance of such are no loss to us', Harrison observed.[2] Soon, however, the Howard incident passed into relative obscurity. In late June and throughout July of 1651 attention was focused instead on one of the major political conflicts of the Rump period: the case of Christopher Love.

In March, the intelligence system run by Thomas Scot and George Bishop had brought off a major coup with the arrest of the royalist agent Thomas Coke. Threatened with death, Coke proved singularly forthcoming under interrogation. Evidence soon emerged of a large network of conspiracy, based on the exiled court and the city of London, and involving a number of prominent city presbyterian ministers. On 2 May three of them, Christopher Love, William Jenkins and Thomas Case, were arrested. So were five laymen, two of whom had links with two of the most important political presbyterians (Denzil Holles and Edward Massey) to have sat in the Commons before the purge.[3] It was widely expected that a number of other min-

[1] *Perfect Account* 28 May–4 June 1651, p. 161.
[2] C.J. 20, 24, 25 June 1651; *Memoirs of Edmund Ludlow*, i. 258–9; H.M.C.R. *De Lisle and Dudley*, vi. 482; Whitelocke Letters (Longleat) x, fo. 169: Darnall to Whitelocke, 31 July 1650; C.C.C., pp. 435, 445; *Perfect Passages* 20–27 June 1651, p. 352; *Several Proceedings* 14–21 Aug. 1651, p. 1520.
[3] The significance of the Love episode has not, I think, been adequately appreciated. For brief accounts see Gardiner, *History of the Commonwealth and Protectorate*, ii. 13–17, 20–1; Underdown, *Royalist Conspiracy in England*, p. 49; Carlson, 'History of the Presbyterian Party from Pride's Purge to the dissolution of the Long Parliament', pp. 115–22. Cf. Lois Spencer, 'The politics of George Thomason', *The Library*, 5th series, xiv (1959),

isters, including even such moderate figures as Stephen Marshall and Edmund Calamy, would be arrested and tried.[1] In June Love was sentenced to death by the High Court of Justice. At first radicals were confident that the sentence would be implemented, but their hopes began to fade as an intensive campaign was launched to quash, or at least to lighten, the penalty.[2] Love's case soon came to symbolise the conflict between on the one hand those for whom Pride's Purge and the execution of the king had been merely the starting point of the godly reformation, and for whom there could be no going back to the 1640s, and on the other all those who were anxious to heal the wounds of the parliamentary cause.

To some the issue was a simple one: no regime as heavily beset as the Commonwealth government by both internal and external dangers could afford to be lenient towards those whom it found guilty of treason. Love's crimes seemed to vindicate those who had argued that royalists and presbyterians were both of the same mould, and who had therefore opposed the Rump's overtures to presbyterians. Love, like his fellow conspirator Jenkins, had been in trouble with the regime before, and had received every warning.[3] As his wife wrote later, he 'had a deep knowledge and was well skilled in the mysteries of the kingdom', and 'publicly declared himself against the horrid murder of the king and against that cursed engagement when it came to be pressed upon his parish'.[4] Vane saw Love's case as a purely political one, finding himself, as he wrote to Cromwell, 'confirmed in my own opinion, that he and his brethren do still retain their old leaven . . . they do not judge us a lawful magistracy, nor esteem anything treason that is acted by them to destroy us, in order to bring in the king of Scots as the head of the Covenant'. Vane's attitude earned him a reputation as a 'back friend to black coats', but he remained firm in his conviction that Love must die.[5] Scot and Bishop were merciless in their exposure of the evidence against Love. In the event Scot opposed the ultimate penalty, but Bishop asked indignantly 'to what end serves all the providence of God . . . in bringing these designs to light, if so be such a malefactor as

pp. 18–20; H. G. Denton, 'The Presbyterian plot of 1651', *Journal of the Presbyterian History Society*, x (1952).
[1] Gardiner, *History of the Commonwealth and Protectorate*, ii. 15; Bell, *Memorials of the Civil War*, ii. 131.
[2] Clarke MS xix, fos. 32, 44ᵛ–5, 46ᵛ, 53.
[3] *C.J.* 4 July 1650; *Mercurius Politicus* 27 June–11 July 1650, pp. 50–3, 66–7.
[4] B.M., Sloane MS 3945, fo. 111ᵛ.
[5] *Original Letters . . . addressed to Oliver Cromwell* p. 84; 9, 11, 15 July 1651.

Mr. Love escape?'[1] *Mercurius Politicus*, having until May 'given a weekly taste of the necessity of a reconciliation between us and our brethren of the [presbyterian] opinion', now changed its tune, perhaps under Milton's influence. 'It is high time', the paper announced, 'to assert the honour and integrity of the parliament against the passion and proceedings of our malcontents of the ministry; who notwithstanding all the levity, moderation and persuasion that hath been used towards them, have continually prostituted the reverence of their function.' *Mercurius Politicus* devoted an almost weekly tirade to the misdeeds of the presbyterian clergy until the Love case closed.[2] Most of the other government newspapers attacked Love in similarly scathing terms and urged the implementation of the death penalty.[3] Their sentiments were widely shared in the army;[4] as one army writer commented on the debates in the Rump over Love, 'if he escape the whole presbyterian [interest] will be a-top of the House'.[5] Feeling in parliament ran high when Sir Henry Mildmay introduced a part of Coke's confession which named twenty-one rumpers, including the Speaker, Bulstrode Whitelocke, Cornelius Holland, William Purefoy and Sir John Hippisley, as parties to the conspiracy.[6] Coke's allegations on this point were soon recognised as specious even by the Rump's enemies.[7] They were readily discounted by parliament, but not before Purefoy and others had threatened 'to move against Sir Henry Mildmay for bringing in so scandalous a report into the House against them'.[8]

Cromwell, although away in Scotland, was looked to as the chief 'balance' to Vane's demand for the implementation of the death penalty.[9] In fact, swayed no doubt by army feeling and perhaps also by Vane's arguments, he did nothing to encourage presbyterian hopes.[10] In

[1] *C.J.* 9 July 1651; C. H. Firth (ed.), 'Thomas Scot's account of his actions as Intelligencer during the Commonwealth', *E.H.R.*, xii (1897), 121; *Original Letters ... addressed to Oliver Cromwell*, p. 75; and see Abbott, *Writings and Speeches*, ii. 654.

[2] *Mercurius Politicus* 12 June–28 Aug. 1651, pp. 863, 879–82, 884, 885–7, 900, 917–19, 928, 933–5, 949–52, 965–7, 983–6, 1013–16.

[3] *Weekly Intelligencer* 24 June–1 July 1651, pp. 210–11; *Perfect Account* 25 June–2 July 1651, p. 196; *Mercurius Scommaticus* 1–8 July 1650, pp. 38–9; *Perfect Passages* 20 June–7 July 1651, p. 1148.

[4] Clarke MS xix, fos. 33ᵛ, 53, 76; Lt. Col. George Joyce, *A Letter or Epistle to all well-minded People* (1651).

[5] Clarke MS xix, fo. 45.

[6] *Ibid.* xix, fos. 12 &ᵛ, 13ᵛ, 14, 15, 18.

[7] *Brief Narration of the Mysteries of State*, p. 109.   [8] Clarke MS xix, fo. 73ᵛ.

[9] *Original Letters ... addressed to Oliver Cromwell*, p. 84.

[10] Gardiner, *History of the Commonwealth and Protectorate*, ii, 20; Whitelocke, *Memorials*, iii. 326; *Gag to Love's Advocate*, p. 22; *Letters from Roundhead Officers ... to Captain A. Baynes*, p. 37.

one letter, which has apparently not survived, he even gave a 'hint . . . for impartial justice', to the pleasure of the soldiery.[1] This, nevertheless, was the kind of issue on which Cromwell could usually be expected to favour moderation, and Love himself appealed to him.[2] So did Cromwell's friend Robert Hammond, who, writing from London, hinted that mildness towards Love might be repaid by his own return to the cause he had deserted at Pride's Purge. To Hammond, the Love case was a first-class opportunity to reconcile the presbyterians to the regime; for leniency, 'according to the frame and temper men who have been exceedingly averse are now in . . . may so gain upon them, that the victory may be greater than winning a field'. Above all, 'the hearts of many, if not most of all good men here of all parties are exceedingly set to save his life, from this ground, that it may be a means to unite the hearts of all good men, the bent of whose spirits are set to walk in the ways of the Lord'.[3]

Hammond did not exaggerate the widespread determination to use the Love case as a means of reconciling presbyterians and independents. The movement for leniency towards Love, supported by daily fasts in the city and by a petition said by an unfriendly source to have attracted over twenty thousand signatures, came not only from presbyterian clergymen, not only from politically neutral divines in Kent and Worcestershire, but also from ministers who preached regularly before the Rump, like John Bond, Joseph Caryl, William Greenhill, Philip Nye and William Strong. John Dury also pleaded for mercy. As one petition to the House put it, 'Consider who they are that plead for [Love], and you will find them the most faithful and knowing Christian friends you have . . . they that do daily pray for you.' Soon after the trial, as one writer reported, a series of weekly meetings was organised between presbyterian and independent ministers, 'to seek God for a happy reconciliation of the difference between them . . . and truly I understand there is great hope of making up that sad breach, even by this means'. One petition on Love's behalf, catching precisely the tone of political moderation, combined with distaste for the army, which was likely to appeal to a large number of rumpers, shrewdly implied that the army's demand for Love's execution was a good reason for quashing the sentence.[4] If rumpers were appalled by Love's methods,

---

[1] Clarke MS xix, fos. 45, 53.
[2] *A Clear and Necessary Vindication of Mr. Love* (1651), p. 42.
[3] *Original Letters . . . addressed to Oliver Cromwell*, p. 75; Gardiner, *History of the Commonwealth and Protectorate*, ii. 20.
[4] *Love's Advocate* (1651), pp. 6, 7, 11–12; *Gag to Love's Advocate*, p. 16; *Clear and Necessary*

many of them must have regarded his aims as less reprehensible. He and his fellow conspirators had planned not a return to unbridled royalism, but the restoration of the Long Parliament as it had been before the purge, and negotiations with Charles II on the lines followed at Newport in 1648.[1] This was a programme with which many rumpers were likely to sympathise.

Those who pleaded for Love seem to have been concerned as often with political strategy as with political morality. Love claimed that the independent divines declined to attend the weekly meetings with their presbyterian brethren unless the latter 'would own the present power, declare against the Scots, and such like hard terms ... so that it seems their aim was more at the bringing over the ministers to join with the state faction, than out of any aim to save my life'. Two moderate independent clergymen, Owen and John Bond, visited Love in the Tower to try to persuade him to render his petition for pardon more conciliatory, a mission in which they may have been helped by the suspected clerical conspirator Edmund Calamy. Love refused to back down, and it was probably Owen and Bond who, between the time the petition left Love's hands and the time of its presentation to parliament, altered the wording to imply that Love had renounced the political aims of the Scots.[2]

Love's case dragged on in parliament for several weeks, and the Rump's undignified indecision earned considerable scorn.[3] The execution was twice postponed, once so late that a huge crowd had already gathered at the scaffold by the time the reprieve was announced.[4] Proposals that Love be merely banished, or even pardoned, received support in the House from religious presbyterians like John Gurdon and Philip Skippon, from conservative politicians like Sir William Brereton and Lord Lisle, and from advocates of religious toleration like Charles Fleetwood and Sir Gilbert Pickering. The motions for leniency were nevertheless defeated, with Vane and Mildmay leading the opposition.[5] Love, with one of the laymen involved in the conspiracy, was executed on 22 August, on 'an evening as fair as

Vindication of Mr. Love, p. 41; *Several Proceedings* 10–17 July 1651, pp. 1147–9 (where the petition from the prominent divines is given, with their names); *C.J.* 11 July, 16 Aug. 1651.

[1] Gardiner, *History of the Commonwealth and Protectorate*, ii. 15.

[2] *Clear and Necessary Vindication of Mr. Love*, pp. 36–7, 41–2; *A Short Plea for the Commonwealth* (1651), p. 11.

[3] *H.M.C.R. De Lisle and Dudley*, vi. 601–2, 607–8.

[4] Clarke MS xix, fo. 60.

[5] *C.J.* 9, 11, 15 July, 15, 16, 23 Aug. 1651.

it was calm'. Next day there was a storm of terrifying proportions, widely interpreted as an expression of divine anger.[1]

Love's execution broke the back of clerical opposition to the Rump. The day of thanksgiving appointed to celebrate the battle of Worcester was observed with a willingness which surprised government supporters.[2] Thereafter there was only occasional trouble from the presbyterian pulpits. William Jenkins, Love's fellow clerical conspirator, was released after submitting and publishing a cringing confession renouncing his former ways.[3] Richard Baxter, nevertheless, described the decision to execute Love as a 'blow' which

sunk deeper towards the root of the new Commonwealth than will easily be believed; and made them grow odious to almost [all] the religious party in the land, except the sectaries (though some Cavaliers said it was good enough for him, and laughed at it as good news); for now the people would not believe that they fought for the promoting of the gospel, who killed the ministers for the interest of their faction . . . After this, the most of the ministers and good people of the land did look upon the new Commonwealth as tyranny, and were more alienated from them than before.[4]

In viewing the execution as a piece of gratuitous malice, Baxter overlooked the political significance of the affair. On the day Love went to the block, Charles II's Scottish army, having marched south through England, was encamping at Worcester.[5] Love would never have died at parliament's hands for his religious views alone. He was executed, at a time of acute political danger, for political misdemeanours. That he was reprieved for so long tells us at least as much about the attitudes of rumpers as does the fact that he was eventually beheaded. Baxter was no doubt right in thinking that the immediate general reaction to Love's death was one of horror; but Baxter's political judgement was not always as sound as it might have been, and his own ecumenical aims may have led him to exaggerate the more lasting consequences of the Rump's decision. Although the combined attempts of presbyterian and independent divines to save Love failed, in the long term they strengthened the movement for reconciliation.

The conflict over the Love case reflected a growing bitterness in Rump

---

[1] *Weekly Intelligencer* 19–26 Aug. 1651, p. 263.
[2] *Ibid.* 21–28 Oct. 1651, p. 330; *Perfect Account* 22–29 Oct. 1651, p. 334; *The Diary* 20–27 Oct. 1651, p. 40.
[3] *Several Proceedings* 9–16 Oct. 1651, pp. 1656–7.
[4] *Reliquiae Baxterianae*, p. 67.
[5] Abbott, *Writings and Speeches*, ii. 450.

politics which can also be seen in other developments between Dunbar and Worcester. In January and February 1651, Algernon Sidney was threatened by 'divers officers of the army' with a court-martial for crimes, whose nature is hidden from us, as governor of Dover. 'Truly', wrote his brother Lord Lisle to their ex-royalist father, 'I think he hath had very hard measure, and I know no grounds of it but his relation to a sort of people who are looked upon with a most jealous eye.' No doubt the memory of Sidney's clash with the 'revolutionaries' in February 1649, over the composition of the first Council of State, played its part in the incident. The charge against him was dropped, but only after what seems to have been an unseemly dispute between parliament and army over jurisdiction in the case.[1] In February, perhaps with a hint of deference to classical models of government, the Rump decided to retain only half the Councillors of State whose term had expired, and to elect new members in their places. John Bradshaw noted 'much talk . . . of persons and things, relating to the succeeding choice'. Much of the talk concerned Bradshaw himself, whom Cromwell was reputedly anxious to have removed from the office of president. Cromwell did not press his objections, but although Bradshaw retained his seat on the council his tenure of the presidency was nearing its end.[2] Lord Lisle, who wrote that 'many of us . . . have a mind to keep our seats',[3] became uncharacteristically energetic in the House in the weeks before the council elections, whether to impress the House with his industry or to protect his brother from the army's criticisms. Nevertheless he lost his seat. So did his equally conservative colleagues the Earl of Salisbury, the Earl of Denbigh (now on very distant terms with the regime), Robert Wallop and Alexander Popham. The inclusion of such men on the previous two councils had provided the 'revolutionaries' with a continual reminder of their tactical defeat in February 1649. Fairfax, now in retirement in Yorkshire, was also dropped from the council. On the other hand Harrison, so pointedly omitted from the previous councils, was now elected, as was his sectarian friend John Carew. Yet the elections were not an unqualified victory for the radicals. Such unrevolutionary figures as Brereton and John Feilder joined the council. Still more surprising was the omission of Marten and of two of his allies, Herbert Morley and Luke Robinson.

[1] *C.J.* 14, 29 Jan. 1651; *H.M.C.R. De Lisle and Dudley*, vi. 488; *Weekly Intelligencer* 28 Jan.–4 Feb. 1651, p. 47; above, p. 181.
[2] *Original Letters . . . addressed to Oliver Cromwell*, pp. 39, 40, 49, 50.
[3] *H.M.C.R. De Lisle and Dudley*, vi. 488.

Ludlow also lost his place, having been appointed in December 1650,
with John Jones, Miles Corbet and John Weaver, as a parliamentary
commissioner to Ireland. Marten had never been the most active of
councillors, and even when he returned to the council in November
1651 he was near the bottom of the list of those elected. The influence
exerted in the Rump by a figure so often unpopular is extraordinary;
indeed, his omission from the council in February 1651 came at a time
when his policies were meeting with considerable success.[1] In general,
however, those dropped from the council had either been among the
less energetic councillors or, if active on the council, then less so in the
House: the jealousy with which parliament controlled the executive
remained undiminished. Equally, most of those newly elected, like
Francis Allen, Richard Salwey and Edmund Prideaux, had been among
the most active rumpers and had perhaps been unlucky not to secure
election earlier. The elections, nevertheless, left a sour taste. 'I am
afraid', wrote a government supporter about this time, 'that too many
study faction; and that self-greatness is too much eyed and aimed at.'[2]

   Another opportunity for factious squabbling was created by the
decision of 23 October 1650 (another of the Rump's concessions to
army feeling after Dunbar) to revive discussion of the issue of elections.
Constituencies not represented in the Rump began to voice their
dissatisfaction openly between Dunbar and Worcester.[3] Once again,
however, parliament expressed a preference for 'recruiter' elections
rather than fresh ones. Again, too, the Rump resolved to postpone
discussion of even the recruitment proposal until the scheme for a
redistribution of constituencies had been worked out;[4] and even by
March 1651 the House had not worked through the list of counties.
There was also the problem of deciding which members should be ex-
empted from re-election when the recruiter elections were held. The
proposal of November 1650 to expel all M.P.s who would not swear
approval of the act of regicide was doubtless intended to open their constituencies to men of revolutionary views. The House, quashing the proposal, agreed to an alternative plan likely to please 'conformists' rather
than 'revolutionaries'. If it had been implemented, some of the members
who had not sat since the purge would, like the rumpers, have been
allowed to retain their seats without re-election in the recruited parlia-

[1] Below, pp. 253–60.
[2] *Mercurius Politicus* 30 Jan.–6 Feb. 1651, p. 568. For the council elections see *C.J.* 7, 10
Feb. 1651.
[3] Cf. above, p. 176 n. 1, and the sources there cited.
[4] *C.J.* 23 Oct. 1650; *Mercurius Politicus* 20–27 Mar. 1651, p. 686.

ment. The Rump, in grand committee, worked through the names of
M.P.s absent since the purge to decide which of them should thus
retain their seats. A proposal to exempt William Pierrepoint from
re-election was defeated, but among the members recommended for
exemption were Sir Benjamin Rudyerd and Sir Richard Onslow, both
of whom had been imprisoned at the purge, Thomas Westrow and
Richard Norton, both to be admitted to the Rump after Worcester,
John Selden, Francis Bacon, and the son of the presbyterian leader
Denzil Holles.[1] The proposal to grant exemption to such members
may have been designed as a bait to lure them to the House, and so
to help fill the benches, rather than as a prelude to recruiter elections;
had the bait worked, indeed, recruitment would presumably have
become superfluous, at least in the eyes of 'conformists'. It may have
been to secure exemption that Gervase Piggot and Brampton Gurdon,
two rumpers admitted in the summer of 1649 apparently without
taking their seats thereafter, returned briefly to Westminster in April
1651. The exemption proposal was not the only attempt made between
Dunbar and Worcester to increase the Rump's active membership.
One member, Hugh Rogers, was admitted on 20 November 1650, and
six days later another, Richard Edwards, who had been admitted in
April 1649 but who had apparently failed to appear thereafter, was
summoned to attend the House. Neither proved an energetic acquisi-
tion.[2] In June 1651, when the order banning judges from sitting in
parliament was revoked, Oliver St John at last returned to the House.
In general, however, the movement to fill up the benches was unsuccessful. Whether men like Onslow and Selden would have been prepared to return we do not know. The question never arose, because in
the summer of 1651, as in the summer of 1650, the whole issue of
elections and membership was put to one side while the threat from
Scotland occupied the centre of the political stage.

The disappointment of the radical hopes raised by Dunbar was
reflected in, and to a large extent brought about by, changes in the
attitudes of Marten, Chaloner and their allies. The growing influence
of these men in the Rump was bought at the expense of their overriding
commitment to social radicalism. It was not that they lost interest in

[1] William Salt Library, MS 454, no. 6: John Trevor to John Swynfen, 7 Jan. 1651 (quoted
by Underdown, *Pride's Purge*, p. 289n.); *H.M.C.R. De Lisle and Dudley*, vi. 486.
[2] Above, p. 72; *C.J.* 10, 25 Apr. 1651. Edward Neville, another rumper who may not
previously have taken his seat, may have reappeared for similar reasons in January 1651
(*C.J.* 24 Jan.), and it is also possible that John Trevor, who had never been formally
admitted to the Rump, briefly appeared in it in December 1650: see below, p. 387.

reform; Marten, as we have seen, remained deeply involved in the movement to reform the law. It was merely that they became more interested in other things, and that it was about those things, rather than about reform, that a growing number of rumpers agreed with them. Dunbar gave a strong fillip to republican sentiment in England. Republicanism remained for the most part a nebulous concept, earning popularity partly because of its very imprecision and partly because it blended so easily with such age-old prejudices as jingoism and hatred of the Scots. *Mercurius Politicus*, in many ways the mouthpiece of the Marten–Chaloner group between the summer of 1650 and the summer of 1651, began almost immediately after Dunbar to proclaim, in a series of weekly editorials, the virtues of a Commonwealth without a king.[1] Soon a series of pamphlets appeared, rejoicing in the successes of the new republic or advocating the commercial policies with which, as will be seen, the republican movement was increasingly becoming associated.[2] Early in 1651 there developed a cult of enthusiasm for the Venetian republic,[3] although radicals soon learned to rebel against so oligarchical a republican model.[4] Milton, too, sang the praises of republicanism, while Robert Blake reportedly told the Spanish king in Madrid that 'all kingdoms will annihilate tyranny and become republics. England had done so already; France was following in her wake; and as the natural gravity of the Spaniards rendered them some-what slower in their operations, he gave them ten years for the revolution in their country'.[5]

Yet one did not need to be a republican to support the policies pur-sued after Dunbar by Marten and Chaloner, whose principal concern was now the strengthening of England's commerce and diplomacy.[6]

[1] See the passage at the beginning of the newspaper for each weekly edition from Septem-ber 1650 onwards.

[2] E.g. H. Robinson, *The Office of Addresses and Encounters* (1650); S. Hartlib, *A Discourse of Husbandry* (1650); *Samuel Hartlib his Legacy* (1651); *London's Blame if not its Shame* (1651); *Several Proposals for the General Good of the Commonwealth*; Thomas Violet, *The Advance-ment of Merchandise* (1651). (There were many others.) I do not mean to imply that the concerns of these pamphleteers were in evidence only after Dunbar. Although the commercial policies advocated outside parliament, and pursued within it, did not make a profound impact on Rump politics until after September 1650, their foundations had been laid earlier.

[3] Cf. Trevor-Roper, *Religion, The Reformation and Social Change*, p. 359n.

[4] E.g. *Mercurius Politicus* 8 Jan.–5 Feb. 1652, pp. 1337, 1367, 1385.

[5] Zagorin, *History of Political Thought in the English Revolution*, p. 112; *Calendar of State Papers Venetian* 1647–52, pp. 169–70. The Blake episode had no doubt grown in the telling.

[6] E.g. *C.J.* 3, 29, 31 Oct., 19, 24, 31 Dec. 1650, 1, 7, 8, 10, 14, 15, 16, 21, 22, 24 Jan., 26, 27 Feb., 10, 11 Apr. 1651.

Before Dunbar the Commonwealth had survived largely because European governments were committed elsewhere. In August 1650, however, Blake had won an important naval victory over Rupert,[1] and Dunbar transformed the Commonwealth from a weak, isolated, defensive body into a much more secure and self-confident one, anxious to display its new-found strength before European courts now obliged to compete for England's favour. In November 1650 the Rump's diplomatic standing improved still further with the death of William of Orange, Stadtholder of the United Provinces, whose pro-Stuart sympathies had caused the Commonwealth considerable unease. His demise reversed a tendency towards Orange domination of the United Provinces, and Holland, which independently of the other provinces had long pursued a policy of amity with England, began to assume the leadership of the States General. The rumper Walter Strickland, England's ambassador at The Hague, had for some time been urging the Rump to support Holland against the Orange household; he argued that an alliance with Holland would 'be a foundation to cut off for ever all the hopes of your greatest enemies'.[2] The wisdom of Strickland's advice was now apparent to all.

By December 1650 and January 1651, when it received embassies from Spain and Portugal, the Rump felt strong enough to play off rival powers against each other. Insisting that foreign envoys pay tribute to its republican credentials, it indulged itself in, and immensely enjoyed, 'the pomps and formalities of receiving ambassadors'.[3] With its triumphant army and navy behind it, the Commonwealth was able to take a much stronger line in negotiations with foreign powers than had any English government for decades. Disagreement arose, however, about just how uncompromising a stance the government should adopt. Bradshaw complained to Cromwell of 'our impotent haste to ingratiate with neighbouring states', but even he felt that the Rump should aim only to 'be independent enough as to others; only [to] do all persons and nations justice, and causelessly provoke none; which would be the best way for subsistence and establishment, and teach nations in time to value us aright, and to do as they

---

[1] Gardiner, *History of the Commonwealth and Protectorate*, i. 303–5.
[2] *Collection of the State Papers of John Thurloe*, i. 115, 117, 118, 121–2, 123–6, 127, 128, 133–4; *Original Letters . . . addressed to Oliver Cromwell*, p. 51; Whitelocke, *Memorials*, iii. 51. See also P. Geyl, *The Netherlands in the Seventeenth Century (Part 2) 1648–1715* (1964), pp. 13–14, 19–25, and (for a fuller discussion) Geyl's *Orange and Stuart, 1641–1672* (1969).
[3] Salt MS 454, no. 6; *H.M.C.R. De Lisle and Dudley*, vi. 485; Whitelocke, *Memorials*, iii. 283; *Original Letters . . . addressed to Oliver Cromwell*, p. 401.

would be done to'.[1] Bradshaw probably toned down his jingoism for Cromwell's benefit, but it is unlikely that anyone in the Rump as yet contemplated an openly aggressive policy in Europe. So long as the Scottish threat remained, European warfare was unthinkable. Even so, the Commonwealth set its diplomatic sights high. There were proposals, first aired in *Mercurius Politicus* early in January 1651, for the subjugation of Scotland to the English Commonwealth, and for a union, both political and economic, with the United Provinces.[2] It was in pursuit of the latter policy that St John and Strickland set out on their ill-fated mission to The Hague in March 1651. The Dutch, interested only in the economic possibilities of union, were unsympathetic to the political aspects of the scheme, and the negotiations broke down. Whitelocke recorded that St John, his vanity wounded by the Dutch, arranged for his 'creatures' in the Rump to secure his and Strickland's recall to England.[3] The mission did far more harm than good to Anglo-Dutch relations, marked as it was by a haughtiness on both sides which contributed much to the outbreak of war between the two nations in 1652. The Rump's proposal for political union, although primarily designed to secure England from the ambitions of other powers, was the boldest manifestation of the government's diplomatic self-confidence after Dunbar.

Marten and Chaloner provided the impetus behind the new diplomacy. Chaloner, lauding the memory of 'worthy Hawkins and the famous Drake', yearned for a return to the glorious era of Elizabethan sea-power.[4] In December 1650 he wrote to Scot, who was visiting Cromwell in Scotland at the time, urging him to beg Oliver to expedite the defeat of the Scots and then turn his thoughts 'towards the sea', where lay 'our main business now'.[5] Chaloner had been the moving spirit, too, behind the Council of Trade set up by the Rump in August 1650.[6] The council's appointed task was to 'maintain and advance the traffic-trade, and several manufactures of this nation', and 'to improve and multiply the same for the best advantage and benefit

---

[1] *Original Letters . . . addressed to Oliver Cromwell*, pp. 39–40. (Possibly 'impotent' should be 'impatient'.)

[2] *Mercurius Politicus* 2–9 Jan. 1651, pp. 508, 512.

[3] Whitelocke, *Memorials*, iii. 287, 301.

[4] See his preface to Thomas Gage, *The English-American his Travail by Sea and Land* (1648).

[5] *Original Letters . . . addressed to Oliver Cromwell*, p. 43. (That the letter was written to Scot is evident from internal evidence.)

[6] *C.J.* 16 Mar., 19 June, 1 Aug., 24 Dec. 1650, 8 Jan. 1651; Firth and Rait, *Acts and Ordinances*, ii. 403–6.

thereof; to the end that the poor people of this land may be set on work, and their families preserved from begging and ruin; and that the Commonwealth might be enriched thereby, and no occasion left either for idleness or poverty'. The House, issuing its instructions to the council, noted that both foreign and domestic trade, 'being rightly driven and regularly managed, [do] exceedingly conduce to the strength, wealth, honour and prosperity' of the Commonwealth, while 'the negligent, irregular and defective management of trade must necessarily prove disadvantageous' to it. The brief given to the Council of Trade required it to draw up schemes to foster economic improvement. It was to discuss means of improving manufacturing techniques, and 'to consider how the trades and manufactures of this nation may most fitly and equitably be distributed to every part thereof, to the end that one part may not abound with trade, and another remain poor and desolate for want of the same'. It was also to procure 'a perfect balance of trade'; to make certain sections of rivers navigable; to debate the issue of free ports; and to ensure that customs and excise dues were 'so equally laid, and evenly managed, as neither trade may thereby be hindered, nor the state made incapable to defray the public charges of the nation'.[1]

After Dunbar both parliament and the Council of Trade busied themselves with proposals designed to answer these needs. There were moves to give the Norwich Weavers Company control of the whole Norfolk cloth industry; to repair the highways of the city of London; to make navigable an important section of the River Wye; to reform abuses in the manufacture of wire thread; to prevent the export both of clay and of lead and iron ore; to promote the melting of iron ore; and to reform the collection of the excise. Convoys were granted to merchant ships not only (as had hitherto been the case) in coastal waters, but in the European seas.[2] Thomas Atkins, M.P. for Norwich and sponsor of the Norfolk Weavers bill, wrote in January 1651 that 'it is hoped that over a short time . . . trading will be revived, and traders encouraged'.[3] In economics as in diplomacy, the clouds seemed to be lifting.

The interest of Marten and Chaloner in commercial matters was shared by many rumpers. Vane, with Chaloner, was one of the warmest

[1] Firth and Rait, *Acts and Ordinances*, ii. 403.
[2] J. P. Cooper, 'Economic regulation and the cloth industry in seventeenth-century England', *Transactions of the Royal Historical Society*, 5th series, xx (1970), 89, 90; *C.J.* 27 Nov. 1650, 10, 22, 29 Jan., 27 Feb., 6 Mar., 29 July 1651; *Perfect Passages* 20–26 Dec. 1650, p. 159. And see Violet, *The Advancement of Merchandise*, pp. 94–124.
[3] B.M., Add. MS 22,620, fo. 142: Atkins to mayor of Norwich, 9 Jan. 1651.

advocates of the Council of Trade.[1] Scot, on intimate terms with Chaloner after Dunbar and a close relation of the prominent city merchant and politician Owen Rowe, energetically cooperated with the merchant community of London in the autumn of 1650 to devise cheaper means of financing and supplying the navy.[2] Heselrige, who accompanied Scot on the latter's visit to Cromwell in Scotland in December 1650, also seems to have been friendly with Chaloner at this time.[3] He had long been an ally of John Price, the city politician and assiduous Commonwealth supporter.[4] The importance and cohesion of M.P.s with commercial interests and experience has already been emphasised. London merchants like George Thomson (brother of Maurice Thomson, one of the most influential overseas traders of the Rump period), George Snelling, Rowland Wilson, Francis Allen, Richard Salwey (one of the founder members of the Council of Trade) and Edmund Harvey sat together on committees concerned with a wide variety of issues. They were frequently joined by west-country merchants like John Dove, John Ashe, Gregory Clement, Thomas Boone (with Chaloner one of the chief advocates of the Council of Trade) and Nicholas Gould. The nexus of merchant M.P.s now grew in political importance as it came to overlap two of the Rump's other groupings. The Marten–Chaloner network was the first. Chaloner was especially active in organising merchant M.P.s, but Marten also played his part. Luke Robinson, one of Marten's closest allies, developed a strong interest in commercial matters at this time,[5] while Ludlow, accustomed to cooperating with his fellow Wiltshire rumper John Dove, was thus brought into the circle of Dove's friend Gregory Clement. The second grouping, controlled by Herbert Morley, consisted of M.P.s from Sussex and the Cinque Ports. Some of Morley's satellites, like William Hay, John Fagge and Roger Gratwick, appeared only rarely in the House, but Morley marshalled them as an effective combine on the Navy Committee. Morley himself was easily the most important member to join forces with the Marten–Chaloner group.[6]

---

[1] E.g. *C.J.* 16 Mar. 1650; Firth and Rait, *Acts and Ordinances*, ii. 403.

[2] *Original Letters . . . addressed to Oliver Cromwell*, p. 28; J. E. Farnell, 'The Navigation Act of 1651. The first Dutch war and the London merchant community', *Economic History Review*, 2nd series, xvi (1963–4), 442.

[3] *Original Letters . . . addressed to Oliver Cromwell*, p. 43.

[4] May, *Anatomy of . . . Lilburne's Spirit and Pamphlets*, p. 11; J. Lilburne, *A Just Reproof to Haberdashers Hall* (1651), p. 5.

[5] Above, p. 39.

[6] Cf. above, pp. 29, 222. It would be impossible to convey by citation the cooperation, cohesion and interconnection of these three groupings in this period. The evidence is

There were a number of other M.P.s who took an informed and lively interest in commercial and naval matters during the Rump period, like Bulstrode Whitelocke, Sir James Harrington, Sir John Danvers, John Trenchard and the Bristol M.P.s Richard Aldworth and Luke Hodges.[1] The Rump was well equipped to discuss commercial policy, not least because of its close relationship with a number of merchants and politicians among the independent congregations of London. These men, coming to power on the backs of the army in December 1648, had thereafter entrenched their authority in the city. Throughout the Rump period they undertook a wide range of administrative responsibilities on the government's behalf.[2]

It is sometimes implied that the Rump's relationship with the merchant community represented a subordination of public to private interests. It is certainly the case that a number of M.P.s, and a number of friends of M.P.s, had private commercial interests, and that some of those interests must have benefited from the government's commercial policies. Yet this is true of almost any period of modern English history. What matters is the manner in which the Rump's decisions on commercial matters were taken. Depending heavily on merchants and trading companies for much of its information, the regime received the usual petitions, and was subjected to the usual pressures, from lobbies representing commercial interests. Those lobbies, however, had to compete for the government's attention, and the government's bargaining position was stronger than that of the men who lobbied it. The only evidence which has been advanced to suggest that the Rump put private before public concerns is a brief statement by a royalist newswriter, who was often ill-informed, to the effect that the navigation act of October 1651 was framed 'by some few men for their interest'.[3] Conceivably it was, although there is no evidence to support the claim. But whoever inspired the navigation act, the important question is why the Rump agreed to it. If one reads the memoranda, the pamphlets,

both extensive and diffuse, pervading the *Journal of the House of Commons*, the *Calendar of State Papers Domestic*, and the records of parliamentary committees.
[1] Again, the evidence is ubiquitous. Interesting evidence on Harrington's commercial activities can be found in B.M., Add. MS 10,114, fo. 31ᵛ, and on Trenchard's in Hartlib MSS, bundles xxxiii (letters of Worsley to Dury, Aug. 1649 and of Wheeler to Worsley, Aug. 1650) and lxi (Strickland to Vane, Sep. 1649).
[2] Farnell, 'The Navigation Act', and 'Usurpation of honest London householders', *passim*; Firth and Rait, *Acts and Ordinances*, ii. *passim* (all acts involving the appointment of commissioners); *C.J.* 15 Dec. 1648.
[3] Gardiner, *History of the Commonwealth and Protectorate*, ii. 120. Cf. Farnell, 'The Navigation Act', p. 449.

and the records of discussions bearing on the formulation of the government's commercial policies, one is reminded time and again of a pervasive and time-honoured concept of the proper relationship between trade and the public interest. The precarious economic circumstances of the Commonwealth period dictated firm economic priorities, clearly reflected in the instructions given to the Council of Trade. The fear of poverty, the need to spread wealth equally through the land, the concern for fiscal stability, the emphasis on strengthening shipping and improving inland communications – these were age-old matters of national economic survival, to which private interests had invariably to be subordinated. The Rump worked closely with merchants who were prepared to assist it, but negotiations were conducted strictly on the government's terms. What is most striking about the M.P.s and the city merchants whose commercial expertise so profoundly influenced government policy is the variety of the private interests, as well as of the political views, which they represented. Few merchant M.P.s stood to gain personally from the policies they advocated. If members with commercial interests were able to form a united pressure group, it was only as exponents of a programme designed in accordance with the House's concept of the public interest.[1]

The interplay between trade and politics became increasingly important in the seventeenth century, because trade itself became an increasingly important part of the national economy. Whether and how far the period of the civil wars and Interregnum hastened these twin developments is a matter for debate. What is clear is that the Rump's preoccupation with commerce reflected rather than created a trend. The government's economic concerns remained traditional. Nothing better illustrates its conservatism than its failure to abolish commercial monopolies and to broaden the social base of the great trading companies. The Marten–Chaloner group seems to have been sympathetic to anti-monopolistic sentiments, and it is likely that Marten's commercial policies after Dunbar, like his advocacy of law reform in the same period, were designed to appeal to 'the middle sort' whom Milton praised so warmly in March 1651.[2] The instructions given by

---

[1] On the general theme of the relationship between English governments and commercial interests, see the sagacious essay by C. H. Wilson, *Economic History and the Historian* (1969), chapter ix. The Rump period seems to me to provide an admirable illustration of Professor Wilson's argument. There is, of course, room for a much fuller analysis of the Rump's commercial policies than I have provided.

[2] *Weekly Intelligencer* 22–29 Oct. 1650, p. 40; *Perfect Passages* 13–20 Sep. 1650, p. 81; Zagorin, *History of Political Thought in the English Revolution*, p. 112. Cf. *Perfect Passages*

the House to Chaloner's Council of Trade on the subject of monopolies were nevertheless cautious. The council was ordered to consider whether it was 'necessary' to 'give way' to 'a more open and free trade than that of companies and societies, and in what manner it is fittest to be done'. Care was to be taken 'that government and order in trade may be preserved, and confusion avoided'. As Professor Underdown has observed, 'There is no sign that the Rump ever seriously contemplated a general loosening of trade in favour of the small traders, the provincial clothiers, or the outports.'[1] This was partly because of the Rump's innate resistance to social change; it was also partly because a government frightened of economic instability could more easily exercise economic control, and protect the community at large, by cooperating with trading companies than it could without them.

The very success of the Marten–Chaloner group in promoting ambitious commercial and diplomatic policies had the effect of disarming its radicalism. The commercial policies which Marten and Chaloner advocated had, for them, a social dimension, but as time went by the group became more concerned with national power and prestige than with social change. Its programme, once taken up by men like Morley, Heselrige and Scot, became respectable; and as an agent of social radicalism the Marten–Chaloner group became increasingly ineffective. Scot's attitude at this time is especially revealing. Despite his commitment to the act of regicide, his radicalism can easily be exaggerated. Like his friend William Purefoy, he may have been among the M.P.s who had resented Pride's Purge. In January 1649 he and Purefoy had sought to preserve the House of Lords. In February 1649 he had taken charge of the five-man committee which had nominated so many 'conformist' members to the first Council of State. He had been responsible for the strikingly unrevolutionary manifesto produced by the Rump during the perilous circumstances of September 1649.[2] Now, in November 1650, organising the government's cooperation with city merchants, he wrote a letter to Cromwell which encapsulated the political philosophy of the Rump's 'juncto', of which he was so prominent a member: 'England is not as France, a meadow to be mowed as often as the governors please; our interest is to

---

25 Oct.–1 Nov. 1650, pp. 104–5; *Perfect Diurnal . . . Armies* 21 Oct.–4 Nov. 1650, pp. 585–6, 600; Stocks, *Records of the Borough of Leicester*, pp. 428–30.
[1] Underdown, *Pride's Purge*, p. 284.
[2] Above, pp. 49, 177, 214–5; *Diary of Thomas Burton*, iv. 453.

do our work with as little grievance to our new people, scarce yet proselytised, as is possible.'[1]

The preoccupation of Marten and his friends with commercial matters also encouraged a growing awareness of the contradiction within the revolution between spiritual and secular radicalism. Had the civil war been fought, as the sects believed, on behalf of the godly elect? Or had its outcome, as Marten and Chaloner argued, been the victory of popular political rights?[2] The radicalism of a Harrison and the radicalism of a Marten became increasingly at odds. Marten, Chaloner and Neville were renowned for their indifference to matters spiritual. Anthony à Wood wrote that Chaloner was 'as far from being a puritan or a presbyterian as the east is from the west; for he was a boon companion, of Henry Marten's gang, was of the natural religion, and loved to enjoy the comfortable importances of this life, without any thought of laying up for a wet day'. Wood wrote of Thomas May, an intimate associate of the Marten–Chaloner group who died late in 1650, that he 'became a debauchee *ad omnia*, entertained ill principles as to religion, spoke often very slightingly of the Holy Trinity, kept beastly and atheistical company, of whom Tho. Chaloner was one'.[3] It was May who had warned, in October 1649, that fear of religious toleration was the chief source of presbyterian hostility to the regime.[4] Perhaps May's comment explains why, after 1649, Marten's concern for religious reform became much less pronounced than his interest in the more secular issues of commerce and the law. Henry Robinson, who found favour with the Rump, had written in 1649 that after seven years of fighting for religious liberty it was time to concentrate on 'civil immunities'; and in October 1650 Robinson's associate Vincent Potter, advancing a programme of economic reform, suggested that 'though heavenly things should beyond all proportion be preferred before earthly, yet where they are both consistent neither ought to be at all neglected'.[5] The distinction between the heavenly and the earthly was beginning to play an important part in Rump politics, whose worldly tenor became ever more disturbing to religious radicals outside the House.

[1] *Original Letters . . . addressed to Oliver Cromwell*, p. 28.
[2] Cf. G. Burnet, *History of Mine Own Time* (2 vols., 1897), i. 120, and Hill, *God's Englishman*, chapter 8.
[3] Wood, *Athenae Oxoniensis*, ii. 295, iii. 531; *Dictionary of National Biography*: Chaloner and Neville; *Diary of Thomas Burton*, iii. 296. Cf. Marvell's poem, 'Tom May's Death'.
[4] Above, p. 232.
[5] James, *Social Problems and Policy*, p. 66; Potter, *The Key of Wealth* (1650), p. 1.

It also upset godly men within it. Vane, who was an old enemy of Marten and who had challenged Neville's election to the Rump, was dismayed by the outlook of 'Tom Chaloner, Harry Neville, and those wits', of 'Tom Chaloner, Tom May . . . and that gang'.[1] For Vane, the year between the victories of Dunbar and Worcester was an unhappy one. Shortly after Dunbar he assured Cromwell that the rumpers 'in general have good aims, and are capable of improvement upon such wonderful deliverances as these'. By the following August, however, he was complaining to Oliver of the 'continual contestation and brabling' among them: they 'will not suffer to be done things that are so plain as that they ought to do themselves'.[2] Vane's influence in the Rump was on the wane, and the 'juncto' which had shaped the government's policies, and whose continuing cooperation depended on the survival of external dangers, was beginning to break up. Vane acted as teller in opposition to Heselrige three times in the first half of 1651, and lost twice. One of his defeats was over the treatment of the Socinian rumper John Fry, whom Heselrige was anxious to punish and whom Vane wished to protect from his clerical enemies. Heselrige, with Fenwick, was regarded by Vane's fellow advocates of toleration as the champion of 'all the priests'.[3] Quite apart from his clashes with Heselrige and from the quarrels in the House over the fate of Christopher Love, Vane was on the losing side as teller four times between Dunbar and Worcester. In December 1650, when Chaloner was complaining of the incompetent management of the fleet, Vane resigned as treasurer of the navy. Early in August 1651 he withdrew testily, albeit temporarily, to the country.[4]

His dismay was symptomatic of the growing feeling that the puritan cause was in decline. Puritanism, thriving on conflict and drama, was gravely jeopardised by the return to relative political security after Dunbar. A fortnight after the battle, William Rowe wrote to Cromwell from London that 'right and useful men are but few here; men grow rusty upon the least interval of stress'. The Rump's apparent worldliness, and its growing religious intolerance, strained its relations with the sects. The separatist Peter Chamberlain wrote to Cromwell from London in December 1650 that 'were there the same integrity with us

[1] *Original Letters . . . addressed to Oliver Cromwell*, p. 43; *C.J.* 11 Oct. 1649, 19 Dec. 1650; Rowe, *Sir Henry Vane the Younger*, pp. 152–3, 156.
[2] *Original Letters . . . addressed to Oliver Cromwell*, pp. 19, 78.
[3] *C.J.* 31 Jan., 1 Apr., 18 June 1651; Rowe, *Sir Henry Vane the Younger*, pp. 199–200; *Complete Writings of Roger Williams*, vi. 255.
[4] *C.J.* 4, 19 Feb., 3 July 1651; Rowe, *Sir Henry Vane the Younger*, pp. 149–50, 169–70.

at home as with you abroad, surely the Lord would bless us; but a secret ease divides us into jealousies, and nothing but a mutual guilt keeps us together. Your counsels, at this distance, are soon forgotten; every man seeks his own.' 'Might it not be accepted now', Chamberlain hinted, 'if one poor man could save the city?' George Bishop, writing in January 1651, was equally dispirited: 'Truly . . . we have too few honest hearts among us, who honour God by their uprightness . . . Upon a narrow survey of the temper of those in the House, and the general frame of things, a tender heart would weep for the day of visitation that is coming.'[1] In the summer of 1651, when Harrison was 'giving encouragement to some well-affected' in the north and in the west, the gathered churches of England, Wales and Ireland began to organise themselves for concerted political action.[2] Only the struggle in Scotland prevented open conflict between the Rump on the one hand and soldiers and saints on the other.

The coalition of interests which had made the Commonwealth government possible was by now under severe strain. Parliament and army scarcely managed to conceal their dislike of each other. Parliament itself was becoming patently divided. Dunbar, hailed as a momentous victory for the new regime, had given M.P.s a breathing space in which to quarrel among themselves. The divisions over the Love case in the summer of 1651 were merely the climax of months of discord. Meanwhile Cromwell's campaign in Scotland, held up for a time by his serious illness in May, moved towards its crisis. In August the government began to panic. There was more talk of an adjournment, and when Cromwell allowed the Scottish army to invade England there was open suspicion at the Council of State of his motives.[3] On 3 September, however, there came the 'crowning mercy'[4] of the battle of Worcester. The Rump, at long last, was secure from its enemies. From now on it was to battle for its survival not against royalists or presbyterians, but against its erstwhile friends.

[1] *Original Letters . . . addressed to Oliver Cromwell*, pp. 21, 36, 50.
[2] *C.S.P.D.* 1651, p. 293; Cary, *Memorials of the Great Civil War*, ii. 202–3; *Mercurius Politicus* 10–17 July 1651, pp. 924–5; *Several Proceedings* 24–31 July 1651, p. 1476, 7–14 Aug. 1651, pp. 1509–10; *Perfect Passages* 6–13 June 1651, pp. 333–4.
[3] Clarke MS xix, fo. 81ᵛ; *Memoirs of Colonel Hutchinson*, p. 287.
[4] Abbott, *Writings and Speeches*, ii. 463.

PART FOUR

PARLIAMENT *VERSUS* THE ARMY, SEPTEMBER 1651–APRIL 1653

REFORM AND REACTION,
SEPTEMBER 1651–MAY 1652

The triumph of Worcester, ending for the foreseeable future the danger of a successful royalist invasion or uprising, left the army officers free at last to concentrate on problems of social reformation and political settlement. Cromwell and his colleagues were repeatedly to recall the hopes they had entertained of the Rump on their return to London after the battle, and the disappointments which it had held in store for them.[1] Initially, victory produced a glow of goodwill. Hugh Peter urged the militia regiments which had fought at Worcester 'to think well of the present government who was so watchful for the whole', and Harrison wrote that God had 'owned and honoured the House in the eyes of all the world'.[2] Cromwell, now devoting himself principally to civilian politics, came from Worcester to Westminster with three aims in mind. First, he wanted the Rump to dissolve and to hand over power to a new representative. Secondly, he hoped to broaden the base of the Commonwealth's support, principally through an act of oblivion. Thirdly, urging the Rump to 'encourage and countenance God's people, reform the law, and administer justice impartially', he called for 'the fruits of a just and righteous reformation'.[3] Over all three aspects of his programme Cromwell was to be at least partially frustrated.

At first, all went well enough. He received an appropriately heroic reception in London, and was immediately added to the Council of State's most important standing committees.[4] On 16 September, when he made his first appearance in parliament for over a year, the Rump revived its long-suspended discussions of both parliamentary elections and the proposed act of oblivion.[5] The issue of elections dominated

[1] E.g. *A Declaration of the Lord General and his Council, showing the grounds and reasons for the Dissolution of the late Parliament* (1653), pp. 1–2; Abbott, *Writings and Speeches*, iii. 54–6, 452; *Mercurius Politicus* 3–10 Feb. 1653, p. 2213; *Several Proceedings* 21–28 Apr. 1653, pp. 2957–8.
[2] Abbott, *Writings and Speeches*, ii. 465; *Several Proceedings* 11–18 Sep. 1651, p. 1584.
[3] *Declaration of the Lord General and his Council, showing the grounds ... for the Dissolution of the late Parliament*, pp. 6, 9.
[4] Abbott, *Writings and Speeches*, ii. 472–6.   [5] *C.J.* 16 Sep. 1651.

parliamentary business for the next two months. Cromwell's exertions initially seemed successful, but the inability of parliament and army to agree soon became apparent. When Cromwell first raised the subject the House merely resumed discussion of the Vane scheme, debated in so desultory a fashion before Worcester, for recruiter elections and for a redistribution of constituencies.[1] Cromwell, however, wanted not recruiter elections but fresh ones. On 23 September parliament, probably at his suggestion, held a fast to contemplate the whole question of elections, and two days later, when Cromwell 'did exceedingly appear in the House for a new representative', the Rump backed down. The recruiting scheme was abandoned, and it was resolved that 'a bill be brought in, for setting a time certain for the sitting of this parliament, and for calling a new parliament'. On the same day a committee, to which Cromwell was added on the 26th, was appointed to draft the bill. As in the Vane scheme which was now set aside, there was to be a redistribution of seats.[2] Cromwell and Scot, the tellers in favour of bringing in the bill, could muster a majority of only seven; and although 'a great many' M.P.s were reported to be 'dejected' by the vote, and to believe that it would be 'in vain to think to avoid' its implementation, stern resistance was correctly anticipated by the army.[3] It is nevertheless important, in view of prevalent misconceptions about the Rump's electoral proposals, to emphasise the significance of the House's decision at this point to jettison the recruiting scheme. That scheme had been the focus of the Rump's discussions of the issue of elections at least since January 1650; but Cromwell's return to Westminster radically altered the position. The recruiting scheme was to be mooted again, but it was never incorporated into the bill framed by the committee set up in September 1651 and intermittently debated by the Rump until its dissolution on 20 April 1653. Throughout this period army as well as parliamentary sources were agreed that the bill provided for the dissolution of the Long Parliament and for a newly elected parliament. The charge that the bill was a recruiting one, which as we shall see has misled historians, was made only after the dissolution, when the army was obliged to justify its actions; and even then it was soon dropped.[4]

The committee which drafted the bill, ordered on 1 October to

[1] *Several Proceedings* 31 July–7 Aug. 1651, p. 1499; *C.J.* 16, 17, 24 Sep. 1651.
[2] Clarke MS xix, fo. 142ᵛ.
[3] *C.J.* 17, 23, 25, 26 Sep. 1651; Clarke MS xix, fo. 142ᵛ, xx, fo. 1; *The Faithful Scout* 12–19 Sep. 1651, p. 272.
[4] Cf. below, Part Five; and see *Faithful Scout* 10–17 Oct. 1651, p. 300.

meet daily, took several days to complete its work, but on the 8th the 'bill for a new representative', as it came to be known, was brought into the House and given its first reading. The second reading followed two days later, when the House resolved to debate the bill in grand committee for a fortnight. This proved to be not long enough, even though it was reported that 'the soldiers quicken [the bill] on apace'. On 25 October came a report that the proposal for a new representative 'now meets with much opposition' in the House, and the debate dragged on into November. The main problem was to persuade the Rump to set a deadline for its dissolution. In mid-October the House had decided 'not to name the time for the dissolution of the parliament', or for the calling of its successor, until the remainder of the bill's provisions had been worked out. But on 14 November Cromwell, making 'a long speech . . . to set a time for the sitting of this parliament', achieved what must at first have seemed an important breakthrough. Although the House still declined to name the day on which it would dissolve, it did concede that it was 'now a convenient time to declare a certain time for the continuance of this parliament, beyond which it shall not sit'. The judges who were also M.P.s were called in from Westminster Hall for the debate, and the motion was passed by only two votes in what was, by the Rump's standards, a packed House. The Rump's next move was eagerly awaited by the army. On 18 November the Commons reached a decision not to sit beyond 3 November 1654, which would be the fourteenth anniversary of the first meeting of the Long Parliament. Reporting the news, an army writer observed that 'it's conceived a short time will give occasion of a vote of dissolving sooner'. His optimism was unfounded. After 18 November the question of elections was evaded by the Rump for over six months. Cromwell's initiative had been successfully parried.[1]

Cromwell emphasised after Worcester the need 'to establish the nation and the change of government, by making the people . . . willing to the defence thereof';[2] and there is no mistaking his enthusiasm for an act of oblivion or his desire to make its terms as generous as possible.[3] He made other moves, too, to broaden the base of the Commonwealth's support. He secured the reprieve on 16 October of Christo-

[1] Gardiner, *History of the Commonwealth and Protectorate*, ii. 72; *Clarke Papers*, ii. 233; Clarke MS xx, fos. 5ᵛ, 19ᵛ, (26), 52ᵛ, and fo. between fos. numbered 55 and 56.

[2] Abbott, *Writings and Speeches*, ii. 463.

[3] *C.J.* 22, 29 Jan., 5, 6, 10, 13, 24 Feb. 1652; Underdown, *Royalist Conspiracy in England*, pp. 58–9.

pher Love's accomplices,[1] and supported the Earl of Leven, one of the most important prisoners taken during the Scottish campaign, in his bid to avoid the confiscation of his estate.[2] The pardon of Love's fellow conspirators encouraged other political prisoners to believe that more lenient times lay ahead.[3] Cromwell also assisted the Rump after Worcester in its plans to reduce the forces and hence the burden of taxation. On 10 September the House decided on the disbandment of four thousand horse and dragoons, and early in October it resolved to disband five regiments, and thirty individual companies, of foot.[4]

The basis of the Rump's debates on oblivion was probably the bill of pardon which had been briefly discussed in the spring and summer of 1649. The matter had been raised at various points thereafter, but the bill only became a serious possibility once the royalists had been defeated.[5] It was not until the decision of 18 November 1651 on the issue of elections had been taken that the Rump gave serious attention to the oblivion bill, and not until 20 January 1652 that the measure was discussed in detail. Then, after five weeks of intensive debate, the act of oblivion was finally passed on 24 February 1652.[6] Designed to end bitterness, the act in fact helped to revive it; as a pamphleteer wrote after its passage, 'in the parliament . . . it is to be wished, that the things henceforth to be debated and voted should look rather forward than backward'.[7] In January and February the House looked backward. The treatment of royalists was an issue on which M.P.s, recalling the bloodshed and the treacheries of a conflict which had so recently been concluded, were rarely capable of balanced discussion. Even in the second protectorate parliament of 1656–7, feelings ran high as soon as the subject was raised.[8] In the prolonged debates on the oblivion bill early in 1652, the alignments of rumpers cut across the divisions between

---

[1] B.M., Add. MS 10,114, fo. 29ᵛ (with which cf. *Mercurius Politicus* 9–16 Oct. 1651, p. 1140); *C.J.* 15 Oct. 1651, 26 Feb. 1652.

[2] Whitelocke Letters (Longleat) xii, fo. 42: Leven to Whitelocke, 10 May 1652. And see *ibid.* xii, fo. 61.

[3] B.M., Loan MS 29/176, fo. 238ᵛ: Sir William Lewis to Edward Harley, 20 Oct. 1651. Cf. *H.M.C.R. De Lisle and Dudley*, vi. 608; Gardiner, *History of the Commonwealth and Protectorate*, ii. 59–63.

[4] *Several Proceedings* 4–11 Sep. 1651, p. 1579; *Mercurius Politicus* 9–16 Oct. 1651, p. 1127; Abbott, *Writings and Speeches*, ii. 483–4.

[5] Cf. above, pp. 193, 201, 240; *C.J.* 5 July 1649.

[6] *C.J.* 16, 26 Sep., 21, 27 Nov., 2 Dec. 1651, 13 Jan.–24 Feb. 1652; Firth and Rait, *Acts and Ordinances*, ii. 565–7.

[7] *The Moderator: endeavouring a full composure and quiet settlement of these many differences, both in doctrine and discipline* (1652), p. 9.

[8] Cf. *Diary of Thomas Burton*, e.g. i. 230–43.

'revolutionaries' and 'conformists': both radicals and moderates were to be found among the most eager supporters of the bill and among its most bitter opponents. There was much feeling in the army and in the radical press in favour of making the terms of the act as generous as possible.[1] Lambert and Desborough favoured it,[2] as did Harrison's rumper and regicide friends John Jones and Nathaniel Rich.[3] Marten, with Cromwell, was the principal advocate of the act, supported by the regicide Sir John Danvers and by Henry Neville. Determined attempts to restrict the generosity of the measure were made by men with equally diverse political records: William Purefoy, Cornelius Holland, Luke Robinson, Thomas Atkins, Denis Bond, and above all that arch-enemy of delinquents,[4] Sir Arthur Heselrige, who after conducting a mopping-up operation against the royalists in the north had returned to Westminster early in October.[5]

The act aggrieved some of the Rump's officials in the localities, where anti-royalist feeling ran even higher than at Westminster. Local commissioners complained that the measure, favouring 'sons of violence, who have enriched themselves by the spoils of poor sufferers', 'exceedingly heightens the spirits of the enemy, and makes them jeer at those whom they have wronged'; no amount of lenity would win the royalists' 'affection', because 'their satanical spirits are still in enmity'. Opponents of the act suspected that it was 'drawn up by the consultation and counsel of the Cavalier party'. Although eventually passed, it was 'clogged with so many provisos' that its possible benefits were seriously diminished. Professor Underdown has rightly commented that 'many individual exceptions were named, so many that the act's title was seriously inaccurate'. As John Jones wrote, 'it will produce but little good; I see no reconciliation in the hearts of men, but rather a spirit of bitterness'.[6] Matters were not helped by the Rump's decision,

[1] Clarke MS xx, fos. 58, 68ᵛ, xxii, fos. (12ᵛ), 19ᵛ; *Perfect Account* 18–25 Feb. 1652, p. 473; *The French Intelligencer* 23–31 Dec. 1651, p. 48; *Faithful Scout* 12–19 Sep. 1651, p. 273, 16–23 Jan. 1652, p. 416, 27 Feb.–5 Mar. 1652, p. 460. Cf. *Kingdom's Weekly Intelligencer* 14–21 Aug. 1649, p. 1470.
[2] *Diary of Thomas Burton*, i. 240, 315–16.
[3] N.L.W., MS 11,440D, p. 10: Jones to Scot, 16 Sep. 1651; *C.J.* 20, 24 Feb. 1652.
[4] Cf. May, *Anatomy of . . . Lilburne's Spirit and Pamphlets*, p. 6; Howell, *Newcastle-upon-Tyne and the Puritan Revolution*, pp. 191–4, 235.
[5] For the attitudes of these rumpers towards the bill see *C.J.* 20 Jan., 24 Feb. 1652.
[6] *C.C.C.*, pp. xviii, 547, 549, 557; *Diary of Thomas Burton*, i. 232, 234; Clarke MS xxii, fo. 19ᵛ; Underdown, *Royalist Conspiracy in England*, p. 58; *Rump: or an exact collection of the choicest poems and songs relating to the late times* (1662), pp. 303–4; N.L.W., MS 11,440D, p. 41: Jones to Scot, 19 Mar. 1652. See also Gardiner, *History of the Commonwealth and Protectorate*, ii. 81–2.

in its attempt to prop up its tottering finances, to undertake extensive sales of royalist estates. The lands of seventy-three 'malignants' had been singled out for confiscation in an act of July 1651. Twenty-nine more were selected in an act of July 1652, and the massive total of six hundred and seventy-eight in an act of November 1652. Such measures fatally undermined the oblivion policy.[1]

Cromwell was soon organising support in the Rump for the third aspect of his programme, the call for social and religious reform. From late December 1651 a group of M.P.s can be seen cooperating in the House to achieve reform measures. Cromwell and Harrison, whose paths had yet to diverge, were acting in unison at this stage, and their respective supporters now joined forces in an efficiently coordinated alliance. Its principal members, apart from Cromwell and Harrison themselves, were Sir Gilbert Pickering, Nathaniel Rich (who was becoming increasingly close to Harrison), John Carew, Charles Fleetwood, Francis Allen, Richard Salwey, Sir William Masham (an old friend of Cromwell), and two members admitted to the Rump only after Worcester, Thomas Westrow, whom Cromwell had long urged to return to the House, and Robert Bennett, a religious radical from Cornwall who had been returned to parliament after one of the Rump's rare by-elections. Bennett had for some time regarded the House's failure 'to relieve the oppressed and to hear the complaints of poor grieved afflicted people' as 'a sad omen ... in these days of pretended reformation'.[2] Although members of the group, which included men of diverse temperament and beliefs, must have differed considerably about how extensive social and religious change should be, they were agreed in wanting at least some measure of reform. They worked together in the house for law reform, for poor relief, for financial retrenchment, for the replacement of certain parliamentary committees by commissioners who were not M.P.s (to allow rumpers more time to discuss reform in the House), and even for the expulsion of the rumper Gregory Clement for adultery.[3] Yet Cromwell's pressure for reform was as unsuccessful as his attempts to secure speedy elections and a generous act of oblivion.

[1] M.G.W. Peacock, *An Index of the Names of Royalists whose Estates were Confiscated* (Index Soc., 1879); Underdown, *Royalist Conspiracy in England*, pp. 57–8.

[2] Folger Library, Add. MS 494, fo. 195.

[3] *C.J.* 26 Dec. 1651, 10, 19, 27 Feb., 19, 30 Mar., 27 Apr. 1652. See also *ibid.* 3, 11 Dec. 1651, 13 Apr., 20 May, 3 June, 2, 15, 22, 27 July, 27 Aug., 28 Sep., 15 Oct., 27 Nov. 1652, 2, 18 Feb. 1653; SP 28/81, fos. 357, 1068. Cf. *C.J.* 29 June, 13, 26 July 1649, 28 Jan., 5, 7, 10, 20 Feb., 16 Mar., 5 July 1650, 5, 6, 7 July 1653.

The bill for the propagation of the gospel at national level was revived on 1 October, but by the end of the month discussion had once again become confined to devising means of improving the maintenance of ministers. The measure was allowed to drop. A bill against 'popery', too, made no progress.[1] There was more chance of persuading the House to introduce measures of law reform, and on 8 October the committee for regulating the law, almost entirely dormant since the previous December, was revived. In late November and early December there were some discussions of a bill, which the Rump had debated previously, for the probate of wills, but this was not enough to placate the army leaders.[2] At a meeting on Christmas Day of the Council of Officers, which about this time was holding regular discussions of 'many good things', it was proposed that the Rump be asked to commission a body, on which no M.P. would sit, to discuss the whole issue of law reform. The House obediently discussed the scheme on the following day. In doing so, it received a grim reminder of the perils of disobedience. As an army writer recorded, 'Col. Pride attended at the door while this was in debate, so that now in good earnest the reforming of the law will be taken into consideration.'[3] The Rump duly resolved to appoint 'persons out of the House, to take into consideration what inconveniences there are in the law, and how the mischiefs that grow from the delays, the chargeableness, and the irregularities in the proceedings in the law, may be prevented, and the speediest way to reform the same'. This was the Hale Commission on Law Reform, a distinguished body of twenty-one men representing a wide spectrum of opinion. The committee instructed by the Rump to nominate members of the commission was headed by the most prominent rumpers among the reforming group: Cromwell, Carew, Fleetwood, Harrison, Westrow and Allen.[4] Only recently has the work of the Hale commission been fully appreciated.[5] In an intensive series of meetings between January and July 1652 it produced reasoned and far-reaching proposals for law reform. Yet not one of its recommendations was implemented by the Rump.

Once parliament had agreed to appoint a commission, there was

[1] *C.J.* 8, 15, 29 Oct. 1651; *Mercurius Politicus* 23–30 Oct. 1651, p. 1172.
[2] *C.J.* 8 Oct., 28 Nov., 5 Dec. 1651.
[3] Clarke MS xx, fos. 73ᵛ, 79&ᵛ.
[4] *C.J.* 26 Dec. 1651.
[5] Cotterell, 'Interregnum law reform', *passim.* See also Veall, *Popular Movement for Law Reform*, pp. 79–84. The commission's report is in John Lord Somers, *A Collection of scarce and valuable Tracts*, vi. 177–245, and its minute-book in B.M., Add. MS 35,863.

much jockeying in the House over its composition, the most radical figures in the original list of nominees eventually being omitted.[1] On 26 December, the day of the House's decision to set up the commission, Sir John Danvers wrote to his old friend[2] Bulstrode Whitelocke a letter which provides a rare glimpse of the calculation which informed the Rump's proceedings and of the resourceful nature of the opposition reformers had to face. Danvers urged the need to appoint to the commission 'persons experimentally known of the greatest ability and faithfulness, and such as should be likely to consort in particular affection as well as in general for the public service'. Three of the men Danvers suggested, William Methold, Samuel Moyer and John Sadler, all prominent city merchants, were in fact appointed. Danvers also wanted two men to be 'reserved to be additional at another time, whilst the present work may be carried on by a lesser number'. The first was the Earl of Denbigh, whose appointment, Danvers thought, would 'temper those reformados who seem to value his worth and magnanimity'. Secondly, Danvers asked

whether Colonel Robert Overton, both rational and learned, and of good estate in land of inheritance, whose forward zeal to justice and right made the Levellers assume to own him as a pillar of theirs, but remaining trusty to the public interest, may not be one, in some regard for the better tempering of any remaining party of the said Levellers.

Danvers also proposed that Cromwell should 'be specially consulted for the choice of one or two of the officers of the army known to be duly sensible and judicious even in the present business'.[3] In the original list of nominees proposed by the Rump's committee, four names were grouped together in a way which suggests that Danvers's advice on this point was followed. They were Hugh Peter and three (at this stage) Cromwellian officers, Desborough, Thomlinson and Packer.[4]

From the beginning the commission was subjected to radical pressure. At its first meeting it received a deputation from the Council of Officers which pointed out 'that divers were punished for their consciences', and which requested that it 'might be the first work to consider those laws the repealing of them'. Such action would encourage

[1] *C.J.* 9, 14, 16, 17 Jan. 1652.
[2] Whitelocke, *Memorials*, i. 521, 532, 544, ii. 11, iii. 53–4; B.M., Add. MS 37,344, fos. 263, 285; *C.J.* 28 Dec. 1652.
[3] Whitelocke Letters (Longleat) xi, fo. 159&ᵛ.
[4] *C.J.* 9 Jan. 1652; Portland MS (Bodleian) N. xvi, no. 104. Cf. Duncon, *Several Propositions of Public Concernment*, pp. 5–6.

Reform and reaction

'the advancement of the gospel'. This was not the only attempt to persuade the commission to exceed its brief; soon afterwards Hugh Peter presented it with 'a model about the poor'.[1] Both moves were deflected, however, and the commission managed to confine its discussions to the issue of law reform. At first the commissioners and the Rump seemed to work well together. A parliamentary committee was appointed to receive the commission's proposals, and arrangements were made for close consultation through the offices of Cromwell and Whitelocke. M.P.s who had drafted bills foreshadowing the work of the commission were invited to help, and the commission's capacity for both moderation and fruitful discussion soon became apparent. On 19 March 1652 Whitelocke presented to the Rump the first of a series of draft bills. One of these was read twice and committed on the same day, and similarly favourable treatment was accorded to three more bills in the following week. It is likely, however, that Whitelocke now ceased to cooperate. No further progress was made in the House until, three weeks later, Augustine Garland took over from Whitelocke the job of reporting bills from the parliamentary committee to the Rump. Then, on 15 April, two more bills were both given two readings. Another was given two readings on the 22nd. Yet at this stage the Rump's enthusiasm for the commission's work began to wane noticeably. Law reform was discussed again on 13 May, when the commission's bill for abolishing duelling was read twice, but another measure, previously given two readings, made no progress when it was brought before parliament on the same day. This was the bill 'for ascertaining of arbitrary fines upon descent and alienation of copyholders of inheritance', a proposal born of concern more for tenants than for landlords. Soon afterwards parliamentary discussion of the committee's recommendations ceased abruptly. Radical agitation in June 1652 persuaded the Rump briefly to renew discussion of law reform, but the subject played little further part in the Rump's proceedings until January 1653. Then, army pressure brought heated debate but few results.[2]

Cromwell has been depicted as a political innocent, unskilled in the arts of parliamentary management.[3] The failure of his policies after Worcester, however, is to be explained less by any incompetence in the use of

[1] Clarke MS xxii, fo. 19; B.M., Add. MS 35,863, pp. 1, 144.
[2] Cotterell, 'Interregnum law reform', p. 696; B.M., Add. MS 35,863, pp. 5, 6, 7, 16, 21, 83, 155; C.J. 19, 25 Mar., 15, 22 Apr., 13 May 1652.
[3] Trevor-Roper, Religion, The Reformation and Social Change, pp. 345–91.

273

political means, at which in some ways he showed himself at this time highly adept, than by his confusion about political ends: by the tension between on the one hand his taste for constitutional respectability, and on the other his hunger for godly reformation.

Despite the hidden moderation of his actions, the events of December 1648 and January 1649 had enhanced Cromwell's stature among religious radicals, who subjected him throughout the Rump period to intense and persistent psychological pressure. From his entry into Scotland in July 1650, when he 'like David . . . went forth against the uncircumcised', the saints kept up a 'continual inquiring after the workings of the Lord with you'. Harrison urged Cromwell shortly before Dunbar to 'run aside sometimes from your company, and get a word with the Lord. Why should you not have three or four precious souls always standing at your elbow, with whom you might now and then turn into a corner?' After Worcester radicals outside parliament turned expectantly to Cromwell as the instrument of reformation. They portrayed him as the Joshua who had slaughtered God's enemies in the field, as the Moses who had led the chosen people out of bondage, and as the Hezekiah who would now 'cleanse the temple'. Walter Cradock told Cromwell of his own 'prayers and praises, which sometimes I make my business in a ditch, wood, or under a hay-mow in your behalf'. 'Great things God hath done by you in war', William Erbury informed Cromwell, 'and good things men expect from you in peace; to break in pieces the oppressor, to ease the oppressed of their burdens, to release the prisoners of their bonds, and to relieve poor families with bread.'[1]

Both the saints and the advocates of radical social reform appreciated Cromwell's vulnerability to such pressure, and he showed himself anxious to sustain his image as a radical reformer, as the champion not only of the elect but of 'the meaner sort of people'. Between September 1651 and December 1652, and especially in late 1651 and early 1652, there developed what can only be regarded as an organised press campaign intended to promote Cromwell's radical following. There is no evidence to suggest that Cromwell initiated it, but it could not have

[1] *Original Letters . . . addressed to Oliver Cromwell*, pp. 10, 23, 61, 85, 88, 89 (and cf. *ibid.* pp. 6, 31, 36); Taylor, *Certain Queries or Considerations*, ep. ded.; William Sheppard, *The People's Privilege* (1652), ep. ded.; *The Last News from the King of Scots* (1651), pp. 4–5; *The Levellers Remonstrance* (1652), ep. ded.; *A Declaration of the Commons of England, to Cromwell* (1652), p. 5; *French Intelligencer* 9–16 Dec. 1652, pp. 29–32; G. Winstanley, *The Law of Freedom* (1652), ep. ded.; *Perfect Diurnal . . . Armies* 29 Sep.–6 Oct. 1651, p. 1345, 27 Oct.–3 Nov. 1651, pp. 1399–1401; etc.

flourished had he not, at the least, approved of it. Radical newspapers, and especially *The Faithful Scout* which had intimate connections with army headquarters, interspersed factual reporting with references to Cromwell's reforming aspirations. His desire to help the poor and to reduce the burden of taxation on 'the meaner sort' was given special emphasis. Readers of *The Faithful Scout* learned in December 1651 that Cromwell, 'to whom, next the Almighty, this nation remains indebted for the preservation of their freedom and liberties', was 'meditating of a way for the ease and freedom of the people, from the heavy burden of taxes, excise etc. An acceptable piece of service, and worthy to eternise his name to all posterity.' In February 1652 the same newspaper reported that Cromwell 'hath declared for liberty and freedom, and is resolved to ease the people of their heavy burdens, and to use means for the increase of trading, etc.'. In April the *Scout* announced that 'several propositions have been presented to his excellency the Lord General Cromwell, for the better regulating of the law'. The 'propositions' consisted of hackneyed, unspecified demands that 'the laws of the Commonwealth of England may be created, enacted, and established, in like manner and form as the laws of the Commonwealth of Israel . . . viz. few, short and pithy'. Nevertheless, the *Scout* reported, 'These proposals being seriously weighed and considered by the General, his excellency declared, that it was his ardent affection and desire, that the law might be so regulated, wherein true and impartial justice may be freely administered, and that he was resolved to the utmost of his power to promote and propagate the same.' In May the *Scout* recorded that Cromwell 'hath visited several committees; and a speedy course will be taken for reducing of the supernumeraries, officers and courts, both in city and country; a fair riddance'.[1]

This, then, was Cromwell's publicised image after Worcester: the champion of the radicals. What was the political reality? On his way to London after the battle he was met at Aylesbury by a four-man parliamentary delegation consisting of John Lisle, Bulstrode Whitelocke, Sir Gilbert Pickering and Oliver St John. He talked with them all, but 'more than all the rest' with St John, the advocate of mixed monarchy who had opposed the purge and the execution and who now sought to repair the breach within the parliamentary party which they had

---

[1] *Faithful Scout* 20–27 Feb. 1652, p. 456, 16–23 Apr. 1652, pp. 518–19, 14–21 May 1652, p. (409). Cf. *French Intelligencer* 23–31 Dec. 1651, p. 48, and *French Occurrences* 17–24 May 1652, p. 409. For the press campaign see also *Perfect Passages* 14–21 Nov. 1651, pp. 319–20, 7–14 May 1652, p. (270); *Moderate Intelligencer* 22–29 Dec. 1652, p. 2630; *Flying Eagle* 25 Dec. 1652–1 Jan. 1653, p. 40; *Last News from the King of Scots*, p. 6.

caused.[1] Shortly before Dunbar St John had urged on Cromwell the policy of conciliating presbyterians.[2] The two men worked in close cooperation in the autumn of 1651. Their alliance was especially noticeable on the two issues of constitutional settlement and parliamentary elections. Both men played a central part in a conference held at the Speaker's house to consider, in Cromwell's words, 'whether a republic, or a mixed monarchical government will be best to be settled'. The date of the meeting is uncertain; it may have been held on 10 December, but an earlier date, probably soon after Cromwell's return to London, seems more likely.[3] Among those present, apart from Cromwell, St John and Lenthall, were the lawyers Whitelocke and Widdrington and the army officers Harrison, Fleetwood, Whalley and Desborough. Whitelocke noted that 'generally the soldiers were against anything of monarchy' – although, he added peevishly, 'every one of them was a monarch in his regiment or company' – while 'the lawyers were generally for a mixed monarchical government'. When Desborough asked 'why may not this, as well as other nations, be governed in the way of a republic', Whitelocke replied that 'the laws of England are so interwoven with the power and practice of monarchy, that to settle a government without something of monarchy in it would make so great an alteration in the proceedings of our law, that you have scarce time to rectify nor can we well foresee the inconvenience which will arise thereby'. Widdrington and Lenthall fully agreed. So did St John: 'It will be found that the government of this nation, without something of monarchical power, will be very difficult to be so settled as not to shake the foundation of our laws, and the liberties of the people.' Cromwell listened patiently to the debate before concluding: 'That will be a business of more than ordinary difficulty! But really I think, if it may be done with safety, and preservation of our rights, both as Englishmen and Christians, that a settlement with somewhat of monarchical power in it would be very effectual.' Before Worcester, the royalist threat had made it unthinkable that the Rump should voluntarily restore monarchy. Now the government could undertake such an initiative on any terms to which it could persuade the army to agree. Charles II was at this stage evidently an unacceptable candidate, but, as Widdrington said at the conference, 'the late king's

---

[1] Abbott, *Writings and Speeches*, ii. 470–1; Whitelocke, *Memorials*, iii. 372–4.
[2] *Original Letters . . . addressed to Oliver Cromwell*, p. 26. Cf. Tanner MS 54, fo. 107.
[3] Whitelocke, the authority for the meeting, retrospectively included it in his Annals under the date 10 December, but his account of it begins 'Upon the defeat at Worcester'. Cf. Carlyle, *Cromwell's Letters and Speeches*, ii. 360 and n.

third son, the Duke of Gloucester, is still among us; and too young to
have been in arms against us, or infected with the principles of our
enemies'. Many others at the meeting 'were for the Duke of Gloucester
to be made king'.[1] There is no way of knowing what royalists might
have thought of the proposal, but Cromwell was said to have floated
the scheme again as late as September 1652.[2] Nothing came of it,
however, and the issue of monarchy was quietly dropped.

St John was named first to the parliamentary committee which drew
up the bill for a new representative, and acted as teller with Cromwell
in favour of the motion of 14 November 1651 to set a time-limit to the
Rump's existence. The two men seem to have agreed that, so long as
the Rump continued to sit, they should try to secure the readmission to
parliament of certain members who had not sat since the purge.
Cromwell had long been anxious to persuade a number of his friends
among the 'middle group' politicians, men like Philip Lord Wharton,
Henry Lawrence, Robert Hammond, Thomas Westrow and Richard
Norton, to return to the cause which, he believed, they had deserted at
the purge. On 1 January 1650 he had written to Wharton: 'You was
desired to go along with us: I wish it still . . . You were with us in the
form of things; why not in the power?' He had made a similar appeal
on the day after Dunbar, and a week before Worcester he wrote to
Wharton again: 'In my very heart, your Lordship, Dick Norton, Tom
Westrow, Robert Hammond (though not intentionally) have helped
one another to stumble at the dispensations of God, and to reason yourselves out of his service.' Hammond was not an M.P., but Norton and
Westrow were. Both were admitted to the Rump in the autumn of
1651, shortly after the revival of the Committee for Absent Members.
John Stephens, another middle group politician, was also readmitted,
as was Sir Thomas Wodehouse.[3] At the same time St John tried to
arrange the readmission of another M.P. of 'middle group' views, the
religious presbyterian John Harington, whom Cromwell had approached in June 1650 and whom he was to invite to dinner in April
1652.[4] St John's move failed, whether because of opposition in the
House or because of reluctance on Harington's part.[5] Harington was
involved in the social network of M.P.s who, as heirs to the middle

[1] Abbott, *Writings and Speeches*, ii. 505–7.
[2] *Nicholas Papers*, i. 310.
[3] *C.J.* 14 Nov. 1651; Abbott, *Writings and Speeches*, ii. 189–90, 328, 453. Cf. Jones, *Saw-pit Wharton*, p. 129, and Underdown, *Pride's Purge*, p. 291.
[4] B.M., Add MS 10,114 fos. 27, 29ᵛ, 31.
[5] Cf Underdown, *Pride's Purge*, p. 291.

group, had worked together in the later 1640s as 'royal independents', opposing political radicalism on the one hand and alliance with the Scots on the other. St John, the only royal independent to sit in the Rump, remained in close consultation with three of the others, John Crewe, William Pierrepoint and Samuel Browne. Cromwell, after his return to London in September 1651, was on easy social terms with the royal independents.[1] Perhaps this was the point of Ludlow's complaint that after Worcester Cromwell 'chose new friends', and of Cradock's warning to Cromwell lest the latter's 'catholic projects (though otherwise fundamentally good) serve to excuse your conscience for letting slip any particular present opportunity to serve the least saint'.[2] The act of oblivion, fresh elections, mixed monarchy, and reconciliation with the middle group and the royal independents – these were Cromwell's 'catholic projects'. His problem was to combine them with his desire for a godly reformation of church, state and society. In political terms he could shelve the problem, if hardly solve it, by his policy of radicalism on the public stage and conservatism behind the scenes. The question was whether he could square his behaviour with the conflicting demands of his conscience.

Cromwell's attempt to identify himself with both radical fervour and middle group respectability, to proceed towards godly reformation through constitutional means, reflected his overriding determination to preserve the unity of the regime. The radical press which proclaimed his reforming intentions also followed a distinctive policy on reform issues. Every move made by the Rump in the months after Worcester towards reform, and particularly towards law reform, the act of oblivion, and the bill for a new representative, was greeted enthusiastically by the radical newspapers, which were evidently kept well informed of proceedings at parliamentary committees. Taking advantage of the newspapers to retain his radical support, Cromwell used that support to press the Rump into moderate reform, while at the same time making use of an ostensibly reforming parliament both to preserve political stability and to mollify the radicals. The Rump thus depended for its survival on its ability to satisfy the reforming ambitions of the army.

It is in Cromwell's advocacy of law reform that his strategy can be

B.M., Add. MS 10,114, fos. 27ᵛ–33. For St John and Pierrepoint see also Clarendon MS 43, fo. 245ᵛ: Hyde to Nicholas, 26 Oct. 1652.
Memoirs of Edmund Ludlow, i. 282; *Original Letters. . . . addressed to Oliver Cromwell*, pp. 85–6.

seen most clearly. The radical press, and especially the army newspapers *The Faithful Scout* and *A Perfect Diurnal*, gave vigorous expression to crude anti-lawyer sentiment, emphasised Cromwell's determination to reform the law, and at the same time reported enthusiastically and in detail every reforming move made by the Hale commission.[1] Cromwell, appointed to act with Whitelocke as go-between from the Hale commission to the parliamentary committee set up to receive its proposals, exploited Whitelocke's susceptibility to flattery. Early in January 1652, during the struggle over the committee's composition, Whitelocke recorded that 'I was often with the L.G. Cromwell, who seemed well pleased with my company and did communicate to me, and advise with me, about matters of greatest concernment.' Or again, later in the same month, 'The L.G. often sent for me, and expressed extraordinary respect and favour to me.' Cromwell was repeating the tactics he had adopted in his dealings with Whitelocke in December 1648.[2] Whitelocke's comments on the Hale commission are best known for his stinging remark about the pretensions of Hugh Peter, one of its members, as a law reformer;[3] but for the first two months of its sitting Whitelocke was persuaded to work closely with the commission, even though many of its resolutions must have dismayed him. If Cromwell were to promote reform through such agents as Whitelocke, however, he would clearly have to tread carefully. On 22 March Cromwell received from the commission quite the most controversial measure it had yet proposed, the bill 'for better regulating clients and their fees'. If passed, the bill would have put a ceiling on counsellors' fees, while at the same time obliging them to pursue their clients' cases to the end, irrespective of financial incentive. It would also have barred practising counsel from sitting in parliament. Cromwell, presented with the bill, announced that he 'feared' lest it 'was mistimed'. Admittedly, 'upon debate of the reasons inducing the commissioners to enter upon such an act, it being agreed to be certainly within the cognizance' of the commission, he agreed to deliver it to the parliamentary committee. The timing, however, was left to his 'wisdom'; and, in contrast to most of

---

[1] The relevant references in the press to law reform, and to the other reform issues, during this period are too numerous to list here, but they can easily be found in the newspapers. (The references are given in my doctoral thesis, 'Politics and policy of the Rump Parliament, 1648–1653' (Bodleian Library), pp. 175 n. 2, 185 n. 3, 186 n. 1.) See also B.M., Add. MS 35,863, p. 7.

[2] B.M., Add. MS 37,345, fos. 174ᵛ–5, 176ᵛ; above, pp. 67–8. (As Whitelocke's Annals show, Cromwell had occasionally adopted similar tactics in the interim.)

[3] Whitelocke, *Memorials*, iii. 388.

the other measures which the commission had discussed, the bill was held back from the House.[1]

The Faithful Scout reported at one stage that the Hale commissioners 'sit constantly to make speedy dispatch of that glorious work. The parliament, council and army are very unanimous, in bringing it to a happy period.'[2] This was precisely the unity for which Cromwell strove. If it ever existed after Worcester, however, it was short-lived; and it was upon the growing divisions within the regime that Cromwell's policies foundered. Pride's appearance at the door of the Commons on 26 December 1651 indicated the dramatic deterioration in relations between parliament and army in the months after Worcester. On 3 November, when feelings were beginning to run high over the bill for a new representative, the rumper Daniel Blagrave asked his horoscope 'whether . . . the parliament shall be broke up suddenly or not'. On 11 November Cromwell was using political threats to bully Blagrave into toeing the line on the issue of elections. In the next few days the House filled rapidly, partly no doubt because of the debates on the dissolution, but partly also because of the impending annual elections to the Council of State, an event which invariably gave a temporary boost to parliamentary attendances.[3] In February 1651, at the time of the previous council elections, it had been resolved that such elections should in future be held in the month of November, probably because matters of defence and diplomacy usually made fewer demands on the parliamentary timetable in the autumn than in the early spring.[4] (Perhaps it was for the same reason that the Rump consistently favoured November as the month in which it would dissolve and in which its successor would meet.) One hundred and twenty M.P.s voted in the council elections of November 1651, and attendances remained relatively high throughout the winter. As usual, high parliamentary attendances resulted in a strengthening of parliamentary conservatism. In November 1651, as in February 1651 and as in November 1652, it was decided to replace half the members of the existing council. The changes thus made provide a telling indication of the House's mood.[5]

Among those newly elected, Herbert Morley topped the poll. Less

---

[1] B.M., Add. MS 35,863, pp. 15, 18, 26, 73, 74, and Add. MS 37,345, fo. 178&[v]; *C.J.* 19, 25 Mar. 1652; John Lord Somers, *A Collection of scarce and valuable Tracts*, vi. 184.
[2] *Faithful Scout* 13–20 Feb. 1652, p. (448).
[3] Josten, *Elias Ashmole*, ii. 591; *C.J.* 14 Nov. 1651.
[4] *Perfect Passages* 21–28 Nov. 1651, p. (2).
[5] *C.J.* 24. 25 Nov. 1651.

than a fortnight earlier he had acted as teller against Cromwell's motion to set a deadline for the Rump's dissolution. Anthony Stapley, one of the Sussex M.P.s in Morley's tow, came third. He had served on the first two councils, where he had distinguished himself only by a *penchant* for interrogating political prisoners. Otherwise he had played little part in Rump politics, and he had made no recorded appearance in the House since April 1651. Also newly elected were two of Morley's other satellites, William Hay, who had played an even less active part in the Rump than Stapley and who had made no recorded appearance since May 1651, and John Downes. Chaloner remained on the council; Marten returned to it; and Neville joined it for the first time. Soon, in cooperation with the Morley group, these three men were to capture the council standing committees responsible for the navy and foreign affairs.[1] Morley and Stapley were prominent landowners. So was Robert Wallop, who despite his previous indolence in Rump politics came second among those newly elected; and so were two equally conservative and equally unenergetic rumpers, Lord Lisle and Alexander Popham, who came fifth and sixth respectively.

The Rump's reactionary mood was similarly reflected in the decision not to include two men who had sat on the previous council. The Earl of Leicester noted that it was 'thought strange' that Sir Henry Mildmay and Thomas Harrison, 'who were so powerful and active the last year', failed to retain their seats.[2] Mildmay had led the attack in parliament on Christopher Love, charging a number of M.P.s with complicity in the plot, while at the same time Harrison, rebuked in March for his patronage of the 'antinomian' preacher John Simpson, had secured the expulsion of Lord Howard of Escrick.[3] By the end of October there were reports, which many rumpers were only too anxious to believe, of corruption among Harrison's followers on the Commission for the Propagation of the Gospel in Wales. Vast sums from tithes were said to be unaccounted for, and Philip Jones and other commissioners were reported to have embezzled funds from sequestered estates.[4] On 17 November, a week before the council elections, one of Harrison's supporters outside parliament wrote from London that 'there is several articles produced to be exhibited against him for several things, and . . .

[1] Below, p. 301.
[2] *H.M.C.R. De Lisle and Dudley*, vi. 609. Cf. Gardiner, *History of the Commonwealth and Protectorate*, ii. 74.
[3] Above, pp. 242, 243, 245.
[4] *C.C.C.*, pp. 495, 517, 2177–8; SP 23/98, pp. 73, 75–8, 85, 87, 89; *Perfect Diurnai . . . Armies* 22–29 Dec. 1651, pp. 1562–4; *Weekly Intelligencer* 6–13 Jan. 1652, p. 317.

he is to be suddenly cast out of the House, as well as out of the Council of State . . . he hath more need of the help of the prayers of saints, than any man I know this day'.[1] Harrison was not expelled from the House, but the implications of his omission from the council were clear enough. There was no challenge to the position of Cromwell, who came top of those re-elected. He was followed, however, by two conservative lawyers, Whitelocke and St John, while a third, John Rolle, was close behind. Only two of the ten re-elected councillors who secured most votes, and only two of the ten newly elected councillors who secured most votes, were 'revolutionaries'.

On 24 December Vane, Richard Salwey and St John made their last appearances at the council before departing as parliamentary commissioners to Scotland. George Fenwick, Heselrige's ally, was another of the commissioners, whose number was completed by two men who were not M.P.s, Richard Deane and Cromwell's friend the city politician Robert Tichborne. Vane did not return until March 1652, St John and Salwey until May.[2] John Jones commented, 'Verily I like the commissioners exceeding well, and I think England hath not another set, but I like not their absence from Westminster where affairs of most concernment are.'[3] Certainly their presence might have been expected to discourage the House, in the weeks after Christmas, from so provocatively mishandling an incident which embittered relations between parliament and army still further. On 23 December the Rump had received, and spent all day debating, a petition from one Josiah Primate. Primate was the owner of a colliery in Durham, where a prolonged dispute had arisen about the lease. The Durham county sequestrators, supported by Heselrige, claimed that the lease was held by a royalist, and was therefore subject to confiscation by the state. There was, however, another claimant, who happened to be John Lilburne's uncle. It was on the issue of the colliery that the long-standing feud between Lilburne and Heselrige reached its climax. Primate, backed by Lilburne, took the part of the Leveller leader's uncle, and the two accused Heselrige of acting shadily on the sequestrators' behalf. An army writer prophesied that Lilburne would 'make [Heselrige] a far higher offender than ever Strafford was'.

On Christmas Day, while the officers were resolving on the need for an extra-parliamentary commission on law reform, a Rump committee debated Primate's petition. Attended by at least fifty members, it sat

[1] N.L.W., MS 11,439D, fo. 8&ᵛ: Hugh Prichard to Morgan Lloyd, 17 Nov. 1651.
[2] *C.S.P.D.* 1651–2, pp. xxxv, xxxviii, xl.　　　　　[3] Mayer, 'Inedited letters', p. 192.

all day until eight in the evening. It met again on the 26th, the day of Pride's appearance at the door of the Commons and of the decision to set up the Hale commission, and probably for several days thereafter. It was evident that the House intended to judge the case itself rather than leave it, as the army wished, to the courts. On the 27th an army writer reported that 'many of the Council of Officers at Whitehall fly high in their debates'. On 6 January the Rump decided, by an overwhelming majority and in spite of the objections of Marten, to investigate the circumstances surrounding the printing of Primate's petition, in which the Leveller John Wildman was suspected of having taken a hand. On 15 January, after a debate lasting well into the evening, the petition was voted 'false, malicious and scandalous'. Primate was imprisoned, fined £3,000, and ordered to pay £2,000 damages both to Heselrige and to some of the Commissioners for Compounding. Lilburne, for whom 'very few spoke', was fined £3,000, ordered to pay similar damages and exiled. Heselrige was wholly vindicated. The contrast between the House's response to the charges against him, and its attitude in the previous November to the accusations levelled at Harrison, was startling. On 20 January a petition from London on Lilburne's behalf 'was very ill resented by the House' as being 'too bold and insolent'. On the 23rd *The Faithful Scout* reported that

divers officers and soldiers of the army have declared to live and die together in the preservation of their fundamental rights and native liberties, and seem to be much troubled at the grievous sentences against Lieut. Col. Lilburne. Many thousands of well affected citizens, and most of the private congregations, are likewise petitioning the parliament, imploring them to recall the said grievous sentence ... and requesting that Sir Arthur Heselrige be referred to take his course at law.

Cromwell declined to lend support to the army malcontents, however, and parliament stuck to its guns. On 26 January, for good measure, Heselrige was made president of the Council of State for the ensuing month. The act for Lilburne's banishment was passed four days later. As an army reporter bitterly noted, the Leveller leader was exiled 'as a troubler of Israel' on the third anniversary of Charles I's execution. The 'new chains' which Lilburne had 'discovered' in early 1649 were being tightened.[1]

[1] *C.C.C.*, pp. 1917–21, 2127–30; *C.J.* 23 Dec. 1651, 6, 15, 30 Jan. 1652; Clarke MS xx, fos. 58ᵛ, 79ᵛ, xxii, fos. 10, (11), (12&ᵛ), 14, 16, 19ᵛ; *Faithful Scout* 23–30 Jan. 1652, pp. 418–19, 422–3, 424, 5–12 Mar. 1652, p. 466; *French Intelligencer* 20–27 Jan. 1652, p. 72; *Perfect Account* 21–28 Jan. 1652, pp. 446–7, 448; *A Declaration of the Army concerning Lieut. Col. John Lilburne* (1652), esp. p. 3; *Lilburne Tried and Cast* (1653), p. 15.

Relations between parliament and army went from bad to worse in the following months. On 3 February Blagrave resorted once more to his horoscope, asking 'whether the soldier shall overcome the parliament or the parliament the soldier'.[1] In January and February Cromwell and Heselrige, around whose growing enmity the events leading to the Rump's dissolution were to turn, were respectively at the forefront of the opposing parties in the debates on the act of oblivion.[2] Primate was released in April and his fine reduced, but the damage had already been done.[3] Old wounds were opened on 5 May, when the Rump considered a bill to give protection to royalists who, in the army's view, were exempt from punishment by virtue of articles of war. Parliament's previous failure to respect the principle of such exemption had long been a sore point in its relations with the army, and the act was introduced so that 'a right understanding may be procured on all sides'. The understanding might have been procured had not Colonel Pride been nominated in the bill as a commissioner. The tellers in Pride's favour were Philip Skippon and Lord Grey of Groby, both of whom had played a central part in Pride's Purge. One of the tellers against Pride's nomination was Henry Neville; the other was Denis Bond, who had acted as teller with Herbert Morley against Cromwell's motion of 14 November 1651 to set a deadline for the Rump's dissolution. Pride's nomination was defeated.[4] Two other incidents in May exacerbated relations between parliament and army. The first came when John Lambert, already aggrieved by arrears in his pay, was upset by the Rump's failure to offer him a sufficiently decorous post in Ireland.[5] Lambert was emerging into a position of major influence in army politics. The second incident came when Harrison and his followers, aiming a blow at the ungodly coalition of Martenites, Morleyites and merchants, persuaded the House to expel Gregory Clement for adultery. Clement's closest parliamentary allies, Thomas Boone and Nicholas Gould, promptly withdrew from Westminster. Boone rarely returned to the Rump; Gould probably never did so.[6]

[1] Josten, *Elias Ashmole*, ii. 605.   [2] *C.J.* 22 Jan., 10, 24 Feb. 1652.   [3] *Ibid.* 7 Apr. 1652.
[4] *Ibid.* 14 Nov. 1651, 5 May 1652; *C.C.C.*, p. 3066; Whitelocke, *Memorials*, iii. 165–6; Clarke MS xxii, fo. 19; SP: 23/101, fos. 1035, 1037; 23/118, fos. 1107–8; *Weekly Intelligencer* 23–30 Mar. 1652, pp. 402–3, 4–11 May 1652, p. 447; *Perfect Diurnal . . . Armies* 18–25 Mar. 1650, p. 143; *Perfect Occurrences* 23 Feb.–2 Mar. 1649, p. 863. The issue was likewise to sour relations between parliament and army in Barebone's Parliament.
[5] *Letters from Roundhead Officers . . . to Captain A. Baynes*, p. 39; *Memoirs of Edmund Ludlow*, i. 346 n. 2. Cf. Whitelocke, *Memorials*, iii. 430–1.
[6] *C.J.* 6, 11 May 1652.

After Worcester extravagant mistrust and envy on both sides came to inform relations between parliament and army. The Rump's dilatoriness over reform convinced the officers that 'this parliament . . . would never answer those ends which God, his people, and the whole nation expected from them'. The rumpers' 'meddling in private matters between party and party', the arbitrary proceedings of their committees, 'the scandalous lives of some of the chief of them', and 'the corruption of some, the jealousy of others, the non-attendance and negligence of many' proved especially irksome, particularly when combined with a genuine fear that the Rump planned to disband the army, and, as Cromwell admitted, with

the inclinations of the officers of the army to particular factions, and to murmurings that they are not rewarded according to their deserts; that others, who have adventured least, have gained most; and they have neither profit, nor preferment, nor place in government, which others hold, who have undergone no hazards or hardships for the Commonwealth; and herein they have too much of truth . . . [1]

The Rump, for its part, came increasingly to resent the army's claims to a say in political developments. Images of natural servitude illuminated the rumpers' conception of the army's proper relationship to parliament. 'The army are our children; they came from us', recalled Heselrige in 1659; 'now the servants rose against their masters', wrote Whitelocke of the 'rash and arrogant action' of the dissolution.[2] Soon after the Rump's expulsion one rumper, probably Henry Marten, complained of 'the ingratitude of the army towards those who . . . raised them'.[3] Attempts to reconcile parliament and army were impeded by the unwillingness of M.P.s to discuss in Whitehall matters which, they believed, should be debated solely at Westminster; for 'when they were in the House they had their yeas and noes'.[4] When the army officers presented an important petition to the House in August 1652, Whitelocke noted, 'many were unsatisfied . . . looking

[1] Abbott, *Writings and Speeches*, ii. 558–9; *True State of the Case of the Commonwealth*, p. 9; *Declaration of the Lord General and his Council, showing the grounds and reasons for the Dissolution of the late Parliament*, pp. 5–6; *Several Proceedings* 21–28 Apr. 1653, p. 902; *Memoirs of Colonel Hutchinson*, p. 292; Williams, 'Political career of Henry Marten', p. 552.

[2] *Diary of Thomas Burton*, iii. 27; Whitelocke, *Memorials*, iv. 6; B.M., Add. MS 31,984, fos. 6ᵛ–7.

[3] Williams, 'Political career of Henry Marten', p. 550.

[4] *Several Proceedings* 21–28 Apr. 1653, p. (2959). Cf. Coates, *Journal of Sir Simonds D'Ewes*, pp. 273–4.

upon it as improper, if not arrogant, for the officers of the army to petition the parliament their masters'.[1]

Such sentiments were generalised and often expressed in retrospect. Yet the significance of the charges levelled at each other by parliament and army lay in their very imprecision. Irrational resentment complicated discussion of specific issues. Hostility between parliament and army cut across all other groupings in the House. In particular the Marten–Neville–Chaloner group, which continued to share many of the army's reforming aims, found itself quarrelling with the military at critical stages, so that the radical share of the vote was reduced still further.[2] In a calmer atmosphere, perhaps, the reform programme might have made more headway: army pressure on the House had been successful in the past, and many of the proposals which the Rump was now asked to consider for reform of law and church were far from revolutionary. Yet the identification of reforming aspirations with the political aims of the army gravely weakened the reformers' hopes. There were, of course, those who continued to work for compromise, and the most prominent M.P.s and officers often managed to restrain their more hot-headed colleagues. An open breach was long postponed, and there were times when both sides seemed prepared to make concessions. Equally, although the growth of extreme radicalism in the army and in the congregations stiffened parliament's resistance to reform proposals, it also restricted its room for manoeuvre in its attempts to woo presbyterians. It is noticeable, for instance, that the Rump, like those who urged it to give support to a settled ministry and worship, now took care to avoid provoking the army by use of the term presbyterian in statements on religious matters. Both reform and reaction, indeed, remained stillborn, and stalemate persisted. The man who tried hardest to break the deadlock, and to effect a compromise, was Cromwell. Until the very morning of the dissolution of the Rump he did everything he could to prevent the polarisation of politics, to restrain parliament and army alike from provocative action. Cromwell was potentially the Rump's strongest ally. Its failure to exploit his innate conservatism, its mistrust of his motives, and, ultimately, its ability to alienate him show how far, in the final year of the Rump period, political advantage was sacrificed to conviction and prejudice. The only possible outcome of a showdown, as the Rump must have known, was armed force. In its latter stages the House seems at times almost to have been possessed of a death-wish.

[1] Whitelocke, *Memorials*, iii. 445–6.   [2] E.g. *C.J.* 14 Nov. 1651, 5 May 1652.

The distorted political perspectives which the ill-feeling between army and parliament created are well shown by the conflict over the bill for a new representative. Cromwell did not handle the issue well. Evidently failing to anticipate the hostility which the army's aims aroused in parliament, he brought the demands for both reform and dissolution into the open immediately after his return from Worcester. A more tactful approach might have been more fruitful. The Rump, required by Cromwell both to reform and to dissolve, had evidently to reform before dissolving, so that any differences of opinion about the correct timing of reform measures assumed an exaggerated importance. The conflict which developed, between an army bent on a new representative and a parliament determined not to bow to military pretensions, sometimes obscured the practical questions raised by the demand for fresh elections. However morally urgent Cromwell and his fellow officers held a new representative to be, it is hard to see how fresh elections could have advanced the cause of reformation. Rather, as St John's support for the bill suggests, a new representative pointed to the conciliation of moderate opinion. The officers had long believed in the desirability of frequent elections, preferably on a biennial basis. Yet what could such elections achieve? Without either a numerical extension of the franchise of a kind which the officers never dared contemplate, or alternatively a political restriction of the franchise so severe as to make nonsense of the ideas of representation on which the officers' views on elections rested, a newly elected parliament could not have satisfied the demand for godly reformation which the army consistently coupled with its call for frequent elections. The army could always try to control the elections itself, but this was a course of action of which Cromwell would never have approved. Whatever the limitations of the Rump as an instrument of reform, it was absurd to suppose that fresh elections, fairly conducted, would produce a better one. Quite the contrary: as 1654 was to show, all that fresh elections would do would be to swell the parliamentary ranks of presbyterians and 'neuters'. In his opening speech to Barebone's Parliament in July 1653 Cromwell recalled how providence had, at Pride's Purge, 'sifted, winnowed, and brought to a handful' the House of Commons.[1] Fresh elections would have scattered the handful to the wind. Unless the officers were prepared to by-pass parliament altogether, they stood only to lose by the Rump's dissolution. After the coup of April 1653 the officers accused the Rump of having planned to hold recruiter elections

---

[1] Abbott, *Writings and Speeches*, iii. 54.

and to perpetuate its membership. The charge, as will appear later in this book, was inaccurate; but even if it had been accurate, what cause would the officers have had for complaint? Recruiter elections, however attractive to members already sitting, would also have provided a compromise between on the one hand the army's desire for elections, and on the other its professed wish to secure reform through parliamentary means; the handful, however meagre, would have retained its political base. The desire to be rid of the Rump came in the army's mind to overshadow the most elementary political calculation. The chief attraction of a new representative, from the army's point of view, was simply that it would involve the demise of the old one.

The dilemma facing reformers who wanted fresh elections did not go unnoticed. The central issue, clearly, was that of the 'qualifications' which would be placed by the bill for a new representative on either voters or candidates in the election of the Rump's successor. The House debated this subject on 25 September 1651, the day on which it ordered the drafting of the bill; it was still discussing the same problem a month later.[1] As John Jones asked in November,

What qualifications will persuade a people sensible of their present burdens, and not of the reasons and necessity of them, to choose those persons that laid the burdens, or their adherents, to be of the next representative? What interest in England is likely to carry the universal vote? Is not that interest, that seeing [the nation] to be in a suffering condition, and to promise ease of burdens, and new impositions, if it were again in power, like to have great stroke in election?

Instead of new elections, urged Jones,

let there be patience used until burdens may be taken off, and the people enjoy some rest and opulency under the new change, let the old weeds that lie dead on the ground have time to rot, let the Commonwealth have some time to take root in the interests of men, before it be transplanted or grafted on another stock, let there be trials made by elections to vacant places, and by adjournments, and then some judgement may be given.[2]

Some of the Rump's supporters in Ireland, Jones told Thomas Scot in December, 'are very much puzzled in the consideration of the eager prosecution which is made in England after a new representative'.[3] It is a supreme irony to find Jones, one of Harrison's most articulate allies, providing so sensible an argument for 'elections to vacant places', in

---

[1] *Perfect Account* 24 Sep.–1 Oct. 1651, p. 298, 22–29 Oct. 1651, p. 344; *Mercurius Politicus* 16–23 Oct. 1651, p. 1156; *The Diary* 20–27 Oct. 1651, p. 35.
[2] Mayer, 'Inedited letters', pp. 190–1; Hill, *God's Englishman*, pp. 207–8.
[3] N.L.W., MS 11,440D, p. 31: Jones to Scot, 16 Dec. 1651. Cf. Clarke MS xx, fo. 21.

other words for recruiter elections. The same reasoning must have occurred to other, less radical members of the Rump. The militant city politician Daniel Taylor, agreeing with Jones that 'it's unlikely, nay impossible, that multitudes should make any good choice at this time', was bolder in his conclusions, arguing in November 1651 that the godly congregations of London, rather than the electorate at large, should determine the composition of the assembly which succeeded the Rump.[1]

Mercurius Politicus argued vigorously for fresh and 'successive' elections until, in November 1651, when the Rump's dissolution momentarily seemed imminent, it was obliged to consider the implications. Then it admitted that

there lies some difficulty in the timing . . . Ruptures there are that must be restored; dislocations that must be reduced; and wounds that must be cured . . . which being seriously considered, it will easily be granted, that none can be more fit to effect this, than the old physicians, that have attended all the fits and distempers, and are best acquainted with the state of the body.

On the other hand, the newspaper hastened to add, 'the patient should have a care by all means to see, that the physicians do not long try practices and conclusions, and by this means deprive the body of health and liberty'.[2] From this point of view the Rump's decision to leave the timing of the dissolution open, but to impose a three-year limit for its survival, was not unreasonable. Like the proposal to hold recruiter elections, which many rumpers continued to advocate, it was not necessarily an act of flagrant self-interest. The announcement of the time limit did not produce universal gloom among radicals, but rather a 'variety of discourses and opinions'.[3] Cromwell himself may have been happy at the decision, which would at least have given the Rump time to reform, and perhaps have enabled the Commonwealth to 'take root in the interests of men', before the parliament were dissolved. If men like Richard Norton, Thomas Westrow and John Harington could be persuaded to return to parliament, and if at the same time the House could be persuaded to pass reform measures, then both respectability and reformation might be compatible with the Rump's temporary survival. Yet the contradictions of Cromwell's policy remained. It would no doubt be possible to devise 'qualifications' which would

---

[1] Taylor, *Certain Queries or Considerations*, pp. 7–8. Cf. *Flying Eagle* 4–11 Dec. 1652, pp. 11–12.
[2] *Mercurius Politicus* 6–13 Nov. 1651, pp. 1189–90. Cf. *ibid.* 25 Sep.–2 Oct. 1651, p. 1095, 23 Oct.–6 Nov. 1651, pp. 1157–8, 1174.
[3] *Ibid.* 4–11 Dec. 1651, p. 1267. Cf. Clarke MS xx, fo. 55ᵛ.

prevent the admission of former royalists to parliament, but much
harder to design restrictions which would exclude the presbyterians
and neuters whom the army so strongly mistrusted. The real problem,
as John Jones saw, was 'Who shall judge whether rules and qualifications appointed be observed in elections? Who shall be of that committee?'[1] Would it be left to soldiers or to M.P.s to scrutinise the
names of the members returned? On this point the lack of confidence
between parliament and army proved an insuperable obstacle to agreement.[2]

The growing hostility of the army was not the only development to
generate anti-radical sentiment in parliament, and it was not only in
parliament that anti-radical sentiment was generated. In the city of
London, the defeat of the royalists ushered in a new era of political and
religious conflict. The position of the radicals who had come to power
in London in December 1648 had been gradually undermined, and in
the city elections of December 1650 men who had opposed the purge
and the execution had begun to return to positions of influence.[3] Their
prominence grew during the remainder of the Rump period. At the
height of the Love crisis in August 1651 the mayor, taking advantage of
the moves occasioned by Love's trial towards reconciliation between
presbyterian and independent divines, had suggested to the (presbyterian) London Provincial Assembly that it might cooperate with him
in enforcing the observance of the sabbath. Anti-sabbatarianism was
becoming increasingly fashionable among certain groups of religious
radicals. Other, more nakedly political issues may also have been discussed between the mayor and the assembly, which in October sent a
circular to the ministers under its supervision, instructing them to
preach in favour of the proper observance of the sabbath. 'It should
be no small encouragement unto us', the document hinted, 'that God
hath prepared the magistrate's heart to accompany us in our distress
and endeavours in this way.'[4] In November William Ames, preaching
before the city government, attacked new-fangled religious notions
and stressed the virtues of harmony among orthodox puritans.[5] In
December the London Provincial Assembly made another attempt to

1 Mayer, 'Inedited letters', pp. 190–1.
2 Cf. C. H. Firth, 'The expulsion of the Long Parliament', *History*, new series, ii (1917–18),
141–2.
3 Farnell, 'Usurpation of honest London householders', *passim*.
4 Minutes of the London Provincial Assembly (Dr Williams's Library), pp. 93–7.
5 W. Ames, *The Saints Security against Seducing Spirits* (1651).

strengthen the presbyterian classical system in the capital.[1] Radicals
were quick to challenge the city's movement towards conservatism.
Plans were laid to prevent aldermen from holding office for more than
one year, and to strip the mayor of 'some duties and perquisites . . .
which did help in some measure to defray the charge' of his office.
Tense scenes followed in the Common Council, which passed an act to
widen the franchise in the mayoralty election. Parliament, evidently
embarrassed by the proceedings, seems discreetly to have prevented
the implementation of the act.[2]

The city radicals, however, were themselves becoming divided.
Independent divines, and prominent members of their flocks, had come
since December 1648 to form the new city establishment. As such, they
had found it increasingly difficult to contain radical aspirations, and
after Worcester long-threatened divisions broke out. There was a
pamphlet war between moderate and radical independents, and soon
the congregations of Thomas and John Goodwin were publicly at odds.[3]
In October a group of London sectaries found themselves 'discouraged'
by 'some great ones'; their work was 'much calumniated, envied and
censured by many that were not our professed enemies few days ago'.
Early in 1652 Walter Cradock and Vavasour Powell left London, 'much
saddened' by such developments. In October 1651 a group of city
radicals centred on Christopher Feake broke away from the 'selfish
sectaries' who attempted to identify themselves with, and to secure
power and influence through, Cromwell and the leading officers.
Feake believed the army leaders to be preoccupied with the promotion
of their own wealth and prestige. He and his friends made overtures
to Cromwell, but were disillusioned by his friendly but unhelpful
response.[4] By 30 December it was being whispered that 'the private
churches begin to call his excellency an apostate'.[5] There are hints that
Cromwell, staying away from the Council of Officers, felt uneasy
about the radical stance adopted by other officers towards the end of
December.[6] In Ireland, too, divisions between moderates and radicals

[1] Minutes of the London Provincial Assembly (Dr Williams's Library), pp. 101ff.
[2] *Perfect Passages* 28 Nov.–5 Dec. 1651, p. 329; Clarke MS xx, fo. 3ᵛ; Journal of the
London Common Council xli, fos. 65, 71, 72&ᵛ; *Perfect Passages* 12–19 Dec. 1651, p.
(338); Taylor, *Certain Queries or Considerations*, p. 16. On the act and the Rump's
evasion of it, see James, *Social Problems and Policy*, p. 232.
[3] *A Model of a New Representative* (1651), pp. 4–6.
[4] N.L.W., MS 11,439D, fo. 4: Prichard to Lloyd, Jan. or Feb. 1652; C. Feake, *A Beam of
Light* (1659), pp. 38–41, 43. See also *A Faithful Searching Home Word* (1659), pp. 5–6;
Clarke MS xx, fo. 13; Capp, *Fifth Monarchy Men*, pp. 58–9.
[5] Clarke MS xx, fo. 79ᵛ. Cf. *ibid.* xix, fo. 70.   [6] *Ibid.* xxii, fos. 14, 79ᵛ.

came into the open. The decisive event was the death of Ireton in December 1651. Much loved by radicals, he had known how to handle Lord Broghil, who was held to be 'ambitious' and 'to be more than ordinarily willing to submit to a royal, or lordly interest'. After Ireton's death, which 'struck a great sadness into Cromwell', conflict developed in Ireland between supporters of the 'royal, or lordly interest' and the Anabaptists. The 'foppery and vain pride' of Ireton's funeral, 'as magnificent as that of the late Earl of Essex', increased radicals' suspicions of Cromwell.[1]

The eclipse of the royalists, and consequently the army's willingness to put pressure on parliament, gave a new volume and intensity to the radical reform movement. Before Worcester, it had been possible to regard the respective demands for moderate and for radical reform as differing only in degree; now it was evident that they differed in kind. Envenomed attacks on lawyers and excise collectors became after Worcester a regular feature of radical pamphlets and newspapers. The growth of extremist religious views was still more alarming. In the 1640s, battles fought over toleration had been conducted on the familiar territory of biblical quotation and counter-quotation: in the early 1650s radicals, turning against the puritans whose attitudes had been formed in opposition but who were now themselves in power, propounded notions which went against the grain of parliamentary puritanism. In February 1652 Henry Lawrence, one of the M.P.s whom Cromwell unsuccessfully tried to reconcile to the Rump, complained of a new 'generation of men' who ignored appeals to scripture and who, instead, 'would subject the wisdom of God to the model . . . of their own wisdom'.[2] Ranters, Quakers and Socinians appealed to sources of authority which, whether human reason or the inner light of the spirit, defied external measurement and which, if widely accepted, might thus prove corrosive of existing social values. M.P.s found their puritan values questioned or taken to extremes they dared not contemplate. The clergy were attacked after Worcester with a new and frightening zeal.[3] So was the equation between learning and

[1] Gardiner, *History of the Commonwealth and Protectorate*, ii. 125–6; N.L.W., MS 11,439D, fo. 4ᵛ, and MS 11,440D, pp. 25–6, 36–7; *Memoirs of Edmund Ludlow*, i. 278–9, 293–6; Clarke MS xx, fo. 68ᵛ, xxii, fo. 22; B.M., Loan MS 636, 11: Burgoyne to Verney, 9 Feb. 1652; *Several Proceedings* 8–15 Apr. 1652, p. 2068; E.S. de Beer (ed.), *The Diary of John Evelyn* (6 vols., Oxford, 1965), iii. 57–8; K. M. Lynch, *Roger Boyle First Earl of Orrery* (Tennessee, 1965), pp. 74–5, 77, 79–80, 82–3.

[2] H. Lawrence, *A Plea for the Use of Gospel Ordinances* (1652), ep. ded.; Abbott, *Writings and Speeches*, ii. 328.

[3] The growth and extremity of religious radicalism in general, and of anti-clericalism in

godliness. 'We are almost at the end of books!' rejoiced William Dell, Master of Gonville and Caius College, Cambridge, in 1652. Dell's outlandish radicalism was discouraged by both Cromwell and John Owen, but encouraged by Harrison.[1] Ranters, or people described as Ranters, continued after Worcester in their unseemly ways. Women stripped naked in church or claimed to have experienced fruitful copulation with the deity.[2] In 1652 there were 'many dissensions and contentions' about both the function and the timing of the sabbath.[3] The roaming missionary, offending settled congregations, became a disturbingly common feature of religious life in the provinces. Soldiers, too, often interfered with established patterns of worship.[4] The celebration of Christmas, that annual target of puritan criticism, was attacked in 1652 with an unprecedented bitterness, until the Rump was driven to take fearful measures to ensure that the London shops remained shut and that the feast was not observed.[5] The demand for the abolition of tithes was expressed with a new vigour after Worcester. By May 1652 there was a growing awareness of the 'controversies as have arisen between the pastor and parishioners almost in every parish throughout the nation'; by August the abolition of tithes had been 'often petitioned for by several counties, and propounded and debated at a meeting not far from London, by divers eminent personages of the Commonwealth, and sundry freeholders and others attending on them'; and by December there was a 'petition walking abroad (and hath been in many counties for hands) for the abolishing of tithes'.[6] In some areas the

particular, can be discerned in a host of pamphlets published in 1652. Good examples of radical anti-clericalism can be found in the editorials of *Perfect Passages* from late May to early July 1652.

[1] *Several Sermons and Discourses of William Dell*: eps. ded. to 'The Stumbling Stone' and 'The Crucified and Quickened Christian'; *C.J.* 28 Jan. 1653. Cf. R.B., *The Triumph of Learning over Ignorance* (1652), and Cary, *Memorials of the Great Civil War*, ii. 372.

[2] *The Naked Woman* (1652); *Faithful Scout* 5–12 May 1652, p. (471).

[3] *The Seventh Day Sabbath* (1652), preface. The subject provoked a pamphlet controversy.

[4] *Original Letters ... addressed to Oliver Cromwell*, pp. 81–2 (with which cf. Howell, *Newcastle-upon-Tyne and the Puritan Revolution*, p. 249); G.F. Nuttall (ed.), *Early Quaker Letters from the Swarthmore MSS* (privately printed, 1952), nos. 3, 6, 10, 12, 13; *Several Proceedings* 26 Feb.–4 Mar. 1652, p. 8; *Perfect Diurnal ... Armies* 8–15 Dec. 1651, p. 1507; *Perfect Account* 20–27 Apr. 1653, p. 953; Latimer, *Records of Bristol*, p. 239; *Autobiography of Henry Newcombe*, pp. 34–40; *Journal of George Fox*, p. 139; J. Besse, *A Collection of the Sufferings of the People called Quakers* (2 vols., 1753), i. 200–1.

[5] *Flying Eagle* 18 Dec. 1652–1 Jan. 1653, pp. 31–2, 33–7; *The Vindication of Christmas* (1652); *C.J.* 24 Dec. 1652.

[6] *Perfect Account* 5–12 May 1652, p. 561, 1–8 Dec. 1652, pp. 806–7; D. Lupton, *The Tithe Takers Cart Overthrown* (1652), passim, and *The Two Main Questions Resolved ... if Tithes be Put Down* (1652), title page; R.B., *A Word of Information and Advice touching Tithes* (1652), p. 1; Whitelocke, *Memorials*, iii. 374, 395.

payment of tithes may simply have ceased.[1] Still more alarming was the mounting demand for a complete separation of church and state. Puritans had traditionally assumed that if the gospel were to be propagated, then one of the agents of propagation would be the magistrate; now they were told that the magistrate had no power in such matters. John Owen bitterly attacked such notions in a fast sermon to the Rump in October 1652. Men, he said, were 'almost taking upon [themselves] to prescribe to the Almighty'. Owen's words reflected the general dismay at the growth of a radicalism now alarmingly out of control:

What now by the lusts of men is the state of things? ... Some say, Lo here is Christ; others, Lo there; some make religion a colour for one thing; some for another; say some, the magistrate must not support the gospel; say others, the gospel must subvert the magistrate; say some, your rule is only for men, you have nothing to do with the interest of Christ and the church; say others, you have nothing to do to rule men, but upon the account of being saints. If you will have the gospel, say some, down with the ministers of it, chemarims, locusts, etc., and if you will have light, take care that you may have ignorance and darkness; things being carried on as if it were the care of men, that there might be no trouble in the world, but what the name of religion might lie in the bottom of. Now those that ponder these things, their spirits are grieved in the midst of their bodies; the visions of their heads trouble them, they looked for other things from them that professed Christ.

Owen's *cri de coeur* echoed his bewildered sense of loss. 'Oh where', he asked, 'is that holy, and that humble frame, wherewith at first we followed our God into the wilderness?'[2]

By the spring of 1652 the pressure on parliament to take a firm stand against religious radicalism had become formidable. In March three of the parliamentary commissioners to Scotland, St John, Salwey and Deane, upset army radicals by negotiating with Argyle.[3] A Commonwealth supporter in Scotland heard at this time 'that the parliament are about some thing for propagation of the gospel. Truly if something

---

[1] E.g. *The Ministers Hue and Cry* (1652), pp. 6–7, 13–14; *Diary of the Rev. R. Josselin*, pp. 55–8, 68; *Mercurius Britannicus* no. 4, p. 32; R.B., *Word of Information and Advice touching Tithes*, p. 1; *A Declaration culled out of the Journals* 29 Nov.–6 Dec. 1652, p. 3; Mayo, *Minute Book of the Dorset Standing Committee*, as indexed under 'tithes'. The payment of tithes was always a contentious issue during times of economic hardship. In the Rump period, ministers whose opposition to the government was well known, or who refused to take the engagement, seem to have found special difficulty in collecting tithes.

[2] Asty, *Sermons of John Owen*, pp. 437, 439.

[3] See e.g. Clarke MS xxii, fo. 80&ᵛ; *Mercurius Politicus* 25 Mar.–2 Apr. 1652, p. 1492. There are many references in the newspapers to the negotiations.

be done to settle authority for the carrying on of that work, that the enemy may not say there is liberty of all opinions to do what they list . . . it will get a great repute'.[1] In the same month a writer in England attacked the separatists and called on presbyterians and independents to unite, 'since the differences' between them 'are very small'.[2] In April Stephen Marshall, pleading for a settled church government and attacking the excesses of the sects, wrote in similar vein of 'my earnest desire to help quench the flames of our church-divisions, which threaten destruction to us all'.[3] In the first week of May, 'many of the old clergy, taking notice of divers petitions and proposals which have been made for pulling down their great Diana tithes', presented a counter-petition to Cromwell.[4] In the same month a Somerset clergy-man dedicated a sermon to the rumper John Pyne, asking 'doth not the parliament very well know, that every county of the land can produce divers ministers that have been true to their cause, ever since they first sat, to this very day?' The notion that 'the Christian magistrate has nothing to do with matter[s] of religion', the minister continued, 'casts a . . . blur upon parliamentary proceedings of that nature, for many years past'.[5] It was in May, too, that Joseph Caryl, sensing an opportunity to bring presbyterians and independents together, called for 'brotherly unity among all Christians, especially amongst the ministers of Christ, being . . . (considering the danger and consequences of our present divisions) so desirable and necessary at this time'. Caryl was giving his blessing to a pamphlet, *The Moderator*, whose author was 'acquainted with the resolutions of some of our leading men, eminent in the prevailing side, to moderate matters, and compose our differences'. In passing, the tract made an intriguing reference to 'the zeal and forwardness of those who in the city gave occasion to the best affected to meet at several conferences, whereof the chief aim was . . . to prevent both in church and state the imminent dangers of tyranny on the one hand, and of anarchy on the other'.[6] There had been similar conferences, as we have seen, during the engagement controversy early in 1650 and during the Love case in the summer of 1651. Ecumenical

---

[1] *Several Proceedings* 18–25 Mar. 1652, p. 2025. Cf. *ibid.* 26 Feb.–4 Mar. 1652, p. 1969.
[2] Gi. Firmin, *Separatism Examined* (1652), title page and pp. 91ff. Cf. Baxter Letters (Dr Williams's Library) iii, fo. 271: Baxter to Thomas Hill, 8 Mar. 1652.
[3] S. Marshall, *A Sermon preached to the . . . Lord Mayor* (1653), esp. ep. ded. and pp. 11–12, 30, 33–4.
[4] *Perfect Passages* 30 Apr.–7 May 1652, p. (263).
[5] F. Fullwood, *The Churches and Ministry of England* (1652), cp. ded.
[6] *The Moderator*, imprimatur and pp. 1, 16.

sentiment was to become still stronger during the final twelve months of the Rump period.[1]

The House proved responsive to the anti-radical sentiments which were so frequently pressed upon it. In February 1652, after hearing a petition from several divines, it apparently dropped the bill introduced after Worcester for the propagation of the gospel, and instead set up a committee to receive alternative proposals. The committee soon opted for the scheme usually attributed to John Owen and adopted in a slightly different form during the protectorate as the system of triers and ejectors. The scheme, drawn up by 'some heads and governors of colleges' at Oxford, was conservative in inspiration, designed to counter the growth of religious radicalism. It was aimed in particular at the *Racovian Catechism*, which reached England early in 1652 and which denied the Trinity and the divinity of Christ. Owen, like the Rump, was appalled by the tract. Shortly after his scheme had been presented to the parliamentary committee appointed to receive proposals for the propagation of the gospel, he drew up a list of fifteen 'fundamentals', attacking the principles to be found in the *Catechism*. The fundamentals were intended to define 'those principles of religion, without acknowledgement whereof the Scriptures do plainly affirm that salvation is not to be obtained'. No one, Owen insisted, should be 'suffered to preach or promulgate any thing' against them.[2]

The Rump's official newspaper, *Several Proceedings in Parliament*, made clear the House's sympathy with the movement towards reconciliation between presbyterians and independents and its alarm at the mounting evidence of religious extremism. In the spring and summer of 1652 *Several Proceedings* hinted subtly but firmly at the need for a return to the ways of sober piety. It printed letters and manifestoes which urged discipline in the church and respect for the established ministry, and advertised pamphlets intended either to unite orthodox puritans or to discredit unorthodox ones. Two letters from Chester, probably by the same hand, were published in the newspaper in the early summer. The first, written on 1 May, spoke for those who rejected 'popery, prelacy and Scottish presbytery' on the one hand, and 'all

---

[1] Above, p. 246; below, pp. 322–4. It is of course conceivable that the reference was to the conferences held in the summer of 1651. For the movement towards conciliation see also *Strength out of Weakness* (1652), ep. ded. and preface (with which cf. *Autobiography of Henry Newcombe* p. 43).

[2] *C.J.* 10 Feb., 26 Mar., 2 Apr. 1652; Gardiner, *History of the Commonwealth and Protectorate*, ii. 98–9, 101; *Several Proceedings* 25 Mar.–1 Apr. 1652, pp. 2037–9; *Proposals for the Furtherance and Propagation of the Gospel in this Nation* (1652), pp. 5–21.

blasphemies, rantings, levellings and abominable iniquities and hypo-
crisies' on the other. The writer continued:

I am strongly persuaded (and not only I, but I perceive it much upon the spirits
of godly men) that if there was but a government settled in the church (though
with all sweet liberty of conscience that might be to tender consciences, so far
as the Word will warrant) that people's affections would be much settled. There
have been some near these parts, as we hear, that have published such sad notions, that have much grieved the spirits of divers godly people. I would some
course were taken to prevent the publishing of blasphemies, and such things as
tend to the beating down of the fundamentals of religion.

The message of the second letter, written on 29 May, was equally plain:

The gathered churches in these parts walk sweetly, but there are some above
churches, or ordinances, who broach damnable opinions, and if some course be
not taken to stop them, it may be of ill consequence . . . It is good that godly
men have all liberty of conscience in the service of God, but that must not give
liberty to looseness, to such as will do nothing decently nor in order. The Lord
direct the parliament in the speedy settling of religion, and propagating the
gospel.

The letter was published in *Several Proceedings* under the date 1 June.
On the same day another letter, sent from Dover on 30 May and too
strikingly similar for coincidence, was also included in the newspaper.
It complained of 'factious loose spirits, that are a great scandal to
religion, and who never took greater heed than now'. The writer urged:
'The Lord direct the hearts of the parliament to settle the great business
of religion. We have heard much of a committee for propagating the
gospel. We should be glad to hear of something done therein . . . The
Lord direct the parliament in this great work.'[1]

It thus comes as no surprise to discover that, also on 1 June, the Rump
revived the committee to receive proposals for the propagation of the
gospel.[2] The committee's task, clearly, would be to disavow radical
aims through a gesture of full support for the orthodox ministry. Yet,
however tempted the Rump might be to take decisive action against
the sects, how could it afford to do so? Unsympathetic to the army's
political stance, and yet not daring at this stage to provoke the army too
far, parliament in the next few months relapsed, on religious matters,
into a nervous, perhaps inescapable, but ultimately fatal inactivity.

In April 1652 the relatively high attendances of the Rump's winter
sessions began to fall away sharply.[3] On 21 April the House admitted a

---

[1] *Several Proceedings* 29 Apr.–6 May 1652, p. 2124, 27 May–3 June 1652, p. 2194. Cf. *ibid.*
26 Feb.–9 Sep. 1652, pp. 1977–8, 2025, 2033–9, 2134, 2150, 2166, 2182, 2294, 2390, 2419.
[2] *C.J.* 1 June 1652.   [3] E.g. *ibid.* 9, 16, 21, 29 Apr. 1652.

new rumper, Sir John Dryden, and debated how 'the House may be supplied with members'. Some rumpers favoured a revival of the recruiting scheme, others the device, which had been mooted early in 1651, of readmitting a selection of hitherto secluded members. The advocates of recruiter elections won the day, but their victory was short-lived. By 12 May St John had returned from Scotland to London, and it may have been as a result of his exertions that the proposal to recruit was dropped once more, and discussion of the bill for a new representative, which had not been debated since the previous November, resumed in its place. The grand committee for 'setting a certain time for the sitting of this parliament, and providing for successive parliaments' was revived and ordered to meet weekly. On 26 May, however, the Rump decided that the need for financial retrenchment, 'to ease the charges of the people', was more urgent than the debate on elections, which was again dropped for some months.[1]

Late April and the first half of May were a tense period in Rump politics. The expulsion of Gregory Clement and the snubbing of Pride and Lambert helped to raise the already high political temperature.[2] On 27 April, when an additional bill for the relief of poor prisoners was passed, Cromwell and Harrison pressed hard for measures of poor relief and for the replacement, effected soon afterwards, of the Rump's Committee of Indemnity by extra-parliamentary commissioners. On 29 April the House was presented with a petition from Middlesex demanding the abolition of tithes. The petition was referred to a committee, but the Rump resolved to declare 'that tithes shall be paid as formerly' until an alternative form of maintenance had been worked out. Reaction was setting in. Law reform, hitherto debated at length, now vanished from parliamentary view. The energies of the committee for the propagation of the gospel seem to have waned markedly at the same time.[3] Then, on 19 May, Dutch and English ships clashed in the Channel.[4] The Anglo–Dutch war of 1652–4 was under way. In the ensuing excitement the cause of reform was quickly forgotten.

[1] *C.J.* 21 Apr., 7, 12, 19, 26 May 1652; *Weekly Intelligencer* 11 May–18 June 1652, pp. 458, 464, 472, 481; *Perfect Account* 12–19 May 1652, p. 569, 2–9 June 1652, p. 596; *Mercurius Politicus* 6–13 May 1652, p. 1592; Whitelocke, *Memorials*, iii. 415, 420, 422; Clarke MS xxii, fos. (88ᵛ), 94, 98; *Several Proceedings* 27 May–3 June 1652, p. 2186; *Faithful Scout* 14–21 May 1652, p. 409; *Perfect Passages* 21–28 May 1652, p. 382, 4–11 June 1652, p. 394.
[2] Above, p. 284.
[3] *C.J.* 27, 29 Apr., 13 May 1652; Gardiner, *History of the Commonwealth and Protectorate*, ii. 102 and n.; Underdown, *Pride's Purge*, p. 274.
[4] Gardiner, *History of the Commonwealth and Protectorate*, ii. 177–9.

14

CONFLICT AND CONFRONTATION, MAY–DECEMBER 1652

The Rump passed its famous navigation act on 9 October 1651, after a debate sandwiched between the first two readings of the bill for a new representative.[1] The main principle of the measure was, broadly, that imported goods must in future be brought directly to England from their country of origin, either in English ships or in ships belonging to the country of their origin. The act, which seems at the time of its passage to have occasioned no publicly hostile comment in England, was steered through the House with a smoothness which contrasts strikingly with the difficulties besetting the advocates of social reform after Worcester.[2] In consequence, little can be learnt of the political manoeuvres surrounding the passage of the act. St John's reputed influence in its drafting is plausible but impossible to prove.[3] There is no indication that anyone in the Rump opposed the measure. It is generally accepted that the navigation act did not directly cause the war of 1652–4, but it was clearly aimed at the United Provinces and at the maritime carrying trade so essential to Dutch prosperity. Like the act of October 1650 prohibiting trade with England's royalist colonies,[4] it increased tension between the two republics. Anglo-Dutch rivalry had provoked bitter jealousy for decades. In this rivalry the English had been outclassed,[5] but the growing diplomatic confidence, commercial assertiveness and naval strength of the Commonwealth encouraged its leaders to challenge Dutch supremacy. The piracy war between England and France, in which the English claimed the right to search and confiscate Dutch vessels suspected of carrying French goods, embittered relations still further. In S. R. Gardiner's view, the English

[1] Gardiner, *Constitutional Documents*, pp. 468–71.
[2] *C.J.* 19, 21, 28 Aug., 4, 11, 18 Sep., 9 Oct. 1651.
[3] L. A. Harper, *The Navigation Laws* (1939), p. 47; C. H. Wilson, *Profit and Power: a study of England and the Dutch Wars* (1957), p. 52.
[4] S. R. Gardiner (ed.), *Letters and Papers relating to the First Dutch War* (Navy Records Society), i (1899), pp. 48–9.
[5] Wilson, *Profit and Power*, esp. pp. 1–10, 25–47.

assumption of the right of search must inevitably have led to war.[1] Hostility between the English and Dutch sea-trading communities became increasingly marked at the end of 1651 and in early 1652, when the radical press in England fanned the flames of discontent.[2] War was predicted at least as early as November 1651[3] and at regular intervals thereafter.[4] An embassy from the United Provinces arrived in England in December 1651 to try to secure the repeal of the navigation act. The failure of the mission soon became apparent, and although negotiations continued until the end of June 1652 they were plagued by ill-feeling.[5] In both England and the United Provinces commercial rivalry became subsumed under nationalist sentiment. It was thus fitting that England's claim to sovereignty over her coastal waters, provoking clashes over the circumstances in which Dutch ships should strike sail to English ones, sparked off the outbreak of hostilities in May 1652.[6] So long as the Dutch ambassadors remained in England there was a reasonable chance of avoiding full-scale conflict, but from July 1652 the two republics were openly at war.[7]

The student of the Rump period is consistently limited by the deficiencies of the available evidence, but of no time is this more true than the year before the dissolution. The *Journal of the House of Commons* becomes increasingly scanty, and other sources become in general more unforthcoming or more unreliable. A solitary attempt by a royalist newswriter in March 1653 to list the rival groupings in the house, for example, is patently far-fetched.[8] At the same time, the patterns of Rump politics become not only harder to detect but more complex and more unstable. Alliances which had previously been reasonably consistent now often broke up. As enmities became more intense, so some members became more hardened in their views; but among others the heightened political temperature, and the growth of political infighting, led to frequent changes of allegiance and frequent changes of

[1] Gardiner, *Letters and Papers relating to the First Dutch War*, i. 49–50, 53.
[2] *Perfect Account* 5–12 Nov. 1651, p. 353, 25 Feb.–3 Mar. 1652, p. 481; *Faithful Scout* 2–9 Jan. 1652, pp. 396–7; *Perfect Diurnal . . . Armies* 9–16 Feb. 1652, p. 1671; *Dutch Spy* 17–25 Mar. 1652, pp. 1–2; *Perfect Passages* 6–20 Feb. 1652, pp. 376–7, 385; *Mercurius Politicus* 18 Sep. 1651–11 Mar. 1652, pp. 1089, 1155, 1250–1, 1387–9, 1471–2.
[3] *Mercurius Politicus* 6–13 Nov. 1651, p. 1200.
[4] E.g. *ibid.* 25 Mar.–1 Apr. 1652, p. 1504; *Perfect Passages* 2–9 Jan. 1652, p. 349, 9–16 Jan. 1652, p. 355, 13–20 Feb. 1652, p. 385.
[5] Gardiner, *History of the Commonwealth and Protectorate*, ii. 169–72, 179–80.
[6] Gardiner, *Letters and Papers relating to the First Dutch War*, i. 170.
[7] Gardiner, *History of the Commonwealth and Protectorate*, ii. 184ff.
[8] C. H. Firth, 'Cromwell and the expulsion of the Long Parliament in 1653', *E.H.R.*, viii (1893), 530.

mind. The attitudes of individual politicians, never easy to detect in the Rump period, now become at times quite inscrutable.

The parliamentary politics underlying English policy in the Dutch war are thus often baffling.[1] Heselrige and Scot made a number of nostalgic statements in 1659 celebrating the Rump's achievements in the Dutch war, and there is every reason to believe that they had been among its more ardent supporters.[2] Influential as Heselrige and Scot were, however, it was not they who provided the drive behind the Rump's foreign policy in its later stages. The initiative, once again, was taken by Marten, Chaloner, Neville, Morley and their assorted allies, who gained control of the council's and the House's committees on foreign and naval affairs. Denis Bond and Bulstrode Whitelocke (both of whom, with Morley, may have been involved in a secret scheme early in 1652 to acquire Dunkirk for the Commonwealth) were also well to the fore in the shaping of foreign policy.[3] Whitelocke vigorously asserted English rights of sovereignty at sea against the Dutch, although he may have regretted the cessation of negotiations with the Dutch ambassadors and the outbreak of war. Later he became a warm advocate of the policy, to which war with the Dutch apparently ran counter, of uniting the Protestant interest in Europe; but his pride in parliament's naval exploits against the Dutch was shared by many rumpers.[4]

Among the opponents of the war, Vane's attitude can be seen the most clearly. In June 1652 he suffered a tactical defeat at the council,

[1] There is, however, opportunity for a much fuller study of them than I offer here. Little is yet known, too, about the government's relations with the major trading companies and with other commercial interests in connection with the Dutch war, or about such matters as the financing or supplying of the navy. The best guides to the Dutch war and to the economic issues relating to it are in Gardiner, *Letters and Papers relating to the First Dutch War*; Wilson, *Profit and Power*; R. W. K. Hinton, *The Eastland Trade and the Common Weal* (Cambridge, 1957); Farnell, 'The Navigation Act'.

[2] Gardiner, *History of the Commonwealth and Protectorate*, ii. 180 and n.; Trevor-Roper, *Religion, The Reformation and Social Change*, pp. 358–60.

[3] For all this see the numerous council committees relating to naval and diplomatic affairs in *C.S.P.D.* 1651–2, pp. 43–497, and the manuscript records of the Navy Committee. See also Rowe, *Sir Henry Vane the Younger*, pp. 272–3. There are frequent signs of the cooperation of these men on other matters in the same period, in *C.J.* and in committee records. On the Dunkirk affair see H. J. Smith, 'The English Republic and the Fronde' (Oxford B. Litt. thesis, 1957).

[4] Gardiner, *History of the Commonwealth and Protectorate*, ii. 188, 202–3; Whitelocke, *Memorials*, iv. 202–3. For Whitelocke's general importance in diplomatic and commercial matters see also B.M., Add. MS 37,345, fos. 20ᵛ, 165ᵛ, 182, 185ᵛ, 188&ᵛ, 198ᵛ–9ᵛ; *C.S.P.D.* 1651–2, pp. 67, 122, 172–3, 244, 282, 318, 321; Whitelocke Letters (Longleat) xi, fos. 47–8, 185, xii, fos. 19, 36, 41, 47, 50, 53, 89–91, 140&ᵛ, 148, 160–70ᵛ, 191&ᵛ, xiii, fos. 1, 15&ᵛ, 17–18, 49–53ᵛ; Whitelocke, *Memorials*, iii. 409, 432.

where Marten, Scot and John Bradshaw (another strong advocate of the war) were entrusted with the wording of a stiff message, which Vane opposed, to the Dutch ambassadors. Vane took the battle to parliament and there defeated Marten heavily, but immediately after the departure of the ambassadors he withdrew from politics for over two and a half months. After his return, however, he committed himself whole-heartedly to strengthening the Rump's naval resources and to the direction of naval strategy.[1] In this he was typical of those rumpers who regretted the outbreak of war but thereafter accepted that there was little to do but to try to win it, or at least to achieve a strong bargaining position against the Dutch. No doubt men's attitudes to the war varied with the successes and failures of the navy and with the growing recognition of the huge strain imposed by the conflict on the Rump's finances. Cromwell's hostility to the war, marked after the dissolution of the Rump, was also in evidence by the last few weeks of the Rump period. In March 1653 he acted as teller with Vane, and in opposition to Heselrige, in favour of peace negotiations. There is other evidence of his anxiety at that time to bring the war to a speedy conclusion.[2] Yet his initial reaction to the war is obscure. It may have been one of confusion rather than of outright opposition. In October 1652, on a fast day held to lament the 'unfortunate breach' with the Dutch, his chaplain John Owen told the Rump that it was 'strange . . . that the Netherlands, whose being is founded merely upon the interest that you have undertaken, should join with the great Antichristian interest . . . Hence . . . are deep thoughts of heart, men are perplexed, and know not what to do.'[3]

Gardiner suggested that a peace party may have been at work in the Rump as early as May 1652, and equated this party with the Rump's more conservative members.[4] Certainly the strengthening of anti-radical sentiment, in both politics and religion, in the spring and summer of 1652 lends plausibility to his thesis. In October 1652 it was reported that English achievement at sea 'doth somewhat allay the presbyterian fire' around Coventry, and in the spring of 1653 petitioners from Hampshire, arguing for moderate religious presbyterianism, expressed opposition to the war.[5] It was the presbyterians, whose ideas

---

[1] Rowe, *Sir Henry Vane the Younger*, pp. 146–8, 150–1.
[2] *C.J.* 10 Mar. 1653; below, p. 331; Gardiner, *History of the Commonwealth and Protectorate*, ii. 181, 187–8.
[3] B.M., 669 f. 16, fo. 65; Asty, *Sermons of John Owen*, p. 437.
[4] Gardiner, *History of the Commonwealth and Protectorate*, ii. 192–3.
[5] *Faithful Scout* 15–22 Oct. 1652, p. (622); B.M., Add. MS 24,861, fos. 67ᵛ, 71.

on church government had much in common with those of the Dutch ruling class, who were most likely to be persuaded of the virtues of the united Protestant interest. Equally, 'conformist' rumpers like Robert Reynolds, who regarded the lightening of taxation as one of their prime political responsibilities, may have opposed the huge fiscal burdens which the war brought with it.[1] The contrast between Vane's defeat at the council at Marten's hands in June 1652 and his subsequent victory over him in the House suggests that opposition to the war may have been strongest among M.P.s least involved in the formulation of policy. The results of the council elections of November 1652 lend weight to the same view.[2] It was the council, rather than parliament, which supplied the impetus behind the war. Perhaps this was why opposition to it was so ineffective. It certainly existed: on 1 July 1652, the day Vane withdrew from politics, Whitelocke noted that 'much discourse was upon the departing of the Dutch ambassadors; some members of parliament being unsatisfied with the dismission of them, and that so high terms were insisted on by the parliament'.[3] Whitelocke rarely recorded the state of feeling in the House except when feelings ran high.

The war clearly aroused some unease both in the navy and in the army. William Penn, one of the Rump's Commanders-at-Sea, wrote to Cromwell on 2 June 1652: 'My lord, I find the most, and indeed those that are best principled and most conscientious of our commanders do much desire some information of the justness of our quarrel with the Hollander, which they do not in the least doubt of; yet I find them somewhat troubled and dejected for their ignorance in that point.'[4] It is notable, however, that the officers of the army, although sharp enough in their criticisms of the Rump on other issues, never seem to have made official representations to the House against the war. In December 1652, after a critical naval defeat in the previous month, the army pledged support for the war effort; and 'the late miscarriages of our fleet' were among the subjects of the officers' self-reproach in January 1653.[5] The failure of the army leaders to oppose the war publicly may have been partly due to the evident enthusiasm for the conflict among groups of religious radicals.[6] The end of the campaign against the royalists had

---

[1] Cf. above, p. 65.   [2] Below, pp. 313–14.
[3] Whitelocke, *Memorials*, iii. 435–6. Cf. *H.M.C.R. De Lisle and Dudley*, vi. 613.
[4] *Original Letters . . . addressed to Oliver Cromwell*, p. 86. On the army's attitude see Gardiner, *History of the Commonwealth and Protectorate*, ii. 187–8, 201; Clarke MS xxii, fo. 95.
[5] *Perfect Passages* 3–10 Dec. 1652, p. 605; *Moderate Publisher* 28 Jan.–4 Feb. 1653, p. 710.
[6] On this point see also Capp, *Fifth Monarchy Men*, pp. 152–4.

deprived the saints of those frequent manifestations of divine approval on which they depended for spiritual fodder. It was all very well for *politique* gentlemen like Whitelocke to sing the praises of the united Protestant interest; to the saints, the war against the 'presbyterian' Dutch brought a renewed sense of eschatological drama. Victories at sea broke what Vane later called the 'great silence in heaven' which marked the period of peace after Worcester.[1] Christopher Feake, close to Harrison at least from the late summer of 1652,[2] and one of the most prominent Fifth Monarchist preachers, claimed afterwards that the negotiations with the Dutch ambassadors from December 1651 had been ill resented by the godly, who had regarded the subsequent outbreak of hostilities as a sign of divine approval.[3] Early in June 1652 'some particular congregations' held a series of fasts in London to implore God's blessing on the English fleet, and later in the same month a writer in Scotland, probably a soldier, welcomed the late 'unavoidable breach' with the Dutch: 'the hand of God is in all these revolutions, and He will bring forth His own glory'.[4] In November 1652, as Harrison joyfully reported, radical congregations in London longed for a fight at sea, 'knowing the cause engaged, and who is for us'.[5] The battle of Portland in February 1653 was eagerly awaited by the saints in London, and divine blessing again anxiously sought.[6] Much of the Fifth Monarchist following came from clothworkers and other manufacturers, who hated the Dutch as economic competitors.[7] In March 1653, when peace negotiations were being considered, Harrison wrote to John Jones:

Our last letters give us to believe that not only the Dutch but France, Denmark and Spain will engage speedily against us. Do not these things import the Lord of Hosts about His threshing-work? Yet we are labouring after a peace with the Dutch, notwithstanding a cross-providence. Whether is most the saints' work, to run after Christ to sea whereon He hath begun to set his right foot, or to men fearing the Lord to be put in all places of power at home?[8]

Yet some of the elect had reservations about the war, as Harrison

[1] John Lord Somers, *A Collection of scarce and valuable Tracts*, vi. 313.
[2] *C.J.* 1 Sep. 1652; Mayer, 'Inedited letters', pp. 215, 217; *Perfect Passages* 3–10 Sep. 1652, p. 489.
[3] Feake, *A Beam of Light*, pp. 42, 44–5. Cf. *A Faithful Searching Home Word*, pp. 3–4.
[4] *Perfect Diurnal ... Armies* 31 May–7 June 1652, p. 1933; *Mercurius Politicus* 1–8 July 1652, p. 1716.
[5] Mayer, 'Inedited letters', p. 217.
[6] *Several Proceedings* 10–17 Feb. 1653, p. (2790); N.L.W., MS 11,493D, fo. 29: Thimelton and Rider to Lloyd, 16 Feb. 1653.
[7] Capp, *Fifth Monarchy Men*, p. 153.
[8] Mayer, 'Inedited letters', p. 200.

admitted shortly after the dissolution of the Rump.[1] The reservations derived partly, no doubt, from the fact that the Dutch – even if akin to the English presbyterians – were Protestants nonetheless. Some Fifth Monarchists, seeing the ultimate goal of foreign policy as a crusade against the Roman Antichrist, and attempting to reconcile this aim with the war against the United Provinces, claimed that the Dutch, once conquered, would be obliged to ally with England in a war against the Catholic powers;[2] but this argument can hardly have entirely convinced even those who made it. There was a further dilemma for the saints, illustrated in a letter written by John Jones to Harrison in August 1652. Although 'all that I have conferred with grant the quarrel on our part to be just', Jones and his saintly colleagues in Ireland were 'afraid that the mind of the Lord hath not been thoroughly sought in that case'.[3] However pleasing to God the renewal of warfare may have been, He can have taken little pleasure in the spirit in which it was conducted. The worldly republicanism of Marten, Neville and Chaloner was not the stuff of which the millennium would be made;[4] and it was embarrassing for a Harrison to find himself supporting the same policy as a Heselrige. The war, disastrously expensive,[5] involving the Rump in endless debates on foreign policy and the raising of money, and plunging the government into still higher taxation and the mass confiscation of estates, was fought by the Rump for material rather than spiritual ends. Worse, conducted at the expense of parliamentary discussion of the army's domestic reform programme, it strained still further relations between parliament and reformers outside the House. The war made complex negotiations with the major European powers necessary, and these bit heavily into the parliamentary timetable. Debates on proposals for the union of the defeated nations of Scotland and Ireland with the English Commonwealth added to the congestion of business. The Rump's foreign policy brought to those who formulated it a new self-confidence and political stature. To men like Whitelocke, Morley and Marten the war was emphatically parliament's triumph rather than the army's; and as a result of their policies the army, whose reforming aims had been obstructed before Worcester by the campaigns

[1] *Ibid.* p. 226.
[2] Capp, *Fifth Monarchy Men*, pp. 152–3.
[3] N.L.W., MS 11,440D, pp. 66–7: Jones to Vane, 10 Aug. 1652.
[4] Cf. Gardiner, *History of the Commonwealth and Protectorate*, ii. 148; *Life and Death of . . . Sir Henry Vane Knight*, p. 96.
[5] H. J. Habbakuk, 'Public finance and the sale of confiscated estates during the Interregnum', *Economic History Review*, 2nd series, xv (1962–3), 80.

against the royalists, now found itself frustrated by warfare once more. Yet perhaps the most remarkable feature of the effect of the Dutch war on Rump politics is that, although it overshadowed them and helped to embitter them, it seems to have had little direct influence on the general course which they took. The war never became a direct source of conflict between the Rump and either the army or the sects, and it seems to have had little immediate connection with the dissolution of the parliament.

The outbreak of war in May 1652 drove the Rump to contemplate ways of lowering expenditure and to order the reduction or suspension of the salaries of certain government officials.[1] Proposals for social reform, however, were rarely discussed until 23 June, when 'divers constant adherers to this parliament, and faithful assertors of the fundamental laws and liberties of the Commonwealth' presented a petition to the House. The document expressed hostility to lawyers, clergymen and politicians, and called for law reform, free trade, annual parliaments and the payment of soldiers' arrears. Parliament's response, which evidently failed to satisfy the petitioners, was to take up the least controversial of their demands, that for the provision of county registers to record land transactions. The Rump, which had earlier debated a bill for county registers, now resolved that the subject should have priority in the House's discussions on law reform.[2] Two weeks later parliament resumed consideration of another relatively contentious issue, the probate of wills.[3] Thereafter, however, law reform was again ignored by the House for several months.

The army's patience was by this time wearing thin. In the second half of July there was 'now again a speech of having a new representative', and on 5 August the radical army preacher William Erbury wrote darkly to a friend that 'the parliament is resolved to sit to perpetuity, but I hope they will have a sooner period than is dreamt of. Be silent in this; you shall hear more.'[4] Whatever Erbury was plotting, the army officers for their part now brought their feelings into the open. Early in August they held a number of meetings to discuss reform proposals, and on the 2nd Cromwell met the Council of Officers from

---

[1] *C.J.* 18 May, 2 June 1652.
[2] *To the Supreme Authority, the Parliament* (1652): B.M., 669 f. 16, fo. 54; *C.J.* 23 June 1652.
[3] *C.J.* 9 July 1652.
[4] Clarendon MS 43, fo. 215: newsletter, 26 July 1652; *H.M.C.R. Leyhourne-Popham*, p. 104. Cf. *H.M.C.R. Sutherland*, pp. 191–2.

nine in the morning until six in the evening. He seems to have been anxious to restrain the radicalism of his colleagues. At some point before 10 August a group of officers, 'having had sundry consultations and conferences' concerning the Rump's dissolution, presented him with a 'model' calling for the election of a new parliament 'forthwith'. The model also demanded a drastic reduction of the law courts and the end of taxes and oppressions, 'that so the poor may no longer be insulted over by the rich', and insisted that the Rump account publicly for the expenditure of 'vast sums'. When the document appeared in print, however, it concluded with a general statement – whose tone contrasts strikingly with what had gone before and which bears the marks of Cromwell's influence – to the effect that reform could not be expected in an instant and that due patience must be exercised. Nevertheless the officers remained, in the words of the army newspaper *The Faithful Scout*, 'very high in their proposals to parliament touching the election of a new representative'. On the 10th Cromwell and his colleagues held another meeting, at which many of the demands advanced in the model were taken up. Two clauses, however, were significantly modified, again probably through Cromwell's influence. On the issue of law reform the officers now substituted a much more measured clause, which merely urged the Rump to resume discussion of the recommendations of the Hale commission. On the subject of the bill for a new representative, too, the revised document was much more restrained. It was now propounded that 'this consideration of putting a period to this parliament be resumed and a speedier time ordered, than was formerly voted (if it be convenient) and that [the House] pass when this parliament be dissolved and when another be chosen'. This relatively mild clause was modified still further when the officers' demands were presented to the House, in the form of a petition, on 13 August. The Rump was now requested only 'that for public satisfaction . . . speedy consideration may be had of such qualifications for future and successive parliaments, as tend to the election of such as are pious and faithful to the interest of the Commonwealth'. Once more, attention had been diverted from the timing of the elections to electoral qualifications. The petition presented to parliament made no mention of a fixed date for the Rump's dissolution.

The army's agitation in August was, nevertheless, of major importance in the development of its relations with parliament. Apart from its demands for law reform and for discussion of electoral qualifications, the petition called for: the propagation of the gospel; the dismissal of disaffected magistrates; the removal of abuses in the collection of the excise; the payment of debts on the public faith; the efficient auditing of soldiers' accounts; a solution to the still troublesome problem of articles of war; an end to public sinecures; better provision for setting the poor on work; and security for ex-soldiers seeking manual employment in corporations. As usual, overt army pressure on parliament for reform excited radical agitation elsewhere. *Mercurius Politicus* supported the army with a well-timed editorial arguing for religious toleration and implicitly attacking Owen's 'fundamentals', and soon the army newspaper *The Faithful Scout* began to print a stream of vituperative social comment. It was about this time, too, that 'divers eminent personages of the Commonwealth' attended a meeting 'not far from London', at which the abolition of tithes was 'propounded and debated'. 'Great actions are abroad', wrote John Jones to Morgan Lloyd on 22 August, 'wherein the honoured of God are greatly concerned. Who knows whether the prayers and graces of the saints are given for such a time as this? But if they stand not in the gap they will not be approved when deliverance cometh.'

The presentation of the army's petition of 13 August caused some resentment in parliament, and Whitelocke advised Cromwell to restrain his officers from 'this way of their petitioning . . . with their swords in their hands'. Yet the Rump was already indebted to Cromwell's restraining influence, and the House's reply to the petitioners was polite enough. A committee was set up to

inform themselves how many of the particulars in this petition are now under consideration; and how far they have been proceeded in; and if there be need of any further power necessary to be given to any of those committees, to whom the same are referred, for the better perfecting the same; as also what other things of public concernment are already under consideration, or lie before the parliament; and to consider what method the same may be put into, for a more speedy expedition therein; and report the same, with their opinions therein, to the parliament for their further consideration.

The composition of the committee provided another indication of the strength of the Cromwell–Harrison group, which had been flexing its parliamentary muscles in recent weeks. Richard Salwey was named first to the committee, and Cromwell second. Robert Bennett and Francis Allen were chosen together. So were Pickering and Harrison, and so were John Carew, appointed chairman of the committee, and Nathaniel Rich. Richard Norton and Thomas Westrow were also appointed.[1] The committee was ordered to meet daily from 17 August, and at least for a time it seems to have done so.[2] In the weeks thereafter the Rump discussed in turn each of the demands put forward in the officers' petition. There were other signs, too, that the House was now willing to adopt a more conciliatory approach. Also on 17 August, after a long debate, it decided not to reappoint as one of the parliamentary commissioners to Ireland the rumper John Weaver, who had offended army officers there (especially Sir Hardres Waller), and who on his return to England in May 1652 had successfully opposed Lambert's nomination as Cromwell's deputy in Ireland.[3] On 27 August the House appointed a committee, headed by Cromwell and Harrison and again colonised by their supporters, to investigate the huge backlog of petitions presented to parliament. Whitelocke, writing of a subject close to his heart, recorded that the committee was instructed to decide which petitions 'were proper for the parliament, and which for courts of justice, and other places; and I was entreated to attend that committee, being one of them, and . . . did as much as I could to further that business, that things might move in their right channel; and to take off particular cases from parliament'.[4]

A further series of concessions to military pressure was made in the following month. On 1 September Christopher Feake, nominated by Harrison, was appointed to preach before the House at a forthcoming fast. Meanwhile Carew's committee addressed itself to the most sensitive of the army's demands, that concerning elections to a new representative. On 14 September Carew reported to the House, which promptly bowed to the committee's recommendations. The grand committee which had discussed elections in the autumn of 1651, and again in May 1652, was dissolved. Instead, 'in order to a more speedy passage of the bill' for a new representative, responsibility for the measure was handed over to Carew's committee. The committee was, however, ordered

---

[1] For all this see *Memoirs of Edmund Ludlow*, i. 348n.; *A Declaration of the Army to his Excellency the Lord General Cromwell, for the Dissolving of this present Parliament* (1652), pp. 3–8; Clarke MS xxiv, fo. 5; *Perfect Account* 4–11 Aug. 1652, p. 670; *Perfect Diurnal . . . Armies* 9–16 Aug. 1652, pp. 2082–5; *Mercurius Politicus* 5–19 Aug. 1652, pp. 1785–9, 1806; *Faithful Scout* 13–27 Aug. 1652, pp. 647–8, 655–6, 3–10 Sep. 1652, pp. 671–2; Mayer, 'Inedited letters', p. 212; *C.J.* 13 Aug. 1652; Whitelocke, *Memorials*, ii. 445–6. My account differs in certain respects from Gardiner's (*History of the Commonwealth and Protectorate*, ii. 233–6). See also Abbott, *Writings and Speeches*, ii. 571–2.

[2] *Perfect Passages* 13–20 Aug. 1652, p. 477; cf. below, p. 310.

[3] *C.J.* 17 Aug. 1652; *Memoirs of Edmund Ludlow*, i. 319; *H.M.C.R. Portland*, i. 671–2. Cf. Clarke MS xxii, fo. 86ᵛ, xxiv, fo. 10ᵛ, xxv, fo. 8ᵛ.

[4] *C.J.* 17 Aug. 1652; B.M., Add. MS 37,345, fos. 217ᵛ–18; above, p. 112.

to leave blank in the bill the date of the Rump's dissolution. Another piecemeal act was passed for relief of poor prisoners for debt, and more concessions soon followed. On the 28th, after a closely fought debate, the House at last backed down to Cromwell, Harrison and Rich on the vexed issue of articles of war. On the same day an army reporter noted that Carew's committee was sitting daily, 'and it's thought will proceed effectually and expeditiously'. The qualifications to be imposed on members of the new representative seem still to have provided the principal subject of debate. On the 30th the Rump considered ways of excluding disaffected persons from holding office under the Commonwealth. On 1 October proposals were discussed for reforming the government's financial administration; on the 8th the committee for the propagation of the gospel was revived and ordered to meet daily; and on the 12th the Rump debated a bill for poor relief.[1]

By this stage the army, too, was showing signs of a more conciliatory attitude. Early in October a pamphlet appeared which attacked religious presbyterians and the prevalence of 'popish books' but also contained a protestation of loyalty, mingled with only the mildest of qualifications, to the Rump. Colonel Pride, normally one of parliament's most outspoken critics in the later Rump period, was among the signatories.[2] Cromwell, anxious as ever for 'healing and settling', sought to take advantage of the more temperate mood. In July 1653, in words tinged with the rancour of retrospect, he recalled how he and the officers,

finding the people dissatisfied in every corner of the nation, and laying at our doors the non-performance of these things which had been promised, and were of duty to be performed – truly we did then think ourselves concerned, if we would (as becomes honest men) keep up the reputation of honest men in the world. And therefore we, divers times, endeavoured to obtain meetings with divers members of parliament; and we did not begin these till about October last. And in these meetings we did, with all faithfulness and sincerity, beseech them that they would be mindful of their duty to God and men, in the discharge of the trust reposed in them. I believe . . . we had at least ten or twelve meetings; most humbly begging and beseeching of them, that by their own means they would bring forth those good things that had been promised and expected; that so it might appear they did not do them by any suggestion from the army, but from their own ingenuity; so tender were we to preserve them in the reputation and opinion of the people to the uttermost.[3]

[1] *C.J.* 1, 14, 28 Sep. 1652; Clarke MS xxiv, fos. 30, 31; Gardiner, *History of the Commonwealth and Protectorate*, ii. 226–7; *Perfect Passages* 3–10 Sep. 1652, p. 489.
[2] *The Beacons Quenched* (1652).
[3] Abbott, *Writings and Speeches*, iii. 55–6.

On 28 October Cromwell was at a meeting of the committee for the Propagation of the Gospel. The rumpers present invited 'the ministers' who were also in attendance to prepare a scheme for 'calling together some who should consult of the way how to proceed towards the reconcilement of differences and the propagation of the gospel'. Cromwell made a plea for discussions between presbyterians, independents and sects. It is unlikely that the more extreme sects would have welcomed such a plan, and John Dury, who took a strong interest in the committee's activities, admitted that some of its members may have countenanced Cromwell's proposals for reasons of political strategy, 'to see the weakness of all sides, and keep them at odds, according to that crafty maxim *divide et impera*'. Nevertheless, Dury continued, 'I really hope and believe (whatever may be thought of some particular men) that the House doth uprightly intend and seek the true way of propagating the gospel.'

Dury should have known better. The committee's deliberations soon melted away, and by 6 January he found 'nothing settled, but a suspension of all proceedings tacitly yielded to'. 'I am afraid', he now admitted, 'that we shall not be so happy by anything of their undertaking, who at present manage public affairs.'[1] The conferences between officers and M.P.s, too, came to nothing. Talk, as the army by now well knew, was no guarantee of action, and the officers were soon disillusioned by the House's response to the August petition. Meanwhile, despite the Rump's show of concessions, relations between parliament and army remained infected by continual tension and occasional bursts of ill temper. One contentious issue involved the city alderman John Fowke, who many years previously had been awarded damages by the House of Lords in a dispute with the East India Company, and who was still seeking repayment. On 15 July Cromwell and Harrison had been tellers for a motion to read Fowke's petition. The tellers against were Algernon Sidney, an increasingly prominent member of the Marten–Morley grouping, and Morley himself. The result was a tie. The Speaker's casting vote went to those who supported Cromwell and Harrison, but many rumpers, holding Fowke's claims to be 'pretences', were consequently unwilling to follow the wishes of the defunct upper house. Fowke's petition was not read until 7 September, when a proposal to

[1] Baxter Letters (Dr Williams's Library) vi, fos. 77, 83ᵛ–6: Dury to Baxter, 29 Oct. 1652, 6 Jan. 1653. Cf. Abernathy, 'The English Presbyterians and the Stuart Restoration', pp. 8–10, and G. F. Nuttall, 'Presbyterians and Independents. Some movements for unity 300 years ago', *Journal of the Presbyterian History Society*, x (1952).

press ahead with the case supported by Harrison and opposed by Neville, was defeated by a single vote.[1]

Cromwell's support for Fowke caused considerable resentment in parliament. So did his patronage of a petitioner who wanted the House to overrule a verdict reached in the law courts. Marten opposed Cromwell when the latter case was brought into the House on 26 August. Cromwell won, but the incident left a bitter taste which must have soured the debate of the following day, when the Rump eventually agreed to Cromwell's and Harrison's demand for a committee to investigate the backlog of petitions. Cromwell's habit of supporting individual petitions, 'all of which', in one rumper's view, 'were not constantly for the most just things neither', was a frequent source of testiness in the House; and Whitelocke's criticism, at the time of the appointment of the committee for petitions, of those who pressed in parliament cases which should have been left to the law courts may have been directed against Oliver. There was to be a similar incident shortly before the dissolution, when Cromwell urged parliament to reprieve three men from Southwark sentenced to death for horse-stealing. According to an account given by a rumper after the House's expulsion, Cromwell was 'so earnest therein, and so impatient to be refused, that some have been of opinion that the government was the shorter lived for it'. Not the least irritating feature of Cromwell's conduct, according to his enemies, was his interference in cases he knew nothing about. When feelings ran so high, army and parliament were quick to accuse each other of putting politics before justice. Whatever the rights and wrongs of the individual cases, of which only inconclusive scraps of evidence survive, the incidents they provoked played their part in the further deterioration of relations.[2] Even when, in late September and early October, the officers seemed anxious for conciliation, they combined reasoned discussion with determined shows of strength. *The Faithful Scout* reported on 29 September that 'there hath been a great Council of Officers ... where the commanders declared their resolution to establish this Commonwealth even from the very shadow of oppression, and to take off taxes, etc.'.[3] The conferences between M.P.s and officers launched by Cromwell in October were soon ruined by ill-feeling, the army leaders 'declaring plainly that the issue would

[1] *C.J.* 15 July, 7 Sep. 1652; Pearl, *London and the Outbreak of the Puritan Revolution*, p. 319.
[2] Williams, 'Political career of Henry Marten', pp. 544–7; *C.J.* 26 Aug. 1652.
[3] *Faithful Scout* 24 Sep.–1 Oct. 1652, p. 701.

be the displeasure and judgement of God, disaffection of the people, and putting of things into a confusion'.[1]

Not for the first time, bitterness at Westminster produced an embarrassing fall in parliamentary attendances. In September, never a good month for attendance figures, they dropped to their lowest level for three years. The House and even the Council of State had difficulty in raising quorums. On the 14th, the day parliament handed over the bill for a new representative to Carew's committee, there was talk of a two-months' adjournment, but once more nothing came of it. As in September 1649, the Rump resolved instead on a call of the House.[2] The call was fixed for 3 November, a date assuming the aura of a symbol in the Long Parliament's history, and at least eighty-two members were present at it. In the weeks which followed the House continued to fill, and one hundred and twenty-one members, if not more, were present at the elections to the fifth Council of State on 24 and 25 November.[3] It is possible to identify twenty rumpers who seem to have reappeared at Westminster in November for the first time for several months, or even for much longer.[4] There were probably many more.

The reappearance of these men did nothing to improve the temper of debates, but it temporarily brought about an important shift in the balance of power in parliament. When the truant members reappeared they found the House immersed in interminable discussions about the names to be included in a bill, eventually passed on 18 November, for confiscating the estates of more than six hundred royalists. The purpose of the measure was to help finance the Dutch war, which was by now becoming increasingly unpopular in the provinces from which the reappearing members came. These backbench M.P.s seem to have regarded the war as a policy pursued by a court in opposition to the interests of the country; and the council elections enabled them to make their views felt. The elections were not fought solely over the war, and men like Morley and Bond, who had stood up to Cromwell over domestic issues and who had permanent bases of support in the House, were safely re-elected. Heselrige and Scot did even better. Morley's protégés, however, were dropped, Stapley, Downes and Hay

1 Abbott, *Writings and Speeches*, iii. 55–6.
2 Clarke MS xxv, fo. 23; Whitelocke Letters (Longleat) xii, fo. 70; *C.J.* 23 Sep. 1652.
3 *C.J.* 3, 24, 25 Nov. 1652.
4 *C.J.* Nov. 1652, *passim*: Aldworth, Andrews, Armyne (jr.), Birch, Boone, Brewster, Brooke, Browne, Burrell, Fell, H. Herbert, P. Jones, Lechmere, Lucy, Millington, Pyne, Reynolds, Vane (sr.), Walton, E. Wylde.

failing to secure re-election – although Morley only narrowly failed with his most impudent nomination to date, that of his client John Fagge, who had made no recorded appearance in the House for nineteen months and who throughout the Rump period was among the rumpers who appeared least often in parliament.[1] Chaloner scraped home near the bottom of those re-elected, but Marten and Neville lost their places. Harrison, excluded the previous year, now returned, but only with the minimum votes needed to secure election. As in the previous year, the 'revolutionaries' as a whole won little favour from the backbenchers who had reappeared in parliament for the council elections. Only two 'revolutionaries' were among the ten re-elected councillors who received most votes, and only three were among the ten most successful newly elected candidates.[2]

The advocates of the Dutch war might have fared even worse had the elections been held a week later. On 30 November the navy suffered a major and humiliating defeat off Dungeness, an event which reduced parliamentary morale to a low ebb. There had recently been evidence of administrative incompetence in the navy, and the Navy Committee, dominated by Marten, Neville, Chaloner and their friends, now received the blame. There are signs that the energy of these men in running the war effort had declined during the autumn.[3] In December the administration of the navy was completely reformed. The Navy Committee was replaced by four commissioners, Vane, George Thomson, and two men who were becoming firm allies, John Carew and Richard Salwey. Whatever M.P.s thought about the war itself, they could now assure themselves that its conduct had at last been placed in godly hands. The careers of Marten and Chaloner as politicians of major stature were ended. The coup which they had achieved in December 1650 with Vane's resignation as treasurer of the navy was now reversed.[4] The newly appointed navy commissioners, given room for manoeuvre by the prevalent feeling that the war had reached its crisis, undertook an immediate overhaul of the fleet. They increased the numbers of sailors, tightened their discipline, and improved their financial incentives. At the same time the Rump, in desperate financial straits, at last resolved to bring its separate treasuries under a single

[1] For his recorded appearances see *C.J.* 14, 20 July 1649, 17, 28, 31 May 1650, 16 Apr. 1651.
[2] *C.J.* 24, 25 Nov. 1652. See also Gardiner, *History of the Commonwealth and Protectorate*, ii. 201–2.
[3] Rawlinson MS A226, *passim*. Cf. *Mercurius Politicus* 10–17 Mar. 1653, p. 2296.
[4] Above, p. 261.

administrative body. Francis Allen, John Downes, Cornelius Holland and Denis Bond were appointed finance commissioners.[1]

Meanwhile the Fifth Monarchists patronised by Harrison were providing the Rump with a problem of growing magnitude. When John Owen, Thomas Goodwin and (as Harrison's nominee) Christopher Feake preached before the Rump on 15 October, there was a repetition of the incident involving Feake's friend John Simpson in March 1651. The act appointing the fast day had anticipated the theme of Owen's sermon by urging the deity to show 'how the saving truth of the gospel may be best advanced and propagated, and whatsoever is contrary to sound doctrine and the power of godliness suppressed'. Owen, attacking the excesses of the new religious radicalism, urged the House to 'know them that are faithful and quiet in the land'. He and Goodwin were informally thanked by the House for their sermons, but Feake, who like Simpson in the previous year 'was very home in his applications', was not. 'The pulpit spoke plain English to the parliament that day', an army writer recorded.[2]

In November both saintly and social radicalism became alarmingly well-organised. Harrison wrote to Jones on the 7th that 'many precious ones think . . . our blessed Lord will shortly work with eminence', and on the 27th that 'a sweet spirit of prayer begins to issue forth, and some think will never again decline'. In late November and early December radical congregations in the city held a series of meetings, at which Harrison and Feake played a prominent part and to which saints were invited from Fifth Monarchist strongholds throughout Britain. One purpose of the meetings was to devise means for the propagation of the gospel; another was to 'pray for a new representative, and to preach somewhat against the old'.[3] *The Faithful Scout*, now in daring mood, likewise began to criticise parliament openly: not only had M.P.s broken their promises, but 'they are inconstant in their counsels . . . they vote and unvote, and what they enact one day, they dare repeal another'. One of the *Scout*'s principal targets was the excise, now the focus of huge resentment.[4] In December the Rump, alarmed by

1 Firth and Rait, *Acts and Ordinances*, ii. 652–3, 688–90.
2 *Perfect Diurnal . . . Armies* 30 Aug.–6 Sep. 1652, pp. 2134–5; Asty, *Sermons of John Owen*, p. 446; *Perfect Account* 13–20 Oct. 1652, p. 745; above, p. 242.
3 Mayer, 'Inedited letters', pp. 214, 217, 218; William Erbury, *The Bishop of London* (1653: part 1), pp. 1, 3–5; Gardiner, *History of the Commonwealth and Protectorate*, ii. 232 and n.
4 *Faithful Scout* 13–20 Aug. 1652, pp. 647–8, 655, 3–10 Sep. 1652, pp. 671–2, 5–12 Nov. 1652, p. 744.

reports of excise riots, attempted to reform some of the abuses in the farming of the tax, although financial necessity obliged it to reimpose the excise for a further two years.[1] The increasingly vitriolic performance of the radical press, now reinforced by a new journal called *The Flying Eagle*, drove the Rump to try to suppress such newssheets. The *Scout* was singled out as especially dangerous. No doubt to appease radicals, the Rump also suppressed *Mercurius Britannicus*, a recently revived newspaper which imitated the *Scout*'s histrionics but employed them to opposite ends: it defended tithes and the established church ministry while attacking the Commission for the Propagation of the Gospel in Wales.[2] The commission's term of office was shortly to come up for renewal, an issue which was to make a decisive impact during the final months of the Long Parliament.

[1] *Mercurius Politicus* 18–25 Nov. 1652, pp. 2025–6, 2–9 Dec. 1652, p. 2071; *Perfect Diurnal . . . Armies* 29 Nov.–6 Dec. 1652, p. 2347, 24–31 Jan. 1653, p. 2476.
[2] *C.J.* 28 Dec. 1652 (and see *Mercurius Politicus* 16–23 Sep. 1652, p. 1896); *Flying Eagle* 4–11 Dec. 1652, pp. 11–13, 15–16; *Mercurius Britannicus* 2 Nov.–28 Dec. 1652, *passim*. The *Scout* went underground until March, when it reappeared in a more sober mood.

15

DISSOLUTION AND DISARRAY,
JANUARY–APRIL 1653

Army pressure on the House escalated dramatically at the turn of the year. On 1 January an army writer reported that 'the officers have been seeking God two days; the grandees fear a design in hand'.[1] Cromwell had a meeting with the Council of Officers on 5 January, when, after extensive debate, a sub-committee was appointed to 'draw up the sense of the council concerning the constituency of the civil authority by successive parliaments, and the just and equal dispensation of justice through the nation for the greatest ease and advantage of the people and concerning matters of religion'.[2] The sub-committee took some time to report, and when the officers met again on 20 January there were signs of division among them. They decided to send a circular to the regiments in England, Scotland and Ireland to enlist their support, but 'could not at present agree' about the document's contents. On the 21st some of the gathered churches of London tried to present the officers with a 'paper of advice', but their offer was refused. The less radical of the officers, Cromwell no doubt among them, seem to have been making a stand against their more extreme colleagues; but by the 28th, after the army leaders had spent 'several days waiting at the throne of grace', the circular was ready. Complaining that 'through the corruption of many in places of authority, some good men are punished for conscience sake', and lamenting (as the Levellers had often lamented in identical words) 'the many inconveniences apparently arising from the long continuance of the same persons in supreme authority', the letter urged the need for 'successive parliaments consisting of men faithful to the interest of the Commonwealth; men of truth, fearing God and hating covetousness'. Forceful demands were also made for law reform, religious toleration and the propagation of the gospel. The document was not as outspoken as the Rump must have feared,

---

[1] Clarke MS xxiv, fo. 98ᵛ. I differ from Firth over his (tentative) dating of the letter: Firth, 'Cromwell and the expulsion of the Long Parliament in 1653', p. 527.

[2] Firth, 'Cromwell and the expulsion of the Long Parliament in 1653', p. 527.

but it marked a systematic attempt to coordinate army discontent.[1]

The officers' deliberations in January stimulated radical agitation among the troops and in London, and brought political tension to a new pitch. For the first time, the forcible dissolution of the Rump seemed an imminent possibility. From now on the House 'lived in perpetual apprehension' of a military coup.[2] Parliament responded with unusual alacrity to intensified army pressure. On 31 December, discussion of two contentious issues was resumed. The first concerned debts on the public faith, and especially those owed to the government's poorer creditors. In recent months Pride and his separatist friend Samuel Chidley had tried to organise public agitation among the state's creditors, 'that so there may be an estimate of the said debts, and effectual applications by petitioning the parliament for the payment thereof'. During the same period Marten had attempted to persuade the House to deal with the problem; he proposed that the money should be raised by a sale of cathedral property. In October Pride and Chidley, apparently mollified by Marten's assurances, had backed down, but they revived the issue in December. Once more they withdrew their demands, but their continued patience depended on the Rump's willingness to provide its own remedy. From 31 December the public faith was intermittently but extensively discussed in the House over a period of weeks.[3] Pride's manoeuvres were but one manifestation of his deep involvement in city radicalism, which was now organising itself for concerted action on a number of reform schemes. One, in which Pride was again implicated, was for the overthrow of the oligarchy which controlled the Saddlers Company; another was for the replacement of Prideaux's lucrative postal system by a cheaper and more frequent service.[4] The second issue raised on 31 December was the

---

[1] Firth 'Cromwell and the expulsion of the Long Parliament in 1653', p. 527; Clarke MS xxiv, fo. 107; *Moderate Publisher* 28 Jan.–4 Feb. 1653, pp. 710–(12).

[2] Williams, 'Political career of Henry Marten', p. 547.

[3] *C.J.* 9 July, 26 Aug., 27 Oct., 30 Nov., 31 Dec. 1652, 6, 11, 18, 25, 27 Jan., 1 Feb., 6, 19 Apr. 1653; Chidley, *Remonstrance of the valiant and well-deserving Soldier, passim; Perfect Diurnal . . . Armies* 30 Aug.–6 Sep. 1652, p. 2141, 24–31 Jan. 1653, p. 2463; *Flying Eagle* 4–11 Dec. 1652, pp. 15–16, 18–25 Dec. 1652, pp. 25–6; *Several Proceedings* 2–9 Dec. 1652, p. 2628; Whitelocke, *Memorials*, iii. 446; *Mercurius Politicus* 20–27 Jan. 1653, p. 2192.

[4] There are numerous references to these and related subjects in the pamphlets and newspapers. See e.g. *Perfect Account* 14–21 Apr. 1652, p. 544, 28 Apr.–5 May 1652, p. 553, 15–22 Sep. 1652, p. 719, 15–22 Dec. 1652, p. 822, 2–9 Feb. 1653, p. 871; *Perfect Passages* 27 Aug.–3 Sep. 1652, pp. 489–91, 26 Nov.–3 Dec. 1652, p. 597; *Mercurius Britannicus* 7–14 Dec. 1652, p. 285; *Perfect Diurnal . . . Armies* 4–11 Apr. 1653, p. 2634; *Moderate Publisher* 14–21 Jan. 1653, p. 698. See also Clarke MS xxv, fo. 10; *Clarke Papers*, iii. 3; *Mercurius Politicus* 13 June–4 Aug. 1652, pp. 32, 39, 58–60; SP 23/118, p. 889.

probate of wills. Probate remained under the jurisdiction of a curious remnant of the days of monarchical rule, the Prerogative Court of Canterbury presided over by Sir Nathaniel Brent. Brent's death on 6 November 1652 gave a new urgency to the Rump's discussions of the bill for probate of wills, which with other proposals for law reform was to occupy much of the Rump's attention in January 1653. Then, on 6 January, the Rump made perhaps the most striking concession of its rule to military pressure. Responsibility for the bill for a new representative was handed over to Harrison, and it was ordered that the bill be brought in 'with speed'.[1] On the same day the House, which on the 5th had issued a proclamation banning papists and Jesuits from England, debated a bill 'explaining' the meaning of certain clauses in the toleration act of September 1650. The bill for poor relief was taken up soon afterwards. On 28 January, the day of the dispatch of the officers' circular, parliament even came within three votes of inviting the outrageously radical William Dell, whose cause had been taken up by Harrison, to preach before it; and on the 29th it resolved to remove excise charges on woollen goods and stuffs.[2] Yet, once again, the Rump's concessions proved illusory. Of the reform proposals discussed at this time only two, those for the probate of wills and for a new representative, were given the House's blessing. In neither case, as will be evident, did the Rump's provisions accord with the army's wishes. As for the public faith, Pride and Chidley were driven to exasperation by parliament's capacity for postponement and delay.[3]

After the completion of the circular of 28 January the House was given a brief respite from intensive army pressure. Parliament, whose demise had seemed imminent earlier in the month, could breathe again.

---

[1] *C.J.* 6 Jan. 1653. The *Journal* states that Harrison was put in charge of 'the bill touching equal representatives'. This is in contrast to the entries for February, March and April 1653, when the Rump debated the bill 'for appointing a certain time for the dissolving of this present parliament, and for calling and settling of future and successive parliaments'. The recruiting scheme debated before Worcester had sometimes been called 'the bill for an equal representative'. The Clerk was often wayward with his entries; yet the possibility remains that Harrison, to whose cause a genuinely new representative would have been so disadvantageous, was on 6 January following the advice of his friend John Jones (above, p. 288), and attempting to revive the recruiting plan. If so, he evidently soon abandoned it; but what irony if Harrison at any point pressed for the recruiting scheme for which the Rump was so vigorously attacked by the army after the dissolution!

[2] *C.J.* 11 Nov., 31 Dec. 1652, 5, 6, 8, 11, 12, 19, 20, 21, 26, 28, 31 Jan., 1, 2, 4 Feb. 1653; *Perfect Diurnal . . . Armies* 3–10 Jan. 1653, pp. (2421)–(2), 27 Jan.–3 Feb. 1653, p. 2194; *Dictionary of National Biography: Sir Nathaniel Brent; Perfect Account* 10–17 Nov. 1652, p. 781.

[3] Chidley, *Remonstrance of the valiant and well-deserving Soldier*, *passim*.

It celebrated its reprieve with a burst of uncompromising reaction. Advocates of law reform bore much of the brunt. Against Marten's wishes, the bill for probate of wills was shelved and replaced by a stop-gap measure. Instead of subjecting probate jurisdiction, as the Hale commission had wanted and as the abandoned bill had stipulated, to county courts, the substitute bill merely handed Brent's job over to the members of the Hale commission. This temporary measure sailed easily through the House, but it was less a reform measure than a successful evasion of reform. Meanwhile one debate on the original bill had brought the whole issue of law reform to the moment of decision. On 19 January the Rump had ordered that the entire report of the Hale commission be brought into the House, in the form in which the parliamentary committee had agreed to it. The report was debated all day on both the 20th and the 21st. On the 26th the House resumed discussion of a bill for setting up county registers to record land transactions, a measure which it had not touched since the previous summer. The Rump's hostility to the bill came into the open in a heated debate on the same subject on 2 February. Chaotic scenes developed as the House argued whether or not to turn itself into a grand committee and as the Speaker was repeatedly called to and from his seat. The incident was closed only when a committee was appointed to redraft the bill in consultation with the Hale commissioners. The committee's composition, however, revealed the remarkable degree of coordination achieved by the House's established lawyers in resisting the movement for law reform. Although the committee was headed by Cromwell and included a fair proportion of both his and Harrison's supporters, its transactions were placed in the special care of four conservative lawyers, St John, Whitelocke, Reynolds and William Ellis. Other lawyers appointed were John Wylde, making one of his few recorded appearances in the Rump, Robert Nicholas, who had made no recorded appearance in the House since his appointment as a judge in June 1649, and Francis Thorpe, who may not have sat in the Rump at least since 1650. On 26 January the M.P.s who were judges had been specially summoned to attend the debate on county registers. In the face of such elaborately organised opposition the bill stood little chance. No more did any of the innovatory proposals for law reform now before the House. Except to debate its emasculated probate bill, the Rump never discussed law reform again.[1]

---

[1] *C.J.* 19, 20, 21, 26 Jan., 2 Feb., 17, 22, 31 Mar., 8, 15 Apr. 1653; Firth and Rait, *Acts and Ordinances*, ii. 702–3.

Until the battle of Worcester the Rump had, in the main, contrived to contain radical demands while at the same time eschewing social policies which would offend political and religious presbyterians. Thereafter the task had become increasingly difficult; and by the spring of 1653 it had become impossible. Radicalism and reaction fed off each other, and presbyterians became more stubborn as sects and social radicals became more vociferous. Parliament, under mounting pressure from both sides, was eventually obliged to choose between them. This is what happened in its decisions on law reform in February and March 1653. A similar process occurred in the same period in its debates on religion. Here, too, the Rump at last made a firm and fateful decision.

One of the favourite scenarios of English historians involves a successful act of concession on the part of an establishment to the forces of dissent. The concession splits the dissenters, and those who matter support the establishment. Yet concession can of course stimulate rather than mollify radical ambitions. The realisation that change is possible is followed by the demand for further change. The Rump's gestures to 'Harrison, Rich and their party'[1] in January 1653, although successful in the short term, were the dawn of the political movement whose noonday was to come with the meeting of Barebone's Parliament. In January there was 'great confusion ... in London owing to the multiplicity of sects'. By March the Blackfriars preachers were successfully cultivating hysteria in the city, and it was reported in the same month that 'the preaching people ... are now very violent against this parliament'. On 15 April a newswriter noted that 'our preaching people rant it very high against the parliament. Sunday last a glazier preached in Somerset House, and told his auditors they should ere long see a greater destruction fall on the parliament then ever befell the Cavaliers.' An intelligent observer had written prophetically at the beginning of April: 'You will wonder much to hear me say such fanatic people will shortly sit at the helm, but really it's the opinion of all that it will shortly come to pass.' Fanaticism was not confined to Blackfriars or to the soldiery; in the words of the Lancashire clergyman Adam Martindale, 'About the beginning of the year 1653 the opinions that were rampant in the army infected also the country.' Such was the political atmosphere in which Harrison, bent on a forcible dissolution, was urging Cromwell 'to do that, the consideration of the issue whereof made his hair to stand on end'.[2]

1 *Memoirs of Edmund Ludlow*, i. 345.
2 Gardiner, *History of the Commonwealth and Protectorate*, ii. 248; Firth, 'Cromwell and the

The temper of the saints was unlikely to sustain the conciliatory tendencies displayed by the Rump in January. Indeed, the House was much more disposed to respond favourably to pressure from a quite different quarter. The records of the Westminster Assembly survive only until March 1652, but it was revived early in 1653, its renewal a symptom of growing presbyterian assertiveness.[1] In late 1652 and early 1653 a number of manifestoes and petitions were drawn up in the south and south-west counties of England, urging the Rump to take a firm stand behind the established ministry and to silence the radical crescendo. The petitioners, praising the Rump's ecclesiastical policies and especially its provision for needy ministers, appealed to the same sentiments in the House as those to which the defenders of Christopher Love had addressed themselves in the summer of 1651. The impetus behind the petitions came from Richard Baxter. Since 1650, and especially since early 1652, he had been trying to bring presbyterian, independent and other divines together, partly through conferences, partly through a parliamentary initiative. In May 1652, taking advantage of the anti-radical mood emerging at that time, and hearing of Owen's proposals for the propagation of the gospel and for the imposition of 'fundamentals', he had cooperated with Dury to set proposals for conferences in motion. One of those whom he wished to win over was Archbishop Ussher, at that time on friendly terms with the royal independents and even, probably, with Cromwell. In September, in his native county, Baxter had launched the Worcestershire Association, later to provide the model for a more extended ecumenical movement.[2] His next step was to draw up and circulate a petition which was eventually presented to the Rump on 22 December, a time when, as he put it, 'Anabaptists, Seekers, etc. flew so high against tithes and ministry, that it was much feared they would have prevailed at last'. Urging an end to 'our sad divisions in matters of religion, especially about church government', the petitioners begged the Rump to 'recommend at least to the people so much of church-order and government as you find to be clearly required by Jesus Christ ... vouchsafing it your public countenance, though you scruple an enforcement'. Let parliament encourage a godly ministry, the document implored, 'that all the world

---

expulsion of the Long Parliament in 1653', pp. 527, 528, 529; Josten, *Elias Ashmole*, ii. 641–2; *Life of Adam Martindale*, p. 110.

[1] *Moderate Publisher* 18–25 Mar. 1653, p. 771; *Mercurius Democritus* 19–26 Jan. 1653, pp. 323–4; B.M., Add. MS 36,792, fos. 60ᵛ, 61, 62&ᵛ, 64&ᵛ, 65.

[2] G. F. Nuttall, *Richard Baxter* (1965), pp. 64–84. Cf. *Autobiography of Henry Newcombe*, pp. 34–5; B.M., Add. MS. 10, 114, fos. 29–33.

... may still see and acknowledge your open and resolved adhering to the reformed Christian religion'. The petitioners were thanked by the House, and the Rump's official newspaper *Several Proceedings in Parliament*, continuing its policy of tacit support for the advocates of pious respectability, published a report from Worcester that

the parliament's answer to the petition from this county, for the preaching of the gospel and the ministry thereof, hath much taken the affections of the people. Some ministers have given God thanks in public, both for putting it into the hearts of the petitioners to send such a petition to the parliament, and also for the parliament's answer; and prayers are earnestly put up for the propagating of the gospel, and settling religion under a pious, painful, able and orthodox ministry.[1]

The same newspaper recorded that when Colonel Bridges, one of those who had presented the petition to the House, returned to Worcester, he met

with the mayor and aldermen of the city, and there was a great meeting ... with the rest that carried up the petition; and they have great visitings, and it is very great encouragement to the godly well-affected ministry; and makes the Cavalier and disaffected party ashamed, who endeavoured to possess the people with an expectation of an answer not so satisfactory.[2]

Baxter's example was infectious. Under the date 6 January 1653, *Several Proceedings* opened its weekly account with the statement: 'The letters that come from several parts do certify that there are in divers counties petitions framing, and hands gathering to them to be sent to the parliament, to the like effect as the late petition from the county of Worcester, touching the ministry of the gospel.' On 22 March the Hampshire divine Henry Bartlett wrote to Baxter that the Worcestershire petition 'did take very much with us ... We have in Hampshire subscribed one to the same effect with 8,000 hands. In Dorset, Wilts., Somerset they are going the same way, but slowly.'[3] Progress was quicker than Bartlett imagined. The Wiltshire petition, 'much of the same nature with that which was presented from the county of Worcester', reached the Rump on 29 March. It attacked 'the undermining of holiness and Christian religion, by a generation of men who cry down learning, ministry, ordinances and almost whatsoever belongs

[1] *Reliquiae Baxterianae*, pp. 69–70, 115; *C.J.* 26 Dec. 1652; *Several Proceedings* 23–30 Dec. 1652, pp. 2644–70, 6–13 Jan. 1653, p. 2697. Cf. *Diary of Thomas Burton*, iii. 113–14.
[2] *Several Proceedings* 6–13 Jan. 1653, p. 2695.
[3] Baxter Letters (Dr. Williams's Library) iii., fo. 183: Bartlett to Baxter, 22 Mar. 1653.

to us as Christians or civil men'. At such a time, the petitioners observed, the Rump's constancy to the cause of godly respectability was admirable; all it needed was unashamed advocacy.[1] The Hampshire petition, described by an army writer as an appeal 'for continuance of tithes', was presented to the House on 8 April. It lamented the widespread destructive designs on the ministry: 'and this so boldly attempted even during the sitting of this parliament (which hath so eminently declared and appeared to the contrary)'.[2] In Sussex, some ministers drafted a document complaining of the widespread confusion in religious affairs, and noting that 'divisions more and more increase, [while] a universal toleration of the grossest errors [is] contended for'. The ministers hoped for 'some seasonable expedients to reconcile our differences'.[3] From Somerset, a radical reporter wrote on 27 March that 'we have a petition on foot in this county on behalf of the ministers . . . the solicitors telling the contents of the petition unto the people as they please. I believe many hands are gained, but few well-affected, it being carried on by most dissenting presbyterian ministers and people to the present government.' The Somerset petition, which was one of the last to be drawn up, did not reach the Rump, but what is evidently a draft of it survives in the Hippisley papers in the Somerset Record Office. The document urged the House to continue its splendid 'support and encouragement of a necessary and comfortable maintenance', and left it to the Rump's 'wisdom to consider whether that of tithes (so much agitated) may not be yet found as fit as any other'. Stressing that 'we do not aim at the straightening or the grieving of consciences truly tender', the petitioners nevertheless warned against 'men who abuse their liberty to licentiousness'; for 'at the same door where the respect of the ministry goes out, the ruin of the state comes in'.[4] It was with pardonable exaggeration that an army newspaper reported on 5 March that 'all the counties (almost) in England are getting hands to the petitions for, and to cross petitions against, forced maintenance for the ministry'.[5]

The appeal in the petitions to presbyterian sentiment in the House

[1] *The Wiltshire Petition for Tithes Explained* (1653), pp. 1–3; *Mercurius Politicus* 24–31 Mar. 1653, p. 2340; Clarke MS xx, fo. 2; *Several Proceedings* 24–31 Mar. 1653, pp. 2890–2.

[2] *C.J.* 8 Apr. 1653; *The Cries of England to the Parliament*, pp. 6–8; *Several Proceedings* 7–14 Apr. 1653, pp. 2918–20; *Clarke MS* xxv, fo. 7.

[3] B.M., Thomason MS E804(4), 'The declaration and agreement of the ministers of the county of Sussex', esp. fo. 1&ᵛ.

[4] *Moderate Publisher* 25 Mar.–1 Apr. 1653, p. (778); Somerset Record Office (Taunton), DD/HP Box 10: 'To the Honourable the Parliament of the Commonwealth of England'.

[5] Clarke MS xxiv, fo 122ᵛ.

raises an interesting but probably insoluble problem. Neither political nor religious presbyterians could ever be expected to love the purged parliament, but there were good reasons why they should now rally behind it. Since the defeat of the royalists it had become increasingly clear that the prime conflict was now between the respective proponents of parliamentary and military rule. However disreputable the Rump's constitutional credentials, its tenure of power was infinitely preferable to the prospect of government by the sword. How far had the Rump, in its defiance of the army, attracted presbyterian support? As early as December 1651 a radical newspaper had written derisively of 'our newly reconciled party of the presbyterian mould'.[1] This was probably to exaggerate, but there are hints that in the final months of the Rump period, when there was talk of 'the growing power of the presbyterians in parliament',[2] conservative puritan opinion may have begun to swing behind the regime. The protestations of enthusiasm in the petitions from the south and the south-west for the restraint and moderation of the Rump's religious policies do not have an altogether convincing ring, any more than do similar sentiments expressed early in 1650 or in the summer of 1651:[3] the petitioners' aim, clearly, was to strengthen presbyterian tendencies in parliament by flattering them. Nevertheless, the dissolution of the Rump brought considerable dismay to both political and religious presbyterians. A writer from Scotland reported that 'the most of this country conceive themselves to be in a worse condition than ever', and referred to 'the little blossoming hopes which the people here (especially the clergy) were beginning to entertain of some favour to the presbyterian party sitting in the House'.[4] In England, too, the coup of April 1653, removing all legal, constitutional and social safeguards, and opening the way for military rule and arbitrary taxation, distressed clergymen, lawyers and 'the nobility and gentry'.[5] How far the Rump's conservative opponents appreciated its virtues before its expulsion, and how far they merely woke up to them afterwards, seems impossible to determine.

The Rump's actions in its final months can hardly have lowered its

---

[1] *Perfect Passages* 12–19 Dec. 1652, p. 331.
[2] *Reasons why the Supreme Authority of the Three Nations . . . is not in the Parliament* (1653), pp. 18–19; Underdown, 'The Independents reconsidered', p. 66.
[3] Cf. above, pp. 230–1, 246.
[4] *Reasons why the Supreme Authority of the Three Nations . . . is not in the Parliament*, p. 1.
[5] See e.g. *Autobiography of Henry Newcombe*, p. 44 (with which cf. *ibid.* pp. 24–5); *Nicholas Papers*, ii. 12; Clarendon MS 45, fo. 434: newsletter, 27 May 1653; *Reliquiae Baxterianae*, p. 70.

reputation in presbyterian eyes. Increasingly the House turned to notably unrevolutionary ministers, like William Ames, Thomas Knight (who had wielded political influence as Fairfax's presbyterian minister) and Stephen Marshall, to preach before it.[1] Meanwhile William Erbury was hauled before a parliamentary committee, just as Thomas Brooks had been a few months earlier. Erbury, suspected of 'Rantism', was charged with 'speaking plainly and boldly to the corruptions of parliament'.[2] On 8 February the Rump did make a token suggestion that the penal laws should again be modified,[3] but a much clearer indication of the House's mood came three days later, when Thomas Scot brought in the report of the committee, of which he was chairman, for the propagation of the gospel. The committee, having previously taken no action on the proposals drawn up at Oxford under Owen's guidance in the spring of 1652, now decided to recommend them. Scot's attitude is obscure. He was to be bitterly upset by the dissolution, and to work closely with Heselrige immediately after it; but he had cooperated with Cromwell over the introduction of the bill for a new representative in the autumn of 1651, and he seems to have been prepared thereafter to lend an occasional helping hand to the reform movement. His behaviour over the Owen scheme suggests a tact which would have been uncharacteristic of his friend Heselrige. Of Owen's fourteen proposals, Scot brought only the first eleven into the House. These included the more positive aspects of a scheme which, like the report of the Hale commission, offered reasoned, moderate and practicable solutions to a contentious reform issue. Again like the report of the Hale commission, however, its implementation would have involved interference by the central government in local activities traditionally controlled by the provincial gentry. Many M.P.s would no doubt have been dismayed by the descent on the localities of the ecclesiastical commissioners for which Owen's scheme provided. The three omitted clauses, on the other hand, were those liable to provoke radical resentment, providing as they did for restrictions on religious toleration. Clause twelve, the implementation of which would have represented a modification of the toleration act of 1650, insisted that anyone dissenting from the established state religion must both attend some alternative form of public worship on the Lord's Day and give due notice of his intentions to the magistrate. Clause thirteen enjoined conformity

[1] *C.J.* 27, 28, 31 Jan., 4 Apr. 1653.
[2] Clarke MS xxiv, fo. 117; N.L.W., MS 11,439D, fo. 29; *Several Proceedings* 27 Jan.–3 Feb. 1653, p. (2758); *Clarke Papers*, ii. 233–9.   [3] *C.J.* 8 Feb. 1653.

to the fifteen 'fundamentals'; and clause fourteen called for the 'suppression of that abominable cheat of judicial astrology': the astrologers' burst of popularity about the time when Owen's scheme was presented, standing 'in flat opposition to the ministry of the word of God', had been causing transparent jealousy among the clergy.[1] The House insisted on hearing these clauses even though the committee had omitted them. Once again, however, parliament held back from provoking the army too far. The toleration issue was effectively shelved when the Rump decided to work through the list of proposals every Friday, beginning with the first clause. The contentious clauses were thus left to the end. So leisurely a pace did the House adopt that only the first three clauses had been debated by the time of the dissolution. Discussion of even the first clause was postponed for three weeks while parliament took it upon itself to wonder whether 'the magistrate hath power, in matters of religion, for the propagation of the gospel'. In the end, of course, it decided that the magistrate was thus empowered. The first of Owen's proposals was passed, in slightly amended form, on Friday 4 March. On Friday the 11th the House, which should have been debating the second clause, discussed the Dutch war instead, but the clause was duly passed on the 18th. Discussion was again postponed on Friday the 25th, but on the succeeding Friday, 1 April, the third clause was brought before the House. At this point a solitary concession was made to radical sentiment. The original version of the Owen scheme had proposed that men 'of [social] eminency' should examine the testimonials of candidates for ordination. Before the presentation of the scheme to the Rump's committee, the wording had been changed to 'of eminency, and known ability and godliness'. Now, on 1 April, the words 'of eminency' disappeared altogether.[2]

1 April was, however, the last day on which the Rump discussed religious matters; and the concession over the words 'of eminency' paled into insignificance when compared with the other decision taken by the House at the same time. On the previous Friday, when the third clause of Owen's scheme should have been debated, the Rump had considered instead the results of an investigation by the Committee for Plundered Ministers into charges of peculation against the Commissioners for the Propagation of the Gospel in Wales. The committee, often more sympathetic to religious radicals than the House,[3] had been

---

1 Ashmole MS 421, fo. 214; *Several Proceedings* 25 Mar.–1 Apr. 1652, pp. 2033–6.
2 *C.J.* 11, 25 Feb., 18 Mar., 1 Apr. 1653.
3 See e.g. Brooks, *Cases Considered and Resolved*, pp. 9, 15–16.

unimpressed by the charges, and its dismissive report was brought into parliament by Harrison's friend Robert Bennett. The House took a different view. The act for the propagation of the gospel in Wales, introduced for a three-year period in 1650, was due to expire at the end of March, and radical agitation in the pulpit mounted as the House considered whether or not to renew it. On 1 April it resolved not to do so. The resolution was a bombshell. It is not mentioned in the *Journal of the House of Commons*, since the Clerk had no occasion to record a decision merely to allow the act to expire. The government press, too, maintained a stony silence. The Commission for the Propagation of the Gospel in the Northern Counties, which had likewise run its course, seems similarly to have been deprived of its powers. Also on 1 April Walter Cradock, one of the most active and radical of the Welsh commissioners, was 'excused' from an appointment to preach before the House later in the same month. Although Cromwell may have been disturbed by the reports of peculation, he was almost as indignant at the decision not to renew the Welsh commission as were the preachers of Blackfriars. Five days after the dissolution he instructed the commissioners 'to go on cheerfully in the work' as if the act had been confirmed. The dismissal of the commissioners by the Rump increased considerably the chances of a forcible dissolution; but in its final decision on religion the House, at least and at last, had owned to its true nature.[1]

The army officers, although temporarily quietened by the dispatch of the circular of 28 January, continued to meet 'about the emergent and weighty affairs of the nation'.[2] On 9 and 10 February the House appointed a committee, headed by Harrison, to investigate the behaviour of Daniel Blagrave as chairman of the Committee for Corporations. A further source of tension was created on the 11th, when Heselrige successfully challenged the House's order to proceed with a bill for poor relief. The measure was never heard of again. A week later the conflict between John Weaver and Sir Hardres Waller was again brought before the House. The case dragged on until 14 April, when parliament, having awarded Waller lands for his services, decided to reward Weaver in the same way.[3]

---

[1] *C.J.* 23, 25 Mar., 1 Apr. 1653; Clarendon MS 45, fos. 204ᵛ, 206&ᵛ: newsletters, 18, 25 Mar. 1653; Abbott, *Writings and Speeches*, iii. 13; Gardiner, *History of the Commonwealth and Protectorate*, ii. 249–51. The fullest discussion of the commission is in Richards, *History of the Puritan Movement in Wales*.

[2] *Moderate Messenger* 31 Jan.–7 Feb. 1653, p. 2.

[3] *C.J.* 9, 10, 11, 18, 22 Feb., 22 Mar., 14 Apr. 1653.

As the conflict between army and parliament moved towards its inevitable crisis, so foreign ambassadors and royalist agents strained their ears for snippets of political gossip. Historians, faced with a dearth of evidence, have snatched eagerly at the stories which found their way to foreign governments or to the exiled court. They have eagerly accepted, too, the recollections of men like Ludlow and Hutchinson, who were far away from London at the time and who learnt only later of the events surrounding the dissolution. The history books are consequently full of stories of attempts by the House to dismiss Cromwell from his command, of moves by Lambert and Fairfax to replace him, and of quarrels between Cromwell and Lambert, between Lambert and Harrison, and between Harrison and Cromwell. Some of the rumours were plausible, others less so; all were sadly imprecise. Ludlow's account of the Rump's final months often has the ring of truth, and can sometimes be confirmed by other evidence; but even some of his assertions must be treated with scepticism. Vigilance is equally necessary in the use of royalist newsletters, whose authors were much better informed on some issues than on others.

Cromwell's own position during the Rump's final months is as shadowy as the surviving evidence. The last full description of his frame of mind before the eve of dissolution dates back to November 1652, when at a meeting with Whitelocke he is said to have asked, 'What if a man should take upon him to be king?' Whitelocke gave a dampening reply, admitting to a secret preference for restoring Charles II on terms laid down by the Rump. Cromwell dropped the issue of kingship but persisted with the subject which had given rise to it, 'the dangerous condition we are all in ... by our particular jarrings and animosities'. Whitelocke confessed that some M.P.s were egging on Cromwell's opponents in the army: Cromwell admitted the 'insolency' of army officers who were stirring up 'discontents and murmurings' among the troops. 'The troublesome people of the army', he later acknowledged, 'by this time were high enough in their displeasures'. What dismayed Cromwell most, however, was the rumpers' 'pride, and ambition, and self-seeking, engrossing all places of honour and profit to themselves, and their friends, and daily breaking forth into new parties and factions'.[1] It was the speech of a weary and profoundly disillusioned man. The zealous optimism with which the army had prosecuted the godly cause in the 1640s, and the high hopes entertained of the Rump after Worcester, had been gravely disappointed. The

[1] Abbott, *Writings and Speeches*, ii. 587–92, iii. 56.

righteous reformation had been allowed to languish while urgent business in the House had become enmeshed in interminable debate, procedural obstruction and factious intrigue. Yet matters became still worse after November 1652, especially when the desperate plans advanced in December for financial retrenchment made a drastic reduction of the forces, the army's persistent fear, a real possibility.

Suffering a crisis of confidence in December and January, the government recovered its poise when between 18 and 20 February Blake pulled off 'a huge crack of a sea victory' at the battle of Portland.[1] Suddenly the Rump, which in recent months had seemed to be losing the Dutch war, appeared to be winning it. After the dissolution M.P.s and their friends, lauding the naval achievements of the final months of their rule, convinced themselves that the Commonwealth had been brought to a new pitch of commercial prosperity and financial solvency.[2] It was an implausible picture which did not go without contradiction; but as the Rump's self-esteem grew after Portland, so the political designs of the army became still more unpalatable to M.P.s. Blake's victory made peace negotiations with the Dutch an honourable possibility, and two provinces, Holland and West Friesland, opened a correspondence with the Rump on their own initiative. A majority of rumpers seemed anxious for a settlement. Others, like Heselrige and Scot, scented the opportunity for speedy and outright victory. Scot claimed in 1659 that the Rump had prolonged its rule 'to end the Dutch war. We might have brought them to a oneness with us. This we might have done in four or five months. We never bid fairer for being masters of the whole world.'[3]

Four or five months was longer than the army was by now prepared to wait for the Rump's dissolution. Cromwell, however, remained determined to avoid the use of force. In August he had restrained the more radical of the officers from publicly demanding an immediate dissolution; in November, in his conversation with Whitelocke, he had stressed the need 'to unite our counsels, and hands and hearts, to make good what we have so dearly bought, with so much hazard, blood and treasure'; and it was probably through his influence that a forcible dis-

---

[1] Staffordshire Record Office, D593/P/8/2/2: Langley to Leveson, 22 Feb. 1653; Gardiner, *History of the Commonwealth and Protectorate*, ii. 215–20.
[2] Cf. above, p. 86; Slingsby Bethel, *The World's Mistake in Oliver Cromwell* (1681), p. 3.
[3] Firth, 'Cromwell and the expulsion of the Long Parliament in 1653', p. 521; *C.J.* 10 Mar. 1653; *Mercurius Politicus* 14–21 Apr. 1653, p. 2377; *Diary of Thomas Burton*, iii. 111–12; Gardiner, *History of the Commonwealth and Protectorate*, ii. 238–9. See also *H.M.C.R. Egmont*, i. 516, 517.

solution had been averted in January and the wording of the circular to the regiments toned down. He was still striving for 'healing and settling' in March. On the 4th his fellow officers met to consider how a new representative could be achieved, 'either by petition or otherwise'. On the 11th, the day after Cromwell and Vane had voted in the House in favour of negotiations with the Dutch,

> the Council of Officers at St. James's had resolved to turn [the Rump] out . . . had not the General and Colonel Desborough interceded, [asking] them if they destroyed the parliament what they should call themselves, a state they could not be; they answered that they would call a new parliament; then, says the General, the parliament is not the supreme power, but that is the supreme power that calls it; and besides, the House is now endeavouring a treaty with Holland (which is the only way that we have left for the destroying of the combinations of our enemies both at home and beyond sea), and if we destroy the parliament neither Holland nor any other prince or state will enter into a treaty with us.[1]

Yet those who knew Cromwell well must have been alarmed by his mood in the weeks which followed. He made only one appearance at the Council of State between 8 March and 7 April, and seems to have been absent from parliament for most of the same period.[2] The familiar pattern of his withdrawal from political activity, followed by a swiftly decisive coup, was beginning to assert itself.

Harrison, too, had lost interest in meetings of the Council of State, and he was no more effective in the House. He ignored the opportunity which had been given him by the House's decision on 6 January to put him in charge of the bill for a new representative. On 16 February, however, the House again ordered that discussion of the subject be resumed, and on the 23rd amendments were reported to 'the act appointing a certain time for the dissolving of this present parliament, and for the calling and settling of future and successive parliaments'. It was not Harrison who introduced the amendments: it was Heselrige. The House decided to debate the bill every Wednesday, and in the following weeks considerable progress was made. The Rump decided on a new franchise, and the date of the dissolution was fixed for 3 November 1653. It had long been agreed that the next parliament should consist of four hundred members, the same number as that envisaged in the Vane scheme of 1650.[3] Now the Rump considered how those seats were to be

---

[1] Firth, 'Cromwell and the expulsion of the Long Parliament in 1653', pp. 527–8; Clarendon MS 45, fo. 204.
[2] Gardiner, *History of the Commonwealth and Protectorate*, ii. 246; *C.S.P.D. 1652–3*, pp. xxxi, xxxii.
[3] Above, p. 149.

distributed. Here again its conclusions were in accordance with the
officers' wishes. The main problem, however, remained the 'qualifications' of the M.P.s to be admitted to the next representative. The question should have been discussed on 6 April, but the bill was not debated
on that day. On the 7th the officers accordingly demanded that the
Rump proceed to define the qualifications. It did so on the following
Wednesday, the 13th, when the decision was taken to restrict membership to 'such as are persons of known integrity, fearing God, and not
scandalous in their conversation'. In addressing Barebone's Parliament
Cromwell scorned these qualifications, 'such as they were', but
whatever their limitations they, like so much of the bill for a new
representative, were incorporated into the Cromwellian *Instrument of
Government*.[1] Former royalists, again as in the *Instrument*, were of
course to be excluded from election. By themselves, however, 'qualifications' were bound to be useless unless a specific oath were tendered
to elected members, something the officers do not seem to have contemplated even in the circular of 28 January. The precise wording of
the qualifications was not important: what mattered was who would
decide whether those elected fell within them. The bill provided for an
adjournment shortly after its passage, and stipulated that the Rump
should meet again in November on the day before the new representative met. Then, clearly, the House would be able to examine the
names of the newly elected members, an alarming prospect from the
army's viewpoint.[2]

Only the finishing touches now remained to be added to the bill, which
was due to pass the House on the following Wednesday, 20 April. It
seems likely that at some stage in the previous weeks there had been
more conferences between officers and M.P.s of the kind initiated by
Cromwell in the previous October; and for at least two or three days
before the dissolution he tried to arrange a further meeting. During
the previous nineteen months he had been the moving spirit behind the
bill for a new representative: now he was desperate to avoid its passage. On 19 April, while the Rump blandly debated Irish affairs, the
Council of Officers 'partly concluded of dissolving this government,
and also of constituting another (by consent of parliament if possible)
till another representative shall be chosen'.

[1] Gardiner, *History of the Commonwealth and Protectorate*, ii. 252-3, and *Constitutional
Documents*, p. 411; Abbott, *Writings and Speeches*, iii. 58. In the *Instrument* the wording
ran: 'such (and no other such) as are . . .'.
[2] Cf. below, Part Five.

At last, on the evening of the same day, a meeting was held at Cromwell's lodgings between the leading officers and about twenty of the most influential rumpers. In Whitelocke's words, there was 'a large discourse and debate . . . touching some expedient to be found out for the present carrying on the governing of the Commonwealth, and putting a period to this present parliament'. The 'expedient' which Cromwell proposed was that 'forty persons or about that number of parliament-men and officers of the army should be nominated and empowered for the managing of the affairs of the Commonwealth till a new parliament should meet, and so the present parliament to be forthwith dissolved'. The 'forty persons or about that number', according to an account given by the officers immediately after the dissolution, were to be

men fearing God and of approved integrity; and the government of the Commonwealth committed unto them for a time, as the most hopeful way to encourage and countenance all God's people, reform the law, and administer justice impartially; hoping thereby the people might forget monarchy, and understanding their true interest in the election of successive parliaments, may have this government settled upon a true basis, without hazard to the glorious cause, or necessitating to keep up armies for the defence of the same.

The premise underlying Cromwell's scheme was that which was later to inform first his decision to summon Barebone's Parliament and then, after the failure of Barebone's, his decision to accept the title of Protector. Before parliamentary elections could be allowed, he seems to have believed, there must be an interim period of government by 'men fearing God and of approved integrity'. Once godly men had shown the way, the electorate would at last be awakened to the virtues of righteous reformation. Barebone's, like the interim 'committee' proposed by Cromwell on 19 April, was designed as a hand-picked assembly of the pious, whose task was to set the process of reformation in motion and then to give way to 'successive' elected parliaments; and in December 1653, when he became Protector, Cromwell insisted on a nine months' period of conciliar government, with godly men at the helm, before the first protectorate parliament was allowed to meet.

At the conference on 19 April Cromwell told the rumpers present that his scheme for an interim council 'had been no new thing when those nations had been under the like hurly-burlies'. The officers, Cromwell later recorded, 'had been labouring to get precedents to convince them of it'. It would have taken much more than precedents to convince Heselrige, who may have attended the meeting uninvited

333

and who was witheringly dismissive of the proposal. Whitelocke, too, recorded that 'it was offered by divers as a most dangerous thing to dissolve the present parliament, and to set up any other government, and that it would neither be warrantable in conscience or wisdom to do so; yet none ... expressed themselves so freely to that purpose as Sir Thomas Widdrington and I then did'. Cromwell had taken care, however, to pack the meeting with those rumpers whom he believed most likely to cooperate. Many of them were evidently prepared to accept the scheme, partly, Whitelocke believed, because they hoped to be among the 'forty persons'. Whitelocke noted that

Of the ... opinion as to putting a period forthwith to this parliament, St. John was one of the chief, and many more with him; and generally all the officers of the army, who stuck close in this likewise to their General ... They and their party declared their opinions, that it was necessary the same should be done one way or other, and the members of parliament not permitted to prolong their own power.

'At which expression' Cromwell, conciliatory as ever,

seemed to reprove some of them; and this conference lasted till late at night, when Widdrington and I went home weary, and troubled to see the indiscretion and ingratitude of those men and the way they designed to ruin themselves.

Whitelocke and Widdrington may have left before the meeting finally broke up, for Whitelocke does not mention a point on which the officers laid great stress and which helps to explain Cromwell's actions the following day. The rumpers present at the meeting, Cromwell recalled in July,

told us that they would take consideration of these things till the morning, that they would sleep upon them and consult with some friends ... At the parting two or three of the chief ones, and very chiefest of them did tell us that they would endeavour to suspend farther proceedings about the bill for a new representative until they had had a further conference. And upon this we had great satisfaction, and we did acquiesce, and had hope ... that the next day we would have some such issue thereof as would have given satisfaction to all.[1]

Cromwell's hopes were to be disappointed; for on the morning of 20 April the Rump, far from 'suspending farther proceedings about the bill for a new representative', decided to proceed with its immediate

[1] Whitelocke, *Memorials*, iv. 4; *Declaration of the Lord General and his Council, showing the grounds ... for the Dissolution of the late Parliament*, pp. 6–9; Abbott, *Writings and Speeches*, iii. 59. Abbott (*Writings and Speeches*, ii. 637–47) and Gardiner (*History of the Commonwealth and Protectorate*, ii. 258–65) have full accounts of the events of 19 and 20 April.

passage. At least part of the explanation of the dissolution of the Rump is to be found in Cromwell's sense of betrayal.

A 'few' of the M.P.s present at the conference on the evening of 19 April returned to Cromwell's lodgings early on the following morning to discuss again with the officers the proposal for an immediate dissolution and the appointment of 'forty persons'; but most of the other rumpers who were in London at this time were already in the House. There had rarely been more than fifty members present during the previous weeks, but at least eighty seem to have attended the fateful debate of 20 April.[1] The meeting at Cromwell's lodgings was soon interrupted by the news that parliament was 'proceeding with a representative . . . with that haste as had never been known before'. The M.P.s present at once departed for the House, but Cromwell, stunned with disbelief, stayed where he was until 'a second and a third messenger' confirmed the news. It was at this point that Cromwell finally abandoned his patient attempts to compromise and to conciliate. Months of frustration, disillusionment and despair at last took their toll. In Whitelocke's words, Cromwell 'commanded some of the officers of the army to fetch a party of soldiers, with whom he marched to the House and led a file of musketeers in with him; the rest he placed at the door of the House and in the lobby before it'.

Three rumpers have left detailed descriptions of what followed: Whitelocke and Algernon Sidney, who were eye-witnesses, and Ludlow, whose main source was probably another of the M.P.s present, Harrison. The three accounts are agreed in their general drift, but they differ over details. Whitelocke, for example, recorded that Cromwell entered the House 'in a furious manner', but on this point Sidney's restrained description is more convincing:

Cromwell came into the House, clad in plain black clothes, with grey worsted stockings, and sat down as he used to do in an ordinary place. After a while he rose up, put off his hat, and spake; at the first and for a good while, he spake to the commendation of parliament, for their pains and care of the public good; but afterwards he changed his style, told them of their injustice, delays of justice, self-interest and other faults; then he said, perhaps you think this is not parliamentary language; I confess it is not, neither are you to expect any such from me; then he put on his hat, went out of his place, and walked up and down the stage or floor in the midst of the House, with his hat on his head, and chid them soundly, looking sometimes, and pointing particularly upon some persons, as . . . Whitelocke . . . Sir Henry Vane, to whom he gave very sharp

[1] Abbott, *Writings and Speeches*, ii. 643.

language, though he named them not, but by his gestures it was well known he meant them. After this he said to . . . Harrison . . . 'Call them in.' Then Harrison went out, and presently brought in Lieutenant Colonel Worsley (who commanded the General's own regiment of foot) with five or six files of musketeers, about twenty or thirty, with their muskets. Then the General, pointing to the Speaker in his chair, said to Harrison, 'Fetch him down.' Harrison went to the Speaker, and spoke to him to come down, but the Speaker sat still, and said nothing. 'Take him down', said the General; then Harrison went and pulled the Speaker by the gown, and he came down.

Sidney himself was in the seat nearest the Speaker's chair, and Cromwell now ordered Harrison to have Sidney evicted. Sidney stayed where he was, however, until Harrison and Worsley had placed their hands on his shoulders, 'as if they would force him to go out'; at which he

rose and went towards the door. Then the General went to the table where the mace lay, which used to be carried before the Speaker, and said 'Take away these baubles'. So the soldiers took away the mace, and all the House went out . . . All being gone out, the door of the House was locked and the key with the mace was carried away . . .

From the accounts of Whitelocke and Ludlow, and from other pieces of surviving evidence, we can add to Sidney's description various details of whose authenticity we can be confident. There was Cromwell's attack on the 'drunkards' and 'whoremasters' in the Rump, Marten and Sir Peter Wentworth being singled out for individual censure. Wentworth was one of the members who unavailingly 'rose up to answer Cromwell's speech'. It is also clear that Cromwell interrupted the debate only at the last moment, when the motion for passing the bill was about to be put. Francis Allen, by the army's own admission, was 'a little while under confinement' for 'some words'. Allen, like his friend Richard Salwey, with whom he was in close touch at this time, had been anxious to cooperate with Cromwell since Worcester; but, again like Salwey, he broke with him over the passage of the bill for a new representative. Cromwell was never more bitter than when rounding on those who had turned against him, and he reserved his sharpest invective at the dissolution for one of his most cherished friends: 'Oh Sir Henry Vane, Sir Henry Vane, the Lord deliver me from Sir Henry Vane.'[1]

[1] Abbott, *Writings and Speeches*, ii. 638, 641–4; Firth, 'Cromwell and the expulsion of the Long Parliament in 1653', p. 532; Staffordshire Record Office, D593/P/8/2/2: Langley to Leveson, 30 Apr. 1653; *Hatton Correspondence* (Camden Soc., 1878), i. 7; SP: 28/91, fo. 530; 28/92, fo. 292.

The dissolution took place around noon.[1] In the afternoon a few rumpers defiantly sought to reassemble the Council of State. Cromwell, hearing the news, took Lambert and Harrison with him to the council chamber, where he told the assembled councillors:

'Gentlemen, if you are met here as private persons, you shall not be disturbed; but if as a Council of State, this is no place for you; and since you can't but know what was done at the House in the morning, so take notice, that the parliament is dissolved.' To this Serjeant Bradshaw answered: 'Sir, we have heard what you did in the House in the morning, and before many hours all England will hear it; but, sir, you are mistaken to think that the parliament is dissolved; for no power under heaven can dissolve them but themselves; therefore take you notice of that.' Something more was said to the same purpose by Sir Arthur Heselrige, Mr. [Nicholas] Love and Mr. Scot; and then the Council of State, perceiving themselves to be under the same violence, departed.

Those who had organised the council's final meeting were probably acting in conjunction with the Rump's friends in the city, who were shortly to remonstrate on their own behalf against the dissolution.[2]

Who was responsible for the House's crucial decision on the morning of 20 April to ignore the promise which Cromwell claimed to have extracted the night before and to press ahead with the bill for a new representative? St John almost certainly had a hand in it. On the evening of the 19th he had favoured Cromwell's compromise proposal; yet he recalled at the Restoration that, 'not being satisfied concerning' the Rump's 'sitting without the Lords and the members excluded', he had 'endeavoured the bringing in of a free parliament; and as the distractions then were, I thought it the best way of healing them, and this was near effecting, when in April 1653, there sitting, I was hindered by Cromwell and the army'.[3] Yet it was Vane, not St John, who bore the brunt of Cromwell's displeasure on the morning of 20 April. According to Sidney, Cromwell told Vane as the members filed out of the House that the latter 'might have prevented this extraordinary course, but he was a juggler, and had not so much as common honesty'.[4] Even so, Vane's failure to prevent the bill's passage, however discreditable in Cromwell's eyes, was not necessarily the same thing as pressing the bill forward. The man who took the initiative in the House on 20 April

---

[1] Cf. Josten, *Elias Ashmole*, ii. 642.
[2] *Memoirs of Edmund Ludlow*, i. 357; *Moderate Publisher* 15–22 Apr. 1653, p. 813; *Nicholas Papers*, ii. 12; below, p. 369.
[3] *The Case of Oliver St. John*, p. 7.
[4] Abbott, *Writings and Speeches*, ii. 642.

was probably neither St John nor Vane. It was Sir Arthur Heselrige.

Ever since his quarrel with the army over the Lilburne–Primate case early in 1652, Heselrige had been the officers' most formidable parliamentary opponent. He had celebrated his growing political eminence with magnificent personal ostentation, acquiring a notoriously lavish coach and even decking out his page in velvet, with 'silver sword and silver buckles upon his shoes, and silk stockings'.[1] It was hardly a picture to delight radicals, and in February 1653 Heselrige had provoked them further by persuading the House to cancel a debate on poor relief. It was Heselrige, too, who had introduced the amendments to the bill for a new representative on 23 February. Thereafter he had kept a firm grip on the House's discussions on the subject. By late March he was evidently commuting between the country and London to attend the weekly debates on the bill, dominating the House's discussions on Wednesday mornings, attending the Council of State on Wednesday afternoons, and then retiring once more to his rural retreat. He appeared at the council on 23 and 30 March and on 13 April, but on no other day within that time: the three dates were the Wednesdays within those weeks on which the House debated the bill. On 6 April, when it should have debated it, Heselrige was away and the debate was postponed. After 13 April he remained in London for at least two more days, but then left once more for the country.[2] There, as he subsequently recalled,

I heard, being seventy miles off, that it was propounded that we should dissolve our trust, and dissolve it into a few hands. I came up and found it so; that it was resolved in a junto at the Cockpit. I trembled at it, and was, after [i.e. on the evening of 19 April], there and gave my testimony against it. I told them the work they went about was accursed. I told them it was impossible to dissolve this trust. Next day, we were labouring here in the House on an act to put an end to that parliament and to call another. I desired the passing of it with all my soul. The question was putting for it, when our General stood up, and stopped the question, and called in their lieutenant, with two files of musketeers, with their hats on their heads and their guns loaded with bullets.[3]

Heselrige had been quite prepared, since February 1653, to steer the bill for a new representative through the House. He had seen the House bring forward the date of the intended dissolution to November 1653, and had evidently approved of decisions, on such issues as electoral

[1] Underdown, *Pride's Purge*, p. 262.
[2] *C.S.P.D.* 1652–3, council attendance tables; *C.J.* for dates mentioned.
[3] *Diary of Thomas Burton*, iii. 98.

qualifications, the franchise and the redistribution of seats, which in the following December the army officers were to consider admirable. What he was not prepared to do, and what on 20 April the Rump was unwilling to do, was to submit to the dictates of 'a junto at the Cockpit'.

The Rump had always been a fragile coalition; and after the dissolution its members went their separate ways. Some immediately committed themselves to Cromwell, who remained as determined as he had been on the eve of the expulsion to separate 'godly' M.P.s from ungodly ones. A newswriter predicted on 23 April that 'some timber of the house pulled down may be of use in the new building', and on the 28th *Several Proceedings*, now in army hands, warned that 'those that shall abuse the godly of the late members of parliament, without a cause, will not be approved of therein, some being such for piety and worth, as probably may be our governors again'. Robert Bennett, Walter Strickland, William Sydenham and Richard Salwey immediately joined the interim council set up by Cromwell after the dissolution, and Carew, Pickering and Stapley (who now broke with Morley) took their places soon afterwards. Salwey, however, withdrew from the council on 3 May; and Ludlow described how about this time Cromwell

sent for Major Salwey and Mr. John Carew, to whom he complained of the great weight of affairs that by this undertaking was fallen upon him; affirming that the thoughts of the consequences thereof made him to tremble, and therefore desired them to free him from the temptations that might be laid before him; and to that end to go immediately to the Chief Justice St. John, Mr. Selden and some others, and endeavour to persuade them to draw up some instrument of government that might put the power out of his hands. To this it was answered by Major Salwey, 'The way, sir, to free you from this temptation is for you not to look upon yourself to be under it, but to rest persuaded that the power of the nation is in the good people of England, as formerly it was.'[1]

After 3 May Salwey also withdrew from the Rump's Army Committee, which continued to sit until, with other of the House's committees, it was 'broken up' early in June. Some of the warrants issued by the Army Committee during these weeks were defiantly headed 'From the Committee of Parliament for the Army'. Twenty-one rumpers attended the committee at various points during May, even Chaloner putting in an

[1] *Clarke Papers*, iii. 4; Firth, 'Cromwell and the expulsion of the Long Parliament in 1653'. p. 533; *Several Proceedings* 21–28 Apr. 1653, p. 2954; Clarke MS xxv, fos. 37, 39ᵛ, Abbott, *Writings and Speeches*, iii. 16.

appearance on the 5th. Salwey continued to act as navy commissioner until 14 May, but not, apparently, thereafter. By the 21st George Thomson, one of his fellow commissioners, had been dismissed. Francis Allen and Denis Bond lost their jobs as treasurers about the same time.[1]

Other rumpers were more discreet. Immediately after the dissolution Vane withdrew 'discontentedly or politiquely' to Lincolnshire, Wentworth to Warwickshire, and 'divers others unto their several houses'. By mid-June Wentworth had 'stepped aside' from public affairs 'to secure himself in some dark corner'. Perhaps he was afflicted once more by the 'sprains and bruises' which had kept him out of London in the weeks before Charles I's execution. Whitelocke, at first remaining at his post as Commissioner of the Great Seal, soon 're-solved to use the best lawful means I could for my own preservation'. He retreated to his home at Henley-on-Thames, discovering, he said, a preference for fresh air and green fields to the sycophancy of courtly life. Few rumpers were better equipped to make the comparison. Thomas Atkins was another who quickly absented himself from London; he resolved 'to apply himself more to his shop traffic than otherwise'. Prideaux wisely resigned as postmaster-general. St John may have been one of those who retired to the country, but Heselrige, who later claimed that there had been an attempt to arrest him shortly after the dissolution,[2] seems to have remained a helpless spectator in London, evicted from the lodgings he had acquired in Whitehall and at Hampton Court. It was observed that he 'blusters much' at the Rump's expulsion. He was to carry on blustering for many years.[3]

Defeat in politics is rarely dignified, and in disarray the rumpers were not a prepossessing band. Many of them, unable to forget the events of 20 April, devoted the rest of their careers to fighting the same battle over and over again; and when the Rump was restored to power in 1659 they devoted themselves to the pleasures of revenge. The memory of the dissolution exercised a profound influence on the remaining course of Interregnum politics. The rumper John Pyne was not alone in 1659 in continuing to see the central political conflict as one between 'the single person men' on the one hand, and 'the appearing and preserving of the true good old cause', after which 'my soul

[1] SP: 18/51, 18/52, 28/92, 28/269, *passim;* Tanner MS 52, fo. 13.
[2] *Diary of Thomas Burton,* iv. 156.
[3] Clarendon MS 45, fos. 334, 366ᵛ, 400ᵛ, 486ᵛ, 498ᵛ; Clarke MS xxv, fo. 13ᵛ; Staffordshire Record Office, D593/P/8/2/2: letters of 30 Apr., 4 May, 18 June; B.M., Add. MS 37,345, fo. 271&ᵛ; Whitelocke, *Journal of the Swedish Embassy,* i. 6.

panteth', on the other.[1] Such attitudes distorted men's impressions, and hence their recorded recollections, of what had taken place between 1648 and 1653. Many rumpers were radicalised by the dissolution, or came subsequently to espouse a republicanism of which they would earlier have fought shy. Yet if the extent of republicanism in parliament before 1653 has sometimes been exaggerated, the Rump's commitment to the principle of parliamentary supremacy has been inadequately acknowledged. The feud with the army could only strengthen that commitment. The terms in which men like Salwey, Bradshaw, Heselrige and Marten expressed themselves to Cromwell either at or shortly after the time of the dissolution testify to their belief that 'no power under heaven can dissolve' parliaments 'but themselves'.[2] The dissolution seems to have taken M.P.s by surprise; yet they must have known that in pressing ahead with the bill on the morning of 20 April they were playing with fire. They would have served their own interests better by agreeing to Cromwell's request for a postponement. Their refusal to do so is not hard to explain. A skilful orator like Heselrige or Marten would have found little difficulty in playing on his audience's hostility to the army. The members who had attended the meeting on the evening of 19 April had held no brief from the House, and the Rump would not have felt itself bound by promises made 'at the Cockpit' without its consent. It was in the House alone that M.P.s 'had their yeas and noes'. The Long Parliament had begun life defending its threatened privileges against Charles I. It ended it defending them against the army. Dorothy Osborne, writing a few days after the dissolution, put it best: 'If Mr. Pym were alive again, I wonder what he would think of these proceedings, and whether this would not appear as great a breach of the privilege of parliament as the demanding the five members.'[3]

[1] *H.M.C.R. Pyne and Woodford*, p. 493.
[2] Above, pp. 337, 338, 339; below, p. 365.
[3] Abbott, *Writings and Speeches*, ii. 654.

PART FIVE

THE DISSOLUTION OF THE RUMP

16

THE ARMY APOLOGIAS

Why did Cromwell dissolve the Rump? At least part of the explanation clearly must lie in the provisions of the bill which, had he not intervened, would have passed the House on the morning of 20 April 1653.
But what were those provisions? The bill has apparently not survived,
so that we can never be wholly sure. Historians, nevertheless, have had
few doubts. The bill for a new representative, they have decided,
provided for the 'recruitment' of the Rump's membership. The existing
members were to continue to sit, while the seats which had been
vacant since Pride's Purge were to be filled by recruiter elections held
under the Rump's auspices and presumably modelled on the precedent
of the 1640s. The 'new representative' would thus have been no more
than a fortified version of the old one.[1] Here I shall contest this view.
First, I shall suggest that the charge that the bill was a recruiting one is
inaccurate; that, on the contrary, the bill provided for completely
fresh elections; and that it follows from this that the generally accepted
view of the Rump as a regime selfishly determined to perpetuate its
power must be abandoned. Secondly, I shall argue that even if the
recruitment charge were accurate, it would not provide the correct
explanation of Cromwell's actions of 20 April. Cromwell's objection
at the time of the dissolution to the bill for a new representative, I shall
contend, was not that it provided for recruiter elections. It was that it
provided for elections at all. The issue of the bill's contents is a com-

[1] D. Masson, *The Life of Milton* (6 vols., 1859–90), iv. 409 and n.; Gardiner, *History of the
Commonwealth and Protectorate*, ii. 254 and n., and *Oliver Cromwell* (1901 edn.), pp. 208–10;
C. H. Firth, *Oliver Cromwell and the Rule of the Puritans in England* (1961 edn.), p. 313;
A. H. Woolrych, 'The calling of Barebone's Parliament', *E.H.R.*, lxxx (1965), 493.
Abbott (*Writings and Speeches*, ii. 633) adhered to the same view, although he was
evidently uneasy about it. Masson countered the argument of A. Bisset, who denied
that the bill had been a recruiting one (Bisset, *History of the Commonwealth of England*
(2 vols., 1867), ii. 469–75). Bisset could hardly have made his case less effectively, but the
case itself was a much better one than either he or Masson realised. See also Christie,
Life of Anthony Ashley Cooper, i. 93n., and William Godwin, *History of the Commonwealth
of England* (4 vols., 1824–8), iii. 473 ff.

plicated one which turns on detailed points of evidence, and discussion of it must therefore likewise be detailed. Yet the conclusions which derive from that discussion oblige us, I believe, to revise prevalent assumptions about the Rump Parliament, about the politics of 1653, and about Oliver Cromwell.

The problem at issue is this. Contemporary sources are agreed that the bill provided for the Rump to adjourn at some point shortly after the measure had become law. The House would then have reassembled at the beginning of November 1653. On the 3rd of that month, it would have made way for a 'new representative'. Thus far there is no dispute. What is in question is the nature of the elections which would have been held during the adjournment. The implication of what may by now be called the traditional view is that the elections would have been 'recruiter' ones and that the members returned by them would have joined the rumpers in the House on 3 November. There is however an alternative interpretation which may be put forward. This is that the 'new representative' would have been a genuinely new one: that on 3 November the Rump would have been replaced by a parliament returned by fresh elections in each constituency, on the basis of the new franchise and the new distribution of seats described earlier in this book. This parliament would have sat for two or, less probably, for three years. So would each 'successive' parliament thereafter. The grounds for advancing this view will become apparent in the pages which follow.

Certain points should be made clear before the evidence is examined in detail. First, the bitter relationship between parliament and army in the spring of 1653, and the breakdown of trust between them, explain some features of the bill and some of the feelings which its contents engendered. It is clear from the apologias issued in defence of the dissolution that the main issue in the army's eyes, on the eve of the Rump's expulsion, was simply whether the House could be made to dissolve immediately. Not all the officers (and not all historians) seem to have distinguished between parliament's determination to remain in the saddle until November and its supposed intention to recruit its membership, or indeed to have taken much interest in the bill's provisions for subsequent constitutional developments. To the more extreme of the officers, indeed, the Rump's desire to remain in office for a further six months, rather than dissolve at once, was a heinous enough offence to warrant its forcible expulsion. In March the officers had demanded an immediate coup. On 19 April they pressed for an immediate dissolution 'one way or other'.[1] On both occasions it took Cromwell's influence to restrain them; and Cromwell's concern to secure agreement between M.P.s and army officers on a form of government to follow the dissolution does not seem to have been widely shared among his fellow army leaders. Shortly before the dissolution Richard Salwey asked the officers that 'before they took away the present authority, they would declare what they would have established in its room; to which it was replied by one of the General's party, that it was necessary to pull down this government, and it would be time enough then to consider what should be placed in the room of it'.[2] In 1654 the Cromwellians publicly acknowledged 'the irresolution and unpreparedness of the army' at the time of the dissolution 'as to any particular way of settlement'; until the Rump was 'actually dissolved, no resolutions were taken in what model to cast the government'.[3] Cromwell's plan for a committee of 'forty persons', although providing an interesting insight into his thoughts, was as it stood no more than a vaguely and hastily conceived compromise which won support because of its very elasticity; there can have been few other occasions when St John and Harrison found themselves in agreement. Harrison can hardly have been worried by the suggestion that there would eventually be the parliamentary elections which he and his fellow Fifth Monarchists had no reason to want: as Dr Hill has observed, the task with which the forty persons were to be entrusted, of setting the godly reformation in motion and of enabling 'the people' to 'forget monarchy', 'sounds a pretty long-term programme for an interim government'.[4] The argument at the conference of 19 April was essentially between those who were 'for putting a period forthwith to this present parliament', and those who argued that 'the way was to continue still this present parliament'. Rumpers who held the latter view, and who on 20 April pressed forward a bill which in Whitelocke's words 'would occasion other meetings of them again and prolong their sitting',[5] were not, as Sir Charles Firth supposed they were,[6] necessarily displaying a determination to recruit their membership: they were merely arguing that the Rump should dis-

---

[1] Above, pp. 331, 334.

[2] *Memoirs of Edmund Ludlow*, i. 351.

[3] *True State of the Case of the Commonwealth*, p. 12; Trevor-Roper, *Religion, The Reformation and Social Change*, p. 363.

[4] Hill, *God's Englishman*, pp. 135–6.

[5] Abbott, *Writings and Speeches*, iii. 59; Whitelocke, *Memorials*, iv. 5; *Declaration of the Lord General and his Council, showing the grounds and reasons for the Dissolution of the late Parliament*, p. 7.

[6] Firth, 'The expulsion of the Long Parliament', pp. 141–2.

solve in November rather than in April. That the two things were not necessarily the same is clear even from the officers' accounts of the meetings of the 19th.[1] At some point in its last months the Rump had agreed to dissolve a year earlier than its stipulation of November 1651 had made necessary, just as it had agreed to the army's wish for a new franchise and a new distribution of seats.[2] Having done so it was clearly unwilling to bow to threats of violence or to abdicate until its self-appointed course were run.

The Rump's resolve to remain in power until November was not born of mere pique. If the House were to dissolve before the new representative met, it would be the army, not parliament, which decided whether those elected fell within the qualifications imposed by the bill on the membership of its successor. By adjourning until November the Rump would ensure that the bill's provisions could not be changed under pressure from the army; by meeting again in November it would be able to supervise the legitimate assumption of power by the new representative. We should also remember Thomas Scot's subsequent claim that the Rump had been anxious to remain in power for a few months after April 1653 in order 'to end the Dutch war'.[3] There was nothing necessarily sinister about the proposal to adjourn. Indeed if, as I shall argue, the bill provided not for recruiter elections but for completely fresh ones, rumpers who wished to stand for re-election would clearly have needed an adjournment in which to do so. Nor is the plan to reassemble in November, which gave the government an insurance policy in case the elections proved disastrous, in itself indicative of a determination to recruit. The Levellers, as suspicious of the officers' intentions as was the Rump in 1653, had in 1649 begged parliament not to dissolve, 'nor suffer yourselves to be dissolved', until a new representative were ready to take its place on the following day; 'by whose immediate succession, without any interval, the affairs of the Commonwealth may suffer no stop or intermission'.[4] The Rump's plan to adjourn and then to reassemble just before the inauguration of its successor had been included in the bill for a new representative since 14 November 1651, a time when all accounts were agreed that the bill provided for wholly fresh elections.[5]

---

[1] Abbott, *Writings and Speeches*, iii. 6–7, 59.
[2] The date of the dissolution had been undecided at least as late as September 1652: *C.J.* 14 Sep. 1652; *Mercurius Politicus* 9–16 Sep. 1652, p. 1880.   [3] Above, p. 330.
[4] *Perfect Occurrences* 23 Feb.–2 Mar. 1649, p. 839; Haller and Davies, *The Leveller Tracts*, p. 284.
[5] *Faithful Scout* 14–21 Nov. 1651, p. 339.

Nevertheless such a scheme, given the breakdown of confidence between army and parliament in the spring of 1653, was bound to arouse the army's suspicions. Indeed, as we shall see, after the dissolution the Rump's opponents frequently hinted that the rumpers had intended somehow to 'delude' the army by circumventing the bill's provisions and thus holding recruiter elections. Such anxiety, however understandable, is clearly incompatible with the charge that the bill itself was a recruiting one. The claim that the rumpers had intended thus to delude the army was made only after the earlier accusation, that the bill contained a recruiting clause, had been dropped, and it bears all the marks of special pleading. It was never specified or substantiated, and no one ever suggested how the Rump could have succeeded in outmanoeuvering an army which had used force on parliament before and which was to do so again.[1]

Some of the army's charges were clearly accurate. The accusation that the Rump had proceeded with the bill only at a dilatory pace, and even then only under pressure from the army, was well-founded. It was also true that before Worcester, and again in the early summer of 1652, the Rump had devoted lengthy discussions to proposals for recruitment. The recruiting scheme was evidently in the air in the weeks before the dissolution, when the poet George Wither, who held office under the Rump and who had friends in high places, observed that the subject 'of late/Hath ground administered of much debate'.[2] There is no need to question the Cromwellians' repeated assertion that a recruiting plan had been propounded, not least to Cromwell, by 'divers of the activest' rumpers, who had been 'labouring to persuade others to a consent therein'.[3] What is in question is whether their labours were successful.

The charges levelled by Cromwell and his colleagues on the subject of the bill for a new representative developed and changed as the passions surrounding the dissolution subsided and as the political purposes of army and Cromwellian apologias altered. It should be noted, first, that

[1] Firth, when in 1917 he came to re-examine the dissolution of the Rump, modified his earlier view in a brief aside, suggesting that the Rump may have planned to pass a bill for wholly fresh elections but subsequently to cancel the writs for constituencies represented by rumpers – a formula resembling that in fact adopted by the restored Rump in 1659. Had the Rump planned such a device in 1653, however, its opponents would surely have said so; and there is no evidence to support Firth's suggestion. (Firth, 'Expulsion of the Long Parliament', p. 142.)

[2] Wither, *The Dark Lantern . . . whereunto is annexed, a Poem concerning a Perpetual Parliament* (1653), p. 38.

[3] *Declaration of the Lord General and his Council, showing the grounds . . . for the Dissolution of the late Parliament*, p. 5.

although army newspapers and newsletters frequently referred to the bill from the time of its introduction into the House in October 1651, at no point before the dissolution did any of them mention a recruiting clause or hint that the bill contained any provisions not positively welcome to the army.[1] One historian has wondered whether the bill debated on 20 April was a different one from that which the House had previously been considering.[2] Both supporters and opponents of the Rump, however, talked consistently of a single bill; and Cromwell's own words make clear that he had been as dissatisfied with that bill on 19 April as he was on the 20th.[3] There is no evidence to suggest that the measure taken up by the Rump on 20 April differed in any way from the bill which had been introduced in October 1651 and which until the dissolution had been consistently supported by the army press. Newsletters sent from army headquarters to the forces in Scotland in the weeks before the Rump's expulsion referred variously to the 'bill for setting a time for dissolving of this present parliament', 'the bill for dissolving of this, and calling and settling of future and successive parliaments', 'the bill for a new representative' and 'the bill for successive parliaments'.[4] The charge that the bill was a recruiting one was made by the army only after the dissolution, when it was quickly dropped.

In fact, it was only made twice; and in neither instance was the accusation officially sanctioned by the army, although it was clearly approved by it. The charge first appeared in an edition, published the day after the dissolution, of *Several Proceedings*, which was now under army control. The newspaper stated that 'the danger of the act was declared as the House was about to pass it, for calling a new representative, it giving so much liberty that disaffected persons might be chosen; and by the said act these present members were to sit and to be made up by others chosen, and by themselves approved of'.[5] *Several Proceedings*, it should be noted, was making two separate charges as if they were one. It was objecting both to the threat that the elections for which the bill provided would have returned 'disaffected persons' and to the rumpers' decision to exempt themselves from those elections. Surely, it might be thought, fresh elections would have been likely to return an even higher number of 'disaffected persons' than would recruiter ones. The

[1] Cf. above, pp. 266, 278.   [2] Williams, 'Political career of Henry Marten', p. 557.
[3] Abbott, *Writings and Speeches*, iii. 58–60. Cf. *ibid*. iii. 6–7.
[4] Clarke MS xxiv, fos. 121, 126, 128, xxv, fos. 1ᵛ, 3ᵛ, 8ᵛ.
[5] *Several Proceedings* 14–21 Apr. 1653, p. 2944. (The newspaper was now entitled *Several Proceedings of State Affairs* rather than *Several Proceedings in Parliament*.)

juxtaposition of the two criticisms of the bill seems curious; yet it is even more marked in the second accusation that the bill had provided for recruiter elections, which is to be found in a letter written by Gilbert Mabbott on 23 April to persuade the armed forces in Scotland of the justice of the dissolution. Mabbott asserted, briefly and in parentheses, that 'the bill to be carried on by parliament was not for dissolving this parliament but recruiting it with such as probably would be disaffected, neuters, lawyers or the like, which would destroy the public interest of the nation'.[1] Mabbott's words were no slip of the pen; on the same day he wrote an almost identical letter, of exactly similar import, to the city government at Hull.[2] The tactic employed by him and by the author of *Several Proceedings*, of intermingling the two issues of recruitment and 'disaffected persons', was to be adopted time and again by subsequent apologists for the dissolution. Yet, although army writers frequently returned to the theme of recruitment, they never repeated the accusation that the bill itself had contained a recruiting clause. The charge is sometimes implied in their accounts, and it can sometimes be inferred from them; but never again is it specifically made. At first the omission may seem accidental, the product of hasty speech or writing rather than of calculation. It is the consistent failure to repeat or to substantiate the charge that arouses suspicion. It soon becomes evident, in fact, that the whole issue of recruitment was a red herring, used by the army sometimes to discredit the dissolved parliament, sometimes for purposes of self-vindication. It was the fear of 'disaffected persons', not of a recruited Rump, which brought about the dissolution.

The army's propaganda was certainly effective. That the bill was a recruiting one became common gossip in the fortnight or so following the dissolution. Both royalists, who were happy to believe anything bad of the Rump, and foreign diplomats accepted the story, and their newsletters adopted the tone and sometimes even the wording of army statements.[3] Gossip and rumour are, of course, often pointers to the truth; but they do not necessarily contain any truth at all. The public silence maintained after the dissolution by the rumpers themselves, a phenomenon to which we shall return, made possible the general acceptance of the army's claims.

The army's first official explanation of its actions on 20 April

---

[1] *Clarke Papers*, iii. 1.   [2] Hull Corporation MSS, L. 565.
[3] These reports are discussed by Firth, 'Expulsion of the Long Parliament', pp. 134–7. See also Staffordshire Record Office, D593/P/8/2/2: Langley to Leveson, 30 Apr. 1653.

appeared in a *Declaration* written two days after the event. Like the account in *Several Proceedings*, it was evidently drawn up quickly. The *Declaration* claims that, in the period before the dissolution, a 'corrupt party' in the House had 'the desire . . . of perpetuating themselves in the supreme government. For which purpose, the said party long opposed, and frequently declared themselves against having a new representative.' Eventually they 'saw themselves necessitated to take that bill into consideration', but even then 'they resolved to make use of it to recruit the House with persons of the same spirit and temper, thereby to perpetuate their own sitting'. There is nothing to suggest that the 'corrupt party' succeeded in its resolve to insert a recruiting clause in the bill. Instead, we meet for the first time the argument that the Rump had planned to delude the army by somehow circumventing the bill's provisions. The only specific charge on the subject of the bill is that the Rump had had an 'intention' to 'make use of' it (a phrase used twice) to recruit. Even on the eve of the dissolution, it seems, the officers had had only 'apprehensions' that 'not any love to a representative, but the making use thereof to recruit, and so perpetuate themselves', was the Rump's 'aim'.[1] If there had in fact been a recruiting clause in the bill it would have been much easier for the author of the *Declaration* to say so.

That his omission was not accidental is suggested by the other evidence relating to the bill which appeared in the fortnight following the dissolution. *The Moderate Publisher* for 22 April, defending the Rump's expulsion, followed the account which had appeared in *Several Proceedings* on the previous day, but omitted the passage containing the charge that the Rump had intended to recruit. *Several Proceedings* returned to the subject of the bill in its issue of 28 April. Its sole comment now was that had the bill been passed there would have been a 'new parliament in November next', which 'would not answer the thing desired'; the rumpers had proceeded with the bill '(as clearly appeared) not so much to answer [the officers'] desires, as to effect their own ends in the thing, by passing several things in that act of dangerous consequence'. What those 'things' were the newspaper did not say. In the *Declaration* of 22 April a further, fuller statement was promised, and by the 25th a 'more large and particular account' was expected to be 'extant tomorrow morning'.[2] The officers obviously had second

---

1 *Declaration of the Lord General and his Council, showing the grounds . . . for the Dissolution of the late Parliament*, pp. 5–7.

2 *Several Proceedings* 21–28 Apr. 1653, pp. 2957–9; *Declaration of the Lord General and his Council, showing the grounds . . . for the Dissolution of the late Parliament*, p. 10; *Moderate Publisher* 22–29 Apr. 1653, p. 1034; *Weekly Intelligencer* 19–26 Apr. 1653, p. 822.

The army apologias

thoughts, for no such document ever appeared, unless we count a *Declaration* of 3 May which portrayed itself as an official army statement but which was probably spurious.[1] Whatever its inspiration, it merely reprinted the comments on the bill which had appeared in *Several Proceedings* on 28 April. So did the issue of *The Army's Scout* published on 6 May.[2]

Two other documents published on 3 May inspire still less confidence in the recruiting charge. The first was a letter, designed to justify the dissolution and to ensure the army's support for it, sent by the officers in London to their colleagues in Scotland and subsequently sent also to the officers in Ireland. The letter makes the familiar charge that the rumpers had wanted to perpetuate their sitting, but the bill itself is described simply as 'an act for a new representative'. Once more there is no sign that there had been a recruiting clause in the bill.[3] The second document appeared in pamphlet form as *A Letter written to a Gentleman in the Country, Touching the Dissolution of the late Parliament and the Reasons Thereof*. It was written, almost certainly at Cromwell's prompting, by the journalist John Hall.[4] At first it seems that Hall is charging the Rump with making specific provision for recruitment: parliament, after postponing the dissolution for two or three years, had at last decided to 'provide the business so, as that their kingdom may stand, and others to sit with them upon the throne, that is to say, like Theseus his ship, perpetually to be pieced, and made into the same'. As we read on, however, the issue of recruitment becomes merged in familiar fashion with another complaint, which enables Hall to shy away at the critical moment from the charge that the bill had contained a recruiting clause. Indeed, the obvious inference from his pamphlet, as from other evidence, is that parliament had abandoned the recruiting scheme under pressure from the army and had agreed instead to fresh elections. The Rump, Hall recalls, had had a 'design' to recruit; but

when they saw that a necessity was upon them to break up at last, they then came down to the 3rd November of this year; but the act which had been three years a-hammering was so warily provided that, what in point of electors and elected, we should have been within a month after the new parliament in a

---

[1] Woolrych, 'Calling of Barebone's Parliament', p. 495n.
[2] *Another Declaration: wherein is rendered a further Account of the Just Grounds and Reasons of the Dissolving the Parliament* (1653), pp. 4, 6; *The Army's Scout* 30 Apr.–6 May 1653, pp. 901–3.
[3] Clarke MS xxv, fos. 48–51; *The Fifth Monarchy, or Kingdom of Christ, in opposition to the Beast Asserted* (1659), pp. 21–4. Cf. Clarke MS xxv, fo. 42.
[4] Abbott, *Writings and Speeches*, ii. 584 and n.

353

worse condition than we had been during this sitting of the old. They that were to be electors, were people that had not forfeited their liberty.

Once again the basis of complaint has shifted surreptitiously from the recruitment charge to the fear of 'disaffected persons'. The 'qualifications' imposed by the bill, Hall observes, had merely required candidates to be 'men that had been constantly true to the Commonwealth', a stipulation so broad that it might have led to the return to power of the presbyterian party – 'which is merely a Jesuit in a Genevan cloak' – and even of former royalists. Hall elaborates: 'This you will say may be prevented by examining the return of writs. Suppose it. But herein first, an impossibility to that end, as who can discover a man's heart? ... Who can judge that a convert is real?' Besides, such supervision, implying a 'power paramount to allow or disallow of this election', would be an invasion of the electorate's liberties. The relevance of these criticisms to the recruitment charge is at best unclear.[1]

There, with the publication of Hall's *Letter*, the matter for the time being rested. It was raised again only on 4 July, when Cromwell delivered his opening address to Barebone's Parliament. Much of the speech was taken up with a lengthy 'exoneration' of the dissolution of the Rump. Cromwell's argument, often closely resembling those advanced in the *Declaration* of 22 April and in Hall's *Letter*, undermines still further the charge that the bill had been a recruiting one.[2] After outlining in by now familiar terms the Rump's political and moral failings, he recalls the army's attempts, through petitions, to persuade the members to mend their ways. These efforts failed; but

At last, when indeed we saw that things would not be laid to heart, we had a very serious consideration among ourselves what other ways to have recourse unto; and when we grew to more closer considerations, then they began to take the act for a representative to heart, and seemed exceeding willing to put it on.

The rumpers' decision to proceed with the bill, however, lacked 'integrity'. Their 'intention' was 'not to give the people right of choice (it would have been but a seeming right); the seeming to give the people [their right] was intended only to recruit the House, the better

---

[1] *Letter written to a Gentleman in the Country*, pp. 10–12.
[2] He had clearly perused the *Declaration* while preparing his speech. He referred his audience to it in his account of the dissolution, and on one important point, relating to the rumpers' statements at the meeting on the evening of 19 April, adopted the *Declaration*'s careful innuendo almost *verbatim*: Abbott, *Writings and Speeches*, iii. 6, 59.

to perpetuate themselves'. Once more there is no indication that this 'intention' was reflected in the bill itself. The Rump is criticised for having aimed to circumvent the bill by holding recruiter elections; there is no suggestion that the bill had provided for them.

It is tempting at first to attribute this omission to mere clumsiness of expression. As Cromwell's speech develops, however, there emerges a separate element of confusion which puts his behaviour of 20 April in a quite different light. Setting aside the recruitment charge, he claims that those rumpers who would 'not hear of this bill before, when they saw us falling into more close considerations, then instead of protracting the bill, did make as much preposterous haste on the other hand, and run into that extremity'. Why was such 'preposterous haste' (a charge which he was to repeat later in the same speech, which had been made in the officers' letter of 3 May to their colleagues in Scotland and Ireland, and which he was to advance again in 1657)[1] as objectionable as had been the sluggish treatment which the Rump had previously accorded the bill? One explanation might be that it was the insertion of a recruiting clause which had so dramatically accelerated the progress of the bill. Neither Cromwell nor his colleagues ever made such a correlation. On the contrary, their evidence consistently suggests that the recruiting scheme had been dropped before the Rump stirred itself into 'preposterous haste'; and as Cromwell's speech to Barebone's continues it becomes clear that he had objected to the Rump's precipitancy not because of any change of mind on parliament's part, but because of a change of mind on his own. Cromwell, hitherto the advocate of open elections, had become resolutely opposed to them.

One of his main concerns during the negotiations with M.P.s over the bill had been the 'qualifications' to be imposed on newly elected members. At the meeting of 19 April between officers and M.P.s, Cromwell informed Barebone's, the army had told the rumpers present

that the way they were going in was impracticable; we could not tell them how it would be brought to pass, to send out an act of parliament into the country, with such qualifications as to be a rule for electors and elected and not to know who should execute this; desiring to know whether the next parliament were not like to consist of all presbyterians? Whether those qualifications would hinder them or neuters?

This was the language in which Mabbott had claimed that the bill would have brought to power 'such as probably would be disaffected,

---

[1] Clarke MS xxv, fos. 48ᵛ–9; *The Fifth Monarchy . . . Asserted*, p. 22; below, p. 362; and see *Another Declaration: wherein is rendered a further Account . . .* (3 May 1653), p. 5.

neuters, lawyers and the like', and in which Hall had argued that it would have resulted in victory for the presbyterian party, 'which is merely a Jesuit in a Genevan cloak'. Cromwell even objected, in words hardly suggestive of a desire for open and frequent elections, to the 'danger' of the bill's provisions 'in drawing the concourse of all people' – much as a politician of 1719 might have argued for the septennial act, and in much the same way as Marchamont Nedham, writing on the Rump's behalf in 1650, had attacked Leveller demands for frequent elections.[1] In its 'preposterous haste' on 20 April, Cromwell claimed, the Rump had resolved to pass the bill 'leaving out all things relating to the due exercise of the qualifications'. We do not know what he meant by this aside, but he had clearly decided before the debate of 20 April that the qualifications themselves would be inadequate, whether duly exercised or not. For 'it did fall obvious to us that the power would be put into the hands of men that had little affection to this cause'. The bill 'would have ... thrown away the liberties of the people into the hands of those who had never fought for it'. It would have led to the 'bringing in neuters, or such as should impose upon their brethren, or such as had given testimony to the king's party'. Indeed 'we had as good have delivered up our cause into the hands of ... interested and biased men; for it is one thing to ... love a person in another judgement ... ; another thing to have any so far set into the saddle upon that account as that it should be in them to have all ... their brethren at mercy'.[2]

In this speech Cromwell was admittedly addressing an assembly many of whose members would have been delighted by his attack on presbyterians, neuters and the advocates of religious intolerance. Yet his argument, however politically felicitous, was no pose. There is a striking similarity between the sentiments he expressed at the opening of Barebone's and those which had inspired him to dissolve the Rump. Indeed Cromwell's performance on 20 April would have done credit to one of the Fifth Monarchist preachers who had so avidly prophesied the Rump's destruction. He told his fellow officers immediately after the dissolution that 'when he went into the House, he intended not to do it; but the spirit was so upon him, that he was overruled by it; and he consulted not with flesh and blood at all'.[3] Railing at the assembled M.P.s for their alcoholic and sexual turpitude, he accused them of having 'espoused the corrupt interest of presbytery and the lawyers, who were the supporters of tyranny and oppression'. It was observed

---

[1] Nedham, *Case of the Commonwealth of England, Stated*, p. 82.
[2] Abbott, *Writings and Speeches*, iii. 55–60. [3] Streater, *Secret Reasons of State*, p. 3.

shortly after the dissolution that Cromwell's 'hate of rotten presbyters and assurance that [the] new representative would have been an inlet to that tyrannical, now sordid tribe' had driven him to destroy the Rump.[1] Within three days of the dissolution the Fifth Monarchist John Spittlehouse was defending Cromwell's action on the ground that the bill would have resulted in the election of royalists and presbyterians, and soon afterwards army sources were asserting that in the assembly which was to replace the Rump 'no professed lawyer is to be of the number'.[2]

Cromwell's affinity to Fifth Monarchist sentiments at the time of the dissolution represented a striking victory for Harrison and his saintly followers. For on 20 April Cromwell abandoned the policies he had pursued so patiently and for so long. Since Worcester he had pressed consistently for fresh elections and for a new representative: at some point shortly before the dissolution he evidently changed his mind. Throughout the crisis in relations between parliament and army he had denounced the call for a violent solution, restrained the more vehement army leaders, and avowed with lachrymose protestations the army's continuing fidelity to the Rump. He would obey parliament's orders, he said, if it 'would command the army to break their swords over their heads, and to throw them into the sea'. Shortly before the dissolution he 'protested to the House, with weeping eyes, that he would as willingly hazard his life against any whatever that should profess themselves [its] enemies, as he had done against those that were public enemies to the Commonwealth'. He assured Barebone's that, to the officers, 'the thinking of an act of violence was to us worse than any engagement that ever we were in . . . so desirous were we, even very tender and desirous if possible, that these men might have quit their places with honour'. The army had proceeded by 'humble solicitations', 'being tender of doing anything against authority'; it had 'refused to meddle, leaving it to the parliament, that all might be done by them'. Even on the eve of the dissolution the officers, according to their own account, had been 'still resolved to use all means possible to avoid extraordinary courses'.[3] These claims, as a summary of the behaviour of the

---

[1] Abbott, *Writings and Speeches*, ii. 642–3; Firth, 'Cromwell and the expulsion of the Long Parliament in 1653', pp. 532, 534.

[2] J. Spittlehouse, *The Army Vindicated in their late Dissolution of the Parliament* (1653), pp. 3–6; *Clarke Papers*, iii. 4. Cf. Clarke MS xxv, fo. 61.

[3] *Memoirs of Edmund Ludlow*, i. 347–8; Firth, 'Cromwell and the Expulsion of the Long Parliament in 1653', pp. 528, 529; Abbott, *Writings and Speeches*, iii. 56; *Declaration of the Lord General and his Council, showing the grounds . . . for the Dissolution of the late Parliament*, pp. 2, 7; *Several Proceedings* 14–28 Apr. 1653, pp. 2944, 2957. Cf. Gardiner, *History of the Commonwealth and Protectorate*, ii. 233, 236.

officers as a whole, were of course unwarrantable; but they were accurate enough as a description of Cromwell's own conduct. As he had told his army colleagues in March 1653, the use of force against the Rump would imply that 'the parliament is not the supreme power'.[1] He had sought before the dissolution to influence the House from within, 'some of the officers being members, and others having very good acquaintance with, and relations to, divers members of parliament'.[2] Indeed, his determination to 'stick close to the House' had offended the sects.[3] The studied conciliatoriness of his behaviour towards the Rump in the period before the dissolution is radically at odds with his conduct on 20 April. Again, throughout the Rump period he had been on intimate terms with leading members of the legal profession and with M.P.s who had ceased to sit at Pride's Purge. Yet on 20 April, throwing his 'catholic projects' to the wind, he joined the chorus of anti-professionalism and of 'hate of rotten presbyters' which had precipitated the crisis and which was to be echoed in his opening address to Barebone's.

The closer we look at Cromwell's actions of 20 April and at his subsequent accounts of them, the harder it is to see how the issue of recruiter elections could be held to have explained the dissolution. By what reasoning did a proposal to recruit justify the House's expulsion by an army intent on godly reformation? Talk of a recruiting clause no doubt helped to strengthen the army's suspicions of the Rump and to create an atmosphere in which the dissolution became possible; but once the dissolution had taken place, such talk could serve only as a pretext for the action the army had taken. Fresh elections would never have produced godly reformation. Unless radicals in the army and the congregations were prepared to by-pass the institution of parliament altogether, they stood only to lose by the Rump's dissolution. By the spring of 1653 they were prepared to by-pass parliament; and by 20 April Cromwell was ready to join them. The way was now open not for the 'successive' parliaments to which Cromwell's colleagues had paid lip-service on the evening of 19 April, but for a hand-picked assembly of saints.

The fact that recruitment was not the issue which provoked the dissolution does not in itself, of course, dispose of the accusation that the bill contained a recruiting clause. The statements we have examined so

---

[1] Above, p. 331.
[2] Abbott, *Writings and Speeches*, iii. 55.
[3] Firth, 'Cromwell and the expulsion of the Long Parliament in 1653', pp. 528, 529.

far – with their failure to specify the charge, their suggestion that the Rump had intended to 'delude' the army by circumventing the bill's provisions, and their claim that the bill would have resulted in the election of a parliament 'like to consist of all presbyterians' – gravely undermine the charge, but it may be felt that they do not by themselves permit us to dismiss it. Evidence which appeared subsequently, however, makes the recruitment charge even harder to sustain.

In February 1654 the protectorate government issued an official apologia entitled *The True State of the Case of the Commonwealth*.[1] In this pamphlet the army's actions of April 1653 are once more defended. The political and moral failings of the rumpers are still stressed, and hints as to their intended deception of the army are still liberally scattered, if without quite the rancour or persistence of earlier statements. The Rump, it is again insisted, had taken up the bill for a new representative only under pressure from the army. Yet there is a marked change of emphasis from the apologias of 1653. The charge or implication that the bill had been a recruiting one is replaced by novel and quite different criticisms of the Rump's intentions. For the recruitment charge had by now served its purpose. The prime aim of *The True State* was to justify not the dissolution of the Rump but the form of government represented by the protectorate. The Rump is accordingly criticised less for the designs or deficiencies of its members than for the weaknesses of the system of government which it embodied. The inauguration of the protectorate, with its provision for parliaments of limited duration, represented a return to more traditional theories of government. The idea of 'a single person and parliament', implying a balance between executive and legislature, stood in direct line of descent from the constitutional position adopted by the parliamentary opposition to Charles I. It is in this light that the charges brought against the Rump in *The True State* should be examined. The real objection to the bill for a new representative, it now appears, is that it had provided for uninterrupted and unlimited parliamentary government, for 'standing' parliaments assuming both executive and legislative powers and responsible to no authority but themselves. Thus 'the supreme powers of making laws, and of putting them in execution, were by that bill to have been disposed in the same hands; which placing the *legislative* and *executive* powers in the same persons is a marvellous inlet of corruption

---

[1] On the official nature of this document see Woolrych, 'Calling of Barebone's Parliament', p. 494n., and Abbott, *Writings and Speeches*, iii. 587. Abbott (*op. cit.* iii. 193) plausibly attributes it to Marchamont Nedham.

and tyranny'. 'Parliaments always sitting', the author concludes, 'are no more agreeable to the temper of the people, than it is to a natural body to take always physic instead of food.'

The True State is the first army or Cromwellian apologia to give more than the vaguest information about the contents of the bill; and the word 'recruit' is nowhere to be found in it. Certainly the 'visible design carried on by some [rumpers] to have perpetuated the power in their own hands' had made the proposal to combine executive and legislative powers in a 'standing' parliament 'yet the more exceeding grievous'; but once again there is no indication that the 'design' had influenced the contents of the bill. Instead, the author of the document provides another revealing glimpse of the bill's true contents. He states clearly that the bill had provided for 'successive', 'biennial' parliaments, which would have 'governed for two years successively'. Later he refers to the Rump's 'biennial bill', which would 'have returned again to representatives'.[1]

This information gives us a much clearer idea of the bill's provisions than do any of the earlier apologias. Recruitment would not of course have been incompatible with 'successive' and 'biennial' parliaments: it is conceivable that the rumpers could have retained their seats in such parliaments, or at least in the first of them, which presumably would have held office from November 1653 to November 1655. Yet there is no evidence in the testimony of anyone whose comments on the bill have survived to suggest that this is what the rumpers had intended. Given the determination of army and Cromwellian apologists to make the case against the bill as black as possible, and given Cromwell's anxiety, which in the protectorate period bordered on the obsessive, to convince both his audiences and himself of the justice of the dissolution, it is almost inconceivable that he and his colleagues would have failed to make such an accusation had there been grounds for doing so. The Cromwellians referred to 'biennial' and to 'successive' parliaments only after they had abandoned the charge that the bill had been a recruiting one. They made no attempt to reconcile the two claims, and by advancing the second they implicitly acknowledged the inaccuracy of the first. There had been every political advantage to be gained by suggesting that the bill had contained a recruiting clause: there was no obvious political advantage to be gained by claiming that the bill had provided for biennial and successive parliaments. The former claim had

[1] *True State of the Case of the Commonwealth*, pp. 9–12, 22, 23, 30. Cf. *ibid.* p. 36, and Firth, *Oliver Cromwell and the Rule of the Puritans in England*, p. 314.

been at once imprecise and self-contradictory: the latter claim was precise and consistent.

The veracity of *The True State*, and the inaccuracy of the recruitment charge, are confirmed by Cromwell's statements on the subject of the bill in his speech to the first protectorate parliament on 12 September 1654. By this time his infection by millenarian elitism had been fully cured. Much of the argument of *The True State* reappears in the speech. The rumpers' 'design' of 'perpetuating themselves', Cromwell claims, had given 'high cause for their dissolving'. But for army pressure, he suggests, the design would have been executed. It is nevertheless clear that the army's exertions were successful: 'It's true, this will be said, that there was a remedy to put an end to this perpetual parliament endeavoured, by having a future representative. How it was gotten, and by what importunities that was obtained, and how unwillingly yielded unto, is well known.' But gotten, obtained and yielded unto it evidently was.

At no point in this speech does Cromwell suggest that the bill had been a recruiting one: on the contrary he acknowledges, as *The True State* had done, that the bill had provided for 'successive' parliaments. Instead he suggests, as had earlier apologias, that the rumpers had intended to delude the army by circumventing the bill; and what he now claims to have objected to is not the bill itself but the lack of any guarantee that it would be put into effect. Discussing the formula for elections laid down by the bill, he asks: 'What was this remedy? It was a seeming willingness to have successive parliaments. What was that succession? It was, that when one parliament had left their seat, another was to sit down immediately in the room thereof, without any caution to avoid that which was the danger, [viz.] perpetuating of the same parliaments.' Once again it seems that the army had been unable to trust the Rump to do on 3 November 1653 what the bill obliged it to do; but the speech leaves little doubt that the bill itself had provided for a newly elected rather than for a 'recruited' parliament.[1] Cromwell makes no reference on this occasion to the dangers of holding elections. This is not surprising. He was speaking now with the experience of Barebone's behind him. He had turned instead to a politically more sober and constitutionally more respectable assembly, an 'Elizabethan' parliament elected on the franchise, and according to the distribution of seats, laid down by the Rump's bill. Aspersions at this time on the dangers of holding elections, or of readmitting to power those 'presby-

[1] Abbott, *Writings and Speeches*, iii. 453–4.

terians' and 'neuters' who were so well represented in the assembly Cromwell was addressing, would hardly have fostered the spirit of harmony which he was so keen to encourage at this time.

Cromwell returned once more to the subject of the dissolution in a speech during the kingship crisis of April 1657. His criticisms of the bill here, emphasising the dangers of 'standing', all-powerful parliaments, are again reminiscent of those made in *The True State* three years earlier. He repeats the claim of 1653 that the rumpers had intended to recruit, but yet again makes clear that the proposal had been abandoned under army pressure. In the place of a recruitment clause, the Rump had substituted a plan which would have taken the puritan cause 'out of the frying-pan into the fire'. The rumpers had conceded that 'a parliament might not be perpetual': instead, they had resolved that 'parliament might be always sitting . . . that as soon as one parliament went out of their place, another might leap in . . . that was pursued with that great heat, that I dare say there was more progress made in it in a month, than was with the like business in four'. Such 'standing', 'perpetual' parliaments would have enjoyed the same arbitrary powers as the Rump.[1]

How seriously should we take the criticisms made in *The True State* and in Cromwell's speech of 1657 of the bill's provisions for 'standing' parliaments and for the continued combination of executive and legislative powers? Such charges were not altogether mere retrospective rationalisation. The son of the rumper Isaac Pennington had objected in 1651 to the Rump's combination of executive and legislature, and a passage in *The True State* stressing the need for the separation of powers was lifted from an editorial published in July 1652 in *Mercurius Politicus*, which had also anticipated the complaint in Cromwell's speech of 1657 that perpetually sitting parliaments would have prevented men from 'learning how to obey as well as govern'.[2] Yet, although concern for the separation of powers may have contributed to Cromwell's dissatisfaction with the Rump, and although its enjoyment and abuse of arbitrary authority certainly dismayed him, the issue was clearly not responsible for the dissolution. Barebone's assembly, like the Rump, combined executive and legislative powers, apparently with Cromwell's blessing. Arguments about the need for the separation of powers

[1] Abbott, *Writings and Speeches*, iv. 486–8.

[2] Pennington, *The Fundamental Right, Safety and Liberty of the People*, ep. ded. and pp. 2, 13, 18–19, 23–5; *True State of the Case of the Commonwealth*, p. 10; *Mercurius Politicus* 29 Jan.–5 Feb. 1652, p. 1381, 1–8 July 1652, pp. 1705–6; Abbott, *Writings and Speeches*, iv. 486. Cf. *Moderate Intelligencer* 13–20 Sep. 1649, pp. 2263–4.

were revived only with the inauguration of the protectorate system of government which both *The True State* and Cromwell were anxious to defend.

Cromwell's speech of 1657 finally demolishes the army's claim that the bill for a new representative had contained a recruiting clause. It also makes it incontrovertibly plain that the charge of intended recruitment had been a red herring. Referring to the dissolution, Cromwell recalls that the 'hasty throwing away of the liberties of the people of God, and of the nation, into a bare representative of the people . . . was then the business we opposed'.[1] On 20 April 1653 the bill for a new representative, opening the door to presbyterians and neuters, would have been rejected whether it had provided for recruiter elections or not; and it is evident that it had not provided for them.

[1] Below, p. 381 n. 3.

17

CONCLUSION

So far, in our discussion of the contents of the bill for a new representative, we have examined the case advanced by the Rump's opponents. It is not an impressive one. Two brief and vague initial accusations, issued unofficially and followed by a prolonged and extensive retreat from them, do not constitute a convincing argument. But what of the case for the defence? What did the rumpers have to say about the bill's provisions? Such of their statements as survive support the argument that the bill had provided for completely fresh elections. But the rumpers did not say very much, at least in public, and what they did say they did not say very strongly. Their behaviour on the subject of the bill, although not as puzzling as that of the Cromwellians, is nevertheless curious. Masson, in his *Life of Milton*, claimed that the rumpers' failure to counter effectively the charges made against them is in itself indicative of their guilt, and his argument is impressive.[1] It must, however, be qualified.

In the first place, so little source material relating to any aspects of the Rump period has survived from the pens of the rumpers themselves that the impression of reticence may very well reflect no more than a chance gap in the evidence. It would, indeed, be quite uncharacteristic of the evidence for the Rump period as a whole if detailed accounts by rumpers of the bill's contents had survived. A document which has come to light since Masson wrote, combined with other material previously available, shows that the rumpers were not, in fact, as reticent as he supposed. C. M. Williams, in the doctoral thesis on Henry Marten which he submitted in 1954, included a transcript of a letter he had discovered among previously mislaid Marten papers. Addressed to Cromwell shortly before the meeting of Barebone's, the letter was written probably by Marten, certainly by someone who held Marten's views on many subjects and who was a member of his entourage, and certainly by someone who had sat in the Rump and who

[1] Masson, *Life of Milton*, iv. 409n.

had attended the House regularly, not least in its final months. Although Williams realised the importance of the document and made brief but helpful suggestions about its implications, his discovery has not hitherto prompted a re-examination of the evidence as a whole concerning the bill for a new representative. What the letter tells Cromwell is clear and unequivocal and comes as a refreshing contrast to the convoluted innuendo of army and Cromwellian apologias:

But let us grant the parliament to have been as unpardonable in all their actions as it is possible to imagine them, yet your excellency will acknowledge that their being sensible of it at ast, and desire to put a cure to all by dissolving, was not crime, and, if it were, it was such a one as the army and yourself were most eminently guilty of . . . They . . . are punished for the best and most honest attempt they ever made, to wit the endeavour they had [that] the settlement of these nations, which they saw themselves not able to accomplish, might be performed by others, and by them only who had the right to do it, and to establish whose right they had struggled with death and dangers near thirteen years; and this is so evident that your excellency hath declared in print that they might have been reprieved if they would have but consented to lay aside the consideration of a new parliament, only you say there that they meant to recruit themselves; whereas if you please to view the bill you took from the Clerk (if it be not burnt) you will be convinced of the contrary, if you are not so already by having been present at the debate of dissolving upon the 3rd of November next, at the very instance of putting which question you did interrupt the parliament.[1]

If the letter is correct, it makes nonsense of the charge either that the bill had been a recruiting one or that the Rump had intended to by-pass the bill and so to recruit. If, as Williams believed, Marten was the author (and the internal evidence is impressive),[2] the case for the letter's accuracy is strengthened; for Marten, whatever his faults, was an inveterate teller of the truth who spent much of his career getting into trouble because he spoke it all too bluntly. Whoever wrote the letter acknowledged with disarming frankness the Rump's failings on other matters, so that it is hard to see why he should have lied on the subject of the bill. There is the possibility that the document was intended for circulation or publication, in which case it would have to be considered as propaganda rather than as a private remonstrance to

[1] Williams, 'Political career of Henry Marten', pp. 548–9. The original is in the Marten-Loder MSS in the Brotherton Library at Leeds.
[2] The authorship of the document is discussed by Williams, 'Political career of Henry Marten', pp. 528 34. It would be possible to take the discussion further and to advance a variety of plausible alternative hypotheses, but Williams's arguments remain, to me, convincing.

Cromwell;[1] but few propagandists concede so readily the deficiencies of the political bodies they are defending. At any rate the letter's import is remarkable enough to warrant a fresh look at the statements of other rumpers involved in the events of April 1653.

One of them was Robert Reynolds, the Commonwealth's solicitor-general, who raised the subject of the bill in parliament in 1659. Williams noted the implications of Reynolds's speech in the light of the letter he had discovered; and, although there are exasperating gaps in the manuscript, Reynolds's words point to the same conclusions:

> I was very pressing for that act to dissolve ourselves. I never desired any earthly thing with more earnestness than to see that parliament fairly dissolved, and another provided to build up what . . . [BLANK] . . . The question being put to dissolve . . . [BLANK] . . . 3 November with a very loud yea. This done persons came to the door . . . This was never known abroad, how near that parliament that conquered others was to conquer themselves.[2]

Reynolds, who had sat in the Rump only under persuasion, and who had had little love for it,[3] had no more motive for lying than had the author of the letter to Cromwell. The tone of both men's statements, so different from that of army apologias, has the confident ring of conviction.

Two of the Rump's other lawyers who were present at the dissolution, Oliver St John and Bulstrode Whitelocke, have left brief comments on the bill. St John, as we have seen, recalled at the Restoration that he had 'endeavoured the bringing in of a free parliament', and that at the dissolution 'this was near effecting when, there sitting', he had been hindered 'by Cromwell and the army'. The statement is unfortunately as terse as the rest of St John's account of his role in Interregnum politics, but it is most unlikely that he meant by a 'free parliament' anything other than completely fresh elections. His commitment to the Rump had always been at best tentative. He had co-operated with Cromwell in the autumn of 1651 in securing the introduction of the bill for a new representative, at a time when everyone agreed that the bill provided for fresh elections, and he had been at one with Cromwell on the evening of 19 April in believing that the Rump must dissolve as soon as possible.[4] Whitelocke's comments on the bill in his Annals are oddly brief and uninformative,[5] but he recorded elsewhere that in January 1654 he told the Swedish chancellor Oxenstierna

---

[1] Williams, 'Political career of Henry Marten', p. 536.
[2] B.M., Add. MS 15,862, fo. 71&ᵛ. (The date, 3 November, is omitted from the printed version (*Diary of Thomas Burton*, iii. 209–10) from which Williams quoted.)
[3] Above, p. 65.   [4] Above, pp. 277, 337.   [5] Whitelocke, *Memorials*, iv. 5.

– in a conversation in which he was merely imparting information rather than seeking to defend the Rump – that the House had arranged 'to put a period to their sitting, and a new parliament to be chosen'.[1] Whitelocke's statement is lightweight as evidence, and perhaps not incompatible with the recruitment charge: a recruited parliament would still have been a 'new' one. The same complaint might also be made against all the testimony bequeathed by rumpers, except for the letter attributed by Williams to Marten. Yet confidence in the veracity of that letter is, in general, increased by the assertions of other rumpers. Scot and Heselrige, for example, both touched on the bill in speeches made in parliament in 1659. Scot, who like St John had cooperated with Cromwell in the autumn of 1651 to secure the introduction of the bill, claimed that the Rump had 'intended to have gone off with a good savour' once the few months necessary for the defeat of the Dutch were over, and that the House had 'provided for a succession of parliaments'.[2] Heselrige, as we have already seen, described the measure debated on 20 April as 'an act to put an end to that parliament and to call another. I desired the passing of it with all my soul.'[3] The brevity of both these assertions seems to have derived not from a desire to slur over the truth but from an unconscious assumption that those who heard them would know them to be well-founded. The history of the Rump period was resuscitated time and again during the debates of 1659, yet the bill itself was rarely mentioned. The statements made in the House by Reynolds, Scot, and Heselrige went unchallenged, and none of the Rump's many parliamentary enemies, derogatory though they were on other matters, revived the recruitment charge. One other piece of negative evidence should also be mentioned. There has been considerable confusion about the role of Sir Henry Vane at the time of the dissolution. He has been represented as arguing throughout the Rump period for recruiter elections.[4] In fact, there is nothing either to suggest that his advocacy of recruiter elections before Worcester was sustained after it, or to connect him with the drafting of the bill for a new representative. After the dissolution, for what it is worth, he argued that 'successive' elections were essential to the people's well-being.[5]

[1] Whitelocke, *Journal of the Swedish Embassy*, i. 310.
[2] Above, p. 266; *Diary of Thomas Burton*, iii. 111–12.   [3] Above, p. 338.
[4] J. Willcock, *Life of Sir Henry Vane the Younger* (1913), pp. 231–2. Cf. Gardiner, *History of the Commonwealth and Protectorate*, ii. 231–2; Abbott, *Writings and Speeches*, ii. 647 and n.; Roots, *The Great Rebellion*, p. 164.
[5] John Lord Somers, *A Collection of scarce and valuable Tracts*, vi. 305.

Marten (or whoever wrote the letter to Cromwell), Reynolds, St John, Whitelocke, Scot, Heselrige and Vane were all present at the dissolution. Records of the impressions of two rumpers who were not then present, Hutchinson and Ludlow, also survive. Mrs Hutchinson, in her biography of her husband, denied that the Rump had planned to perpetuate itself, and claimed that before the dissolution its members 'had prepared a bill to put a period to their own sitting, and provide for new successors'.[1] Ludlow claimed that before its expulsion the House had been 'hastening with all expedition to put a period to their sitting, having passed a vote that they would do it in the space of a year', and that the act was 'for their own dissolution'. He dismissed as a 'calumny' Cromwell's charge that the rumpers had aimed to perpetuate their own authority.[2]

Finally, one voice from the army spoke up in the Rump's defence. Immediately after the dissolution John Streater, recently returned from service in Ireland, distributed among the officers a document which claimed that the choice Cromwell had had to make on 20 April had been between on the one hand allowing the nation 'to elect a new representative' which would 'sit six months', and on the other entrusting power (as the army wanted) to a select few. In 1659 Streater drew up an account of the events surrounding the dissolution which accords well with what is known of his own statements and actions in 1653. His narrative suggests that on 20 April Cromwell had found it as difficult as he was to find it in his subsequent speeches to distinguish between the rumpers' desire 'to perpetuate themselves' and the threat provided by 'disaffected persons'. Thus on the morning of the dissolution Cromwell told the officers both that the rumpers were 'designing to spin an everlasting thread', and that if the Rump were permitted to pass the bill and so 'put the people to elect a new parliament, it would tempt God'. Streater had 'credible information' at the time of the dissolution that the Rump was 'in consultation about the putting a period to their sitting, and also providing for a succession of parliaments', with sufficient 'qualifications' to ensure the Commonwealth's survival. He also attacked Cromwell for arguing, at the time of the dissolution, that 'the people' were 'not fit to be trusted with their own liberty', an assertion which ties up with a statement in the letter discovered by Professor Williams that Cromwell, when he broke up the abortive meeting of the Council of State on the afternoon of 20 April, told his audience that

[1] *Memoirs of Colonel Hutchinson*, pp. 292–3.
[2] *Memoirs of Edmund Ludlow*, i. 345, 350–3.

'the people shall not have their liberty, I say the people shall not have their liberty' to hold elections.[1]

Yet if Masson exaggerated the reticence of the rumpers and their supporters on the subject of the bill, it remains true that there is in the main a lack of vigour, of a sense of outrage, about their statements which contrasts strangely with the emotional investment which such rumpers as Scot and Ludlow came to place in the halcyon days of the Long Parliament and with the bitterness with which they recalled the dissolution. It is possible to suggest contributory reasons for this relative quiescence. In the weeks following the dissolution there was particularly good cause for the rumpers' public silence. Rumours abounded that the army would prosecute individual M.P.s for 'corruption', and the fear of reprisals must have inhibited a spirit of contradiction. So must the arrest of Francis Allen on 20 April and the attempt to arrest Heselrige. The fate of those who did dare to remonstrate against the dissolution can hardly have encouraged further opposition: the prominent city politicians who presumed to urge Cromwell to restore the Rump, so that it could dissolve itself in an orderly fashion, were dismissed from their posts, while Streater was imprisoned for his protests.[2] When Colonel Hutchinson came to London shortly after the dissolution he found the rumpers whom he met resolved to hold their peace and await better days.[3] Many of them had already retired to the country. To others, who accepted or angled for office under Cromwell, the prospect of advancement may have provided as strong a motive for silence as did caution or cowardice. Early in May a royalist newswriter heard that 'some of the late parliament, or some body of them, are putting out a declaration against those of the General and army',[4] but no such document ever got into print. It is not hard to see why: as a perusal of the pamphlet and newspaper material of the weeks following the dissolution makes clear, the new regime was in full control of the press.[5]

---

[1] B.M., Thomason MS E693(5), 'Ten Queries: by a friend to the new dissolved Parliament'; James Heath, *Flagellum* (1665), p. 130; Streater, *Secret Reasons of State, passim*.

[2] Farnell, 'Usurpation of honest London householders', p. 42; *Dictionary of National Biography*: Streater.

[3] *Memoirs of Colonel Hutchinson*, p. 295.

[4] Clarendon MS 45, fo. 366ᵛ: newsletter, 6 May 1653.

[5] If there was little overt hostility to Cromwell in the weeks after the dissolution, it may simply have been, as a royalist suggested, because his opponents – rumpers and presbyterians alike – were too 'cowed' to protest. Cromwell later claimed that 'so far as I could discern, when [the Rump was] dissolved, there was not so much as the barking of a dog, or any visible repining at it'. 'That', retorted Thomas Scot, 'is according to the

The rumpers' failure to deny the army's charges at a later date is initially more disconcerting. It may be that the use of force at the dissolution came to enjoy an imaginative hold on the men who had been driven from power in 1653 which overshadowed in their minds the issue of the bill's contents. This certainly seems to have happened to Whitelocke; and it is remarkable how little attention is given in any of the contemporary descriptions of the dissolution to the actual contents of the bill. By the later 1650s, too, the idea of a recruited (or more precisely of a rotating) membership had attained respectable appeal, not least among some of the most influential rumpers, who may therefore have been disinclined to deny the charge that they had made provision in 1653 for a political manoeuvre which they were now prepared to advocate. The charge itself had of course been abandoned by the Cromwellians in 1653, so that it could be said that there was no longer a case to answer. Finally, it is worth noting that the restored Rump ordered an (unsuccessful) search for the bill in 1659 – something it would surely not have done had the rumpers had something to hide.[1]

By themselves, however, these observations inflict relatively limited damage on Masson's argument from silence. Much more important is the fact that it can be stood on its head. Cromwell took the bill away with him from the House on 20 April 1653.[2] He had every opportunity to print or otherwise to relate in detail those parts of the document which made it the transparent example of the Rump's self-interest that he said it was. He ignored these opportunities.[3] Instead, he resorted to confused and interminable accounts of the dissolution in which he never particularised the bill's contents. We are left with two possible explanations of his conduct. The first is that, from the moment of the dissolution, he and his army colleagues deliberately set out to create a misleading impression of the bill's contents and of the Rump's intentions. If so, they succeeded in convincing both contemporaries and subsequent historians. This theory would not, however, explain why

company men keep. Men suit the matter to their lips.' (*Nicholas Papers*, ii. 12; Abbott, *Writings and Speeches*, ii. 654.)

[1] *C.J.* 9 Aug. 1659.
[2] Abbott, *Writings and Speeches*, ii. 644; above, p. 365.
[3] Bisset (*History of the English Commonwealth*, ii. 469–74) claimed that Cromwell's failure to publish the bill suggested that there was no recruiting clause. Bisset's argument was itself reversed by Masson, but Cromwell's public silence is at least as curious as that of the rumpers. Bisset's only positive support for his thesis, however, lay in the statements of Scot, Ludlow and Mrs Hutchinson. Masson argued that such statements were 'too general to be worth anything'. So, by themselves, they would be. (Masson, *Life of Milton*, iv. 409n.)

the army at first specifically charged the Rump with including a recruiting clause and then so quickly dropped the claim and replaced it with the accusation of intended 'delusion'. It would not explain, either, why army propaganda in the fortnight following the dispatch of Mabbott's letter of 23 April 1653 was so remarkably silent about the bill's actual provisions. Besides, anyone who studies Cromwell will have reservations about such a theory. Cromwell may have been a devious politician, but he was not a cold-blooded one. His art was in deceiving himself, not others. Although in his statements on the bill Cromwell criticised the Rump in aggressive terms, the purpose of those statements was clearly defensive. They make sense only as exercises in self-vindication or even self-persuasion, addressed as much to himself as to his audiences.

The second possible explanation, on the other hand, has the virtue of consistency both with the evidence as a whole and with the injured tenor of Cromwell's speeches. It is that Cromwell acted on 20 April under a genuine misapprehension about the bill's contents. His speeches make it plain that he had been under no such misapprehension at the meeting on the evening of the 19th; but it is quite possible that one of the army 'messengers' who brought him the news on the 20th that the Rump was pressing ahead with the bill gave him to understand that the House had now decided to insert a recruiting clause. The accounts of Cromwell's behaviour in the House at the dissolution suggest that he was not in a mood to listen to or to inquire about the bill's provisions. This explanation would give point to the remark, in the letter probably written by Marten, that Cromwell would realise that the recruiting charge was inaccurate 'if you please to view the bill you took from the Clerk'. It would also account for the contrast between the confident nature of the charges made against the bill immediately after the dissolution and the confused backtracking of subsequent apologias.[1] The turning point, in this case, would presumably have come when Cromwell was 'pleased to view the bill'. If so, he must have discovered his error at some point between the time the issue of *Several Proceedings* of 21 April went to press and the writing of the officers' *Declaration* on the following day. Admittedly Mabbott, writing on the 23rd, was under the impression, or sought to foster the impression, that the bill was a recruiting one, but this was not a view Cromwell ever seems to have discouraged. At any rate, inquiry as to the subsequent fate of the

[1] Is this also the explanation of Cromwell's words, in the passage quoted in the penultimate paragraph of this chapter, 'as well as they were thought to love their seats'?

371

bill must begin with Cromwell. Perhaps, as the letter attributed to Marten hinted, he burnt it. If this is what happened, his discovery of the bill's true contents did not destroy in his mind the justification for the action he had taken on 20 April, which lay as we have seen in his hostility to presbyterians and neuters. It merely robbed him of his pretext.

What conclusions may be drawn, then, about the provisions of the bill for a new representative? Historians have been as reluctant as were the Cromwellians to discuss the bill's arrangements for parliamentary developments after 1653, yet it is here that the evidence is in some ways most clear. First, there were to have been 'successive' parliaments (a phrase taken up, like so much else in the bill, in the *Instrument of Government*),[1] elected on the basis of the reformed electoral system which was in fact put into effect in the elections of 1654. *The True State* asserted that these parliaments were to have been biennial. Cromwell said in 1657 that they were to have been triennial, but here, understandably but ironically, he may have been confusing the bill with the *Instrument of Government*.[2] *The True State*, a considered manifesto of 1654, seems a more reliable guide than Cromwell's improvised blustering of 1657.

For how long was each of the 'successive' parliaments to sit? Streater claimed in May 1653 that they were to 'sit six months'; and Ludlow declared that the Rump had

resolved to leave as a legacy to the people the government of a Commonwealth by their representatives, when assembled in parliament, and in the intervals thereof by a Council of State, chosen by them, and to continue till the meeting of the next succeeding parliament, to whom they were to give an account of their conduct and management.[3]

The Cromwellians, on the other hand, objected strongly to the bill's provision for 'standing', 'perpetual' parliaments. A conceivable resolution of these apparently contradictory assertions is that the Cromwellians meant, by standing or perpetual parliaments, not parliaments in perpetual session but the permanent investment of power in parliamentary authority. On this score a proposal that future parliaments

[1] Gardiner, *Constitutional Documents*, pp. 406, 407.
[2] Abbott, *Writings and Speeches*, iv. 488.
[3] *Memoirs of Edmund Ludlow*, i. 351. It is just conceivable, however, that Streater meant by a parliament 'to sit six months' not a parliament of six months' duration but a parliament called to sit in six months' time, i.e. in November 1653.

should, between parliamentary sessions, entrust authority to councils responsible solely to themselves or to their respective successors would have been as objectionable as parliaments in permanent session. Yet the vigour of expression in *The True State*, and in Cromwell's speech of 1657 (not, admittedly, a document automatically to be trusted on points of detail), impels scepticism of this view. So, still more, does the Rump's behaviour during its tenure of power. It is conceivable that the rumpers had come to feel that permanent parliamentary sessions were inadvisable: they had, after all, frequently attempted to arrange adjournments during the Rump period, and they provided for an adjournment in the bill for a new representative. Equally, the bill anticipated the *Instrument of Government*, which provided for short parliaments to be followed by long periods of conciliar government, on so many other issues that it would not be altogether surprising if it likewise anticipated it on this point. Yet the Rump's previous adjournment proposals had all failed, not least because of the House's reluctance to give the Council of State too free a rein. It is hard to believe that a parliament which, as the dissolution approached, had become ever more solicitous of its privileges would have contented itself with limiting its successors to sessions of short duration. This is a point on which no firm conclusion is possible.

A firm conclusion is, I believe, possible in relation to the recruitment charge. The evidence, it seems to me, points decisively to the conclusion that the bill provided for fresh elections, and renders insupportable the claim that it provided for recruiter ones. Of course, the evidence is not as full as we could wish. Yet when the army and Cromwellian apologias are examined, it becomes clear that it is precisely because of the relative shortage of other evidence that the recruitment charge has stuck for so long. For the unanswerable objection to the charge is not that the assertions of the Rump's enemies are contradicted by the surviving evidence of its friends: it is that the army and Cromwellian statements themselves show the accusation to be untenable. The Rump's opponents, in seeking to justify the dissolution and to show that the issue of recruitment had in some way been responsible for it, were hoist by their own petard.

Whatever view we take of the recruitment issue, one thing at least is plain. The conflict of 20 April 1653 was not between a parliament determined to perpetuate its power and an army resolved to hold elections, but between a parliament which had resolved to hold elections

373

(of whatever kind) and an army determined to prevent it from doing so. The dissolution was not a victory for St John and the advocates of open elections: it was the triumph of Harrison and the prophets of the imminent millennium. At some point before the dissolution, in other words, the roles of parliament and army were reversed. Previously the army had pressed for a speedy dissolution while the Rump had resisted it: now the Rump was arranging elections while the army tried to stem the House's 'preposterous haste'.

There are two possible reasons why the Rump resolved to press ahead with the bill in the spring of 1653. The first is that it intended to delude the army by abusing the measure. We have seen that the only support for this view is to be found in army and Cromwellian apologias, which never substantiated the claim and which adopted it only after the accusation that the bill was a recruiting one had been abandoned. To explain the charge of duplicity we need look no further than the need felt by the Rump's opponents to retreat from the original charge without loss of moral ground. What, in any case, did the 'delusion' charge explain? On 20 April the Rump was clearly in a mood to follow its own wishes and to ignore those of the army. It resolved on that morning to pass a bill to which the army, on grounds quite separate from the issue of recruitment, was bitterly opposed. Why, then, should the House have proceeded with a measure which did not correspond to its own intentions? If the Rump intended to recruit, why did it not pass a recruiting bill?

The Cromwellian explanation of the Rump's behaviour is, indeed, riddled with inconsistencies. There is, for example, Cromwell's claim that the Rump had proceeded with the bill with 'preposterous haste'. The House's decision to press ahead with the bill seems to have been taken on 23 February 1653, with Heselrige's introduction of the amendments and the resolution to debate them weekly thereafter. By what standards did weekly debates in the spring of 1653 on a bill given its first two readings in the autumn of 1651 constitute 'preposterous haste'? Only on 20 April did the Rump try to outwit the army through speed; yet Cromwell claimed that the Rump had proceeded with 'preposterous haste' for a period of at least a month before the dissolution.[1] During that month the House had in fact failed on one

---

[1] Above, p. 362. Cromwell also claimed (Abbott, *Writings and Speeches*, iii. 60) that on 20 April the Rump 'resolved to pass [the bill] only in paper' without engrossing it, for the quicker dispatch of it'; but there are grounds for doubting this assertion. See *C.J.* 9 Aug. 1659.

occasion to hold its weekly debate on the amendments: it had promptly been rebuked by the army for its negligence. By adopting the charge of preposterous haste Cromwell was able to accredit his behaviour in the weeks before the dissolution with a consistency it had simply lacked; but he never gave any indication why the Rump should have behaved so irresponsibly. All we can tell from his wording is that the reason had had nothing to do with recruitment. The explanation of the Rump's actions which Cromwell's accounts require us to accept is that M.P.s who for seventeen months had wilfully, selfishly and obstinately refused 'to period themselves' suddenly became possessed, in February 1653, with a reckless desire to betray the cause by yielding their seats to presbyterians and neuters.

If this explanation were compatible with the evidence, we might be obliged to take it seriously. Since the evidence contradicts it, we can safely dismiss it. The closer we look at army and Cromwellian apologias, indeed, the further do we travel from a convincing explanation of the Rump's decision to proceed with the bill in the spring of 1653. Yet there is a perfectly satisfactory explanation which is fully compatible with the evidence. It is that the Rump attempted to pass a bill for fresh elections for the simple reason that it wanted to hold them; and that its desire to hold them, far from representing a profound or sudden change of heart, was consistent with the attitudes its members had always held and with the policies they had always pursued.

The evidence bequeathed by rumpers on the subject of the dissolution is meagre, but on one point, at least, it is consistent. As Cromwell said, the rumpers proceeded on 20 April 'with all the eagerness they could'. There is Reynolds's 'I never desired any earthly thing with more earnestness'; there is Heselrige's 'I desired the passing of [the bill] with all my soul'; and there is the claim, in the letter attributed to Marten, that at the dissolution the rumpers were 'punished for the best and most honest attempt they ever made' to achieve the kind of settlement for which they had 'struggled with death and dangers near thirteen years'. Marten's views on representation were more strongly held than those of most rumpers, whose commitment to a speedy dissolution was no doubt of more recent origin; we can see how the hostility between parliament and army must have infected the attitudes of M.P.s in the days before the dissolution, so that men like Reynolds and Heselrige came to regard fresh elections as an urgent moral necessity. In April a number of members who do not seem to have taken their seats at least for several months returned to the House,[1] and the views of back-benchers were likely to increase the House's determination to hold elections. Yet if the conviction and the passion with which the House proceeded on 20 April were novel, its resolve to hold elections was much older. The Rump had never regarded itself as anything other than an interim government, and it had always acted on the assumption that it would eventually make way for a newly elected parliament. In all its resolutions on the subject of elections, from March 1649 onwards, it implicitly acknowledged that by postponing them it was compromising between the ideal and the necessary: elections were desirable, but they were not yet practicable.[2]

Before Worcester, this attitude had the support of the army officers. After Worcester, the attitude was hardened by the army's hostility to the Rump; the demand for a speedy dissolution met with resentment and obstruction, and attempts were made, in May 1652 and early 1653, to revive the recruiting plan. Yet Cromwell's assertion on the evening before the dissolution that fresh elections were undesirable until the electorate should 'forget monarchy' reminds us, as does John Jones's warning in the autumn of 1651, that there were eminently sensible reasons for postponing fresh elections and for contemplating recruiter ones. That historians automatically attribute to mere selfishness the Rump's prolonged reluctance to dissolve is due entirely to the imbalance in the surviving evidence. The most plausible explanation of the Rump's behaviour after Worcester is that it intended to delay elections until the army had been disbanded or at least reduced to impotence, and until, in Jones's words, 'burdens' had been 'taken off' and the Commonwealth given 'some time to take root in the interests of men'.[3] The way would thus have been cleared for the civilian, constitutional settlement for which the Rump had always striven. In January 1653, however, it at last became clear that the Rump would be obliged to dissolve before the army were disbanded. Faced with this realisation the House changed not its heart, but its strategy. The recruiting scheme, never seen as more than an interim solution, was

---

[1] Abbott, *Writings and Speeches*, ii. 643. Fourteen members who rarely attended the Rump or who do not seem to have taken their seats at least for many months can be identified as sitting in April 1653: Aldworth, Brereton, Constable, H. Darley, Dormer, Dunch, Hallowes, Hay, Heveningham, Hill, L. Hodges, Hussey, Nutt, Sydenham. The *Journal of the House of Commons* is very thin by this stage, and it is likely that the number was considerably higher.

[2] Cf. above, pp. 157–8, 176–7, 188–9, 221; and see *A Declaration of the Parliament of England, in answer to the Letters sent to them from Commissioners of Scotland* (1649), p. 16.

[3] Above, pp. 268, 285, 288, 330.

finally abandoned, and the decision to proceed with the bill for a new representative taken. That decision, although initially welcomed by the army, was of course not in the army's interests. For by resolving to hold elections before the Commonwealth had 'taken root in the affections of men', the rumpers were jeopardising the Commonwealth's survival. That they were prepared to do so is a reminder of their continuing lack of commitment to the form of government which had emerged after the execution of the king. There is no doubt that the bill would have led to the election of members who had not sat since December 1648 and of men of similar views. What the Rump was plotting on 20 April was not the perpetuation of its authority: it was revenge for Pride's Purge.

Although it is unlikely that the Rump would have debated the bill in the spring of 1653 but for army pressure, the form taken by those debates shows that the House was not acting from mere panic. The decision to proceed with the bill was taken at a time when the army's agitation of January had subsided and when the House was firmly resisting army demands on such matters as law reform and poor relief. The amendments were introduced the day after news had come through of Blake's crucial victory off Portland, an event which gave a considerable boost to parliamentary morale. The resolution to debate the bill at weekly intervals (a customary procedure) typified the Rump's determination to proceed as if the army simply did not exist. On 20 April the rumpers, hitherto so bitterly divided, spoke with a single voice. That they did so is remarkable, for different groupings in the Rump must have had different requirements of the bill, and it must have been hard to word 'qualifications' which would have satisfied both 'revolutionaries' and 'conformists'. In their determination to enact their own settlement rather than to dissolve at the army's bidding, the rumpers were prepared to sink their differences. Or rather, perhaps, they were prepared to postpone consideration of them; for in November the battle between 'revolutionaries' and 'conformists' over parliamentary membership would no doubt have been resumed. But it was in parliament, and in parliament alone, that the battle would have been fought.

Because of the nature of the army and Cromwellian charges against the Rump, any explanation of the dissolution which does not accord with those charges is bound to raise questions about the correct distribution of moral opprobrium. With those questions we need not concern ourselves; we are simply obliged to find the explanation of the Rump's behaviour which tallies with the evidence. If it is clear that the Rump did not act selfishly on 20 April, there is no need to suggest that its decision to pass the bill was a move of astounding selflessness. The Rump merely behaved in accordance with the principles and attitudes which had informed the proceedings of the Long Parliament since its inception. All M.P.s knew that parliament was supposed to be the representative body of the nation, and that therein alone lay its claim to authority. They knew that membership of parliament was a public trust involving public service. The rumpers had differed from other members of the Long Parliament in believing that they could best fulfil that trust by sitting in a blatantly unrepresentative parliament and by implicating themselves in a coalition for which they had little if any enthusiasm. To explain their decision they had found themselves arguing that the M.P.s who had ceased to sit at the purge had betrayed their trust, or adopting theories justifying government by conquest; but these claims, which can rarely have convinced even those who advanced them, were designed merely to justify the Rump's tenure of power, not to perpetuate it. No doubt many rumpers enjoyed the experience of power and developed a taste for it, but there is no reason to suppose that they believed they had an exclusive right to it. Their decision in April 1653 to pass a bill from which, as individuals, they had nothing to gain and everything to lose suggests the opposite.

Before Worcester, the Rump had served its purpose: the royalists had been defeated; army radicalism had been contained; the threat of social revolution had been averted; constitutional forms had been preserved. The country, if not governed in the way either rumpers or soldiers would have liked, had at least continued to be governed. After Worcester, however, the Rump had to concern itself not only with its own short-term survival but with long-term problems of political settlement; and the fracture of the coalition between parliament and army, the increasing stagnation and bitterness of politics, and the hardening of both presbyterian and radical opinion in the country made it plain that settlement could never be achieved so long as the Rump remained in power. Accordingly, in the words of the letter attributed to Marten, it was the rumpers' 'endeavour' that 'the settlement of these nations, which they saw themselves not able to accomplish, might be performed by others'. However radically rumpers had differed in the past, they had come by April 1653 to agree with St John that, 'as the distractions then were', fresh elections were 'the best and justest way of healing them'.

Most rumpers, like most members of the Long Parliament of the 1640s, belonged to the ship money generation. The 1630s, when there had been no parliaments and no elections, had been decisive in the formation of their attitudes. Circumstances, admittedly, obliged the Long Parliament to sit for a period even longer than the eleven years' personal government; indeed, it was the Long Parliament's dilemma that it frequently found itself resorting to means which ran counter to its ends. But the ends themselves remained consistent. They were, indeed, the ends of all seventeenth-century parliaments: order, peace, plenty, protection of property rights, exclusion of central governments from local affairs. With these ends the rule of the sword was as incompatible as was arbitrary kingship. Parliament's objection to both Charles I and to the Cromwellian army was that they had policies: that they wished to change the world rather than leave it as it was. The seventeenth century showed that the world could remain as it was only if parliaments met frequently and if those who sat in them were prepared to extend the scope of their political activity. The rumpers, many of whom evidently enjoyed political activity, found themselves imposing on their countrymen the very marks of tyranny from which they had fought to deliver them. Nevertheless, the aim of the Long Parliament after Pride's Purge was the aim of the Long Parliament before it: to create, through political means, a world safe from politics.

What, lastly, of Cromwell himself? Why, at some point before 19 April, did he change his mind about the bill for a new representative and oppose the elections he had demanded for so long? We need not imagine that his conversion was a sudden one, but its consequences were dramatic. The key to the explanation, I believe, lies in his extraordinary performance in the House on 20 April, and in the charges he brought both at and after the dissolution against rumpers, presbyterians and neuters.

Cromwell's capacity for self-conviction always depended on his emotional ties with his radical followers. Yet since December 1651 both the gathered churches and the more radical army officers had found it difficult to persuade him to enter the spirit of their deliberations, and by the spring of 1653, staying away for long periods from both parliament and the Council of State, he seems to have become, as so often before his more decisive political interventions, a lone figure. His relations with his radical followers were severely strained. His continuing loyalty to the Rump, it was reported shortly before the dissolution, 'causeth him to be daily railed on by the preaching party, who say they must have a new parliament and a new General before the work be done'.¹ The mantle of patron of the sects was passing to Harrison. The virtue of Cromwell's action on 20 April was partly, no doubt, that it released him from his confusion about the respective advantages and disadvantages of open elections. Perhaps more important, however, it restored his position as the hero of radicals both in the army and in the congregations. Hearing of the dissolution, the godly of Hereford exulted to Cromwell, 'Oh! my lord, what are you, that you should be the instrument to translate the nation from oppression to liberty, from the hands of corrupt persons to the saints?' Their kindred of Durham were still more enthusiastic. On hearing of the coup, 'we were at first like men in a dream, and could hardly believe for rejoicing, to see the wonderful goodness and kindness of God, in renewing a remembrance of your former engagements for this poor nation'. As the words 'renewing a remembrance of your former engagements' suggest, such adulation was not automatic. In their despair before the dissolution, the saints of Durham recalled, 'that which did very much add to our sorrow was the fear of God's presence withdrawing from you, which fear was caused by your long silence; but now to see the Lord hath again quickened you, is as life to our dying expectations'.² The dissolution of the Rump marked the capture of Cromwell by the chosen.

Of course, that is not all it marked. Cromwell did not need Fifth Monarchist fanaticism to disenchant him with the Rump, whose failings had long distressed him; and the news on 20 April that his intimate friends Vane and St John had betrayed him was no doubt the final blow. We need not suppose that Cromwell, throughout the crisis leading to the dissolution, was in the grip of a millenarian trance. The reforms for which he had pressed in the House had been limited ones, drafted by men as moderate as Matthew Hale, John Owen and John Dury, and supported in the House by such equally moderate figures as Gilbert Pickering, Charles Fleetwood and Thomas Westrow. To those who put reform before parliamentary supremacy, the Rump had failed disastrously; and there is no doubting the Rump's ability to offend moderate reformers – or, indeed, its capacity for sheer cussedness. On

¹ Firth, 'Cromwell and the expulsion of the Long Parliament in 1653', p. 528; Gardiner, *History of the Commonwealth and Protectorate*, ii. 251.
² *Original Letters ... addressed to Oliver Cromwell*, pp. 90–1, 92. Cf. Clarke MS xxv, fos. 44ᵛ–5. The Durham letter was addressed to Cromwell 'and the rest of his Council of Officers', but it was clearly Oliver whom the authors had in mind.

the evening of 19 April Cromwell used the Fifth Monarchists' arguments against the bill, but not their vocabulary. His tone was conciliatory and almost calm. Very shortly after the dissolution, too, he
returned to the ways of compromise, not least in his approach to St
John; and it was to be largely through Cromwell's influence that the
saintly element in Barebone's was leavened with men of more moderate
views and temper.[1] Equally, he cannot have been unconcerned on the
evening of 19 April, any more than he had been when in January 1649
he agreed to the trial and execution of Charles I, by the threat of army
disunity. More often than not, Cromwell managed to adjust himself to
the army's wishes when they reached their most formidable expression.
Yet he acted on his own initiative on 20 April, and the accounts of his
behaviour in the House suggest that by that stage he had passed far
beyond the realms of political calculation. The dissolution, as he told
the officers immediately after it, was unpremeditated, an act of spiritual
intoxication[2] – and, we may surely add, the resolution of a prolonged
and private spiritual drama. The compromise proposal he had advanced
on the evening of the 19th had been his final attempt before the dissolution to reconcile his competing concerns for godly reformation
and constitutional propriety. Once the compromise attempt had broken
down, he had to choose between the two. By the evening of the 19th
he was already entrenched in his opposition to presbyterians and neuters.
He had abandoned his long-held commitment to speedy elections; and
on the 20th he adopted the only course still available to him which
could prevent the Rump from providing for them. It was a course which
went directly against the grain of his constitutional scruples. Indeed, his
belief in the rule of law found its most ironic expression in his refusal to
dissolve the Rump by force until the very moment when it was about
to pass a decisive act of parliament; for he would have found any act of
parliament almost unbearable to disobey. Even then, it seems, it was
only by adopting the language and the histrionics of the Fifth Monarchists that he could steel himself to an action which, as his speeches show,
was to trouble his conscience for the rest of his life.[3]

[1] Above, p. 339; Woolrych, 'Calling of Barebone's Parliament', *passim*.
[2] Above, p. 356.
[3] See especially the tortured passage in the speech of April 1657: 'For give me leave, if
anybody now have the face to say, – and I would die upon this, – if any man in England
have the impudence or face to say, that the exceptions of the parliament to dissolve
themselves was their fear of hasty throwing of the liberties of the people of God, and of
the nation, into a bare representative of the people, – which was then the business we
opposed, – if any man have the face to say this now, who did then judge it, and I will
say more, ought then to have judged it, to be a confounding of the whole cause we had

Whatever view we take of Cromwell's relations with the saints, it was the saints who triumphed on 20 April 1653. According to White-locke, 'divers fierce men, pastors of churches, and their congregations' took immediate delight in the dissolution.[1] The 'major number' of the rumpers, claimed the gathered churches up and down the land, had been 'no better than a knot of persons in power, from whom most men were impatient of any good'. The Rump 'for the most part, had wearied God and man, and provoked the Almighty to depart from them'.[2] Yet the men who held power in the spring of 1653 were the men who had held power, with the sects' blessing, in 1649. There had in the interim been developments in Rump politics which may have diminished the regime's right to respect from the godly. But such developments were marginal; and by the spring of 1653 the Rump had become to the saints not marginally but wholly unacceptable. By and large the rumpers came from the same social spectrum, and held the same social convictions, as the other members of the Long Parliament. Like all parliamentarians of the early modern period they believed debate and disagreement in the Commons to be a central and natural part of the political process. It is when we see the alternative convictions of the saints that the charges levelled at the Rump of dilatoriness, division and corruption fall into place. There was, of course, a social dimension to the agitation of the sects, expressed in the demand that, in the choice of the assembly which was to succeed the Rump, 'godly prudent men, though of mean estates, may be looked to', and 'that not the eminency of their persons, but the excellency of their spirits may be looked at'.[3] More important, however, the saints judged the Rump by wholly apolitical criteria. This is well illustrated by a saddening letter written from Ire-land by John Jones to Harrison in August 1653, when disputes in Bare-

fought for, – which it was, – I would look upon that man's face! I would be glad to see such a man! I do not say there is any such here: but if any such should come to me, – see if I would not look upon him, and tell him he is an hypocrite! I dare say it, and I dare die for it, he is an hypocrite.' This tirade, apparently unprovoked and delivered four years after the event, succeeded only in emphasising the contradictions of the army's attitude to the bill for a new representative. (Carlyle, *Cromwell's Letters and Speeches*, iii. 336–7. The passage is an editor's nightmare: I prefer Carlyle's version to Abbott's.)
[1] Whitelocke, *Memorials*, iv. 6. I cannot, however, accept the argument of J. E. Farnell ('Usurpation of honest London householders'), who seems to regard the dissolution as a coup engineered by city Baptists. Farnell provides no evidence for his claim, and he is surely mistaken in regarding national politics as a mere extension of city politics. The same criticism is made in what seems to me an otherwise unconvincing article by Tai Liu, 'The calling of the Barebones Parliament reconsidered', *Journal of Ecclesiastical History*, xxii (1971).
[2] *Original Letters . . . addressed to Oliver Cromwell*, pp. 95, 114.   [3] *Ibid.* pp. 93, 95.

bone's were becoming intense. Jones had always been one of the more tolerant and less fanatical of the saints, and he had often been dismayed by their exclusiveness and want of charity;[1] but only during Barebone's did his moment of disillusionment arrive. In his words to Harrison, the members of Barebone's had been chosen 'upon the account of being more religious, more meek in spirit, and more self-denying than those that went before them'. Through their work Jones had hoped to see

occasions of divisions removed . . . by the sweet and pleasant stream, those rivers of pleasures, the powerful love of God in Christ to the saints begetting in their spirits an overflowing of perfect love towards one another . . . But dear friend it hath been declared unto us, to the exceeding great grief of some, that there are contentions and divisions among you; the choicest and most singularly elected parliament that ever was in England.

Jones was appalled by the thought that the saints might be quarrelling over 'those civil interests which divided counsels formerly'.[2] Even the elect, it seemed, were subject to the mortal failings, the 'contentions and divisions', which beset all political assemblies. For many of the saints, the realisation marked a sobering advance in self-knowledge.

When we understand Jones's perspective, we grasp too the roots of Cromwell's indignation at the difficulty, as he put it to Barebone's, of pushing any measure through the Rump 'without making parties, without practices indeed unworthy of a parliament'.[3] Making parties was, to rumpers, an essential part of politics, even if the term 'party' was one they tried to avoid. 'Perhaps you think this is not parliamentary language', Cromwell told the Rump during his outburst on the morning of 20 April.[4] Indeed it was not; it was the apolitical language of the saints. As a result of it, the bill for a new representative was consigned to oblivion, perhaps to the fire. Yet that bill, so much of which was incorporated into the *Instrument of Government*, embodied a large part of the programme which Cromwell had propounded since Worcester; and to this paradox events were to give an ironic twist. The first parliament for which the *Instrument* provided met in September 1654. Cromwell greeted it with his customary optimism: 'You are met here on the greatest occasion that, I believe, England ever saw.' Not for the first and not for the last time, his hopes of parliament were to be

[1] N.L.W., MS 11,440D, pp. 44–5, 131–2, 137–9; Mayer, 'Inedited letters', pp. 199–200, 209–10, 212–13, 213–14, 215, 235.
[2] *Ibid.* pp. 238–9.
[3] Abbott, *Writings and Speeches*, iii. 57.
[4] Above, p. 335.

dashed. Procedural obstruction prevailed, factions and 'parties' were 'made', and the military basis of Cromwell's authority was challenged. It was like the Rump all over again. Or was it? When Cromwell dissolved the first protectorate parliament he addressed it in terms which suggest that, in comparison, even the Rump might seem to have had its virtues:

> I will say this to you in behalf of the Long Parliament, that had such an expedient as [the *Instrument of Government*] been proposed to them, and that they could have seen the cause of God thus provided for, and had by debates been enlightened in the grounds by which the difficulties might have been cleared, and the reason of the whole enforced, the circumstances of time and persons, with the temper and disposition of the people, and affairs both abroad and at home when it was undertaken, well weighed (as well as they were thought to love their seats) I think in my conscience that they would have proceeded in another manner than you have done, and not have exposed things to those difficulties and hazards they are now at, nor given occasion to leave the people so dissettled as now they are . . .

'As well as they were thought to love their seats': the harder Cromwell tried to justify the dissolution of the Rump, the more his own words condemned him. When we remember how much the *Instrument* owed to the bill for a new representative, his tribute in this speech seems at best a grudging one. It was, nevertheless, a far cry from the attack on the drunkards and whoremasters of April 1653.[1]

In the traditional view of the Rump there is a hiatus. The rumpers, it has seemed, were energetically radical in 1649; yet by 1653 they had become intolerably oligarchical, dilatory and corrupt. Both the initial radicalism and the subsequent decadence of the regime have been exaggerated. The explanation of the Rump's demise lay less in any change in its character, which had been largely determined in infancy, than in the changing requirements Cromwell made of it. Cromwell, the destroyer of the Commonwealth regime, had also, more than anyone else, been its architect. The Rump was his conservative solution to the problems of 1648–9. Thereafter it never displayed the reforming idealism he demanded of it. The wonder is that he ever imagined that it would.

[1] Abbott, *Writings and Speeches*, iii. 434, 587. Cf. above, p. 371 n. 1.

APPENDICES

APPENDIX A

THE RUMPERS

The composition of the Rump's membership is discussed by Brunton and Pennington (*Members of the Long Parliament*, pp. 41–2), and there is little to add to their account. The list of rumpers which follows is almost, although not quite, identical with that to be found on pp. 226–45 of their book. No list of rumpers could be definitive. A number of contemporary lists of rumpers survive, some apparently reliable, others patently less so. The lists are mainly useful in confirming that the *Journal of the House of Commons* gives a fairly accurate picture of the Rump's membership (cf. below, p. 393). One of the contemporary lists of rumpers is an erratic document drawn up under parliament's auspices in May 1652 (perhaps as a result of the recruitment proposal mooted at that time). It contains six M.P.s whose names do not appear in the *Journal* for the Rump period. I agree with the implied view of Brunton and Pennington (*op. cit.* pp. 41, 245) that these men probably did not sit in the Rump. There might be a case for adding to my list of rumpers the name of Edmund Weaver (cf. Brunton and Pennington, *op. cit.* p. 244n.) or for subtracting that of John Trevor. Trevor appears only once in the *Journal* during the Rump period (*C.J.* 17 Dec. 1650, where the entry accurately reproduces the MS), and the circumstances of that entry suggest that the Clerk may have been in error.

It will be evident from this book that to describe an M.P. as a rumper is not, in itself, to tell us much about his political attitudes. The categories into which Professor Underdown divides the rumpers in *Pride's Purge* enable students of the secondary sources for the period to gain a clearer idea of the outlook of a particular M.P. than was previously possible. Here I provide another set of categories intended similarly to aid the student tracing the careers of individual M.P.s. The number beside each name in my list of rumpers is designed as a guide to the extent of the parliamentary activity of the member concerned (cf. chapter 1, above). I have devised a grading system whereby the most active members of the Rump are given six points, the least active members one point, and the other members appropriate scores in between. The breakdown is as follows:

> 6: 9 members
> 5: 23 members
> 4: 29 members

387

3 : 36 members
2 : 58 members
1 : 50 members

Six members are given a '?' instead of a number: these are men who were given permission to sit in the Rump but who may not have done so, at least after the dates of their admissions.

The points system I have devised is, it must be emphasised, the most rough-and-ready of guides. It is impossible to be more exact. The grading is based primarily on the record of each member's activity supplied by the *Journal of the House of Commons*, and to a lesser extent on the records of the Council of State and of the Rump's standing committees. All these sources are fallible guides. Measuring parliamentary activity (in which I include activity on the council and on standing committees) is of necessity a largely unscientific and speculative exercise, whose accuracy and worth partly depend, as so often, on whether the historian has the feel of the available evidence. (One particular problem is to know how much weight to attach to the composition of *ad hoc* parliamentary committees. It is likely that in many cases a high proportion of those appointed to such committees failed to attend them: indeed, when the matter committed was a relatively trivial one, the House sometimes tended to appoint a large number of members to the committee, presumably in the hope that if enough members were appointed a few might actually attend. But committee lists do have their uses, not least – as we shall see – in giving us an idea of the composition of the Rump's active membership during particular periods; and I have normally assumed that members who were frequently appointed to committees took a more active part in the House's affairs than those who did not – a rule to which there were, no doubt, individual exceptions.)

Members given the number 1 in the list below made very few recorded appearances in parliament during the Rump period. Members given the number 2 were present slightly more often, but still only rarely. Members given the number 3 were a little more active, and members given the number 4 were in general present as often as not. Members given the numbers 5 and 6 were almost full-time politicians, rarely away from Westminster unless on government business. The dividing lines between the categories are, of course, wholly artificial. The boundary between 2 and 3 is often hazy, and that between 3 and 4 still more so. And there are two complicating problems. The first is that on numerous occasions the *Journal*, like other sources, gives only the surname of a member whose namesake also sat in the Rump, so that it is not always clear which member is meant. (This difficulty also presents itself in the use of committee lists to establish attendance figures over a particular period: it is sometimes impossible to know whether one or both members with the same surname were present during the period concerned.) The second problem is that various rumpers were often away from the House on military, naval, diplomatic or other government business. Other members died, or were expelled from the

House, during the Rump period. I have assumed that members who for any of these reasons were involuntarily absent from Westminster for extended periods, and who were energetic M.P.s when they were at Westminster, would have been similarly energetic throughout the Rump period had they had the opportunity. Finally, it should be stressed that the gradations I have used refer to the activity, and not to the influence, of the members concerned. The two things were not necessarily equal.

I have also used the following symbols:

d: known to have died during the Rump period
e: expelled from the Rump
w: signed Charles I's death warrant.

RUMPERS ELECTED TO THE LONG PARLIAMENT BEFORE PRIDE'S PURGE

Aldworth, Richard	2	Chaloner, Thomas	5 *w*
Allanson, Sir William	3	Clement, Gregory	3 *ew*
Allen, Francis	6	Constable, Sir William	2 *w*
Alured, John	1 *dw*	Corbet, John	4
Andrews, Robert	1	Corbet, Miles	5 *w*
Anlaby, John	2	Crompton, Thomas	1
Apsley, Edward	1 *d*	Cromwell, Oliver	4 *w*
Armyne, Sir William	4 *d*	Danvers, Sir John	5 *w*
Armyne, William	1	Darley, Henry	3
Arthington, Henry	1	Darley, Richard	4
Ashe, Edward	3	Dixwell, John	2 *w*
Ashe, James	2	Dormer, John	3
Ashe, John	4	Dove, John	4
Atkins, Thomas	3	Downes, John	5 *w*
Bacon, Francis	?	Dryden, Sir John	?
Bacon, Nathaniel	1	Dunch, Edmund	1
Baker, John	1	Earle, Erasmus	1
Barker, John	1	Edwards, Humphrey	5 *w*
Baynton, Sir Edward	1	Edwards, Richard	1
Bingham, John	1	Ellis, William	2
Blagrave, Daniel	4 *w*	Eyre, William	1
Blake, Robert	1	Fagge, John	1
Blakiston, John	5 *dw*	Feilder, John	5
Bond, Denis	5	Fell, Thomas	2
Boone, Thomas	3	Fenwick, George	2
Bosvile, Godfrey	4	Fleetwood, Charles	3
Bourchier, Sir John	4 *w*	Fleetwood, George	1 *w*
Brereton, Sir William	4	Fry, John	2 *e*
Brewster, Robert	1	Gardiner, Samuel	1
Brooke, Peter	1	Garland, Augustine	6 *w*
Browne, John	2	Goodwin, John	4
Burrell, Abraham	2	Goodwin, Robert	4
Carent, William	?	Gould, Nicholas	2
Carew, John	4 *w*	Gratwick, Roger	2
Cawley, William	3 *w*	Grey, Thomas Lord	5 *w*
Chaloner, James	3	Gurdon, Brampton	1

Appendix A

Gurdon, John	5	Norton, Sir Gregory	2 *dw*
Hallowes, Nathaniel	3	Norton, Richard	2
Harby, Edward	1	Nutt, John	2
Harrington, Sir James	5	Oldsworth, Michael	3
Harrison, Thomas	5 *w*	Palmer, John	2
Harvey, Edmund	3	Pelham, Peregrine	2 *dw*
Hay, William	2	Pennington, Isaac	3
Herbert, Henry	2	Pickering, Sir Gilbert	4
Herbert, Philip Lord	2	Pierrepoint, Francis	2
Heselrige, Sir Arthur	6	Piggot, Gervase	1
Heveningham, William	3	Popham, Alexander	2
Heyman, Sir Henry	2	Popham, Edward	1 *d*
Hill, Roger	4	Prideaux, Edmund	5
Hippisley, Sir John	3	Purefoy, William	5 *w*
Hodges, Luke	3	Pury, Thomas, sr.	3
Hodges, Thomas	1	Pury, Thomas, jr.	1
Holland, Cornelius	5	Pyne, John	2
Hoyle, Thomas	2 *d*	Reynolds, Robert	4
Hussey, Thomas	2	Rigby, Alexander	4 *d*
Hutchinson, John	2 *w*	Robinson, Luke	3
Ingoldsby, Richard	2 *w*	Rogers, Hugh	?
Ireton, Henry	5 *dw*	Rous, Francis	2
Jervoise, Sir Thomas	2	Russell, Francis	1
Jones, John	5 *w*	St John, Oliver	2
Lascelles, Francis	2	Salwey, Humphrey	3 *d*
Leman, William	4	Salwey, Richard	6
Lenthall, John	2	Say, William	5 *w*
Lenthall, William (Speaker)	6	Scot, Thomas	6 *w*
Lisle, John	5	Searle, George	1
Lister, Thomas	4	Sidney, Algernon	3
Livesy, Sir Michael	3 *w*	Sidney, Philip (Lord Lisle)	3
Long, Lislibone	3	Skinner, Augustine	2
Love, Nicholas	4	Skippon, Philip	4
Lowry, John	1	Smith, Philip	1
Lucy, Sir Richard	2	Smyth, Henry	2 *w*
Ludlow, Edmund	3 *w*	Snelling, George	2 *d*
Mackworth, Thomas	1	Stapley, Anthony	2 *w*
Marten, Henry	6 *w*	Stephens, John	1
Martyn, Christopher	2	Stephens, William	3
Masham, Sir William	5	Stockdale, Thomas	1
Masham, William	2	Strickland, Walter	3
Mauleverer, Sir Thomas	1 *w*	Strickland, Sir William	3
Mayne, Simon	1 *w*	Temple, James	2 *w*
Mildmay, Sir Henry	6	Temple, Sir Peter	1
Millington, Gilbert	4 *w*	Temple, Peter	2 *w*
Moore, John	1 *dw*	Thomson, George	5
Monson, William Lord	3	Thorpe, Francis	2
Morley, Herbert	4	Toll, Thomas	1
Moyle, John	3	Trenchard, John	4
Nelthorpe, James	2	Trevor, Sir John	3
Neville, Edward	?	Trevor, John	1
Nicholas, Robert	1	Valentine, Benjamin	1 *d*
North, Sir Roger	1 *d*	Vane, Sir Henry, sr.	2

Vane, Sir Henry, jr.	6	Whitaker, Lawrence	3
Venn, John	5 *dw*	White, William	1
Wallop, Robert	2	Whitelocke, Bulstrode	5
Walsingham, Sir Thomas	1	Widdrington, Sir Thomas	3
Wastell, John	1	Wilson, Rowland	4 *d*
Waite, Thomas	2 *w*	Wodehouse, Sir Thomas	1
Walton, Valentine	4 *w*	Wogan, Thomas	1 *w*
Weaver, John	4	Wroth, Sir Thomas	2
Wentworth, Sir Peter	4	Wylde, Edmund	1
West, Edmund	2	Wylde, George	1 *d*
Weston, Benjamin	2	Wylde, John	2
Westrow, Thomas	2		

RUMPERS ELECTED (OR HAVING THEIR ELECTIONS CONFIRMED) ONLY
AFTER THE PURGE

Bennett, Robert	3	Rich, Nathaniel 3
Birch, Thomas	2	————
Fairfax, Thomas	?	William Cecil, Earl of Salisbury 2
Jones, Philip	2	Philip Herbert (fourth) Earl of Pembroke
Neville, Henry	3	2 *d*
Raleigh, Carew	4	Edward, Lord Howard of Escrick 2 *e*

THE PURGED MEMBERS

The Rump's enemies often claimed, especially in retrospect, that at Pride's Purge the army forcibly denied entry to as many as two hundred members, and perhaps to even more. Yet if we consult the accounts drawn up at the time – most of them in newspapers, and most of them hostile to the army – it becomes clear that the number (including the forty-five members who were imprisoned) cannot have been higher than about one hundred and ten. Other members were doubtless – in Clement Walker's words – 'frighted away', but there were many others who stayed away of their own volition: some of the army's supporters, indeed, were angered by the behaviour of M.P.s who 'would not attend the House when they might'. (Walker, *History of Independency*, ii. 31, 46, 81; N.L.W., MS 11,434B, fo. 3.) I am thus wary of Professor Underdown's category, in *Pride's Purge*, of 'secluded' members, which contains one hundred and eighty-six members (a figure which does not include the imprisoned members). Their names are derived from two lists of purged members drawn up between the purge and the king's execution. One of them is patently unreliable: Underdown acknowledges its failings but still makes extensive use of it. The other list is Prynne's, which contains a suspiciously high proportion of members whose names do not appear in the *Journal of the House of Commons* at any time during the autumn of 1648. Even if Prynne's list is accurate, it is still much smaller than Underdown's category. It seems to me that (apart from those of the imprisoned members) we know the names of only about twenty of the members turned away by the army. Thus the overwhelming majority of Underdown's 'secluded' members might equally well appear, I believe, in his 'abstaining' category. And if the categories are suspect, then so may be the conclusions Underdown derives from them. This difficulty is related to the more general one confronting those examining Underdown's categories: that some of them consist of men who belong to them as a result of choices they made for themselves, and the others of men who belong to them as a result of choices which the army made for them. Given the state of the available evidence, such problems of classification are inevitable and probably insoluble.

Underdown – unlike Brunton and Pennington, *Members of the Long Parliament*, pp. 42–3 – wisely ignores the lists of secluded members drawn up in 1659 and 1660, when all members who had ceased to sit at the purge, whether by compulsion or by choice, were regarded as secluded: see Prynne, *A Full Declaration*, pp. 29–30.

ATTENDANCES

Attendance patterns in the Rump are very hard to gauge. The obvious evidence to use consists of the voting figures at divisions of the House. (These figures do not include the four members who acted as tellers on each occasion; nor, of course, do they include the Speaker. But they probably do include all other members present, since – at least in theory – members were not allowed to abstain.)[1] Voting figures are often useful, especially for periods when the House divided frequently, but they do not tell the whole story. They give the numbers present at particular times on particular days: they are not necessarily reliable as guides to attendance patterns over particular periods.

The evidence of voting figures needs to be combined with that supplied by the names of members referred to in the *Journal of the House of Commons* over particular periods. Such names appear most often in the lists of committees appointed by the House. Committee lists, unlike voting figures, give an indication not only how many members were present but which members were present. Yet the lists raise two problems. First, can we assume that a member appointed to a committee was in the House at the time of his appointment? Secondly, can we assume that a member present during a particular period was likely to be appointed to a committee, and so have his name recorded in the *Journal*, in that time?

It was a rule of the House that members could be named to committees only if they were present (cf. below, p. 400). We know that the rule was sometimes broken: the question is how often. We can gain a fairly clear idea, from sources other than the *Journal*, of the whereabouts of certain M.P.s for most of the Rump period, and such evidence suggests that it must have been extremely rare for members to be named to a committee when they were not present at, or at

[1] Snow, 'Attendance trends and absenteeism', p. 303.

least about, the time of the committee's appointment. I have detected very few exceptions to this rule, and the exceptions fall into a pattern. Augustine Garland was appointed to a committee on 12 April 1649, when he was not present in the House. This, however, was evidently regarded as an exceptional case; so was the appointment of Whitelocke and Widdrington to a committee in December 1648 when neither was in the House. It was because these cases were regarded as exceptional, indeed, that we know about them. There were three occasions in 1649, too, when Whitelocke was appointed to a committee when he was probably absent, but in each case there were special reasons for his appointment. Vane the younger was appointed to a committee in January 1649, and claimed afterwards to have been absent at the time, but there are strong grounds for believing that he was lying; he certainly had good cause to do so.[1]

Whitelocke, Widdrington and Garland were all lawyers, and it is possible that it was only in the case of lawyers, who were in great demand on committees, that exceptions were allowed. There was of course little point in appointing men to committees, most of which were appointed for short-term purposes, unless they were likely to be able to attend them. In general, then, the evidence confirms what common sense might suggest.

More difficult is the question whether members active in the House over particular periods are likely to have been named to committees during those periods. In the Rump's earlier stages the House appointed committees with remarkable frequency and evidently sought to employ as many members on them as possible.[2] The number of members appointed to committees during each of the earlier months of the Rump period was usually much higher than the average attendance during the same months at divisions of the House. It is thus likely that, in the Rump's earlier stages, the *Journal* supplies the names of all members who made more than the most fleeting appearances. For later periods, the problem is more complicated. Although committees tended to become larger, they were appointed much less often. Indeed, in the case of fifteen individual months (ten of them after Worcester), the number of members appointed to committees was smaller than the number present at the best attended division. We clearly do not have the names of all members present in those months.

In general, then, appreciably more members attended the House over particular periods than attended the average division. In every year except 1652, the number attending over particular periods was also significantly higher than the number present at the best-attended divisions. It may well be, however, that committee lists and division figures both give too gloomy a picture of attendances after 1649. Especially towards the end of

---

[1] *C.J.* 7 Mar., 12 Apr., 21 Dec. 1649; Clarendon MS 34, fo. 17; Underdown, *Pride's Purge*, pp. 197n., 211n.; B.M., Add. MS. 37,344, fos. 268ᵛ–9ᵛ, and Add. MS 37,345, fos. 33ᵛ–4.

[2] Some of the most important committees, which tended to be small and over whose composition there were evidently occasional conflicts, were exceptions.

Appendix A

Monthly averages

	1649	1650	1651	1652	1653 (Jan.–Apr.)
Named in *Journal* (committees, etc.)	87	81	72	69	68
Present at divisions (incl. tellers but not Speaker)	53	56	57	56	49
Present at best-attended division (incl. tellers but not Speaker)	70	64	67	71	56

the Rump period, there are frequent examples of members attending standing committees but not being recorded as present in the House. Of course, they may not have attended the House, but even if they did not, the number of members active in parliamentary affairs is still more impressive than the *Journal* suggests. There is, unfortunately, no way of knowing whether or not attendances in the House declined as the Rump period wore on. The monthly average of members present at divisions remains reasonably consistent throughout the Rump period, and the fall in the number of names in the *Journal* is, as we have seen, related to the decline in the number of committees appointed. It therefore seems unlikely that there was a marked decline in attendances. Yet it is true of almost every month in the Rump period that any member who was pulling his weight in the House was likely to find his way, in some capacity, into the *Journal*. We probably know the names of all the more energetic members present during most periods; but members who attended only rarely were much more likely to find their way into the *Journal* in the earlier Rump period than they were later on.

One of the most striking features to emerge from a study of the Rump's membership is the degree of fluctuation in the size and in the composition of the House's active membership, both over short periods and over long ones.

ELECTORAL REFORM

(cf. above, chapter 8)

TABLE I

KEY

Column 1   The representation of each county (both county and borough
(1640)   seats) at the beginning of the Long Parliament. The figures in
            parentheses are designed, as are the figures in parentheses in
            columns 2 and 3, to facilitate comparison between the various
            columns. As there were 507 seats in 1640, and as both Rump
            schemes provided for only 400 members, I have multiplied the
            representation of each county (and each region) in 1640 by $\frac{4}{5}$,
            and placed the resulting figures in parentheses.

Column 2   The representation awarded to each county by the Leveller
(Lev 48)   scheme. That scheme provided for only 300 members, so I have
            multiplied each figure by $\frac{4}{3}$, and placed the resulting figures in
            parentheses.

Column 3   The representation awarded to each county by the officers'
(Offs 49)   scheme. As the officers made provision for only 351 seats, I have
            multiplied each figure by $\frac{8}{7}$, and placed the resulting figures in
            parentheses.

Column 4   The number of seats to which each county was entitled on the
(Assess 49) basis of its share of the assessment tax imposed in 1649.

Column 5   The representation awarded to each county by the 1650 scheme.
(Rump 50)

Column 6   The number of M.P.s for each county entitled to sit in the Rump
(Rumpers)   at the times – January 1650 and March 1653 – when the two

Rump schemes were brought into the House. (Thus in the latter figures I have included those members admitted after January 1650 and omitted those known to have died or to have been expelled between January 1650 and March 1653.)

Column 7
(1653)

The representation awarded to each county by the 1653 scheme, i.e. that contained in both the bill for a new representative and the *Instrument of Government*.

For the convenience of the reader who wishes to investigate the redistribution schemes further, I have listed the various counties under the regional headings adopted in Snow, 'Parliamentary reapportionment Proposals'.

	1640	Lev 48	Offs 49	Assess 49	Rump 50†	Rumpers 50	Rumpers 53	1653
SOUTH WEST								
Cornwall	44(35)	6(8)	8(9)	9	10	9	8	12
Devon	26(21)	14(19)	17(19)	18	20	4	5	20
Dorset	20(16)	6(8)	8(9)	8	8	9	8	10
Somerset*	18(14)	11(14)	12(14)	16	14	11	11	18
Wiltshire	34(27)	8(11)	8(9)	11	13	16	15	14
	142(114)	45(60)	53(60)	62	65	49	47	74
SOUTH EAST								
Hampshire	26(21)	7(9)	10(11)	12	13	9	10	14
Surrey	14(11)	7(9)	7(8)	10	7	5	4	10
Sussex	20(16)	7(9)	9(10)	11	14	9	7	13
Kent	10(8)	12(16)	13(15)	21	18	5	5	16
Cinque Ports	16(13)	—	3(3)	—	—	6	7	3
	86(69)	33(44)	42(48)	54	52	34	33	56
EAST								
Cambridgeshire	6(5)	6(8)	8(9)	8	8	4	4	8
Essex	8(6)	11(14)	13(15)	20	14	2	2	16
Hertfordshire	6(5)	8(11)	6(7)	8	6	1	1	7
Huntingdonshire	4(3)	3(4)	3(3)	4	4	2	2	4
Lincolnshire	12(10)	11(14)	13(15)	16	15	4	3	16
Middlesex	8(6)	16(21)	14(16)	37	13	2	2	12
Norfolk	12(10)	11(14)	14(16)	16	14	4	3	16
Suffolk	16(13)	11(14)	13(15)	21	16	5	5	16
	72(58)	77(103)	84(96)	130	90	24	22	95
MIDLANDS								
Bedfordshire	4(3)	5(7)	4(5)	5	6	0	0	6
Berkshire	9(7)	7(9)	6(7)	6	6	6	5	7
Buckinghamshire	14(11)	8(11)	6(7)	7	9	9	9	8
Derbyshire	4(3)	6(8)	6(7)	5	5	1	1	5

	1640	Lev 48	Offs 49	Assess 49	Rump 50†	Rumpers 50	Rumpers 53	1653
MIDLANDS								
Leicestershire	4(3)	6(8)	6(7)	6	6	4	4	6
Northamptonshire	9(7)	6(8)	6(7)	8	8	2	3	8
Nottinghamshire	6(5)	5(7)	5(6)	5	6	5	5	6
Oxfordshire	9(7)	6(8)	8(9)	6	6	1	1	8
Rutland	2(2)	2(3)	1(1)	2	2	2	2	2
Warwickshire	6(5)	6(8)	7(8)	7	7	3	3	7
	67(54)	57(76)	55(63)	57	61	33	33	63
WEST								
Cheshire	4(3)	6(8)	7(8)	5	5	1	1	5
Gloucestershire*	8(6)	8(11)	9(10)	10	8	6	7	9
Herefordshire	8(6)	5(7)	5(6)	7	6	1	1	6
Monmouthshire	3(2)	3(4)	4(5)	3	3	2	2	3
Shropshire	12(10)	6(8)	7(8)	8	8	4	4	8
Staffordshire	10(8)	5(7)	6(7)	5	6	2	2	6
Worcestershire	9(7)	6(8)	6(7)	7	7	6	4	7
	54(43)	39(52)	44(50)	45	43	22	21	44
NORTH								
Cumberland	6(5)	2(3)	3(3)	1	4	4	3	3
Durham	—	3(4)	4(5)	1	4	—	—	3
Lancashire	14(11)	7(9)	7(8)	5	12	5	3	8
Northumberland	8(6)	4(5)	6(7)	1	8	2	2	5
Westmorland	4(3)	2(3)	2(2)	1	3	2	1	2
Yorkshire	30(24)	16(21)	20(23)	18	24	22	19	22
	62(50)	34(45)	42(48)	27	55	35	28	43
WALES	24(19)	16(21)	31(35)	20	20	4	5	26

* Snow puts Bristol under Gloucestershire: I follow the reapportionment schemes, which place it in Somerset.
† Although the 1650 scheme envisaged 400 seats, it made specific provision for only 386.

TABLE 2 *Proportion of County to Borough Representation*

	1640	Levellers 1648	Officers 1649	1653
Borough seats	413	41	72	131
University seats	4	2	4	2
County seats	90	257	275	267
Percentage of borough (with university) seats	82	14	20	33

APPENDIX C

A NOTE ON SOURCES

At various points in this book I have drawn attention to the limitations of the evidence available to the student of Rump politics. In seeking to make use of that evidence, I have found myself applying techniques of investigation some of which do not seem to have been previously adopted. They do not represent any seminal methodological breakthrough: they would, I think, suggest themselves to anyone confined by the same material. But they could perhaps be used to advantage in studies of other periods of parliamentary history. The specialist reader will want to know something of them if he is to trust certain of the references given in my footnotes to supporting evidence. Other readers may also, I hope, find interest in the observations which follow.

The chief difficulty in studying Rump politics is not the amount of available evidence but its nature. There is plenty of institutional, formal evidence. What is in short supply, at least by comparison with the evidence for the earlier years of the Long Parliament, is a fund of informal material – of diaries, letters and memoirs – to give flesh and blood to the dry bones of institutional records, to tell us not only what men did but why they did it. It is interesting to speculate on the reasons for this relative dearth. The fashion for compiling parliamentary diaries, prevalent in the earlier 1640s, seems to have died out well before the Rump period. Many politicians who have bequeathed private papers were excluded from power, and hence from an intimate knowledge of political developments, after Pride's Purge. Much evidence was destroyed, for fear of reprisals, at the Restoration of Charles II in 1660. Even so, far more evidence survives for the later 1650s than for the Rump period, although even here the chance survival of a mere two parliamentary diaries, and the still more fortuitous preservation of the invaluable *Thurloe State Papers*,[1] remind us how much difference even a small number of individual sources can make. The Rump, of course, included a much higher proportion than did other Interregnum parliaments of men who had been implicated in Charles I's execution, and who are therefore likely to have destroyed incriminating evidence. Perhaps, too, the dissolution of the Rump in 1653, when army reprisals against individual members were confidently predicted, helps to explain the shortage of informal material for the Rump period. Whatever the explanation, the consequences for

[1] W. C. Abbott, *A Bibliography of Oliver Cromwell* (Cambridge, Mass., 1929), p. xvi.

the Rump's historian are clear: he must reconcile himself, for most of the time, to forgoing the pleasures of reading other people's letters, and concentrate his attention on the institutional evidence, especially that furnished by parliament, by its committees and by the Council of State. If the task sometimes resembles an attempt to draw blood from a stone, it is frequently rewarded by surprising and substantial gains.

The order books of the Council of State, preserved in the Public Record Office and efficiently (if not always comprehensively) summarised in the printed *Calendar of State Papers Domestic*, provide an almost uninterrupted record of its decisions. They also give the names of members who attended its meetings and to whom particular tasks were entrusted. Like the surviving records of some of the Rump's and of the council's standing committees, however, the order books are in general more useful to the student of administrative achievement than of political conflict.

The *Journal of the House of Commons* is more forthcoming. The famous eighteenth-century printed version is an accurate reproduction of a contemporary fair copy which survives in the House of Lords Record Office. It is not, however, quite complete. At various times, but especially in 1660, the Commons ordered that certain of the entries for the Rump period be deleted from the *Journal*. The passages accordingly deleted do not appear in the printed version. Some of them, however, had already been copied by Clement Walker and William Prynne, and survive in their printed works.[1] Of the others, not all were deleted as effectively as they might have been, and it is possible, and often fruitful, to read some of them through the scores on the fair-copy. This exercise, however, in general adds only marginally to the bulk of information which can be derived from a thorough examination of the printed *Journal*.

Seventeenth-century historians have recently been rebuked, by the most rigorous historian of the sixteenth, for their primitive approach to parliamentary records and for their ignorance of the rudiments of parliamentary procedure.[2] There is much justice in the charge, but the failings are almost as hard to remedy as to deny. Contemporary manuals of parliamentary procedure often tell us what ought to have happened rather than what did happen, and there is little evidence with which to supplement them. This is especially true of the Rump period, which is in many ways so atypical a phase of parliamentary history: the abolition of kingship and the House of Lords led to a number of procedural adjustments whose details are hard to unravel. Yet there are aspects of the procedure of all seventeenth-century parliaments about which we are ignorant. Little is known of the manner in which the House of Commons organised its daily business or compiled its records. It is, however, possible to make some sense of the two aspects of the *Journal* which most help us to understand the political attitudes and behaviour of M.P.s.

[1] E.g. Walker, *History of Independency*, ii. 48–9; Prynne, *A Full Declaration*, pp. 20–4.
[2] G. R. Elton, 'Studying the history of Parliament', *The British Studies Monitor*, ii (1971).

First, there are the names of the tellers for and against the motions on which the House divided. Professor Hexter made extensive use of the names of tellers in his doctoral thesis and in his *Reign of King Pym*. They are equally useful to a student of the Rump period. It is clear that the tellers were chosen by the Speaker from the supporters and opponents respectively of the motions concerned:[1] it is unfortunately not always clear what was at stake in a particular motion. In any case, the motives which impel one man to vote one way on a single issue may be incalculably various. He may act from deeply held conviction; he may be influenced by the decision of his friend *A*, his cousin *B*, or that sound-thinking man *C* to support one side, or of the tiresome and wrongheaded *D* to support the other; or he may simply want to end the debate as soon as possible and eat his dinner. There were more than 350 divisions in the Rump period, yet only a minority of them can be trusted to tell us anything helpful about Rump politics.[2] Only when a consistent pattern emerges, or when the names of tellers can be related to knowledge derived from other sources, are those names reliable guides to M.P.s' opinions or allegiances.

Secondly, there are the lists in the *Journal* of the members of committees appointed by the Rump. Some were standing committees, but most were set up either for the drafting or amendment of particular legislation or for other *ad hoc* purposes. Little can be learned of the manner in which parliamentary committees were appointed. In theory, each M.P. present in the House could name two other members to a committee, provided his nominees were also present and provided they were not opposed in principle to, nor had any private interest in, the measure which was to be committed. The Clerk noted down as best he could the names of committee members as they were appointed.[3] In practice, the procedure was evidently haphazard. M.P.s sitting far away from the Clerk sometimes failed to secure their nominations,[4] while other members occasionally appeared twice on the same committee list or were even added to a committee to which they already belonged; and as a number of committees were open to all members whether or not they had been appointed to them, their true membership is not easy to determine.

We do not know how the order of names on committee lists was determined. What we can see, from a close scrutiny of the lists, is that a number of pairs and groups of names are repeatedly to be found bunched closely together; and an awareness of this tendency can provide a number of insights into Rump

[1] Coates, *Journal of Sir Simonds D'Ewes*, pp. 120, 130, 152, 275; Scobell, *Memorials of the Method and Manner . . . of Passing Bills*, p. 26. Comparison between the *Journal* and informal evidence confirms the point.

[2] There are, in any case, signs that the Clerk may on occasion have got the names of tellers (and of members of parliamentary committees) wrong.

[3] D. H. Willson, *Privy Councillors in the English House of Commons 1604–1629* (Minneapolis, 1940), pp. 238–9. See also Notestein, *Journal of Sir Simonds D'Ewes*, p. 214; Scobell, *Memorials . . .*, pp. 46–7.

[4] Willson, *Privy Councillors*, p. 240; Notestein, *Journal of Sir Simonds D'Ewes*, p. 163.

politics. The persistence of such pairings and groupings, far outstripping the claims of chance or coincidence, leads to the firm conclusion that the members concerned were regularly naming each other, or being named together, to committees. The phenomenon becomes especially interesting when familiar groups of names appear near the head of a committee list or include the member or members given special responsibility for the workings of the committee concerned.[1] If there were any cause for doubting the significance of the groupings, it would be dispelled by the frequency with which allegiances reflected in committee lists are confirmed by other, usually informal, evidence. Committee lists, like the names of tellers, tend indeed to be especially helpful only when they can be related to other evidence, for while repeated groups of names make it clear that members were cooperating, they do not in themselves make clear the purpose of their cooperation. It is of course by no means certain that all the alliances at work in the House were reflected in committee lists. Those lists, nevertheless, are our most informative guide to the nature, timing and extent of parliamentary allegiances. Once the groupings have been identified, we can learn more about them from the records of standing committees, where groups of allies tended to congregate, and of the Council of State. Allies tended to arrive together at council meetings (as can often be seen from the council's order books, although not from the printed *Calendar*), and to be appointed together to the small council sub-committees.

Although the use of institutional evidence to detect parliamentary allegiances can be wearisome, it is not particularly difficult. Nor is it hard to comb the *Journal* for references to particular subjects. It is much more difficult to get the feel of the day-to-day activity of the House and to sense its changing moods and conflicts. This is the main challenge facing any historian using the *Journal* as his main source. The task is not, I believe, impossible, but no one could write the parliamentary history of the Rump period from the *Journal* (and the other institutional evidence) alone. Where else can the student of Rump politics turn?

Private correspondence, although often quite invaluable, usually exists only in snatches. Royalists and diplomats, sending newsletters to their masters on the continent, were rarely well informed. We might be able to learn more about Rump politics if the manuscripts of the *Milton State Papers* ever came to light: the printed version, a very useful source, is professedly only a selection. The memoirs of Edmund Ludlow, whose career in the Rump ended with his departure to Ireland in December 1650, are disappointingly unforthcoming on the intricacies of parliamentary politics; so, still more, is Lucy Hutchinson's biography of her husband, who rarely, if ever, sat in the Rump after May 1651. Whitelocke's manuscript Annals (in the British Museum) are a dull compendium culled largely, as he often admitted, from the newspapers, but sometimes illuminated by personal narrative and comment, much of it omitted from the

---

[1] It is clear both that members named near the top of a committee list were often closely involved in the matter committed, and that they were by no means always so.

printed versions.[1] The Clarke MSS at Oxford, and the Plas Yolyn MSS at Aberystwyth, are also more revealing than the extracts which have been printed might suggest. There is a considerable amount of retrospective evidence from the later 1650s and from the Restoration, much of it useful but much of it impaired, like the memoirs of rumpers, by hindsight, wishful thinking, distortions of memory and the desire for self-exculpation or self-justification.

More valuable, and indeed with the *Journal of the House of Commons* our major source, is the massive corpus of tracts and pamphlets of the period, most of them collected at the time by George Thomason and preserved in the British Museum,[2] and many of them providing more political information – as opposed to mere political polemic – than we might expect. Above all there are the weekly newspapers, which afford opportunities to the historian which have barely been appreciated. The newspapers which attacked Pride's Purge and the king's execution found themselves thereafter gradually more isolated from useful sources of information, and although two of them, *Mercurius Elencticus* and *Mercurius Pragmaticus*, continued to embarrass the government well into 1650, they were a mere shadow of their former informative selves. More valuable are the newspapers founded or taken over by men supported and encouraged by the new regime. There is no point in pretending that they make stimulating reading. Their authors, severely handicapped by the secrecy in which the government shrouded so much of its activity and by the sycophantic posture which was the price of such information as they did acquire, concentrated primarily on events in Ireland and Scotland and on the continent. Thomas Scot, writing afterwards of the intelligence system which he had created during the Rump period, recalled that 'my correspondents did little but inform common news from Sweden, Poland and Muscovia and fit to help to fill the Gazettes'.[3] He was probably thinking particularly of *A Brief Relation*, the dreariest of all the Rump's newspapers, with which he clearly had direct links[4] and which announced in its second issue that 'to have no news is good news; it is a symptom of a placid and quiet state of affairs'.[5] Thereafter it subjected its readers to a tedious weekly narrative of events abroad, interrupted only by rare and similarly dampening editorial comment. Newspapers more attentive to events in England were for the most part equally reluctant to spice their chronicles with

---

1 Carlyle (*Cromwell's Letters and Speeches*, ii. 360) aptly observed that Whitelocke's *Memorials* display 'a kind of dramaturgical turn . . . indeed an occasional poetic friskiness; most unexpected, as if the hippopotamus should shew a tendency to dance'.

2 See G. Fortescue (ed.), *Catalogue of the Pamphlets, Newspapers, and Manuscripts relating to the Civil War, the Commonwealth, and Restoration, collected by George Thomason* (2 vols., 1908).

3 Firth, 'Thomas Scot's Account', p. 122; with which cf. B.M., Stowe MS 185, fo. 182.

4 See my doctoral dissertation, p. 11n.

5 Joseph Frank, *The Beginnings of the English Newspaper* (Cambridge, Mass., 1961), pp. 200–1. Frank makes many valuable comments on Rump newspapers, and I have drawn on his observations here; but he does not always appreciate the full political significance of the material.

revealing comment. The aim of *The Weekly Intelligencer*, its editor virtuously avowed, was to provide 'matter of intelligence, and not to declare my judgement'.[1]

Nevertheless, as both Rump and army politicians quickly learned, the press provided a convenient vehicle for the discreet dissemination of political views, and there is plenty of evidence to suggest close cooperation between politicians and journalists, each newspaper cultivating its special contacts. Newspapers sometimes acknowledged the source of an anonymous M.P. or Councillor of State, and in July 1650 *The Weekly Intelligencer* announced in its first edition that 'the parliament this day sat not, and thereupon letters directed from several places to several members could not so easily be acquired'.[2] Although we are rarely able to identify the politicians involved, there were two periods in the Rump's history when journalists were prepared to insert occasional comment evidently representative of the views of a particular group of M.P.s, and when we can learn from the press something of the tensions and rival policies in the House.

First, there were the months from February to September 1649, when a number of newspapers were allowed to flourish which sometimes presented differing versions of events. It is indicative of the Rump's character that the four pro-government newspapers of these months whose bias is most distinctive, *A Modest Narrative*, *A Perfect Summary*, John Dillingham's *The Moderate Intelligencer* (known to royalists as a 'presbyterian' paper[3]) and, above all, Henry Walker's *Perfect Occurrences* (the parliament's official mouthpiece), all showed scant sympathy for the purge and the execution and advertised moderating tendencies within the new regime. These newspapers were all suppressed, however, after the censorship act of September 1649, to be replaced by news-sheets still more uncontroversial and still more closely controlled by the regime. As a royalist observed in January 1650, the government newspapers had 'grown so dull of late, and [do] so timorously . . . intermeddle with the public concernments of the infant Commonwealth, that they hardly deserve the expense of so much time as to read them'.[4] A further batch of government newspapers was founded in the summer and autumn of 1650, but for some months *Mercurius Politicus* was the only one of them prepared openly to advocate a partisan line. Others began to follow its lead in the summer of 1651, but it was only in the spring of 1652 that the second period of relative independence in the press began. As the army's criticisms of the Rump became more overt, so newspapers sympathetic to the army began to incite their readers to social radicalism and to hostility to parliament. Unfortunately for the historian none of the Rump's newspapers was equally provocative, but *Several Proceedings in Parliament*,

---

[1] *Weekly Intelligencer* 23–30 Mar. 1652, p. 399.
[2] *Ibid.* 16–23 July 1650, p. 7. For fuller documentation on this and related points, see the introduction to my doctoral dissertation, and the sources cited there at p. 82, n. 2.
[3] *Mercurius Elencticus* 15–22 Oct. 1649, p. 194. Dillingham was a client of St John.
[4] B.M., Loan MS 331, fo. 23ᵛ: newsletter, 12 Jan. 1650.

which under Henry Walker's guidance had taken over from *Perfect Occurrences* as the House's official gazette, began to give expression to the moderating policies favoured by a majority in the House. Even at their worst, the newspapers of the Rump period can sometimes make clear the purpose of a parliamentary action whose intention is left obscure by the *Journal*. At their best, they are as valuable to the historian as are *Pravda* and *Izvestya* to a Kremlinologist attempting to discern developments and changes in power and policy: in other words, although we cannot trust editorial comments to be accurate, we can learn much from the fact that the comments were made. Of course, the use of newspaper material presents the same trap as does all printed material, namely the danger of paying too much attention to the sentiments of people who published their views and too little to those of people who did not. And in any case one should, no doubt, beware of believing everything one reads in newspapers. In general, however, I believe that on matters of information mid-seventeenth-century newspapers were more trustworthy than are their twentieth-century counterparts.

BIBLIOGRAPHICAL GUIDE

What follows is neither a comprehensive bibliography nor a complete list of works cited in this book. It is rather a guide for readers consulting footnote references. The manuscripts I have cited are listed below, with their locations. Also listed are those printed works – primary and secondary – which are cited more than once in the footnotes, and which thus appear, after the first citation, in shortened form and/or without the date of publication. The only newspapers listed below are those which are given abbreviated titles after the first footnote reference. Most of the newspapers of the Rump period, and most of the pamphlets and newspapers I have cited, are listed in the *Thomason Catalogue* (see above, p. 402). For a comprehensive – although not infallible – guide to the primary printed sources of the period see D. Wing, *Short-Title Catalogue of Books Printed . . . 1641–1700* (New York, 1945). For secondary material, there is a good bibliography in Ivan Roots, *The Great Rebellion* (1966). It can be supplemented by M. F. Keeler, *Bibliography of British History, Stuart Period, 1603–1714* (1970 edn.), and by the *Annual Bulletin of Historical Literature* published by the Historical Association.

I. MANUSCRIPTS

Bodleian Library
    Ashmole 421, 423
    Bodleian 328–9 (Committee for Plundered Ministers)
    Clarendon 34, 39, 43, 45 (mainly royalist newsletters)
    Portland: Nalson xvi, xxii
    Rawlinson A224–6 (Navy Committee)
    Tanner 52, 54, 56, 57/2

British Museum
    Additional: 10,114 (Diary of John Harington)
            15,862 (Diary of Thomas Burton)
            15,903 (Norfolk collection)
            22,546 (Ordnance papers)
            22,620 (Norwich collection)
            24,861 (Richard Major papers)

28,002 (Oxinden papers)
31,984 (Whitelocke's history of his 48th year)
35,332 (Ordnance papers)
35,863 (Hale commission minute-book)
36,972 (Presentations to benefices by Commissioners of the Great
  Seal)
37,344–5 (Annals of Bulstrode Whitelocke)
53,728 (Whitelocke's sermons)

Egerton: 1048 (collected papers, 1620–60)
          2618 (collected papers, 1556–1753)

Harleian: 454 (Diary of Sir Humphrey Mildmay)

Loan: 29/123, 176 (Harley papers)
          Film 331 (Northumberland MS, Fitzjames letter-book)
          Film 636, 9–11 (Verney MSS)

Sloane: 3945 (Life of Christopher Love by his widow Mary)

Stowe: 184, 189, 333

Thomason: E537(8), E693(5), E804(4)

Dr Williams's Library (Gordon Square, London)
Letters of Richard Baxter
Minutes of the London Provincial Assembly (typed transcript)
Minutes of the Westminster Assembly (microfilm)

Folger Library, Washington
Additional MS 494 (Bennett papers)

Guildhall Record Office, London
Journal of the London Common Council, xli

Holkham Hall
Holkham MS 684 (commonplace-book of William Heveningham: microfilm
  in Bodleian Library)

House of Lords Record Office
Journal of the House of Commons, xxxiii–xxxviii
Main Paper Series, 1649–50

Hull Corporation MSS
Letters, 1640–60 (L)

Lambeth Palace
MS 1019 (Day-book of trustees for the maintenance of ministers)

Longleat, Wiltshire
Whitelocke Letters, x–xiii, xxvii

National Library of Wales, Aberystwyth
Plas Yolyn: 11,434B (Morgan Lloyd)
 11,439D (Morgan Lloyd)
 11,440D (John Jones's letter-book)

Public Record Office
Commonwealth Exchequer Papers, SP classmarks:
 18 (Navy Committee)
 19 (Committee for Advance of Money)
 22 (Committee for Plundered Ministers)
 23 (Committee for Compounding)
 24 (Committee of Indemnity)
 25 (Council of State order-books; Committee for Trade and Foreign Affairs)
 28 (Army Committee; Committee of Revenue)
 46 (Navy papers)

Somerset Record Office, Taunton
DD/HP (Hippisley papers)

Sheffield University Library
Hartlib, bundles xxxiii, lxi

Staffordshire Record Office, Stafford
D593/P/8/2/2 (letters of John Langley to Sir Richard Leveson)[1]
D868/5 (original letters, 1641–61)

William Salt Library, Stafford
454 (Swynfen)

Worcester College, Oxford
Clarke, xix, xx, xxii, xxiv, xxv

2. PRINTED SOURCES

A. *Primary*

Another Declaration: wherein is rendered a further account of the Just Grounds and Reasons of the Dissolving the Parliament (1653)

---

[1] Extracts from some of these letters are printed in D. A. Johnson and D. G. Vaisey (eds.), *Staffordshire and the Great Rebellion* (Stafford, 1965), pp. 72–8.

The Anti-Levellers Antidote (1652)

Arbitrary Government Displayed (1682)

Ashhurst, W. *Reasons against Agreement with* ... *The Agreement of the People* (1648)

Asty, J. (ed.) *A Complete Collection of the Sermons of the Reverend and Learned John Owen, D.D.* (1721)

Aubrey's Brief Lives (ed. O. Lawson Dick, 1949)

The Autobiography of Henry Newcombe (ed. R. Parkinson, Chetham Soc., 1852)

R.B., *A Word of Information and Advice touching Tithes* (1652)

Bacon, R. *A Taste of the Spirit of God* (1652)

Bell, R. (ed.) *Memorials of the Civil War: comprising the Correspondence of the Fairfax Family* (2 vols., 1849)

Blencowe, R. W. (ed.) *The Sydney Papers* (1825)

A Brief Narration of the Mysteries of State carried on by the Spanish Faction in England (The Hague, 1651)

A Brief Relation of some Affairs and Transactions, Civil and Military, both Foreign and Domestic (newspaper: 1649–50)

Brooks, Thomas *Cases Considered and Resolved* (1653)

   The Hypocrite Detected, Anatomised, Impeached (1649)

The Buller Papers (ed. R. N. Worth, Plymouth, 1895)

Calendar of State Papers Domestic

Calendar of State Papers Venetian

Calendar of the Committee for Advance of Money

Calendar of the Committee for Compounding

Carlyle, T. *Cromwell's Letters and Speeches* (3 vols., 1846)

Carte, T. (ed.) *A Collection of Original Letters and Papers concerning the Affairs of England from the year 1641 to 1650* (2 vols., 1739)

Cary, H. (ed.) *Memorials of the Great Civil War in England* (2 vols., 1842)

The Case of Oliver St. John (1660)

Certain Proposals of Divers Attorneys of the Court of Common Pleas (1651)

Chidley, S. *A Remonstrance of the valiant and well-deserving Soldier* (1653)

The Clarke Papers (ed. C. H. Firth, Camden Soc., 4 vols., 1891–1901)

A Clear and Necessary Vindication of Mr. Love (1651)

Coates, W. H. (ed.) *The Journal of Sir Simonds D'Ewes from the First Recess of the Long Parliament to the Withdrawal of King Charles from London* (New Haven, 1942)

Cobbett, W. (ed.) *The Parliamentary History of England* (36 vols., 1806–20)

Cockayne, W. *The Foundations of Freedom Vindicated* (1649)

A Collection of the State Papers of John Thurloe (ed. T. Birch, 7 vols., 1742)

Complete Writings of Roger Williams (7 vols., New York, 1964: vol. vi, ed. J. R. Bartlett)

The Cries of England to the Parliament (1653)

A Declaration of the Lord General and his Council, showing the grounds and reasons for the Dissolution of the late Parliament (1653)

Diary of the Rev. R. Josselin (ed. E. Hockliffe, Camden Soc., 1908)
Diary of Thomas Burton (ed. J. T. Rutt, 4 vols., 1828)
Duncon, Samuel *Several Propositions of Public Concernment, presented to . . . Cromwell* (1652)
Dury, John *Considerations touching the present Engagement* (1649)
The Engagement Vindicated (1650)
A Faithful Searching Home Word (1659)
Feake, C. *A Beam of Light* (1659)
The Fifth Monarchy, or Kingdom of Christ, in opposition to the Beast Asserted (1659)
Firth, C. H. (ed.) 'Thomas Scot's account of his actions as intelligencer during the Commonwealth', *E.H.R.*, xii (1897)
Firth, C. H. and Rait, R. S. (eds.) *Acts and Ordinances of the Interregnum* (3 vols., 1911)
Fry, John *The Accuser Shamed* (1649)
A Gag to Love's Advocate (1651)
Gardiner, S. R. (ed.) *Constitutional Documents of the Puritan Revolution* (1958 edn.)
  Letters and Papers relating to the First Dutch War (Navy Records Soc., 6 vols., 1899–1930)
Goodwin, T. *Christ the Universal Peace-Maker* (1651)
Grey, E. *Vox Coeli, containing Maxims of pious Policy* (1649)
Haller, W. and Davies, G. (eds.) *The Leveller Tracts, 1647–1653* (Gloucester, Mass., 1964 edn.)
His Majesty's Declaration and Remonstrance (1648)
Historical Manuscript Commission Reports:
  De Lisle and Dudley vi (1966)
  Egmont i (1905)
  Hodgkin (1897)
  Kenyon (1894)
  Leybourne-Popham (1899)
  Loder-Symonds (in *H.M.C.R. Rye and Hereford, etc.*, 1892)
  Lord Hatherton (1877)
  Portland i and iii (1891, 1894)
  Pyne and Woodford (1884)
  Southampton and King's Lynn (1887)
  Sutherland (1877)
The Hull Letters (ed. T. Wildridge, undated: 1887?)
The Humble Petition and Appeal of John Feilder (1651)
Josten, C. H. (ed.) *Elias Ashmole, 1617–1692* (5 vols., Oxford, 1966)
Journal of George Fox (ed. J. C. Nickalls, Cambridge, 1952)
Journal of the House of Commons
The Last News from the King of Scots (1651)
Latimer, J. (ed.) *Annals of Bristol* (Bristol, 1900)

Letters from Roundhead Officers . . . *to Captain A. Baynes, July 1650–June 1660* (Edinburgh, 1856)

A Letter written to a Gentleman in the Country (1653: by John Hall)

The Life and Death of . . . *Sir Henry Vane Knight* (1662)

The Life of Adam Martindale (ed. R. Parkinson, Chetham Soc., 1845)

J. Lilburne, *The Legal, Fundamental Liberties of the People of England* (1649)
  London's Liberty in Chains Discovered (1646)
  Rash Oaths Unwarrantable (1647)
  The Second Part of England's New Chains Discovered (1649)

Love's Advocate (1651)

Marshall, S. *A Sermon preached to the* . . . *Lord Mayor* . . . *tending to heal our Rents and Divisions* (delivered 1652 but published 1653)

M[ay], T[homas] *An Anatomy of Lieut. Col. John Lilburne's Spirit and Pamphlets* (1649)

Mayer, J. 'Inedited letters of Cromwell, Colonel Jones, Bradshaw and other regicides', *Transactions of the Historical Society of Lancashire and Cheshire*, new series, i (1860–2)

Mayo, C. H. (ed.) *Minute Book of the Dorset Standing Committee* (Exeter, 1902)

Memoirs of Colonel Hutchinson Governor of Nottingham by his widow Lucy (ed. C. H. Firth, 1906)

Memoirs of Edmund Ludlow (ed. C. H. Firth, 2 vols., 1894)

Memorandums of the Conferences held between the Brethren scrupled at the Engagement, and others who were satisfied with it (1650)

Milton, J. *The Tenure of Kings and Magistrates* (ed. W. T. Allison, New York, 1911)

The Moderator: endeavouring a full composure and quiet settlement of these many differences, both in doctrine and discipline (1652)

A Modest and Clear Vindication of the Serious Representation (1649)

A Modest Narrative of Intelligence (newspaper: 1649)

Nedham, M. *The Case of the Commonwealth of England, Stated* (1650)[1]

The Nicholas Papers (ed. G. F. Warner, 4 vols., 1886–1920)

Notestein, W. (ed.) *The Journal of Sir Simonds D'Ewes from the Beginning of the Long Parliament to the Opening of the trial of the Earl of Strafford* (New Haven, 1923)

Original Letters and Papers of State . . . *addressed to Oliver Cromwell* (ed. J. Nickolls, 1743: often known as the *Milton State Papers*)

Overton's Defiance of the Act of Pardon (1649)

'The parliamentary diary of John Boys' (ed. D. E. Underdown) *Bulletin of the Institute of Historical Research*, xxxix (1966)

Patterson, F. A. (ed.) *The Works of John Milton* (18 vols., New York, 1931–8)

Pennington jr., Isaac *The Fundamental Right, Safety and Liberty of the People* (1651)

A Perfect Account of the daily Intelligence from the Armies (newspaper: 1651–?)

---

[1] There is a modern edition of this work, edited by T. A. Knachel (Charlottesville, 1969).

A Perfect Diurnal of some Passages and Proceedings of, and in relation to, the Armies (newspaper: 1649–53)

A Perfect Diurnal of some Passages in Parliament (newspaper: 1649)

Perfect Occurrences of Every Day's Journal in Parliament (newspaper: 1649)

Perfect Passages of Every Day's Intelligence (newspaper: 1650–2)

A Perfect Summary of an Exact Diary of some Passages in Parliament (newspaper: 1649)

Price, J. *The Cloudy Clergy* (1650)

Prynne, William *A Full Declaration of the true State of the Secluded Members Case* (1660)

Raines, F. R. and Sutton, W. C. (eds.) *Life of Humphrey Chetham* (Chetham Soc., 1903)

Reasons against the Bill entitled an Act for County Registers (1653)

Reasons why the Supreme Authority of the three Nations . . . is not in the Parliament (1653)

Reliquiae Baxterianae: or, Mr. Richard Baxter's Narrative of the most Memorable Passages of his Life and Times (ed. M. Sylvester, 1696)

A Remonstrance of his Excellency Thomas Lord Fairfax, Lord General of the Parliament's Forces, and of the General Council of Officers (1648)

Russell, T. (ed.) *The Works of John Owen* (21 vols., 1826)

Scobell, H. *Memorials of the Method and Manner of Proceedings in Parliament in Passing Bills* (1689)

Several Proceedings in Parliament (newspaper: 1649–53)

Several Proposals for the General Good of the Commonwealth (1651)

Several Sermons and Discourses of William Dell (1652)

A Short Discourse between Monarchical and Aristocratical Government (1649)

Some Advertisements for the new Election of Burgesses (1645)

Somers, John Lord *A Collection of scarce and valuable Tracts* (ed. W. Scott, 13 vols., 1809–15)

Stocks, M. (ed.) *Records of the Borough of Leicester* (Cambridge, 1923)

Streater, John *Secret Reasons of State* (1659)

T[aylor], D[aniel] *Certain Queries or Considerations, presented to the view of all that desire Reformation of Grievances* (1651)

The Traitor's Perspective Glass (1662)

The Trial of Lieut. Colonel John Lilburne (1649)

The True State of the Case of the Commonwealth (1654: by Marchamont Nedham?)

A Tuesday's Journal of Perfect Passages in Parliament (newspaper: 1649)

Violet, T. *The Advancement of Merchandise* (1651)

Walker, C. *Complete History of Independency* (4 vols., 1661)

Warren, A. *Eight Reasons Categorical* (1653)

    The Royalist Reformed (1649)

The Weekly Intelligencer of the Commonwealth (newspaper: 1650–3)

Whitelocke, B. *Journal of the Swedish Embassy* (2 vols., 1855)

    Memorials of the English Affairs (4 vols., 1853)

Winstanley, G. 'England's spirit unfolded' (ed. G. E. Aylmer, *Past and Present*, 40 (1968))

Wolfe, D. M. (ed.) *Leveller Manifestoes of the Puritan Revolution* (1967 edn.)

Wood, A. à *Athenae Oxoniensis* (3 vols., 1692)

Woodhouse, A. S. P. (ed.) *Puritanism and Liberty* (1938)

B. *Secondary*

Abbott, W. C. *Writings and Speeches of Oliver Cromwell* (4 vols., Cambridge, Mass., 1937–47)

Abernathy, G. 'The English Presbyterians and the Stuart Restoration, 1648–1663', *Transactions of the American Philosophical Society*, new series, 55, part 2 (1965)

Ashley, M. *Financial and Commercial Policy under the Cromwellian Protectorate* (1962 edn.)

Bisset, A. *History of the Commonwealth of England* (2 vols., 1867)

Brunton, D. and Pennington, D. H. *Members of the Long Parliament* (1968 edn.)

Capp, B. S. *The Fifth Monarchy Men. A Study in Seventeenth-Century English Millenarianism* (1972)

Carlson, L. H. 'A history of the Presbyterian party from Pride's Purge to the dissolution of the Long Parliament', *Church History*, xi (1942)

Christie, W. D. *A Life of Antony Ashley Cooper, First Earl of Shaftesbury* (2 vols., 1871)

Cotterell, M. 'Interregnum law reform: The Hale Commission of 1652', *E.H.R.*, lxxxiii (1968)

Dictionary of National Biography

Everitt, A. M. *The Community of Kent and the Great Rebellion 1640–60* (Leicester, 1966)

Farnell, J. E. 'The Navigation Act of 1651. The First Dutch War and the London Merchant Community', *Economic History Review*, second series, xvi (1963–4)

'The usurpation of honest London householders: Barebone's Parliament', *E.H.R.*, lxxxii (1967)

Firth, C. H. 'Cromwell and the expulsion of the Long Parliament in 1653', *E.H.R.*, viii (1893)

'The Expulsion of the Long Parliament', *History*, new series, ii (1917–18)

The House of Lords during the English Civil War (1910)

Oliver Cromwell and the Rule of the Puritans in England (1961 edn.)

Gardiner, S. R. *History of the Commonwealth and Protectorate* (4 vols., 1893)

Gentles, I. J. 'The debentures and military purchases of crown land' (London Ph.D. thesis, 1969)

Hexter, J. H. *The Reign of King Pym* (Cambridge, Mass., 1941)

Hill, C. *God's Englishman. Oliver Cromwell and the English Revolution* (1970)

Holmes, C. A. 'The Eastern Association' (Cambridge Ph.D. thesis, 1969)

Howell jr., Roger *Newcastle-upon-Tyne and the Puritan Revolution 1640–1660* (Oxford, 1967)

James, M. *Social Problems and Policy in the Puritan Revolution 1640–1660* (1930)

Johnson, A. M. 'Buckinghamshire 1640–1660' (Swansea M.A. thesis, 1963)

Jones, G. F. T. *Saw-pit Wharton* (Sydney, 1967)

Keeler, M. F. *The Long Parliament 1640–1641* (Philadelphia, 1954)

Macpherson, C. B. *The Political Theory of Possessive Individualism* (Oxford, 1964 edn.)

Masson, D. *The Life of Milton* (6 vols., 1859–90)

Niehaus, C. R. 'The issue of law reform in the Puritan Revolution' (Harvard Ph.D. thesis, 1957)

Pearl, V. *London and the Outbreak of the Puritan Revolution* (Oxford, 1961)
    'Oliver St. John and the "Middle Group" in the Long Parliament', *E.H.R.*, lxxxi (1966)
    'The "Royal Independents" in the English Civil War', *Transactions of the Royal Historical Society*, 5th series, xviii (1968)

Richards, T. *A History of the Puritan Movement in Wales . . . 1639–1653* (1920)

Roots, I. *The Great Rebellion 1642–1660* (1966)

Rowe, V. A. *Sir Henry Vane the Younger* (1970)

Snow, V. F. 'Attendance trends and absenteeism in the Long Parliament', *Huntington Library Quarterly*, 18 (1954–5)
    'Parliamentary reapportionment proposals in the Puritan revolution', *E.H.R.*, lxxiv (1959)

Trevor-Roper, H. R. *Religion, The Reformation and Social Change* (1967)

Underdown, D. E. 'The Independents again', *Journal of British Studies*, viii (1968)
    'The Independents reconsidered', *Journal of British Studies*, iii (1964)
    'Party management in the recruiter elections', *E.H.R.*, lxxxiii (1968)
    Pride's Purge. Politics in the Puritan Revolution (Oxford, 1971)
    Royalist Conspiracy in England (Yale, 1960)

Veall, D. *The Popular Movement for Law Reform 1640–1660* (Oxford, 1970)

Wallace, J. M. *Destiny his Choice. The Loyalism of Andrew Marvell* (Cambridge, 1968)
    'The engagement controversy 1649–1652', *Bulletin of the New York Public Library*, 68 (1964)

Wedgwood, C. V. *The Trial of Charles I* (1964)

Williams, C. M. 'The political career of Henry Marten' (Oxford D.Phil. thesis, 1954)

Willson, D. H. *Privy Councillors in the English House of Commons 1604–1629* (Minneapolis, 1940)

Wilson, C. H. *Profit and Power: a study of England and the Dutch Wars* (1957)

Woolrych, A. H. 'The calling of Barebone's Parliament', *E.H.R.*, lxxx (1965)

Yule, G. *The Independents in the English Civil War* (Cambridge, 1958)

Zagorin, P. *A History of Political Thought in the English Revolution* (1954)

INDEX